HENRY HOLT EDITIONS IN PSYCHOLOGY

Egon Brunswik: 1903-1955

The
Psychology
of
Egon Brunswik

EDITED BY

KENNETH R. HAMMOND

UNIVERSITY OF COLORADO

A HENRY HOLT EDITION IN PSYCHOLOGY

HOLT, RINEHART AND WINSTON, INC.
NEW YORK · CHICAGO · SAN FRANCISCO · TORONTO · LONDON

Preface

Every scientist who makes a strong effort to contribute to his discipline must, in the small hours at the desk or in the laboratory, have at least a fleeting wonder as to what his legacy to that discipline will contain. He knows well the legacies of the gods in his field—how they left numerous ideas and discoveries to numerous disciples working feverishly in their image—but he knows more intimately those who departed from the scene unnoticed and left the trend of events undisturbed. What will his own legacy consist of—and who will be the heirs?

Psychology, of course, is no different in this respect from other fields. It has had its heroes, if not gods, and undoubtedly will have more of them. Recently, these flourished during what Koch has called the *Age of Theory,* and certainly left their mark on psychology. Brunswik was one of them, but his legacy was far different from the others. Whereas Tolman, Hull, and Lewin left their ideas and doctrine to a sturdy and determined second generation, there were, in effect, no heirs present at the reading of Brunswik's intellectual will.

This is a fact worth reflecting upon. It makes one wonder how Brunswik's influence could have been so large. For strange as it may seem, the first chapter in this book is the only paper ever written in America that declares an open alliance with Brunswik's probabilistic functionalism on all points. During his lifetime he found not a single prominent psychologist who actively supported his views as a whole. True, there were some like Campbell, for example, who found their work touching upon areas that Brunswik had already explored, and who made their indebtedness to Brunswik clear. But there was never a prominent psychologist who frankly declared himself to be a "Brunswikian," as there were "Hullians," "Lewinians," and the like. The edifice that Brunswik erected became a significant landmark—but it was virtually empty; there were visitors, it is true, but no one stayed.

The absence of protagonists was matched by the indifference of antagonists. Certainly there were those who thought Brunswik was all wrong; indeed, their numbers were, and perhaps are, legion. But apparently he was thought to be *so* wrong that it was hardly worthwhile to attack his position—even if one could understand how this could be accomplished. Again, there are minor exceptions, but the only full-scale attacks on Brunswik's point of view came in the 1941 symposium with Hull and Lewin, and the 1953 symposium with Hilgard, Krech, Feigl, and Postman. Interestingly,

v

both symposia were held in connection with the unity of science movement, and if the first symposium was not arranged by Brunswik, the second certainly was. It is as though he were forced to make his own provisions for other psychologists to give serious attention to his ideas in published form.

And although Brunswik seems to have had many students when he was in Austria, he never had a group of students in America who fashioned their work after his and who carried out their doctoral dissertations under his direction. There were many vigorous and enthusiastic graduate students during Brunswik's eighteen years at the University of California, but Max Levin is the only one who completed his dissertation under Brunswik's supervision.

The essential fact remains that his ideas continue to be seen as important, and they continue to affect psychologists. The edifice he erected is still there; it gives promise of a long life, and there is some evidence that it is attracting an increasing number of visitors.

It is this situation that prompted the editor, with the assistance of Edward C. Tolman, Donald T. Campbell, and Jane Loevinger to prepare this volume. It has been rather long in the making (it did not get underway until after Tolman's death) perhaps because some of the contributors knew their indebtedness to Brunswik and wanted to make it clear, but hardly understood what their relation to him was. For some of the contributors— Bailey, Campbell, Jarvik, Loevinger, Hochberg, and myself—it was relatively easy because we were students at Berkeley during Brunswik's time, and were profoundly moved by him. For other contributors—Barker, Crow, Cronbach and Azuma, Hake and collaborators, Sarbin, and Smedslund—it was not so easy. For although each recognized that his work was influenced by Brunswik, it often seemed difficult for them to know precisely of what the influence consisted, and sometimes their response to his influence was one of ambivalence.

Heider and Leeper were Brunswik's contemporaries; they are writing about a colleague whom they respected and admired. Heider has made it clear how close he and Brunswik were on certain fundamental issues, which is the reason we chose to include an excerpt from his book (1956). And Leeper, in his role as critic and reviewer, found it important and useful to get his own thinking straight as to what Brunswik was after.

A final word. Because this book is a memorial volume for Egon Brunswik our readers will no doubt be surprised to find that we have included three papers that are, on the whole, critical of his work. In most memorial volumes, we agree, this would be in poor taste. But, as we explained above, Brunswik never really got the informed criticism he deserved. All three of the critics here, Hochberg, Leeper, and Smedslund are well acquainted with Brunswik's work, and their words are worth attending to. The reader, therefore, will be able to learn, not only what Brunswik's position was and how it influenced certain psychologists, but what sort of criticisms are maintained by informed psychologists. Certainly Brunswik worked hard enough to invoke criticism—there should be no reason to walk softly now. Brunswik cannot reply, however, so the reader will have to form his own conclusions. If these happen to take the form of a compromise, that would have been no surprise to Brunswik—for that is much as probabilistic functionalism would have predicted.

K. R. H.

Boulder, Colorado
October 1965

Contents

I. ESSAYS AND STUDIES

II. CRITICISMS

III. SELECTED PAPERS BY BRUNSWIK

Eulogy: [1]

EGON BRUNSWIK: 1903–1955

Egon Brunswik was born in Budapest, March 18, 1903. His father was Hungarian—an engineer in the Austro-Hungarian government; his mother was Austrian. His childhood tongues were Hungarian and German. When only eight, he was sent to Vienna to be educated at the famous Gymnasium of Theresianische Akademie as preparation for entering government service in the Austro-Hungarian Empire; and from this early age, he was almost always on his own. The boys at the gymnasium came from all parts of the empire and received training in science, the classics, mathematics, and history. Some of the teaching was in the boys' own respective, provincial languages (Hungarian, in Brunswik's case). This meant, for example, that he studied the history of the empire both in Hungarian and in German and early noticed the discrepancies between the two accounts. Perhaps it was this early experience that gave him his initial insight into the merely probabilistic character of one's knowledge of his environment.

After the First World War, he was sent with his sister for some months to Sweden to recover from the malnutrition of the war years. He returned and graduated from the Theresianische Akademie in 1921. He then spent two years, 1921–1923, at the Vienna Technische Hochschule studying to become an engineer, passing the first state examination required at the end of that period; however, he then decided to transfer to the University of Vienna to study psychology. Here he worked under Karl Bühler and came under the influence of Moritz Schlick and the Vienna Circle of logical positivists. In 1926 he passed the state examination for gymnasium teachers in mathematics and physics.

After he received his Ph.D. in 1927, Brunswik became an Assistant in Bühler's *Psychologisches Institut*. He also taught concurrently for a year in a Real Gymnasium and later for several years in the Vienna

1. Reprinted from the *American Journal of Psychology*, 1956, *69*, 315–342. With the kind permission of the Editor.

1

Pedagogical Institute and the Vienna Volkshochschule. In 1931–1932 he spent a year as a visiting lecturer in the School of Education at Ankara, Turkey, where he established the first psychological laboratory. He became Privat-dozent at the University of Vienna in 1934. In 1933–1934, the present writer, during some months in Vienna, became acquainted with Brunswik. In 1935–1936 Brunswik received a Rockefeller Fellowship and spent the year as visiting lecturer and research fellow in psychology at the University of California, Berkeley. In the fall of 1937, he returned to Berkeley as assistant professor, where through the normal course of events, he became professor in 1947.

In 1938 he married Else Frenkel, who had been a fellow student in Vienna and also an assistant in Bühler's Institut. They were married in New York upon her arrival from Austria and both became American citizens in 1943. In 1942–1943, during a sabbatical leave, Brunswik underwent a sympathectomy for hypertension. This reduced his blood pressure, which had become dangerously high; but later, the hypertension became active again. In recent years, he had to restrict his social contacts greatly, both professional and otherwise. His death on July 7, 1955, came, nonetheless, as a complete surprise and terrifying shock and sorrow to his friends, colleagues, and students.

In Brunswik's personality, on the one hand there was a mixture of outgoing warmth and friendliness, and on the other, of basic reserve. He was a delightful and courteous host. Although sometimes seemingly withdrawn in company, he was intensely interested in persons and very acute in his estimation of them. He was most generous to students and supportive of them and had a tremendous influence on them—even upon those who did only minor work under him. His mind was unique, stimulating, and dedicated, and this was felt by all who came in contact with him. Although he had the highest intellectual and scholarly standards for himself, he had considerable understanding of and tolerance for those less gifted.

Brunswik's own interests in psychology lay primarily in the fields of perception, cognition, methodology, and theory, but he was always intensely informed of, interested in, and sympathetic towards the wider psychoanalytical and sociological studies of his wife, Else Frenkel-Brunswik, and he took enormous pride in her achievements.

His psychological and scientific interests can perhaps be summarized under seven somewhat overlapping and interlocking rubrics:

1. his early envisagement of perception as in the nature of a focused and more or less successful "intentionalistic attainment" (Erreichung) of environmental entities

2. his translation of this notion of intentionalistic attainment into more general and more behavioristic terms, so that it came to cover not merely the cue-object relations in perception but also the means-end relations in instrumental behavior and his emphasis on the merely probabilistic character of both of these types of relations
3. the growth in his thinking of the complementary doctrines of representative design and ecological validity
4. the basic development of the two doctrines of probabilism and functionalism with an accompanying plea against too premature a concern with problems of mediation
5. his analyses of the differences between perception and reasoning
6. his suggestions for future investigations
7. his encyclopedic interest in the historical development of psychology

1. *Perception as an intentionalistic attainment*   In an early book, Brunswik (1934) summarized some fifteen experiments carried out by himself and his students in Vienna. These were concerned with the general topic of object constancy (*Dingkonstanz*) as it was then being much studied in Europe; but Brunswik approached the topic from a somewhat new angle. He began by drawing a distinction between a quality or quantity as immediately given in experience (a *Gegebenheit*) and the same quality or quantity as an independently measurable environmental object—a *Gegenstand*. Influenced by Brentano, he conceived of perception as a process in which the immediately given (the *Gegebenheiten*) *intended* the independently measurable objects, which later might, in perception, be more or less successfully attained (*erreicht*). Later, of course, as he became more of an objectivist, the *Gegebenheiten* or the immediately given became merely the physicophysiological processes or cues on the subjects' sensory surfaces.

Further, Brunswik pointed out that in the usual object-constancy experiment the organism can, on the one hand, be set by the instructions, or by innate propensity, to "intend" (be focused upon) the relatively independent, *distal* object such, for example, as: inherent object-size, independent of distance; inherent object-shape, independent of angle of regard; or inherent object-brightness (albedo) independent of the momentary amount of light then falling upon the object's surface. Or, on the other hand, the subject can be set for, intend, a more artificial, *proximal* object, more closely related to some immediate partial pattern of stimulation on the organism's receptor surface. Such proximal objects would be the size of an object as projected on a plane, a given standard distance in front of the eyes; or the shape of an oblique surface as projected on a screen, perpendicular to the line of regard; or the actual intensity of light reflected from an object's surface, abstracted from any further cues indicating the amount of light being shone onto that surface from an independent light source.

Three findings appeared. (A) If left without instructions or artificial set, the independent distal object is the one which the organism seems primarily to "intend" (to be focused upon) and to come nearest to attaining. (B) Even when instructed by the experimenter, or by itself, to achieve this independent distal object or quality, the organism's perceptual response is pulled slightly in the direction of the more immediate proximal object. (C) When set to achieve this more proximal object, however, the organism's perceptual response will be pulled (and to a greater degree) in the direction of the independent, distal object. In a word, perception in all cases tends to achieve merely some *compromise* between these two different poles of intention.

It should be pointed out here that the notion of "intending" or "focusing upon," as thus treated by Brunswik, loses its subjective connotation and becomes merely a statement of the degree to which the organism's perceptual responses do tend to approximate one or another purely objectively measurable environmental entity, or to compromise between them or to do both.

Finally, Brunswik expanded this concept of perceptual poles, between which the organism's achievement could fall, to new problems outside the narrow range of thing-constancy. Thus, in one experiment, the subject had to compare cards with groups of dots. The groups were made to vary both in numerosity of dots and in sizes of the individual dots, and hence in the total area covered by them (the total amount of paint required). It was found that, if the subject was instructed to equate cards on the basis of numerosity, he was pulled somewhat towards equating them on the basis of the total areas covered; whereas, if he were instructed to equate the total areas covered, he was pulled somewhat towards the pole of numerosity.

Brunswik also investigated cases of three poles—for example, numbers, areas, and monetary values. In one experiment this was done with groups of coins. The subject could be told to equate the groups on the basis of numbers of coins in them, or on the basis of total area covered by the coins or on the basis of their total monetary value. It appeared that, whenever the subject attempted to equate on the basis of one of these three poles, his responses were deflected (compromised) in some degree by each of the other two. Thus Brunswik anticipated the more recent American studies of motivational factors in perception. But his own interest seems to have been more in measurements of the degrees of veridical perception *per se* than in the resulting motivational distortions as such.

2. *Cue-object and means-end relations: Probabilism*   After coming into contact with American behaviorism, Brunswik translated the concept of the relation of givens (*Gegebenheiten*) to objects (*Gegenstande*) in perception into the more objective terms of the relation of perceptual cues to the to-be-perceived objects (whether proximal or distal). He developed the additional notion of a similar relation of means-objects to goals on the instrumental side (Tolman and Brunswik, 1935). The organism on its perceptual side receives and selects among cues in order perceptually to attain objects, and on its instrumental side it selects and manipulates means-objects in order to reach (attain) goals. So he came to put great emphasis upon the fact that both cue-object relations and means-goal relations, to which the organism has thus to adjust, have usually only varying degrees of "probable" applicability or validity. For example, one single cue for perceiving the albedo of a surface is simply the amount of light reflected from that surface, but under special conditions, where other cues are impoverished, the subject may be misled by this one cue and overevaluate it. Thus, for example, it was found (Gelb) that a black disk in a dim room reflecting a large amount of light may, if the source be hidden, be seen as relatively white. Without adequate other cues the organism overevaluates this one cue of reflected light. If however, a bit of white paper be added and the light also reflects from this really white paper, then the black disk is immediately seen as black.

Similarly, Brunswik became impressed with the fact that in the normal environment given means-objects are apt to lead to given goals with only certain degrees of probability. He conceived a new sort of experiment in animal learning to illustrate this point (1939). Up to that time, in most of the orthodox instrumental learning experiments, the probability that a given means would lead to the reward had usually been set as 1.00 and the probability that an alternative means would lead to reward had been set at 0.00. This all-or-none relation was felt by Brunswik to be an artificial, nonrepresentative situation. Specific means, as well as specific sensory cues, lead in real life to given goals (and given to-be-perceived objects) with varying degrees of probability. In the means-end case there may also enter in a second factor. In the real environment there is also a tendency for a given goal (for example, food) to become exhausted after repeated gettings to it. Hence a given means (for example, a given location) may become less good (principle of exhaustible supply) with repetition.

Brunswik's experiment illustrated the first point. In a simple T maze the correctness of the one side and the incorrectness of the other were given different probabilities with different groups, such as: 100 percent —00 percent; 75 percent—25 percent; 67 percent—33 percent; 100 percent—50 percent and 50 percent—00 percent. He discovered that, whereas 67 percent—33 percent was below threshold, the other probability-combinations led to the choice of the more probable side with increasing frequency in the order 100 percent—50 percent; 75 percent —25 percent; 50 percent—00 percent and 100 percent—00 percent (the last combination being the best). A brief (inadequate) summary of these results would be that above a certain threshold the rats were governed by, and in some degree responded appropriately to, the increasing differences in probability values of the two alternative means-routes.

Several additional experiments, somewhat similar to this rat experiment but using human subjects, may be briefly mentioned. Brunswik and Herma (1951) early did an experiment in Vienna in which the subject had to judge which was the heavier of two weights, one presented to each hand. In a semi-randomized fashion the weight on one side was in 67 percent of the paried lifts heavier than that on the other side. In a series of interspersed test-trials where both weights were equal—either both heavy or both light—the subjects showed a first increasing, and then an unexplained somewhat decreasing tendency (when both weights were equal) to judge the one on the 67 percent side as lighter (contrast). In other words, the contrast illusion could be set up on the basis of merely probable and not univocal relations between positions and weights.

Levin (1952) repeated the Brunswik-and-Herma experiment with similar results. Jarvik (1951) did an experiment on the building up of the relative expectations of two alternative symbols attached with different probabilities to orally presented words. His results, although using such different materials, were nonetheless also similar to those of Brunswik and Herma.

3. *Representative design and ecological validity*   As time went on, Brunswik became more and more concerned with general principles of experimental design (1947; 1952; 1955). He pointed out that, in the classical and, as he saw it, overcontrolled laboratory sort of experiment, many of the important, independent stimulus-determiners in a perception experiment or a learning experiment become artificially "tied" (made to covary in an unnatural fashion) or artificially untied (prevented from covarying—some of them held artificially constant

and only one or two allowed to vary). He thus became more and more impressed with the need for a wide sampling over a natural *ecological* array of total stimulus-situations and over a natural ecological array of total-means-end situations. He argued, in short, that we must substitute *representative design* for what he called the classical, nomothetic, or *systematic design*. If we wish to generalize how well an organism actually attains its perceptual or its instrumental goals, and this he felt was the true aim of a proper psychology, we must study the organism in its natural ecology.

As an early empirical step in this direction, he devised a perception experiment in which the subject (a woman graduate student) was followed about by an experimenter off and on during four weeks and questioned in nineteen sessions, every few minutes, to judge the most obvious linear dimension (vertical, horizontal, or oblique) of whatever frontal surface she happened to be looking at at that moment (1944). She was asked to judge under various attitudes—the only two we shall consider here being that for distal size and that for proximal size. She was also asked to judge the distances of the given surfaces that she was looking at. It turned out that the relative goodness of her judgments of distal sizes exceeded that of her judgments of projected or proximal sizes. Also it turned out that her judgments of distance were very highly correlated with the actual objective distances. Two reasons why this experiment was important were that it first made use of the notion of truly representative sampling and, secondly, it led Brunswik to his first extended use of correlation statistics. The questions to be answered were: how highly over a wide sample of situations do a subject's perceptual estimates of size *correlate* with distal sizes and with the proximal sizes, and how highly do estimates of distances correlate with true distances. The correlations (using logarithms of sizes and distances and of estimations of sizes and distances) were 0.98, 0.85, and 0.99, respectively. There were many other important questions asked and answered which, however, are too detailed for presentation here.

Brunswik likewise initiated a series of experiments (these were first begun in Vienna) in which the subjects were asked to judge, relative to schematic faces, such social characteristics as: intelligence, mood, age, character, likeability, beauty and energy (1956). Again he used correlations as measures of the degree to which the perceptual judgments of these social qualities were determined by the various different cues presented by the faces, such as length of nose, height of forehead, distance between the eyes, and so forth.

It was these experiments in "social perception" that, perhaps more than any others, led him to arrive at the notion of *"ecological validity."* Actually, in the true ecological environment of human observers, what are the real correlations, *if any,* between such factors as length of nose, distance between the eyes, and so forth, and say, the intelligence of individuals having such faces? Probably they are very small. It thus became obvious that in a complete "probabilistic functionalism" (see below) one would want to compare the experimentally obtained correlations between cues and perceived social character with the true correlations actually existing in the environment—against, that is, the real *ecological validity* of such cues. Furthermore, by the use of partial and multiple correlations, it could also be discovered that cues were given by the perceptual apparatus more or less weight than their true ecological validity, and what cues, if any, tended by perception to be given ecologically appropriate weightings.

There should also be mentioned here a couple of experiments in which the aim was to measure objectively the ecological validity of visual cues as these occur in the normal environments of our culture. Brunswik and Kamiya, using photographs from *Life* magazine of "stills" from a moving picture, measured the degree to which the proximity (nearness together) of pairs of parallel lines in the picture could be taken as a cue that the two lines were boundaries of a single object (1953). It was found that, the greater the proximity of the two lines, the more probable it was that they indicated the boundaries of a single object. The correlations were small but significant. Brunswik and Kamiya believed that this objective probability-relationship means that proximity is a cue that the organism can *learn* to depend upon and that proximity is presumably not an innate, autochthonous cue, as orthodox Gestalt psychology would hold.

Seidner did a similar experiment on the ecological validities of the respective vertical positions of two points as cues for positions in the third dimension (Brunswik, 1956). He also found a definite relationship. The higher points tended to belong to objects further away.

In short, it is to be emphasized again that the probability-values of objective ecological relations are the standards *against which* the probability of responses are to be evaluated.

    4. *Probabilistic functionalism*   Given the above sorts of findings and his own general point of view, Brunswik came more and more to conceive the nature of a proper psychology as being what he called a "probabilistic functionalism." It would be a functionalism (in the sense of American functionalism) because it would be a study of the organism's successes and failures, both in the perceptual at-

tainment of objects and in the instrumental reaching of goals. It would also be a probabilism because in the organism's environment the objects to be perceived and the goals to be reached usually have only probable and practically never univocal relationships to their respective cues and means.

Furthermore, in this study of the organism's functionalistic and probabilistic achievements, he felt that at the present time a consideration of what he called "mediational problems" (1952) such as the detailed investigation of the specific sensory, motor, and cerebral activities involved should be postponed. In this connection he adopted Boring's slogan of "the psychology of the empty organism" (1952) not as an ontological, but rather as a purely programmatic, proposal. We need first, he argued, to find out what the general successes of the organism's perceptual and goal-reaching attainments are and the general environmental conditions underlying these attainments, before we get involved in too detailed an investigation of the physiological or other mediational mechanisms involved.

Further, as a merely illustrative pedagogical device, he developed what he called the "lens model" (1952). This was a pictorial way of suggesting that a unit of behavior (whether perceptual or instrumental) could be conceived as if it operated by a double convex lens that brought a wide-spreading array of influences issuing from one focus, through the interposition of either the perceptual or the means-end apparatus of the organism, together again at a second focus. All the rays radiating out from a to-be-perceived object in the form of an array of sensory cues are brought together to a second focus in a perceptual response. All the rays (radiating out from a goal-oriented focus within the organism in the form of possible alternative means-routes) are brought together again to a second focus upon the actual goal to-be-reached.

Finally, most importantly in his thinking was the notion of *vicarious functioning*. That is, he always emphasized the frequent equivalence and intersubstitutibility of cues and of means-routes. Different rays can be substituted one for another. But he also emphasized the fact that these cues and means form *hierarchies* in that they come to be rated by the organism in orders of relatively better and relatively poorer.

    5. *Perception versus reasoning*   Throughout both his earlier and his later studies Brunswik was intrigued by the rapid but usually only approximate attainments of perception. He envisaged perception as a primitive and relatively autonomous function within the total cognitive system of the human being. He contrasted it with reasoning,

in which the subject tends either to hit the solution on the nose, or else to be far off. The differences in the distributions of errors would thus be a distinguishing criterion of whether the case was one of perception or one of reasoning. This was a concept that early fascinated him and an area of research to which he was beginning to pay much attention just prior to his death.

Thus in a recent experiment two partially overlapping groups of subjects were presented first in the laboratory with a perceptual problem in size-constancy (distal size) (1956). Subsequently they were presented with the necessary data in the same situation and asked to find arithmetically the distal size of the same object at the same distance. The perceptual laboratory judgments yielded a normal distribution about the correct distal size, with the mode close to this distal value though slightly deflected toward the proximal size. The solutions in the reasoning (paper and pencil test) yielded, on the other hand, a bimodal distribution. They tended to be either completely correct and fall exactly at the distal size or completely incorrect and fall exactly at the proximal size.

6. *Brunswik's suggestions for future investigations*   As has been indicated, after he came into contact with American psychology, Brunswik conceived that the relations of means-routes to goals have, in a normal environment, an analogous probabilistic character to that of perceptual cues to objects. His own experiment with the rats, his study with Herma and the studies of Levin and Jarvik were steps in this direction. In a sense, of course, all the various studies in other laboratories under the heading of partial reinforcement bear upon the issue. But they do not usually, as Brunswik wanted, confront two or more differentially probable means-routes, one against another. What he really wanted were studies in which the alternative means-routes and their respective probabilities would correspond to their natural values in the organism's normal ecology. This neither he nor his students had yet really achieved, although several beginnings had been made. It is, of course, the difficulty of deciding what is a normal instrumental ecology for a given organism, which to date has proved the major problem in the way of attempts at such experiments. Yet, he was keenly desirous that such further experiments be done. For underlying Brunswik's whole thesis was a well-founded scepticism as to the *generalizability* of the laws of learning and of memory (as well as of those of perception) as we now have them as a result of our traditional, artificial, nomothetically overcontrolled laboratory conditions.

A second suggestion as to possible further work lies in the area of clinical psychology. Here Hammond (1955) and his students have made a beginning. These workers have pointed out that an adequate ecological sampling means that not only subjects, but also a wide range of interviewers or projective-test-interpreters or both, must be sampled, if we are to make any true generalizations as to the ecological validity of interview results or projective-test results. They considered, for example, how well Rorschach protocols predict IQ (as defined by some independent measure such as the Wechsler-Bellevue test) and found that this could be answered only if Rorschach interpreters as well as Rorschach protocols were widely sampled. When this was done, partial and multiple correlations indicated which Rorschach factors were actually the more ecologically valid and also which Rorschach factors the various interpreters actually depended upon—which ones they weight properly, which ones they overweight and which ones they underweight. The results were illuminating both theoretically and practically.

The above are, however, only two inadequate suggestions of the types of further work that should stem from Brunswik's genius.

7. *History of psychology*   Finally, Brunswik had an encyclopedic knowledge of and interest in the history of psychology and of its relations to the other sciences. He emphasized especially that psychology, while obeying all true scientific canons, must not slavishly follow the nomothetic thema of classical physics. In other words, while championing the unity of science in relation to its basic objectives, he also advocated diversification of content and of method. Much of his teaching (and he greatly enjoyed giving a course in the history of psychology) was devoted to the thesis that true progress in science has come from the various and imaginatively conceived different developments in the several disciplines. His interest in the "Unity of Science" was an interest in appropriate diversities as well as in common objectives. He also believed that in the history of psychology itself he could discern specific and to some degree logically sequential trends: away from dualism, away from sensationism, away from molecularism, away from encapsulated centralism, away from nomotheticism; but towards monism, towards distal-achievementism and towards molarity —that is, towards his own doctrine of functionalism and probabilism.

This account of some of the more salient of Brunswik's concepts and their experimental implications by no means adequately portrays the complexity, the richness and the creativity of his thinking. The present report appears thin and bare when one turns from it to the perusal of Brunswik's own writings. There is a brilliance, a depth, a subtlety in

his language and in his ideas that both dazzles and baffles. The reader
is intrigued, stimulated, flounders, but is enormously challenged and
enriched.

In the coming years, Egon Brunswik will hold an ever increasingly
significant and important position in the history of psychology. His
posthumous monograph (1956) will help to hasten this increasing recognition. Those of us who knew and loved him can but be glad that such
ever-greater recognition lies ahead, though we grieve that he did not
live to see it happen.

EDWARD C. TOLMAN

University of California

REFERENCES

Brunswik, E. *Warnehmung und Gegenstandswelt.* Vienna: Deuticke,
1934.
Brunswik, E. Probability as a determiner of rat behavior. *J. exp.
Psychol.,* 1939, *25,* 175–197.
Brunswik, E. Distal focusing of perception: size constancy in a representative sample of situations.
Psychol. Monogr., 1944, (Whole
No. 254.)
Brunswik, E. *Systematic and representative design of psychological
experiments.* Berkeley, Calif. University of California Press, 1947.
Brunswik, E. *The conceptual framework of psychology.* Chicago:
University of Chicago Press, 1952.
Brunswik, E. Representative design
and probabilistic theory. *Psychol.
Rev.,* 1955, *62,* 193–217.
Brunswik, E., and H. Herma. Probability learning of perceptual cues
in the establishment of a weight

illusion. *J. exp. Psychol.,* 1951, *41,*
281–290.
Brunswik, E., and J. Kamiya. Ecological cue-validity of "proximity"
and of other Gestalt factors.
Amer. J. Psychol., 1953, *66,*
20–32.
Hammond, K. R. Probabilistic functioning and the clinical method.
Psychol. Rev., 1955, *62,* 255–262.
Jarvik, M. E. Probability learning
and a negative recency effect in
the serial anticipation of alternative symbols. *J. exp. Psychol.,*
1951, *41,* 291–297.
Levin, M. M. Inconsistent cues in
the establishment of perceptual
illusions. *Amer. J. Psychol.,* 1952,
65, 517–532.
Tolman, E. C., and E. Brunswik.
The organism and the causal texture of the environment. *Psychol.
Rev.,* 1935, *42,* 43–77.

I
ESSAYS
AND STUDIES

1

Probabilistic Functionalism: Egon Brunswik's Integration of the History, Theory, and Method of Psychology

KENNETH R. HAMMOND [1]

The purpose of this chapter is to introduce the reader to Egon Brunswik's approach to the science of psychology. The chapter is addressed more to the student, or better, to those curious about Brunswik's effort to change the nature of psychology, than to those already satisfied with and committed to conventional views. But there are already at least two excellent discussions (Allport, 1955; Postman and Tolman, 1959) of Brunswik's probabilistic functionalism. Why another?

First, Allport's treatment is highly curtailed. Second, Postman and Tolman's discussion bears more of a reportorial stamp than that of enthusiastic explication. And that was as it should have been. Prior to their paper there was no place where the student could find a digest of Brunswik's theory and research. Moreover, their paper is authoritative, objective, and quite complete, although it does not, of course, cover all of the ideas that Brunswik contributed to psychology.

This chapter, however, intends to do both less and more than the Postman-Tolman paper. It intends to accomplish less since it is not as complete, nor as objective in approach. It intends to do more for it is openly identified with Brunswik's position. The attempt is made to persuade, to convince, to show the shortcomings of other views and the superiority of Brunswik's. Its tone is frankly partisan. Its content includes

1. The author wishes to express his appreciation to Donald T. Campbell, Jane Loevinger, Robert MacLeod, and Frederick J. Todd for reading early drafts of this chapter, and the Council on Research and Creative Work of the University of Colorado for their assistance.

Brunswik's views on the history of psychology, his conceptual framework, and his methodology.

Brunswik's psychology is Darwinian; it is a form of functionalism because its main focus is on the adaptive interrelation of the organism with the environment. As Brunswik saw it, the task of psychology is to study and to understand how these two complex systems come to terms with one another. In all of Brunswik's writings this view was never stated more clearly than in his final paper, which was read at the Colorado Symposium:

... both organism and environment will have to be seen as systems, each with properties of its own, yet both hewn from basically the same block. Each has surface and depth, or overt and covert regions ... the interrelationship between the two systems has the essential characteristic of a "coming-to-terms." And this coming-to-terms is not merely a matter of the mutual boundary or surface areas. It concerns equally as much, or perhaps even more, the rapport between the central, covert layers of the two systems. It follows that, much as psychology must be concerned with the texture of the organism or of its nervous processes and must investigate them in depth, it also must be concerned with the texture of the environment as it extends in depth away from the common boundary. (1957, p. 5.)

The definition of psychology's task as the analysis of the interrelationship between two systems in the process of "coming-to-terms" with one another, the assertion that psychology must treat each system with equal respect, the directive that psychology ". . . must also be concerned with the texture of the environment as it extends in depth away from the common boundary" of the two systems—these are the buttresses of Brunswik's theory and methodology, and they must be kept in mind. Moreover, it is Brunswik's concern with the "texture" of the environment which separates him from almost all of the prominent theoreticians psychology has ever had.

Brunswik's students were made keenly aware of the fact that his point of view concerning the role of psychology in the world of science was not in the least arbitrary. One could hardly fail to see that his conception of psychology's task emerged from his close analysis of the history of science and the history of psychology. As a result, Brunswik's writings constitute an organic whole—a history, a comprehensive theory, and a methodology. This is an intellectual feat as yet unparalleled in twentieth century psychology—and it may remain so. We turn first to his history of psychology.

STRUCTURAL HISTORY

In 1939 Brunswik read a paper before the History of Science Club at the University of California in which he noted with apparent approval that Bergmann had compared his (Brunswik's) "structural history writing" with the "pragmatic tracing of historical influences in terms of intellectual biography, which characterizes the customary historical narrative." (1959.) Brunswik's history is indeed structural. It possesses form, and therefore, principle. It is no mere longitudinal compendium of names, dates, places, ideas; it is a theory of history. As a result, those who are willing to cope with it will find that structural history has a capacity for prediction of the future as well as for explication and recapitulation of the past.

In order to understand Brunswik's approach, it is first necessary to understand how he classified the variables that enter into psychological research (see Fig. 1). Note that variables are classified in terms of regions relative to an organism. Such "regional reference," as Brunswik called it, is absolutely essential; the analysis, over time, of the relations between regions constitutes his structural history.

Reading from left to right in the upper part of Figure 1 we encounter first *distal* variables. These require definition from a source independent of the behaving organism. Examples of distal variables are sizes of physical bodies, or the measured intelligence or personality traits of a stimulus person. In general, objects provide distal variables, but events or other phenomena may also provide distal variables. Furthermore, as these variables become more remote from the organism, that is, as they become more embedded in time and in layers of the environment, in short, as they become less susceptible to direct measurement, they become more distal in nature. One further distinction: the size of a physical body is an *overt* distal variable because it is susceptible to direct measurement; the intelligence of a person-object is a *covert* distal variable because measurement of it is indirect. Brunswik speaks of "investigating the environment in depth" as one moves from a consideration of overt distal variables to covert distal variables.

Moving to the right, *proximal* variables are defined in terms of physical stimuli impinging on the sensory surface of the organism. As indicated in the same diagram, adjacent to these are *peripheral* variables. These refer to physiological excitation and neural transmission. Brunswik later

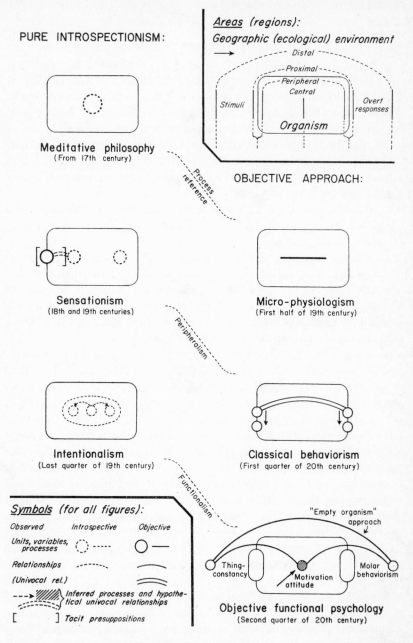

Fig. 1. Major stages of introspective and objective psychology. Reprinted from *The Conceptual Framework of Psychology 1952* by E. Brunswik by permission of the University of Chicago Press.

broadened this concept to include all physiological variables and put all of these under the rubric of *mediators*.

In the center of the diagram is the *central* region. This is the repository for all those hypothetical intraorganismic dispositions and constructs such as motivation, attitude, set, and so forth, that purport to account for and control behavior from the inside. The right hand, or output side of Figure 1 is a mirror image of the left or input side. The peripheral region here refers to the physiological mediators of responses, the proximal region refers to output events on the surface of the skin, and the distal region involves the more or less remote goals that the organism may be seeking to achieve.

With such a classification of variables it becomes possible to ascertain and to describe those regions whose relations to one another come under scrutiny by psychologists during a given period of history, and to locate trends or shifts of emphasis with respect to such relations, as well as to uncover changes in the approaches to their analysis. As Figure 1 illustrates, the analysis of such changes over time makes up Brunswik's structural history. Unfortunately, the full details of his history were never written for publication, and therefore, only the students who listened to Brunswik's lectures will ever appreciate how carefully he wove the particulars of history into a single fabric. Although his monograph "The Conceptual Framework of Psychology" (1952; see also "The Conceptual Focus of Psychological Systems," 1963) contains a certain explication of his history, even here we find what is essentially an outline, indeed, a "framework." In the next few pages we provide merely a paraphrase of Brunswik's manner of looking at the historical development of psychology with respect to psychophysics, Gestalt psychology, and probabilistic functionalism. It is important to observe the emergence of Brunswik's own approach.

Sensory psychology was in at the start of experimental psychology and found a favored position because of its intrinsic tie with micromediational physiologism. Proximal stimulation and peripheral physiological excitation, together with neural transmission formed a basis for scientific research. However, because the "declared core of the classical approach in psychology is structurally to analyze, inventorize, and classify the basic elements of consciousness" (1952, p. 52) a place must therefore be found for consciousness. And it is psychophysics that does so. Brunswik described psychophysics as:

concerned with a functional relation which, although short-arc (see Fig. 2) and thus elementaristic by comparison with later types of research, establishes the principle of studying a gross stimulus-response relationship, while prob-

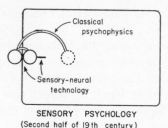

SENSORY   PSYCHOLOGY
(Second half of 19th century)

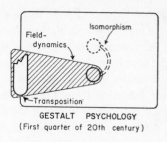

GESTALT   PSYCHOLOGY
(First quarter of 20th century)

Fig. 2. Part-objective stages of experimental psychology. Reprinted from *The Conceptual Framework of Psychology 1952* by E. Brunswik by permission of the University of Chicago Press.

lems of sensory and nervous technology are removed to a secondary position. One of the terms of the relationship, here the response, is conceived of as conscious content, sensation; verbal or other expressive behavior is interpreted as a tool of introspection. The programmatic outlook of psychophysics is thus physicalistic with respect to the stimulus, while it remains mentalistic concerning the response; in short, it proposes to be S-objective, R-subjective. (1952, pp. 52–53.)

Brunswik summed up his reaction to psychophysics by saying that it was "narrowly confined;" because ". . . this type of approach concentrates on relations with the proximal stimulus impact, it does not reach the biologically most relevant layer." And this "most relevant layer," or region, is that of "manipulable and social objects." Psychophysics was, therefore, dismissed by Brunswik as "comparatively insignificant from a functionalist point of view. . . ." (1950, p. 57.)

Brunswik saw Gestalt psychology as taking a step in the direction of the relaxation of the narrow proximal-peripheral focus that characterized psychophysics. He found this freedom from concern with point-for-point proximal-peripheral correspondence to be a step—but only a step—toward the development of a molar psychology. (Brunswik's representation of the emphasis on Gestalt patterning is indicated in Figure 2 by an oval at the proximal-peripheral region—thus indicating the importance of the phenomena of transposition (phenomenal equivalence of "stimulus patterns that possess intrinsic geometric or melodic similarity").) The relaxation of the strictures dealing with stimulus identification at the "skin" was appreciated by Brunswik, but he found Gestalt psychology to be "encapsulated" for Gestalt psychology does not deal with *objects*. As Heider has pointed out, there is an inconsistency in the Gestalt position toward distal determinants of perception. For although "The original program was to make 'meaning' dynamically real and to give a solution to the problem of the coordination of the organism to the object world . . . in the psychology of perception the environmental distal determination is disregarded." (Heider, 1939.) [2]

At this point the reader should be able to anticipate the developing trend of events. If Gestalt psychology refuses "to reach out into the environment," if it refuses to deal with objects, a different approach must attempt to do so. Functionalism does just that; its tradition stems from Darwin, and its main concern is the relation between the organism and its environment—an environment, however, that must be described in terms of distal objects, events, and persons. And *probabilistic* functionalism not only recognizes, but advances to full respectability, the uncertain relations among environmental variables—an uncertainty that requires an organism to employ probabilistic means in order to adapt and thus to survive. In Brunswik's terms, ". . . recent developments in psychology emerge as a combination of the de-emphasis of the peripheral region and the establishment of a central-distal or at least a central frame of reference that takes cognizance of the predominately central-distal focusing of behavior itself." (1952, p. 67.) Just as the distinction between distal and proximal variables led to the concept of environmental *depth,* the recognition of the uncertain relations among environmental variables led to the concept of environmental *texture.*

Probabilistic functionalism, then, is the necessary culmination of psychology and a proper fulfillment of its promise. Both the narrow proximal-peripheral focus of psycho-physics on the input side and narrow focus of classical behaviorism on motor responses on the output side forego too much in the way of scope in their effort to acquire the respectability of rigor. And although Gestalt psychology demonstrated the inutility of considering point-for-point stimulation, it turns toward physiology; Gestalt psychology fails to deal with objects. Brunswik, therefore, urged psychology to expand its framework to include distal-central regions and to place primary emphasis on an object-centered psychology. Thus, he advocated three things: that distal variables embodied in objects and/or persons should be employed in psychological research; that cen-

2. Hochberg emphasizes the tendency of Gestalt psychologists to turn inward in his review of nativism and empiricism in perception as follows: "Most Gestaltists seemed willing to postpone any further application of the organizational laws until investigators could succeed in following the 'law of isomorphism' backward, and from the careful examination of what we see, to understand the underlying principles of physiology." More specifically, "It is also clear that Gestaltists are not free from the classical tendency to refer (and defer) the problems of behavior to speculative underlying physiological mechanisms." (1962, p. 308.)

tral states such as motivation, set, attitude, or personality characteristics should be varied; and that distal effects such as goal achievement should be observed. And here at last we find those "wide-arched dependencies," (see Fig. 1) which Brunswik found to be the ultimate source of problems for psychology—the dependencies between distal causes and distal effects. As a corollary, it will be noted that the study of mediational problems, which captured the enthusiasm of the Gestalt psychologists, should be postponed.

Summary

Ours, of course, has been merely the sketchiest description of what Brunswik pursued with vigor and in complete detail. What is to be observed here, however, is the historical unfolding of a general line of development that necessarily proceeds toward probabilistic functionalism. It seems fair to say that no other modern psychologist struggled so hard to find the historical roots of a point of view, and that no other psychologist sought so earnestly to develop his conceptual framework from his historical analysis. Finally, as we shall see, Brunswik's theoretical and historical analyses compelled him to inquire into the most fundamental aspect of scientific psychology—its experimental method.

CONCEPTUAL FRAMEWORK

The first point to be emphasized in connection with Brunswik's conceptual framework is that he did indeed present a comprehensive theory of behavior. It may appear strange that this point needs to be made, but it does, for many psychologists appear to believe that Brunswik offered a methodology, but not a theory. Consequently, his methodological arguments were criticized in isolation from his theoretical aims. And, quite naturally, his methodological position failed to be understood when he introduced it, and fails to be understood today. One finds few, if any, critical discussions of Brunswik's methodology in relation to his theory of probabilistic functionalism; the few criticisms of his unorthodox methodological suggestions that one does find are made in terms of orthodox theoretical aims.

This unfortunate state of affairs seems to have occurred because Brunswik's principal theoretical work was written in difficult German before he came to the United States, (Brunswik, 1934) [3] and has been

3. An excerpt from this book, translated by Lewis Brandt, is provided in Chapter 18 so that the reader may learn how Brunswik thought about certain fundamental issues prior to the development of his methodological suggestions. This is the only translation made so far of any of Brunswik's publications in German.

largely unknown by Americans. The first presentation in English of Brunswik's theoretical views appeared in the joint paper with Tolman (published in the *Psychological Review* in 1935 and reprinted in this volume). This paper is important, for it shows (despite Tolman's fluid prose and Brunswik's formidable German neologisms) the parallel development of their ideas. Also, a digest of Brunswik's theoretical position was presented in "Psychology as a science of objective relations." (1937; reprinted in Marx, 1951.) Brunswik refers to this paper as a "short outline of the more general considerations" set forth in his 1934 book. Significantly, no mention of methodological issues is made in either paper.

Brunswik's concern about methodology apparently began shortly after he came to America, probably about 1937.[4] And his first call for a revision of methodological orthodoxy was presented in the 1941 Symposium with Hull and Lewin (Brunswik, 1943). In this paper Brunswik dwelt on the question of the nature of the environment to a considerable extent and explained that he did so ". . . because I believe that the probability character of the causal (partial cause-and-effect) relationships in the environment calls for a fundamental, all-inclusive shift in our methodological ideology regarding psychology." (1943, p. 261.) With this remark Brunswik became the first probability theorist in modern psychology as well as the first psychologist to challenge the precepts of orthodox experimental design.

The failure to recognize that Brunswik's methodological heresy stems from his theoretical position has led to unfortunate criticism of his methodology—unfortunate because it fails to consider Brunswik's derivation of method from theory. Method and theory in Brunswik's system are logically and *explicitly* linked, as we shall see. And, we cannot help but note, psychological theory, in the main, has been *implicitly* based upon conventional views about what constitutes appropriate methodology. Ironically enough, the failure to recognize Brunswik's theory led to criticism of him for putting method before theory, whereas in actuality it is conventional psychology that has done this from the start.

Brunswik's theoretical approach is best introduced by a reminder of what he considered psychology's task to be—the analysis of the interrelation between two systems, *the environment* and *the behaving subject.* The importance of this definition of purpose must not be glossed over because of its large generality, however, for it has major and concrete

4. The author recalls that in 1946 Brunswik remarked to him that he first saw fundamental methodological problems in psychology after he had presented a paper to a faculty seminar at Berkeley shortly after his arrival there.

implications for both theoretical program and subsequent methodological task.

One way to grasp the importance of this point of departure is to notice what psychologists consider their domain of investigation should properly be. The orthodox approach is to look at the organism with the aim of discovering the laws that govern its behavior. Ordinarily, we take the organism as given, speculate about its nature, and then devise ways and means of getting into contact with it so as to decide on the correctness of our speculations. And, of course, we "get into contact" with the organism by giving it a test or devising an experiment. Whatever the technique used, two criteria must be met: (1) the technique must be adequately scientific; and (2) it must test our speculations about the organism. It should be noted that just that fraction of the environment necessary to test our speculations about the organism is brought to the investigation.

Brunswik, however, urged that the task of the psychologist should include both theoretical and empirical research concerning the environment, and that the parts of the environment that are brought to the investigation must be as relevant to environmental theory as the parts of the organism that are brought to the experiment are relevant to organismic theory. That is why he said, ". . . much as psychology must be concerned with the texture of the organism or of its nervous processes and must investigate them in depth, it must also be concerned with the texture of the environment as it extends in depth. . . ." (1957, p. 5.)

But considering organisms in depth has become virtually habitual with psychologists; only a few fail to construct hypothetical variables within the organism to account for observable behavior. Research is carried out by bringing highly organized, albeit fragmented, parts of the environment to the subject—whether these be Rorschach-blot cards brought to the clinic patient or white-black cards brought to the laboratory rat—in order to test the explanatory power of the unobservable construct. Carefully-woven speculations about what goes on inside both patient and rat, however, are confronted by not-so-carefully unwoven strands from the environment. That is what Brunswik meant when he said, "Both historically and systematically, psychology has forgotten that it is a science of organism-environment relationships, and has become a science of the organism." (1957, p. 6.) He was expressing regret that psychologists had become preoccupied with the organism, were failing to give thought to the nature of the organism's environment, and, as a consequence, were failing to achieve sufficient generality for their findings.

Psychologists were failing to achieve the generality they wanted, for two reasons: (1) psychologists were confronting organismic theories with arbitrarily extracted fractions of the environment; this led to results that were highly contingent upon the arbitrary character of the stimulus arrangements; and (2) psychologists were employing a "double standard" in their application of the criteria for safe inductive inferences; for although adequate sampling was acknowledged to be mandatory for inductive generalization to subjects other than those used in the experiment, all statistical logic about sampling was cast aside when it came to generalizing about stimulus presentations. Brunswik tried to call the attention of psychologists to this double standard on sheer technical grounds when he pointed out that "generalizability of results concerning . . . the variables involved (and here he meant environmental variables) must remain limited unless at least the range, but better also the distribution . . . of each variable, has been made representative of a carefully defined universe of conditions." (1956, p. 55.) [5] Indeed, his book on *Perception and the Representative Design of Psychological Experiments* is a detailed explication of the technical issues involved in the making of safe inductive generalizations with respect to the environment as well as to subjects.

Later we shall deal with Brunswik's methodological suggestions. At this point we turn to the more important issue that Brunswik was trying to bring within the scope of psychology; that issue is environmental conceptualization, the problem of how the environment as well as the organism is organized in depth.

The Nature of the Environment

In order to see how this problem becomes important we must first note that experimental psychologists typically define environmental presentations in terms of data that lie on the surface of the physical world. That is, they typically define stimulus presentations in terms of the physical operations used to measure stimuli; for example, "a line eight inches long . . . ." And all arrangements or displays of such stimuli are made with two things in mind: (1) the requirements of experimental design; and (2) the theory of organismic behavior to be tested. What is not kept in mind, however, in fact, what is given no consideration whatever, is the question of *what relation the stimulus arrangement has to the distal objects in the ecology in which the organism has evolved and to which it has adapted.*

As we shall see below, it has become increasingly clear that organisms

5. This is the core of his methodology and explains why he called his methodological approach "representative design." The word "representative" refers to the environment.

must behave in relation to objects and object-properties in their environment, not in relation to isolated proximal data. Not only had research made this clear, but, Brunswik argued, if organisms did react to momentary proximal stimulus events they would be at the mercy of a semierratic environment. This observation raises a question: What is the relation between the nondirectly-observable properties of distal objects (to which organisms react) and the proximal data produced by these objects? Conceptualization of this relation is a primitive step; it is a necessary and fundamental one, however, for unless it is taken, psychologists will continue to be theoretically capricious about the form in which they present the stimulus arrangements of their experiments to their subjects. Another way to say this is that without such conceptualization they will continue to be arbitrary in the way in which they *simulate* the environment. (See Barker and Crow, this volume, for research involving this point.)

Brunswik's first step toward a conceptualization of the environment was to make a clear distinction between the surface of the environment and its depth. He urged that we address ourselves first to the question of the relation between the distal layers of the environment and their proximal counterparts. His position with respect to this relation is as clear as it is fundamental—the relation between distal variables and proximal data, or proximal *cues,* is a fallible, uncertain relation. Both the physical and social world of distal objects provide an irregular, less than completely dependable system of offshoots; "nature scatters its effects . . . irregularly." Thus, "the most important feature of the general relationship between distal and proximal stimulus variables is its lack of univocality." (1943, p. 256.)

For example:

Firstly, there is ambiguity from cause to effects. Inventories of possible "cues for third-dimensional distance" have been compiled from the beginning of psychological inquiry. Current textbooks list something like ten depth criteria, such as binocular parallex, convergence of the eye axes, accommodation, linear and angular perspective, interception of far objects by near objects, atmospheric effects, number of in-between objects, vertical position. The list could be extended considerably further. The necessity for becoming so involved derives from the fact that none of these proximal variables can be considered *the* distance cue in the sense of an effect which could be present without exception wherever the distal condition should obtain. Some of the cues will more often, others less often, be present, depending on circumstances. . . . (1943, p. 256.)

Let us examine the matter of cues more closely. In order for the organism to perceive correctly (that is, to achieve) the intended object, the organism must have information about it. Information is provided by stimulation at the proximal layer; a stimulus in this region is referred to as a sensory *cue*. Such cues are the physical stimuli impinging on the surface of the organism. But they are more than that. They are *local signs* that have a referent in the world of objects. Put otherwise, proximal stimuli are *local representatives* of distal objects or distal variables.

"By means of such local representatives the organism comes to operate in the presence of the local representative in a manner more or less appropriate to the fact of a more distant object or situation, that is, the *entity represented*." (Tolman and Brunswik, 1935, p. 43.) The proximal stimulus, then, is a local representative that provides only a "hint" in an uncertain situation as to the nature of the object.

Not only must the organism have information in order to achieve the distal object, it must have a means for achieving its goals. It is at this point that Brunswik and Tolman complement one another. Their joint paper, written while Tolman was staying in Vienna, describes their discovery of mutual views concerning the over-all nature of behavior-environment interaction despite the fact that Brunswik had concerned himself almost entirely with perception and Tolman with learning. Brunswik had emphasized the equivocal nature of cues, Tolman had emphasized the equivocal nature of environmental means-objects with respect to ends.

It appears also that, whereas one of us, Tolman, was led to emphasize these two facts of *local representation* and of *equivocality* by a study of the relations of *means-objects* to *ends* in the learning activity of rats, the other, Brunswik, was led to emphasize those same concepts as a result of an examination of the relation of *stimulus-cues* or *signs* to *Gegenstände* (distal variables) as a result of a study of the relations involved in the constancy phenomenon in human perception.

We observe animals making and using tools, entering paths, ingesting food, avoiding dangerous objects, and the like. But in each case the tools, the paths, the foods, the dangerous objects are behaved to only because of their role as means-objects. They are behaved to, that is, in their roles as the most probable "local representatives" whereby to reach or avoid such and such more ultimate, "represented" positive or negative, goals. For it is the reaching or avoiding of these more distant represented goals which are of the final importance to the organism. And further, we also observe these same animals, responding selectively, (and perhaps in the ordinary case relatively correctly), to immediate entities (for example, the detailed structure of light-wave bundles, and the like) in their turn, as the most probable local representatives, that is, cues, for such tools, paths, foods, dangerous objects, and so forth. And here, also, it is the character of these more distant "represented" objects which has the greater determining significance for the organism. Light-wave bundles, and the like, are to be correctly selected as the most probable local representatives, that is, as cues, for such and such object-characters, just as the latter must themselves be correctly selected as the best local representatives (that is, as means-objects) for the finally to-be-reached or to-be-avoided goals. Without the ability to rely on these two successive types of local representation no higher forms of organism could have developed and successfully survived. (Tolman and Brunswik, 1935, p. 44.)

Because cues (and means-objects) have an equivocal (or as Brunswik later put it, *probabilistic*) relation to the object intended, it follows that this relation should be described in terms that permit quantitative measures of the degree of relationship. Brunswik employed the correlation coefficient for this purpose, and the correlation between distal and proximal variables describes the *ecological validity* of the cue. Thus,

Any fairly consistent rapport, be it intuitively perceptual or explicitly rational, with distal layers of the environment presupposes the existence of proximal sensory cues of some degree of ecological validity to serve as mediators of that relationship. (1956, p. 48.)

Brunswik went to considerable pains to measure the ecological validity of various distance cues under conditions representative of human ecology. His book *Perception and the Representative Design of Experiments* (1956) summarizes his experimental work on this problem and illustrates the ecological validity of various cues to distance in the normal unrestricted ecology of humans. For example:

Preliminary results . . . suggest the following ecological validities, that is, correlations of the real distances in the situation photographed . . . with the actual location, color, and so forth, of their projectures in the photographs.

About .6 (later revised to .4) for the cue of "vertical position," that is, for the probability of greater real distance for objects appearing higher up in the picture.

About .4 (later revised to .2) for "filling of space" (measured by the number of items, that is, distinguishable steps, between the projection of two objects), more items between objects being associated with greater differences in real depth.

About .2 (later revised to .4) for color (that is, on the achromatic pictures used, the local brightness of a spot) greater brightness increasing the chances of greater real distance—as would blue versus red. (1956, p. 49; see also p. 123.)

Brunswik was almost alone during the 1940's in his emphasis on the need for conceptual and empirical analyses of the environment. Except for the mutual recognition of the parallels between Brunswik's position and that of Tolman's, Heider was the only theoretical psychologist to come to grips with the vagaries of the relation between object and cue.

Note how Heider describes in almost poetic terms the problem of environmental conceptualization:

A certain arrangement of stimuli, of cues, can help us very much in perceiving the general meaning of an event or structure. In some cases it is very hard to see this general meaning. We don't see anything beyond the superficial layer—the skin, so to speak. (Note that Heider is referring to the "skin of the world" here, not to the skin of the organism—Ed.) In other cases we seem to see right through to deeper layers, and I think it is not chance that the movements of the planets or the free fall were the points where a more rigidly systematic physics started. These are the points where the laws of gravity show through on the surface. It is as if some of the skeleton of nature were exposed at certain points where we can have access to the underlying generalities more or less directly. In psychology, the subject matter is structured in such a way that the generalities are very deep, buried in the ground, so that some people merely give up digging and say, "Let's stay on the ground." (1957, p. 73. See also (1958, 1959) for a full presentation of Heider's views.)

Brunswik always made a point of acknowledging and underscoring Heider's (1939) thoughtful analysis of the ambiguous relation between "thing and medium." Heider, furthermore, made the lack of univocality between object and cue a cornerstone of his own major contribution concerning the psychology of interpersonal relations. Thus, for example, in his conclusion he says:

We started out with the observation that the person is located in a complicated causal network of the environment. It is useful to distinguish two parts within this network: on the one hand, the mediation, the part that is close to the skin of the organism, comprising the proximal stimuli which impinge on the organism . . .; on the other hand the distal environment made up of the vitally relevant persons and things. The person is separated . . . from the contents of the distal environment [by] the *variable manifold* [italics ours] of mediating events. (1958, p. 296.)

It was the mutual recognition of vicarious mediation between distal and proximal layers of the environment that led Brunswik and Tolman to use the title "Causal texture of the environment" for their joint paper. The environment has *texture* because it is not clear-cut; it is not merely a series of hard and fast one-to-one relations. Rather, the environment involved partial causes and partial effects in its own ecological relations, independent of the behaving organism. That is, not only are there less-than-perfect relations between distal object and proximal cues, but correlations of less than one between various cues for the same object. The term "ecological validity" refers to the correlation between proximal cue and distal object; "intra-ecological correlation" refers to the relation between various features (cues) of the environment. If the intra-ecological correlations between the cues for a given object are high, the environment is *redundant* with respect to the object in question.

Note that studies of the texture of the environment do not involve or require a *subject*. Research without subjects will undoubtedly seem to be a strange sort of psychological research, but we must remember that the task of psychology is to understand the interaction of *two* systems—the environment and the organism, and we must, therefore, concern ourselves with the dynamics peculiar to each. It is for this reason Section XVI in Brunswik's 1956 book is entitled "Textural Ecology as a Propaedeutic to Functional Psychology." Here, of course, we find studies that are concerned with ecological validity only. "Since they deal with interrelationships among external variables which have to do with the causal texture of the environment, they may be labeled studies in textural ecology." And organisms' responses must be "totally ignored" (1956, p. 119), in such studies (one of which is described below, see p. 32).

Suppose, however, that studies of the ecology that do not include subjects are carried out. How can such studies possibly be of interest to psychologists? Brunswik's answer is in the following context:

One of the comparatively neglected tasks of a molar environmental psychology is to find out the extent to which environmental hierarchies of probabilities of object-cue as well as means-end relationships do find a counterpart in similar hierarchies of evaluation by the organism. . . . We shall discuss the question of the significance of such a "counterpart" below.[6]

First, we must see that to be able to study the relation between "environmental hierarchies of probabilities of object-cue as well as means-end relationships" would require that

. . . the environmental probabilities be first ascertained for all of the cues or means involved, with say, the "normal" life conditions of the organism taken as the defining reference class. This part of the research would be strictly environmental and preparatory in character and would not involve any reference to organismic reaction. Very little has been done thus far in the direction of such an environmental analysis. (1943, p. 259.)

With the exception of Roger Barker's work (see chapter 9, this volume) little was done in the intervening twenty years. For as Gibson observed:

6. Certain of Brunswik's theoretical considerations relating the texture of the environment to the form of the organism's processes are of interest to probability theorists. For example, the question of whether environmental probabilities find a "counterpart," that is, are matched, in the organism's probabilities preoccupied statistical learning theorists during the '50's.

The problem of the connection between stimuli and their natural sources has not been taken seriously by psychologists. Stimuli have not even been classi- fied from this point of view, but only with respect to the sense organs and the types of energy which carry stimuli. It is a problem of ecology, as Brunswik realized when he wrote about the "ecological validity" of cues. (1960, p. 699.)

Environmental research and theory-testing ecological analyses, then, are primary (Brunswik's term is "propaedeutic"). Moreover, studies of the ecology without a subject are fundamental because they describe the nature of the environment and provide hypotheses as to the nature of the organisms that have adapted to it. Brunswik felt that it was clear enough that vicarious mediation, that is, intersubstitutability of cues in the environment, is a fact of Nature. And his research with Kamiya on the ecological validity of the Gestalt factor of "proximity" provides an example of how theoretical issues can be confronted by such propaedeutic studies. We now turn to a discussion of this example in order to show that Brunswik's aims were indeed theoretical ones, and not, as some critics have claimed, merely empirical ones. The research to be described contests the nativistic Gestalt theory of perception.

Brunswik's interpretation of the Gestalt position was that it implied that the effectiveness of such factors as proximity in organizing sensory data into percepts "rests on dynamic processes inherent in the brain field. . . ." Such factors ". . . are a condition for—rather than a result of —learning." (1953.) According to a functionalist view, however, factors such as proximity are cues to object-character, that is, they are environ- mental "guides to the life-relevant physical properties of the more remote physical objects." Note that the Gestalt psychologists begin with a stimu- lus configuration and carry it *inward*—beneath the skin of the subject, so to speak—whereas Brunswik carries the investigation *outward*. Thus, "Our aim is to take the guesswork out of the ascertainment of (environ- mental) frequency relations. . . . This is to make up for the resistance intrinsic to Gestalt psychology, against extrapolations into the 'causally remote strata' on the basis of probabilistic cue validity." (1953.)

The next two paragraphs from the Brunswik-Kamiya study are re- produced in full to show his insistence on the necessity for adequate empirical analyses of the "connection between stimuli and their natural sources" as Gibson put it.

Any study of ecological validity can be no more than propaedeutic to psy- chology; concern is limited to a survey of statistical relations among variables as typical of the natural or cultural habitat of an individual or group while the question of the actual utilization of cues or of other aspects of organismic response is left untouched. In short, such studies deal with *potential* cues, not with cues actually employed. Yet ecological surveys are indispensable not only for an understanding and appraisal of responses but, as is especially true in our particular case, *for general problems in psychological theorizing as well* [italics ours].

There can be no doubt that the ecological validity of the Gestalt factors, when seen as potential perceptual cues, could likewise be of no more than very limited value. In part perhaps for this reason, but certainly at least in part by virtue of their predilection for dynamic rather than learning-type explanations, Gestalt psychologists were prone to brush aside suggestions of "generalized experience" as the possible source of the laws of perceptual organization. Thus they were pointing out that there are "in nature . . . *fully as many* obtuse and acute angles . . . (for example, branches of trees)" as there are right angles [Brunswik quoting Wertheimer]. This statement was made to explain preference for rectangularity as a *prägnant* form of organization. Or they were pointing out that "my general experience is that, *as often as not,* similar members of a group are movable, and move, independently" [Brunswik quoting Köhler]. "This is a broad presentation of similarity proximity, and other organizational factors as allegedly autochthonous principles. In effect, statements of this kind atomize reality by playing down regularity in our surroundings or by asserting ecological zero correlations." (1953, p. 21.)

It is very likely that Brunswik undertook this research because these specific statements about the environment by Wertheimer and Köhler were casual observations unsupported by evidence. And these statements are what led him to say, "Our aim is to take the guesswork out of the ascertainment of (environmental) frequency relations. . . ." (1953.)

The problem, then is to discover whether proximity contributes to the organizing process of perception quite independently of environmental "frequency relations" as the Gestalt psychologists would have it, or whether, in a sample of conditions representative of our ecology, proximity is a cue that *could* provide a basis for probabilistic inferences about the "mechanical coherence" of objects. Put otherwise, is there a relation between the proximity or "nearness" of parallel lines and the probability that these lines bind a mechanical object? To what extent is proximity a dependable cue to mechanical coherence? After examining a sample of 892 pairs of parallel lines, taken from pictures (see Hochberg, this volume, for a discussion of this point) the answer is that there is a point biserial correlation of $\pm.34$, (which is modified by certain conditions). In short, Brunswik argued, proximity *is* a potential cue to mechanical coherence, and, he argues, Wertheimer and Köhler were wrong when they asserted, in effect, that the environmental correlation between proximity and object character was zero.

But this ecological research demonstrates only that the cue is of *potential* use. The question now arises—to what extent is proximity actually utilized by various organisms? Brunswik assumed that good adjustment would require that the functional validity of the cue for the organism be approximately the same as its ecological validity. (Note again his assumption of "matching" behavior.) That is, the organism should utilize the cue to whatever extent it is ecologically valid or useful, if the organism is to make a successful inference. It is at this point that subjects will be required for research.

He wrote:

The successful demonstration . . . of the ecological validity of a Gestalt-factor does not automatically imply the legitimacy of its interpretation as a learned cue. It merely shows that an objective basis for probability learning is offered the individual within the framework chosen. Since, however, all ecological validities represent a challenge to the organism for utilization, and since probably many cues are actually being utilized roughly in proportion to the degree of their validity, our findings lend plausibility-support to the reinterpretation of proximity as a cue acquired by generalized probability learning. If this should become possible for other Gestalt factors also, they could all be seen as externally imposed upon, rather than innately intrinsic to, the processes in the brain; they would then appear as functionally useful rather than as whimsically autochthonous." (1953.) [7]

It is important to observe from the foregoing not only what Brunswik meant by the analysis of "the environment as it extends in depth . . ." and "the relation between the distal layers of the environment and their proximal counterparts," but also the part that such *representative* ecological analyses play in relation to theoretical questions. Some psychologists and philosophers have assumed that Brunswik's insistence on environmental studies proves that he was a Baconian empiricist—interested only in enormous sampling operations—the entire focus of which is merely adequate sampling. On the contrary, Brunswik saw representative ecological studies such as the one just described as "indispensable for . . . general problems in psychological theorizing."

In summary, Brunswik developed a conception of the nature of the environment available to the behaving subject; he had a far more differentiated view of the organism's ecology and a far greater recognition of the need for the theoretical and empirical analysis of the environment than any of his contemporaries, with the exception of Heider. It is

7. It is worth noting how his next comment brings him close to the ethologists: "It goes without saying that such an interpretation would lose much of its cogency if it would turn out that proximity has similar organizing effects in individuals, groups or species in whose habitat or culture it has no (or opposite) ecological validity." (1953.) See Campbell (1964) for a Brunswikian analysis of cultural differences in the Müller-Lyer illusion.

instructive to note how one psychologist reacted to Brunswik's emphasis on the necessity for ecological studies. Osgood, in commenting upon Brunswik's paper in the Colorado Symposium on Cognition, remarks:

My last point concerns Brunswik's early statement that "if there is anything that ails psychology," it is the neglect of investigations of ecological or environmental structure. I think I know the cause of this ailment. It is simply that psychologists have not as yet solved the problem of the *descriptive units* of their science—*in fact, they haven't worried about it much* . . . [italics ours] (1957, p. 38.)

Worrying about the description of environmental systems was precisely what led Brunswik to develop a network of concepts such as vicarious mediation and ecological validity, and eventually led to his insistence on research procedures which permitted adequate description and representation of the organism's environment.

Before leaving this point, it should be observed that psychology may no longer be able to afford the luxury of ignoring the environment. Ashby points out that in the effort to develop computer simulations of cognitive processes the problem of the environment must be faced:

This type of analysis *forced* a recognition that to model an organism that would adapt to an environment implied that one must also *model an environment*—the situation is meaningless, otherwise. Here the modelmaker must seriously consider what sort of an environment he is thinking of, whether it is properly representative of some biological environment, and if not, of exactly which set of environments it *is* representative. Hence, it is true to say that today we not only understand better what is meant by "brainlike," but we can also see more clearly the peculiar and pervading features of the world we live in—the world that has imposed so many special characteristics on the creatures that have evolved in it. (1962, p. 457.)

These remarks certainly vindicate Brunswik's concern about the proper representation of the organism's environment, voiced twenty years earlier.

The Nature of the Organism

Brunswik's view of the organism derives directly from his conception of the environment, for the environment is historically and logically prior. Having developed the rudiments of a conceptual system for describing the environment, the next task is to derive from these the nature of adaptation and survival, and to determine what it should signify for a theory of the organism. Brunswik's derivation is quite clear:

Survival and its subunits, which may be defined as the establishment of stable interrelationships with the environment, are possible only if the organism is able to establish compensatory balance in the face of comparative chaos in the physical environment. Ambiguity of cues and means relative to the vitally relevant object and results must find its counterpart in an ambiguity and flexibility of the proximal-peripheral mediatory processes in the organism. (1943, p. 258.)

Why must the ambiguity of the environment "find its counterpart in an ambiguity and flexibility" at the proximal-peripheral layer of the organism? Because although the environment may be controlled by strict universal law, it *hides* its lawfulness behind a semierratic medium of probabilistic cue-object relations. Therefore, higher organisms must have sufficient flexibility in their proximal-peripheral mediational processes to cope with such ambiguity between cause and effect. Because "nature scatters its effects irregularly," the organism must insure its survival by achieving stable relations with the hidden regularities of a lawful world. It achieves such stable relations by means of a perceptual apparatus that weights environmental cues according to their probable association with the distal variable, and by weighting environmental means according to their probable association with success. As Brunswik put it:

The universal lawfulness of the world is of limited comfort to the perceiver or behaver not in a position to apply these laws, and he therefore must rely largely on whatever snitches of particular or semigeneralized information he may be able to assemble. This is what we meant . . . by the assertion that ordinarily organisms must behave as if in a semierratic ecology. (1955 (b), p. 209.)

Given access to unstable, changing, in a word, probabilistic, rather than completely determined sets of cue-object relations, we therefore expect to find the organism also to be probabilistic at the proximal-peripheral layer. Because "nature scatters its effects irregularly" the surviving organism adapts to the irregularity of Nature's *effects;* but the organism is also able to establish "stable interrelationships with the environment"—more specifically, stable interrelationships with Nature's *causes,* that is, variables in the distal region. The fact that the organism manages to achieve such stable relationships with the distal layer "in the face of comparative chaos" at the proximal-peripheral boundary is a key problem for psychology. It is best illustrated by the problem of the constancies, which Brunswik perceived to be the empirical cornerstone of the study of behavior. As Osgood puts it, "Constancy has fundamental biological significance: it is to particular objects (food, enemies, implements, possessions) that the organism must react, not to momentary stimulus qualities." (1953, p. 271.)

Reacting to objects, then, is what organisms do. Put otherwise, behavior focuses on objects, not proximal data. And, as Brunswik liked to say, "Research should focus where behavior focuses." In one of Brunswik's major papers entitled "Organismic Achievement and Environmental Probability," he addresses himself to this issue:

The point I should like to emphasize especially in this connection is the necessary imperfection, inflicted upon achievements—as relations between classes—by the ambiguity in the causal texture of the environment, which remains apparent as long as single variables, that is partial causes and partial effects, are considered under otherwise not specifically controlled conditions. Because of this environmental ambiguity, no matter how smoothly the organismic instruments and mechanisms may function, relationships cannot be foolproof, at least as far as those connecting with the vitally relevant more remote distal regions of the environment are concerned. This intrinsic lack of perfection, that is of univocality, will on the whole be the greater the more wide-spanning the relationships involved are. The only way in which perfection could be secured would be by control over all the remaining conditions which could possibly become relevant in the given case. This however is something the reacting organism cannot do for lack of time if not for other more serious reasons—and thus something which the psychologist who wishes to catch and rationally to reconstruct organismic adjustments at large, with all of its faults and fallacies, should also not do. All a finite, sub-divine individual can do when acting is—to use a term of Reichenbach—to make a posit, or wager. The best he can do is to compromise between cues so that his posit approaches the "best bet" on the basis of all the probabilities, or past relative frequencies, of relevant interrelationships lumped together. (1943, p. 258.)

Perhaps the best way to see how Brunswik theorized about the way in which the organism copes with the ambiguity of the causal texture of the environment is to consider three of his main ideas: *vicarious functioning, the lens model,* and *compromise.*

Vicarious functioning

In an ecology "that is of essence only partly accessible to . . . foresight," an ecology that provides intersubstitutable, uncertain cues to objects, we should expect to find organisms that cope with such an ecology by a complementary system of vicarious mediation, or better, vicarious functioning. And, Brunswik argues, the empirical facts of molar psychology all point in this direction (that is, insofar as our restricted experimental methods will permit such findings to emerge). The *one-many* relation, rather, than the *one-to-one* relation is, as far as Brunswik was concerned, an empirical regularity, an empirical block upon which a science of molar behavior must build. Feigl endorsed this point of departure with these remarks (1955, p. 232): "The mutual substitutability ('vicarious functioning') of the mediating processes in organisms is indeed a striking feature. Biological thinking has borne its imprint for a long time." [8]

The scattering of effects in the environment is matched by the principle of vicarious functioning in the organism. Indeed, Brunswik repeatedly referred to vicariousness (both with respect to cue-object relations and means-end relations) as the "foremost objective criterion of behavioral purposiveness" (1956, p. 93) and noted with approval that Hunter had much earlier "elevated vicarious functioning to the role of the defining criterion of the subject matter of psychology." (1952, p. 17.) Organisms, then, find a counterpart to the vicarious mediation of a "semierratic" environmental medium by means of vicarious functioning.

The lens model

Because the data received via the various intersubstitutable receptor functions must be combined, or "recollected" by the organism, the entire process from distal causes to central effect can be represented by the manner in which a convex lens functions. As a result Brunswik referred to his theory as a "lens model" of behavior.[9] (See Fig. 3.) The distal cause in the environment scatters its effects and the organism "re-combines" them.

The general pattern of the mediational strategy of the organism is predicated upon the limited ecological validity or trustworthiness of cues. . . . This forces a probabilistic strategy upon the organism. To improve its bet, it must accumulate and combine cues. . . . Hence the lens-like model . . . which may be taken to represent the basic unit of psychological functioning. (1955(a), p. 297.)

In 1943 Brunswik had indicated that the response of the organism was based on "past relative frequencies of interrelationships *lumped* together." [italics ours—Ed.] (1943, p. 258.) By 1955, however, he had

8. Brunswik frequently noted with regret the decreasing role of the "habit-family-hierarchy" concept in Hull's work because of its clear relation to vicarious functioning. (See Brunswik, 1952, p. 82.) Leeper expressed the same regret: ". . . we psychologists have neglected the processes that permit an individual to express the same underlying motives in quite divergent ways—even sometimes in seemingly opposite ways—under different circumstances. Among the stimulus-response or *S-R* psychologists, Hull's concept of habit-family-hierarchies is a partial attempt to explain such cases. But, this concept has been virtually unmentioned by Hull's group ever since it was first proposed in 1934." (1951, p. 38.) When dealing with the complexities of human behavior in the late '50's, however, it was evidently necessary for *S-R* theorists to bring this concept to life.

9. Evidently Brunswik was among the first model-builders of the twentieth century.

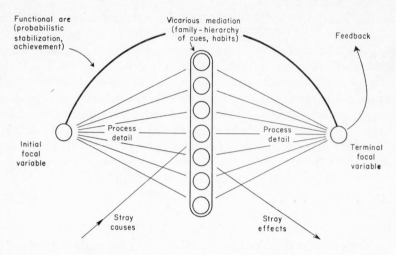

Fig. 3. The lens model: Composite picture of the functional unit of behavior. Reprinted from *The Conceptual Framework of Psychology 1952* by E. Brunswik by permission of the University of Chicago Press.

coined the term "ratiomorphic" to represent the organism's process of coordinating uncertain data in order to make an inductive inference from them. Perception is a ". . . ratiomorphic subsystem of cognition. . . ." The process is, in other words, "reasoning-like." A more specific suggestion was that the organism behaved much like an "intuitive statistician." (1956, p. 80; see Peterson and Miller, 1964, for a study of man as an intuitive statistician;) had Brunswik lived five years longer, he surely would have had much to say about the use of mathematical models and computers to simulate the organism's ratiomorphic processes.

Even in 1952, he was alert to the analogies between cybernetics and probabilistic functionalism, as well as to the relation between Shannon and Weaver's telecommunication theory and his own point of view. Thus,

. . . vicarious functioning of psychological cues and means may be viewed as a special case of receiving or sending messages through redundant, repetitive channels, thus reducing the probability of errors, that is, the set of possible causes, or effects, that could result in, or be reproduced by, the type of event in question. Vicarious functioning is thus indeed the essence of behavior. (1952, pp. 91–92.)

We shall have more to say about Brunswik's conceptions of the ratiomorphic process below. Before doing so, however, we must pause to note that toward the end of his life Brunswik began to see that his colleagues believed his system to be methodological rather than theoretical in nature. He rose to the defense of the lens model at the 1953 Unity of Science meetings with a vigorous statement in which he made it clear that he felt that his colleagues had failed to see the theoretical nature of the lens model. First he pointed out that present connotations of the concept of "theory" are too narrow, and then he proceeded to argue that the lens model did in fact meet the requirements of theory.

We must include within the scope of theory proper the substantive part of functional considerations also, involving primarily the structure of the lens model as a ratiomorphic explication of achievement rather than merely its reduction to physiology or physics. This model involves focal points, areas of unspecificity, mechanisms of substitutions, and other devices of multiple mediation. When Feigl demands generality of theory, the lens model has it; in fact, the very essence of generalized achievement is incorporated within it, and it can be transported from perception to action and other psychological functions. It even may be used for "explanation" in the sense of subsuming a single act under a generalized "wish," ascertained by the probabilistic application of operational criteria of "purposiveness" such as those of Tolman. The lens model also has productivity: predictions concerning the efficiency and foolproofness of functional attainment, concerning other areas or dimensions of the ecology, and so forth, may be "derived" from it, and the probabilistic character of these derivations should not detract from the potential rigor and objectivity of the procedures involved (1955(b), pp. 237–238.)

The lens model, then, was the fundamental, theoretical basis of Brunswik's position.

Compromise

Although his defense of the theoretical capacity of the lens model did not include a reference to the principle of *compromise* (attributed by Brunswik to Hering; see also Thouless (1931)), this was an important aspect of his theory.

Brunswik measured the potential ecological validity of a cue in terms of the relative frequency of its association with a distal variable and measured the functional validity of the cue in terms of the relative frequency of its association with a response. Since relative frequency plays such an important role here, it is fair to ask at this point whether Brunswik was an associationist. The answer is: yes and no. Yes, in the sense that the relative frequencies of association between cue and distal variable form the basic information available to the organism and lead directly to the weights attached to a cue. No, because different relative frequencies pull the organism's response in different directions—the principle of compromise must also be involved.

Brunswik's experimental work on size constancy led him to focus on this principle. It is apparent that there are at least two sets of determiners of the subject's attainment of the correct bodily size of an object: (a) proximal data, for example, retinal size, and (b) object size. Although size constancy is the rule over a wide variety of conditions, it does not reach perfection—the subject's estimation of the physical size of a body forms a compromise between the two sets of determiners.

The principal aim of Brunswik's study of size constancy (1944), which was carried out over a representative sample of a subject's ecology, was generalizability of this principle. The results were convincing—at least to Brunswik. As he put it: "The ecological applicability . . . of the principle of perceptual compromise has thus been adequately demonstrated." (1956, p. 48.) The compromise principle was not intended to be limited to size constancy, however. In that area, Brunswik thought of it ". . . as primordial as any theoretical principle in psychology proper is ever apt to become." (1951, p. 215.) The question of its extension to other areas remains, but positive evidence was obtained, and a considerable portion of his final work (1956) is devoted to documentation of this principle. The perceptual compromise between object-size and object-value provides an example.

In Brunswik's early work in Vienna on the perception of stamps, and with Fazil in Ankara on the perception of coins (see also Ansbacher's 1937 study on the perception of stamps), one set of determiners is object *size,* and the other set is object *value*—thus providing a forerunner to the work of Bruner and Postman in the 1950's that precipitated a rash of studies on the perception of coins and a theoretical position that earned the label of the "New Look." (See the primary "New Look" study by Bruner and Goodman (1947) for an explicit acknowledgment of Brunswik's early work.) Brunswik concluded that "Value constancy is considerable, but there is some compromise with area and/or number. In turn, the latter variables are affected by value. . . ." (1956, p. 78.) Thus, the principle of compromise was extended successfully.

We must note, however, that despite the similarities between Brunswik's pioneer studies in this field and the research of the New Look decade, there were marked differences. Brunswik, with his never-failing focus on the stable relations between organism and environment, has this to say in 1956:

To those of us who see in functionalism mainly an avenue to the study of *veridacality* [italics ours—Ed.] in perception the emphasis is shifted from the value-induced error [as emphasized by the New Look,—Ed.] to the positive aspect of value constancy. From this latter point of view the monetary value of such objects as stamps or coins is a distal variable worth knowing in its own right. The intriguing part of the problem is that monetary value exists by *fiat* of the "laws" of a cultural ecology only; thus it is of a different, more limited and more temporary character than are purely physical object characteristics and the natural or geometric laws by which they are interconnected. This in turn means that value-cues must be acquired cues. In consequence, the study of value constancy as well as that of the interference of values with the perception of other object properties may shed light on the role of learning or familiarity in intuitive perception." (1956, p. 78.)

A similar point of view had been expressed in 1950 (q.v.) shortly after the New Look had been initiated.

In brief, Brunswik was not content with simply emphasizing the fact that central variables such as motive could produce something less than verdical perception. He wanted to quantify the effect of various sets of determiners on the correct achievement of the distal variable. Perceptual compromise "states the fact of dynamic field-interaction. . . ." (1951, p. 215;) Brunswik presented a variety of evidence on this point (pp. 61–87, 1956) and urged that it remains to discover and to measure the effect of the ecological as well as central determiners in this dynamic situation.

To summarize, the organism meets the vicarious mediation of the environment with vicarious functioning on its own part; the lens model provides an analogy for the recombining of "nature's off-shoots" and the principle of compromise governs the nature of the perceptual response. We turn now to the explication of Brunswik's views concerning central processes.

Central Processes

Brunswik's interest in central, "ratiomorphic" processes increased in the last few years of his life. Earlier he had argued that if psychology was to move ahead, it must ignore whatever processes take place inside the organism in favor of distal-distal studies. Thus, for example, in the 1943 symposium with Lewin and Hull, he noted a difference in attitude between himself and Tolman toward intervening variables.

An important difference, though one of secondary order, between the type of molar approach represented by Tolman and that proposed by the present writer is that the former seems to put much additional emphasis upon inferences regarding the intra-organismic "intervening variables" (which bring him close to Lewin), e.g., a hunger drive as inferred from maintenance schedule; whereas the latter [Brunswik, Ed.] would tend, at least in principle, to discard for the moment intervening variables wherever they are not directly accessible. By representing an organism's or species' achievement system in terms of attained objects and results, such a psychology would in a sense be *without* the organism (that is, would neglect all but a few focal details of organismic structure and intra-organismic processes), yet would let us know much *about* the organism. . . . (That is, its relationships to the environment, in both cognition and action.) (1943, p. 271.)

Brunswik, then, differed from Tolman in that he wanted to go as far as he could in terms of a psychology of objects without inventing intervening variables. We can assume that there were two reasons for this: (1) that psychology was already far too entangled in the "texture of the organism," and (2) that distal-distal studies should come first. It is these studies that should provide the proper point of departure for theories about central processes.

Both these points may be illustrated by his criticism of Lewin's position as being "encapsulated in the central region." A psychology in terms of objects, Brunswik argues, "would be the direct counterpart to that represented by Lewin; it would not be post-perceptual and pre-behavioral but perceptual and behavioral." (1943, p. 27.) That is, Lewin's psychology was confined to the central region because it concerned the organism's *perception* of an event (there being no concern for an independent measure of the event itself), as well as behavior *prior* to action, (there being no concern for whether the organism achieved his intended goal). Too little concern for the environment had led to encapsulation in the central region.

Fortunately this characterization of Lewin's approach had an effect. Note what Cartwright, Lewin's close associate, had to say about this point in 1959:

. . . it may be instructive to consider the statement made by Brunswik that the lifespace is "post-perceptual and pre-behavioral." It seems to me that Brunswik pointed here to an important issue concerning Lewin's use of the term, life space. This statement can be accepted, however, only by ignoring certain features of Lewin's theorizing, the modifications he suggested in response to Brunswik's characterization, and the actual procedures he employed in conducting research. Nevertheless, I believe Brunswik was correct insofar as he referred to the more explicitly developed parts of Lewin's treatment. (1959, p. 69.)

Cartwright then describes the efforts made to meet Brunswik's criticism, among which he points to studies of psychological ecology carried out by Barker (see Chapter 9 of this volume). And Cartwright notes that "Work of this sort will rapidly clarify the many theoretical and methodological problems involved in psychological ecology and will help field theory from being 'encapsulated' in the sense that Brunswik feared it might." (1959, p. 74.) Thus Brunswik's succinct, powerful description of Lewin's approach contributed toward the psychological ecology (distal-distal studies) illustrated by Barker and his associates' research on *behavior settings* (see pp. 325–337).

Some ten years after his remarks on "encapsulation" Brunswik reaffirmed his emphasis on studies that would be *about* the organism yet would be *without* the organism; that is, studies that "would neglect all but a few focal details of organismic structure and intra-organismic processes."

> The present writer has spoken of a "psychology in terms of objects" in which organisms are described and differentiated from one another by reference to the—predominately distal—stimulus or result variables with which they have attained stabilized relationships. By applying this approach to distal-distal functional arcs bridging over the entire organism without descending into it, one may further gain scope and at the same time get around the construction of intervening variables. Such an approach may be characterized as "without, yet about, the organism" in that it is concerned with relationships established by the organism although not with their organismic anchorage. (1952, p. 72.)

Distal-distal studies, then, are intended to relate remote causes and remote effects without reference to central variables—except perhaps to mention the species involved. One example of such a "wide-arched dependency," as Brunswik liked to put it, is provided by Harlow (1962) in which he found that monkeys deprived of natural mothers during infancy failed to provide maternal care for their offspring. A distal cause, maternal deprivation, is found to be related to a distal effect, namely, a second generation of infant monkeys deprived of maternal care. No reference need be made here to central or mediating variables, and the behavior of the organisms involved is not manipulated or restricted by the experimenter, except for the cage surround.

In general, then, Brunswik looked forward to studies that minimize reference to central variables, such as the one just mentioned. But he was not hostile to inferences concerning central variables so long as the ultimate relation sought was a *central-distal* one. For example, he was always quite benign in his attitude toward psychoanalysis. Moreover, he gave several illustrations of his own ideas of how central-distal relations should be studied. As noted above, the approach is always from the "outside-in." Thus, in 1947 (1956, Part I), the discussion of his ecological study of size constancy was followed by remarks suggesting that if a similar

. . . program were carried out on a variety of functional topics, a subject (or patient) would then be described in his relationship to the world by a set of correlation coefficients (or other measures achieving the same end). That is to say, he would be psychologically characterized "in terms of objects" (ecological variables) he is capable of attaining rather than just in terms of his responses or in terms of relatively short-range achievements under specific conditions as in the classical experiment and test. His psychological portrait would thus emerge in terms of the stabilized, generalized object relationships established and maintained by him cognitively or in overt behavior, up to and including such wide-spanning covert distal adjustment features as, say, "social perceptual alertness and differentiation" versus "social blindness. . . ." From the coefficients describing these relationships one would, of course, not be able to predict correctness of orientation in the environment with certainty for any particular instance. But they definitely would give an over-all relative frequency ("probability") of adequate contact with vitally relevant variables, which may be a much more relevant type of information than certainty with respect to relatively insignificant instances or details. (1956, p. 48.)

These remarks not only illustrate Brunswik's approach to central variables from the outside-in, they also show that Brunswik had already laid the groundwork for the large number of American studies on interpersonal perception that occurred during the '50's. His own studies of the role of physiognomic cues in the perception of other persons, which began in the '30's (1956, pp. 99–119) as well as his later studies on social perception (1956, pp. 26–39) were fundamental steps. Certainly it is clear from the above remarks concerning "social-perceptual alertness" that he perceived the central-distal possibilities inherent in probabilistic functionalism.

To mention only two studies that proceeded directly from Brunswik's approach, Crow and Hammond (1957; see also Hammond and Kern, *et al.,* 1959), followed up his suggestion that ". . . a subject (or patient) could be . . . described in his relationship to the world by a set of correlation coefficients . . ." in their studies of medical education. They found that the investigation of medical students' "social-perceptual alertness" with respect to individual differences among patients, for example, was a rewarding field of inquiry. In a different effort to illustrate Brunswik's suggestion concerning the investigation of a subject's ability to attain "accurate" perceptions of distal variables, Hammond and O'Kelly (1955) studied two groups of schizophrenic patients (those who had had psychotherapy and those who had not) in order to discover whether the patients who had the benefit of psychotherapy were better able to achieve the same perception of certain social situations as certain nonhospitalized members of the community than patients who had not received psychotherapy. It was found that a "psychological portrait" could indeed "emerge in terms of the generalized, stabilized object relationship established and maintained by . . ." the patient. Rommetveit's (1960) detailed investigation of interpersonal perception also starts from an explicit consideration of Brunswik's views.

As a result of his increased interest in central-distal relations in the later part of his life, Brunswik gave some attention to projective tests (1956, pp. 131–139). These pages were first presented as a paper read to the Veterans Administration Research Conference in Clinical Psychology in 1953. Because of his careful historical, systematic, and conceptual analysis of the stimulus materials used in the Rorschach and Bender-Gestalt tests, the paper should have, but regrettably did not, precipitate a sorely-needed fresh approach to the whole matter of projective testing. We include some of his remarks on this topic to demonstrate the application of Brunswik's ideas to clinical research, as well as his focus on the *outside-in* approach to central variables.[10]

Brunswik begins his analysis by pointing out the close relation between Gestalt psychology and projective testing.

Gestalt psychologists share with projective testers the view that all illusory perception is not only illusion *away from* some ideally accurate or veridical type of response but at the same time is illusion *toward* something else, that is, assimilation toward some preferred pattern of organizations. In projective testing most of the assimilative power is seen as coming from the inner motivational stratum with its richness of personal figures and themes. (1956, p. 132.)

Further:

The Gestalt psychologist and the Rorschach (psychologists) must also be assumed to be akin in a rather deep-seated attitudinal respect. Their efforts and those of all projective techniques have in common that they are based on the recognition of what such precursors of the modern Gestalt movements as Benussi and his friends at Graz have called Gestalt "ambiguity." (1956, p. 133.)

However, Brunswik points out that most Americans are familiar only with the Berlin school of Gestalt psychology (Koffka, Köhler, and Wertheimer), and they do not recognize that several rival points of view existed. One of these, the Leipzig school, is represented by Sander

10. See Sarbin, Taft, and Bailey (1960) for an application of Brunswik's approach to clinical psychology. See also Hammond (1954, 1955), Grebstein (1963); Hammond, Hursch and Todd (1965), Hoffman (1960), and Hursch, Hammond, and Hursch (1964).

(1928), in which he argues that the perceptual act is made up of three stages. "A most primordial, feeling-like stage is said to be followed by a second 'geometric-ornamental' stage and eventually by a third 'realistically meaningful' (sinnhafft-bedeutungsvoll) stage." (1956, p. 133.) Brunswik notes that it is the second "geometrical-ornamental" stage that has pre-occupied Gestalt psychologists and provides the stimulus material upon which the law of Prägnanz is developed and based. The Leipzig school, however, also emphasized the third stage, characterized by pressures to perceive "in terms of palpable objects or 'things' " rather than in terms of "pure nonrepresentational geometry" which characterizes the second stage. Having shown that a choice exists as to which type of stimulus materials will be employed, and that the choice has important theoretical implications, Brunswik, consistent with his interest in object relations then goes on to say:

Remembering that the law of Prägnanz refers to but one of at least two major types of preferred patterns of organization in the perception of form, both the Berlin research techniques and the Rorschach inkblots appear lop-sided when held against the requirements of representative stimulus design. Their onesidedness tends in diametrically opposite directions, quite in the same spirit of splendid isolation that exists between the various sub-varieties within the academic Gestalt movement.

The standard stimulus fare offered by Wertheimer (1923), Gottschaldt (1926), Wulf (1922) and others of the Berlin school consists of arrays or patterns of dots, straight or angular lines, and smoothly drawn curves. All these patterns are extremely provocative of geometric-ornamental or eidotropic tendencies while giving little chance to representational meaning or even to the factor of familiarity to make itself felt.

The Rorschach inkblots, on the other hand, with their peculiar tying of bilateral symmetry with irregularity and blurredness—as well as subsequently designed inkblots and the less well-known cloud-pictures which K. Struve has used under the stimulus of William Stern (1938)—give the inside track almost exclusively to the realistically meaningful tendencies. They even prove conducive to very specific types of objects (animals, anatomy, and so forth) so that the natural balance of the world view is threatened even within the domain of existing physical or social objects. With an eye again on the more general controversy concerning eidotropic vs. ontotropic tendencies with which we are here primarily concerned we may note the fact that even in the more volumi-nous lists and catalogues of Rorschach responses no more than a handful of abstract "squares," "triangles" or other purely geometric formations could be discovered; this goes so far that even the giving of such responses by a subject is viewed with alarm in the standard evaluation of protocol. (1956, p. 134.)

Brunswik then went on to show that the Bender-Gestalt test was made up directly from typical Gestalt geometrical figures, which ignored the realistic-meaningful tendencies so strongly emphasized by the Rorschach test. Brunswik, in short, was attempting to point out the traditional arbitrariness in the selection of stimuli practiced by clinical psychologists as well as by experimental psychologists. And by relating both tests to Sander's theory, he was illustrating the traditional lack of concern for theory about stimuli.

Nothing could illustrate better the trivial consideration given to stimulus materials used for inferences concerning central variables than the uncritical acceptance for nearly a half-century of the ten inkblot stimuli offered by Herman Rorschach. Anything is acceptable as stimulus materials, it appears, as long as such materials provide individual differences in responses. Theoretical analysis of stimulus materials has seldom occurred. It is hardly surprising that clinical psychologists should be oblivious to the importance of the theoretical derivation of stimulus materials; their academic teachers were equally oblivious to the problem.

Thinking and Perception

Brunswik's concern with central processes is also illustrated by his interest in the distinction between thinking and perception. He had concerned himself with the problem in Vienna before coming to the United States, and in 1943 tempered his criticism of Lewin's overconcern with central processes with this remark: "But in the end, it seems that none of the various aspects just discussed can be dispensed with in a completely rounded-out system of psychology." (1943, p. 27.)

Again proceeding from the premise that psychology must be concerned with the texture of the environment, Brunswik described the properties of these two forms of cognition and carried out an experiment, or more properly, a demonstration, of the different results obtained by the two processes. The results are expressed in terms of distributions of errors; this was done to show the kind of interaction with the environment produced by each process.

Brunswik's first papers on this subject were not read in America until 1948. And the full development of his thoughts did not appear until the 1954 meetings of the International Congress of Psychology in Montreal where he read a paper entitled "Ratiomorphic Models of Perception and Thinking." This paper was never published, but Professor Robert Leeper has kindly made a copy of the paper available for publication in this volume and it appears in Section IV. The ideas in this paper were developed in somewhat more depth in the 1956 book in Section XIV (pp. 89–99) entitled "Perception and Thinking."

Brunswik saw perception as a probabilistic, intuitive, continuous, highly adaptive and rapid process—though not without its occasional stupidities. In contrast, thinking is at the opposite pole—deterministic, analytic, discontinuous, with sudden attainment and lengthy pauses, and frequent maladaptive twists. Perception, in short, is "uncertainty-geared;" thinking is "certainty-geared."

The more perceptual-like the process, the greater the importance of empirical near-regularities, the greater the expectation of being right in the long run, and the more likely is the subject to achieve "smallness of error at the expense of the highest frequence of precision." Analytical thinking gains in rigor—but its errors are greater and more likely to be catastrophic.

The 1948 paper reported an experiment that illustrated a statistical separation between perception and thinking in terms of the distribution in errors. Perceptual errors provided a normal distribution centered on zero; errors resulting from thinking were distributed in an irregular fashion. And although the results are of great interest, Brunswik noted that the experiment that was presented as an illustration was not intended to be more than that.

Ending on a note of caution, we should like to stress that the representativeness of our two versions of a common cognitive task is open to some doubt. Many specific conditions could be listed under which it is perception which is bizarre while it is thinking which is mellow and given to compromise. Aside from deductive considerations, only representative design could definitely prove us right or wrong in our conjecture that the juxtaposition we have proposed is more typical than its reverse. (1956, p. 93.)

Because of vicarious functioning in perception, Brunswik wrote that perception

must appear as the more truly behavior-like function when compared with deductive reasoning with its machine-like, precariously one-tracked tight-rope modes of procedure. The constantly looming catastrophes of the intellect would be found more often developing into catastrophes of action were it not for the mellowing effect of the darker, more feeling-like and thus more dramatically convincing primordial (that is, perceptual) layers of cognitive adjustment. (1956, p. 93.)

As early as 1952, Brunswik saw a risk in the possible inappropriate use of computers as thinking machines, or decision-makers, upon which our lives depend today and will depend in the foreseeable future.

To take for granted univocal interrelations among different types of events is to a certain extent justified so long as one has in mind only the psychological texture typical of "thinking" in the sense of explicit logical reasoning. It ceases to be adequate when we include the less ideally executed patterns of thought or the compromise type of probabilistic quasi-reasoning on the basis of insufficient evidence which is implicit in the more primitive form of cognition usually called "perception." Ideal rational thinking manages to isolate cues of highest dependability and thus is enabled to switch from vicarious to single-track functioning with not only no loss but even a gain in univocality. This lends a narrowly machine-like quality to discursive thinking; it is precisely this quality which is represented in the "machines that think" of cybernetics and in some of the concepts of mathematical biophysics. (1952, p. 90.)

The significance of Brunswik's remarks concerning the distinction between perception and thinking, or between intuitive and analytical modes of cognition can hardly be overemphasized. Yet even in the early 1960's when psychologists once more have taken up the problem of cognition, no one has seen fit to investigate Brunswik's assertions concerning cognitive modes (other than those who still pursue personalogical typologies; see, for example, Messick and Ross, 1963).

Summary

We have presented some of the essential elements of Brunswik's conceptual framework. It was our intention to show that his conceptual framework does indeed have the degree of generality, specificity, and deductive potential, which he spoke of with some force in 1953. We tried to show that his theory of behavior has considerable scope, encompassing both a theory of the environment, a theory of the organism, and the form of their interaction.

The environmental theory is general in that it proposes vicarious mediation between depth and surface; it is specific in that it leads directly to studies of the texture of the environment; it demonstrates its deductive potential by showing how such experiments can confront theory with data. The theory of the organism rests on the concept of vicarious functioning—a highly generalized process that forms a counterpart to the vicarious mediation of the environment. The ratiomorphic nature of cognition with its intuitive, perceptual character, and its analytical, "thinking" character, together with the principle of compromise lend specificity to the system. The deductive potential of the theory of the organism is indicated by the large number of ingenious and unorthodox experiments carried out by Brunswik and his students in Austria.

Finally, the lens model provides the basis for studying the relation between organism and environment. It lends itself to prediction without reduction; thus, it makes possible the attainment of adequate complexity without loss of rigor. But in order to accomplish that aim, we must free ourselves from methodological orthodoxy, as Brunswik did when he discovered that he would have to invent a methodology appropriate to his broadened conception of psychology's task. Let us turn now to that problem.

METHODOLOGY

Because Brunswik set forth his methodological system in detail in 1956, and because a description of his position may be found in his paper in the Symposium on the Probability Approach in Psychology (1955b), as well as in an overview by Postman and Tolman (1959), it is unnecessary to present an abridgment of the principles of "representative design" here. However, the basis for his methodological suggestions will be discussed in detail.

Brunswik's main arguments are two: (1) that if we are to understand fully how organisms capable of vicarious functioning behave, we shall have to place them in situations that permit vicarious functioning to occur; and (2) the logic of statistical inference is just as applicable to stimulus situations as it is to subjects, and its application is just as necessary. Both points are included in this statement:

According to the much-stressed requirement of "representative sampling" . . . individuals must be randomly chosen from a well-defined population; in the same manner, the study of functional organism-environment relationships would seem to require that not only mediation but also focal events and other situational circumstances should be made to represent, by sampling, or related devices, the general or specific conditions under which the organism studied has to function. This leads to . . . the "representative design of experiments." (1952, pp. 29–30.)

The point is:

Situational instances in an ecology are analogous to individuals in a population of responders. Both may be considered as sets of more or less incidental variate packages. The difference is that instances can be taken apart and created at the spur of the moment while individuals usually cannot. But . . . a program of functional research demands that they too be left as they come. We must resist the temptation of the systematic experimentalist to interfere. . . . (1955, p. 198.)

We are, therefore, urged to extend the concept of representativeness (applied so frequently to subject sampling) to the stimulus side of the experiment in order to permit the study of vicarious functioning and to permit the logic of statistical inference to be applied in both directions.

With only this much of the concept of representative design in mind, we turn first to Brunswik's emphasis on probability laws—the natural outcome of his insistence on vicarious mediation in the environment and vicarious functioning in the organism. Following this discussion we shall make some general observations on the problem of generalization of research findings.

Representative Design and Probability Laws

Brunswik was the first psychologist to take the probability point of view. Although he urged this point of view on grounds of principle on numerous occasions and in varying contexts (see especially 1952, pp. 21–25), he was persistently misunderstood. The primary misunderstanding occurred in the Symposium with Hull and Lewin; Hull implied that Brunswik's advocacy of probability laws was not merely wrong, but a step backwards. Hull's misunderstanding was founded on the notion that probability laws intrinsically have something like second-class status—acceptable, but only as temporary expedients, and therefore with apologies. Consequently, to argue for statistical laws is akin to urging a retreat. Thus in 1940 (but far less so in 1960) one could hear it said that further research would, or at least *should,* take the probability out of the law. The essence of this position may be found in Hull's remark (1943) that "uncertainty may lie entirely in the conditions and not at all in the rules or laws." Uncertainty, in brief, derives from mere technological problems.

The implication that anything short of the search for unequivocal relations was a retreat is indicated by Hull's suggestion that "Brunswik . . . is convinced that no such uniformities exist, and that the best we may hope for is to find correlations among phenomena which will always lack appreciably of being 1.00." Moreover, "if the quest (for uniform laws) appears hopeless, all of us may as well give it up, *as Brunswik seems already to have done.*" [italics ours] (1943, p. 274.) In short, scientific psychologists will overcome the more technical difficulties that stand in the way of discovering uniformities. But those who are already discouraged, those who have already given up the struggle for a scientific psychology, will settle for whatever statistically significant correlations they can get.

This was a serious distortion of the probability view for two reasons. First, the plain fact is that the probability view stems directly and logically from the theoretical and empirical cornerstones of Brunswik's position. Nowhere had Brunswik made a prior judgment as to whether technical problems could or could not be overcome. In fact, Brunswik

recognized that his approach offered even more serious technical difficulties than the conventional approach. The search for statistical laws is,
therefore, not a retreat in the face of formidable technical problems;
rather, it follows directly from premises different from those dear to the
classical behaviorists about the interaction of organism and environment.
The probability view, moreover, has led directly to scientifically respectable Brunswikian concepts (for example, ecological validity), as well as
those introduced by other psychologists, not to mention those long accepted in biology and physics. To confuse the issue here is, as Brunswik
put it, to confuse the "univocality of observation and communication,"
upon which we all insist, with the "univocality of prediction"—which
some of us may insist is theoretical wrong-headedness, to which anyone
may subscribe, of course, provided he does not in turn *proscribe* an
alternative point of view. Brunswik urged us to remember that ". . . a
statistical correlation coefficient or any other probability law is just as
exact, that is to say, just as public and palpable in its meaning as a strict
law." (1952, p. 37.)

Second, Brunswik did *not* suggest that uniformities or invariances
would not or should not be found by psychologists. On the contrary, he
argued that "Survival . . . may be defined as the establishment of stable
interrelationships with the environment. . . ." (1943, p. 258.) The point
is that such "stability," or invariance, is ". . . possible only if the organism is able to achieve compensating balance in the face of comparative
chaos in the physical environment." In short, invariances are to be found
between scientific constructs in the *distal* region of the environment and
the *central* region of the organism; the probability, the uncertainty lies
in the mediational processes of the physical world (from the surface of
the environment to its remote causal layers) and in the mediational
processes of the organism (from the surface of the organism to its central layers).

Brunswik apparently never really succeeded in making his position
concerning probability understood, although it emerges clearly in these
short paragraphs written in his rebuttal presented at the Berkeley Unity
of Science meetings (1955).

The term "uniformity point of view," which I myself have never used, erro-
neously suggests that being a probabilist excludes the belief in uniformity,
perhaps in the way in which some of the quantum physicists—or in quite another way the vitalists—do not believe in uniformity. The allegation which
Hull made in the same vein at the beginning of this paper [1943, Ed.] asserting that I do not believe in the "existence" of laws applicable to behavior, is
thus based on misunderstanding. The same holds for the present remarks of

Krech. Contrary to what he imputes, I do believe "that God does *not* gamble;" I fully realize that the impasse of quantum physics is irrelevant to our case, uncertainty being for all practical purposes wiped out at a level of physical macrolaws—which are still microlaws to us psychologists—and that vitalism is mere dogma.

But the crucial point is that while God may not gamble, animals and humans do, and that they cannot help but to gamble in an ecology that is of essence only partly accessible to their foresight. And although an infinite and omniscient intellect could operate by law and ratiocination alone, as a psychologist even such a being would have to follow the methodological postulate of behavior-research ismorphism, and operate at the probabilistic level of discourse. As in geography or textural ecology, this does not entail the negation of law; it merely entails relinquishing attention to law within certain contexts. As these disciplines do not go "beyond" law, we do not either; and as they are sciences, so is probabilistic psychology. (1955, p. 236.)

Probabilistic functionalism, then, seeks to describe certain behavioral phenomena in statistical terms, not because it has settled for something less, but because the probability view combined with its methodological counterpart, representative design, provides the tools for something more —the understanding of variance and invariance at an adequate level of complexity.

Whatever credence may have been attached to Brunswik's plea for the necessity for consideration of probability laws, it is evident that many psychologists still look upon such efforts as regrettable; not only are they perceived as a retreat from loftier aims, but also as somehow depressing. Gibson, for example, put it this way:

He [Brunswik] asks us, the experimenters in psychology, to revamp our fundamental thinking and to adopt a consistent functionalism in which the organism survives—when it does—by adapting its behavior to a world of merely probable objects. It is an onerous demand. Brunswik imposed it first on his own thinking and showed us how burdensome it can be. His work is an object lesson in theoretical integrity. (1957, p. 35.)

And Barker asserted:

I stand with Brunswik so far as the breadth of psychology is concerned, and take the whole span from the environment to the environment, the *E-E* unit, as the basic psychological entity. . . . [But] I cannot accept his macro-probabilistic . . . treatment.

He further notes:

It is true too that some systematists would like to include the whole *E-E* unit in their psychology, but finding no way to do so without accepting the *discour-*

aging [italics ours] conclusion of Brunswik that only empirical probability laws are possible, they withdraw into what Brunswik has called encapsulated psychologies. (1960.)

The search for exactitudes of the one-to-one variety evidently has a firm place in the value systems of psychologists. Stevens is probably right in his observation:

. . . even a phenomenological existentalist would cherish a natural law if he found one. Perhaps the psychologists' questing for nomological principles ought to get extinguished for lack of frequent reinforcement, but it obviously does not. Maybe it comes with the organism, like native curiosity, wired in from the start. Whatever it is that motivates inquiry, we can be sure that psychologists will not renounce the experimental search for simple and powerful principles of behavior. (1962.)

Fortunately Brunswik did not shrink from the methodological implications of his theoretical position however onerous or demanding they appeared to others. Because Brunswik's view of the history of psychology and his conceptual framework directed his methodological efforts, all three constituted an organic whole; the methodological aspects of his conceptual framework could not be arbitrarily set aside. Beginning with an historical and conceptual analysis as he did, Brunswik was *forced* to re-examine psychological methodology. This is why Gibson said "his work is an object lesson in theoretical integrity." And when he found that orthodox methods simply were not congruent with what history required of psychology in the twentieth century, nor were they congruent with his conceptual system, he developed (set forth in 1947 and expanded in 1956) certain methodological principles derived from his general outlook. In doing so, he accomplished two extremely important things: (1) he provided the first detailed, systematic, scholarly, comprehensive methodological analysis psychology has ever had, and (2) he provided psychology with an "indigenous" methodology (to borrow a term from Koch)—a methodology *derived* from what he considered psychology's task to be, not merely *borrowed* from traditional canons of logic, or older sciences. Brunswik was not merely a critic; he was a creator.

Brunswik's creativity is what makes his unorthodoxy different. For although protests against psychology's methodological premises have been heard for some time, the protests have generally consisted of general complaints, rather than alternative programs. Prior to Brunswik's effort, there had never been such a searching examination of psychological methodology within the context of a statement of the scope and aims defining the study of behavior. The criterion of methodological simplicity, which served the primary scientific disciplines long and well, and which finds its culmination in Mill's Canons, was taken over directly and uncritically by psychology. Prior to Brunswik, there had never been any *detailed* criticism documenting the hidden implications for psychological theory that stem from adherence to historical notions of what constitutes scientific research. There was no *documentation* of the fact that assumptions concerning proper method were indeed emulations of the rules of older disciplines rather than directives evolving from the requirements of a task. Most important, no one had ever presented a concrete alternative that did, in fact, meet the essential criteria of science, which did present an explicit logical relation between method and task, and which escaped from the overenthusiastic application of the criterion of simplicity.

Brunswik asserted that ". . . psychology has tried to copy not only the basic methodological principles but also the specific thematic content of physics, thus nipping in the bud the establishment of (appropriate) methodological directives. . . ." Brunswik saw "emulative physicalism" as a millstone around the neck of a psychology trying to free itself from its molecular, nomothetic biases. ". . . emulative physicalism springs from an overawed 'me too' attitude of a psychology struggling in the wake of an outdated image of the older natural sciences."

. . . nomothetic behaviorism overexpands physicalism beyond the necessary observational and procedural core and includes unessential borrowings from the specific thema of physics. A functionally oriented objective psychology, on the other hand, dealing as it does with organismic-environment relationships at the more complex level of adjustment, may be seen as falling in line with a more searching interpretation of the historical mission of psychology. (1952, p. 36.)

Regardless of how many other protests against a "me too" attitude might have been voiced, no other alternatives were ever set forth in full detail prior to Brunswik's exposition of representative design because of the deeply-rooted implicit assumption of the generally regular, lawful character of nature, and of the physical environment in particular. Given an environment whose essential characteristic, according to scientists from the eighteenth century on, was lawful regularity, what could be more natural than the application of Mill's Canons, the essential elements of which are directives for paring away the irregular entanglement of partial causes and effects in the natural ecology until the singular, fundamental regularity becomes apparent? Under the (then) all too obvious fact of the necessity for exposing the hidden regularity of nature, what better methodological model could a scientist have than Mill's Canons? (See Gillis and Schneider, this volume.)

It was Brunswik's genius that perceived that although Nature, in some sense was regular, that is, could be described in terms of the nomothetic laws of physics, *this aspect of Nature was not immediately available to the behaving organism.* The Nature with which the behaving organism must deal "scatters its effects irregularly." Although the physicist is now able to construct a macroscopic description of the world which consists of regularities, the fact remains that ". . . the environment to which the organism must adjust presents itself as semierratic. . . ." And

So long as the organism does not develop, or fails in a given context to utilize completely, the powers of a full-fledged physicist observer and analyst, his environment remains for all practical purposes a semierratic medium; it is no more than partially controlled and no more than probabilistically predictable. The functionalistic approach in psychology must take cognizance of this basic limitation of the adjustive apparatus; it must link behavior and environment statistically . . . rather than with the predominate emphasis on strict law which we have inherited from physics. (Chapter 17, this volume, p. 509.)

It was his focus on partial causes that separated Brunswik from all other psychologists (until the advent of statistical learning theory). Traditional psychology was imbued with man's effort to discover nature's regularity—the most pre-eminent feature of science until very recently. Given this point of departure, nothing could be more reasonable than to proceed in terms of a classical, systematic, isolate-one-variable-at-a-time methodology. Pavlov, Hull, and the psychophysicists illustrate this approach at its best. But, no matter how regular the world may be when described in terms of physical laws, the fact remains that the behaving subject does not have access to these laws. As a result, ". . . the environment to which the organism must adjust presents itself as semierratic. . . ." It follows, therefore, as Brunswik argued, that "all functional psychology is probabilistic . . ." and therefore, probabilistic functionalism

. . . demands a "representative" research design of its own, and leads to a special type of high-complexity, descriptive theory. This program provides not only the necessary thematic diversification from the classical natural sciences but leads to the long overdue internal unification of psychology. (1955, pp. 193–194.)

We turn now to an example of how the uncritical application of systematic design can prevent fulfillment of a theoretical program that implies vicarious functioning.

Experimental Restriction of Vicarious Functioning within the Multiple Mediation Framework

Earlier it was pointed out that, in principle, representative design cannot meaningfully be used in conjunction with theories that do not involve the concept of vicarious functioning. As a result, it is hardly to the point for us to examine in detail any specific study unless it gives some consideration to the question of vicarious mediation, or at least multiple probabilistic cues. It remains true, however, that a second aspect of representative design (application of the statistical logic of inductive inference to the situation-side as well as to the subject-side of an experiment) can be applied to *any* experiment, if for no other reason than to demonstrate that the generality of the conclusions may often be drastically restricted when representative design is applied. An example of this sort follows later.

More relevant, however, is the examination of approaches that incorporate in principle the notions of multiple mediation and vicarious functioning, but which are prevented from fulfilling their aims by the uncritical adherence to the ideals of simplistic, systematic, isolate-one-variable-at-a-time research procedures. The following example, then, is not intended to illustrate a double standard of inductive logic, rather, its purpose is to show a poor fit between a theory that supports the multiple mediation point of view and a test of it—the poorness of the fit being brought about by systematic design. Harlow's research on learning was chosen for this purpose, for it is clear that although he subscribes in principle to the multiple-cue concept, and to the multiple-means concept, the systematic research procedures he has chosen in the past, at least, have prevented a full-fledged realization of a program that attempts to cope with vicarious functioning.

In Volume II of the series edited by Koch (1959), Harlow argues that monkeys learn through the elimination of errors. He says, "It is a reasonable hypothesis that the suppression of all EF's (error factors) defines perfect learning, and that learning is nothing but the suppression or inhibition of EF's." What are the error factors which must be suppressed? Harlow identifies four of them: stimulus-perseveration, differential-cue, response-shift, and position-habit.

Stimulus-perseveration refers to the fact that ". . . certain classes of stimuli, including large stimuli, tall, unstable stimuli, and many-pointed, bright metallic stimuli characteristically elicit avoidant, hesitant behavior." *Differential-cue* refers to the fact that ". . . on any particular trial of a nonspatial discrimination there is ambiguity between the object rewarded and the position rewarded." *Response-shift* is described as ". . .

a strong tendency to respond to both stimuli in the object-discrimination learning situation." Response-shift is a powerful EF for ". . . no investigator has found response-shift to be completely suppressed or inhibited even though hundreds of problems involving thousands of trials may have been completed by every subject." *Position-habit* errors are "consistent responses to either the right or left . . . regardless of the position of the correct object . . ." and are considered relatively unimportant for primates. Other error factors are known or surmised, but we will consider only those mentioned above.

Quite in keeping with traditional research procedures as well as the premise that learning is nothing but the suppression of error factors, Harlow measures the effect of various error factors by holding constant (or otherwise eliminating) in turn all EF's but one. Suppose the interest lies in the question of whether variable Number 1, say, stimulus-perseveration, is indeed an error factor that can be suppressed. Variable Number 1 is allowed to appear in the experiment *as an error,* all other error factors are absent due to control, and one stimulus variable is permitted to correlate perfectly with the food reward. The extent to which the EF (more precisely, the stimulus variable which produces the EF) is allowed to correlate with the food reward is not always perfectly clear, but it is clear that the correlation is close to zero. This condition *defines* variable Number 1 as an error. The relation between irrelevant stimulus variable Number 1 and the response is then examined after a series of trials and if a positive relation is observed, it is concluded that the irrelevant stimulus does indeed produce an error factor. Its persistence over trials is taken as one indication of its relative strength. Next EF Number 1 is eliminated and hypothetical EF Number 2 is introduced in the same way and its endurance is ascertained. And so on.

As a result, error factors and their hypothetical relative strengths are identified and described. Under what conditions? Under conditions in which one EF is relatively "untied" from the food reward, one variable is perfectly "tied" to the food reward, and all other EF's are eliminated. Under these conditions, what does the animal learn? In the main, the animal indeed learns to suppress error factors, and to respond regularly to a certain stimulus, or stimulus pattern.

Now from the point of view of probabilistic functionalism this is a strange kind of learning to ask of a monkey, or any other animal one of whose defining characteristics is possession of a rather high capacity for vicarious functioning. The interesting point here is that Harlow not only recognizes the monkey's capacity for vicarious functioning, but also clearly recognizes the adaptive, that is, positive functional value of error factors themselves. As he puts it, "Progressive reappearance of previously suppressed EF's following protracted failure in a problem-solving situation would appear to be a mechanism of high adaptive value."

But it is entirely plausible that each EF is a mechanism of high adaptive value (even without protracted failure) when conditions are not restricted to the Wisconsin General Test Apparatus. Even in the WGTA, the phenomenon of response-shift, for example, provides evidence that the monkey cannot entirely give up his "bias of exhaustible supply" in favor of the experimenter's "bias of inexhaustible supply." Adapted, in a genetic sense, to a semierratic environment, response-shift shows that the monkey evidently cannot rid himself completely of a probabilistic bias even after "thousands of trials" in the WGTA. It is true, of course, that when the environment tends to be made up of fixed regular relations between cues and rewards, response-shift is adaptive only under conditions of desperation—protracted failure; but in a semierratic environment response-shift can be an adaptive mechanism even when things are going well. The monkey in his natural habitat should not suppress a response tendency to shift, nor must he subscribe to the "bias of inexhaustible supply." In short, "errors" such as those described by Harlow are errors only because they are *made* to be errors by the nature of the experimental environment and by the nature of the learning task. Suppression of such error factors can be defined as learning only when the task presented requires that the animal suppress completely those responses carefully arranged by the experimenter to be "errors." *If* the environment did indeed provide *only* those situations in which the monkey must learn to suppress all response tendencies but one, then, and only then, would these experiments be of more than passing interest, for only then would they provide something more than the results of a special and strange case.

But if one begins with a point of view that recognizes that monkeys are capable of vicarious functioning—that is, are capable of using various intersubstitutable means of achieving a goal, why, then, deprive the monkey by experimental means of just that capacity which makes his behavior interesting? The answer seems to lie in a prior commitment to "legitimate" research procedure.

Consider the situation now free from the bias of simplistic design, free from the necessity for eliminating partial causes, and free from the bias of searching for absolute regularities except between distal-distal regions. We need not begin by assuming that our scientific effort, our research design, must pare away partial relations that supposedly obscure perfect lawful relations. We can begin instead with the reasonable premise that the monkey does not have "the powers of a full-fledged physicist observer and analyst," and that the environment that controlled the monkey's phylogenetic history "remains for all practical purposes a semierratic medium . . . no more than partially controlled and no more than probabilistically predictable." (Brunswik, 1959.)

Rather than assert that "learning is nothing but the elimination of errors" in a situation arranged so that learning can be nothing else, probabilistic functionalism would argue that *learning involves the increasingly effective utilization of all the available intersubstitutable perceptual and response dispositions available to a member of a given species.*

Note that from this point of view the effort must not be to eliminate all partial relations among stimulus conditions in the environment, but to allow the animal to have access to them, and to permit the animal to utilize these partial relations so that it can attain the maximum degree of achievement of the distal variable that the environment will allow. Similarly for the response side; rather than successively eliminating the utility of various response tendencies and allowing only *one* to attain *perfect* utility, the proper course is to permit the animal to bring all his response processes to bear on the situation. The hoped-for laws of learning should not be restricted to conditions that deprive an animal of its capacities for vicarious functioning on either the perceptual or motor side.

As Brunswik noted after comparing the techniques of the successive accumulation and successive omission of factors:

> More abstractly, the major difference between the two techniques may be formulated as follows. In the classical tradition, situational cues are gradually introduced, starting from one cue or factor which later—if not fully eliminated in an opposite alternative, reduction to zero—is enriched by the admittance of further factors in a process of increasing complexity that may be called "successive accumulation." In contrast to this, the modern touch is given by a start from fully, or at least approximately, lifelike conditions, working downward in a process of decreasing complexity that may be called "successive omission" (in the sense of removal, or factual exclusion) of a cue or other condition.
>
> It seems from these results, more clearly than may be possible from other types of sources, that the classical experimentalist used channeled mediation in his experiments primarily because he tacitly assumed actual mediation to be likewise one-track, or one-cue. This may have given him the illusion of proceeding in a representative manner. The intersubstitutability of cues in the over-all biological function of stabilized orientation shows the inadequacy of such a conception. (1956, pp. 25, 26.)

Representative Design and Generalization

No discussion of Brunswik's methodology would be complete without mention of this fundamental point concerning generalization—that the logic of inductive inference must be applied to both subjects and objects. Psychology is replete with examples of the application of a double standard concerning the rules of inductive inference, where careful attention is given to the logic of statistical inference concerning subjects, but little or no consideration is given to the matter of sampling and generalizing over conditions. As Brunswik put it, "Generalizability of results concerning . . . the variables involved must remain limited unless at least the range, but better also the distribution . . . of each variable, has been made representative of a carefully defined set of conditions." (1956, p. 53.)

As an example, consider once more the matter of Harlow's error factor, stimulus-perseveration; "Tall, unstable stimuli . . . elicit avoidant, hesitant behavior." Reflection on the nature of the monkey's natural habitat must make such a statement seem peculiar indeed. For monkeys live in trees that are "tall" in some sense or other, and "unstable" in some sense as well. What, then, could "tall" and "unstable" mean? The best guess is that "laboratory-tall" means something quite different from "tall" in the sense of, say, two standard deviations above the mean of a distribution of heights of objects in the monkey's natural environment. In fact, without the data, one cannot help but surmise that what is "tall" in the monkey laboratory is actually much below the mean of the distribution of the heights of objects usually encountered by monkeys. And "laboratory-unstable" must mean something quite different (falls over when touched?) from "unstable" in the sense that a branch of a tree, a rope, or a swing, is "unstable." Without a specification of the range or distribution of the variable in question, or the specification of relation between the distribution of the variable and *some* set of conditions, results are masked in doubts. Indeed, without such specification one might come to exactly the wrong conclusions—such as asserting that monkeys avoid "tall stimuli."

If one is not to be arbitrary about the choice of the range and distribution characteristics of the stimulus variables of an experiment, what criteria should be employed? Brunswik's answer was always to the effect that the choice should be such that the experimental environment is made representative of the animal's natural habitat. Consequently, ecological analyses are required in order to develop the appropriate laboratory environment to present to the organism. In the case of the monkey, one might begin with an analysis of photographs of typical monkey environments and carry out studies in the spirit of the Brunswik-Kamiya (1953) experiment concerning the relation between nearness of parallel lines and mechanical coherence. Similarly one might study the relations between the tallness-instability dimension and food. It seems rather apparent that a positive correlation of considerable magnitude would be found between preference and tallness, provided one included trees among the environmental objects embodying height. It is thus likely that the antipathy of Harlow's monkeys for "tall, unstable stimuli" would be seen instead to be indifference to, or lack of preference for, *"small"* (that is, WGTA-size "large") objects. At what point Harlow's "unstable" objects might be found on the stability-instability continuum is difficult to say.

Resistance to Brunswik's Methodology

Koch (1959a, pp. 729–788) has recently asserted that there is a "stubborn refusal of psychological findings to yield to empirical generalization." A statement of this sort in the context of the Epilogue to Study I of "Psychology: The Science of Behavior" clearly defines a crisis, a crisis that Brunswik had persistently tried to call to the attention of his colleagues, and a crisis for which he had proposed a constructive solution in terms of both theory and methodology. Earlier we discussed the resistance to his emphasis on probability laws. Why were his assertions concerning the "stubborn refusal of psychological findings to yield to generalization" ignored, and why were his methodological suggestions disregarded? There are many answers to this question, but we wish to call attention to three: (1) the prevalence of an organismic-centered psychology; (2) the indoctrination of students in classical methods of experimentation, and (3) the technical problems associated with representative design. (We have earlier called attention to a fourth reason: his concern for experimental design was not examined in the context of probabilistic functionalism.)

Organismic-centered psychology

It is interesting to note that Koch (1959a) finds that the authors of Study I see the principal difficulty concerning generalization of findings to lie with the intervening-variable paradigm so widely used in the 1930's and 1940's. While agreeing with Koch's definition of the locus of the problem, we feel that he has not gone far enough. What he fails to note is that the principal characteristic of the intervening variable paradigm is its directive to focus on the organism. The experimental specification of stimulus conditions (ordinarily arbitrary, occasionally theoretical, almost never situationally representative) and response forms are sufficient to define an intervening variable, the locus of which is in the organism. Given such an organism-focused methodology, one should hardly be surprised to find that modern psychology possesses a rich assortment of intervening variables intended to account for the behavior of the organism.

But our affluence with respect to *organismic* concepts is exceeded only by our poverty with respect to *environmental* concepts. For the problem of conceptualizing the environment in which the organism must behave has been virtually ignored. Indeed, on the infrequent occasion when a psychologist does wish to describe an environment, he is apt to select a concept from his repertoire of organismic concepts; thus he may speak of a "hostile" environment, but beyond that he is virtually helpless. Explicit theories of the environment are rare; implicit assumptions about its form and content are the rule. As Brunswik put it, ". . . psychology has forgotten that it is a science of organism-environment relationships, and has become a science of the organism." (1957, p. 6.)

The problem of generalization, therefore, is more fundamental than a discussion of the intervening variable paradigm would imply. In pursuance of the difficulty, however, it is useful to ask *why* this paradigm found such ready acceptance. Our answer is that it is perfectly congruent with psychology's over-riding methodological paradigm—classical, one-variable design. Because classical design *cannot* be representative with respect to environmental circumstances (indeed, it shuns the notion), it therefore directs all attention to the organism. The essence of classical design is planned, systematic arrangement of stimulus conditions so that inferences may be drawn concerning the organism. Such systematic stimulus arrangements are made either with an eye to convenient antecedent and consequent conditions, or with an eye to antecedents and consequents that are important to organism-centered theories; the environment toward which generalization must ultimately point is simply ignored.

The situation is accurately described by the diagram in the textbook by Chaplin and Krawiec (1960) (see Fig. 4). Note that in this diagram, all variables save one are "prevented from acting on the organism." This design clearly predisposes the psychologist to focus on the intervening variable, that is to say, the organism. As Chaplin and Krawiec put it, "Irrespective of the psychologist's attitude toward the reality of intervening variables, his research programs are devoted to the study of such 0 variables. They are the meat of psychology." (1960, p. 160.)

In short, under the rules of classical methodology it is obvious that the only place to put a theoretical concept is between S and R. Psychology did not forget that it was a "science of organism-environment relations" and thus become a "science of the organism." Under its methodological rules that force a devotion to the intervening variable paradigm, it has no choice. Commitment to a specific procedural rule of design precluded the choice. The florescence of the intervening variable procedure, with

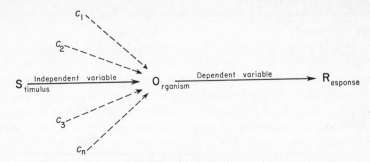

Fig. 4. Schema of an experiment. The independent variable or stimulus acts on the subject, who gives a response, the dependent variable. C_1, C_2, C_3, C_n represent controlled variables. They are shown in dotted lines to indicate that they have been prevented from acting on the organism (Adapted from Chaplin, J., and T. Krawiec. *Systems and Theories of Psychology*. New York: Holt, Rinehart, and Winston, Inc., 1960).

its concomitant proliferation of organismic concepts, together with the absence of environmental theory, are direct consequences of classical experimental methodology—and all of these prevent generalization of psychological findings. Psychological findings, in short, do not generalize over conditions because differences among conditions are given no place in classical methodology.

Indoctrination of students

All introductory courses in psychology, as well as courses in statistics and experimental psychology, place a large emphasis on systematic control. The reason for such emphasis is clear—the demonstration of systematic control of variables competing with the theoretically favored independent variable of study is the essence of psychology's claim to a place in the scientific sun. *Every* psychologist, and *every* student of behavioral sciences has been taught that without the ability and intent to control variables, that is, without the ability and intent *systematically* to include and exclude, and *systematically* to vary as the experimenter deems appropriate, there could be no science of psychology. As an example of the enthusiasm with which psychologists introduce students to our first methodological commandment, it is interesting to note that one reviewer in 1962 complains of a new textbook that "Even an untried freshman may feel that repetition becomes tedium, however, when he reads the definition of the rule of one variable fifteen times in one twenty-five-page section."

Graduate students, no less than undergraduates, are given to understand that the rule-of-one-variable is beyond analysis, evaluation, or criticism. In his textbook for graduate students Underwood makes this point as clearly and as vigorously as it has ever been stated.

> . . . I think it is well to note the basic design problem present in all stimulus-oriented research. Obviously, if we are going to vary a given stimulus condition, and observe changes in behavior, the essential dictum is that only one such condition (be it a very simple or a very complex condition should be allowed to vary systematically. This is commonly said to be holding all conditions constant except one. Some comments have appeared in recent literature which imply that this basic principle of experimental procedure is outmoded. This is not true. One may vary more than one stimulus condition in a given experiment (multivariate designs) and it is very efficient to do so. But to draw a conclusion about the influence of any given variable, that variable must have been systematically manipulated alone somewhere in the design. Nothing in analysis of variance, co-variance, Latin squares, Greco-Latin squares, or Greco-Arabic-Latin squares has abrogated the basic principle. These powerful designs and statistical tools may save wounded experiments, and they may provide remarkable levers for extracting variances, but in actual operation there are no laws resulting from their use which obviate the necessity of holding all factors constant except one if we expect to conclude anything about the effects of the factor. From *Psychological research* by Benton J. Underwood. Copyright © 1957 by Appleton-Century-Crofts, Inc. Reprinted by permission of Appleton-Century-Crofts, pp. 35–36.

The point here is not so much that factorial designs are essentially rule-of-one-variable designs. The important point is that Underwood provides no justification for "the necessity of holding all factors constant except one." Instead he offers an "essential dictum"—a dogma. Underwood has chosen his words well; such rules *do* rest on dogmatic principle. But dogmatic principle about what is to be considered a legitimate research procedure must be examined carefully with an eye to psychology's task. Furthermore, when dogma stands in the way of fulfilling that task, it must be seen for what it is—an obstacle based on ideas as to what is proper, respectable, and legitimate in science—ideas which rest on the faith and intuition that what proved to be successful in the natural sciences *must* be successful in psychology. Not only have psychologists restricted themselves to simplistic models of man because of a commitment to what is believed to be legitimate science, we have restricted ourselves to simplistic models of the environment as well. The first point has been obvious to nonpsychologists for some time; it is Brunswik to whom we are indebted for bringing the second point to our attention.

The above quotation from Underwood will serve its purpose if the reader perceives in it the factual essence of Koch's remark that "man's stipulation that psychology be adequate to science outweighed his com-

mitment that it be adequate to man" (1959b). We must go further than
Koch, however, and ask the reader to perceive that the stipulation that
psychological research be adequate to science also outweighs the commitment that it be adequate to either man *or* his environment. I think it
fair to say that there was no basis for this observation until Brunswik
formulated the proposition that ". . . both organism and environment
will have to be seen as systems, each with properties of its own . . ."
and that psychology ". . . also must be concerned with the texture of the
environment as it extends in depth away from the common boundary"
with the organism.

In view of the persistent indoctrination of students in what is considered to be the fundamental ground rule of scientific psychology, one
could hardly expect enthusiasm about a theoretical approach that required the abandonment of this rule; therefore, when Brunswik argued
that psychology was pursuing a false image in searching for absolute
one-to-one laws such as those described in high school physics, and when
he combined this argument with statements of this sort: "The deliberate
replacement of systematic by representative design for stimulus variation
and co-variation is the key to further progress in functional stimulus-
response psychology" it is not hard to see that psychologists (particularly
graduate students fully persuaded by the virtues of conventional methodology) would wonder what he could possibly mean. Failure to understand developed into an opposition characterized more by indifference
than vigor.

If Koch's assertion that there is a "stubborn refusal of psychological
findings to yield to empirical generalization" is to be taken seriously,
then the question of student indoctrination must be taken seriously. For
whatever may be unique to various graduate and undergraduate programs in psychology, there is a single unifying element—commitment to
the classical methodological paradigm. Every student learns how to do
the research that has not yielded findings that can be generalized. Indeed,
if generalization is our goal, would it be too extravagant to say that it
follows that every student is taught how to fail? [11]

Technical problems associated with representative design

In the final analysis we must come to grips with the technical, procedural feasibility of representative design. Can it be done?

To begin with, we must note that psychology not only has a wide
variety of concepts it is willing to employ to account for the behavior of

---

11. See Kuhn (1963) for a discussion of the role of scientific paradigm and
dogma in the education of scientists. Of more general interest is his analysis of
scientific change (1962), in which the above is included.

organisms, it also has an elaborate technical apparatus available for testing the generality of its findings with respect to these organismic concepts. Parallel to our conceptual poverty concerning the environment, however, is our *technical* helplessness with respect to testing our generalizations over conditions.

Our ability to generalize over organisms rests on our ability to select our subjects randomly and the technical apparatus of the statistical method to legitimize our inductive generalizations over subjects. But we have no procedural counterpart with respect to inductive generalizations over situations. Hence, the technical apparatus of the statistical method cannot be used. (For examples of its misuse see Hammond (1954).) Yet we know of no other defensible method of induction.

The reason that the technical problem looms so large is that psychology has never directed itself to this problem. There is no well-developed literature on the topic—only scattered references to it—aside from Brunswik's determined, but largely unheeded, efforts (1943, 1952, 1956). The best illustration of this point may be found in the field of person-perception. Here, if anywhere, it should have been apparent that statistical tests must be a part of the inductive process concerning person-objects presented as stimuli. For if the stimulus materials provided for the subjects are persons, then, of course, the usual procedures of subject sampling can be, indeed, must be, applied to person-*objects,* just as they are applied to person-*subjects.* Object-persons must be sampled, and statistical tests concerning generalizations must be made over object-persons as well as subjects. So firm is the organismic focus in psychology, however, that a definite lag has been evident even in grasping this point; seldom are statistical tests made over person-objects. The reader will find numerous examples of claims and generality of findings despite failures to make statistical tests over person-objects taken from the literature concerning person-perception in a paper by Crow (1957). The current literature on person-perception can be counted upon to provide a rich yield of similar applications of the double standard of the logic of inductive inference.[12]

The logic of representative design was developed not only with the express purpose of combatting the organismic focus of psychology, but also to provide the technical means for generalizing over situations. Brunswik was among the first to point out the "stubborn refusal of psychological findings to yield to generalization" *over conditions.* He knew

12. See Bieri (1962) for a recent example of a double standard of induction reported in a symposium of sophisticated measurement theorists. Bieri employed 350 *subjects* who were asked to rate a *single person-object.* Will the results generalize to a second person-object?

why generalization was failing, and set forth the methodological principles of representative design in 1947 and 1956 for remedying matters —principles based firmly on the fact that if statistical logic was the basis for inductive generalization over subjects, the same logic had to be the basis for induction over situations. It is impossible to estimate how convincing the logical argument was. Unfortunately, however, it is perfectly clear that his proposals were unconvincing from a technical, procedural standpoint. For although Brunswik was able to carry out certain studies involving situational sampling (for example, 1944) these experiments evidently failed to convince psychologists that true ecological, or situation, sampling was feasible. However much Brunswik argued the logical point about induction, the technical problems of sampling situations seemed insurmountable. (See Hochberg, Chapter 12, for comments on ecological sampling.)

It must be said that at this time, the question of feasibility remains open. When considered as a *substantive* problem precisely parallel to subject sampling, situational induction (over and beyond the obvious case of person-object sampling) offers technical problems concerning the definition of a population of situations and objects, and procedures for sampling therefrom which appear enormously difficult at present. *Formal* situational sampling however has recently been made possible by the electronic computer. Each is discussed in turn below.

Substantive situational sampling

However difficult sampling of real ecologies is, it is not impossible, as Barker's work (this volume) with children's ecologies shows. And the *simulation* of real ecologies is now becoming practical, as Crow's work in internation simulation shows.

Once outside the traditional realm of either the perception of object-sizes or interpersonal perception, the definition of the "object" and the functional ecological "cue" becomes a central problem, however. Brunswik was certainly aware of the problem of the definition of the stimulus, its consequences for psychological problems in general and ecological sampling problems in particular. One of the first points he addresses himself to in Part I of "Perception and the Representative Design of Experiments" (first published in 1947) concerns identification of the stimulus variable. Thus:

Many of the environmental stimulus variables mentioned by psychologists, such as "physical size" or "physical color," seem at first glance simply to be taken over from physics or chemistry. Others, such as "food," "sit-upon-ableness" (William James), "likability of a person," and so forth, are obviously conceived with an eye to potential effects upon organisms. In both cases the "dispositional" character of the definition (Carnap) is maintained, the psychological slant of the latter type of variables notwithstanding. Upon closer inspection, however, even the former often reveal psychological entanglement when they appear in the context of a psychological experiment. For example, the "sizes" of physical objects (more precisely, of physicist's objects) figuring as one of the major stimulus variables in the statistical survey of size constancy (see § VII/3) are in fact to be specified as "sizes of objects of attention, that is, of potential manipulation or locomotion, of a certain human being."

Considering the arbitrariness with which objects, spaces between objects, or parts thereof may be subjected to physical measurement, sizes *per se* can hardly be thought of as possessing a finite range or distribution. Sizes attended to in perception or behavior, however, although likewise strictly determined by external measurement (and not to be confused with perceptual size estimates) delimit a much more closely circumscribed reference class or "universe" of sizes; we must therefore not be surprised if they show a definite central tendency. Actually, their logarithms even seem to tend toward a normal distribution. (See Brunswik, 1944, Fig. 1.) This feature is of the utmost importance in the present context, since it allows, and in fact demands, an application of the principles of representative sampling to variables which at face value may not appear capable of being sampled. It is the type of organism-centered specifying redefinition mentioned above which may be summarized by saying that *stimulus variables are "ecological"* rather than purely "physical" or "geographic" in character.

The above "organism-centered specifying redefinition" of the stimulus, that brings Brunswik away from the arbitrary physicalistic definition of the stimulus, also brings him close to Lewin's response-centered definition, yet avoids "encapsulation into the central region," which made Lewin so vulnerable to criticism. However, such a definition by no means makes the task of ecological sampling any easier.

It is our view that the feasibility of substantive ecological sampling that meets all the statistical requirements of the logic of inductive inference must remain an open question until a direct and forthright attack is made on the problem. But we also believe that technical advances in capturing and reproducing ecologies on film and tape will make the future application of representative design inevitable. And if we may be permitted a further surmise, such application will first become standard in a "psychology eager to do work of practical significance without having to wait for sanctioned academic methods to catch up with their problems." (Brunswik, 1956, p. 26.)

Formal situational sampling

Aside from substantive situational sampling, there is the possibility of *formal* situational or ecological sampling. *Formal* situational sampling concerns the *relations between environmental (stimulus) variables* (with content ignored).

It will help to clarify matters if the reader will consider the Chaplin and Krawiec diagram once more. This is the model that governs all experimental design—every textbook agrees. But what every textbook does not say, is that all such experiments are *formally identical* with respect to the relations between stimulus variables. Thus, although the classical experimental model permits the psychologist to disentangle the effects of various substantive stimulus variables, it does not permit the analysis of the *relations* between such variables. It cannot, because the classical model requires the psychologist to present the same formal relations between stimulus variables in every experiment, despite variations in content.

Note, for example, that Chaplin and Krawiec indicate that all independent stimulus variables except one are "prevented from acting on the organism." Brunswik observed:

The chief advantage to be gained from this technique, envisaged in J. S. Mill's "method of difference," is the exclusion of a condition as a possible contributor to variations in the response which then, if present, must be attributed to other causes. It is in this sense that variables held constant do enter the scope of the experiment in question. But they do so only in a negative way, without actually being given a chance as a potential factor. (1956, p. 8.)

In effect, variables are controlled by setting their correlations with the independent stimulus variable at *zero*. Thus, in no way can the response variable be interpreted to have been "caused" by, that is to say, to be a function of, or statistically dependent on, the controlled variables.

Contrast the Chaplin and Krawiec diagram with Brunswik's lens model. The lens model clearly offers numerous possibilities for varying the relations among environmental variables, and thus offers the researcher a choice: at a minimum, he may vary (1) the *number* of stimulus variables to be presented to the subject, (2) the *degree of relation* between the stimulus variables, and (3) the *degree of relation* between the stimulus variables and the distal variable. Thus, once freed from the straitjacket of the classical design of experiments, psychologists can *vary* the formal characteristics of the environments presented to subjects—a variation crucial to the problem of situational generalization.

In order to give adequate consideration to varying the formal characteristics of the stimulus arrangement, however, psychologists would first have to consider seriously the nature of the environment, and to pursue such considerations free from the restrictions of simplistic design. More specifically, psychologists would have to develop more highly differentiated conceptions of the environment. It would be necessary to ask *what kind* of environment an organism is coming to terms with. Functionalism requires a theoretical consideration of the environment in terms of its *form* as well as its content.

It must be emphasized that it is the theory of probabilistic functionalism coupled with representative design that opens up the question of what form the environment should take in an experiment. Under the rule of simplistic, systematic design this question will ordinarily never be considered, because the form of the environment is predetermined by the design itself. It is the *design* that demands that one variable be permitted to vary independently of all others, not a psychological *theory* (compare Underwood, p. 65 above). More broadly, it is the conception of what is legitimate scientific procedure that determines the form of the environment rather than thought, or reflection, on the kind of environmental form theoretically desirable. Probabilistic functionalism, on the other hand, asserts that the researcher should make an explicit choice regarding the formal characteristics of the stimulus display.

Once having made a choice, however, the researcher needs to know as much as possible about the statistical properties of the probabilistic environment, or stimulus array, which he presents to his subjects. Because there has been virtually no concern with the statistical properties of probabilistic multiple-cue environments, little such knowledge is available. Hursch, Hammond and Hursch (1964) examined six cases (within the framework of multiple regression analysis) and have shown the limits of achievement imposed on the organism by the statistical properties of the environment. In general, when achievement of a distal variable is measured in terms of a correlation coefficient (r_a) calculated between the subject's inference of the value of the distal variable and its actual value, it is shown that:

$$r_a = \frac{R_e^2 + R_s^2 - d}{2} + C \sqrt{1 - R_e^2} \sqrt{1 - R_s^2}$$

where

r_a = the correlation between subject's judgments and the variable estimated
R_e = the multiple correlation between the cues and the variable estimated
R_s = the multiple correlation between the cues and the subject's judgments
Σ_d = the sum of the products $(r_{e_i} - r_{s_i})(\beta_{e_i} - \beta_{s_i})$ where

$\quad r_{e_i}$ = the correlation between cue_i and the variable estimated,
$\quad r_{s_i}$ = the correlation between cue_i and the subject's judgment,
$\quad \beta_{e_i}$ = the beta weight for the correlation between cue_i and the variable estimated and β_{s_i} = the beta weight for the correlation between cue_i and the subject's response.

C = the correlation between the variance unaccounted for by the multiple correlation in the ecology and the variance unaccounted for by the multiple correlation in the subject's response system.

The above equation demonstrates that achievement is indeed a function of the statistical properties of the environment (R_e^2), as well as the statistical properties of the subject's response system (R_s^2), the extent to which the linear aspects of the two systems match one another (Σd), and the extent to which the nonlinear variance of one system is correlated with the nonlinear variance of the other (C). If a major purpose of probabilistic functionalism is to appraise the ". . . interplay and relative contribution of environmental factors in the (organism's) adjustment to a given ecology" (1956, p. 143), this equation is of utmost importance because it permits the precise analysis of the "interplay."

Brunswik assumed that achievement would be at a maximum if the correlation between each cue and the distal variable was matched by the correlation between each cue and the response. ("Ideally cues should be utilized according to their validity." 1956, p. 141.) The above equation shows that if the subject exactly matches ecological validities with utilization coefficients, his achievement will be equal to R_e^2 (providing $C = 0$). But if a subject maximizes the linearity ($R_s^2 = 1.00$) of his response system in the best possible manner, then his achievement will be equal to R_e. Since $R_e > R_e^2$, it is, therefore, possible for subjects to attain *greater* achievement if they maximize linearity, rather than match their utilization of cues with the ecological validities of cues. However, the greater achievement resulting from maximizing linearity is bought at a price that depends on the characteristics of the environment. If the environment offers useful *non*linear variance as well as linear variance, the matching subject can achieve *perfect* performance, provided he can detect and utilize correctly the nonlinear aspects of the environment. The extent to which the subject accomplishes this is indicated by C in the above equation. The important point here is that the above equation opens up a type of complexity that follows directly from the analysis of Brunswik's lens model.

A critic might reply "Granted that the above equation makes it possible to analyze behavior in a multiple-cue probabilistic situation—the question is, what can we learn from it about the 'interplay' of organism and environment?" Such a question deserves an answer and three examples will be given briefly.

(a) *Multiple-probability learning.*   Summers (1962) carried out a multiple-cue probability learning experiment in which R_e, the multiple correlation of cues with the distal object, was equal to 1.00, although the highest validity of a single cue was .74. Applying the above equation, Hursch, *et al.,* report:

During the first block of trials, the manner in which Subject No. 6 combined the data from the stimulus array essentially could be represented by the multiple correlation procedure; the multiple correlation (R_s^2) between the cues and his response being .970. Thus, Subject No. 6 functions in almost the identical manner in which the environment, about which he must learn, functions. But note also that although Subject No. 6's process-form closely matches the form in which the environment functions, it is badly applied—the difference between ecological validities and utilization coefficients (d_r^2) being very large (3.002). As a result, achievement in the first block of trials is poor; r_a is a fairly large *negative* coefficient, −.516. However, by the time Block V is reached, Subject No. 6 has largely given up a linear, additive procedure $(R_s^2 = .203$ instead of .970); also, d_r^2 has been markedly reduced (from 3.002 to .634), and as a result achievement has increased (r_a now equals +.284 instead of −.516). No marked change took place in Block VI. In short, an increase in achievement came about as a result of *decreasing* the match between the subject's response process-form (R_s^2) and the environmental function-form (R_e^2), and *increasing* the match between utilization coefficients and ecological validities.

Thus, when the above equation was applied to Summer's data, a new kind of information about subjects' interaction with the environment was uncovered. (See also Smedslund, 1955, Uhl, 1963, and Azuma and Cronbach, this volume for studies of multiple-probability learning within the Brunswikian and multiple regression framework.)

(b) *Clinical inference.* The above analysis was also applied to the problem of clinical inference. When data from Grebstein's (1963) study of "naive" and "sophisticated" clinical psychologists were analyzed by Hammond, Hursch and Todd (1964), it was learned that

. . . there were statistically significant differences between Grebstein's groups with respect to Σd; this component becomes progressively smaller, as it should, as the experience of the clinician increases. Furthermore, Σd is highly related to *achievement* within groups; the smaller Σd, the higher the achievement. (Rank difference correlations for the Naive, Semisophisticated and Sophisticated groups are −.90, −.90, and −.72 respectively.) Σd, therefore, clearly has promise as an important component of clinical inference.

It was also learned that the correlation between patient's IQ and the "sophisticated" clinical psychologists' estimates of IQ were very nearly at the maximum possible—given the statistical properties of the task, a fact not previously ascertainable.

Moreover, the above equation provides a specific term for the relation between nonlinear variance in the task and the nonlinear variance in the subject's response system. This makes the equation appropriate for analyzing subjects' capabilities with respect to tasks that have both linear and nonlinear relations. In the clinical situation in particular, the equation makes it possible to ascertain what the clinician adds to the accuracy of prediction over and beyond what the multiple regression equation provides. If the task of clinical prediction involves nonlinear relations, the term (C) in the equation denotes the intent to which such nonlinear relations are detected and correctly utilized by the clinician. In short, the value of C in any specific tasks denotes the special properties of the clinician that are missing in the multiple regression equation.

Hursch, *et al*. (1964) and Hammond *et al*. (1964) showed that clinicians were not making effective use of nonlinear relations in predicting IQ from Rorschach protocols. It is pointed out that the magnitude of C specifies the extent to which the clinician effectively uses those special properties which distinguish him from the multiple regression equation. Of course, if the task does not provide the opportunity, he cannot use these special properties.

Hammond and Summers (1965) arranged a quasi-clinical task in which fifty per cent of the variance in the criterion variable was predictable from a cue *linearly* related to the criterion, and 50 percent of the variance was predictable from a cue that was *nonlinearly* related to the criterion variable. The empirical significance of C was illustrated by showing, first, that ideal subjects (actually mathematical equations) with the proper performance characteristics would indeed improve their performance by maximizing C, and, second, that real subjects can learn under the proper instructions to utilize nonlinear relations between the cue and criterion variable.

(c) *Lens model feedback.*   Newton (1965) carried out a study of clinical inference in which his subjects estimated Freshman grade averages on the basis of four cues, as indicated above. Each subject was then assigned to one of five different conditions in which different forms of feedback were provided. The results indicate that those subjects who were told what the ecological validities in the sample were, and what their utilization coefficients were, improved (not substantially, but to a statistically significant degree) in their second set of fifty-three trials.

Todd and Hammond (1965) carried Newton's procedure a step further and compared the effect of three types of feedback on learning in a multiple-cue probability study. Here it was found that subjects who were provided with the ecological validities of cues and with their own utilization coefficients after blocks of twenty-five trials learned more rapidly than those provided with traditional outcome-after-each-trial feedback. These findings were obtained with an environment which presented cues of equal validity and were replicated with an environment of unequal cue-validities. Thus, the lens model itself provides a basis for new methods of informing subjects about their achievement—methods that have a definite enhancing effect on performance.

Extensions of formal situation sampling to two-person studies

Rappoport's (1964) study of two-person conflict provides an example of how the lens model lends itself to applications to social psychology aside from social perception studies. In an effort to study conflict between two persons that arises purely as a function of cognitive differences, Rappoport made use of the lens model to develop the technique for carrying out such studies. Person A was given one form of training in a multiple-probability learning task in which the subject developed a set of cue-dependencies different from Person B. Person A learned that cue 1 was most dependable, cue 2 next, and cue 3 the least dependable. The subjects were then brought together, assuming that their training was identical, and were asked to work on a new task, which they assumed to be identical with the training task, but which was actually equally different from the two training tasks. This situation is depicted in terms of the lens model in Figure 5. Thus Rappoport was able to analyze the situation in which two persons "reared" in different environments deal with a new environment different from those in which each was trained. Rappoport's study clearly demonstrates the heuristic role of the lens model.

Summary

In the beginning of this chapter (p. 16) we argued that the essence of Brunswik's theory and methodology could be seen in his "definition of psychology's task as the analysis of the interrelationship between two systems in the process of 'coming-to-terms' with one another, the assertion that psychology must treat each system with equal respect, the directive that psychology '. . . must also be concerned with the texture of the environment as it extends away from the common boundary' of the two systems."

The above equation (p. 71) shows that this entire conception may

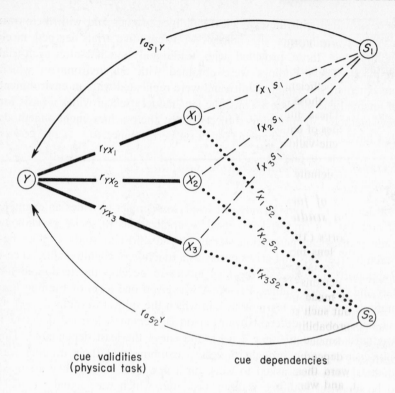

cue validities
(physical task)   cue dependencies

Fig. 5. Brunswik's lens model applied to two-person conflict.

be stated in quantitative terms. The environment and organism are indeed specified as "two systems," each with its linear and nonlinear components, and the extent to which they "come-to-terms" is indicated not only by r, (the correlation between the central layers of the two systems), but also by Σd, which indicates the relation between the "surface areas" of the systems. Each system is "treated with equal respect" for each system is analyzed and described in exactly the same terms, and each has equal significance in the equation. The "texture" of the environment is indicated by the relative contribution of linear and nonlinear components to it, as well as by the specific statistical properties of these components.

Too much should not be claimed from this equation, for it will undoubtedly be reformulated in many ways in the near future. The main point is that it has proved possible to explicate Brunswik's general and massive statement into mathematical terms, which permit precise, quantitative analyses of behavior. Moreover, the behavior analyzed is behavior in those various probabilistic situations *formally* representative of various life-like conditions of uncertainty.

Noteworthy is the fact that none of the above studies could have been carried out without the aid of modern computers. These machines now make *formal* situational sampling possible, and increase the feasibility of carrying out research involving various relations among stimulus variables—a form of research heretofore unavailable to us. Further technological development will undoubtedly bring substantive situational sampling as well as formal situational sampling within the realm of practicality.

CONCLUSION

What does the future hold for Egon Brunswik's probabilistic functionalism? What part will it play in the unfolding of the science of behavior? All those who knew Egon Brunswik agreed that he was a brilliant man and an earnest scholar. The question is—was he a brilliant man who wasted his life on ideas that were so tangential and so unorthodox that they could be of no use to the graduate student, the young professor, those who are carving the new face of psychology? Or did he lay the groundwork for a new point of departure, slow to be recognized but sure to be overwhelming in its final impact? Only history, of course, can give the final answer.

We know, however, that the history of every scientific discipline provides an admonition that credence, wary though it may be, must be given to those who re-examine the fundamental concepts of the discipline in a responsible and particularistic way. For it is the relentless scrutiny of the least-questioned, most-apparent truths that uncovers the greatest scientific gold. But such efforts are dangerous, for failure at this venture is complete failure—or what may be worse, one's work may be reduced to a curiosity and a warning to the timid. Moreover, history may be slow to provide its judgment. As a result, we must prejudge the issue. Because some of us who were Egon Brunswik's students caught a glimmer of gold, we believe that the fundamental changes he envisioned will occur. Even more important, perhaps, we were inspired to investigate thoughtful unorthodoxy, to admire the scholarly unconventional, and given courage to lend credence to the new idea—a result worthwhile in its own right.

REFERENCES

Allport, F. *Theories of perception and the concept of structure.* New York: Wiley, 1955.

Ansbacher, H. Perception of number as affected by the monetary value of the objects. *Arch. Psychol.,* N. Y., 1937, No. 215.

Ashby, W. Simulation of a brain. In H. Borko (Ed.), *Computer applications in the behavioral sciences.* Englewood Cliffs, N.J.: Prentice-Hall, 1962.

Attneave, F. Some informational aspects of visual perception. *Psychol. Rev.,* 1954, *61,* 183–193.

Barker, R. Ecology and motivation. In M. Jones (Ed.), *Nebraska symposium on motivation.* Lincoln, Neb.: University of Nebraska Press, 1960. Pp. 1–50.

Bieri, J. Analyzing stimulus information in social judgments. In H. Messick and J. Ross, (Eds.), *Measurement in personality and cognition.* New York: Wiley, 1962. Pp. 223–239.

Bruner, J., and C. Goodman. Value and need as organizing factors in perception. *J. abnorm. soc. Psychol.,* 1947, *42,* 33–44.

Brunswik, E. *Warnehmung und Gegenstandswelt.* Vienna: Deuticke, 1934.

Brunswik, E. Psychology as a science of objective relations. *Philo. Sci.,* 1937, *4,* 227–260.

Brunswik, E. Probability as a determiner of rat behavior. *J. exp. Psychol.,* 1939, *25,* 172–197.

Brunswik, E. Organismic achievement and environmental probability. *Psychol. Rev.,* 1943, *50,* 255–272.

Brunswik, E. Distal focusing of perception: size constancy in a representative sample of situations. *Psychol. Monogr.,* 1944, Whole No. 254.

Brunswik, E. Remarks on functionalism in perception. In J. Bruner and D. Krech (Eds.), *Perception and personally.* Durham, N.C.: Duke University Press, 1950. Pp. 56–65.

Brunswik, E. *The conceptual framework of psychology.* Chicago: University of Chicago Press, 1952.

Brunswik, E. In defense of probabilistic functionalism: a reply. *Psychol. Rev.,* 1955, *62,* 236–242. (a)

Brunswik, E. Representative design and probabilistic theory. *Psychol. Rev.,* 1955, *62,* 193–217.   (b)

Brunswik, E. *Perception and the representative design of experiments.* Berkeley, Calif.: University of California Press, 1956.

Brunswik, E. Scope and aspects of the cognitive problem. In H. Gruber, R. Jessor, and K. Hammond (Eds.), *Cognition: The Colorado Symposium.* Cambridge, Mass.: Harvard University Press, 1957. Pp. 5–31.

Brunswik, E. Ontogenetic and other developmental parallels to the history of science. In H. Evans (Ed.), *Men and moments in the history of science.* Seattle: University of Washington Press, 1959. Pp. 3–21.

Brunswik, E. The conceptual focus of psychological systems. In M. Marx (Ed.), *Contemporary theories in psychology.* New York: Macmillan, 1963. Pp. 226–239.

Brunswik, E., and J. Kamiya. Ecological cue-validity of "proximity" and of other Gestalt factors. *Amer. J. Psychol.,* 1953, *66,* 20–32.

Campbell, D. Distinguishing differences in perception from failures of communication in cross-cultural studies. In F. S. C. Northrup (Ed.),

Epistemology in anthropology, New York: Harper & Row, 1964. Pp. 308–336.

Cartwright, D. Lewinian theory as a contemporary systematic framework. In S. Koch (Ed.), *Psychology: a study of a science.* Vol. 2. New York: McGraw-Hill, 1959. Pp. 7–91.

Chaplin, J., and T. Krawiec. *Systems and theories of psychology.* New York: Holt, Rinehart, and Winston, Inc., 1960.

Cronbach, L. Processes affecting scores on "understanding of others" and "assumed similarity." *Psychol. Bull.,* 1955, *52,* 177–193.

Crow, W. The need for representative design in studies of interpersonal perception. *J. consult. Psychol.,* 1957, *21,* 321–325.

Crow, W., and K. Hammond. The generality of accuracy and response sets in interpersonal perception. *J. abnorm. soc. Psychol.,* 1957, *54,* 384–390.

Estes, W. The statistical approach to learning theory. In S. Koch (Ed.), *Psychology: a study of a science.* Vol. 2. New York: McGraw-Hill, 1959. Pp. 380–491.

Estes, W. Learning theory and the new "mental chemistry." *Psychol. Rev.,* 1960, *67,* 207–223.

Feigl, H. Functionalism, psychological theory, and the uniting sciences. *Psychol. Rev.,* 1955, *62,* 232–235.

Gibson, J. Survival in a world of objects. (A review of "Perception and the representative design of experiments.") *Contemp. Psychol.,* 1957, *2,* 33–35.

Gibson, J. The concept of the stimulus in psychology. *Amer. Psychologist,* 1960, *15,* 694–703.

Grebstein, L. Relative accuracy of actuarial prediction, experienced clinicians and graduate students in clinical judgment task. *J. Consult. Psychol.,* 1963, *37,* 127–132.

Hammond, K. Representative vs. systematic design in clinical psychology. *Psychol. Bull.,* 1954, *51,* 150–159.

Hammond, K. Probabilistic functioning and the clinical method. *Psychol. Rev.,* 1955, *62,* 255–262.

Hammond, K., Kern, F., *et al. Teaching comprehensive medical care: a psychological study of a change in medical education.* Cambridge, Mass.: Harvard University Press, 1959.

Hammond, K., Carolyn Hursch, and F. Todd. Analyzing components of clinical inference. *Psychol. Rev.,* 1964, *72,* 438–456.

Hammond, K., and L. O'Kelly. A note on adjustment as achievement. *J. abnorm. soc. Psychol.,* 1955, *51,* 371–374.

Harlow, H. Learning set and error factor theory. In S. Koch (Ed.), *Psychology: a study of a science.* Vol. 2. New York: McGraw-Hill, 1959. Pp. 492–537.

Harlow, H. The heterosexual affiliation system of monkeys. *Amer. Psychologist,* 1962, *17,* 1–9.

Heider, F. Environmental determinants in psychological theories. *Psychol. Rev.,* 1939, *46,* 383–410.

Heider, F. Discussion. In H. Gruber, R. Jessor, K. Hammond (Eds.), *Cognition: The Colorado Symposium.* Cambridge, Mass.: Harvard University Press, 1957. Pp. 71–74.

Heider, F. *The psychology of interpersonal relations.* New York: Wiley, 1958.

Heider, F. On perception and event structure. *Psychol. Issues,* 1959, *3,* 1–123.

Hochberg, J. Nativism and empiricism. In L. Postman (Ed.), *Psychology in the making.* New York: Knopf, 1962. Pp. 255–330.

Hoffman, P. The paramorphic representation of clinical judgment. *Psychol. Bull.*, 1960, *57*, 116–131.

Hull, C. The problem of intervening variables in molar behavior theory. *Psychol. Rev.*, 1943, *50*, 273–291.

Hursch, Carolyn, K. Hammond, and J. Hursch. Some methodological considerations in multiple-cue probability studies. *Psychol. Rev.*, 1964, *71*, 42–60.

Koch, S. Epilogue. In S. Koch (Ed.), *Psychology: a study of a science.* Vol. 3. New York: McGraw-Hill, 1959. Pp. 729–788.   (a)

Koch, S. Toward an indigenous methodology. (mimeo.), 1959.   (b)

Kuhn, T. *The structure of scientific revolutions.* Chicago: University of Chicago Press, 1962.

Kuhn, T. The function of dogma in scientific research. In A. Crombie (Ed.), *Scientific change.* London: Heinemann, 1963. Pp. 347–369.

Newton, J. R. Judgment and feedback in a quasi-clinical situation. *J. Pers. soc. Psychol.*, 1965, *1*, 336–342.

Osgood, C. *Method and theory in experimental psychology.* New York: Oxford, 1963.

Osgood, C. Discussion. In H. Gruber, R. Jessor, K. Hammond (Eds.), *Cognition: The Colorado Symposium.* Cambridge, Mass.: Harvard University Press, 1957. Pp. 71–74.

Peterson, C., and A. Miller. Mode, median, and mean as optimal strategies. *J. exp. Psychol.*, 1964, *68*, 363–367.

Postman, L. The probability approach and psychological theory. *Psychol. Rev.*, 1955, *62*, 218–225.

Postman, L., and E. Tolman. Brunswik's probabilistic functionalism. In S. Koch (Ed.), *Psychology: a study of a science.* Vol. 1. New York: McGraw-Hill, 1959. Pp. 502–564.

Rappoport, L. Non-competitive conflict in a probabilistic situation. University of Colorado, Behavior Research Laboratory Report No. 38 (mimeo.), 1964.

Rommetveit, R. *Selectivity, intuition, and halo effects in social perception.* Oslo, Norway: Oslo University Press, 1960.

Sarbin, T., R. Taft, and D. Bailey. *Clinical inference and cognitive theory.* New York: Holt, Rinehart, and Winston, Inc., 1960.

Sells, S. (Ed.) *Stimulus determinants of behavior.* New York: Ronald, 1963.

Smedslund, J. *Multiple probability learning.* Oslo, Norway: Oslo University Press, 1955.

Stevens, S. The surprising simplicity of sensory metrics. *Amer. Psychologist*, 1962, *17*, 29–39.

Summers, S. Learning the utilization of multiple cues which vary in weighting. *J. exp. Psychol.*, 1962, *64*, 29–34.

Thouless, R. Phenomenal regression to the "real" object. *British J. Psychol.*, 1931, *21*, 339–359.

Todd, F., and K. Hammond. Effect of feedback and set on performance in a multiple-cue probability learning task. *Behav. Sci.* (in press).

Tolman, E., and E. Brunswik. The organism and the causal texture of the environment. *Psychol. Rev.*, 1935, *42*, 43–77.

Uhl, C. Learning of interval concepts. I. Effects of differences in stimulus weights. *J. exp. Psychol.*, 1963, *66*, 264–273.

Underwood, B. *Psychological research.* New York: Appleton, 1957.

2

Pattern Matching
as an Essential in Distal Knowing[1]

DONALD T. CAMPBELL

To establish the setting and the problem, this paper first deals with Egon Brunswik's concept of distality in terms of behavior theory and evolutionary development. Even here, knowing in science is introduced as in continuity with those modes of knowing on the part of organisms described by biologists and psychologists. The problem is then introduced: How is distal knowing achieved? How are the proximal threads tied in a distal knot? The thesis is advanced that pattern matching is one of the recurrent attributes. This is illustrated first at the level of stereoscopic perception of objects and the coordination of motor behavior. Further illustrations come from the diagnosis of inferred entities in science. Finally, the perspective is used to summarize an emerging consensus among philosophers of science as to the relationship between theory and data.

Joining analytic philosophers since Hume, both scientific knowledge and ordinary knowledge of the common-sense objects of the external world are recognized as analytically unjustified, highly presumptuous, and fallible. This recognition seems basic to both philosophical and psychological approaches to the problem of knowledge. But if to the problem of knowledge, the philosopher answers in a specific instance or in general that "knowledge is impossible," he has answered a different question than was asked. For the question, "How is knowledge possible?" usually implies that knowledge, corrigible though it may be, has in some instances been achieved to a sufficient degree to make the question worth asking. It presumes that instances of valid knowing and of mistake both occur and are in some instances discriminable. How are such discriminations made? How can one identify new instances as "the same"

1. Supported in part by U. S. Office of Education Project C-998, Contract 3-20-001, under provisions of Title VII of the National Defense Education Act.

as old ones so that "knowledge" may be applied? How do knowers choose between the interpretation of sense data as indicating a new entity versus connoting an old entity from a changed perspective? It is the problem of knowledge at this level to which the present inquiry is addressed.

Distal knowledge means, in particular, knowledge of external objects and events, knowledge of predictable processes reidentifiable as the same, hypothetical knowledge optimally invariant over points of observation and observers. Perhaps in the truest connotations of the word, all knowledge is distal, and our title has a needless redundancy. Perhaps there is no sense in which punctiform raw sense data unidentified as recognizable recurrents, uninterpreted as diagnostic of external events, should be called knowledge.

Both psychology and philosophy are emerging from an epoch in which the *quest for punctiform certainty* seemed the optimal approach to knowledge. To both Pavlov and Watson, single retinal cell activations and single muscle activations seemed more certainly reidentifiable and specifiable than perceptions of objects or adaptive acts. The effort in epistemology to remove equivocality by founding knowledge on particulate sense data and the spirit of logical atomism point to the same search for certainty in particulars. These are efforts of the past, now increasingly recognized to be untenable, yet the quest for punctiform certainty is still a pervasive part of our intellectual background. A preview of the line argument as it relates to the nostalgia for certainty through incorrigible particulars may be provided by the following analogy. Imagine the task of identifying "the same" dot of ink in two newspaper prints of the same photograph. The task is impossible if the photographs are examined by exposing only one dot at a time. It becomes more possible the larger the area of each print exposed. Insofar as any certainty in the identification of a single particle is achieved, it is because a prior identification of the whole has been achieved. Rather than the identification of the whole being achieved through the firm establishment of particles, the reverse is the case, the complex being more certainly known than the elements, neither, of course, being known incorrigibly.

THE OPERATIONAL DISTINCTION BETWEEN DISTAL AND PROXIMAL *S-R* LAWS

It is today fashionable in the psychology of learning to acknowledge that molar responses and molar stimuli are involved in the empirical regularities upon which behavior theories are based. But usually this is presented as the scientist's arbitrary choice of a convenient level of analysis, rather than in recognition of the empirical fact that it is at a molar level rather than at the molecular level that *S-R* laws can be obtained. This recognition is fundamental to Brunswik's similar distinction between the distal and proximal levels. Examination of his "lens model" in Figure 1 will help make this clear.

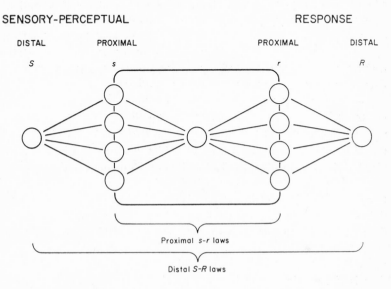

SENSORY-PERCEPTUAL   RESPONSE

DISTAL   PROXIMAL   PROXIMAL   DISTAL

S   *s*   *r*   *R*

Proximal *s-r* laws

Distal *S-R* laws

Fig. 1. Brunswik's "lens model." The box represents a conceptual organism, with a sensory-perceptual surface (to the left) and a response surface (to the right). The radial lines indicate the multifarious proximal channels alternatively (vicariously) mediating the distal achievement. On the stimulus side, these could be illustrated by the multiple inter-substitutable proximal cues for distance or for object color, and so forth. On the response side these could be illustrated by the multiple specific muscle contractions by which the rat might depress a lever, or locomote a runway, and so forth.

Brunswik recognized the scientific legitimacy of the search for proximal *s-r* laws, relationships between single retinal cell activation and specific muscle contraction, for example. However, he summarized psychology's experience with the higher vertebrates by the general induction that such laws did not exist; that when computed, these correlations (between presence-absence of stimulus and presence-absence of muscle contraction over a population of occasions) were of zero magnitude. He did not deny the possibility of discovering such laws in any programmatic or logical sense, and in fact emphasized that the behavioral regularities of the lower animals, such as Uexküll's (1934) sea urchins, were of this proximal sort (Brunswik, 1956, p. 62). For such coelenterates, the activation of a given tactile receptor cell dependably activates a specific muscle. But for man, the significant S-R correlations are to be found at the distal, object-act level, rather than at the proximal level. These significant and impressive (if never perfect) correlations are a major fact that psychological theory must accept. A major self-deception of traditional behaviorisms has been the use of these distal correlations in specious support of theories adequate only to explain proximal ones. A major achievement of Brunswik's perspective is that of maintaining a positivistic, behavioristic orientation without denying the flexible, purposive adaptedness which is characteristic of the perceptual and motor systems of the higher organisms. Smedslund (1953) and Campbell (1954), in defense of a Brunswikian point of view on the problem of "what is learned" and in summary of the research in learning showing the distal character of most learned habits, have emphasized that such distal foci are operationally distinguishable from the proximal.

The achievement of such a point of view meant overcoming special temptations for a person of Brunswik's positivist background. The positivist's militant attack upon vitalism and upon the metaphysical baggage of pseudoproblems made them prone to overlook or deny these less tangible facts of perception and behavior. The particular form that their quest for certainty took was in seeking a certainty of communication, that is, in seeking unequivocally specifiable terms. Proximal stimuli and proximal responses seem much more appealing in this sense than do distal ones. It was Brunswik's achievement to make objective the facts that necessitated the renunciation of this approach to certainty, facts to which many positivists within psychology are still blind. It was his achievement to have retained both his vigorous positivism, and to have harnessed these "organismic" and "vitalistic" facts as positivistically demonstrated laws. His empirical law of distal achievements through vicarious mediation I accept as established, setting the problem for this essay.

EVOLUTIONARY PERSPECTIVE
UPON DEGREES OF DISTALITY

In the primitive coelenterate, the nervous system connects each specific tactile sense organ with a specific muscle. The s-r reflexes are adaptive, in that the muscle response changes the relationship between the organism and environment (in some instances leading to tenacle with-drawing, in other instances, contraction and grasping, depending on location, and so forth). While these are distal effects, there is but a single means of mediating them—there are no alternative channels for vicarious mediation. Thus at the proximal level, the correlation holds. Higher forms, even locomotor forms, may possibly preserve this proximal consistency. Loeb (1918) described an ingenious mechanical bug with presumed animal counterparts that flexibly tracked a light. The left eye or photocell activated the right hind leg or wheel, and the right eye, the left hind leg. Thus when both eyes were equally stimulated, locomotion was straight ahead toward the light. If the initial orientation was to one side, the eye receiving the greater amount of light activated the opposite side the more, leading the bug to turn in the direction of the light, up to that point where the eyes were equally stimulated.

But the major stable relationships in the world available for organismic exploitation are consistencies adhering to other objects than the organism itself—consistencies adhering to food objects, shelters, predators, locomotor obstacles, throughways, and so forth. Due to the fluctuating illumination and the variable distance of such objects, proximal stimuli are not optimal indicators of these, nor are proximal responses optimal effectors. Somewhere in the evolutionary hierarchy the available distal relationships come to be exploited, and with this comes a renunciation of rigid one-to-one reflexes at the proximal level. Presumably this has been achieved by the evolutionary level at which image-forming eyes appear. The organism at that point tries out the strategy of hypothesizing stable external objects mediately known, or of behaving in a manner consistent with such hypothesizing.

This is awkwardly conveyed on two counts. On the one hand, the statement is atrociously anthropomorphic. On the other, we so unquestioningly assume the existence of specific external objects—objects with a stability independent of our movements—that we find it hard to accept these as merely the hypotheses of a fallible cognitive apparatus, at best mediately known. We find it hard to comprehend an organism that does not live and locomote in a world of objects. Yet this feature of animal life is clearly dependent upon distance receptors and, in any high degree, upon perceptual constancy mechanisms.

S-R consistencies, whether instinctive or habitual, are dependent for their establishment and maintenance upon consistencies in the environment, inasmuch as selective survival or selective reinforcement are essential. Initially, only environmental contingencies at the skin of the organism are involved. At higher stages, environmental contingencies at some remoteness from the skin can be diagnosed, and the diagnostic inference becomes to some degree independent of the position of the observing organism. Since it is ecologically true that these less self-centered, more "objective" contingencies are stronger statistically (provide better predictions) there is a selection-pressure in evolution leading to their exploitation, and to the increasingly complex perceptual-loco-motor apparatus that makes this possible.

Students of science and epistemology have long found it appropriate to tease out the hidden premises underlying the reasoning of scientists and laymen. These premises are often for convenience stated in a language of conscious contents: the scientist presumes order (or partial order) in nature, he presumes that there are fewer causal laws than there are events, and so forth. These premises are unconscious until thus explicated. It is in a similar vein that I use a conscious experience terminology of "hypothesizing" in discussing the implicit presumptions about the nature of the world built into animals at various evolutionary stages (Lorenz, 1941; Campbell, 1959). These presumptions, these synthetic hypotheses (ontogenetically a priori or a posteriori), increase with the adaptive radius, the range of correspondences of the organism (Spencer, 1896), and represent the increased "knowledge" of the laws of the world, of the "causal texture of the environment." (Tolman & Brunswik, 1935.) In these terms, the proximal-level organism in his inherited reflexes modestly assumes some degree of order, some deviation from pure randomness in his environment. At some later level, his ambitious presumptiveness goes so far as to presume the existence of external objects. At this stage, the organism's cognitive apparatus becomes a diagnoser of external entities and processes. At this stage, the puzzling fact of distality and of purposive behavior emerges in full degree. From the standpoint of an amoeba, this is a wondrous, if very presumptive, procedure.

Continuing the evolutionary paradigm, we can note that the higher the level of development the higher the degree of distality achieved, the greater the magnitude of the Brunswik constancy ratio, and the greater the degree to which external events and objects are known in a manner independent of the point of view of the observer. Thus Brunswik (1928; 1956) found the degree of constancy achieved to be higher in older children than younger ones, reaching a maximum around fourteen or fifteen years of age. Thus Piaget (for example, Flavell, 1963; Piaget, 1957) finds his youngest children failing to reify external objects as having continuing existence and motion when out of sight. With increasing age come not only increasing hypostatization of external objects, but also of increasing presumption of the conservation of weight and volume, as the child more and more imputes to the world stability under transformations of his point of observation. Thus, within the historical span of human experience, the distality of man's knowledge has been increased by learning and reason over that provided by visual perception. Brunswik both emphasized the marvelous constancy mechanisms of the visual and auditory systems, and at the same time spoke of the "stupidity" of the perceptual apparatus relative to thinking in its rigidity and susceptibility to illusion under ecologically atypical conditions (for example, Brunswik, 1934; 1956, pp. 88–92). Piaget provides similar evidence. Man's introduction of measuring rods constructed of relatively inelastic quasi solids has freed his knowledge of objects from the ubiquitous compromise with retinal size found in unaided vision (Brunswik, 1956, p. 88 and *ad passim*).

The course of science has this over-all trend. The intricacies of measuring instruments and laboratory equipment show a development analogous to that of the vertebrate eye. The addition of specific compensating devices and control features lead meter readings to reflect more and more purely the attributes of the object of study, uncontaminated by the irrelevant specifics, vagaries, and rigidities of the measuring instrument. The concept of a compensated or of an automatically self-calibrating instrument, and the need for continually recalibrating a more primitive one, convey the general spirit of this development. (See Wilson, 1952, for specific illustrations.)

Similarly, physical theory has provided in each generation a model of the universe more independent of man's particular position of observation. In the shift from Ptolemy to Kepler this is clear; some see the contributions of relativity and quantum theory and the complementarity principle as reversals in this direction. This is not the position taken here, however. What these developments have done is to convince man that his knowledge of the world is not as completely distal or objective as he had thought, that it is still contaminated by a certain degree of astigmatism (Bachem, 1951), and that there are limitations upon the degree of objective knowledge that he can obtain. But note that in many specifics, if not all, the errors of the Newtonian system become correctible when an Einsteinian relativity is adopted, achieving a greater degree of distality, independence of point of observation, and predictive efficacy than that previously held. Oppenheimer (1956) has presented a parallel development in early science. He contrasts Babylonian astronomy with the later Mediterranean versions of Ptolemy and Copernicus. Babylonian astronomy was able to predict the movement of the heavenly bodies with great accuracy, including such subtleties as the eclipses of the moon, without any model of celestial mechanics. This achievement was the product of centuries of bookkeeping, and was based upon vast libraries of detail from which identical sequences and spatial contingencies could be identified as a base for prediction. The great advantage of the model-building astronomies was not one of accuracy (at least initially) but rather one of library space. The same repertoire of predictions could be encompassed with one one-thousandth of the written records. Similarly, while it is conceivable that instinct or learning provide an animal with a fixed response tendency for each possible proximal pattern of stimulation, the central nervous system storage requirements involved for an animal like ourselves with proximal stimulus receptors numbering in the millions, are such as to argue the economy of the more presumptive strategy of creating an approximate model of the environment as a base of prediction. The phenomenal reality of separate external objects for myself, and reputedly for other men, helps convince me that my near relatives probably use this presumptive strategy.

TYING THE PROXIMAL THREADS IN A DISTAL KNOT

In the laboratory research on thing constancy, the distal thinghood of the object being judged is never in question—rather only some attribute of it—as its size, shape, or distance. Starting from this setting one misses some of the wonder of the achievement that would be more apparent if one examined an instance in which even the positing of a single thing was equivocal. For note, there is always the alternative of inferring several independent causal sources for the several proximal data, rather than inferring a single common source (Heider, 1959).

"Triangulation" is an attractive model (for example, Feigl, 1958; Campbell, 1959). The "lens model" suggests it. From several widely separated proximal points, there is a triangulation upon the distal object, "fixing" it and its distance in a way quite impossible from a single proximal point. Binocular vision can be seen quite literally as such a triangulation.

As Brunswik emphasized, each proximal stimulation is equivocal when interpreted as evidence of a distal event. For each, there is a subinfinity of possible distal events to which it could be witness. We could if we wished add to the lens model a radiation of lines from a heterogeneity of distal events to a single proximal one. How does the cognitive apparatus decide on the distal focus, decide in what distal bundles to tie the proximal particulars? How do the two proximal sources "know" when they are fixing on one single object rather than two separate ones? Or rather, under what conditions do they "presume" one rather than two? The tentative and partial answer is that this is achieved through a pattern matching. The tentative theme of this paper is that such a pattern matching is involved in all instances of distal knowing, including the achievements of scientific theory. In making this suggestion I join many others. For example, it is an important theme in Craik's (1943) *The Nature of Explanation*. Konrad Lorenz has made a similar point in his recent paper on "Gestalt Perception as Fundamental to Scientific Knowledge" (1959), a paper which, like the present one, emphasizes the epistemological significance of the evolution of the perceptual constancies. Bertrand Russell has been particularly explicit.

In Russell's (1948) *Human Knowledge: Its Scope and Limits* he starts out as though writing a summary of epistemological problems for laymen. And in the section on language, he seems little changed from his earlier logical atomism. But in the subsequent parts of the book he is again creatively thinking about the problems that have always troubled him. Particularly in his final section on "The Postulates of Scientific Inference" he offers a synthetic theory of inductive knowledge quite in keeping in spirit with that essayed here. While the list of implicit hypotheses about the nature of the world which he offers differs in particulars from one that I might develop, the general effort is similar.

In his "structural postulate" Russell states the principle with which the present paper deals: "When a number of structurally similar complex events are ranged about a center in regions not widely separated, it is usually the case that all belong to causal lines having their origin in an event of the same structure at the center" (p. 492). His illustrations include multiple copies of photographs, the similar percepts of people viewing a given scene or hearing a given sound, the multiple copies of a given book, the identification of which shadow goes with which man, the assumption of a common culprit in the "brides-in-the-bath" murders, and so forth (Russell, 1948, pp. 460–475).

STEREOSCOPIC VISION

As a first example, let us examine binocular vision via the stereoscope. The stereoscope is ecologically a very unrepresentative sample of possible environments, and is one in which the distal-perceptual apparatus goes awry, in that two separate distal events (the separate pictures each eye views) are misinterpreted as one. In the process, the cues by which oneness is inferred are made more evident.

There are three typical outcomes, if heterogeneous pairs of pictures be allowed: Binocular fusion into a single image, double-image super-imposition, and a domination of one eye's content to the exclusion of the other. If one starts out with similar simple line drawings that will fuse, this resolution can be destroyed by making one of the drawings more and more different from the other. If there is little detail in the drawings, the failure of fusion may lead to a superimposition of the two contents. For example, if each side has only two vertical lines, under the fused condition only two are seen. If the separation of the two is greatly increased beyond the capacity of binocular resolution, then three or four lines may be seen. If, on the other hand, each eye's view is rich in detail (as when two photographs are used), lack of common contour in the two pictures results in a total suppression of one or the other. It seems clear that the fusion of the two proximal sources into a distal inference is made possible through a process of pattern matching, and does not occur in the absence of a high degree of pattern similarity. Once this high degree of similarity is present to guide fusion, then minor disparities of the correct kind can produce a distal increment through the inference of the third dimension. But without an overwhelming similarity of pattern, such discrepancies cannot be utilized, as the inference of a single common source does not take place.

The above contrasts the matching of congruent patterns with the condition under which patterns are incompatible. We can draw a similar conclusion by comparing the presence of congruent patterns with the absence of any pattern. Consider the use of the stereoscope in connection with a separate reduction screen for each eye, so that a punctiform view of each image is obtained. Under these conditions, no convergence takes place, even though each eye be viewing positions that would be fused if the total patterns were to be seen. Similarly, triangulation upon one of several distal light sources of heterogeneous distance and location would be impossible in a system consisting of two mechanical eyes each made up of a single photocell. Under such conditions, triangulation would be unusable just because of the unresolvable ambiguity as to whether both eyes were looking at the same source. While pattern identity can be misleading, it seems in this setting to be a minimum essential. The multiple-celledness of the retina becomes an essential requirement. No doubt it is true that the greater the degree of pattern similarity the more certain the fusion and the more inappropriate angles of optical convergence that it will overcome. From the point of view of inductive theory, the more elaborate the pattern, the more statistically unlikely a repetition of it through independent chance events becomes, and hence the more implausible the rival hypothesis of twoness becomes, in competition with the hypothesis of oneness.

Monocular processes of distal inference contain upon examination the same dependence upon pattern, and through the utilization of memory, the assumption that repetitions of pattern in time come from a common source. In Wertheimer's phi phenomenon of perceived movement, where two separate events are presented (under certain conditions of spatial and temporal proximity and sequence), the visual system shows bias toward a single-object interpretation so great that the hypothesis of one object in motion becomes more plausible than that of two discrete events. No doubt this effect is the stronger, and occurs over the wider spatial and temporal intervals, the more elaborate the shared pattern of the two stimuli. The recognition of visual events as similar to past ones, and hence the use of memory at all, is dependent upon pattern similarity, and is unavailable to homogeneous fragments. Similarly for patterns extended in time. (Russell calls these "event structures" as distinct from the spatial patterns or "material structures," 1948, p. 464.) Auditory recognition and memory are obviously dependent upon this. In animal brains at least, it seems probable that memory access or memory search is only possible on the basis of some pattern-matching resonance process (Pringle, 1951). In mechanical brains, all outcome-controlled processes including memory search are based upon a matching process, in the older machines called "comparing relays." The detail of the pattern involved depends upon the magnitude of the alternative set within which equivocality could take place.

"IMAGE" AS A PATTERN OF OBJECT, GUIDING DISTAL RESPONSE

So far our focus has been on the perceptual side of distality, on human perceptual performance where verbal response effectively makes the response unproblematic. But in fact, distal responses too show imperfect mediation via equivocal proximal responses. The learned memories or instinctive guides that provide the comparison base against which motor feedback is checked must be quite multidimensional. For this multidimensional thermostat setting, for this "input reference set" as a servosystem engineer might put it, for this blueprint of desired outcomes, or criteria against which to check the sensory inputs representing the status quo, the use of the term *template* seems appropriate (for example, Campbell, 1963, pp. 143–144).

Without in any way suggesting how or in what form such a central nervous system record might be carried, it nonetheless seems logically required that there be stored templates or maps for each distal, object-consistent segment of behavior. A further problem enters here. In the servomechanism model in its simplest form, the template operates in terms of feedback *after* response. But such a model does not seem to be complicated enough for the typical guided distal response. For these there seem to be a perceptual search and a perceptual checking of perceptual objects against a template in terms of the discrepancy from which motor responses are guided. For organisms with vision one needs either one template against which both vision and motor feedback are compared, or else separate templates somehow coordinated. The checking of a perceptual pattern against the template (which very obviously must take place even in instinctive behavior, as in the insect recognizing a mate, or the baby chick pecking at grains of wheat) brings us closer to concepts of the storage of behavioral dispositions in terms of *images*. Note Uexküll's (1934) use of the concept of "search image," Tolman's (1948) "cognitive map," and Holst's and Mittelstaedt's "efference copy." (For example, Holst, 1954; Mittelstaedt, 1962; Lorenz, 1959.) Mowrer (1960), and Miller, Galanter, and Pribram (1960) have also been influenced by cybernetic considerations to reintroduce the term *image*. The traditional concept of *schema* as used by Head (1920), Bartlett (1932), and Piaget (for example, Flavell, 1963) has a similar function.

TRIAL-AND-ERROR OF PATTERN MATCHING

In the present writer's previous contributions to a potential "psychology of knowledges processes" or "psychological epistemology," two themes have dominated. One is a perceptual theme (Campbell, 1958; 1959, pp. 172–179; 1964; Campbell & Fiske, 1959) and the other is of a trial-and-error nature (Campbell, 1956; 1959, pp. 163–172; 1960b). Since many find these two themes incompatible, and since the present paper is in the perceptual vein, it seems well to emphasize that I do not at all see the points of view in disagreement, and do indeed regard both as essential. Distal knowing when involving discovery of new distal objects, or the recognition of old ones from among a set, is a trial-and-error of pattern matchings. The trial-and-error component is, of course, missing in settings in which—through other sources of knowledge—no selection is required. It is often overlooked when actually present due to the utilization of human links in a communication system, whose rapid and subtle processes are assumed but not specified.

Let us consider a possible map-guided postal missile, designed to home on a city and airport via radar pictures. Let us conceive of the system as designed to operate under conditions of ambiguity as to city, distance, and approach angle. For such a system to operate mechanically, there would have to be a trial-and-error of matchings of the current scope reading with a stored criterion map. This would have to include a mechanism for expanding and contracting the current radar picture, shifting it horizontally and vertically, tilting and rotating it, and so forth, comparing it with the criterion under all conditions. Some summation of discrepancy process would be involved, as through the use of a "negative" image of the criterion projected upon the "positive" of current reading, so that when the net reached a low, some guidance-locking impulse was transmitted. While the practical details are overwhelming, and might require a mechanism too large to transport, the general system is possible. In considering such a system, the blind surveying of possibilities (whether systematically, as in a radar beam, or randomly) is an essential process, only reduced insofar as already achieved knowledge, and/or reduction of potential equivocalities, is built in.

Probably for our postal missiles such a spatial or "visual" homing system is too expensive and too uncertain. The city maps, for example, might not be distinctive enough. So the engineer would probably be tempted to employ homing on a radio beam. (The problem of contraction of pattern magnitudes with greater distance is avoided, inasmuch as the temporal "spacings" do not expand with distance from source as do the spatial ones.) If we now envisage a purely mechanical system that can "recognize" its own appropriate homing beam from among the inappropriate ones designating different systems, we see that again a pattern matching, and a trial-and-error of pattern matching is involved. Being no electrical engineer, I shall not attempt to indicate an efficient system but merely sketch out a crudely plausible one that makes explicit the problems involved. For a pattern-comparator, let us again use a subtractive procedure of combining energies, with a selector system picking out minimum energies. (Lorenz, 1959, citing Holst, has pointed to the ubiquity of these image-cancellation processes in perceptual phenomena.) Or a resonator generating a derived energy when two inputs maximally matched could be used. The process would be a "selective retention" one in that all inputs picked up would be tried out, only those which happened to resonate being "selected." It would save a lot of hardware if the total system were master-clocked so that the correct homing sender and the criterion model contained within the missile were always in perfect synchrony once the missile came in range. However, "auditory" recognition systems are not usually so restricted. To remove this restriction, a trial-and-error of lags of the criterion pattern is required, such as might be achieved by having multiple resonator units each with a recording of the criterion at a different time of onset. The received input would be blindly matched against all of these, resonance magnitude or over-all pattern similarity measures selecting the optimal one.

In creative knowledge processes involving exploring new areas of knowledge, there is not only a try and fit of extant patterns against some input, but there is also a trial-and-error of novel patterns, novel gestalten, or recenterings (Campbell, 1960b, pp. 389–390).

Pattern Matching in Astronomy

Astronomy, our oldest successful science, deals with the most remote and unknowable of objects. It is, therefore, an appropriate place from which to select samples of the utilizations of pattern matching in science.

Consider first the remarkable assurance with which man assumes that he can identify "the same" star upon successive nights, even with the unaided eye. This is the more remarkable (and the more presumptive) because the stars for such instrumentation are so homogeneous a set of objects as to be mutually indistinguishable. It is further remarkable because a given star is continually changing its location, and because the average star is out of range of observation some three-fourths of the time (that is, when below the horizon, when in ascendance during the daytime, and when eclipsed by clouds). It is the rigid pattern of the so-called "fixed" stars that make this possible, or which makes this the preferred interpretation. If indeed the stars were transient events, destroyed each dawn and constituted afresh each evening, then the recurrence across the observed ages of "the same" pattern would be a set of coincidences beyond our credulity. If there were indeed permanent stars, but these moved on a time and space scale corresponding to an enlarged Brownian movement, so that each evening a novel pattern were apparent, then astronomy would not have been the first science to emerge, nor would the confident reidentification of "the same" star on successive nights have taken place. If all the visible "stars" had been planets of our sun (a system that we now understand as simpler and more orderly than that of the fixed stars), the manifest pattern would have been so much less obvious and compelling as to have postponed the hypothesis of reidentifiable sameness for many centuries. It was the grid of the "fixed" stars that facilitated the observation of the patterned meanderings of the "wandering" stars, and enabled their reification as stable particulate substantial entities.

Astronomy's entities at this stage were diagnosed almost entirely (except for the sun and the moon) by external pattern. Each star was unidentifiable in isolation. The frame of the other stars, each in itself unidentifiable, provided the identification through its fixed pattern. In the ecology of our normal vertebrate development, most external entities are diagnosed by recurrence of internal pattern. Today with telescopes, we can so identify nearby planets, and potentially with refined spectroscopes extended into the radio frequencies, we may find internal patterns marked enough to justify the hypothesis of stable thing for some of the fixed stars without the crutch of external pattern. The external pattern of the fixed stars is so strong and redundant that minor discrepancies can provide 3-D gains from successive comparisons, and through such triangulations the distances of stars and the movements of the sun itself have been inferred.

The first achievement of radar reflection from Venus (Price, *et al.,* 1959) provides another illustration. It provides a good example because the knowledge process utilized an extremely noisy and fallible channel, and yet was so clear-cut in outcome as to make possible a correction of the prior computations of the distance of the target. Note in ordinary radar (and in television) an interchangeable transition between temporal pattern and spatial pattern, the latter being made possible by the lag in the decay of the phosphorescence on the picture tube. For ordinary uses of radar, the output beam need not be temporally patterned, but can be a constant emission in amplitude and frequency. Its figure-ground patterning comes through the contrasting reflection from object and nonobject as the antenna sweeps and resweeps the area. (A single punctiform and unmoving antenna's reception would be uninterpretable, due to the numerous extraneous sources of radio waves.) For the first radar reflection from Venus, this spatial patterning was not used, as not enough contrast to be visible would have resulted, the small angular size of the target and the small energy reflection being parts of the problem. Instead, a temporal pattern was imposed upon the emitting wave. The reception of a radio telescope antenna focused in the direction of the Venus was then searched for a matching pattern. The reflected signal was so weak relative to the radio frequency noise of the background that such pattern matching could only be ascertained by a cross-correlation of broadcast and reception which used two-millisecond pulses, present or absent on a fixed quasi random pattern for four and one-half minutes of transmission. When the cross-correlation was computed with a lag appropriate to the speed of light for the astronomically computed distance, the correlation was not above chance levels. A trial-and-error survey of shorter and longer lags located the optimal lag at a point some 5.0 milliseconds less than expected. At this lag a highly significant cross-correlation repeatedly

appeared, indicating a small but significant error in the previous computation of distance. This achievement is a most impressive evidence of the
power of pattern matching in identifying recurrences of "the same"
thing even when the initial instructions as to "where to look" were in
error.

Further Notes on the Ubiquity of Pattern Matching

The above are, of course, but a small fraction of the relevant illustrations that might be drawn of this most ubiquitous ingredient in cognitive
achievements. And the present paper is, of course, only one of many
appeals for the recognition of its centrality. Acknowledgment should
again be made of the important paper by Lorenz (1959) on this topic.
Polya (1954), Oppenheimer (1956), and Jones (1957), among others,
have called attention to the important role of analogy in scientific
thought. Jones has provided a bibliography on the theory of the use of
models and analogues and discussions of the concept of similarity under
such conditions. The concentration of efforts on pattern recognition in
the computer simulation of cognitive process is further testimony to the
widespread recognition of the problem (for example, McCulloch and
Pitts, 1947; Clark and Farley, 1955; Dineen, 1955; Selfridge, 1955;
Unger, 1959; Rosenblatt, 1960; Uhr, 1963).

THE PATTERN MATCHING OF SCIENTIFIC THEORY AND DATA: IMPLICATIONS FOR OPERATIONAL DEFINITIONS AND VERIFICATION OF THEORY

Science is the most distal form of knowing. Scientific theories are
distal achievements. The processes and entities posited by science (for
example, radio stars, neutrinos, atoms, molecules, genes, cells, and so
forth) are all very distal objects very mediately known via processes
involving highly presumptive pattern matchings at many stages. Such is
a summary of the preceding pages. The present section extends this by
identifying the over-all relationship between a formal scientific theory and
the relevant accumulations of empirical data as one of pattern matching.
The resulting interpretation is felt to be compatible with, and to summarize something common among those several modern philosophies of
science that have attempted to retain the "posit" and "put-up-or-shut-up"

hard-headedness of pragmatism and logical positivism, without making the error of exhaustive-definitional-operationism (Campbell, 1960a). We will but sample from these philosophies, and will not argue here their equivalence upon any grounds other than this one.

It has long been a common property among logical positivisms to describe scientific theory as an internally consistent formal logic (analytically valid) which becomes empirical (gains synthetic truth) when various terms are interpreted in a data language. A variant of this general model is accepted here. The formal theory becomes one "pattern," and against this pattern the various bodies of data are matched, in some overall or total way. These empirical observations provide the other pattern, but somewhat asymmetrically. The data are not required to have an analytical coherence among themselves, and indeed cannot really be assembled as a total except upon the skeleton of theory. In addition, the imperfection or error of the process is ascribed to the data pattern, for any theory-data set regarded currently as "true," and except for quantum theory. Theories "known" to be in need of revision, or accepted only as convenient oversimplifications are conceptually allowed to share the residual matching error. It is as though in the radar reflection from Venus we regarded the known or intended output as the "true" pattern or theory, and the noisy reception as the data. (The asymmetrical conceptual allocation of error between experimental and dependent variables is, however, another problem, receiving explicit treatment in modern statistics.)

This variant of the "interpreted logic" version of logical positivism is in disagreement primarily with those applied variants that have taken an extreme position on "operational definitions." For the "exhaustive-definitional-operationist" if we take his "operational definitions" as defining terms in his formal theory, no error is allowed in the interpretation of theory by data. For him, the admitted imperfection of all scientific theory is located in the strength of the theoretical laws stated, that is, within the kind of relationships which the theory posits. In such a case, it seems doubtful if a formal, analytically consistent theory is possibly utilizing such terms.

While the categorization may seem to fit, Bergmann (1957) should not be identified as an "exhaustive-definitional-operationalist" in any simple manner, for note his criticisms of a similarly extreme operationism (1954) and his condoning of the reification of concepts in physics (1943). Nor should Bridgman (1927), in spite of his temptingly clear expression of this point of view in this quote: "If we have more than one set of operations we have more than one concept, and strictly there should be a separate name to correspond to each different set of operations." (p. 10.) The exposition of this paper will not be hindered by regarding the "exhaustive-definitional-operationalist" as a straw man or ideal type useful in clarifying the issues but not to be identified with the position of any actual philosopher of science. While some have indirectly advocated it when arguing against the errors of other positions, the obvious weaknesses of the position as here presented have probably kept any from direct advocacy.

In contrast to definitional operationism, in the position here advocated the error in matching theory to data is allocated to the imperfect representation of the theoretical concepts by the data series. Where the measurements used by a science have a negligible proportion of error, as in macrophysics and astronomy, the difference in the points of view may be unnoticeable. In any case, focusing the difference upon a decision in the allocation of error makes it obvious that there is no analytically correct choice between the two points of view. As a description of how science has operated, I prefer the present variant, at least as the model of those segments of the physical and biological sciences that have achieved useful formal theory.

Among the logical empiricists, Feigl's critical-realistic version (for example, 1950) is compatible with that here advocated. Hempel (1952, pp. 29–50) states the "interpreted logic" position clearly, and has attempted to preserve the values of operationism without accepting a construct-defining version of it. He calls for operational *interpretations* of scientific terms, allowing these to be partial interpretations. His version of the operationist requirement becomes the requirement that theory be testable, that is, interpretable so that at many points its matching with data be ascertainable. Were he to have explicitly emphasized the inherent mediateness and imperfection of all measurement processes, or to have explicitly recognized the interpretations of theory-terms as fallible, or to have explicitly located the errorfulness on the data side of the matching, his position would be indistinguishable from the one here advocated. Margenau (1950) while not a member of the logical positivist camp has a point of view regarding the relationship between theory and data that is equivalent on these points. So also are judged to be the positions of Popper (1935; 1959), Quine (1953), Hanson (1958), and Kuhn (1962), some aspects of which will be discussed in more detail below.

Note particularly that there are *two* patterns to be compared—that of theory and that of data, even though in an iterative fashion each has developed in contact with the other. This is in disagreement with those views of science in which theory is viewed simply as a summary of data, that is, as the simple product of inductive generalization. Popper (1959) has effectively discredited such a point of view. Hanson (1958) has emphasized this duality through his stress upon the perceptual aspects of relating theory to data, that is, how differences in theory lead scientists to perceive the world differently, how corrections of outmoded theories must await the availability of an alternative theoretical structure. While there is a subjectivist flavor to much of Hanson's protest, descriptively his portrait of science is a pattern matching one. His discussion of Kepler's struggles to match theory and data are of particular value, as also are his detailed citations on the shifts in status of specific scientific constructs from empirical law to analytic tautology. The replacement of an old and unsatisfactory theory by a new one has in many instances the characteristic of a trial-and-error process in which total theoretical systems are tried out, being accepted or rejected as a whole. In practice, no theory that has been judged useful in the past of a science is ever rejected simply upon the basis of its inadequacy of fit to data. Instead, it is only rejected when there is an alternative that fits better to replace it. And the fit of the new theory is not perfect, only better. Kuhn (1962) presents similar episodes in the history of science.

Of course, even for theory in physics, the above description has exaggerated the analytic (logical, mathematical) internal consistency of the theory. As Quine (1953) has pointed out, analytic systems contain hidden empirical assumptions. Where the logical or mathematical form of the theory is not complete, considerable revision of specific terms of a theory is possible without necessitating an over-all accept-reject decision. What is important is the recognition of the two-part, two-patterned nature of the process, and the acceptance or rejection of the theory or model upon the basis of some over-all criterion of fit. This is particularly clear in total-theory shifts in science (Kuhn, 1962). The model of piecemeal theory revision in its extreme form makes the "theory" no theory at all, but simply a restatement of the data in its full complexity. Theory must instead be a separable pattern from data, with the fit to data problematic, otherwise testability, predictive power, and parsimony all are lost.

Fringe Imperfection

It is fundamental to the general epistemology here argued that all knowledge is indirect, that all proximal stimulation is equivocal or fallible as a basis for inferring distal objects. This leads to the rejection of those epistemologies based upon any incorrigible sense data or other phenomenal givens, and a parallel rejection of a purely "proximal" science in which scientific constructs be defined in terms of (exhaustively known through) specific meter readings. Instead, all specific meters are regarded as fallible, corrigible instruments. On theoretical grounds alone, any specific meter can be seen to involve many physical laws other than the construct-relevant one. Keeping these other laws inactive through specific compensations (as in the control of inertial forces in a galvanometer) or through constant conditions is never achieved to perfection. Wilson (1952) in instance after instance provides specific illustrations of such limitations. Yet this obvious fact is apt to be negated implicitly in a *definitional* operationism. This negation is induced by the need to make explicit the essential relationship of scientific theory to experimental data, overdetermined by a psychic need for certainty. The pattern matching model for the fit of theory to data provides an explanation of that essential relationship which nonetheless avoids the assumption of certainty for any of the specific data. The imperfection of fit is conceptualized so that any specific meter reading can be regarded as in error, as judged by the pattern matching that minimizes error in general.

Let us consider a case in which we graph together a set of empirical points and a theoretically derived curve and achieve a good correspondence. Some of the points lie above the line, others below, but in general they fit well, and some lie "exactly" on the line. If there is no systematic deviation, we interpret the point by point deviations where they occur as error, and would expect such error to occur on some of the "perfectly fitting" points were the experiment to be replicated. While an over-all fit has been required, no single observation point has been taken as an infallible operational *definition* of a theoretical value—all rather are partial and fallible operational representations. Were each taken as "operational definitions," the "theory" would have to be multiple parametered enough to fit each point exactly—and if selected upon that basis one would need a new "theory" for each new set of data.

In the pattern matching of theory to data we reduce the fringe of error as much as possible, we center theory in the data points so that the fringe occurs without systematic deviation from theory, and we distribute the fringe of error over all of the observational points, potentially. We may end up saying that one observation was "right on," and that another was probably in error. A priori, however, any of the points could be wrong. It is through such a process that physicists can throw away "wild observations," an impossibility for a rigid operationist (Kruskal, 1960; Campbell, 1964). It is through such a process that physics has been able to refine its measuring instruments, a paradoxical event from the standpoint of exhaustive-definitional-operationism. Physics has at any period assumed that the great bulk of its "knowledge" was correct. From this floating platform of over-all pattern, it has then challenged and re-examined a particular measurement process. As Neurath said "We are like sailors who must rebuild their ship on the open sea" (1932.) The "anchoring" of theory to data has not at all been achieved through a *perfect* correspondence at any particular point, but rather through a pattern matching of the two in some over-all way. The matching of the noisy radar reception from Venus with the ideal transmission pattern shows how such a pattern matching process as cross-correlation can powerfully recognize pattern while still distributing the large fringe of error over every data point. Actual statistics for estimating degree of pattern matching are, of course, not generally available, and the estimate of the human eye from graphed results is still the commonest criterion. The correlation coefficient sets a good example, however, by its equitable allocation of error.

Although Quine doubts the value of the traditional analytic-synthetic distinction which it has been convenient to employ here, he states a perspective upon the relation of theory to data quite compatible with that presented here on a number of points, but in particular, in the handling of fringe imperfection:

Taken collectively, science has its double dependence upon language and experience; but this duality is not significantly traceable into statements of science taken one by one. The idea of defining a symbol in use was an advance over the impossible term-by-term empiricism of Locke and Hume. The statement, rather than the term, came with Frege to be recognized as the unit accountable to an empiricist critique. But what I am now urging is that even in taking the statement as a unit we have drawn our grid too finely. The unit of empirical significance is the whole of science.

The totality of our so-called knowledge or beliefs, from the most casual matters of geography and history to the profoundest laws of atomic physics or even of pure mathematics and logic, is a man-made fabric which impinges on experience only along the edges. . . . A conflict with experience at the periphery occasions readjustments in the interior of the field. . . . But the total field is so undetermined by its boundary conditions, experience, that there is much latitude of choice as to what statements to re-evaluate in the light of any single contrary experience. . . . A recalcitrant experience can . . . be accommodated by any of various alternative re-evaluations in various alternative quarters of the total system, . . . but . . . our natural tendency [is] to disturb the total system as little as possible. . . . Physical objects are conceptually imported into the situation as convenient intermediaries—not by definition in terms of experience, but simply as irreducible posits. . . . Science is a continuation of common sense, and it continues the common-sense expedient of swelling ontology to simplify theory. (Reprinted by permission of the publishers from Willard Van Orman Quine from *A logical point of view*. Cambridge, Mass.: Harvard University Press, Copyright 1953, 1961, by the President and Fellows of Harvard College. Pp. 42–45.)

Confirmation and Falsification of Theory

In the positivists' early effort to root out pseudo problems and metaphysics, they produced a testability criterion of meaning, so stated that confirmability of a proposition through the agreement of theory and data become its typical form. But since theories posit general laws whose verification can only spottily be sampled, and also because of the ambiguity introduced through error in data collection processes, this criterion has been challenged, particularly by Popper (1935; 1959). A strict and rigid form of it shares many of the problems of a definitional operationism, and we may regard it as an unsatisfactory statement of how experimental outcomes strengthen our belief in theory.

Popper has advocated instead a falsifiability criterion, in which a theory becomes scientifically meaningful if it is capable of being falsified by empirical data, and in which a theory becomes the better established the more experimental opportunities for falsification that it has survived and the more exacting these probes. Our established scientific theories at any time are thus those that have been repeatedly exposed to falsification, and have so far escaped being falsified. Because of its evolutionary and selective retention analogies, this criterion has appealed greatly to the present writer. As Popper explicitly recognizes (for example, 1959, pp. 80–81), falsifiability cannot be held too strictly, as every observation refutes theory if carried out to enough decimal points. Instead, it is a selective retention of theories in competition with other theories, with the magnitude of the tolerable fringe of imperfection dependent upon the sharpness of that competition.

Note that in the pattern-matching model, the theoretical pattern is complete and continuous (with the exception of quantum theory), but the data series may be spotty and incomplete. Kepler actually had data on only a few segments of the path of Mars. If the data confirm the pattern insofar as tested, the theoretical pattern as a whole is made more tenable, including the nontested segments of the pattern. The fact that theories go beyond the as-yet-observed would not require the rejection of a confirmation criterion in a pattern-matching model, as it would in a more traditionally inductive empiricism. Further, the selective-survival of theories is now perceived to be a selection taking place *in competition with other extant theories.* As Popper (1959), Hanson (1958), and Kuhn (1962) all make clear, it is the absence of plausible rival hypotheses that establishes one theory as "correct." In cases where there are rival theories, it is the relative over-all goodness of fit that leads one to be preferred to another, not the absolute degree of fit of the better.

SUMMARY

Ordinary and scientific knowledge of the external world is an analytically unjustified, highly presumptuous, and fallible process. As Egon Brunswik has pointed out, the strategy of distal knowing, that is, the positing of external objects mediately known, is characteristic of knowledge processes at all higher levels. In distal knowing, proximal particulars are equivocal and intersubstitutable, raising the problem of how recognition, reidentification, and confirmation are achieved. The thesis of this paper is that in all distal knowing, a pattern-matching process is involved. This thesis is sampled at various levels including visual perception and the diagnosis of specific entities in science. As a model for the fit between scientific theory and data, pattern matching makes data relevant to the acceptance or rejection of theories without committing the error of a definitional operationism. In this, it points to an emerging consensus among philosophers of science, a common denominator among such varied philosophers as Feigl, Hempel, Margenau, Popper, Quine, Hanson, and Kuhn.

REFERENCES

Bachem, A. Brain astigmatism: a discussion of space and time. *Amer. Scientist*, 1951, *40*, 497–498.

Bartlett, F. C. *Remembering*. London: Cambridge, 1932.

Bergmann, G. Outline of an empiricist philosophy of physics. *Amer. J. Physics*, 1943, *11*, 248–258, 335–342.

Bergmann, G. Sense and nonsense in operationism. *Scient. Mon. Monogr.*, 1954, *79*, 210–214.

Bergmann, G. *Philosophy of science*. Madison, Wis.: University of Wisconsin Press, 1957.

Bridgman, P. W. *The logic of modern physics*. New York: Macmillan, 1927.

Brunswik, E. Zur Entwicklung der Albedowahrnehmung. *Z. Psychol.*, 1928, *109*, 40–115.

Brunswik, E. *Wahrnehmung und Ge-genstandswelt*. Wien: Deuticke, 1934.

Brunswik, E. Psychology as a science of objective relations. *Phil. Sci.*, 1937, *4*, 227–260.

Brunswik, E. The conceptual framework of psychology. *Int. Encyc. unif. Sci.*, *1*, No. 10. Chicago: University of Chicago Press, 1952.

Brunswik, E. *Perception and the representative design of psychological experiments*. Berkeley, Calif.: University of California Press, 1956.

Campbell, D. T. Operational delineation of "what is learned" via the transposition experiment. *Psychol. Rev.*, 1964, *61*, 167–174.

Campbell, D. T. Perception as substitute trial and error. *Psychol. Rev.*, 1956, *63*, 330–342.

Campbell, D. T. Common fate, similarity, and other indices of the status of aggregates of persons as social entities. *Behav. Sci.,* 1958, *3,* 14–25.

Campbell, D. T. Methodological suggestions from a comparative psychology of knowledge processes. *Inquiry,* 1959, *2,* 152–182.

Campbell, D. T. Recommendations for APA test standards regarding construct, trait, or discriminant validity. *Amer. Psychologist,* 1960, *15,* 546–553. (a)

Campbell, D. T. Blind variation and selective retention in creative thought as in other knowledge processes. *Psychol. Rev.,* 1960, *67,* 380–400. (b)

Campbell, D. T. Social attitudes and other acquired behavioral dispositions. In S. Koch (Ed.), *Psychology: a study of a science.* Vol. 6. *Investigations of man as socius.* New York: McGraw-Hill, 1963. Pp. 94–172.

Campbell, D. T. Distinguishing differences of perception from failures of communication in cross-cultural studies. Chapter 18 in F. S. C. Northrop & H. H. Livingston (Eds.), *Cross-cultural understanding: epistemology in anthropology.* New York: Harper & Row, 1964. Pp. 308–336.

Campbell, D.T., and D. W. Fiske. Convergent and discriminant validation by the multitrait-multimethod matrix. *Psychol. Bull.,* 1959, *56,* 81–105.

Clark, W. A., and B. G. Farley. Generalization of pattern recognition in a self-organizing system. *Proc. Western Joint Computer Conf.* I.R.E., 1955, pp. 86–91.

Craik, K. J. W. *The nature of explanation,* London: Cambridge, 1943.

Dineen, G. P. Programming pattern recognition. *Proc. Western Joint Computer Conf.,* I. R. E., 1955, pp. 94–100.

Feigl, H. Existential hypotheses: realistic versus phenomenalistic interpretations. *Phil. Sci.,* 1950, *17,* 35–62.

Feigl, H. The "mental" and the "physical." In H. Feigl, M. Scriven, and G. Maxwell (Eds.), *Concepts, theories, and the mind-body problem.* Vol. II of Minnesota studies in the philosophy of science. Minneapolis: University of Minnesota Press, 1958.

Flavell, J. H. *The developmental psychology of Jean Piaget.* Princeton, New Jersey: Van Nostrand, 1963.

Hanson, N. R. *Patterns of discovery.* London: Cambridge, 1958.

Head, H. *Studies in neurology.* London: Oxford, 1920.

Heider, F. On perception and event structure and the psychological environment. *Psychol. Issues,* 1959, *1,* no. 3, 1–123.

Hempel, C. G. *Fundamentals of concept formation in empirical science.* Chicago: Univer. Chicago Press, 1952.

Holst, E. von. Relations between the central nervous system and the periphery. *Brit. J. Anim. Behav.,* 1954, *2,* 89–94.

Jones, R. W. Models, analogues and homologues. In G. Miller (Ed.), *Reglungstechnik: Moderne Theorien und ihre Verwendbarkeit.* München: R. Oldenbourg, 1957. Pp. 326–329.

Kuhn, T. *The structure of scientific revolutions.* Chicago: University of Chicago Press, 1962.

Kruskal, W. H. Some remarks on wild observations. *Technometrics,* 1960, *2,* 1–3.

Loeb, J. *Forced movements, tropisms, and animal conduct.* Philadelphia: Lippincott, 1918.

Lorenz, K. Kants Lehre vom apriorischen im Lichte gegenwärtiger Biologie. *Blätter für Deutsche Philosophie,* 1941, *15,* 94–125. Translation in L. von Bertalanffy & A. Rapoport (Eds.), *General Systems, Yearb. Soc. Gen. Systems Res.,* Vol. VII. Soc. for Gen. Systems Res. Ann Arbor, Michigan (205 N. Forest Ave.) and New York (787 United Nations Plaza), 1962. Pp. 23–35.

Lorenz, K. Gestaltwahrnehmung als Quelle wissenschaftliche Erkenntnis. *Z. exp. angewandte Psychol.,* 1959, *6,* 118–165. Translation in L. von Bertalanffy & A. Rapoport (Eds.), *General Systems. Yearb. Soc. Gen. Systems Res.,* Vol. VII. Soc. for Gen. Systems Res. Ann Arbor, Michigan (205 N. Forest Ave.) and New York (787 United Nations Plaza), 1962. Pp. 37–56.

Margenau, H. *The nature of physical reality.* New York: McGraw-Hill, 1950.

McCulloch, W. S., & Pitts, W. How we know universals: the perception of auditory and visual forms. *Bull. Math. Biophysics,* 1947, *9,* 127–147.

Miller, G. A., E. Galanter, and K. H. Pribram. *Plans and the structure of behavior.* New York: Holt, Rinehart and Winston, Inc., 1960.

Mittelstaedt, H. Control systems of orientation in insects. *Annu. Rev. Entomol.,* 1962, *7,* 177–198.

Mowrer, O. H. *Learning theory and the symbolic processes.* New York: Wiley, 1960.

Neurath, O., Protokollsätze. *Erkenntnis,* 1932–1933, *3,* 204–214. Translation in A. J. Ayer *Logical positivism,* New York: The Free Press, 1959, 199–208.

Oppenheimer, R. Analogy in science. *Amer. Psychol.,* 1956, *11,* 127–135.

Piaget, J. The child and modern physics. *Scient. Amer.,* 1957, *196,* 46–51.

Polya, G. *Mathematics and plausi-* *ble reasoning.* Vol. I. *Induction and analogy in mathematics.* Vol. II. *Patterns of plausible inference.* Princeton, N.J.: Princeton University Press, 1954.

Popper, K. *Logik der Forschung.* Vienna: Springer, 1935.

Popper, K. *The logic of scientific discovery.* New York: Basic Books, 1959.

Price, R., P. E. Green, T. J. Goblick, R. H. Kingston, L. G. Kraft, G. H. Pettengill, R. Silver, and W. B. Smith. Radar echoes from Venus. *Science,* 1959, *129,* 751–753.

Pringle J. W. S. On the parallel between learning and evolution. *Behaviour,* 1951, *3,* 175–215.

Quine, W. V. *From a logical point of view.* Cambridge, Mass.: Harvard University Press, 1953.

Rosenblatt, F. Perceptual generalization over transformation groups. In M. C. Yovits and S. Cameron (Eds.), *Self-organizing systems.* New York: Pergamon, 1960. Pp. 463-484.

Russell, B. *Human knowledge: its scope and limits.* New York: Simon and Schuster, 1948.

Selfridge, O. G. Pattern recognition and modern computers. *Proc. Western Joint Computer Conf.* I. R. E., 1955, pp. 91–93.

Smedslund, J. The problem of "what is learned?" *Psychol. Rev.,* 1953, *60,* 157–158.

Spencer, H. *Principles of psychology.* Vol. I., Part III, General synthesis. New York: Appleton, 1896.

Tolman, E. C. Cognitive maps in rats and men. *Psychol. Rev.,* 1948, *55,* 189–208.

Tolman, E. C., and E. Brunswik. The organism and the causal texture of the environment. *Psychol. Rev.,* 1935, *42,* 43–77.

Uexküll, J. von. *Streifzüge durch die Umwelten von Tieren und Menschen.* Berlin: Springer, 1934.

Translated in C. H. Schiller (Ed.), *Instinctive behavior*. New York: International Universities, 1957. Pp. 5–80.

Uhr, L. "Pattern recognition" computers as models of form perception. *Psychol. Bull.*, 1963, *60*, 40–73.

Unger, S. H. Pattern detection and recognition. *Proc. I. R. E.*, 1959, 1737–1752.

Wilson, E. G. *An introduction to scientific research*. New York: McGraw-Hill, 1952.

3

Psychological Tests in the Conceptual Framework of Psychology[1]

JANE LOEVINGER

The volume of the *Psychological Review* that carried Tolman and Brunswik's (1935) "The organism and the causal texture of the environment" contained an article by Willoughby that set forth, among other things:

A homogeneous, closely knit test, in which each item is highly correlated with the others and thus makes a strong contribution to the total, is to be suspected of measuring, with them, a really existent trait; although it may not measure the trait we wished, it is nevertheless apparent that we have succeeded in selecting from all possible human responses a group which forms a natural constellation. Such a trait would be reliable in the sense of having high inter-item correlation, and valid in the sense of genuine or corresponding to some psychological reality. (1935, p. 163.)

Willoughby may not have seen any connection between his thesis and the Tolman-Brunswik article. Brunswik and Tolman, although not at that time explicitly relating their ideas to the problems of individual differences and test construction, did indicate, in text and in title, that they believed they were expounding principles of great generality.

The purpose of the present essay is to relate some current issues in psychometrics to the systematic views of Tolman and Brunswik, particularly as those views were subsequently developed by Brunswik. Psychological tests will be shown, by the same reasoning which relates them to Brunswikian principles, to provide under certain circumstances particularly incisive instruments for investigating personality. Particular emphasis will be laid on the principle, common to Brunswik's methodology

1. This research was supported by Grant M-1213 to Jewish Hospital and Grant M-5115 to Washington University from the National Institute of Mental Health, Public Health Service.

and the above quotation from Willoughby, that the structural character- istics of the data are important in clarifying substantive issues.

Because of the complexity and abstruseness of the subject, a somewhat redundant exposition will be followed. The first section is concerned with expounding some major Brunswikian principles and gives a preview of the areas of psychometrics where they apply. The second section con- siders in detail some psychometric problems as they are related to Bruns- wikian principles. The final section recapitulates the most important points running through the consideration of several psychometric problems.

SOME BRUNSWIKIAN PRINCIPLES

The Lens Model

The systematic position of the "causal texture" paper (1935) was later expanded in a number of directions by Brunswik and Tolman. In particular, Brunswik (1952) expounded a "lens model" (Fig. 1) to cover both the perception paradigm, with which he had been working,

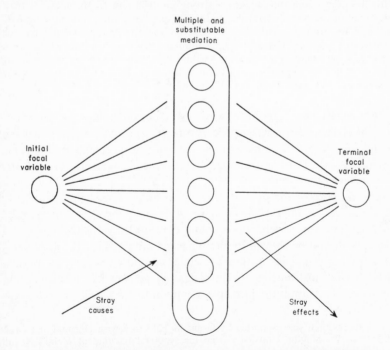

Fig. 1. Then lens model. Reprinted from *The Conceptual Frame- work of Psychology 1952* by E. Brunswik by permission of the University of Chicago Press.

and the purposive behavior paradigm, with which Tolman had been working. In perceiving, one typically reconstructs something very like the perceived object, more or less independently of the many alternative retinal images and other cues that mediate the perception. Similarly, in purposive behavior, there are many alternative paths to a given goal; the correlation between goals and achievements is much higher than that between goals and particular pathways to the achievement. The lens model depicts abstractly the vicarious mediation that Brunswik (1952) showed to be the defining characteristic of behavior, and hence of the subject matter of psychology. The lens model was intentionally made sufficiently general to cover other aspects of psychology in addition to learning and perception; in the present chapter it will be applied to test items as representative of traits and to criteria.

In applying the lens model, Brunswik (following Heider, 1926, 1930) differentiated the functional unit of behavior into regions: distal, proximal-peripheral, and central (Fig. 2). Objects to be perceived on the

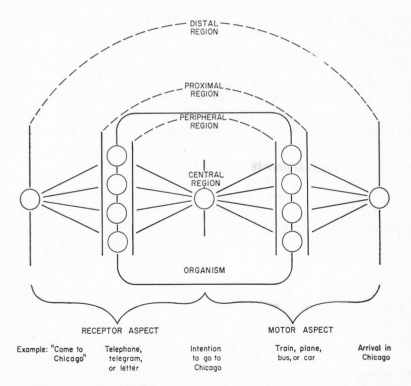

Fig. 2. The functional unit of behavior. Reprinted from *The Conceptual Framework of Psychology 1952* by E. Brunswik by permission of the University of Chicago Press.

one side and achievements on the other are distal, their local representatives are proximal, sensory projections and motor impulses are peripheral, and perception, purposes, traits, and so forth are central. Typically the foci of the lens are found in the distal and central regions, while the lens itself, that is, the vicarious mediation, is typically found in the proximal-peripheral region.

Closely related to the lens model is the principle, central to Brunswik's systematic position, that the focus of our psychological constructs should coincide with the focus of the correlations of behavior: "Psychology has to focus its descriptions on what the organisms have become focused on, not on events systematically located at the interstices between these foci. Ordo idearum sit idem ac ordo rerum." (Brunswik, 1951, p. 136.)

This principle, that the order of ideas should be the same as the order of things, will be occasionally abbreviated below as the structural principle, since it is the structural aspect of the data that reveals focuses of correlation. It is an aspect of what Brunswik later (1952, p. 25) called the methodological postulate of isomorphism between behavior and research.

The outstanding recent development in test theory is exegesis of the concept of construct validity as a mode of evaluation and also of test construction (Cronbach & Meehl, 1955; Jessor & Hammond, 1957; Loevinger, 1957; Campbell & Fiske, 1959). The central thesis of the several expositions of construct validity may be summarized as: To validate a test and the corresponding construct, one must show the convergence of many different lines of evidence. This thesis is only one step removed from the postulate of behavior-research isomorphism.

The slogans of construct validity have been adopted with surprising speed and disconcerting painlessness; sure enough, the protagonist of every test finds some lines of evidence to support his concept. Typically, journal articles purporting to show the construct validity of a test depend on a single thin line of evidence, such as a set of factor loadings or verification of a single deduction from a theory. But as all the major expositions of construct validity have emphasized, no single line establishes construct validity; only the convergence of many lines of evidence on a single explanation or theory does so. More specifically, to establish the construct validity of a test one needs both convergent and discriminant validation, that is, there must be several independent lines of evidence that the test does indeed measure a given trait (convergent validation), and the test must be shown not to be a measure of other traits, such as intelligence, or other variables, such as age and education (discriminant

validation). One formalization of a program for convergent and discriminant validation has been proposed by Campbell and Fiske (1959)
and will be discussed below.

The construct validity view, if pursued to its logical conclusion, demands not simply that some evidence support the conception, not merely
that all known evidence be somewhat in accord with the given construct,
but that the given construct accord with all known evidence better than
alternative constructs. The world is full of intercorrelated things; one
must seek not merely correlation but the focus of correlations. This
criterion—let us call it *salience*—whether or not it has been clearly stated
in the construct validity literature to date, is consistent with and a necessary addition to that literature. With that addition, the pursuit of construct validity becomes an instance of the search for focuses of correlation that Brunswik argued is a major task of psychology.

Items as Cues to Traits

If the problem of test construction is cast in the form of the perception
paradigm, the test constructor, or the test construction process, stands
in the place of the perceiving organism, and the testee is the environmental object (*hantierbarer Körper*) whose properties or *Gegenstände*
are to be ascertained (Fig. 3). In this context, rendering *Gegenstände* as
traits hardly stretches its meaning. Responses to test items then become
local representatives of the traits, those traits being even more inacces-

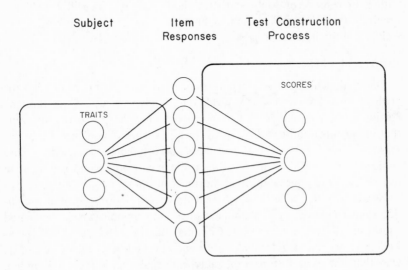

Fig. 3. Test construction as a receptor process.

sible to direct manipulation than chocolate is to the child in the crib, to use an example from Tolman and Brunswik (1935).

Consider for a moment, as Tolman and Brunswik did, the problem of the infant in building up his image of the world about him. His ideas of thingness are constructed by a study of concomitances between visual, tactual, and other bits of information. Piaget (1954) has shown in many ways how the verification of predictions contributes to building up a stable world of objects. The apprehension of concomitances and the verification of predictions—these are the keystones in building up the perception of objects.

Looking now at the test construction process, we see that it is built on the same two steps in a foreshortened version. The apprehension of concomitances is, in this context, the search for statistically homogeneous clusters of items. That such correlated sets of items are clues to the existence of traits was stressed in the above quotation from Willoughby. Here the emphasis is on the fact that they serve as what Brunswik (1952) called "cue-family hierarchies," by analogy with what Hull, speaking of the learning paradigm, called "habit-family hierarchies."

As will be discussed in more detail later, there are alternative conceptions of test homogeneity. One view, currently espoused by protagonists of Guttman's scale analysis, stresses similarity of manifest item content and (almost) univocal relations between items. Another view, that of the present essay, stresses the greatest possible diversity of content consistent with achievement of some statistical homogeneity. As will be shown, precisely this diversity of content enables us to infer something about traits from the item responses.

Equivocal Character of Cues

One of the chief points of the Tolman-Brunswik argument was that the environment characteristically yields only equivocal cues. Since the perceiving organism cannot find univocal cues for the properties or traits that interest it, it must make do with probable cues. Some cues are better (more probably correct) than others, but, typically at least, all are subject to error. This point has direct application to current problems in test methodology, particularly in the study of internal consistency.

Nowhere is the belief stronger that univocal relations are more scientific than equivocal or probabilistic ones than among certain dedicated psychometricians (for example, Coombs and Kao, 1955). The Tolman-Brunswik argument, later elaborated and clarified by Brunswik (1952), was that the search for completely univocal relations is misguided. Equivocality is part of the environment that the organism must master and certainly part of the environment that one organism provides for another. There is no merit in setting up univocal models for which no psychological counterpart exists. Many test theorists, to be sure, have felt intuitively that models that postulate univocal relations between trait level and item response are inappropriate for their data, but the point has perhaps not been specifically related to the Tolman-Brunswik argument.

In all fairness to Brunswik and Tolman on the one side and to their opponents on the other, one must acknowledge an alternative view widely held among psychologists who aim, as they did, for theoretical and experimental rigor. The alternative view, of which Hull and Spence are proponents, seeks deterministic laws of behavior. The classic statement of the deterministic position occurred in LaPlace's *Essai Philosophique sur les Probabilités* of 1814:

Given for one instant an intelligence which could comprehend all the forces by which nature is animated and the respective situation of the beings who compose it—an intelligence sufficiently vast to submit these data to analysis—it would embrace in the same formula the movements of the greatest bodies of the universe and those of the lightest atom; for it, nothing would be uncertain and the future, as the past, would be present to its eyes. (Newman, 1956, v. 2, p. 1325.)

Brunswik stated his view equally clearly:

The probabilistic character of behavioral laws is not primarily due to limitations in the researcher and his means of approach but rather to imperfections inherent in the potentialities of adjustment on the part of the behaving organism living in a semi-chaotic environmental medium. In this sense even an omniscient infinite intellect, when turning psychologist, would have to adopt a probabilistic approach. (1952, p. 28.)

In relation to the study of test homogeneity, the question is whether models postulating univocal relations among items or between trait level and item responses are worthy of major emphasis. (Examples of such models are Guttman's scale analysis [1944] and the scaling models of Coombs [1952].) To be consistent with Brunswik's systematic position of probabilistic functionalism, primary or even exclusive emphasis must be put on models postulating only probabilistic relations. (Examples are usual methods of test construction and the homogeneous keying method of Loevinger, Gleser, and DuBois [1953].) Actuarial models are seen not as temporary expedients to be replaced when more and better data are available but rather as being the only appropriate ones for psychological data.

Test Behavior as Purposive: Ecological Representativeness

Test responses can also be viewed within the paradigm of purposive behavior. Tests of ability depend for their validity on the examinee's acceptance of the purpose "to do as well as possible." There is clear agreement on this aim between examiner and examinee. The aim of the subject taking a personality test is more nebulous. Some personality tests depend on a spurious ability orientation to conceal the examiner's aim of studying more or less unwitting response tendencies. Other tests are given their distinctive character largely by presenting no clearcut aim to the subject.

Brunswik was dubious, particularly in regard to laboratory studies of perception, whether psychologists are asking the right questions, setting those tasks for subjects that optimally reveal life-important capacities and traits. He used the term ecological or situational representativeness to signify this question (Brunswik, 1952, 1956). The principle of ecological representativeness has had little attention in test theory except in the naive version that would have every test be simply a sample of the behaviors to be predicted. Two possible applications are developed in the present chapter. Ecological representativeness can be used as a principle for constituting the pool of items that will be analyzed later in terms of homogeneous subtests. The nature of the task posed by a given item format can also be examined in terms of its ecological representativeness. Is it true, as one might suppose, that tests that pose familiar, ordinary tasks, tasks with real-life verisimilitude (*Lebensnähe*), enlist most dependably the traits that are highly determinative of everyday behavior? The question is at least worth asking.

Summary of Brunswikian Principles

The basic model for Brunswik's system is that of the lens (Fig. 1). The behavior that is the subject of psychology exhibits multiple, diverse, vicarious mediation (the lens) between those elements (the focuses) that display functional relation. Typically, the functionally related aspects of behavior are in the distal and central regions, while the proximal and peripheral regions are those of vicarious mediation, or the lens of the lens model (Fig. 2).

Closely related to the lens model is the structural principle, which Brunswik adapted from Spinoza: Let the order of ideas be the same as the order of things. In psychology, the focus of our constructs should be where the focus of correlations is.

Correlations between events at initial and terminal focuses of the lens are high compared to correlation of either with mediational events. But all behavior, in Brunswik's view, is essentially probabilistic. Thus models for psychological events, including the models of test theory, should be essentially actuarial. Given the nature of behavior, actuarial models are potentially more exact as representations of psychological traits and their manifestations than are mathematically exact models.

Responses to test items are peripheral bits of behavior. Seen from one side, they are clues to the traits of the respondent. From this angle, test construction is like a perceptual process, reconstructing the respondent's traits from imperfect cues (Fig. 3).

Seen from another side, item responses are samples of achievement-oriented behavior. Their goodness as clues to traits probably depends in part on their representativeness as samples of behavior. Imaginative adaptation to test construction of Brunswik's principle of situational representativeness offers a possibility of new insights into problems of test construction.

SOME PSYCHOMETRIC PROBLEMS

The Criterion

In constructing psychological tests, there have been three types of methods:

1. those relying on a criterion, formerly called empirical keying but here more precisely called criterion keying;
2. those relying on internal consistency;
3. and those relying on a priori judgments as to content.

Recently emphasis has been put on construct validation as a method of test construction; it utilizes data from all three sources. Although the term is new, Binet's work can be considered an instance of construct validation.

A critique of criterion keying as a method of test construction can be found elsewhere (for example, Loevinger, 1957). In this essay, only those aspects directly applying Brunswikian principles will be considered. These are:

1. Criterion keying ignores Brunswik's structural principle, while construct validity is an application of it.
2. Criterion keying is pseudo-behavioristic.
3. Because of the imperfection of available criteria, in general, multiple criteria must be used. Since this point has been discussed in a general way

by Cronbach and Meehl (1955) and in a specific context by Holt and Luborsky (1958), it will not be developed at length here.

4. When multiple criteria are used, structural characteristics of the data again must be taken into account.

Criterion keying and the structural principle.   One of the most conscientious and systematic instances of test construction based on differentiation of criterion groups was that of the Minnesota Multiphasic Personality Inventory (MMPI) (Hathaway & McKinley, 1940). The reasoning underlying the method was essentially as follows. A scoring key was constructed for each of several recognized diagnostic syndromes. Items were keyed that differentiated at a statistically significant level between a group with the given diagnosis and a standard normal control group. The hope was that one could then turn the process around, administer the test, and assign each individual to that diagnostic category corresponding to his highest score. Many details of the research not relevant to the present discussion were conducted with exemplary care, exceeding standards generally adhered to at that time.

While the MMPI remains probably the most widely used of objective personality tests, it has not achieved its original aim. It cannot be used in place of a psychiatric diagnostic study. Indeed, Hathaway and Meehl (1951) have gone so far as to recommend that the original scoring keys be referred to by number rather than by the name of the syndrome used to construct the key. The latter recommendation is an indication of how far criterion keying as an enterprise failed to achieve its goal in this instance.

When constructing a test by criterion keying, one is in effect committed to a fortuitous construct, that embodied in the totality of differences between the chosen groups. This set of differences is unlikely to correspond to any intuitively intelligible psychological trait or to interrelations among responses existing in other groups. Something of the sort seems to have been a major source of the deficiencies of the MMPI, as its authors probably came to realize. The nosology that served as basis for the scoring keys is no longer accepted by some psychiatrists as germane to their work, though a notably superior nosology has not yet appeared.

An alternative approach to constructing a multiphasic test would involve searching for the patterns of response intrinsic to the data matrix, that is, homogeneous keying. (In evolving the K scale, Meehl and Hathaway [1946] used a form of homogeneous keying plus convergent evidence of other kinds, thus providing an early instance of construct validity. Psychological interpretation of K scores is unfortunately obscured by the large element of response bias.) A homogeneous keying approach is consistent with the Brunswikian doctrine of letting the focuses of research coincide with those of behavior. At the time the first MMPI keys were being worked out, there was no accepted method for producing homogeneous keys, though the quotation cited from Willoughby (1935) shows that the idea was in the air. In raising these questions again, the purpose is not to castigate those such as Hathaway whose careful work has helped us attain present insights, but to profit from the history of the testing movement. Criterion keying still has ardent advocates, besides numerous practitioners who may never have considered thoughtfully alternative modes of test making.

Criterion keying as pseudo-behavioristic.   Hathaway is deeply committed to behaviorism, as Brunswik was. Close examination reveals, however, that criterion keying is only pseudo-behavioristic. A common method of test construction at the time the MMPI was being evolved was to write a set of items having a priori validity for such a trait as introversion-extroversion or dominance-submission and to set up the scoring keys in advance. Certainly such a method involves reification of the psychologist's pet theories in a way that criterion keying avoids. But criterion keying is not anchored in the subjects' behavior; rather it is rooted in whatever divides the criterion groups. In the case of the MMPI, the criterion groups were differentiated in terms of psychiatric diagnosis. As nosology represents the preconceptions and theories of psychiatrists, one can hardly claim for it a firmer basis than that provided by the trait theories of psychologists. Homogeneous keying, though not without difficulties of its own, is anchored in the responses of subjects rather than preconceptions of psychiatrist or psychologist; in this sense it represents a more thoroughgoing behaviorism.

Multiple criteria and differential prediction.   The MMPI continues to be widely used, which use testifies to the fact that it aids some kinds of predictions. Where it falls down is in differential prediction, particularly the kind of differential prediction that its originators probably thought they could not fail to achieve. That is, to give one manifestation of the failure of differential prediction, those with a particular diagnosis such as schizophrenia will not necessarily have their highest score on the corresponding scale. Differential prediction is also the criterion, as yet largely unmet, of the proposed alternatives to criterion keying. Some attention must therefore be devoted to it.

One paradigm of differential prediction can be drawn as follows: the Nonesuch Differential Test has a verbal and a mathematical score. Success in English and history courses is highly correlated with score on the verbal subtest and only slightly correlated with score on the mathematical subtest. The situation is reversed for success in engineering, physics, and chemistry. Similarly, one might imagine a test for psychopathology such that psychotics and neurotics make somewhat similar scores on General Maladjustment, while psychotics but not neurotics would score high on Loss of Contact with Reality, and neurotics but not psychotics would be high on Oppressive Superego, or whatever. Such differential prediction as has been reported in psychometric literature is modest in the extreme, and unlike that of the foregoing fictitious tests, usually not coordinated to other information about the syndromes or performances to be differentiated. Super's collation (1957) of evidence concerning multi-factor tests shows little differential prediction of abilities from the best known tests based on factor analyses. Meehl's advocacy (1956) of a cookbook approach to differential prediction with the MMPI is an admission of failure of a more rational-theoretical approach.

The most widely advocated alternative to criterion keying has been factor analysis. The factor analysts reason somewhat as follows. A limited number of abilities and other common traits will serve to describe most individual differences. Predictive indices for various performances can be derived from weighted sums or other functions of scores on these "primary" traits. Thus a new prediction should require not a new test but merely another regression equation. Advocacy of a factor analytic approach to test construction has been specifically tied to promises of differential prediction.

There can be little doubt that tests of ability have some predictive efficiency; repeatedly, however, studies have shown that most of the prediction is carried by some measure of general ability, most or all of which are in the direct line of descent from Binet's pioneer work. If factor analytic test construction is justified, it must be by some further contribution in the direction of differential prediction. This is precisely what has failed to materialize to any significant extent (Super, 1957). There are many technical difficulties in the factor analytic approach, some of which have been more or less solved only recently. In searching for clusters among items rather than tests, homogeneous keying (Loevinger, Gleser, and DuBois, 1953) may have some advantages. The present discussion is not intended to cover such technical matters, however.

The position being advocated here is that no device, no formula or technique, can take the place of a thorough examination of evidence from many disparate sources. A collation of evidence from diverse sources cannot be reduced to a formula; only a scientist can integrate all the evidence and evaluate it. To establish that a test is valid for a significant trait is a major undertaking requiring many kinds of convergent evidence; it is questionable whether any other kind of test construction is worthwhile. Factor analysis, homogeneous keying, differences among criterion groups, analysis of content are all germane to the enterprise but none suffices to take the place of the whole. The situation must be embraced in its full complexity. Undoubtedly the long popularity of the classical method of criterion keying resulted from reducing test construction to the apparently simple procedure of maximizing a single correlation or its equivalent. But as Brunswik used to remark to his classes, "Nature doesn't answer simple questionnaires."

Since the argument here is somewhat complex, let us recapitulate. Criterion keying has not been as successful as its advocates originally thought it must be. In examining criterion keying in terms of Brunswik's principles, one notes that the focus of test construction is the criterion, which embodies the test constructor's preconceptions and usually also fortuitous features of the environment, that is, differences that are accidentally associated with the differences in criterion performance. This method violates Brunswik's structural principle, since the focus of test construction does not lie where the focus of correlations is. At the same time, it is pseudo-behavioristic, since the investigator's preconceptions rather than the data determine the crucial point, choice of criteria. The imperfections of any given criterion can be met in part, as they are in the construct validity approach, by means of multiple criteria. But multiple criteria are also used in what at first seems an entirely separate problem, the problem of differential prediction. In the former case, interest lies in what the criteria have in common, which it is hoped is the construct one wishes to test. In the latter case, interest lies in the differences among the criteria, which are what one wishes to predict. Differential prediction has not been notably successful, whether based on criterion-keyed tests or tests derived from factor analyses. In the next section a study will be discussed that began with the apparent aim of predicting differentially different aspects of psychiatric competence but ended by discovering that what was predictable was exactly what the several criteria of competence had in common. Thus when multiple criteria are used, whether one primarily wishes to take them as separate measures of a single trait or as differentiable performances, one must take into account the actual interrelations among them. For research to be effective, the focuses of conceptions must correspond to the focuses of correlation in the data.

Structural aspects of multiple criteria. In principle, each trait of an individual influences many if not all of his performances, and each criterion performance is influenced by many if not all of his traits. The situation may be viewed as a complex instance of Brunswik's "lens model." But while there are potentially large numbers of intercorrelated criteria and predictors, the focuses of correlation can be expected to be much more limited in number. Further, focuses of correlation within the individual, that is, abilities and traits, should be reflected in and discernible through focuses of correlation among the criterion performances. While factor analysis at first seems the ideal method of tracing such focal correlations, technical requirements for application of factor analysis are typically not met by criteria. The fact that we know how well a candidate has done in medical school precludes our finding out how well he could have done in engineering school. Ordinarily it will not be possible to obtain a series of criterion scores on a single set of individuals, which is a minimal condition for application of factor analysis. The data for studying focuses of correlation in a set of criterion measures will usually be varied and will need to be combined by a variety of statistical and inferential means.

In a recent study predicting success in psychiatric training at the Menninger School of Psychiatry, Holt and Luborsky (1958) displayed unusual sensitivity to the many difficulties in use of criteria. Many excellent aspects of their work will not be discussed here; the study as a whole can be taken as a valuable dissertation on use of multiple criteria. One feature of their study is exceptional. They were able to get a considerable number of criterion measures on the same individuals. Moreover, they factor analyzed these data and reported the structural features clearly:

A statistical study of the correlations between the criterion ratings themselves found them to be minor variations on one main over-all impression of how good a man a resident was; and the same was true of the predictive ratings. . . . Under such circumstances, one would expect a prediction of one variable (say, Psychotherapeutic Competence) to correlate about as well with one criterion rating as another—e.g., it might even correlate better with Management Competence, than with therapeutic competence. That is exactly what happened; with few exceptions, the predictors showed no consistent tendency to correlate best with the appropriate criterion. (Holt and Luborsky, 1958, p. 211.)

Their best single predictor was the blind rating of likeability, which had originally been included for use as a suppressor variable. Surprisingly, the same structural observation obtained in this case:

It is true only of Judge III (whose validities were generally among the lowest in the study) that his Liking ratings correlate at about the same level with the criterion raters' Liking as they do with Over-all Competence. For the other three raters, the validities of predictive ratings and of their personal Liking ratings are consistently *higher* than the correlation between their Liking and the criterion raters' Liking. (Holt and Luborsky, 1958, p. 219.)

In noting the structural features of their data with clarity, Holt and Luborsky have performed a service for those who wish to study the implications further. They missed the possibility, however, that the structural features per se clarify substantive issues. To say this is not to criticize them, for the methodological principles involved are of recent origin and certainly were not widely known at the time of their work.

The problem at issue is a subtle one which can only be clarified by a digression and some anticipation of the argument of later sections of this essay. Suppose we have several items of behavior which are univocal manifestations of a single trait. Then Guttman's model of a perfect scale will ordinarily describe the interrelations of the items. The nature of behavior, however, is that it is not simply or univocally determined. Every bit of behavior is multiply determined and related only probabilistically to any of its determinants.

To predict anything, including classical criterion performances, one needs to make use of the comparatively stable determinants, here traits, rather than the less predictive but more observable proximal bits of behavior. These determinants, or traits, are never available directly but only through cues to which they are probabilistically related. Thus we are constantly concerned with probabilities of varying magnitudes.

In this context, how can one say that two or several items of behavior are manifestations of a single trait? Lazarsfeld refers to what is here called a trait as a *latent continuum*. His definition of a pure test of a single latent continuum is: "All interrelationships between the items should be accounted for by the way in which each item alone is related to the latent continuum." (Lazarsfeld, 1950, p. 367.)

Loevinger has pointed out, as a consequence of this line of reasoning, "Such inferences as can be drawn from test behavior will not be based on direct correspondence between individual items and particular behaviors outside the test situation, except in so far as both are related to a central trait." (Loevinger, 1957, p. 662.)

Returning to Holt and Luborsky, let us equate predictive ratings with test items and criterion ratings with behavior outside the test situation. Precisely the structural situation described by Lazarsfeld and Loevinger obtains. The pattern of correlations among predictive and criterion ratings indicates that a single "latent continuum" or trait is responsible.

Figure 4 is an attempt to clarify the matter. Consider the psychiatric candidate at the time he applies for training. The predictive ratings are,

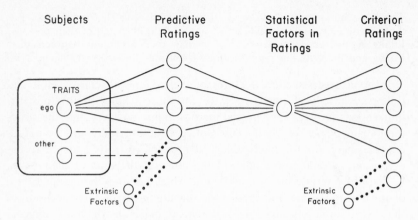

Fig. 4. Single factor in multiple criteria. Hypothesized scheme for data of Holt and Luborsky (1958).

so to say, immediate effects of his traits and behavior, and thus are represented in Figure 4 in a manner similar to item responses in Figure 3. The criterion ratings represent long-term effects of the same traits, to the extent that they are predictable. Some factors other than the subject's traits also affect the ratings (for example, the raters' traits), and they are simply referred to as "extrinsic factors." Holt and Luborsky found no direct connections between immediate effects (predictive ratings) and corresponding long-term effects (criterion ratings). This situation is exactly analogous to the one in which the immediate effects are item responses and the long-term effects are behaviors outside the test situation. That there is but a single common factor in the predictive ratings is evidence that a single trait is responsible for all the correlations between predictive ratings. The evidence is that this same common factor is responsible for all covariance between predictive and criterion ratings. Thus all prediction depends on a single trait.

The structural aspects of the data concerning the Menninger trainees can be accounted for best by postulating a single trait that mediates all predictions, including that based on likeability. Holt and Luborsky, although obviously dissatisfied with "general competence as a psychiatrist" as the concept to mediate their predictions, forbore to conclude that a single trait was indicated by their data. Had they stated the problems in Brunswikian terms, they would have seen that over-all psychiatric competence describes a focus of correlation in the achievement layer. It is not appropriately descriptive of a trait in the central layer but is indication that such a trait should be postulated. The construct of ego development seems to be the one called for by their data, but to argue the point would lead afield.

What must be added is that the conclusion, which they forbore to draw, is one of the most important consequences of their study. If ego development, or whatever, is indeed the trait that mediates all the prediction they could achieve, then future prediction of psychiatric success should start with analysis and study of that central trait. The less inclusive traits that had some validity are undoubtedly related to the central one either as aspects, such as insight into self, or as consequences, such as likeability. Thus, besides being intrinsically interesting and theoretically illuminating, the discovery of a single trait that mediates these predictions is of practical importance for future predictions.

A commitment to objectivity, to behaviorism of the Tolman-Brunswik kind, leads to use of the focuses of correlation in criteria to illumine the nature of internal focuses, or traits. All available data utilizing the chosen universe of predictors and criteria must be examined; the data should be combined by a variety of statistical and inferential means. The resultant conclusions, or second-order data, must then be integrated into a single interpretation or a set of interpretations very much smaller in number than the sets of data that gave rise to them. If each new set of data requires a new twist of interpretation to bring it into line with previous work, no powerful explanations have been evolved.

Consider a single psychological test. Let us take into account all its correlations with various criteria for several populations, its pattern of correlations with other predictors, and indications of the extent of instrumental error and spurious relations due to other systematic causes such as age. If a single explanation or a parsimonious set of explanations can be found to account for all such data, we are well advanced in pursuit of construct validity. But if this is construct validation, it is also behaviorism of the Tolman-Brunswik stamp. It is a search for the focal correlations that are the optimal loci for our constructs, which is the program of Brunswik's methodology.

The Structural Model for Tests

Although the predominant trend in test theory, until recently, involved validation against a single external criterion, there has been simultaneous interest in the internal consistency of tests. As indicated by the quotation from Willoughby with which this essay opened, assembling into a single test or scoring key items that are somehow consistent derives from a wish to make tests instruments of substantive psychology rather than merely psycho-technology. The consistency of the items is taken as evidence for the operation of an underlying determining tendency or trait, at least under certain circumstances. Thus the statistical cluster of items becomes the lens of the lens model, with the prior focus a trait of the organism. The final focus may be an achievement or criterion performance or more likely a common element in a set of achievements or criteria, when one is concerned primarily with the relation between test behavior and achievement (Fig. 4). When one thinks about test construction as a process, then the lens model, in a different application, shows how scores reconstruct traits. The test construction process is considered to be like a perceiving organism. Responses to individual items are now a "cue-family-hierarchy" used to reconstruct the characteristics of an environmental object, in this case the subject's trait level. The test score then corresponds to a percept within the test construction process viewed as a synthetic organism (Fig. 3).

Use of structural properties of tests to clarify trait constructs is an excellent illustration of the Brunswikian motto, Let the order of ideas be the same as the order of things. Item responses, as distinct from other responses of the organism, are peculiarly adapted to just this kind of analysis, since they are discrete and thus supply an unambiguous unit of behavior lacking in many other instances. Moreover, when certain technical requirements are met, which will be discussed later, they are peculiarly amenable to statistical analysis of structure. Thus test analysis may, under appropriate circumstances, be an especially favorable instrument for analyzing traits.

A first step in this use of test responses is selecting a statistical model for test structure. Many aspects of this problem are explored elsewhere (Loevinger, 1957, and in references given there). Here a single question will be taken up: Should a nomothetic-deterministic or an actuarial-probabilistic model be utilized? To accord with the probabilistic character of human behavior, only a probabilistic model suffices. Since a prestige entirely disproportionate to any psychological usefulness has accompanied development of univocal models, they are worth some consideration.

The most important univocal model historically has been Guttman's (1944) scale analysis, which is similar to Loevinger's (1947) technic of homogeneous tests. Coombs and others have worked out a number of other univocal models which (like the technic of homogeneous tests) have not come into wide use, for reasons that may be apparent from the discussion of scale analysis.

Both Guttman's definition of a perfect scale and Loevinger's definition of a perfectly homogeneous test are equivalent to stating that for each total score there is one and only one pattern of item responses. Obviously, the implication is that for each trait level there is one and only one pattern of response. Guttman's original program was that the investigator set up a group of items that, in his judgment, sampled a given "universe of content." He then used his data to evaluate the degree of scalability of that universe of content, either with no item selection or with rejection of only an occasional item.

What has happened in practice is entirely different from Guttman's program, though it is not clear that he has disavowed these practices. Scale analysis has in large part superseded more conventional methods of test construction in sociology, and its use in that discipline will be taken as typical (Stouffer *et al.*, 1952). The investigator does indeed set up a group of items that are similar in content and that he designates as being from his universe of content. The scale model is then used to select four or five out of a larger number of items, which are taken as representative of the original universe of content. In order to preserve the appearance of scalability, these four or five items must be widely dispersed in difficulty or its equivalent. In many instances the items so chosen are highly redundant in content and thus not provocative of new insights. Loevinger (1954a) has shown that both of these steps, reduction in number of items and dispersion of their difficulties rather than use of items with difficulties concentrated at about the 50-50 point, will operate to reduce the validities of the resultant tests in the case of any data likely to be available to psychologists or sociologists. Guttman's papers are not relevant to the point, since the steps he postulated are not at all those actually followed by users of scale analysis.

Apparently sociologists have been purchasing scalability at the price of validity. Why? Brunswik (1952, p. 36) wrote of "misconceptions of exactitude in psychology," and this would seem to be an instance. The apparent precision of the scale model has led some investigators to feel that its use conferred a precision upon research. But the perfectly scalable universes that Guttman supposed were waiting to be discovered have not turned up for they do not exist in human responses with their many contingencies and cross-currents of causes. In order to produce even a crude semblance of scalability, it has been necessary to gerrymander the data, discarding many items and keeping only those that are (usually) redundant in content and dispersed in difficulty. Surely the failure to discover perfect scales without selection of items confirms Brunswik's insights into the essentially probabilistic nature of the causal texture of human behavior. The virtue of a statistical model is not that it should be as precise as possible in the sense of univocality, but that it should be as precise as possible in the sense of having the properties of the thing modeled.

An answer to a test item is a proximal manifestation of one or more traits. Proximal effects are in general many, varied, and more or less mutually substitutable. Moreover, any particular proximal act is likely to have many determinants, of which the trait to be measured is only one. In order for the search for items univocally related to each other or to a trait to be reasonably successful, variations in response to the items must be solely a function of a single trait or a constantly weighted composite of traits, and each level of the trait or trait composite must be uniquely connected with one item response. If one person with trait level k gets an item right, all others with the same trait score must get the item right. In principle, there might be tests of ability for which such a paradigm is useful, though certainly not tests of the Binet type. As regards personality traits, everything we know about their manifestations in the small details of life contradicts such assumptions. A single test answer is given by different people for different reasons and hence, in some cases at least, manifests different traits. Two people very similar with respect to some trait or even a given person at different times will manifest the trait in variable ways. If these observations are true for everyday behavior, why should they not be true of test behavior?

Since the relations between traits and their proximal manifestations, whether in a test situation or elsewhere, are in general probabilistic, the statistical model for test structure should also be a probabilistic one. The enthusiasm among psychologists and sociologists for Guttman-type scales, an enthusiasm that has not been rewarded by noteworthy substantive discoveries, can only be taken as an instance of the attempt to emulate in a superficial way the precision of the physical sciences. Brunswik and other like-minded psychologists and philosophers of science have noted that such emulation is basically fallacious.

Substantive Implications of Structure

The theme of this essay is that structural aspects of test data can illuminate trait structure (under certain circumstances to be specified in succeeding sections). Two different programs of drawing such inferences will be discussed in the present section, in one instance using the interrelations of items, in the other that of tests or subtests. There are, however, many other ways of relating structure to content. More general treatments have been given by Loevinger (1957) and Jones (1960).

The factorial problem. Broadly speaking, concern here is with the factorial problem. It must not be supposed, however, that the factorial problem is coextensive with the problems for which factor analysis is a solution. The techniques that are subsumed under the heading of factor analysis are only one group, albeit the best known and most widely exploited, of the possible approaches to the factorial problem. Alternative techniques include the latent structure analysis of Lazarsfeld, Guttman's circumplex theory, the molar correlational analysis of Jones (1960), and many others. In the present context the factorial problem can be formulated simply as finding the traits accounting for a given set of behaviors. There is no loss of generality in specifying that the behaviors be test responses, since if the behavior does not occur in a situation that is ordinarily thought of as a test setting, it may nonetheless be arbitrarily defined as constituting a test.

Let us consider for a moment the classical approach, factor analysis. Its history, particularly that of the school that grew up around L. L. Thurstone, reveals an enormous superstructure of theory yet only the most meager returns to substantive psychology. The failure of the often-promised differential prediction has already been mentioned. More generally, a valuable technique should yield results intuitively plausible, not completely reducible to common sense, and verifiable by methods independent of itself and its assumptions. Factor analysis, however, has with rare exceptions yielded results verifiable if at all only by other factor analyses. The most intuitively plausible results, such as the distinction between verbal and numerical abilities, antedated formal factor analytic methods. Technically sophisticated uses often yield factors with no intuitive appeal or ones not verifiable by nonfactorial methods. The continued devotion of generations of competent psychometricians to factor analysis, despite its evident sterility for psychology, requires some explanation.

Psychologically, this situation appears to be another instance of what Brunswik called "misconceptions of exactitude in psychology." The elaborate and involved mathematical derivations hide from view the tenuousness of the basic assumptions and the poverty of the results. Repeated declarations that factor analysis must be the road to differential prediction take the place of demonstration. Defense of schemes of axis rotation in the past often relied on the assertion that results were independent of the particular tests used and therefore psychologically meaningful. Actual use of the techniques led to an unwieldy multiplicity of factors, one shading into the next, and often to factors that the investigator could not interpret.

The exactitude of factor analysis is thus at least partly spurious. Methods that keep the investigator closer to an intuitive grasp of the data and do not depend on questionable assumptions, particularly that of additive effects due to the several factors, may be, in sum, just as rigorous. Two such methods are discussed presently, though it is premature to claim that they will prove more fruitful than factor analysis.

Any factorial method, including factor analysis, is in effect a method of examining the behavioral lens to determine where its prior focus must lie. That is, item responses or test scores are examined in terms of their structural relations, such structures then serving as basis for inferring traits. To state the matter another way, the limits of vicarious mediation indirectly yield the limits and hence the definition of the trait measured.

A psychological trait to be of importance must be manifest in many aspects of behavior. Surely the manifestations of a trait that occur in the psychologist's testing room are, by themselves, the least consequential ones. They derive their importance only from their reliable service as cues for what goes on in life-important situations. Convergence of evidence from many disparate manifestations has been emphasized as a criterion for a trait construct in recent literature on construct validity. In seeking common themes or threads in diverse behaviors as a means of disentangling the nature of traits, one is precipitated into a major dilemma. The many different kinds of data do not lend themselves to any single statistical treatment; indeed, one often cannot reduce the data from different kinds of behavior to common units. But a precise statistical treatment is exactly what is needed. For the many crosscurrents of causation have the result that all sorts of behaviors are correlated somewhat, but at the same time two different behaviors are rarely highly correlated. How then shall we discern just those groups of behaviors whose interrelations qualify them to serve as signs and measures of a single trait? Apparently the most acute statistical analysis is required.

Test responses can be made to provide discrete bits of behavior that can be handled rigorously. By themselves, however, they provide access to too narrow a segment of behavior to stand alone as definers of traits. Various means serve to palliate these difficulties. For one, the test format should be such as to minimize factors specific to the test situation but not of equal importance elsewhere, for example, response biases. This point is elaborated in a later section. For another, the manifest content of the items should be as diverse as possible. Only at that point can the limits of the trait be tested. Indeed, many items not to be included in the test must be tried out to set those limits adequately. Finally, to confirm that it is indeed the test content and not the test format or the testing situation which defines the trait, one must show appreciable correlation with other measures of the same trait by different testing methods and discrimination from measures of different traits by the same test methods.

Homogeneous keying as a clue to trait structure. Guttman's (1944) scale analysis was proposed originally as a means of evaluating the statistical homogeneity of a set of items preselected by the investigator for apparent homogeneity of content. Use of the scale model for further selection of items from the original pool was not part of the program proposed by Guttman, though it seems to be practiced more or less universally by those who claim to be applying scale analysis. What happens, then, is that items are first selected for similarity of content, then a small subset is selected that also is statistically homogeneous in some sense.

By contrast, the homogeneous keying method of Loevinger, Gleser, and DuBois (1953) is intended as a model for selection of items. (Properly, the degree of homogeneity of the subtests selected must then be evaluated with a new sample. The latter point is obscured in scale analysis by the confusion over whether it is or is not used for item selection.) As expounded by Loevinger (1957), the substantive value of homogenous keying depends on precisely the reverse of the scale analysis situation, that is, the evidential value depends on the apparent diversity of content of the original pool of items.

The minimum condition for the homogeneity of a set of items to be evidence for the existence of a corresponding trait is that the items be selected from a pool whose content is defined more broadly than that of the selected set. This principle can be extended in two ways. The pool can contain items representing all theories or conceptions of the putative trait; then the pattern of interitem correlations will help to clarify the construct. Alternatively, the pool can contain items sampling as broadly as possible some area of life. The last statement is an application of Brunswik's principle of situational representativeness (Loevinger, 1957).

In constructing homogeneous keys for a personality test for women, Loevinger *et al.* (1962) provide illustration of the foregoing points. They used the Family Problems Scale, Research Edition II, which is a pool of 213 items. Each item is a pair of more or less contradictory statements about some problem of family life; the subject is to choose the preferable one from each pair. Subtests were evolved by a modification of the homogeneous keying method of Loevinger, Gleser, and DuBois. The pool of items that constitutes Research Edition II of the Family Problems Scale was constructed to sample problems of everyday family life as they occur in all the activities of the day and night and with reference to the entire life cycle from infancy through grandparenthood, with emphasis, however, on problems of childhood. Different theories of child-rearing and child development were also kept in mind when writing items, ranging from superficial conceptions such as punitiveness-permissiveness to deep ones, such as level of psychosexual development.

Let us consider a few of the results, as illustrations of how homogeneous keying aids psychological inference. A subpool of items all classified a priori as referring to sex roles yielded two statistically homogeneous clusters when analyzed blindly, that is, without knowledge of the content of the items beyond the fact that they were in that subpool. One cluster referred to acceptance of woman's social role, one to acceptance of woman's biological role. These clusters were, moreover, negatively correlated to a slight degree, a finding confirmed in a cross-validation sample. By itself, this finding does not establish either or both of these clusters as important traits, but it is evidence against a frequent assumption that "acceptance of the feminine role" refers to a more or less unitary trait or set of dispositions. Apparently acceptance of social aspects of the feminine role tells nothing about acceptance of biological aspects; the negative correlation, too small for predictive use, nonetheless sharpens our sense of the difference of these dispositions.

A subpool of items, all of which were classified a priori as referring to punitiveness-permissiveness, yielded a single strongly homogeneous cluster of items that included many but not all of the items in the subpool. Except for the use of a probabilistic rather than a univocal statistical model, the procedure at this point resembles that of the users of scale analysis, that is, the apparent content of the original pool of items and of the set selected for statistical homogeneity are both described in terms of punitiveness-permissiveness. Comparable procedures are used whenever psychologists construct tests by methods stressing internal consistency. Results such as were obtained at this stage are taken as indicating support for punitiveness-permissiveness as a construct describing the child-rearing attitudes of mothers.

In the present instance the research was carried further, giving results which led to a different conclusion. A new pool of items was created from what seemed to be the most promising items from all the pools, regardless of their a priori content, and again examined blindly for statistical clusters. What emerged as the central and most salient cluster in this analysis had the punitive-permissive items of major importance, but the inclusion of many items with no direct reference to that theme and the exclusion of some items directly referring to punishment challenged the original interpretation.

Table 1 presents part of a worksheet used in constructing the subtest, showing the first items in the test; Table 2 presents the content of the items whose covariances are shown in Table 1. The method of test construction involves selecting first a triplet of items with high covariances *inter se,* then adding items one at a time in order to keep the homogeneity (Kuder-Richardson formula 20) a maximum. The diversity of content in the three best items, referring to striking mother, teenage gratitude, and pants-wetting, is apparent. Moreover, following through items 83 and 98, which are rather similar references to toilet training, one sees that their covariance with each other (.073) is slightly less than their covariances with an item referring to thumbsucking (.084 and .077). Apparently whatever leads a woman to have strict attitudes about toilet training also leads to strictness about thumbsucking and food training.

TABLE 1. COVARIANCES OF 10 OF THE BEST ITEMS IN CLUSTER AFI, FAMILY PROBLEMS SCALE

Item	P	68	130	197	70	83	55	98	108b	33b	118
68	.60		89	87	52	71	62	74	72	69	62
130	.43			80	53	55	58	36	63	57	40
197	.37				47	63	59	62	53	56	57
70	.13					49	38	18	31	6	11
83	.58						84	73	39	73	33
55	.48							77	78	40	48
98	.63								44	56	60
108b	.45									50	51
33b	.60										44
118	.72										

Note: .0 omitted before each entry.
$N=202$ women.
$P=$proportion answering in scored direction.
KR-20 for these 10 items$=.76$.

Let us consider now the problem of punitiveness. Item 70, referring to hating mother, has no direct reference to punishment. Another excellent item, which does not appear in Tables 1 or 2 for technical reasons, is, "A father should be his son's best pal," which refers neither to punishment nor to permissiveness. On the other hand, an item with direct reference to corporal punishment, "Hitting a child is one thing a mother

TABLE 2. ITEMS REFERRED TO IN TABLE 1

68a. No child should be permitted to strike his mother.
68b. A mother should not be harsh with a small child who strikes her.
130a. After all the sacrifices parents make, teen-age children should be grateful to them.

130b. Teen-agers cannot be expected to be grateful to their parents.

197a. A three-year-old who wets his pants should be made to feel ashamed of himself.

197b. There is no use making a child feel ashamed when he wets his pants.

70a. There is something wrong with a child who hates his mother.

70b. Most children have times when they hate their mothers.

83a. A child of five should be reminded every day to have his bowel movement.

83b. Parents should not ask about a five-year-old's bowel movement unless he is sick.

55a. If a three-year-old still sucks his thumb, his mother should prevent it or punish him.

55b. A mother should not prevent a three-year-old from sucking his thumb, or punish him for doing so.

98a. It is up to the parents to train a child to have regular toilet habits.

98b. If too much fuss isn't made, a child's toilet training will take care of itself.

108a. Parents should not pay any attention when small children use naughty words.

108b. Parents should punish small children when they use naughty words.

33a. Mothers should prepare good meals and let children eat what they like.

33b. Mothers should teach children to eat everything on their plate.

118a. A five-year-old should be taught not to tell big stories that aren't true.

118b. It is fun to hear a five-year-old tell big stories.

---

should never do," is unrelated to the cluster. Thus punitiveness-permissiveness is a misnomer. There is indeed a behavioral tendency closely related to what those terms suggest, but its limits are incorrectly indicated by the usual designation. Authoritarian family ideology is a more exact term, for reasons developed elsewhere (Loevinger *et al.,* 1962).

The point here is that if only items prejudged to be measures of punitiveness-permissiveness had been analyzed, no revision of the conception would have seemed necessary; in scale analysis and other methods of analyzing tests for internal consistency, such a restriction of content for the initial pool is practiced. In the study cited, the lack of redundancy in the items, the diversity of their apparent content, is what persuades us that a trait of some general significance for behavior outside the test situation is being tapped. An examination of the limits of the content included within the statistical cluster, and the contrast between included content, and the content of items clearly unrelated to the cluster serve as clues to the nature of that trait. This is an instance of examining the behavioral lens to determine its prior focus.

The multitrait-multimethod matrix and instrumental error. Coming at the problem of the evidential value of structural test data from the point of view of tests rather than items, Campbell and Fiske (1959) have brought together a number of arguments and a sampling of data that clarify the requirements of the situation. They argue that we cannot draw conclusions about validity from intertest correlations unless we have at least two traits measured by at least two, and preferably very different, methods. Their requirement that the several traits measured by a given method should intercorrelate less than their "reliabilities" is essentially the same as, but less explicit than, one requirement for homogeneous keys for a multiple-score test. The Kuder-Richardson formula 20, a measure of homogeneity, is the proper diagonal ("reliability") value (Loevinger, Gleser, and DuBois, 1953). Measures of stability over time are irrelevant in this context. Campbell and Fiske go on to show that this is only one of a series of requirements, all of which can be displayed in terms of a multitrait-multimethod matrix of correlations. Measures of a given trait by two methods should be more highly correlated than measures of different traits by different methods. Further, one might reasonably require that measures of a given trait by different methods would be more highly related than measures of different traits by a single method.

What is astonishing is how little evidence there is for valid trait measurement by these criteria. Many studies claim to have validated tests when in fact their data did not satisfy the weakest of the Campbell-Fiske requirements. Both the Campbell-Fiske argument and the tables of data to which they refer show again the importance of the Brunswikian structural principle, that is, of the search for focuses of correlation. Many matrices of correlations contain a series of values all significantly different from zero. Customarily the investigator will cite one or two of these values as evidence for "the" validity of the test. Their discussion shows that single validity coefficients cannot be interpreted out of context. What emerges from many tables of test data is that while ostensible content does account for some variance, the focus of correlation is the method rather than the trait. An argument of their paper to which insufficient attention has been paid is that for such analyses the arrangement and inspection of data that they propose may be clearer and more convincing than factor analysis.

Of the sources of instrumental error, probably the most important and certainly the one to which psychologists are currently paying most attention is response bias. It was known and described by several psychologists in the 1930's; yet tests are still being constructed whose purposes are clearly destined to be vitiated by use of a format susceptible to response bias. Consideration of the sequence of reasoning will show that the test constructors have been concerned with too small a portion of the multitrait-multimethod matrix.

One of the first studies to recognize the problem of response bias was

Rundquist and Sletto's attempt (1936) to measure morale during the depression. They constructed a pool of items half of which were slanted so that positive answers represented good morale, half, negative answers. They found, however, that items calling for negative answers appeared much "better" by what criteria they could muster. External criteria of good morale were few and dubious, so they necessarily fell back chiefly on the criterion of internal consistency. They even noticed that it was not so much whether the keyed response was yes or no but rather whether it was socially approved which accounted for the goodness of the item. Thus, while having a fairly sophisticated understanding of the problem of response bias, Rundquist and Sletto were perhaps the first in a long line of test constructors to be beguiled by the greater internal consistency of tests heavily weighted with response bias. They failed to appreciate that the high internal consistency and high correlation with other tests weighted with the same method variance were purchased at the price of systematic distortion, more detrimental to the measurement endeavor than random error would be.

To sum up, interrelations of items can clarify our constructs, but internal consistency by itself can be, indeed has been, misleading and has resulted in tests unduly weighted with systematic distortions or instrumental error. To state this conclusion in Brunswik's terms, what is important is not that items or tests be significantly correlated, nor even that they be highly correlated; what is important is the focus or focuses of correlation. Thus the Campbell-Fiske matrix is again an application of the Brunswikian principle that our constructs must follow the structure of the data. Some consideration will now be given to the technical requirements that must be met in order that test structure will reflect trait structure.

Item Format

Uncritical acceptance of the desirability of raising the absolute level of internal consistency probably, then, has done much to bring objective personality measurement to its present low estate, where method variance obscures and largely predominates over valid trait variance. The present section will follow a suggestion of Jessor and Hammond (1957) that the format of items be examined in relation to the aim of measurement. Items differ in statistical properties, that is, the formal nature of the data they yield, and in psychological properties, that is, the nature of the task they pose for the subject. The former aspect will be considered in the present section, the latter in the next section.

Principal types of objective personality items are degree of agreement, checklist, and forced choice. Each has distinctive subtypes. The Berkeley F scale is an example of a degree of agreement test. Three degrees of agreement and three of disagreement are permitted; no indifferent or neutral choice is given. Other such tests differ in the number of degrees of agreement and in giving a neutral choice. The MMPI is an example of a checklist of statements, though they are often administered as cards to be sorted rather than literally being checked. In the case of the MMPI one possible answer is "?" Some similar tests do not permit the evasive or uncertain alternative. The Edwards Personal Preference Schedule (EPPS) (Edwards, 1957) is an example of a forced-choice scale where items are paired on a statistical basis. In the Family Problems Scale alternatives are paired logically or psychologically. Some forced choice scales use more than two alternatives, but these have not been markedly successful and will be disregarded in this survey, along with the Q sort approach.

Response bias as proximal behavior. Recent literature on the foregoing types of tests has concentrated largely on response bias as the principal and most obvious form of instrumental error. The three main types of response bias are 1) acquiescence vs. denial, 2) tendency to choose extreme alternatives vs. tendency to choose moderate or evasive alternatives, and 3) tendency to describe oneself in a socially acceptable light. Particular response biases are not connected with particular item types; rather, several response biases may be called forth by a given kind of item in such a way that the relation between the tendencies is built into the test. Thus if a set of items presents a group of symptoms that one admits to or denies having, denial will be in accord with a socially approved stereotype. One cannot acquiesce to and deny the same statement, but a given person can deny symptoms and acquiesce to banal, conventional statements. Denial and acquiescence seem to be specific to content, since Welsh (1956) found two independent scales within the MMPI, each of them keyed almost entirely in one direction. One of the first and best attempts to deal systematically with the problem of response bias was the devising of the K scale for the MMPI (Meehl and Hathaway, 1946). All but one of the items are keyed false, and almost all of them are keyed in the socially accepted direction. The original use of the key was as a suppressor variable in interpreting other scales, but it is sometimes given an interpretation along the lines of defensiveness.

The importance of response bias in both the California F scale and the MMPI has been well known for some years. One is not surprised that they continue to be important and widely used tests, since they represent an enormous investment in completed research. What is surprising is that they continue to be widely imitated. For example, the California Psychological Inventory is similar to the MMPI, while the Dogmatism and Opinionation scales of Rokeach (1960) and the Parental Attitude Research Instrument of Schaefer and Bell (1958) preserve the item format of the Berkeley F scale.

Those who defend such tests either ignore the problem of response set or argue that response bias is itself known to contain valid variance and thus assists in measurement. In part, this argument takes us back to Rundquist and Sletto and the problem of increasing internal consistency, though at times it takes a far more sophisticated form. Gage, Leavitt, and Stone (1957) argue that acquiescence is an important part of the authoritarian syndrome. Jackson and Messick (1958) argue for response bias as an indication of personal style.

Tests are being considered here as instruments of psychology, as clues to the nature and organization of traits. We must remember that response bias does indeed contain some valid variance and yet that it operates as a distortion, that is, as a source of systematic error correlated with similar errors in other tests as well as with true factors in tests and in other variables.

Now every voluntary action of a human being contains valid variance with respect to some underlying traits—actions are not uncaused. Thus the statement that response bias does so is trivial. Actions are not only caused; they have multiple causation. In life the components of variance for most kinds of conduct are confounded, that is, the various causes exist simultaneously and are complexly intertwined in behavior. The task of psychometrics is precisely to assess separately the traits that in life are manifest in conjunction with each other. The principle of this deciphering is that the trait to be measured shall be common to all items but the sources of error shall not be repeated. This principle has been recognized and used at least since the early work of Spearman. By its means items with only a small proportion of valid variance may be parlayed into highly valid tests, provided only that there are enough of them. As soon as there is a constant source of error, such as response bias, running through many or all items, no increase in number of items will eliminate it. Its variance will increase with addition of items just as true variance increases (Loevinger, 1954b).

If response bias is indeed the only thing we wish to measure, then we need only make sure that there is no other systematic source of variance. Obviously, outside of an occasional methodological study, response bias in itself will not be what psychologists want to measure. Conceivably, response bias is perfectly correlated with some trait worth measuring.

But no such thing has ever been demonstrated. Indications are rather that it is somewhat correlated with and logically connected with other traits of greater intrinsic psychological interest. To measure psychologically interesting traits without a systematic bias, therefore, requires removing the effects of response bias either statistically or experimentally. While statistical removal is by no means a difficult task conceptually, as a number of papers on "suppressor variables" have shown, it can only be achieved probabilistically. Thus the correction itself must be based on simplifying assumptions and must also introduce a new random error.

A more serious difficulty in statistical removal of response bias is that some individuals are much more subject to stereotypy of response than others. Most likely this fact is the source of such valid variance as response set yields. While acquiescence to banal and stereotyped ideas marks the high scorer on the Berkeley F scale, one should note that the lowest possible score is obtained by marking "Strongly disagree" for every item. The latter is surely a completely stereotyped response. The California group, to be sure, recognized such "rigid lows" among those who tested very nonauthoritarian. Rokeach (1960) picked the point up and made it the starting point for his work on general opinionation, following in many respects a precedent set much earlier in a study of fair-mindedness by Goodwin Watson (1925).

Some kinds of stereotyped responses are certainly very common, stereotyped agreement to conventional and authoritarian sentiments, denial of symptoms, and painting a socially acceptable self-portrait. Stereotyped responses in the opposite direction, while less common, are not necessarily markedly different in their significance. Tendency towards stereotypy, as such, is more central to personality but more difficult to measure. Adherence to a particular stereotype is easy to measure, but vacillating between two opposite stereotypes as, for example, adolescents frequently do in their self-concept, is by no means equivalent to not answering stereotypically, though the two modes of response would be difficult to differentiate objectively.

The situation when viewed systematically is again familiar. Response bias is an aspect of surface or proximal behavior. As such, it is unlikely to be uniquely tied either to more distal effects of behavior or to underlying personality traits. "Tendency to respond in a stereotyped fashion," which begins to be more of a psychological trait than "high MMPI K score," is not uniquely connected with high or low scores on any particular test. There is no reason at present to suppose that response set is any more univocal in its significance than, say, keyed response to self-report inventories, notoriously ambiguous in significance. Thus, insofar as the situation can be assessed with present incomplete evidence, it seems better to measure personality by methods that contend in a straightforward fashion with the probabilistic character of proximal behavior than to search for crumbs of valid variance in the all-too-consistent instrumental error.

Forced choice and experimental dependence. Forced choice items have been developed explicitly in an attempt to eliminate response bias experimentally. Forced choice between pairs of alternatives has been particularly important. With this format everyone agrees to the same number of statements, so acquiescence does not appear as a response set. While, of course, some alternatives will express more extreme positions than others, any expression of a tendency to choose extremes will be manifest in terms of item content rather than in terms of stereotypy. There remains the problem of "social desirability," and two ways of handling this problem have resulted in rather different items.

One kind of forced choice item is constructed by first giving all the alternatives as a checklist type of test. The forced choice pairs are assembled of alternatives as different as possible in validity and as similar as possible in at least one other characteristic, such as social preference value, susceptibility to distortion, or simply popularity. This method of item construction is based on the assumption that the characteristics of the alternatives when presented singly are the same as their characteristics when presented as a forced choice pair, an assumption that has been questioned several times recently (Loevinger, 1959).

One of the best known tests of this type is the EPPS. A sample item is:

(A) I like to judge people by why they do something—not by what they actually do. (B) I like my friends to show a great deal of affection toward me.

If the (A) alternative is checked, one point is added to the Intraception score; if the (B) alternative is checked, a point is added to the Succorance score. Every choice, although obviously giving but one bit of information, is in effect scored twice. There results a statistical interdependence of items and of scales that renders impossible the study of structural relations of the behaviors elicited. Whatever concepts the test constructor begins with he must stick with; there is no clearcut way to utilize data from such a test to sharpen conceptions, in the fashion cited above by which parental authoritarianism was shown to be a more precise characterization of response trends than punitiveness.

Edwards, apparently influenced by the psychophysical method of paired comparisons, has chosen to use each alternative a number of times, in combination with other items taken from the several scales. This feature is not a necessary one in the forced choice format, but it is a feature that other testers have imitated. The result is a psychological task peculiarly onerous to many people, probably especially those not accustomed to the vagaries of psychologists. Parenthetically, many uses of the Q sort technique are subject to some of the same objections, namely, interdependence of subscores, no opportunity for item selection and consequent sharpening of concepts, and irksomeness. In a test well-established to have high validity, one might ignore the complaints of subjects, but in tests of questionable value ignoring complaints is not done so easily. The possibility that the unpleasantness is causally connected with the weakness of the test is worth exploring. The next section will pursue a related point.

There is a quite different kind of item that is also a forced choice between a pair of alternatives. Perhaps the term paired choice should be used, since the distinguishing mark is that the arbitrary pairing of the forced choice technique is eschewed. In this kind of item the two alternatives are composed together as a logical or psychological disjunction. The format is so straightforward and unaffected that one hesitates to say who might have been the first user. Certainly one of the most ingenious as well as one of the first uses was by Hammond (1948). Hammond constructed a pseudo-information test for which the two alternative choices were equally wrong but in opposite directions, one likely to coincide with prejudices of labor, the other of business. A twenty item test of this sort differentiated a union from two business groups with almost no overlap.

Owens (1947) changed a neurotic inventory from a thirty item checklist form to twenty-seven items of the paired choice form with a great increase in validity.

Use of the paired choice form in the Family Problems Scale lies between the pseudo-information items of Hammond and the self-report items of Owens. The items in Table 2 illustrate the use of two statements that have been composed as a pair rather than assembled by some arbitrary statistical criterion. In some cases the statements are logically contradictory, in others psychological alternatives. The influence of the authors of *The Authoritarian Personality* (Adorno *et al.,* 1950), who stressed allowing people to express themselves with their defenses and rationalizations intact, is clear in the Family Problems Scale. In such a test there is no occasion to try out the separate statements in preliminary studies. The item is composed as a pair of statements and all its properties are assessed in this form. That the interrelations of such items can be psychologically fruitful is suggested by the results already quoted.

The proportion of method variance in any particular item of whatever format may not be markedly different from that of items of other formats. Personality tests are swamped with method variance because they use formats that permit the same source of error to operate in every item. Checklist and degree of agreement items, the most popular types, seem particularly susceptible to response set. Promising results have been obtained with paired choice items in several instances, suggesting that this and other methods of reducing response set are worthy of further investigation.

A final word may be added about the statistical properties of different formats. Most of test theory has been evolved for dichotomous items, and only such items can be treated rigorously. Where an item offers more than two choices, if it is scored numerically, as in the Berkeley F scale, there is introduced an unwarranted assumption of quantitative equality between steps of the scale. Where each of three or more choices is scored as a separate item, there is introduced an experimental dependence between such separately scored items. In the case of the EPPS and some uses of Q sort there is also such an experimental dependence.

The argument of this essay is that answers to test items are bits of proximal behavior. As such they have only probabilistic relation to the enduring traits that are more promising predictor variables. Item families or clusters can constitute an important clue to the nature of those traits. But certain formal requirements must be met for data to be used in this fashion. Obviously experimental dependence, that is, a necessary, built-in relation between items, precludes the use of the data to study psychologically meaningful relations.

In sum, for personality tests to contribute to substantive psychology it is desirable, perhaps even necessary, to use items that are experimentally independent and to plan to avoid repetition of the same source of error variance in several items. Use of item formats minimally susceptible to response bias seems highly desirable. Since test items are discrete, clearly defined, easily scored bits of proximal behavior, their structural characteristics can be studied precisely. They may under proper conditions thus provide unique insights into traits.

The Nature of the Task

While we are viewing tests in the framework of psychology, we may stop to ask what is the nature of the tasks that different tests present. How does the nature of the task determine or affect the traits called forth by a test?

Ability and achievement tests are entirely straightforward. To the subject as well as the psychologist, a correct answer is an achievement. The aim is at all times to do as well as possible. The aim of giving right answers on a test is a thoroughly familiar one for most people in our society, certainly for all more or less educated ones. Consequently, when presented with a "test" that has any other purpose, most people will assimilate the situation to the familiar one and construe it as a situation involving right and wrong answers. This may contribute to the observed tendency to describe oneself in socially desirable terms.

There are, however, marginal individuals who never adjust to the competitive, achievement-oriented *Geist* of our society. Sarason and Gladwin (1958) believe that this fact accounts for much of the feeble-mindedness that is present at school ages but apparently disappears in later ages. The failure to have an easily evoked achievement drive operates, then, as instrument error in such tests.

Most factorial studies of ability have depended in large part on speed tests. The reason is probably that only with speeded tests can a sufficient number be administered in a reasonable time. But the speed factor or factors introduced may be an additional instrumental error factor (though of course also in a sense a true factor) adding to the difficulties of those lacking achievement drive and creating difficulties for those achievement-oriented persons who are not willing or are not able effectively to work against time. Thus the speed factor or factors may have been as important in vitiating some ability measurements as response bias has been in personality measurements.

At the other extreme, the Rorschach test poses an extremely ambiguous task to the subject. Schafer (1954) has written at length on this aspect of the Rorschach test. The ambiguity of the task or purpose, quite as much as the ambiguity of the stimuli, challenges the subject, upsets him, and leads him to respond largely in terms of deeper-than-ego-level traits. (That the Rorschach, unlike ability tests, does not tap ongoing or habitual mental processes may contribute to the paradox of Rorschach validation. For there is little doubt that gifted and experienced clinicians can often attain remarkable insights by its means; yet correlational studies of its validity produce only slight favorable evidence.) Mobilizing oneself to meet a deeply but ambiguously challenging task is itself a task, and one which different people may meet with different traits, or even different kinds of traits. The individual clinician can adapt himself intuitively to the level from which the subject's response springs, and temper his interpretation accordingly. A given sign need not always have the same meaning; interpretation in terms of context is standard procedure for the Rorschach tester. Hammond (1955) has discussed this characteristic of clinical judgment as an instance of what Brunswik called vicarious functioning. In a correlational study such flexibility is difficult to achieve.

Ability tests and the Rorschach represent extremes of a continuum. Other tests can be ranged along this continuum in accordance with how closely the task that the test poses approximates the tasks of life outside the test situation. One thing at stake is the reasonableness and face validity of the task for the subject. Logically, the prima facie validity for the subject has no connection with its actual validity, but psychologically there may be some connection. The contention is not that every man is capable of judging for what trait a test is valid; even psychologists have a poor record in that regard. The contention is rather that the realistic appearance, the verisimilitude (*Lebensnähe*) of the task is a favorable circumstance for measurement of some sort to take place.

Pseudo-ability attitude tests, such as the one devised by Hammond to measure attitudes toward labor and business, are the closest to true ability tests of all other types. Campbell (1950) believes that the nature of the task in this case is ideal for the revelation of basic attitudes and recommends such tests as a paradigm for attitude measurement. Clinicians have frequently noted that attitudes and personality traits affect answers to ability tests, though not necessarily in those aspects usually scored. Tests such as the Family Problems Scale and the Berkeley F scale partake somewhat of the character of pseudo-judgments but are often, perhaps always, seen by subjects as self-reports. Instructions for this type of test usually stress that what is wanted is the subject's opinion and that there are no right or wrong answers. However, such instructions do not seem to impress many people, who indicate by their questions, comments, and conversations with others taking the test that they are searching for the right answers.

Self-report tests, such as the MMPI, originated as a kind of substitute for an interview. Certainly, many of the items are similar to those of the standard psychiatric anamnestic interview. The paper and pencil situation, of course, presents a sufficiently different task from the interview to make data from the two sources not comparable. Psychologists were long in adjusting themselves to the discrepancy, but there are other similar examples easy to see. The ten-year-old child who talks incessantly can rarely be persuaded to write a letter of more than three or four sentences, usually more banal in content than his conversation. Among projective techniques, sentence completion tests seem to tap a level close to the ego-syntonic one primarily tapped by self-report inventories; story completion tests such as the TAT represent a somewhat more threatening situation and more or less in consequence tap a deeper level of personality; while tests such as the Rorschach seem to cut deepest of all (Stone and Dellis, 1960).

The whole matter of the nature of the tasks posed by tests has been given too little attention to justify any summary statement or conclusions. One may, however, entertain hypotheses, of which the following is one: Tests that tap ongoing tendencies or pose familiar and not uncongenial tasks will tend to elicit more stable responses and, other things equal, will have higher validities than tests that pose unfamiliar problems or that cannot be answered in line with habitual trends. Forced choice tests such as the EPPS ask the subject to compare two arbitrary statements, statements which in ordinary life would be deemed noncomparable. This is a new task, not solvable by habitual response tendencies. According to the hypothesis, such tests would be expected to attain less validity than tests such as the Family Problems Scale whose language and alternatives are chosen to imitate so far as possible the manner in which people really think about problems they really face.

Two fragments of research illustrate the point somewhat obliquely though they are far from proof.

Items of the Family Problems Scale that present the subject with a choice between a pair of alternatives both of which are objectionable (1) drew protests, (2) were omitted (contrary to instructions) by more women than were other items, and (3) did not correlate significantly with other items. Pumroy (personal communication) in studying maternal attitudes by a test similar in format to the EPPS also found that items offering two unacceptable alternatives worked less well than items offering acceptable alternatives.

Jensen (1957) studied the Thematic Apperception Test as a means of differentiating boys considered not aggressive, aggressive in a socially acceptable way, and aggressive in a socially unacceptable way. The projective content of the stories had no discriminating value, but the test response when viewed as a behavior sample was discriminating. The rules for behavior in school are well-known and present issues on which the boys have already taken stands, whether to use obscenity or forbidden sexual references in the presence of adults, and so forth. As to the content of the stories, however, there are no rules either habitual or in the test presentation. The more habitual aspects of response are the more predictable and hence more predictive.

To date the successes of the entire psychological testing movement have been sufficiently limited that one can only hope for increased ingenuity in the invention of tests. If the hypothesis here proposed is correct, that ingenuity will be best expended not in inventing intrinsically novel tasks, and certainly not objectionable ones, but rather in capturing, realizing, and rendering countable aspects of familiar, everyday behavior. The point is not exactly the same as Brunswik's principle of ecological representativeness, which is his admonition to perception psychologists to make their experiments less artificial and more representative of real life. The foregoing consideration of the nature of test tasks is, however, in keeping with his program of taking account of ecological aspects of behavior, that is, of viewing all behavior within a larger matrix of the subject's life situation.

CONCLUSION:
THE PSYCHOMETRIC MISSION

The purpose of the present essay is to show how principles of Brunswik's methodology and systematic psychology apply to current problems in psychometrics.

In terms of the functional unit of behavior, current psychometrics employs proximal responses (answers to items) to make inferences about the central layer of the organism (traits and abilities), and hence to predict distal effects (criteria). Test responses, like other bits of proximal behavior, are the lens of Brunswik's lens model. They are many, varied, and more or less mutually substitutable in some sense. Each response is influenced by many traits; each trait influences many responses.

This confounding of effects at the proximal level is the problem of psychometrics. Its mission is to sort out the variance, to draw inferences about traits at a higher level of accuracy than that corresponding to single responses. The principle of measuring one trait at a time is not finding items without error, for that is impossible. Since univocal relations between proximal aspects of behavior and more enduring dispositions are rarely or never found, parlaying of low probability items into high probability (highly homogeneous) total scores must be accomplished by having the same true factor in every item but no correlated errors running through any appreciable number of items. Instrumental errors, such as the speed factor in tests of ability and response bias in personality tests, vitiate this effect. Test construction makes use of item-family-hierarchies, the structural aspect of response, to draw inferences relative to the central layer.

The belief that univocal structural models are somehow more scientific than actuarial models is an example of what Brunswik called misconceptions of exactitude in psychology. Psychometrics should use statistical models that have the properties of the behavior to be represented. Since behavioral regularities are at best probabilistic, our models must be actuarial.

Many of the deficiencies of current personality tests are traceable to taking too small a segment of behavior into consideration in test construction, such as use of a single criterion or sole reliance on maximizing internal consistency. But "nature doesn't answer simple questionnaires." A broader and more representative sampling of data is needed for fruitful test construction, as many psychologists, such as Binet and Terman, recognized long ago. The demonstration of convergent and discriminant validity by the multitrait-multimethod matrix is an explicit example of the more general requirement. A broad segment of data is needed to apply Brunswik's structural principle, that the order of ideas should correspond to the order of things. Behavior with its many confounded sources displays innumerable correlated facets. A single correlation has little or no evidential value. *Not correlation but the focus of correlations shows where the focus of constructs belongs.*

Construct validity is a name recently applied to the program of basing test construction and evaluation on the convergence of many diverse lines of evidence. While construct validation is consistent with the structural principle, the latter clarifies what has not been altogether clear in some of the literature to date: Our constructs must be not only consistent with some data, not only consistent with all available data, but more consonant with available data than alternative constructs. Without this principle of salience one of the objections to classical criterion-oriented validity, that it leads to an infinity of tests, is not answered by construct validity. For there is surely an infinity of constructs more or less consistent with psychological data. Thus the program of construct validation is supported, extended, and clarified by the structural principle.

Because test responses are discrete, easily obtained, numerous, and quantifiable, they offer a particularly favorable opportunity to study structural aspects of response. However, not all test data can be interpreted in terms of trait variance. Experience has shown that where an item format susceptible to response bias is used, the focus of correlation lies as much or more in the method than in traits. In meeting the problem of response bias, some methods have been used that introduce experimental dependence among items. But experimental dependence, even more than response bias, precludes drawing substantive conclusions from item structure.

While a number of principles of Brunswik's psychology have been applied to psychometrics in this essay, the most important of these principles is the structural one: The focus of our constructs should lie where the focus of correlation is. The same reasoning that shows the application of this principle to psychometrics shows that when appropriate technical requirements are met, psychometric data provide a particularly incisive instrument for carrying out a program of psychological investigation based on the structural principle.

REFERENCES

Adorno, T. W., Else Frenkel-Brunswik, D. J. Levinson, and R. N. Sanford. *The authoritarian personality*. New York: Harper & Row, 1950.

Brunswik, E. The conceptual focus of systems. In M. H. Marx (Ed.), *Psychological theory*. New York: Macmillan, 1951.

Brunswik, E. The conceptual framework of psychology. In *International encyclopedia of unified science*. Vol. 1, part 2. Chicago: University of Chicago Press, 1952.

Brunswik, E. *Systematic and representative design of psychological experiments*. Berkeley: University of California Press, 1956.

Campbell, D. T. The indirect assessment of social attitudes. *Psychol. Bull.*, 1950, *47*, 15–38.

Campbell, D. T., and D. W. Fiske. Convergent and discriminant validation by the multitrait-multimethod matrix. *Psychol. Bull.*, 1959, *56*, 81–105.

Coombs, C. H. *A theory of psychological scaling*. Ann Arbor: Engineering Res. Inst., University of Michigan, 1952.

Coombs, C. H., and R. C. Kao. *Nonmetric factor analysis*. Ann Arbor: Engineering Res. Inst., University of Michigan, 1955.

Cronbach, L. J., and P. E. Meehl. Construct validity in psychological tests. *Psychol. Bull.*, 1955, *52*, 281–302.

Edwards, A. L. *The social desirability variable in personality assessment and research*. New York: Holt, Rinehart & Winston, Inc., 1957.

Gage, N. L., G. S. Leavitt, and G. C. Stone. The psychological meaning of acquiescence set for authoritarianism. *J. abnorm. soc. Psychol.*, 1957, *55*, 98–103.

Guttman, L. A basis for scaling qualitative data. *Amer. sociol. Rev.*, 1944, *9*, 139–150.

Hammond, K. R. Measuring attitudes by error-choice: an indirect method. *J. abnorm. soc. Psychol.*, 1948, *43*, 38–48.

Hammond, K. R. Probabilistic functioning and the clinical method. *Psychol. Rev.*, 1955, *62*, 255–262.

Hathaway, S. R., and J. D. McKinley. A multiphasic personality schedule: I. Construction of the schedule. *J. Psychol.*, 1940, *10*, 249–254.

Hathaway, S. R., and P. E. Meehl. *An atlas for the clinical use of the MMPI*. Minneapolis: University of Minnesota Press, 1951.

Heider, F. Ding und Medium. *Symposium*, 1926, *1*, 109–157.

Heider, F. Die Leistung des Wahrnehmungssystems. *Z. Psychol.*, 1930, *114*, 371–394.

Holt, R. R., and L. Luborsky. *Personality patterns of psychiatrists*. New York: Basic Books, 1958.

Jackson, D. N., and S. J. Messick.

Content and style in personality assessment. *Psychol. Bull.*, 1958, *55*, 243–252.

Jensen, A. R. Aggression in fantasy and overt behavior. *Psychol. Monogr.*, 1957, 71, No. 16.

Jessor, R., and K. R. Hammond. Construct validity and the Taylor Anxiety scale. *Psychol. Bull.*, 1957, *54*, 161–170.

Jones, M. B., *Molar correlational analysis*. U.S. Naval School of Aviation Medicine, Monogr. No. 4. Pensacola: U.S. Naval Aviation Medical Center, 1960.

Lazarsfeld, P. F. The logical and mathematical foundation of latent structure analysis. In S. A. Stouffer et al. (Eds.), *Measurement and prediction*. Princeton: Princeton University Press, 1950. Pp. 362–412.

Loevinger, Jane. A systematic approach to the construction and evaluation of tests of ability. *Psychol. Monogr.*, 1947, *61*, No. 4.

Loevinger, Jane. The attenuation paradox in test theory. *Psychol. Bull.*, 1954, *51*, 493–504. (a)

Loevinger, Jane. Effect of distortions of measurement on item selection. *Educ. psychol. Msmt.*, 1954, *3*, 441–448. (b)

Loevinger, Jane. Objective tests as instruments of psychological theory. *Psychol. Rep.*, 1957, *3*, 635–694.

Loevinger, Jane. Theory and techniques of assessment. *Annu. Rev. Psychol.*, 1959, *10*, 287–316.

Loevinger, Jane, Goldine C. Gleser, and P. H. DuBois. Maximizing the discriminating power of a multiple-score test. *Psychometrika*, 1953, *18*, 309–317.

Loevinger, Jane, Blanche Sweet, A. Ossorio, and Kitty LaPerriere. Measuring personality patterns of women. *Genet. Psychol. Monogr.*, 1962, *65*, 53–136.

Meehl, P. E. Wanted—a good cookbook. *Amer. Psychologist*, 1956, *11*, 263–272.

Meehl, P. E., and S. R. Hathaway. The *K* factor as a suppressor variable in the Minnesota Multiphasic Personality Inventory. *J. appl. Psychol.*, 1946, *30*, 525–564.

Newman, J. R. *The world of mathematics*. Vol. 2. New York: Simon and Schuster, 1956.

Owens, W. A. Item form and "false-positive" response on a neurotic inventory. *J. clin. Psychol.*, 1947, *3*, 264–269.

Piaget, J. *The construction of reality in the child*. New York: Basic Books, 1954.

Rokeach, M. *The open and closed mind*. New York: Basic Books, 1960.

Rundquist, E. A., and R. F. Sletto. *Personality in the depression*. Minneapolis: University of Minnesota Press, 1936.

Sarason, S. B., and T. Gladwin. Psychological and cultural problems in mental subnormality: a review of research. *Genet. Psychol. Monogr.*, 1958, *57*, 3–290.

Schaefer, E. S., and R. Q. Bell. Development of a parental attitude research instrument. *Child Develpm.*, 1958, *29*, 339–361.

Schafer, R. *Psychoanalytic interpretation in Rorschach testing*. New York: Grune & Stratton, 1954.

Stone, H. K., and N. P. Dellis. An exploratory investigation into the levels hypothesis. *J. proj. Tech.*, 1960, *24*, 333–340.

Stouffer, S. A., E. F. Borgatta, D. G. Hays, and A. F. Henry. A technique for improving cumulative scales. *Publ. Opin. Quart.*, 1952, *16*, 273–291.

Super, D. E. The multifactor tests: summing up. *Personnel & Guidance J.*, 1957, *36*, 154–161.

Tolman, E. C., and E. Brunswik. The organism and the causal texture of the environment. *Psychol. Rev.,* 1935, *42,* 43–77.

Watson, G. B. The measurement of fair-mindedness. *Teach. Coll. Contr. Educ.,* No. 176. New York: Teachers College, Columbia University, 1925.

Welsh, G. S. Factor dimensions A and R. In G. S. Welsh and W. G. Dahlstrom (Eds.), *Basic readings on the MMPI.* Minneapolis: University of Minnesota Press, 1956. Pp. 290–337.

Willoughby, R. R. The concept of reliability. *Psychol. Rev.,* 1935, *42,* 153–165.

4

Personal and Impersonal Causality [1]

FRITZ HEIDER

INTENTION, THE CENTRAL FACTOR IN PERSONAL CAUSALITY

What we have designated as personal causality refers to instances in which p causes x intentionally. That is to say, the action is purposive. This has to be distinguished from other cases in which p is a part of the sequence of events. For example, p may cause x unintentionally merely because his physical or social being exerts some influence on the environment. He may cause a board on which he stands to break or he may act as a social stimulus for others. Sometimes the statement, "He did it" is really a short cut for "It was the weight of his body that caused the board to break." But unless intention ties together the cause-effect relations we do not have a case of true personal causality.

A more complicated case, which is also excluded from personal causality, occurs when p causes x because x is an unintended consequence of a change y which is intended; p may or may not be aware that y leads to x. For instance, p may acquire an object that o also desires. If the true goal of p is only to obtain the object, then the fact that this has negative consequences for o is not part of p's intention. Of course, the fact that the aftereffects of the action were not intended by the person does not mean that we can neglect them in the analysis of action, or that they are irrelevant for psychological processes. The person himself and other persons will react to these effects in a specific way which will derive precisely from the fact that they are not intended. A case in point is an outcome that is very injurious to the person and is the aftereffect of an action from which the person hoped to gain great benefits. This often

1. The material in this chapter is reprinted from Fritz Heider's "Psychology of Interpersonal Relations," 1958, with the permission of John Wiley & Sons, Inc., and Professor Fritz Heider. It is included here because it shows the strong similarity in approach between Brunswik and Heider, and because from 1934 onward Brunswik consistently acknowledged his intellectual indebtedness to Heider.

produces the impression of tragic fate. An element in many tragedies is that the person causes his own destruction. (Reardon, 1953).

Yet this is not the only characteristic of personal causality, for we must distinguish the equifinality in this case from that which sometimes occurs in physical systems, for instance, a system like a pendulum or a marble in a bowl that, in the end, will always come to rest at the lowest point regardless of where it started. In the inorganic world where a particular end state may be enforced, the forces leading to that unitary effect are not controlled by any part of the system. There is no power hierarchy, no leader-led distinction between the parts, and the process is understood in terms of the whole system. On the other hand, in the case of personal causality, the invariant end is due to the person. Because the person controls the causal lines emanating from himself, he not only is the initial source of the produced change, but he remains the persistent cause. Here, if anywhere, one can speak of a local cause, the second characteristic of the causal network in personal causality. Actually, within a wide range of environmental conditions, the person may be thought of as the one necessary and sufficient condition for the effect to occur, for within that wide range the person changes the means to achieve the end, the end itself remaining unaltered. However, equifinality is characteristic of personal causality only within certain limits, and these limits define what the person "can" do if he tries.

On the other hand, in the case of impersonal causality, a wide range of environmental conditions will lead to a wide range of effects. Since no one condition bears the responsibility for creating other conditions necessary for a particular effect, any specific effect of a complex process requires the presence of a great many specific conditions. The more conditions required, the more unlikely it is that the same effect will occur. Thus, if I see leaves on the ground arranged in the form of a neat square, I will conclude that a person created this effect and not that it was an accident of nature. The same is true when we find pictures of bisons in caves, or statues buried in the ground. In some places little piles of stone are used to mark a path. In all these cases we are confronted only with inorganic matter; but this inorganic matter is distributed in a way that would be most unlikely to occur except through the agency of a person with intention and with the possibility of guiding effects in accordance with this intention. Attribution to personal causality reduces the necessary conditions essentially to one, the person with intention, who, within a wide range of environmental vicissitudes, has control over the multiple of forces required to create the specific effect.

It is possible to use topological terms to represent the meaning for p of personal causality that has its source in another person. The goal of being in a certain state or producing a certain effect can be represented by what Lewin has called the "hodological" space, the space of the paths toward the goal (Lewin, 1938). This hodological space represents the fact that wherever p is located in the space, a force will act on p in such a way that he will take the means that most quickly bring him to the goal. Again we see that within a wide range of environmental conditions, the person is the sufficient condition to effect the change. If there are obstacles in his way, the goal-directed person will circumvent them. Moreover, his own actions will take into account changes in the environment.

In an analogous way one can represent the fact that it is o's goal for p to be in a certain state. Then, wherever p is located in the space o controls, o will apply a force on p in such a way that p will be most quickly pushed toward that state. One can say that p is then caught in a field of push forces all of which are directed toward the same point and have their source in the acting person, and especially in the intention of the acting person.

This, then, is the essence of personal causality. It is characterized by equifinality and local causality. Not only is the end state enforced by a convergence of independent forces to a unitary effect, but also, the convergence is effected by a unique part of the totality of conditions involved in the events that transpire, namely the person and especially his intentions.

PERSONAL CAUSALITY COMPARED WITH PERCEPTION

The distinguishing features of personal causality become even more outstanding when we compare purposive action with the impersonal causality involved in another function of the organism, namely perception. Instances of impersonal causality previously considered involved the effect of things on things. The aspect of perception that belongs to impersonal causality is confined to the effect of things (the environment) on persons. We do not consider here that the person's needs and personality may affect what he perceives.

Let us start by comparing the initial focus (the stimulus conditions that set off the train of events), the terminal focus (the end point), and the conditions mediating them.

Initial Focus

In perception it is the environment; in personal causality it is the intention.

Terminal Focus

In perception it is the person's awareness of the environment; in personal causality it is the change that is produced by the action.

Mediation

In both personal causality and perception we find what Brunswik (1952) has called a "wide-arched dependency" of the terminal focus on the initial focus (p. 19). In both, the mediation is characterized by the following three features:

1. The mediation is "atomistic"—that is, the parts of the mediation in themselves are relatively independent of each other. They do not, in the ideal case, form what may be called internally conditioned units (Heider, 1926; Barker and Wright, 1955, pp. 182ff.). With action, for instance, the way I move my fingers to shingle the roof is only in small measure directly determined by my previous finger movements. It is more closely conditioned by my intentions as related to the demands of the task. In fact, to the extent that the sequence of finger movements is determined by its own properties, that is, internally conditioned, to that extent the hand fails as an ideal mediator of intentions. For this reason the hand is generally much more efficient as an action medium than is the foot whose movements are relatively less responsive to the intentions of the person. In a case of perception, the separate light rays emanating from the tree are relatively independent of each other. They are produced by the properties of the tree and the surrounding illumination. The character of one light ray is not affected by the neighboring rays.

2. In spite of the atomistic mediation the terminal effect can be described as a unitary entity. When someone builds a wall the many part actions that are independent in themselves are combined by the intention of the person to produce the unitary object. This is what may be called "concerted action," the causal lines of the part action converging toward the outcome of the action. In perception, the mediating causal lines that are independent of each other bring about the unitary percept of the object.

3. The mediation is vicarious—that is the same terminal focus may be reached by different paths. With action, for instance, the intention to have the roof fixed (initial focus) and the actual roof in repair (terminal focus) may be bridged by such diverse routes as doing the work oneself, paying to have it done, using wooden shingles or asphalt, and so on. Likewise with perception, the tree outside my window (initial focus) and the awareness of that tree (terminal focus) may be mediated by different intensities of illumination, a reflecting surface, and so on.

This relation of focuses to medium has been described by Brunswik as follows:

... both for reception and for action, it turns out that the special manner in which anything is mediated (or done), is not especially essential or significant. One and the same means-object may be represented at different times by very different stimulus configurations. And one and the same goal may be reached equally well by very different kinds of movements and means-object manipulations. (Brunswik, 1936, p. 125.)

Thus there are two kinds of convergence in personal causality: (1) On the one hand, there is the convergence of different means by which the same goal may be reached. This can be called equifinality, since the converging lines represent a number of different instances of reaching the goal; (2) on the other hand there is the convergence of different part actions of a single means toward the goal. In this case the convergence, which might be designated unifinality, refers to the fact that the part actions all combine to produce a unitary effect.

One of the most important differences between perception and purposive action concerns the control over and responsibility for the events that transpire, that is, with local causality. This can most pointedly be seen if we divide the sequence of events in both perception and purposive action into two parts: a divergent part, that is, the initial phase in which the mediating events emanate or radiate outward from the initial focus; and a convergent part, that is, the second phase in which the mediating events are brought together towards their final outcome. Let us make these phases concrete by considering the processes involved when a man see a wall and when a man builds a wall.

In the case of perception, the relation between the initial focus, the objective wall, and the medium manifold of atomistic light waves, the "offshoots" that diverge from it, is one of coordination rather than control. The offshoots are coordinated to the objects according to simple physical laws. But the objects do not guide the offshoots. The waves that are sent out are entirely independent of the object in their further fate. This means that the initial focus has nothing to do with the second phase of the causal network. As we know, the offshoots are not guided by the wall in such a way that they converge on a person in front of it and are converted into a percept of the wall.

If purposive action were like perception in this respect, that is, if only the divergent part of the causal network were coordinated to the initial focus, then we would only have to make a plan visible to the world and let effects of it radiate out into the environment; the things would perceive our intention and would obediently change in such a way that the intention would be realized. Instead, where purposive action occurs, the initial focus, that is, the plan, the intention, controls both the divergent and the convergent phases in guiding the mediation to a unitary effect. In some way the initial focus is responsible for the whole arch. The entire mediation from start to finish is guided by it. If this were true of perception, if both the divergent and convergent parts of the process were controlled by the initial focus, it would mean that the objective thing would have to paint a little image of itself in the life space.

In short, the organism controls the convergent part of the process in perception, whereas in action it controls both the convergent and the divergent parts. To put it another way, the initial focus in perception controls nothing, though the divergent part of the process is coordinated to it. In purposive action, the initial focus controls everything, that is, both the convergent and divergent parts of the action sequence. It is true that very often with action, part of the sequence of events that terminates in the goal change is also not directly guided by the organism. We have to distinguish between two types of action that may be exemplified by putting and by throwing. In both, the motion of an object is caused by a person. But when someone puts a stone in a certain place, he controls the motion of the stone along the whole path, imposing it by the movements of his hand which is in contact with the stone. On the other hand, when a person throws a stone in order to get it to a certain place, he controls the motion of the stone by direct contact only up to the moment when the stone leaves his hand. He imparts kinetic energy to the stone, after which the environment takes over; the events then run off without further interference by the person. The person sets the stage, plants the conditions, initiates the change, and then thinks he is assured, or at least hopes he is assured, of the intended terminal effect. Examples of only part of the sequence of events leading to an intended effect being directly controlled by the person are: telling o about x because we anticipate that when he knows he will do something about it; benefiting a person because he will in turn benefit p; instances of ulterior motive. The true goal in these cases is a necessary or probable consequence of the changes we directly influence: we sow in order to reap.

One might think the causal structure of this kind of "throwing" action is, after all, not so very different from that of perception, for is it not true that only the divergent but not the convergent part of the process controlled by p? However, though the person, when he throws a stone, does not guide it the whole length of its course, he does, nevertheless, in an important sense, control the motion of the stone even after it has left his hand: he plants the conditions in such a way that the intended aim is reached; the further conditions that might influence the movement are taken into consideration (wind, gravity); the person, surveying the situation, gets a feedback from it by way of perception, and he imparts to the stone such speed and direction of movement as will get it where he wants it to be.

Of course, the more variable the conditions that influence the course of events following the person's direct action, the smaller will be the probability that the goal will be reached. We know that the person cannot control the outcome in throwing to the degree that he can in placing it. Even a very skilled person is often unable to throw a stone in such a way that it lands exactly in a certain position. In building a wall, the person will not throw the bricks on it from a distance; he will place them so that the end position of the brick is exactly controlled by direct or proximal influences. A certain stability in the coordination between starting conditions and outcome is necessary to make actions reach distant goals with better than chance probability.

But in spite of this, as we have seen, there is a certain control by the person over the whole course of events in actions that have been exemplified by throwing, through the purposeful planting of the starting conditions. This is not true for perception; there the initial focus, the perceived object, does not plant the light rays in such a way that they are bound, or even likely, to produce a percept in a person. When the light process has left the object, it is completely uninfluenced by the object; it is neither guided step by step, nor have its conditions been set in such a way that a certain result is probable. In "throwing" actions, however, though part of the process is not directly controlled by the person, it is still controlled to such a degree that we again have to ascribe the outcome to the person as the local cause.

DIAGRAMMATIC SUMMARY OF PERSONAL-IMPERSONAL CAUSALITY

We have stressed that personal causality represents a certain kind of structure of events in the system comprising the organism and the environment, namely, a structure in which equifinality and local causality both appear. These characteristics typically do not describe the causal network in impersonal causality. Where equifinality characterizes an instance of impersonal causality, it represents the function of the entire system rather than any local part of it.

The main differences between personal and impersonal causality are

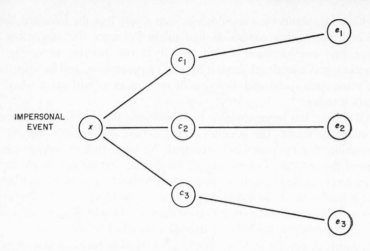

Fig. 1. Multifinality in the case of impersonal causality (Adapted from F. Heider. *The Psychology of Interpersonal Relations*. New York: Wiley, 1958).

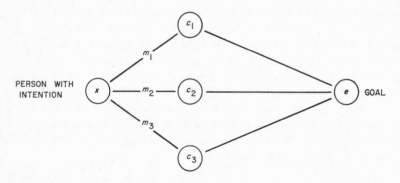

Fig. 2. Equifinality in the case of personal causality. In the particular case depicted, each single means with its circumstance represents a sufficient condition for the goal change. In the case of what may be called "concerted action," that is, where several different actions in combination are required to produce the effect, the diagram would have to include a corresponding differentiation within the causal lines connecting x with e. (Adapted from F. Heider. *The Psychology of Interpersonal Relations*. New York: Wiley, 1958).

represented in Figures 1 and 2. The diagrams show only a few conditions and a few effects. In reality, of course, there are always a great many possibilities. Figure 1 depicts the case of impersonal causality. Here x

stands for an impersonal event which, with circumstance c_1 leads to effect e_1, with circumstance c_2 leads to effect e_2, and so forth. Notice that the effects are all different; for example, a falling stone, depending on the conditions, will hit a man (e_1), fall on the ground (e_2), start an avalanche (e_3). Equifinality does not occur. We are excluding the special case of equifinality in physical systems, where multifinality is the typical situation.

In Figure 2, x represents a source of personal causality, that is, a person with the intention of producing e. If circumstance c_1 is given, x will choose means m_1 to reach the goal e. If circumstance c_2 prevails, he will choose means m_2, and so forth. The means are variable, the end the same. Equifinality exists. Moreover, the equifinality rests upon local causality. The causal lines are seen to emanate from x and to be controlled by x to their final outcome e.

The consequences of the represented differences are significant. For example, in the case of impersonal causality, a source outside the given situation can influence the outcome by altering any one of the circumstances c_1 to c_3. Thus, if a person exposed to the effects of x does not like e_1, he can change c_1 to c_2, as when he steps aside in order to avoid the falling stone. On the other hand, where personal causality operates, a source outside the situation cannot as simply change the outcome. The outcome will not be altered merely by changing c_1 to c_2 or to c_3. Another person will succeed in influencing e only by altering x, that is the intention of the agent, or by creating a circumstance c_4 that makes it impossible for the agent to produce e.

It should be clear that the intention of the person, that is what he is trying to do, usually refers to the point where the causal lines that represent vicarious means-actions converge. Any aftereffect that results, even if it is an inevitable consequence under a variety of intervening circumstances, cannot strictly be considered a part of personal causality.

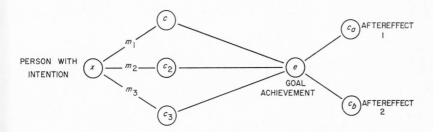

Fig. 3. Multifinality following goal achievement (Adapted from F. Heider. *The Psychology of Interpersonal Relations.* New York: Wiley, 1958).

Figure 3 represents the causal lines leading to the aftereffects. They diverge and produce different consequences under different circumstances. If the circumstance c_a is given, the goal change will have aftereffect 1. If circumstance c_b is present, aftereffect 2 will result. The causal lines beyond the goal change do not show the convergence of equifinality.

REFERENCES

Barker, R. G., and H. F. Wright. *Midwest and its children: the psychological ecology of an American town*. New York: Harper & Row, 1955.

Brunswik, E. Psychology in terms of objects. *Proc. 25th Anniversary Inaug. Grad. Stud. Univer. So. Calif.* Los Angeles, 1936. Pp. 122–126.

Brunswik, E. *The conceptual framework of psychology*. Chicago: University of Chicago Press, 1952.

Heider, F. Ding und Medium. *Sympos., 1*, 109–157.

Lewin, K. The conceptual representation and measurement of psychological forces. *Contr. Psychol. Theor., 1, 4*. Durham, N.C.: Duke University Press, 1938.

Reardon, J. Tragedy and unintended effects of actions. Unpub. term paper, University of Kansas, 1953.

Tolman, E. C. *Purposive behavior in animals and men*. New York: Century Company, 1932.

5

The Immediacy Postulate in the Light of Modern Cognitive Psychology [1]

THEODORE R. SARBIN
DANIEL E. BAILEY

"It is only by an operational approach that we may discover that cognition may be sometimes right and sometimes wrong, and that therefore our treatment of the cognitive problem must be probabilistic. As we will see, cognitive absolutism is still rampant in modern perception psychology, and it appears in a variety of rather treacherous disguises."

Egon Brunswik (1957, p. 12)

One of the basic notions in the philosophy of logical positivism has been that of the primitive or immediate sense datum. This fundamental postulate holds that there exist sensations that, in virtue of their unadulterated purity, can be used as criteria in the verification of empirically meaningful statements. Emphasis is placed on the purity of sensations: for use in verification, sense data must be free of all adulteration, whether by beliefs, interpretations, inferences, and so forth.

Our present concern with this philosophical notion stems from psychological considerations. Two effects, opposite in kind, of the immediacy postulate in psychology may be identified.

1. The recurrent rejection of the study of such psychological processes as cognition, valuation, beliefs, and inference.
2. The acceptance of intuition and phenomenal reports as criteria in testing psychological hypotheses.

THE PHILOSOPHICAL ISSUES

These general effects derive in large part from the philosophy of science formalized by the members and students of the "Vienna Circle," notably Schlick (1936), Carnap (1935), Ayer (1949), Pap (1949), and Lewis

1. This paper is an extension and application of aspects of the theory and methodology developed in Sarbin, Taft and Bailey, *Clinical Inference and Cognitive Theory,* New York: Holt, Rinehart and Winston, Inc., 1960.

(1950), as well as their counterparts in England, G. E. Moore (1932) and Bertrand Russell (1949). In these philosophical movements verifiability of propositions plays a central role. In order for a statement to have scientific meaning it must be verifiable, in principle at least, by *direct confrontation with experience*. Not every experience is appropriate, however, and appeals are made to such constructs as the "immediate data of sensation" (Ayer, 1949), the "immediate apprehensions of sense" (Lewis, 1950), and the "hard data of sense." (Russell, 1949.) Lewis states the proposition succinctly: "When this direct awareness of the given is separated from any interpretation put upon it, it becomes evident that such apprehension neither has nor calls for any verification." (1950, p. 26.)

From these quotations and the general theoretical structure of positivism it is clear that the concept of immediacy with its corollary, the certainty of sense-data, function as primitive elements in the positivistic philosophy. We propose that a resonably accurate statement of the postulate is as follows:

The Postulate of Sensory Immediacy and Guarantee of Certainty:

1. There exist sensations that are immediately presented to awareness without interpretation or any other mediating transformation.
2. Because they are immediate, they carry a guarantee of certainty or infallibility.

The more recent writings of the logical positivists, particularly those of the main stream of the unity of science movement, reflect a more psychologically realistic point of view. The sources cited above, although very recent in the perspective of the history of ideas, according to H. Feigl (personal communication) are "now an antiquated and superseded early form of logical positivism." Drastic revisions of logical positivism (or the new logical empiricism) in the direction of a probabilistic epistemology are evident in the recent books on the philosophy of science.

These reforms are not complete however, and as Brunswik found (see the introductory quotation), we find today evidence of the operation of the concept of the absolute and primitive sense datum in logical empiricism. At the risk of belaboring our point we cite three separate papers indicating the seriousness of the question today.

P. K. Feyerabend charges that there has been a:

tacit withdrawal from the pragmatic theory of observation. It is responsible for the fact that this philosophy, despite the apparent progress that has been made since the thirties, is still in accordance with the assumption that observational meanings are invariant with respect to the process of explanation and perhaps even with full meaning invariance. . . . (1962, p. 42.)

. . . the unwitting and partial return to the ideology of sense data is responsible for many of the "inner contradictions" which are so characteristic of contemporary empiricism as well as for the pronounced similarity of this philosophy to the "school philosophies" it has attacked. . . . (1962, p. 43.)

Other authors in the same collection of papers find it useful to defend themselves in curiously vigorous and *ad absurdum* language against the belief in "sense data." Hilary Putnam's and Grover Maxwell's statements lead one to wonder how unimportant the concept of the sense-datum is in the struggle for synthesis and structure in the philosophy of science.

I don't happen to believe that there are such objects as "sense data"; so I do not find "sense-datum language" much more interesting than phlogiston language or leprechaun language. But even if sense data did exist and we granted the possibility of constructing sense-datum language, I do not think that the expression "chair," although it is synonymous with "movable seat for one with a back," is in the same way synonymous with any expression that one could in principle construct in the sense-datum language. This is an example of the type of "hidden" synonymy or "philosophic" synonymy that some philosophers have claimed to discover and that does not exist. (Putnam, 1962, p. 362.)

. . . let me emphasize that I am not among those philosophers who hold that there are no such things as sense contents (even sense data), nor do I believe that they play no important role in our perception of "reality." But the fact remains that the referents of most (not all) of the statements of the linguistic framework used in everyday life and in science are not sense contents, but, rather, physical objects and other publicly observable entities. Except for pains, odors, "inner states," etc., we do not usually observe sense contents; and although there is good reason to believe that they play an indispensable role in observation, we are usually not aware of them when we visually (or tactilely) observe physical objects. (Maxwell, 1962, p. 13.)

. . . How is it that we can (sometimes) quickly decide the truth or falsity of a pertinent observation sentence? and, What role do sense contents play in the appropriate tokening of such sentences? The heart of the matter is that these are primarily scientific-theoretical questions rather than "purely logical," "purely conceptual," or "purely epistemological." If theoretical physics, psychology, neurophysiology, etc., were sufficiently advanced, we could give satisfactory answers to these questions, using, in all likelihood, the physical-thing language as our observation language and treating sensations, sense contents, sense data, and "inner states" as theoretical (yes, theoretical!) entities.

It is interesting and important to note that, even before we give completely satisfactory answers to the two questions considered above, we can, with due effort and reflection, train ourselves to "observe directly" what were once theoretical entities—the sense contents (color sensations, etc.)—involved in our perception of physical things. As has been pointed out before, we can also come to observe other kinds of entities which were once theoretical. Those which most readily come to mind involve the use of instruments as aids to observation. Indeed, using our painfully acquired theoretical knowledge of the world, we come to see that we "directly observe" many kinds of so-called theoretical things. After listening to a dull speech while sitting on a hard bench, we begin to become poignantly aware of the presence of a considerably strong gravitation field, and as Professor Feyerabend is fond of pointing out, if we were carrying a heavy suitcase in a changing gravitational field, we could observe the changes of the $G\mu_v$ of the metric tensor.

I conclude that our drawing of the observational-theoretical line at any given point is an accident and a function of our physiological make-up, our current state of knowledge, and the instruments we happen to have available and, therefore, that it has no ontological significance whatever. (Maxwell, 1962, pp. 14–15.)

In view of these comments it would perhaps be fair to assert that our target in this paper is the philosophy of the sense datum, not logical positivism. However, as the position we are attacking is traditionally associated with logical positivism, we shall continue to refer to "positivism" in our arguments. There seems no question, however, but that it is a live issue in the philosophy of science and will continue to be so until the epistemological principles involved are brought into line with the modern cognitive psychological principles. This is being done in some circles to be sure, but the progress has been neither swift nor sure. This paper is an attempt to hasten the demise of sense-datum theories of science by presenting it in the light of a model of cognitive psychology based on findings from contemporary psychological research.

It should be noted at this point that the fruitfulness of the positivistic theory of science does not depend necessarily on the truth of the sense data postulate. The main structure of *methodological* positivism is undisturbed by the removal of this postulate from the structure of *doctrinal positivism*. The nature of the doctrinal aspects of the positivistic movement would, of course, be altered by the negation of the postulate. However, these doctrinal aspects of positivism serve the function of an articulate and generally convincing rationale for the procedures, attitudes and evaluations that characterize the work of methodological positivists. They do not logically *determine* methodological positivism. The principles of reducing statements to empirically meaningful propositions and empirical verification are carefully derived by the positivists from their general postulational system. Thus, they may *seem* dependent on that postulate system that includes the immediacy postulate. However, it is clear that the same methodological principles could have been derived from quite different doctrinal systems. Indeed, one could cast a historical argument to the effect that the contribution of the Vienna Circle was to systematize and rationalize an already widely established practice of scientific method.

Regardless of the implicit or explicit status of the postulate in psychology, it is clear that the positivists performed the difficult and invaluable task of clarifying the structure of "positivistic" methods and of furnishing a *philosophical apologetic* for them. However, it would be a mistake to interpret the implication between the positivistic postulates and logical derivations as an *if and only if* implication. The postulates are a set of givens from which, by logical-philosophical argument, one may derive the principles of methodological positivism. *If* we accept the truth value of the postulates, *then* methodological positivism is implied. However, *if* we accept the truth value of methodological positivism, the postulates are *not* necessarily implied.

The point is, of course, that we may dispute the status of the body of postulates, metaphysical, epistemological, and quasi-psychological, that are proposed by the positivists as the rationale for the methodological principles of positivism. And this need not shake our faith in the methodological principles. The thesis of this chapter is that the immediacy postulate is not tenable and that its removal from the framework of positivism will clarify and, hopefully, rectify two serious misconceptions in modern scientific psychology. The foundation or axiomatic basis for this argument is the body of theory and "regulations" comprising methodological positivism stripped of its underpinnings in doctrinal positivism.

The motivations for developing this thesis at length are:

1. To reopen the philosophical questions involved in the immediacy postulate to psychologists and lead to a firmer theoretical foundation;
2. to understand the two effects of the acceptance of the immediacy postulate, that is, rejection of broad areas of inquiry and employment of unsound methods. Psychology, at its contemporary stage of development as a science, is too impoverished to afford to reject broad areas of potential interest or to risk using unwarranted methods on the basis of an untenable postulate.

Our argument is based in large part on the empirical and theoretical work of Egon Brunswik (1937, 1944, 1949, 1952), himself strongly influenced by the Vienna Circle and an enthusiastic participant in the activities of positivism in America through the Unity of Science Movement. Brunswik (1952, p. 66) felt that the distinction between methodological and doctrinal positivism was crucial. The former, under

Brunswik's skillful application in empirical and theoretical researches in perceptual constancies produced results that are contrary to what would be required by the immediacy postulate of doctrinal positivism. The theoretical argument is based preponderately on Brunswik's theory of perception and cognition. His research provides the primary empirical foundation.

In order to focus more readily on the sensory postulate we shall first sketch some of the possible meanings of "immediacy" and "guarantee" as asserted in the postulate.

Immediacy: An Ambiguous Term

For our purposes we may identify two notions:

1. *psychological immediacy*—which was basic to the British empiricists and later to the structural psychology of Wundt and Titchener; and
2. *phenomenological immediacy*—the point of departure of the Gestalt psychologists.[3]

In the former usage, immediacy refers to pure, raw, unrefined sense-data, unadulterated by association, memory, learning, inference or kindred cognitive activities. In the latter usage, immediacy refers to the pre-reflective experience *including* any meanings, associations, and qualities that appear to be a part of the phenomena under scrutiny. In the traditional psychological meaning of immediacy, the report of the "givens" of sensation is primarily in terms of sense words such as "patch of red," "grey flash," "circular form," and so forth. In the phenomenological meaning, the report may contain a series of apparently unmiscible qualities drawn from sources in physical science such as "heavy," "coarse," and "fast," along with qualities drawn from the arts and common sense, such as "inspiring," "grasping," "delicate," and "coy."

We shall first investigate the notion of psychological immediacy, upon which the methods and the theory of structuralism were based. It is unnecessary here to repeat in detail Boring's (1953) history of introspection

3. Wallraff (1953) has written a stimulating paper, "On immediacy and the contemporary dogma of sense-certainty," which parallels to a certain extent the arguments of the present essay. He identifies two additional meanings of immediacy: (1) *Spatio-temporal:* "the immediate contiguity of knower and known in space-time. . . ." "Immediate objects of sense-perception can only be states of the nerves which are felt as sensations by the sensorium." (2) *Pre-inferential:* "Scientific protocol statements are (for example) immediate relative to the inductive conclusions which they yield. . . ." Although of interest in epistemology, these meanings are currently less central for psychologists. Where "Pre-inferential immediacy," as defined by Wallraff, is relevant to this essay, we have included it in the category of Psychological immediacy.

or to belabor the failure of trained introspectionists to agree on what is psychologically immediate. Classical introspection became, says Boring, "a dull taxonomic account of sensory events which suggest almost no functional value for the organism. . . ." Further, the time interval required to report the "contents of consciousness" made it impossible really to deal with the psychologically immediate; the introspective psychologist found himself adding a good deal of memory and inference to the "raw, untrammelled, untouched sensory experience." There was no way of making good Titchener's dictum, that the quality of a sensation "always remains itself through all changes of intensity and of time and space." (1953, p. 38.)

The attempts to make a sense-datum a special kind of object was a natural development from the "psychophysical" dualism that pervaded the thinking of the founders of modern experimental psychology. Ryle's pithy comment apropos of this development is worth quoting here:

. . . to say that an object is green is to say something about the visual sensations of the particular observer who reports that it is green. It was supposed that "green," "bitter," "chilly," and the rest are adjectives which properly apply to sensations and are only improperly applied to objects. And then, as it is obviously absurd to say that a sensation is a green thing . . ., It seemed necessary to allot to sensations their own peculiar objects, so that "green" might be suitably applied not to the having of a sensation but to a peculiar object internally nursed by that sensation. The ban on characterizing common objects of anyone's observation by Secondary Quality adjectives led to the invention of some counterpart, privy objects to carry those adjectives. Because Secondary Quality adjectives would not behave except as predicates in observation reports, sensations had to be construed as being themselves observations of special objects. (1949, pp. 219–220.) . . . it . . . follows that we need erect no private theaters to provide stages for these postulated extra objects, nor puzzle our heads to describe the indescribable relations between these postulated objects and everyday things. (1949, p. 222.)

Thus it is clear that the concept of the sensation as a substantive object has outlived its usefulness. At present the concept of sensation may be identified as a complicated set of functions mapping the world of energy gradients (through several stages) into the world of experiencing, perception and cognition.

THE PSYCHOLOGICAL ISSUES

The Stimulus Error

At the height of European introspectionism and American structuralism a major empirical and theoretical activity in psychology was the isolation and decomposition of the "sensation." The experiments performed toward this end were intended to produce descriptions of the "elements of sensation." However, the extra-organismic object presented as a stimulus constantly intruded in such a way that the descriptions were of the stimulus object as it is functionally relevant to the subject. These descriptions were labeled "stimulus errors" because the subject was not accomplishing his goal of describing the sense data, the raw, untrammeled, pure, stimulus elements.

Since the decline of structuralism, the history of psychology has led to the axiom, almost universally accepted among psychologists, that human organisms, with the doubtful exception of the neonate, respond to "sense-data" against a ground of prior experience, habits, dispositions, expectations, sets, attitudes, values, and so forth, so that the "stimulus error" seems the usual mode of perception and characterizes the normal functioning of the higher mental processes. In this interpretation, sense-data are used by the organism primarily as the selector of the "errors" the organism is to make. A sense-datum may, however, take on a different significance when it is adaptively inadequate or misleading to the organism. If the "error" set off by some sense-datum is not the "correct error," that is, does not lead to functionally valid achievements, then the organism will resort to closer scrutiny of the datum or utilization of a wider variety of data. For example, a person having entered an automobile similar to his own will scrutinize his ignition key carefully when it does not fit. Finding that this is not the source of difficulty, he will correct the stimulus error by a more detailed inspection of the stimulus—the similar, but mistakenly-identified motor car.

Only the acceptance of the doctrines of immediacy and guarantee make this confusing round of sophism about "correct" and "incorrect" errors possible or necessary. Had the doctrine not been so strongly intrenched, the stimulus error might have been more readily recognized for what it is. *The stimulus error is the primary indication of behavioral adaptiveness in that it refers to the behaviorally stable ecology instead of the shifting flux of energy impinging on the organism.* The same level of adaptiveness could be attained without the "stimulus error" via "pure sense-data" only at greater organismic cost and hazard, if it could be attained at all. For example, walking on a sidewalk imbedded with ventilators and skylights, and encrusted with various oddments of human traffic would be impossible without the stimulus error—that the conglomerate is suitable for confident strolling. Drawing the same conclusion from "pure sense data" would require an extravagant amount of scanning, discrimination and exploration at each step.

In spite of the widespread recognition that the stimulus error resists "correction" the postulate of immediacy (especially psychological immediacy), with its implied special theater of awareness, continues to operate as a silent assumption in contemporary philosophy and psychology.

Phenomenology

The idea of phenomenological immediacy is, with a correction, more tenable than that of psychological immediacy because no attempt is made to reduce the personal experience to strange or artificial units. However, when we examine the operations by which the phenomenologically-immediate is made known to self or others, it is at once apparent that the reported phenomenal experience is attenuated in some way by language habits, and that we are dealing with *retrospective* self-report. The introduction of the word retrospective is a necessary correction following from the implication that the immediate is instantaneous, equivalent to the specious present, and that the act of verbally reporting the experience occurs *after* the experience. Thus, phenomenological immediacy, strictly speaking, is a misnomer. Although we shall use the term in the paragraphs that follow, the qualifier "retrospective" is implied.

The presence of the notion of the phenomenological immediacy is seen in attempts at formulating the laws of reason through an analysis of phenomenological reports (for example, Wertheimer, 1945.) On the basis of retrospective reports, the phenomenologist infers the process by which the subject reaches conclusions, formulates plans, solves problems, and so on. Hidden in the assumptions underlying such an approach is the belief that one's own thinking is an aspect of a private shadow world; and, further, that *only* the subject has privileged access to it. To discover the natural laws of the higher mental process, given these assumptions, it is required that the subject report what he is "experiencing."

As an example of the use of a method in which the phenomenologically-immediate is taken as a point of departure for setting up principles of behavior, we can point to the interesting experiments of Michotte (1950). A set of geometrical figures in movement were presented to observers. The reports of the observations were made in terms of human "dynamic-causal relationships." That is, the translocations of inert objects were interpreted as approaching, departing, throwing, pushing, and so forth. Such factors as speed of movement, uniformity of movement, direction, uniformity of direction, and so forth, for each object separately and for pairs of objects, produced these various "phenomenological-givens." Asch (1952), using this experiment as an example, along with a similar experiment reported by Heider and Simmel (1944), concludes that "when we perceive a given act issuing from a person, it is represented phenomenally as a motive, need or intention." (p. 156.) It would be incorrect to assert, says Asch, that the reports of Michotte's subjects "were due solely to past experience. . . . For past experience would have been of no value if the observers had failed to note definite qualities in the present visual situation similar to those of which they already had knowledge. . . . The movement forms of the figures were perceptually similar to actual movement-forms of persons." In short, the phenomenologist asserts that the "impression" is an irreducible given, and something, for example, causation, is "revealed" in the sensations. Would not a more parsimonious explanation be that the observers reported their observations in the vocabulary of common objects? And, the vocabulary of common objects includes words which have, for example, "causal" reference. In fact, Michotte reports the use of "as if" statements by his subjects. The fact that some observers did not use explicit verbal devices, such as the as-if formula, does not mean that for those people some kind of revelation occurred.

One wonders in what terms Samoans and Trobriand Islanders would have interpreted the experiments. According to Mead (1928), Samoans do not use motivation concepts in describing each other's behavior. Lee's linguistic analysis (1957) of Malinowski's observations on the Trobriand Islanders indicates "no temporal connection between objects . . . not for the purpose of; there is no *why* and no *because*."

The phenomenologically-immediate, like the psychologically-immediate, leaves much to be desired as the ultimate source of data for psychological theory and practice. In their retrospections, be they only a matter of milli-seconds following the apprehension of a stimulus object, even sophisticated judges report inferences that—after the variance attributable to the physical properties of the object are accounted for—demonstrate the operation of mediational processes within the responding organism. The fact that a person is unable to isolate the "immediately-given" from the mediately-compounded, of course, points to the inutility of relying upon phenomenal data, at least for the scientific purposes intended by the positivistic philosophy. The inability of the subject to direct or isolate the events taking place on an assumed private stage of awareness is clearly illustrated by experiments on perceptual constancy.

Demonstrations through Constancy Experiments

Experiments on perceptual constancy demonstrate that reports of "immediate experience" may ignore a substantial part of the physical stimulus world and also a substantial part of the intrapersonal contribution. That is to say, responses or behavioral indices based on the perception of an object may belie the object's measurable physical properties and also may match imperfectly the perceiver's prior "knowledge" and the sensory information at the receptor level. Stock examples of the resulting compromise are the approximate constancy in the perception of brightness, size, distance, and so forth. For example, when a piece of white chalk is presented in the shade and a chunk of coal is presented in brilliant sunshine, the sensory information provided is predominantly "overcome." An example of ignoring aspects of one's knowledge, of the subjective reference, is when the observer "knows" that the lights do not move in the *phi* phenomenon yet he perceives them in motion.

This lack of effectiveness of certain rational determinants in perception, pointed out by Helmholtz in 1860, accents the inapplicability of methods based on immediacy notions for solving problems involving directed thought and other higher mental processes (see Helmholtz, 1867). Helmholtz' overemphasis of the mechanical features of inference was modified by Brunswik (1956) who demonstrated that thinking and attitudes influence the results of certain perceptual activities.

Particularly illustrative of the principle that perception is a compromise are the studies cited by Brunswik (1956) showing that the relationship between objective states and estimates of those states is dependent in part on the "attitude" or subjective reference of the estimator. For example, the distribution of estimation errors, in a Muller-Lyer experiment (see Fig. 1), shifted toward objective accuracy rather sharply (but remained a broad distribution) when the subjects took "critical" attitudes in their task. An even sharper shift resulted when the estimates were made after a demonstration of the principles involved in the Muller-Lyer illusion and the subjects took critical attitudes in making their judgments. In addition, the error distributions did not shift back to the same location when the subjects "returned" to their naive attitudes. In view of the shifting of the error distributions under instructions, attitudes and demonstrations in this experiment and in the legion of other experiments Brunswik discusses, we might ask, "where is the evidence of a basic 'pristine-pure' sensory datum in these experiments?" and "which sort of attitude shall we take in establishing the criteria of verification by sensory data?"

The Immediacy Postulate in Psychology

These points indicate clearly that the doctrine of immediacy, psychological or phenomenological, has no utility for scientific theory, whatever its utility in the philosophy of doctrinal positivism. *It is curious that the*

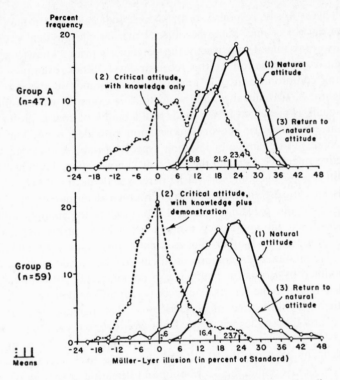

Fig. 1. The effect of attitudes and knowledge on the distribution of errors in a perceptual illusion experiment is indicated in these graphs. These data indicate that with no experience or knowledge, that is the "natural attitude," the Muller-Lyer illusion induces an average error of 23.6 percent of the standard. Introducing a critical attitude on the part of the subjects (Group A) and a description of the illusory character of the stimuli decrease the average error to 8.8 percent of the standard but increases the individual differences quite markedly. If the subjects (Group B) make the judgments with a critical attitude after having been given information *and* a demonstration of the illusion the error nearly vanished (average of 0.6 percent) and the individual differences in errors were *reduced* markedly. A return to the "natural attitude" (immediacy?) was less successful for the group having the practical demonstration of the illusion. (Adapted from E. Brunswik, 1956)

doctrines of psychological and phenomenological immediacy have led to diametrically opposed positions in psychology. The assumption of psychological immediacy has led to the rejection of the behavioristic study of higher mental processes. The assumption of phenomenological immediacy has led to a sort of poetic license in "scientific" description of the higher mental processes through retrospective report. This contradiction of interpretation and use of the immediacy doctrine signifies its positivistic and empirical meaninglessness.

The guarantee doctrine also is curious when viewed positivistically. The guarantee of infallibility suggests an alternative—fallibility. This, however, raises the question of a criterion for deciding what is infallible and what is not. Using a good positivistic approach, we would perform some sort of operation to decide this question. But, within the framework of doctrinal positivism, what could this operation be? We could not check the results by applying the various possible criteria against the real world because the latter concept is metaphysical and thus rejected explicitly by positivistic doctrine. On the other hand, we might confront each such application of the criterion directly with experience, that is, comparing them with the "immediately-given sensations." This is not a valid approach because we would be using in the proof the proposition to be proved.

Dropping any pretense of applying only the criteria of doctrinal positivism in defining infallibility we can guess what the immediacy doctrine tacitly implies. There is a tacit axiom of metaphysical and epistemological realism basic in doctrinal positivism, in spite of the fact that the positivists, especially those of the Vienna Circle, state explicitly that they reject these notions. The epistemological presupposition concerns the representation of reality to the confirming organism—through direct confrontation in sensation, that is, through a one-to-one transformation from the metaphysically-real world to direct experience by way of sense data. Ironically, it is clear that *methodological positivism* has demonstrated that the one-to-one transformation in the sensory system required by *doctrinal positivism* is nonexistent.

In short, neither phenomenological nor psychological immediacy will serve as the construct needed to make the immediacy postulate empirically meaningful. It appears then that the primitive element in doctrinal positivism is not available. At least, psychologists have not been able to find such elements even though a large portion of the history of experimental psychology has been devoted to the attempt to find "pure sensory elements" or the "indubitable givens of awareness." Of course, one may always advance the sophistic argument that psychology just has not been able to find them but they really exist. It is unnecessary to take refuge in such arguments. Instead, we accept the assumption that the higher mental processes are within the realm of study *without resorting to introspection* or to arguments based on the notion of intuition. By testing such an assumption, we can determine whether the immediacy postulate is necessary for a consistent picture of the higher mental processes.

A PSYCHOLOGICAL MODEL

Our argument is derived from a general model that does not depend on assumptions about immediacy, about privileged access to a private shadow world, nor does it use introspection as a method. The model assumes only that mediational processes are, in principle, knowable. Such a model is, theoretically, a sufficient counter-argument against the immediacy postulate. Moreover, the model has empirical implications from which confirmatory experimental findings can be demonstrated to strengthen the argument. In the following paragraphs, we shall turn to empirical evidence after we have developed the model.

We hold that a consistent and empirically useful model can be derived without resorting to notions of immediacy or intuition. We believe that our argument will show that the specific psychology demanded by the immediacy doctrine is such as to have a vanishing degree of credibility.

The proposed model is divided into three primary segments:

1. the ecology in which the organism is placed,
2. the organism, and
3. systems of response indicators which have the same extra-organismic status as the ecology.

The model, in particular that segment having to do with the organism, is formulated without reference to an immediacy postulate or to notions of intuition.

The foundation for the model and much of the empirical evidence for it are a result of Egon Brunswik's work (1952, 1956). The *lens model,* Figure 2, is an adaptation of Brunswik's schematic representation of the macro-detail of the psychological model. The significant and salient features of the argument we shall develop in the following sections are all implied, in the large, by the structure of the lens model. We have applied Brunswik's general model to one special problem and have introduced some new terminology. The emphasis will be on the transition from one segment of the model to another. However, this is done in such a way as to preserve the over-all design and purpose of the lens model. The argument proceeds roughly from left to right within the schema of Figure 2.

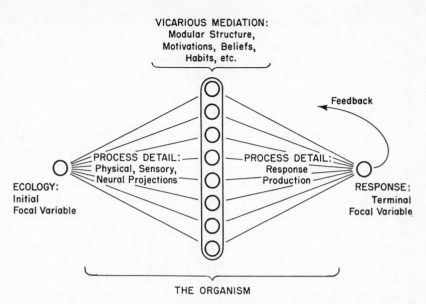

Fig. 2. The lens model. Reprinted from *The Conceptual Framework of Psychology 1952* by E. Brunswik by permission of the University of Chicago Press.

The Ecology

It is necessary first to define the organization of the universe in which organisms function. This is no less important in the study of the higher mental processes than in the study of manipulative processes. We make the assumption of a well-organized independent ecology. If this assumption were not made, the higher mental processes could have no basis outside the solipsistic, fantastic creation of a monistic "mind" or would not exist as "knowable" processes. To evaluate the course of events in the higher mental processes, one must have knowledge of the bases of these processes in the organismically-independent ecology. That is, a well-developed theory and empirical knowledge of the ecology is required.

At any rate, both organism and environment will have to be seen as systems, each with properties of its own, yet both hewn from basically the same block. Each has surface and depth, or overt and covert regions. As in any marriage, the interrelationship between the two systems has the essential characteristic of a "coming-to-terms." And this coming-to-terms is not merely a matter of the mutual boundary or surface areas. It concerns equally as much, or perhaps even more, the rapport between the central, covert layers of the two systems. It follows that, much as psychology must be concerned with the texture of the organism or of its nervous processes and must investigate them in depth, it also must be concerned with the texture of the environment as it extends in depth away from the common boundary.

It will have been noted that by environment we mean the measurable characteristics of the objective surroundings of the organism rather than the psychological environment or life space, in the sense in which Lewin has used this term. We may specify the sum total of these objective surroundings as the "ecology" of an individual or species. (Brunswik, 1957.)

If judgments, diagnoses, reactions, and so on, are the "consequent" terms of psychological processes, the "antecedent" terms of the processes must be understood in order to achieve an understanding of the processes themselves. The "consequent" terms, taken by themselves, have at times been taken as self-subsistent in explaining all lawful behavior. This fallacy, as well as the fallacy of the contrasting "complex process" interpretations of the intuitionists, phenomenologists, and Gestaltists, was forceably pointed out by Egon Brunswik (1952, 1956), whose "science of objective relations" offers a starting point in our attempt to find a well-defined antecedent to behavior. This science, the science of the ecology, is an attempt to describe the objects and events that make up the cognizing organism's universe.

In general, the ecology is made up of objects, events, and relationships between objects and events constituting the cognizing organism's universe. The distinction of what constitutes the ecology as contrasted with the organism is difficult to make in practice. However, there are two useful ways of looking at the problem that give, in principle, the needed distinction. The first is based on the change of lawful relationships when attention is shifted from the "inside" characteristics of the organism to the characteristics of the things "outside" the organism. Barker (1960) stresses this aspect by noting that

As we move from any discriminable thing to more remote, surrounding parts, a point is reached at which the governing laws, so far as we know them, become incommensurate, yet the linkage remains. This point marks the boundary of the entity [organism] and the beginning of the environment [ecology]. By these standards, an automobile and trailer, for example, constitute a single entity; they are discriminable parts coupled by single-level laws; the trailer does not constitute the environment of the car; it is part of the total machine. On the other hand, unattached cars traveling the highway in a caravan are in each other's environment; their coupling is mediated by different-level phenomena and laws, namely, the perceptual and motor systems of the drivers rather than by drawbar or chain. And this has nothing to do with the closeness of the coupling; it can happen that a towed vehicle will correspond less closely to the movements of the towing vehicle than do cars in a caravan. (1960, p. 8.)

Brunswik (1956) emphasizes a different aspect by defining the ecology as that part of the geographical, physical, social, and so forth environment that is *functionally* important to the psycho-biological organism. That is, the ecology is that part of the organism's surround toward which the organism directs its activities. In this sense the ecology is "a causal texture . . . in which events are regularly dependent upon each other. And because of the presence of such causal couplings . . . actually existing in their environments, organisms come to accept one event as the local representative for another event." (Tolman and Brunswik, 1935.) The word ecology is intended:

to designate, not complete environmental objects or bodies in their concrete totalities, but single object-characters abstracted from such total bodies. . . . From this standpoint the properties of means-objects, characterized by Tolman as *discriminanda, manipulanda, utilitanda* are to be conceived as groups of "Gegenstände" [ecological objects], which are different with respect to their abstract relevancy for the organism.

Further, because of its generality and abstractness this word . . . [ecology] can be used not only for the properties of means-objects but also for cue-properties of peripheral stimulation processes (e.g. intensity, form, or size of the projection of an object on the retina, the visual angle, etc.) as well as for such internal events or states as goal-satiation, and the like—in short, for anything which can be defined in terms of physics (or geometry, etc.) and which is therefore capable of objective measurement. Tolman and Brunswik, 1935, pp. 44–45.)

Any attempt to build a theory of behavior that has generality and explanatory power must take into account the ecology. The attempts to define psychological processes exclusively in terms of the peripheral receptor systems, central processes and peripheral effector systems or simply in terms of proximal stimuli and proximal response behavior are doomed to be partial and unsatisfactory theoretical and empirical systems. Barker (1960) states the case very elegantly: "Some find neither of these solutions [organismic encapsulation or excapsulation] very comfortable. The empirical facts keep intruding: whether we like it or not, all the sectors of the total [psychological; scientific] unit [distal objects, proximal stimuli, peripheral receptor systems, central processes, peripheral effector systems, proximal response behavior, distal achievements] *are* linked." (p. 11). Thus, in order to be able to make adequate evaluations of the meaning, effectiveness, and so forth, of behavior and to formulate theories of behavior, we must have a description of the ecology against which behavior can be compared in ascertaining organismic achievements in terms of functional efficiency.

Degree of Calibration

Clearly, the view we attain of the ecology is determined by:

1. the objective nature of ecological variations;
2. the tools and techniques used in assessing the objects; and
3. the working assumptions of the ecologist.

In this respect, the nature of the ecology determines, in large part, the degree of possible independence of the ecological findings and the "personal-social" biases introduced by the ecologist. Where the ecology is primarily defined in terms of the constructs of physics, that is, where highly calibrated measurement techniques are available, this is a very minor problem. On the other hand, where no such physicalistically defined pointer reading techniques are available, such as in most situations where the ecology is social or personal-psychological, independence of the ecologist as an organism and his findings are much more difficult to achieve. Assessors and diagnosticians in psychology have become increasingly aware of "stereotype" effects, interactions of assessor and assessee, transference phenomena, and other factors that obscure the relationships among their objects defined in strictly ecological terms. Thus, it might be argued, when we are dealing with objects not physically defined by a well-calibrated physical process, that the results are merely the ideas, stereotypes, and immediate givens of the assessor or cognizor, and that the phenomenological or psychological givens are the only "real" things involved. However, with the development of psychological technology the degree of organismic dependence in defining the ecology is being decreased to reasonable degrees. There are well-defined segments of the social and psychological ecology existing in the literature today. Much of this is in semantics (for example, Brown, 1958, and Osgood, 1957), which has opened up a wide area important in the specification of the social ecology. Another social-personal example is the general theory of roles, positions, statuses, duties, rights, and other properties of social units. (Sarbin, 1954.) [4]

These examples suggest that the metaphysical and epistemological simplicity of the positivistic criterion of confirmation is illusory. The

4. Since writing this chapter, we have seen *On the Epistemology of the Inexact Sciences* by Helmer and Rescher (1960). They point out that some of the newly-developing branches of the physical sciences recognize the same problems of calibration and exactitude as the behavioral sciences. The general conclusion is that the exact-inexact distinction is not attributive but dimensional.

contrary, indeed, is suggested. In the first place, when "pointer reading" responses are made by subjects with regard to "objective" quantities such as the size of physical objects, they may be shown to be complicated functions of many variables in addition to the "objective" quantity. For example, judgments of distance have been shown to vary with such "non-physical" variables as object interposition, color, linear perspective, and vertical position (Brunswik, 1956). The concept of "the objective" has not been satisfactorily specified by the positivists, but is left as a more-or-less unanchored notion. Unless we retreat into the morass of solipsism we find the only criterion available consists of sets of organismic responses representing the subject terms of meaningful statements, metaphysically real or not. Ultimately, when the question of scientific verifiability is involved, the only reality is in operationally defined constructs. The "immediate givens" of sense data are not, in this sense, operationally defined constructs.

In some branches of science, the "responses" can be precisely controlled with the use of highly calibrated instrumentation. In this sense a great deal of knowledge about "reality" already exists and has been translated into gadgets and devices to stabilize organismic responses required in the final stages of verification. In addition, precise calibration optimally defines operations and allows the substitution of mathematical models for "reality." But where there is imprecise or loose calibration, operations must be defined in terms of sets of organismic or verbal responses and "reality" becomes a collection of universes of equivalent sets of "objects."

Phenomenological indicators are probably the least precisely calibrated. The argument favoring the use of phenomenological reports loses ground when such reports contradict behavioral indicators. *Perhaps phenomenological reports, rather than providing indicators for general theories of behavior, will on closer inspection become an object for behavioral study rather than the criterion as proposed by the theorists asserting the immediacy of the phenomenological awarenesses.*

The question of two sorts of calibration procedures and models, one familiar as the physical science methods, the other based on response indicators, suggests an operational dualism, or pluralism. That is, depending on our operational procedures we may get variations in confirmatory criteria. In the well-calibrated areas the criteria will follow the laws of the calibration model and the mathematics underlying that model. Variability within those areas will be small, depending on how well the mathematics of the model fit the operations involved. In the areas with poor calibration, the criteria will follow the laws of response indicators. In this particular case, no fully appropriate mathematical model is known.[5]

Thus, it follows that the study of higher mental processes has the same general status as the study of physical processes except for the lag in the calibration. Despite this lag, we can build a model of the higher mental processes though not with the esthetically pleasing "minimal-error" variability of the physical sciences.

History provides a well-known instance of the "sloppiness" of human response indicators. In the realm of the well-calibrated physical sciences, the interaction of organism and ecology led Maskelyne, the astronomer, to dismiss Kinnebrook, his assistant, in 1796. For many decades thereafter, personal equations were computed for individual astronomers for the purpose of correcting their observations so that observations of different astronomers could be compared (see Boring, 1950). The problems of the personal equation are largely the same for psychology except for differences between the "astronomical" ecology and the adaptively-relevant ecology of behaving organisms.

Ecological Space

The central concept of ecological science is that of a mathematical space, in particular the ecological space. One of the most widely used models in psychology dealing with the concept of mathematical spaces in a general way is that of factor analysis. The axes in a factor analysis (that is, the factors) are the dimensions of the space and each variable or object being factored is represented as a point in the factor space by the coordinate values on those dimensions (that is, the factor coefficients).

We can illustrate the concept of ecological space with one specific form of space and one restricted class of ecological objects. Boxes, for example, can be represented as points in a three dimensional euclidean space. The three dimensions in this space correspond to the width, depth and length of the boxes. Given a particular box, it can be represented in the space as the point specified by the "length, width and depth dimensions" of the box. That is, for a box of x units in length, y units in width and z units in depth we can specify a point to represent the box x

5. Some parts of probability theory come close. However, it cannot handle, for example, the nontransitivity and nonadditivity found in behavioral indices. Most mathematical-statistical models will not do as the calibration models in the behavioral sciences because of their dependence on transitivity, additivity, and so forth.

units from the origin on the "length" axis, y units from the origin on the "width" axis, and z units from the origin on the "depth" axis of the abstract euclidean "box" space. If we should select a large number of boxes at random from the sorts of boxes that are used commercially and plot a point for each box on this abstract space we may perhaps discover some general characteristics about this restricted class of ecological objects. From our general knowledge about boxes we can make some guesses, in lieu of an actual sample of boxes, about the distribution of the points in the "box" space. The points will be more densely packed in some regions of the space than in other regions. For example, we would find relatively few points within one inch of the origin on each of the three axes. This is due to the fact that most boxes will have all three dimensions in excess of one inch or so. Similarly, the farther from the origin we go, beyond certain limits, the fewer points we can expect to find—boxes just do not come in unlimited sizes. We might find, more importantly, that we could, with some degree of success, predict the magnitude of two of the dimensional characteristics of a given box by knowing the magnitude of the other dimensional characteristic. This is intimately connected with the tendency for boxes of a given width to be made such that they are restricted in depth and length—boxes four feet deep and four feet long but only one inch wide would be "specialty" items and not frequently represented among a sample of boxes. This characteristic can be interpreted geometrically: the points representing the preponderance of the boxes will fall in a sausage-shaped cone along the diagonal of the space cutting equal angles with each of the three axes of the space.

Other general characteristics of this space are of interest to our ecological study. A particular example is the definition of a probability measure on the space. We can split up the "box" space into small cubes, each cube being specified by a small segment on the three axes respectively. For example, one such cube would include all boxes having x between 5 and 5.5 inches, y between 11 and 11.5 inches, and z between 3.5 and 4 inches (this cube would be the locus of the points representing, for example, a standard women's shoe box). Now, for each of these cubical segments of our space we can take the ratio of the number of points in the cube to the number of points in the space as a whole as the probability that a box chosen at random would belong in that cube. Doing this for each separate region in the space we have constructed a probability distribution over the box space and we may then use the tools of mathematical probability theory in studying the characteristics of this segment of the ecology. This example makes clear the wide range of possible analyses that can be performed within our basic ecological model.

This model can be extended to any class of ecological objects and any number of dimensions. For example, if we had "independent" measurement of intelligence, socioeconomic status, age, sex, physical health, ambition, adequacy of grade school training, and emotional stability on each of a number of college students we could study "students in eight dimensions" instead of "boxes in three dimensions." Each student would be represented as a point in the eight-dimensional space. The space could be covered with a probability distribution and other analytic functions could be defined on the set of points using some or all eight dimensions. For example, the relative amount of time spent studying by each student might be given by

$$t = a \text{ (socioeconomic status)} + b \text{ (ambition)} + c \text{ (adequacy of grade school training)} + d \text{ (emotional stability)}$$

where a is likely to be negative (reflecting the financial freedom to do things that detract from study time), and b, c, and d are likely to be positive with b being larger than c and d. Thus, for each point in the "student" space we have attached a specific value that is a function of four of the dimensions of the space. Other functions defined on the space, for example, academic success, may be difficult to define. However, our formulation of the ecology leads directly to an elegant solution of this problem. For example, if we have a "student" space composed of students for whom we have measures of academic success we may assign to the points in that space the respective measures of academic success. Then we may solve for the function of the seven dimensions that comes closest to matching the known criterion at each point. If all the points for students having a given degree of success fall in, say, a plane cutting across all the dimensions, the degree of success for a given student can be expressed as a simple weighted sum of the coordinate values locating that student in the student space. If the regions of points in the space, with respect to some particular value of success, are not so regular, there are powerful methods (for example, least squares linear regression) of finding optimal equations for determining the values of the criterion at sets of points in the space. The equations that result from such an analysis amount to rules for determining the criterion value that is associated with each point. Such a rule specifies a transformation of the student space into the criterion. The result of such a transformation is called a mapping. For example, the transformation corresponding to taking a weighted sum of coordinate values (measurements) on the seven "student" dimensions results in a mapping of all the points on a hyperplane (specified by the value of the weighted sum) in the student space into a single number (point) on the dimension "academic success." If only two dimensions X (say, intelligence) and Y (say, motivation) could unfailingly predict Z (say, academic success) through the transformation

$$aX + bY = Z,$$

for fixed values of a and b, we could picture the mapping by Figure 3.

These examples are, of course, trivial but they have the simplicity needed in presenting a nontechnical exposition of "space" and what can be done with it. The specific example of the boxes was motivated in part by the well-known "Thurstone box problem." Thurstone (1947) derived twenty-six different measurements on a set of boxes including the three basic dimensions of the boxes and performed a factor analysis on the intercorrelations among the measurements. This analysis "discovered" the dimensions of width, length and depth that we began with in our example. This "discovery" points up the usefulness of the factor analytic techniques in reducing the masses of measurements the ecologist is likely to have to make in the early stages of defining the salient dimensions of variation in the ecology.

The Organism: "Sensory" Functions

Having thus sketched a proposal for depicting the ecology, we can turn to the task of getting the organism into the picture. We do this in much the same way as the ecologist who becomes acquainted scientifically with the ecology. The organism "takes a sample" of the ecology. That is, a number of dimensions are assessed for a number of points in the ecological space. This sampling, however, is accomplished differently. The ecologist uses physical instrumentation where possible, or he may watch a number of organisms reacting to the objects in which he is interested, or he may make linguistic analyses of verbal descriptions of the objects, and so forth. The organism, as distinguished from our impersonal ecologist, has built-in measurement devices in the form of his sensory organs, and the sampling is made merely by exposing these organs to the relevant portions of the ecology (this may require manipulation and "changing" the ecology). In both cases the observations on the ecology can be represented abstractly as a transformation of the ecological space with the mode of measurement and observation specifying the character of the transformation. In the case of the organism, the transformation is specified by the nature of the sensory receptors, and the limited, concretely defined physiological organs that transform the

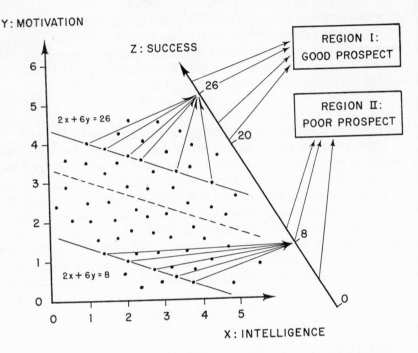

Fig. 3. *Schematic Representation of a Mapping.* Each student is indicated by a point, located by the student's intelligence and motivation "scores." In order to find the value of "success," z, for each point in the (X, Y) plane (that is, for each student) the equation $z = 2x + 6y$ is applied to the co-ordinates of the point. This corresponds to a transformation of 1) the "student" space into the "success" space, and 2) the two-dimensional space of X and Y into the one-dimensional space Z. Since this example is a linear transformation, a line may be drawn through the points having a given value of Z. All of the points through which that line passes are mapped by the transformation into the point of the Z space corresponding to the value of z, as, for example, the mapping of the points on the line $2x + 6y = 26$ into $z = 26$. We will call this transformation T_1. A different transformation, T_2, of the Z space is likewise possible. For example, all points on the success dimension may be mapped into regions, I: GOOD PROSPECTS, and II: POOR PROSPECTS. Region I is defined by $z \geqq 20$ and may be obtained directly by applying a new transformation $T_3 = T_2(T_1)$. Transformation T_3 is a rule stating simply, "all students having scores x and y satisfying $2x + 6y \geqq 20$ fall in Region I." This means that all students represented by points falling above the broken line on the (X, Y) plane belong in Region I. These points are the points that would be mapped into Region I by performing transformation T_1 and then transformation T_2.

Fig. 4 (a). Photograph of village street.

Fig. 4 (b). Village street photographed through a screen.

Fig. 4 (c). The same village street as seen by the eye of the fly.

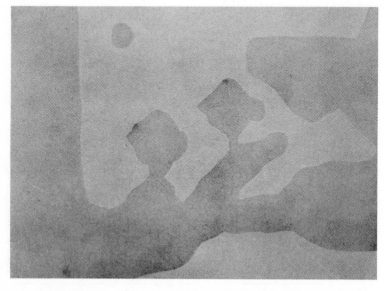

Fig. 4 (d). Village street as seen by the eye of the mollusc.

projections (be they light beams, sound waves, chemical reactions or what) into signals at the neural level. The signal structure of the input from the "projections" on the sensory surfaces may be represented abstractly as a space similar to the ecological space. We not only need to consider the momentary input, but also the continuing sequences of input constellations. Thus, at a given moment, we have a "projection" of the ecological space (or more correctly, a subspace of the ecology) into the input space. These projections correspond to the physical projections of energy from the ecology onto the receptor surfaces. They are such that some of the ecological relationships among the projected objects are preserved while some are lost. For example, the ordering of objects in the ecological space on the basis of physical size, hue, location, and so forth, may or may not be reflected in the input space. More radically, some objects represented in the ecological space may not be represented in the input space at all. For example, the surface of the moon may not be represented in a person's visual input subspace at daytime but may be represented to that person in his nonvisual input subspace.

Figure 4 (a, b, c, and d) graphically illustrates the mappings achieved by four media as discussed by von Uexküll and Kriszat. Their description of these figures illustrates our points that the mapping of the ecology into input is a function of the characteristics of the sensory apparatus.

The eye, in moving about, spreads over all objects in the environment a fine mosaic of points. The fineness of this mosaic depends on the number of visual elements available for focussing on the same section of the visual surround.

Since the number of visual elements in the eyes of different animals varies greatly, the mosaic of points imposed on their environment must necessarily reflect similar differences. The coarser the mosaic, the fewer the details that can be distinguished. The world seen through the eyes of a fly must appear considerably less detailed than the same world seen through human eyes.

The so-called screen method offers the possibility to illustrate the differences in the mosaics created by the eyes of different animals. For this purpose, a photograph may be transformed into a mosaic of points by superimposing upon it a fine screen.

The photograph is progressively reduced in size, photographed repeatedly through a screen of given coarseness and then enlarged again. The photograph may thus be changed into an increasingly coarser mosaic. With successive reproductions, the screen begins to interfere and the coarser mosaics are therefore reproduced as water colors. Figures 4a–d illustrate the method. They enable us to obtain a view of the environment of an animal whose number of visual elements is known. Figure 4c corresponds approximately to the picture obtained by the eye of the common fly. One can easily see that in an environment offering so few details, the threads of a spider net, for example, are lost altogether. We may therefore conclude that the spider produces a net which remains completely invisible to its prey.

The last plate (4d) corresponds approximately to the visual impression received by the mollusc eye. It is clear that the visual space of these animals contains only a number of dark and light surfaces. (Uexküll, J. and Kriszat, G. Streifzuge durch die Umwelten von Tieren und Menschen. Berlin: Springer Verlag, 1934, pp. 21–23. Freely translated.)

In more general terms, there is a transformation (that is performed by an operator, for example, the reaction of sensory surfaces to energy projected onto them) from the ecological space to the input space. This transformation maps the points and regions of the ecological space into (perhaps different) points and regions of the input space. This input space is largely determined by the character of the sensory organs. Some of the possibilities of such a transformation or mapping are presented in Figure 5. We must emphasize that such a mapping is probabilistic in nature. That is, each point is mapped from the ecological space into the input space with certain probabilities. Those ecological points having transformation probabilities equal to zero *will not* be mapped. This, of course, is the case from "nonvisual" subspaces of the input space.

In a fashion corresponding to the relationship between ecological objects and the points in ecological space, each point in the input space is an abstract representation of the state of affairs on the sensory surfaces. This is complicated by the flux of energies at the sensory surfaces over time, the many sensory "modalities," and the special characteristics of the receptors.

The model, as presented, has consequences for our consideration of the immediacy and guarantee doctrines. The immediacy interpretation applied to this ecology-to-input transformation would be that there is a one-to-one correspondence between the two spaces. That is, the transformation would be, under the positivistic doctrine, an identity (or at least a mathematically homomorphic) transformation. We maintain that such a one-to-one transformation has a vanishingly small probability of occurrence. The complexity of the physiology of sensory surfaces alone is enough to require a nonidentity transformation. The nature of this transformation is not known and thus we cannot specify in a deterministic way the mapping from ecological space to the input space, but we can specify the transformation probabilistically. *Until the transformation can be deterministically specified, there is no way of having any guarantee, immediacy or not, that the given points in the input space correspond to particular points in the ecological space.* For example, if two sets of input observations (a sample from the ecological space) are mapped into the same point in the input space, it is possible that they represent different points in the ecological space. Further, if the mappings occur with probability, there never can be any guarantee laws, but only probability laws

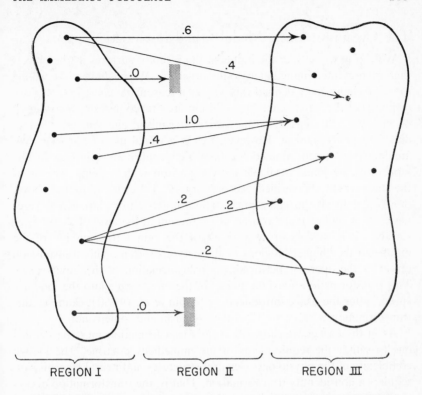

Fig. 5. *Schematic representation of a point-to-point mapping.* Region I: A subspace of the ecological space. Region II: The transformation mapping points into Region III, showing the probability that a point is mapped by the transformation into a given point in Region III. Mappings of zero probability are shown in only two cases. Region III: A subspace of the input space.

in confirmation of statements about the ecology based on a particular realization of the input space.

Our analysis to this point may seem trivial as it is unlikely that any contemporary would espouse a doctrine of spatio-temporal immediacy. However, we have accomplished two things: our method of analysis has been established, and a possible point of refuge and equivocation with regard to the immediacy doctrine has been covered.

To what, then does the immediacy postulate refer? We have barely touched the organism and if immediacy is to have organismic reference, and surely it must, then we must burrow deeper. To make our point, we must push the argument through the entire process—through all regions of the lens model.

The Organism: Cues, Modules, and Instantiations

We can now consider the inputs at the receptor surfaces as the objects that are presented immediately to the organism. We might even be willing to accept immediacy defined this way as a reasonable construct. Regions or points of the input space by definition are "reactions" or "recordings" of energy on the sensory surface of the organism, and thus are "immediate" to that organism. However, this is a trivial use of the term. We are interested in the immediacy on which confirmation is based. The input must be made available for comparison with the implications of the statements to be verified. According to C. I. Lewis, as quoted above, this availability is through a presentation of the sensory input in "awareness." Now, unless that "awareness" is present at the level of the sensory surfaces, it must develop as a result of the neural transmission of the input into the "higher" regions of the nervous system. This transmission serves as the operator performing a transformation of the input space. This transformation maps the points of the input space into the modular space,[6] after the usage introduced by Sarbin *et al.* (1960). Some of this transformation is "accessible" to the organism and some is not.

As in the earlier transformation, this transformation must be one-to-one to satisfy the requirements of the immediacy doctrine. The known complexity of the physiology of neural structures and neural transmission requires a non-identity transformation. That is, the transformation occurs in the context of the partial control by central processes of receptor and afferent tracts, and thus, the specific character of the transmitted input (that portion of the input space mapped into modular space) is determined by both the impinging energies and the concurrent central processes. It seems likely that there are four basic conditions determining the character of central intervention in the mapping:

1. the frequency in the past with which points in input space have been mapped into the points in modular space;
2. the just prior (in time) mappings;
3. the beliefs and values of the organism, and
4. the motivational and homeostatic factors in operation at the time of instantiation.

These factors operate to enhance or depress the probabilities of a given mapping. These in turn are super-imposed on the probabilistic nature of

6. Modules and modular spaces are the cognitive counterparts of ecological objects and ecological spaces. The general mathematical characteristics of the two kinds of spaces and objects in both realms are parallel. For a detailed discussion of these concepts see Sarbin, *et al.*, especially Chapters 4, 5, 6, and 7.

the neural transmission. In addition, the organism is active in searching out, utilizing, and rejecting input available from the ecology.

Frequently, and especially with regard to social ecology, manipulation of objects and events is necessary to make available the relevant inputs. That is, it may be necessary to *probe* the subsurface ecology. Such probings change the mappings from the ecology into modular space on the basis of certain characteristics of the modular space. This suggests that perduring and transitory characteristics of the modular space determine in part the nature of the transformation from input to the modular space. When a given point in input space in mapped into the modular space, that point (in both spaces) takes on a special significance. The input elements that are mapped are taken by the organism as *cues* to the location of points in the modular spaces. The ecological objects corresponding to these points are said to be *instantiated* by the mapping. That is, an object becomes an *instance* of a class.

The main factors determining the acceptance of inputs as cues are the potency, multiplicity, and relevance of the input units. The potency of a unit of input refers to the salience among the collection of input units concurrently available, for example, a golf ball in a sack of tomatoes, or a fully-dressed woman on Bikini Beach. The higher the degree of potency of input, the more likely it is to be accepted as a cue. Independently of this factor, the greater the number of inputs having significance for a particular incipient instantiation, the greater is the probability of instantiation. The third factor, relevance, refers to a characteristic of the modular space involved when the input is used as a cue. If the input variables (that is, axes of the input space) do not correspond to axes of the modular space, they will then not be involved in determining cues.

Our discussion of cues so far implies varying degrees of functional validity and reliability of cues and instantiations. That is, the transformation and mappings involved may be inconsistent from occasion to occasion. Particularly important in this connection is the signification of cues, that is, the way cues differ with respect to the degree that they validly represent the corresponding ecological occurrences. In general, cues vary with respect to their degrees of validity, misleadingness, ambiguity, and nonsignification. These characteristics may be completely described by two orthogonal coordinates representing the correlation between the cue and the specified occurrences, and the correlation between the cue and irrelevant occurrences. Figure 6 indicates these characteristics schematically. Unless a cue falls in the coordinate system at the point $(X=1.0, Y=0.0)$ it does not represent with certainty the ecological object corresponding to the module involved. All other points in the

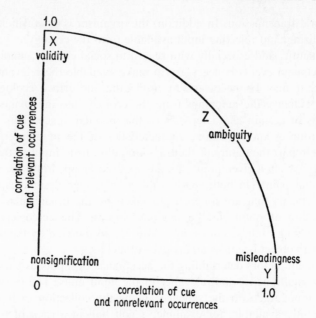

Fig. 6. Ambiguity, validity, nonsignification, and misleadingness in terms of correlations between cue and
relevant (criterion) occurrences and between cue and
nonrelevant occurrences. Maximum replicability is represented by points on the arc. The points low on the arc
may be depended on to be misleading. The points at the
top of the arc represent cues which *may be depended on
to lead to adaptively efficient behavior.*

coordinate system refer to cues for which there is some degree of uncertainty of signification. Instantiations based on the cues will be characterized by the same uncertainty and will thus bear probabilistic terms.
These probabilities are superimposed on the probabilities imposed on the
process at earlier stages.

All stages in the transformation from input to full-blown instantiation,
which presumably is the closest that present-day psychology can come
to the "experiencing" required by the immediacy doctrines, are thus
fraught with probabilistic considerations. These probabilities are cumu-
latively effective in arriving at an instantiation. That is, to the uncertainties
and deformations of input transmission are superimposed the uncertainties and deformations entailed in the redintegrative, motivational,
and valuational factors at work in cue formation. Thus, the likelihood
of a direct "immediate" presentation of the input at the stage of instan-

tiation is vanishingly small. The doctrine of immediacy and certainty would require that all units of input to be transformed into cues would have to fall precisely at the point of perfect validity in our signification diagram ($X=1.0$, $Y=0.0$). The probability of this occurring, even, for example, in the restricted time intervals and structured stimulus situations of pointer readings, is so infinitesimal that we may confidently reject the immediacy postulate.

The immediacy notion we have just shown to be unacceptable *is* the notion intended by doctrinal positivism (that is, psychological and pre-inferential immediacy). Thus, from our theoretical argument, which construes psychological processes in the most general way and allows for the immediacy doctrine within the general theory and without prejudice, the specific psychology demanded by the positivistic doctrine is shown to be beyond credibility. Combining this abstract argument with the empirical findings (see below), the case against the validity of the (psychological) immediacy doctrine is overwhelming.

The Organism: Response System

Our argument to this point covers the domain of the usual referents of the term "immediacy." All of the varieties of immediacy identified by Wallraff (1953) among psychological and philosophical writings are covered. However, there exists one more abstract possibility: occurrences in the response system of the organism could conceivably be argued as the points of immediacy needed in positivistic theory. This argument would require some rewording of the postulate and further derivations to conform with our customary usage of the words "sensation" and "response." No such argument is at present clearly identifiable in the literature. It seems unlikely, also, that such an argument will be proposed.

The main substance of our argument has been the discussion of two families of transformations or mappings. The transformation mapping the ecology into the sensory apparatus of the organism resulted in an input space. This in turn was mapped into the cognitive apparatus of the organism by a second family of transformations. The probabilistic character of these transformations, at both levels, led to rejection of the immediacy postulate with a high degree of confidence. This argument can be applied once again. The elements with which we begin are now modular spaces.

In order for the modular spaces and psychological activities based on the spaces to have utility outside the privacy (phenomenology) of the individuals' access to his own modular organization, they must be expressible in terms other organisms can utilize. This expression, in its most general form, can be described in the "transformation" language used above. That is, the accessible portion of the modular space must be transformed by the response systems of the organisms into overt responses. This transformation, again, may be described as a mapping of the modular space into a space corresponding to the abstract organization of responses. The immediacy notion requires in this case a one-to-one transformation of the accessible part of modular space to the response space. However, probability considerations enter this process as in the previously described transformations. Further, the restriction that only the accessible part of the modular space be mapped further reduces the likelihood of the necessary one-to-one transformation. Thus, as with psychological immediacy, we may confidently reject the notion of a phenomenological immediacy.

The language of our argument may seem to suggest that the degree of functional efficiency must be very small in view of the many probability considerations. The opposite is demonstrated in many studies we cite as basic empirical foundations of the model. This apparent paradox is dissolved with an application of the principles of inter-substitutability and cue-hierarchies. The statistical analogue is the multiple correlation coefficient. A *combination* of variables can correlate perfectly with another variable even if the combined variables individually have low reliabilities and validities.

Applying this directly to our model, we can use the example of distance. Distance (from the organism to an object) cannot be input "directly" as can, say, brightness or color—there are no "distance receptors." However, there are many variables or "cues" related to distance that can function as input via the sensory apparatus. Each of these cues "overlaps" or is correlated with distance to a certain degree and thus better than chance accuracy can be achieved by basing judgments on distance on one of the cues. Further, if the cues are not completely overlapping with one another, with respect to their correlation with distance, then accuracy of judgment will improve as we add new cues to the set. This is illustrated in Figure 7. Thus, the model leads us to expect flexibility with respect to cue utilization and ecological achievements in the face of uncertain but multiple cues.

In short, our model formalizes the process of passing from the antecedents to the consequents of behavior as a series of transformations of the ecological space into the response space. This series of transformations or mappings involves, at each stage, the loss of certain characteristics of the transforming system—the organism. Each transformation is

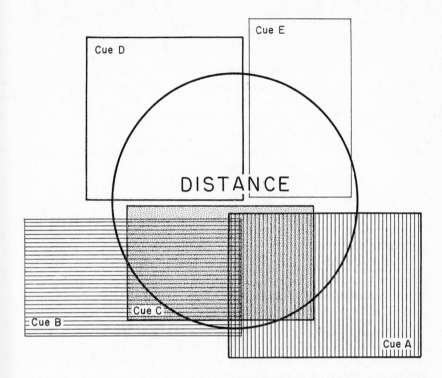

Fig. 7. A diagram showing the multiple determination of distal variables indicating the inter-substitutability of cues. The distal variable, distance of a target from the organism, is represented to the organism by a system of cues, which, when properly combined, give nearly perfect estimability of distance. Cues B and C are very good surrogates of each other when cue A is present but cue C is more desirable (for accuracy) than cue B if cue A is not present.

characterized by probability laws instead of deterministic laws. Thus, the possibility of the series of transformations being one-to-one, that is, identity transformations, from ecology to response systems is so slight as to be negligible. Because the identity transformation required by the postulate of immediacy cannot be demonstrated, the conclusion follows, for both psychological immediacy and phenomenological immediacy, that "sensations," "sense-data," "impressions," and so forth, are untenable as the raw data for verifying propositions. With our rejection of these notions we need no longer take seriously those who assert that the study of higher mental processes is impossible as well as those who take refuge in methods based on intuition and phenomenological analysis.

THE INTUITIONIST'S ARGUMENT

The immediacy postulate is employed, often unwittingly, as the key-stone of the intuition doctrine of knowledge. As the philosophical support for the intuition doctrine, the immediacy notion seems to have been formed from two implausible beliefs, both related to psychophysical dualism: The first of these is that premises inhabit a private theater of awareness, and the second is that only the subject himself has privileged access to his premises (Ryle, 1949). Because some judgments, conclusions, assessments, or knowings occur in the absence of articulated premises, then, argue the intuitionists, no premises exist. In short, goes the argument, "If I cannot witness the mental contents in my private shadow world, then the judgment or conclusion must be formed *directly* without the intervention of mediating premises."

The immediacy postulate as a support for intuition has been rationalized in several ways. At one time, a mind-to-mind leap, as in clairvoyance, was acceptable as an explanation of intuition. At another time, a sense-datum-to-conclusion simulacrum was acceptable, and, more recently, a perception-to-knowledge isomorphism. Behind each of these explanations of intuition lies the immediacy postulate: that certain knowings arise in the absence of other knowings. Stated alternately, knowledge achieved in the absence of awareness of cues and premises is considered to be a *qualitatively* different class than knowledge achieved through processes that are subject to self-examination.

Since we have tried to demonstrate that modern psychological theory is not dependent upon the immediacy postulate, how can we fit intuition in the generalized lens and transformation model? In an analysis of what is purportedly intuition, it is clear that its distinguishing feature is non-accessibility to self-examination. But it is unwarranted to resurrect the immediacy postulate simply because we recognize that some cues and some premises may be nonaccessible to self-examination or report.

It is unwarranted because modern psychology has demonstrated that a person's judgments are predictable from a knowledge of his postulate-system and of the inputs available to him even though the person cannot report which inputs nor which postulates were employed. The evidence for this assertion is multiple: studies of the influence of subliminal stimulation on thought and conduct from the classic report of Peirce and Jastrow (1884) to recent experiments on subception (Lazarus and McCleary, 1951); experiments on learning without awareness (Postman, 1947); experiments stimulated by the microgenetic conception of per--

ception where an apparently unseen stimulus influences the perception of a simultaneously presented occurrence (Flavell and Draguns, 1957); experiments on problem solving, where "hints," inaccessible to the subject, are utilized in his solutions (Maier, 1930). In all these experiments, of course, the inputs were accessible to the experimenters. Observations of this kind, which could be multiplied many times, lend support to the inference model. No immediacy postulate is required to give scientific status to events labeled intuition.

To complete our analysis, it remains to be demonstrated that, within the framework of our general model, one can indeed study the higher mental processes and such study can be performed without resorting to unconfirmable intuitions. To make such a demonstration we shall cite several experiments illustrative of the successful study of one form of the higher mental processes—clinical inference.

SOME EMPIRICAL EVIDENCE

We shall look at a few examples of experiments demonstrating the feasibility of the study of higher mental processes. Such specific examples are readily available. The experiments are more or less imperfect experimental realizations of our idealized model.

These experiments make no assumptions about immediacy, about privileged access to a private shadow world, nor do they employ introspection as a method. They are framed over the assumption that the mediational processes are in principle, knowable. We shall strengthen our argument that the immediacy postulate is unnecessary by employing the criterion of confirming predictions through observation and experiment.

We can observe, say, the conduct of psychologists or others who attempt to diagnose and predict the behavior of other human beings. Behavior in manifold situations, ranging from psychoanalytic interviews to simple reaction time exercises, is observed. From these observations come the data that enter into the formulation of a diagnostic or prognostic statement. The data are manipulated and judgments and inferences recorded. The diagnostician or predictor may record his own retrospections of how he combined the data—that is, he may remember some of the cues and some of the conceptual determinants which were utilized. However, if we can generalize from the constancy experiments, this latter step may be misleading. Further, it is not necessary, as we shall presently see.

The interested behavior analyst now steps into the picture. He correlates the information cues *available to the inferring person* with the judgments or inferences made by the inferring person. That is, he determines the degree to which the variability in the ecology accounts for the variability in the judgments or inferences. What usually results is that the coefficients of correlation between cues and judgment makes public the subtle, and often unreportable, inferential activities of the inferring person. That is, the coefficients reveal the relative degrees that the judgments depend on the various sources of information available to the judge. Frequently, the relationships thus discovered have little resemblance to the retrospective view of the "private world" of the inferring person. The same sort of analysis can be made of psychophysical judgments, perceptual constancy judgments, valuation behavior, and many other forms of behavior reflecting higher mental processes. In the terms of our basic model outlined above, the *behavior analyst,* not the subject, records the transformation involved in going from the ecological space to the judgment space. We shall illustrate with several experiments that are especially relevant in the context of clinical inference.

The subjects of one study (Sarbin, 1944) were five psychologists working in a university counseling center who made predictions of the behavior of college freshmen on the basis of a large assemblage of cues. The predictions were made in terms of college grade point averages. Cues were made available to the inferrers through an interview, several questionnaires, scores on aptitude tests, and an index of high school achievement. After the predictions were made, the correlations between the predictions and those cues available to the predictors that could be easily quantified, that is, test scores, presence or absence of certain social criteria, and so forth, were computed. The correlations showed that nearly 50 percent of the variance of the judgments was accounted for by two variables: an index of achievement in high school and the score on a college aptitude test. These same two variables accounted for only 30 percent of variance in the actual criterion. The judges took data with known weights and assigned other weights with the resulting decrease in accuracy. Although the psychologists in their retrospective reports talked about systematically weighting other cues such as personality test scores, as a matter of fact they did not.

Interested in how people make inferences about others, Levine (1954) correlated available cues with reported inferences. He also correlated the inferences with certain characteristics of the judges, for example, sex, age, professional experience, self-conceptions, and so forth. One of his findings is that, on the basis of the same information, clinical psychologists postdict events in the subject's history considered negative for adjustment; while nonpsychologists postdict events in the subject's history considered positive for adjustment. Thus, dispositional characteristics of the inferring person may enter into the judgment. However, such characteristics are normally not included in the subject's retrospections about his inductions.

The conclusions from these studies are similar to those drawn from experiments on constancy. The "immediately-given" assemblage of data, in this case certain occurrences, ignores or distorts some items of information that were demonstrably associated with the criterion. More important, the psychologists ignored their own knowledge of correlations between certain tests and the criterion because of the "compelling nature" of other tests or information that were invalid for predicting the relevant criterion.

Hammond (1955), Todd (1954), and Hoffman (1960) extended the same basic approach to some broader questions. For example, in Hoffman's research, which directly confirms the results obtained by Sarbin (1944) and by Todd (1954) and the analysis by Hammond (1955), judges were presented with psychological test profiles of person-objects and were asked to make judgments of intelligence and judgments of sociability. The only information available to the judges was contained in the profiles. From these data Hoffman determined the optimal weightings of the scores to predict the judgments. These weights corresponded to the degree the judge used the respective scores in arriving at the judgments.

The resulting multiple correlation coefficients and the fractional weightings indicate, respectively, the over-all linear dependence of judgments on the profiles and the piece-wise linear dependence of judgments on individual variables in the profiles. The multiple correlations for the cases reported by Hoffman were surprisingly high (R's of .948, .829, .901, and .770 when corrected for shrinkage). Thus, it is evident that Hoffman's judges depended in surprisingly high degree on linear combinations of the variables in the profiles in making their judgments. However, by a neat device, Hoffman demonstrated that the judges could not report accurately the characteristics of their judgment model. The judges were asked to indicate the simple weights they used to arrive at their judgments. For some of the judges, the weights reported were strikingly different from those determined statistically. In such cases, by the very nature of the multiple correlation coefficient, the subjective weights, when substituted for the statistically determined weights, would result in smaller multiple correlation coefficients. In fact, since the statistical weights are optimal in predicting the judgments, the subjective weights would have to be identical to the statistical weights to do as well.

It might, of course, be objected that it is too much to ask of the judge to be completely accurate in the reporting of the weights used in his judgments. We would agree emphatically! This is no sort of thing to ask a harassed judge or clinician! But it is just what is required of introspection when attempting to get at a basic substratum of the "mind," and is required of phenomenology in the search for the *phenomenal givens* of awareness.

In finding the weights actually used by the judges in these experiments, nothing was assumed about the doctrines of immediacy of guarantee of certainty; considerations of the privacy of the "inner life" of the judge were not necessary. Yet, within the framework of the linear model, it was demonstrated that the person making judgments could do no better than the "statistician" in describing the way in which he, the judge, put together the information available to make a judgment. These experiments exemplify empirical studies contradicting the derivation based on the immediacy postulate. The process of arriving at a judgment is shown to be open to analysis without resorting to phenomenology and introspection in the search for "immediately-given data of sensation." Some psychologists believe that the process of combining scores from a psychological test battery is so complicated and subtle that it cannot be described, much less accomplished, in the formal language of logic and mathematics. However, the experiments of Sarbin, Todd, Hammond, Hoffman, and Martin (1957) just cited, for example, have uprooted this belief. Such experimental demonstrations, which are dependent on a well-defined ecology, contradict the claims that the ecology and the higher mental processes are not open to objective formal analysis.

In the experiments just discussed, the judgment process is presumed to correspond to the operation of a linear prediction model. When such a model is applied statistically to the input and output (test profiles and judgments respectively), the output is shown to be almost completely recoverable statistically. This, of course, does not prove the model is a "true" picture of the mental process. The assumption of the linear model probably is not strictly justified. However, in general, it leads to clear results and little or no improvement is made by using a more complicated model. It is an important issue nevertheless, and a great deal is being made currently of "nonlinear" models, particularly "configurational" models. However, any "configurational model" can be translated directly into general statistical or mathematical form without loss of efficiency.[7] However, claims that there is no statistical model that can be adequate to describe the process of judgment or prediction, diagnosis, and so forth, are simply erroneous. Judgments based on patterns, interactions, level, and the like can be expressed quite elegantly in analytic-mathematical form. Ultimately the linear model may prove inadequate, but this lends no credence to the argument that no mathematical model is appropriate.

In this connection, Martin (1957) made a direct comparison of the linear model with two "indigenous" models. The linear model, Model I, was the familiar multiple correlation model in which the predictor variables were weighted so that the sum of the weighted variables was correlated maximally with the judge's ratings. The other two models were based on statements made by judges. They stated their impressions of how they had combined eight scales with which they were familiar to arrive at a final numerical judgment of "sociability." From these statements Martin constructed, for each individual clinician, a mathematical model reflecting the combinations the judge claimed to be using. For example, for one judge, the "indigenous" variables formed from the simple raw variables consisted of two of the simple variables and the pair-wise products of five simple variables (Judge B). Model II treated these indigenous interaction variables as if they were simple variables and combined them in a fashion identical to that of Model I. That is, the indigenous variables were weighted by multiple correlation procedures so that the sum of the weighted indigenous variables was correlated maximally with the judge's ratings. The equation for Judge B was, where X stands for the rating predicted by the equation and $x_1, x_2, \ldots, x_8$ for the simple raw variables,

$$X = .31x_1 + .8x_2 + .48(x_3x_4) + .01(x_4x_5) + .25(x_6x_7).$$

In Model III the weights were supplied by statements from the judges as to the importance or "weight" they attached to each of the indigenous variables in making their judgments. For Judge B the equation in Model III was

$$X = .25x_1 + .25x_2 + .20(x_3x_4) + .15(x_4x_5) + .15(x_5x_8).$$

To compare the relative efficiency of the three models in predicting the ratings made by the judges from the simple raw score profiles the correla-

7. For example, a general polynomial in the given number of variables to a certain degree (power) expresses the multiplicative and additive combinations of the variables in all the degrees specified. Our comment refers equally to the simple linear model, the simple linear interaction model, and so on. The appropriate generalized model requires more attention than we can give here.

tion between the judge's ratings and the predicted ratings were computed. These values are equivalent to the multiple correlation coefficients between the judge's ratings, and, for the respective models, the simple raw variables or the indigenous variables. The correlation coefficients for the three models for each of five judges are given in Table 1. From these data it is seen that the simple linear combination of the raw variables weighted according to a least squares criterion of optimality was the best predictor

TABLE 1.* MULTIPLE CORRELATION COEFFICIENTS, R BETWEEN PREDICTOR VARIABLES AND FIVE JUDGES RATINGS

Judge	Model I Linear	Model II Indigenous: Optimal Weights	Model III Indigenous: Subjective Weights
A	.93	.88	.79
B	.89	.77	.69
C	.89	.88	.86
D	.91	.88	.87
E	.83	.66	.64

* Data from Martin (1957).

of the judges' ratings. Model II likewise was, in all cases, the next best while the indigenous model embodying the judges subjective weights was the poorest of the three models. The differences in the multiple correlation coefficients were not consistently significant statistically, and some of the differences were very small numerically. The table of probabilities of the statistical significance of the differences are presented in Table 2.

TABLE 2.* LEVELS OF SIGNIFICANCE OF DIFFERENCES IN MULTIPLE CORRELATION COEFFICIENTS FOR THE DATA OF TABLE I

Comparison	Judge				
	A	B	C	D	E
$P(R_I \leqq R_{III})$	.0001	.0001	.12	.10	.002
$P(R_{II} \leqq R_{III})$	.009	.14	.27	.71	.76
$P(R_I \leqq R_{II})$	.02	.0006	.66	.18	.005

* Data from Martin (1957).

This analysis suggests that the appropriate degree of model complexity which most efficiently indicates the process of combination of the cues to arrive at a judgment (certainly one of the "higher mental processes") is left open, but that the simple linear model remains as the most likely candidate for the ultimate description of the process.

SUMMARY

The effect of the assumption of sensory immediacy and guaranty has been to entrench two unfortunate and opposite effects on psychology:

1. rejection of the study of higher mental processes, and
2. justification for the use of intuition in investigating the higher mental processes.

These effects are due to the postulate that sensations may be presented directly in experience without mediation and are thus the only infallible criteria in the context of confirmation.

A logical analysis of the postulate indicates the source of the opposite effects on psychological theory. The term "immediacy" may on one hand refer to sensory data prior to "adulteration" by association, inference, and so forth (psychological immediacy), or on the other hand may refer to "prereflective" experience regardless of its source (phenomenological immediacy). This duality, and the implied contradiction, greatly reduce the credibility of the immediacy doctrine.

The doctrinal nature of the postulate has shielded it from *direct* empirical argument. However, consequences derived from doctrinal positivism may be investigated within the framework of methodological positivism. The history of experimental psychology is replete with such *indirect* investigations of the postulate. In particular, we may cite the futile attempts at discovering the postulated "pure sense data." The structuralists' difficulty with "stimulus errors" illustrates the empirical intractability of the doctrine of psychological immediacy. In addition, application of methodological positivism in the study of the perceptual constancies have demonstrated the heavy contribution of the redintegrative and rational processes in the so-called "pure sensory functions." The appeal to phenomenological experience as the "immediately given" offers a criterion that is no more satisfactory, and involves both empirical and logical difficulties. The ambiguities and contradictions of retrospective report required in the empirical study of "phenomenological immediacy" attests to the unsatisfactory character of those data in the context of confirmation.

A strong argument against the immediacy doctrine can be made in two steps by,

1. formulating a general psychological model along lines suggested by empirical findings, and

2. testing the postulate against implications drawn from the model.

To insure an unbiased argument, the model is formulated in terms that are non-prejudicial to the immediacy doctrine. After applying the model, we are left with the implication that the immediacy doctrine is acceptable with only an infinitesimal degree of credibility.

The model is an adaptation of Egon Brunswik's lens model. It is stated generally in terms of mathematical spaces and transformations of the spaces that result in the mapping of the points of one space into another space. The spaces are determined by the functional and substantive character of the organism-ecology interaction and the intra-organismic processes. In particular, an ecological space is defined as a space in which ecological objects are represented as points, the locations of which are determined by the functional and substantive character of the organism-ecology interaction and the intra-organismic processes. In particular, an ecological space is defined as a space in which ecological objects are represented as points, the locations of which are determined by objective characteristics of the objects. The projection of the ecology onto sensory surfaces corresponds roughly to the transformation of the ecological space into a sensory input space. Thus, when an organism makes exploratory or confirmatory moves in the ecology it "samples" the ecology; as a result, points in the ecological space are mapped into the input space. This mapping is determined by the nature of the sense organs involved and the segment of the ecology sampled.

This general transformation process is repeated at a higher level in transforming the input space into modular spaces. Again, the transformation behaves like a sampling process, mapping certain points from the input space into the modular space. The determination of this mapping can be attributed primarily to four sources:

1. the frequency in the past with which points in input space have been mapped into the points in modular space;
2. the just prior (in time) mappings;
3. the beliefs and values of the organism, and
4. the motivational and homeostatic factors in operation during the mapping.

One further transformation is required to include the functions subsumed under phenomenological immediacy. Since a phenomenological report refers to a fullblown instantiation, the instantiations are regarded as immediate. However, to have any value in the context of confirmation, instantiations must be accessible and communicable. To this end, the modular space must be mapped into a response space to provide indicators of the instantiations. The primary characteristics of this transformation and the implied probability distributions are determined by the efferent or response system of the organism. The nature of response systems prevent complete mapping in the response space—some instantiations may be inaccessible to the mapping (response) process (or, in the older language, "unavailable to consciousness").

The immediacy postulate may be fitted nicely into this general model. The postulate is, in fact, a specification that each of the respective transformations must be *identity* transformations. That is, each point in the ecological space must be mapped on a one-to-one basis with the points in the modular space. For psychological immediacy the input space must be a replica of the ecological space, and the points in the input space must be mapped without fail and without distortion into the modular space.

The likelihood that these two requirements can be met is virtually nil. The characteristics of the unstable sources of physical projection of the ecology on to sensory surfaces, the sensory system, neural transmission, and the process of instantiation are primarily probabilistic. The immediacy doctrine requires that the probability of each point being mapped is equal exactly to 1.0. The hypothesis that this indeed is a description of the natural phenomena may be rejected with utmost confidence. The same argument and conclusion may be advanced in the case of phenomenological immediacy. The probability of a transformation in the series being one-to-one is so small that it is negligible. It may be concluded that the doctrine of immediacy is invalid.

The logical argument stands by itself. However, empirical evidence with regard to the validity of the model is introduced *a fortiori*. This evidence is readily accessible in the psychological literature. For example, the research area concerned with clinical inference provides abundant data attesting the validity of the model in general and in many particulars.

REFERENCES

Allport, G. W. The psychologist's frame of reference. *Psychol. Bull.*, 1940, *37*, 1–28.

Allport, G. W., and J. S. Bruner. Fifty years of change in American psychology. *Psychol. Bull.*, 1940, *37*, 737–777.

Asch, S. E. *Social psychology*. Englewood Cliffs, N.J.: Prentice-Hall, 1952.

Ayer, A. J. *Language, truth and logic*. (2nd ed.) London: Gollanez, 1949.

Barker, R. Ecology and motivation. In M. Jones (Ed.), *Nebraska Symposium on Motivation*. Lincoln, Neb.: University of Nebraska Press, 1960. Pp. 1–50.

Boring, E. G. A history of introspection. *Psychol. Bull.*, 1953, *50*, 169–186.

Boring, E. G. *A history of experimental psychology*. (2nd ed.) New York: Appleton, 1950.

Brunswik, E. Psychology as a science of objective relations. *Phil. Sci.*, 1937, *4*, 227–260.

Brunswik, E. Distal focusing of perception: size-constancy in a representative sample of situations. *Psychol. Monogr.*, 1944, No. 254.

Brunswik, E. *Systematic and representative design of psychological experiments.* Berkeley, California: University of California Press, 1947.

Brunswik, E. *The conceptual framework of psychology.* Chicago: University of Chicago Press, 1952.

Brunswik, E. *Perception and the representative design of psychological experiments.* (2nd ed., rev. & enl.) Berkeley: University of Calif. Press, 1956.

Brunswik, E. Scope and aspects of the cognitive problem. In H. Gruber, R. Jessor, and K. Hammond (Eds.), *Cognition: the Colorado symposium.* Cambridge, Mass.: Harvard University Press, 1957. Pp. 5–31.

Carnap, R. Testability and meaning. *Phil. Sci.*, 1937, *4*, 1–40.

Feyerabend, P. K. Explanation, reduction and empiricism. In H. Feigl and G. Maxwell (Eds.), *Minnesota studies in the philosophy of science,* Vol. III. Minneapolis: University Minnesota Press, 1962. Pp. 28–97.

Flavell, J. H., and J. Draguns. A microgenetic approach to perception and thought. *Psychol. Bull.*, 1957, *54*, 197–217.

Hammond, K. R. Probabilistic functioning and the clinical method. *Psychol. Rev.*, 1955, *62*, 255–262.

Heider, F., and E. Simmel. A study of apparent behavior. *Amer. J. Psychol.*, 1944, *57*, 243–259.

Helmer, O., and N. Rescher. *On the epistemology of the inexact sciences.* Santa Monica, Calif.: Rand Corp., 1961.

Helmholtz, H. von. *Handbuch der physiologischen optik.* Hamburg: L. Voss, 1909–1911.

Hoffman, P. J. The paramorphic representation of clinical judgment. *Psychol. Bull.*, 1960, *57*, 116–131.

Lazarus, R. S., and R. A. McCleary. Autonomic discrimination without awareness: a study of subception. *Psychol. Rev.*, 1951, *58*, 113–122.

Lee, Dorothy. Codifications of reality. *Psychosomatic Med.*, 1950, *12*, 89–97.

Levine, M. S. Some factors associated with clinical prediction. Unpublished doctoral dissertation, University of California, Berkeley, 1954.

Lewis, C. I. *An analysis of knowledge and valuation.* La Salle, Ill.: Open Court, 1950.

Maier, N. R. F. Reasoning in humans. I. On direction. *J. comp. Psychol.*, 1930, *10*, 115–143.

Martin, H. T., Jr. The nature of clinical judgment. Unpublished doctoral dissertation, Washington State College, 1957.

Maxwell, G. The ontological status of theoretical entities. In H. Feigl and G. Maxwell (Eds.), *Minnesota studies in the philosophy of science, Vol. III.* Minneapolis: University of Minnesota Press, 1962. Pp. 3–27.

Mead, Margaret. *Coming of age in Samoa.* New York: Morrow, 1928.

Michotte, A. E. The emotions regarded as functional connections. In M. L. Reymert (Ed.), *Feelings and emotions.* New York: McGraw-Hill, 1950. Pp. 114–126.

Moore, G. E. *Philosophical studies.* New York: Harcourt, Brace and Company, Inc., 1922.

Osgood, C. E., G. J. Suci, and P. H. Tannenbaum. *The measurement of meaning.* Urbana, Ill.: University of Illinois Press, 1957.

Pap, A. *Elements of analytic philosophy.* New York: Macmillan, 1949.

Peirce, C. S., and J. Jastrow. On small differences of perception.

Mem. Nat. Acad. Sci., 1884, *3,* 73–88.

Postman, L., and R. F. Jarrett. An experimental analysis of learning without awareness. *Amer. J. Psychol.,* 1952, *65,* 244–255.

Putnam, H. The analytic and the synthetic. In H. Feigl and G. Maxwell (Eds.), *Minnesota studies in the philosophy of science,* Vol. III. Minneapolis: University of Minnesota Press, 1962. Pp. 358–397.

Russell, B. *Philosophy.* New York: Norton, 1927.

Ryle, G. *The concept of mind.* London: Hutchinson, 1949.

Sarbin, T. R. The logic of prediction in psychology. *Psychol. Rev.,* 1944, *51,* 210–228.

Sarbin, T. R. Role theory. In G. Lindzey (Ed.), *Handbook of social psychology,* Vol. I. Cambridge,

Mass.: Addison-Wesley, 1954. Pp. 223–258.

Sarbin, T. R., R. Taft, and D. E. Bailey. *Clinical inference and cognitive theory.* New York: Holt, Rinehart and Winston, Inc., 1960.

Thurstone, L. L. *Multiple-factor analysis.* Chicago: University of Chicago Press, 1947.

Todd, F. J. A methodological study of clinical judgment. Unpublished doctoral dissertation, University of Colorado, 1954.

Tolman, E. C., and E. Brunswik. The organism and the causal texture of the environment. *Psychol. Rev.,* 1935, *42,* 43–77.

Wallraff, C. F. On immediacy and the contemporary dogma of sense-certainty. *J. Phil.,* 1953, *50,* 29–39.

Wertheimer, M. *Productive thinking.* New York: Harper & Row, 1945.

6

The Historical Preconditions
of Representative Design

JOHN GILLIS
CAROL SCHNEIDER [1]

A necessary adjunct to understanding the methods of any science is an awareness of the rationale underlying them. It is important to look at not only *what* we are doing methodologically, but *why* we are doing it. There are several possible approaches to appreciating more fully the what and why of scientific methods. One may, for example, learn a great deal by addressing himself to the concrete problems that science is presently attempting to solve. Certainly, however, some valuable insights might also be gained through an historical approach. Indeed, it would seem that a thorough appreciation of current methodology could hardly be gained without some perspective on how things came to be as they are.

We have chosen in this paper to investigate historically psychology's most basic method—classical experimental design. This method insists that experiments should be so designed that all variables but one are controlled. The effects of that variable can thus be assessed independently of confusing, and possibly contaminating, influences.

One of the many aspects of experimental psychology that might profitably be studied through an historical approach, the classical paradigm, was particularly compelling to the writers. Certainly this paradigm is a most basic notion in current experimental thinking, and for this reason alone, we were curious about its origins and its role in the development of psychology. More importantly, perhaps, it represented to us a methodological *choice* rather than an inevitability. It did not appear perfectly obvious that this was the only way to do psychological

1. The authors wish to thank Professor Edwin G. Boring for his suggestions as to relevant historical sources and Professor Thomas S. Kuhn for his critical comments on the manuscript. The research for this paper was supported in part by the Council on Research and Creative Work of the University of Colorado.

experiments, yet clearly, it is the accepted way, and has been throughout psychology's brief history. If the classical paradigm were the result of certain methodological decisions, we were interested in who might have made these decisions, and why they were made.

The focus of our paper is actually two-fold. First, in Section I, we have sought to trace the mainstream of thinking concerning one-variable experimentation up to the time it was adopted by psychology. Secondly, in Section II, we have considered the reactions of a developing psychology, and its principal methodological thinkers, to the paradigm. In tracing the latter trend, we see the fundamental problem that faced the experimenter as that of dealing with multiple causation in nature. Experimenters have chosen to discover the lawfulness in nature by disentangling multiple causes from multiple effects. Their method is to allow one variable at a time to have its effect.

We have, then, attempted to trace the emergence of the idea of disentanglement of causes from the Greeks to the present time, and to show how Wundt and other psychologists brought this idea to psychology. But we have also sought to show the development of dissatisfaction with the disentanglement theme, which culminated in Brunswik's efforts to formulate an indigenous methodology for psychology. Thus, in Section III, we describe the methodological position suggested by Brunswik as a useful alternative to classical design. The purpose of the paper is not, of course, to develop Brunswik's argument in any detail. It is hoped, however, that the presentation of the historical context of psychology's principal experimental method, will enable the reader better to appreciate Brunswik's methodological position.

ANCIENT ORIGINS AND DEVELOPMENT THROUGH EARLY MODERN SCIENCE

The influence of the early Greeks on experimentation and experimental methods was considerable. Such men as Pythagoras, Archimedes, Hero, and Ptolemy were important experimenters, but it was Aristotle who had the greatest influence on methods. His thought served as a model to be investigated, criticized, and expanded. In the *Posterior Analytics* (c. 350 B.C.), he attempted to show how demonstrations can proceed from clearly defined first principles to particular conclusions.

One of the main criticisms leveled against his methods is that, once he found something that he believed was the cause of a phenomenon, he did not develop a way of testing other conclusions that might have been deduced from the same observation. That is, Aristotle appears to have failed to recognize that the same phenotypical effect might have been the result of any of several causes or combinations of causes. It was the later cognizance of multiple causation and attempts to deal with it that led to the stress on controlled experimentation and ultimately to classical design. What was necessary, it seemed, was that the possible causes—or possible contaminants of actual causes—be experimentally separated so that the essential causal factors could be identified. The environmental intermixture of causes must be disentangled, and the crucial variable highlighted. Probably the first to be concerned with the need to disentangle the causal matrix were the medieval English and Italian philosophers. The need for controls of some sort, however, was recognized far sooner, in the early work of Galen (127–200 B.C.).

Galen discussed the necessity of controls in medical experiments with drugs in his *de Methodus Midendi*. Some excerpts from this book will follow, so that his fairly modern conceptions concerning methods can be shown. Galen suggested that the effects of medicines should be noted in the three cases of a perfectly healthy person, a slightly ailing patient, and a really sick man. Furthermore in the last case one should note their varying effects as the disease is marked by any excess of heat, cold, dryness, or moisture. Also, care should be taken that the samples themselves are free from any admixture of a foreign substance. One condition to be observed in experimental investigation of critical days is to count no cases where any step has been made by physician or patient or bystanders or where any other foreign factor has done harm. He also advocates the idea that observation of one or two instances is not sufficient, but that oft-repeated observation was needed with conditions remaining the same on each occasion. And yet with the insight of genius, he points out that one of the difficulties of medical experimentation is the extreme unlikelihood of ever being able to observe in even two cases the same combination of symptoms and circumstances. (Thorndike, Vol. I, p. 161.)

These excerpts do not show that Galen was an advocate of one-variable experimentation; they do indicate, however, that he appreciated the importance of control, which is the essence of classical design. Yet the excerpts are scattered throughout various pages, and nowhere does Galen formally or systematically consolidate his views on method, nor realize that his methods have general applicability for experiments in every field of endeavor.

Toward the end of the twelfth century there was a sudden resurgence of experimentation and discussion of methods, almost concomitant with the availability of translations of Aristotle and Galen for the first time. Possibly the first to discuss scientific method after the work of the

Greeks was Robert Grosseteste (1175–1253). He was impressed by Aristotle's description of how to arrive at a theory or principle to explain repeatedly observed facts by a "leap" of intuition. But Grosseteste considered the problem which Aristotle had missed—namely, how can one properly evaluate the real cause of a phenomenon? He clearly saw the implications of multiple causation. As he writes in Book 2, Chapter 5, of his commentary on Aristotle's *Posterior Analytics:* "Can one effect have many causes? For, if one determinate cause cannot be reached from the effect, since there is no effect that has not some cause, it follows that an effect, just as it has one cause, so may it have another and so may there be several causes of it." (Crombie, Vol. II, 1959, p. 15.)

Because he realized that several causes could account for the effect observed, he goes on to say that in natural sciences there is only "minor certitudo." Natural science offers its explanations "probably rather than scientifically. . . . Only in mathematics is there science and demonstration in the strictest sense." And it is necessary to do specially arranged experiments in order to more closely approach a true knowledge of the causal principles really responsible for the events in the world. As far as we can discover, Grosseteste was the first to speak of the importance of disentanglement of causes.

How he proposed to effect this disentanglement is clear from his commentary on Aristotle's *Posterior Analytics,* Book I, Chapter 14. (italics ours.) "When someone frequently notices that the eating of scammony happens to be accompanied by the discharge of red bile . . . he is led to the conclusion that the scammony is the cause that withdraws red bile. The functioning reason begins to wonder whether things really are as sensible recollection says, and this leads the reason to the experiment, namely, that he should administer scammony *after all other causes purging red bile have been isolated and excluded.* When he has administered scammony many times with the *sure exclusion of all other things that withdrew red bile,* then there is formed in the reason this universal, namely, that all scammony of its nature withdraws red bile, and this is the way in which it comes from sensation to a universal experimental principle." There can be little doubt that Grosseteste is here urging the use of a manipulated independent variable as a means of disentangling causes.

Another early writer on method is Petrus Hispanus (c. 1210–1277), a physician who later became Pope John XXI. His contribution is a presentation of the proper method of medical experimentation, which in some respects can be considered a systematization of Galen's views.

" 'First,' said Hispanus, 'the medicine should be free from all foreign substances. Second, the patient taking it should have the disease for which it is especially intended. Third, it should be given alone without admixture of other medicine. Fourth, it should be of the opposite degree to the disease. Fifth, we should test it not once but many times. Sixth, the experiments should be on the proper body, as on the body of a man and not of an ass.' " (Thorndike, Vol. II, p. 509.)

A contemporary of Hispanus, John of St. Amand, provided seven rules resembling those of Petrus. But Thorndike has evidence that shows they were derived directly from Galen, as were those of Petrus. Since St. Amand's rules are so similar to the ones of Petrus, they are not listed here in their entirety except to note that his first requirement is that "the medical sample which is being tested should be pure and free from every extraneous quality, lest by such extraneous quality the proper operation of the medicine be impeded, and in consequence experimental knowledge." (Thorndike, Vol. II, p. 511.) Here is the idea that without disentanglements, the progress of advancing knowledge is impeded.

Little better evidence of the effect of the recent translation of Galen could be offered than this instance of two contemporaries independently arriving at similar methods. It should be noted that these men were physicians interested in medical experiments, and so did not seek to make their method a general one. It is only the medieval philosopher who tells us of the general necessity of identifying the essential cause of a phenomenon, of disentangling it from its environmental nexus. Thus, William of Ockham (c. 1284–1349) was looking for causes, and like Grosseteste, he realized that the same effect might have different causes. It was necessary to eliminate rival hypotheses. Ockham states his method in general terms, by saying that we do experiments in order to test for causal connections and "I say that this is sufficient for something being an immediate cause, namely, that when it is present the effect follows, and when it is not present, *all other conditions and dispositions being the same,* the effect does not follow." (Crombie, Vol. II, 1959, p. 31, italics ours.) Crombie has pointed out that this method is very similar to J. S. Mill's method of agreement and difference, posited some 500 years later.

So far we have presented the English efforts to formulate a workable experimental method. The Italians were working on such a formulation at about the same time. The work of Italian methodologists is important because Galileo did his work in Italy. He was the first to apply the newly formulated methods to a science other than medicine, and to discuss how this method applied to something other than herbs or drugs curing diseases. The philosophers who formulated the methods, which he used, worked at Padua in Italy. Randall (1940) has described the approach of the Paduan methodologists as translating the logical method of demonstrative proof into an empirical strategy of discovery.

Zabarella (1533–1592) formulated the classic version of the Paduan method *in the very terms* that Galileo was to use about ten years later. Zabarella took pains to distinguish between scientific experiment and mere observation, which he called the accidental or planless collection of cases. The basis for this distinction is that scientific experimentation proceeds to the identification of the essential cause-effect relationship. Such a method, he said, ". . . proceeds from a rigorous analysis of a few selected instances which do not take all the particulars (variables?) into account, since after certain of them have been examined, our mind notices the *essential connection* to be tested, and afterwards, *disregarding the remaining particulars,* proceeds to the universal." (Randall, 1940, p. 191, italics ours.) Although the language is somewhat different from Ockham's, and the explication is not nearly as clear, the idea seems the same. The implication here is that the particulars must be controlled in order to get at the true cause.

Galileo's Dialogues (1632), certainly a bench mark in the history of experimental science, put the methodological notions of Padua to work. Galileo stressed, as had Zabarella and Grosseteste, the rigor necessary for useful experiments and the importance of stripping unessential elements from the design, "since it was impossible to deal at once with all the observed properties of a phenomenon. . . ." (Crombie, Vol. II, 1959, p. 144.) That Galileo was aware that causes must be separated, or disentangled, to be assessed is amusingly illustrated in a passage from *Il Saggiatore:* "If Sarsi wishes me to believe, on the word of Suidas that the Babylonians cooked eggs by whirling them in a sling, I will believe it; but I shall say that the cause of such an effect is very remote from that to which they attribute it and to discover the true cause I shall argue as follows: If an effect, which has succeeded with others at another time, does not take place with us, it necessarily follows that in our experiment there is something lacking which was the cause of the success of the former attempt; and, if we lack but one thing, that one thing is alone the true cause; now we have no lack of eggs, nor of slings, nor of stout fellows to whirl them, and yet they will not cook, and indeed, if they be hot they will cool the more quickly; and since nothing is wanting to us save to be Babylonians, it follows that the fact of being Babylonians and not the attrition of the air is the cause of the eggs becoming hard-boiled, which is what I wish to prove." (Crombie, Vol. II, 1959, pp. 137–138.)

Galileo, Crombie tells us, felt the ". . . first business of science was to

establish regularities, to discover proximate causes, that is, those antecedent events which *when other conditions were the same,* always and
alone produced the same effect." (Crombie, Vol. II, 1959, p. 136.) Again,
Galileo comments in the *Dialogue:* "Thus I say that if it is true that
one effect can have only one basic cause, and if between the cause and the
effect there is a fixed and constant connection, then whenever a fixed and
constant variation is seen in the effect, there must be a fixed and constant
variation in the cause. . . . If we then wish to preserve the identity of the
cause, we must find the changes in these additions and subtractions that
make them more or less potent at producing those effects that depend
upon them." (Galileo, 1952, p. 247.) This is what Mill was later to
refer to as the method of concomitant variations, while the Babylonian-
and-egg anecdote demonstrates the method of differences.

Later scientists and philosophers of science were less explicit about
precisely what was acceptable as an experimental methodology.[2] It was
clear, however, that they were dissatisfied with the loose and uncontrolled—Gilbert calls them "vague and indecisive"—methods of their
predecessors. For many, it is difficult to ascertain whether the directions
they took with respect to disentangling causes, were precisely those
advocated by Galileo.

Most of the active experimentalists—Gilbert, Huygens, Harvey—did
not define their experimental standards beyond calling for cautions and
repeated observations. On those occasions when they did present their
views on more general scientific considerations, it was to justify experimentation as the means to scientific progress. During a period when
experimentation was yet fighting for its scientific life, one might be an
apologist for rigor if he but advocated experimentation over metaphysics.

Those whose principal concern was the philosophical basis of science
were likewise involved with the problem of experimental rigor. Perhaps,
however, because they were encouraging others rather than proposing
standards under which they themselves would frequently labor, their
methodological stipulations are somewhat more easily identified. Francis
Bacon, generally considered the foremost proponent of scientific method
during the seventeenth century, defended at length the role of an inductive, experimental science. Bacon argued that even accurate ob-

2. One possible explanation of this fact is that Galileo began his work at Padua
just after Zabarella had written his summary of the 300 years work on methodology by Italian philosophers. Due to the nature of this work and Galileo's own interests, it is likely that he was influenced by it. Most of the other major experimenters were English or French and were 300 years removed from the work of
Grosseteste and Ockham.

servations were insufficient avenues to the laws of nature. "Artificial" experiments, requiring apparatus and expenditure, were necessary.

Francis Bacon never explicitly supported the classical experimental design. He did stress rigor and simplicity and his general inductive scheme was certainly an encouraging framework for the single-variable approach. He appears never to have actually taken the step—as did Mill—of recommending a single-variable paradigm for experimentation. This fairly accords with Crombie's general evaluation of Bacon as a ". . . philosopher with a clear grasp of the function of the empirical principle but almost none at all of the technical procedures necessary, not only to solve problems but even to formulate them in a scientifically significant manner." (Crombie, Vol. II, 1959, p. 289.)

Although Descartes was not disinterested in experimentation, his primary scientific influence derived, as did Bacon's, from his philosophical system. As did his contemporaries, Descartes placed the source of scientific knowledge in the observation of elementary units. His "Rules for Direction of the Mind" (1630) thus state that: "Inquiries should be directed to what one can clearly behold and deduce with certainty" and that one should: "Reduce involved propositions to continually more simple ideas." Since certainty was the goal, "crucial" experiments would be required. As Descartes said, "I do not know any other plan but to try to find experiments of such a nature that their result is not the same if it has to be explained by one of the methods, as it would be if explained by the other." (Descartes, 1952, p. 62.)

Such an involvement with "experimentum crucis" does not imply advocacy of one-variable design. It does suggest an awareness of the need for control of spurious factors in experimentation. It was just such a concern for controls, when dictated by the *need for certainty*, which gave credence to maximally controlled one-variable experiments.

While Bacon and Descartes can hardly be said to have directly encouraged classical design, their goals and strategies of scientific discovery were certainly congruent with such a methodology. They did not apparently direct themselves to the need for disentanglement; they did assume that essential singular causes existed and concerned themselves with the strategy for detecting these. Though neither spelled out the required design as specifically as Mill was to do some 300 years later, the practicing experimentalists were urged to do unequivocal experiments in which the relationship of single causes and single effects might be correctly slotted into broader schemes of nature. Galileo, of course, sought to carry out such experiments.

Perhaps the experimentalist whose work we might most expect to follow Galileo and the one-variable model was William Harvey. Harvey had spent some time at Padua with Fabrizio of Aquapendente, a colleague of Galileo's, and was thus thoroughly familiar with Galileo's methods. Where Harvey was able to experiment he took considerable care ". . . to render our experiments more undeniable." His procedural methods of hypothesis testing are perhaps nowhere better illustrated than in his work on circulation of the blood. Attempting to demonstrate that the blood flowed in a single direction, a serpent whose vessels might be easily observed, was utilized. Harvey demonstrated that: "When the vena cava was pinched with forceps, the heart drained and became pale, whereas when the aorta was similarly closed (the vena cava being left open) the heart became distended and purple."

In the utilization of such techniques it is apparent that Harvey intended to work with single independent and dependent variables, for example, curtailing of blood flow through the aorta—distended heart. While Harvey does not mention the control of variables at all in his major works, it certainly appears that he was cognizant of a need for disentanglement, that is, for separating the essential from the non-essential factors in the observed relationships. And while one may accuse Harvey of some naïvete in the use of controls—he never questioned that any variable other than that he manipulated could account for the effect [3]—it is clear that his intention was to relate single essential causes to single essential events.

The same might be said of Gilbert's work in the sixteenth century and that of Newton and Huygens in the latter part of the seventeenth century. These investigators conducted orderly, carefully-considered experiments in which their purpose was clearly to interrelate isolated causes and effects. Consider one of Gilbert's elementary demonstrations that even unmagnetized iron assumes a north and south direction: "A straight rod of iron six feet in length and as thick as one's finger is . . . suspended in equilibrium with a fine but strong silk thread. The thread, however, should be composed of several silk filaments, twisted differently and not all in one direction. Let the experiment be made in a small room with doors and windows all closed, to prevent currents of air in the room. Hence it is not well to experiment on windy days or when a storm is brewing." (Gilbert, 1952, pp. 18–19.)

With such extensive controls effected one can expect the iron to act according to its properties and point north and south. Obviously, Gilbert is taking great pains to eliminate all spurious factors that might confuse

---

3. This is, in fact, the point on which Descartes challenged him.

the effects he is seeking. It is indeed the case that, outside of his experimentation with magnetic properties, Gilbert seems hardly to have been aware that controlled experimentation was necessary or even possible. He accepts, for example, evidence of the most magical of medicinal roles for the loadstone without ever questioning the nature of the experiments by which such evidence was derived. (Gilbert, 1952, p. 20.) Despite these lapses, it is our impression that when Gilbert considered it most vital to work as a scientist, he worked within a one-variable model.

Newton's work has the same flavor. Although his experiments in the latter two books of his *Optics* are too complex to be presented here, a brief reading will indicate Newton's rigorous concern with controlling all factors that might possibly effect the phenomena he wishes to observe.

Harvey, Newton, and Gilbert were, of course, personages of tremendous influence in the scientific era before Mill, and it is probably safe to assume that the methods they actually used were of more relevance for future scientists than the methods less explicitly encouraged by Bacon and Descartes. At any rate, we have found general congruency in the more-or-less defined methodological criteria of all of these. And it is our conclusion that by the outset of the eighteenth century, it was clear that if one were to attempt to contribute to science, he must accomplish this by working within that framework defined by scientists, inclusive of those notions we have come to recognize as "classical design."

Another interesting example of the kind of methodological thought that was part of the fabric of single-variable experimentation is found in Lavoisier's work. In his *Elements of Chemistry,* written near the end of the eighteenth century, the great chemist describes his own strenuous efforts to eliminate all possible contaminating factors. "In performing experiments, it is a necessary principle which ought never to be deviated from, that they be simplified as much as possible, and that every circumstance capable of rendering their results complicated be carefully removed. Wherefore in the experiments which form the object of this chapter, we have never employed atmospheric air which is not a simple substance. It is true that the azotic gas, which forms a part of its mixture, appears to be merely passive . . . but if we are not certain but it may alter their results in some circumstances; for which reason I have thought it necessary to remove even this possible cause of doubt by making use of only pure oxygen. . . ." (Lavoisier, 1952, p. 22.) Clearly, Lavoisier was concerned with disentangling the essential causes from all disturbing influences.

It must be borne in mind that Lavoisier defined his experimental standards in 1789, some fifty-eight years before Mill's "Canons" had been published. The same manner of experimental procedure can be observed in the work of Faraday (for example, Faraday, 1839, p. 775 ff.), although this investigator never formulated his methodological criteria as clearly as did Lavoisier.

Considerable ground had thus been laid in the three preceding centuries for Mill's "Canons" of induction when they appeared in 1847 as part of his *Logic*. William of Ockham had formulated the methods of agreement and difference. Bacon had based his natural system on these same methods. Galileo, using the method of the Paduan philosophers, utilized the system of concomitant variation in his experimental work. Harvey, Newton, and Gilbert had performed their experiments with a view toward obtaining data about separate factors. What Mill was to achieve was an ordering of the standards by which scientific experimentation of that day was in fact being judged. Irrespective of Mill's effects on the physical scientist of his day or the future, his achievements had a long and lasting effect on psychological research. Specifically, the effect of Mill's work was to make it quite clear that the one-variable experiment was the acceptable and indeed requisite means of scientific procedure.

Mill's work on methods culminated in his canons of inference. The most important canon in the development of classical design in his method of differences: "If our object is to discover the effects of an agent A, we must procure A in some set of ascertained circumstances, as $A B C$, and having noted the effects produced, compare them with the effect of the remaining circumstances $B C$, when A is absent. If the effect of $A B C$ is $a b c$, and the effect of $B C$, $b c$, it is evident that the effect of A is a." (Mill, 1882, p. 280.)

CLASSICAL DESIGN IN EXPERIMENTAL PSYCHOLOGY

Mill's canons of induction were not the only influence on the experimental methods of the "new" psychology. The early proponents of psychology, for example, had come from medical and physiological fields where these methods were already in application. There is little danger of overstating the role of Mill's canons, however, as psychologists forty and fifty years subsequent to their publication (see below) were still to refer directly to them for the "method of psychology."

The availability of a methodology sufficiently delineated to be represented in experimental canons, must surely have affected the relation of an investigator to his material. There was no longer the problem of how one could most effectively deal with the material at hand. Rather, the task of the experimenter was one of somehow arranging his data that they might be treated by the formulated rules. The template had been provided. The problem remained to adapt one's concerns to it. If the subject matter could not be made to fit the methodological template in any fashion, an investigator would best seek more agreeable topics, or content himself with being something less than a scientist.

There was, then, much to persuade the leaders of the budding nineteenth-century psychology of the advantages of the experimental approach, and the particular version of this approach that was urged in the canons of inference. The "new" psychology was to be experimental and as it was in large part a reaction against the metaphysical preoccupations of past centuries, it meant to be experimental in every sense of the term. Its early leaders had come from natural science and carried a methodological rationale and conviction at little variance from that of Stuart Mill himself. Cognizant of its tenuous scientific status, envious of the preeminence of physics and biology, the new psychology set about vigorously to establish for a skeptical world its kinship in purpose and procedure with the established sciences. Ebbinghaus highlighted the nature of this struggle, and those aspects of it that were most vital to psychologists, in 1885:

The method of obtaining exact measurements—that is, numerically exact ones—of the inner structure of causal relations is, by virtue of its nature, of general validity. This method, indeed, has been so exclusively used and so fully worked out by the natural sciences that, as a rule, it is defined as something peculiar to them, as the method of natural science. To repeat, however, its logical nature makes it generally applicable to all spheres of existence and phenomena. Moreover, the possibility of defining accurately and exactly the actual behavior of any process whatever, and thereby of giving a reliable basis for the direct comprehension of its connections depends above all upon the possibility of applying this method.

We all know of what this method consists: an attempt is made to keep constant the mass of conditions which have proven themselves causally connected with a certain result; one of these conditions is isolated from the rest and varied in a way that can be numerically described; then the accompanying change on the side of the effect is ascertained by measurement or computation. (1913, p. 7.)

The widespread influence of Ebbinghaus' *Memory* makes this stand regarding experimental methods of special significance. Of equal interest, however, is the thinking of the psychology of Ebbinghaus' day, insofar as he can be said to be a spokesman for this thought. First of all, the fact is unequivocal that the spirit of Mill's canons has been totally accepted. There is, for Ebbinghaus, but a single road to scientific truth, the road of one-variable experimentation. That the subject matter of science might be diverse is of no real concern, since "any process whatever" might, and must, be susceptible to exploration via this system.

Of equal note in Ebbinghaus' plea is the justification for this methodological emulation. The case for psychology's adoption of this experimental design is not allowed to rest on its success in natural science—although one can hardly doubt that Ebbinghaus is enamored of this success. Rather, however, the paradigm is defended in much the same way as Mill proposed it—as the rational, logical method of experimental procedure. Further, it is the method that assuredly gets behind the complex, misleading flux of psychological phenomena to the imminent causal features therein. If we are to realize the relationship between any causal unit and its consequent, between any "A" and "a," we must first unravel the camouflage in which it is intermeshed, that is, to *know* we must first isolate suspected causes from the "mass of conditions" surrounding them.

While the above quote vividly captures the bent and desires of an infant psychology, it does not, of course, indicate the reception that was accorded "canonical" design. Particularly does it touch only briefly—Ebbinghaus was later to remedy this in the first chapter of his 1908 *Text-Book*—that aspect of the rationale which, as we shall attempt to document, became the most accepted basis for the one-variable design. This is the notion that the method disentangled causes; the notion that the classical paradigm was the only method that could make scientific sense of the confusion that nature inevitably presents to individual experience. It was within this confusion, as Ebbinghaus suggests, that the elementary linkages, the "absolute and inevitable subjection to law" of *all* natural and psychological phenomena, was thought to reside. As physics and biology had approached lawfulness by teasing out these invariances, so now it was to be psychology's task to do the same.

In passing from Mill to Ebbinghaus we have, of course, avoided some thirty-eight years of psychological and nearly-psychological thought. These were crucial developmental years for experimental psychology and contained methodological decisions seldom again pursued and even more infrequently contested. It is incumbent upon us to consider the methodological notions of at least a few of the decision-makers of that time.

The giant of the period and, for many years the unchallenged leader of experimental psychology, was, of course, Wilhelm Wundt. What Wundt did in the way of content and design of experiments was vital, and what he said about what he did was perhaps even more significant. Experimental psychology was, as Boring notes, defined by Wundt for much of the latter half of the nineteenth century. The way experiments far beyond Leipzig were run would be determined by Wundt's carefully delineated suggestions.

Even if one were to place himself back in the period before Wundt began to write material specifically psychological in nature, it would not have been difficult to anticipate his general methodological position. Wundt's physiological legacy was strong and all the rigor that marked the efforts of Helmholtz, Fechner, and himself might be expected to generalize to his psychological laboratory. Wundt was convinced that psychology, if it were to be an empirical science, must behave as did the other empirical sciences. In all sciences, the elements of experimental isolation, variance, and control were essential. As he put it: ". . . wherever experiment is possible it is always used in the natural sciences; for under all circumstances, even when the phenomena in themselves present the conditions for sufficiently exact observation, it is an advantage to be able to control at will their rise and progress, or to isolate the various components of a composite phenomena." (1897, pp. 18–19.)

As a study of consciousness and associations, Wundt's psychology was systematic and elementary. Although the description hardly does justice to the complexity of his methodological thinking, Wundt's notions were roughly these: what is elemental is perfectly lawful and what is lawful is ascertainable only by using the "probe" of classically designed experiments. Now this elemental lawfulness of consciousness was derived in part from the regularity which the environment presented to individual experience. Wundt perceived that the "concatenation of events" was "regular" only in a limited sense, however, and here his thinking justifies a lengthy reference.

This opinion . . . rests obviously on a mistaken use of the conception of the law. We are only allowed to consider those regularities in phenomena as according to law, which always repeat themselves in the same manner. But there are in reality no such laws, not even in the natural sciences. For this principle is valid here: laws determine the course of phenomena only insofar as they are not annulled by other laws. Now because of the complex nature of all phenomena in general each process stands under the influence of many laws and so it happens that just the most universal natural laws can never in experience be demonstrated in their full power. There is no law of dynamics that has more universal validity than the so-called 'law of inertia' of Newton's first law of motion . . . *It is obvious that this law can never and nowhere be realized in experience, since a case of independence from other external forces, which alter the motion, never and nowhere exists.* (italics ours) (1912, pp. 155–156.)

Wundt saw, therefore, that nature, as it presented itself to the be-having organism, was anything but a clear pattern of perfectly regular relationships. Still, at some level there was strict lawfulness. "Now if we cast a glance, while keeping firmly to this criterion over the manifold processes of consciousness, which have been touched upon in this book, we see at once that all these processes bear the character of a stern regularity. Not in the sense that these laws are fixed rules without ex-ceptions (such laws as we have seen above do not exist, because of the never-failing interference from other influences), but in the only sense permissible, that is, that each complex phenomenon can be reduced to a lawful cooperation of elements." (1912, p. 158.)

Recognizing, then, that there existed both a regularity in nature that was inaccessible to the organism, and a complex, irregular pattern to which he was customarily exposed, Wundt was faced with a methodo-logical choice. He could choose to investigate the organism-environment relationship as the former actually experienced it, or he could choose to seek out those relationships that he believed obtained somewhere beyond the organism's ken. He chose, of course, the latter. And that choice re-quired the use of an experimental technique that served to disentangle causal influences. With a regularity to be obtained, and with an ad-mittedly artificial means required to obtain it, the one-variable paradigm —which had served just such a function for natural science—was clearly suggested.

Let us now seek . . . to recall the general impression which any particular mental experience has left upon us. The impression will always be that of a composite process . . . It is certainly true that these elements of mental life never occur separately, but always in connection with, always in dependence upon, one another. Nevertheless, it seems absolutely necessary, at the begin-ning of a psychological investigation, . . . to separate out the most important factors of this complex inner life and subject each of them in turn to a special analysis. (1896, p. 13.)

And again, regarding the unconscious realm of psychological data: "How can we descend into this secret laboratory where thought has its hidden spring? How separate the thousand threads that make its tissue? . . . experiment is, in psychology, the necessary guide to the hidden foundation where the conscious life has its rise. Internal observation, as observation in general, gives only complex phenomena. By experiment, on the contrary, *we strip the phenomenon of all its accessory conditions,* which we can change at will, and measure. *Everywhere and always, experiment conducts to natural law,* because it exhibits cause and effect simultaneously." (italics ours) (Ribot, 1886, p. 192.)

For Wundt then, the rationale behind one-variable experimentation is little different than that later presented by Ebbinghaus. At its essence lie the assumptions of the lawful regular functioning of nature—conscious and unconscious thought included—a lawfulness that is accessible only through rigorous experimentation, in which every possible causal element is separately assessed. The problem is one of segmenting, of disentangling the causal cobweb—the identical task which natural science had set itself. How better to "disentangle" causes than that inductive method that had already established its scientific utility?

Wundt, of course, wrote copiously throughout all of his career and the materials from which the above comments were selected encompass the period of 1863 to 1911. There appears to have been little alteration in his methodological position, however, and the view we have described was doubtless communicated directly to his many students and indirectly —through the *Philosophische Studien* as well as the teachings of his students—to the entire world of experimental psychology. Methodological leadership came from Leipzig.

While Wundt's statements and practice of experimental methods were undoubtedly the principal spur for the rapidly developing "new" psychology, there came support for the classical paradigm outside of Leipzig and indeed outside of genuine experimental psychology. Some of the strongest support came from the writings of Alexander Bain who had succeeded Hobbes as the chief spokesman for the British associationists. Although Bain's most memorable contribution was his two-volume system of psychology written in the 1850's, his methodological ideas were most clearly set forth in the *Logic* of 1870. Bain, as Boring tells us, had worked with Mill on the latter's *Logic* and had praised the effort extensively. So we might anticipate much of Mill in Bain's own comments regarding the methods of science and this is precisely what we find. The canons are there, together with a rationale for them very similar to that of Mill. And, regarding the notion of one-variable experimentation, the thinking is at little variance from that of Wundt.

Bain assumed, as had Wundt, as underlying regularity of nature, the causal lawfulness of which could only be ascertained by the experimental assessment of isolated variables. "The extended machinery of Inductive research, constituting the Logic or Method of induction, is thus nearly confined to causation. The greatest resources for eliminating accidental accompaniment and for seizing the real concomittances of fact—the so-called 'Experimental Methods'—have their full application only to Cause and Effect." (1870, Vol. II, p. 10.)

For Bain, the task of science, and of psychology as a science, was to analyze all phenomena into their simplest components and to evaluate each component separately as to causal significance. Particularly must essential causal links be distinguished, be disentangled, from the inevitable "inert and otiose accompaniments" of natural phenomena.

The different antecedents and consequents being separated in thought, we have to ascertain which antecedent is connected with a given consequent. Having usually a plurality of antecedents, or a plurality of consequents, or both, we need to single out the connected couples of antecedent and consequent. Thus in order to ascertain which of the gases of the atmosphere supports combustion, or animal life, and what are the elements that bring about putresence and decay, we must, by means of experiments, separate artificially one or another of the gases from the rest; *such separation not being provided for us in nature.* (italics ours) (1870, p. 43.)

Regarding the latter part of this comment, we shall have more to say in a moment. First, however, it is worth mentioning that Bain's position regarding the essential lawfulness of nature and its "discovery" via the methods of eliminative experiment are developed in the *Logic* to their rational extremes. Thus, Bain proposes the establishment of absolute lawfulness, of certainty, through the perfectly-executed one-variable design:

Now it follows (given the "uniformity of sequences") that wherever an agent is introduced into a quiescent state of things, and when certain changes follow at once on that fact, the sequence happening once will happen always. . . . Nature in the matter of sequences is uniform; and a single case, cleared of ambiguities, establishes a law. By the stroke of an axe the block is cleft; the same effect will always follow the cause. Hence a single experiment in a laboratory may establish forever a causal property. (1870, p. 47.)

The disentanglement of causes, as the seemingly avowed purpose of classical design, is always oriented toward certainty. And where it involves an area of investigation where one must be concerned with certainty, it appears to be the reasonable, indeed, the only, way to proceed. But the gap between the perfectly unequivocal experiment to which Bain points, and the chaotic flux of circumstances that Wundt and Ebbinghaus agreed characterizes psychological life is exceedingly large. And yet the latter investigators—and Bain himself—saw the experimental task of science as necessarily striving for unambiguous results. It was a curious paradox, even for an infant psychology.

Bain had some interesting insights regarding multiple causation and even recognized the need for (at least temporary) acceptance of a certain degree of probabilism. With regard to the former he noted that the "Methods of elimination suppose different effects to remain separate as indistinguishable; whereas cases arise where the effects of different causes unite in a homogeneous total." (1870, p. 80.) (This is essentially the argument that Whewell (1860), although he approved emulation of the methods of established science, had urged against the canons from a logical vantage point.) For example, Bain suggested that many rivulets feed a stream and the effects of each single rivulet could hardly be isolated. "A still more perplexing situation," he continues, "is the conflict of opposing agencies. In an equal balance nothing is seen, and yet great powers have been at work . . . The patient may be under various healthy stimulants, each working its proper effect; but some one noxious agency may counteract the whole." (1870, p. 81.) Here the technique of concomitant variations is suggested as the only one of the available experimental methods that might be used to advantage in such cases. The recognition that many causes can contribute to an effect is important. So is the notion that one can handle this state of affairs on occasion not by forcibly effecting the isolation of separate variables, but rather by noting the accord of distinguishable phenomena within their given context of conditions. Bain here seems willing to take at least a half-stride away from the strict experimental-isolationist position. It is at best a reluctant step, however; for the method of concomitant variations was being recommended only when the customary "methods of elimination" are incapable of being implemented. And the essential role of concomitant variations for Bain is, in fact, little more than that of a tool in searching for isolation where such cannot be experimentally obtained. He thus sees its maximal utility in a situation such that "If a cause happens to vary alone, the effect will also vary alone, and cause and effect may thus be singled out under the greatest complications." (1870, p. 83;) where experimental isolation is impossible, statistical isolation is acceptable.

Now, we have made the point that for early psychology the principal asset of the single-variable design was in its use as a strategy for disentangling the causal complexity of nature. Bain, as did Wundt, recognized fully this circumstance of complexity, as witness the above-mentioned awareness of *"separation* (of causes) *not being provided for us in nature."* Bain's position regarding nature's apparent chaos represented, however, rather a novel one among the psychologists of his day (although, as we shall see, Galton was shortly to carry this same position to a meaningful statistical conclusion). Bain thus notes that "The complications of the phenomena of Mind prevent us from attaining laws of universal application. In many instances, we must state our position as more or less probable." (1870, p. 286;) thus:

> There are certain cases, where a cause fails to produce its effect, being counteracted by some other cause. *A B C* is followed by *a b c,* from which the inference, by Agreement would be, that *A* is not the cause of *a.* Bark is administered to a patient in ague, but the symptoms are not alleviated. The strict application of the Method of Agreement would lead to the inference that bark does not cure ague. Yet we do not, in practice, lose faith in medicines from individual failures. We are prepared to encounter exceptions to cases of complicated causation. (1870, p. 85.)

What Bain is advocating, of course, is the acceptance of probabilistic descriptions of nature and statistical criteria of lawfulness.

> In the generalizations of co-inhering attributes, in Physics and in Chemistry, there is often a want of perfect agreement in the details: yet the agreement is too extensive to be the product of chance, and hence we must admit the existence of a law, which, in the complications of phenomena, is occasionally crossed or counteracted. . . . The law does not become waste paper because of this exception. The coincidence is one that mere chance cannot account for. (1870, p. 87.)

The necessity for accepting probabilism suggests a more compromising attitude regarding the disentanglement of causes than Wundt had preferred. For if one is "content" with probabilistic relationships, there need be no quest for that elemental regularity that lies somewhere beyond the appearance of things. Disentanglement—and the methodological analogue of disentanglement—is no longer essential if we are willing to do without this regularity, and if we are willing to settle for something less than certainty.

Bain, it would then seem, is advocating the reasonableness—for his book is a *Logic*—of a probabilistic view of nature and the formulation of lawful systems based on this probabilism. We have already seen, however, that Bain was fundamentally an advocate of lawfulness via disentanglement and of experimental designs implementing the isolation of variables. Wherein the congruity of Bain's position? Very simply, it lies in the pro tem respectability accorded probabilism. Faced with chaos, we must deal with whatever regularity emerges from chaos. Always, however, the assumption of hidden regularity is maintained as the ultimate goal of science. When an exception appears to an otherwise lawful relationship, Bain's primary concern is to "reconcile the discrepancy"—

and the reconciliation is but a matter of time. Thus, Bain's cognizance of probabilistic functioning does not alter his final conclusions concerning methods. Still, he was perhaps more insightful regarding the "scattering of nature's effects" than had any been before him and laid some minimal groundwork for those who might care to develop the implications of such a framework.

Three years after Bain's *Logic* had been published, William Jevons' *The Principles of Science* appeared, a volume which was to have considerable and long-lasting influence on psychological method (Baldwin's *Dictionary,* 1901, cites the *Principles* concurrently with Wundt regarding the method of psychology). Jevons was concerned with quantitative experimentation and there was little in his ideas that was dissimilar to Wundt's. Thus:

Almost every series of quantitative experiments is directed to obtain the relation between the different values of one quantity which is varied at will, and another quantity which is caused thereby to vary. We conveniently distinguish these as the *variable* and the *variant*. . . . Experiments may indeed be made with accuracy, provided we can exactly measure the variable at the moment when the quantity of the effect is determined. But if we have to trust to the action of some capricious force, there may be great difficulty in making exact measurements. . . . (1873, pp. 440–441.)

The publication of works on, and discussions about, psychology seems to have progressed geometrically in the last decades of the nineteenth century. Most of the important writers had something to say about experimental methods; and most of what was said involved rationales similar in all their essentials to those of Wundt, Bain and Ebbinghaus. We had reached a stage, of course, where this might have been expected. If the methodological notions of psychology were only embryonic near the end of the century they were at least past conception. The earliest leaders had done much of the molding and inevitably their notions, methodological and otherwise, would persist.

The continuity of the rationale for "isolated" variable designs was evident in many places during the 1890's. Perhaps the most circumscript packaging of this rationale was achieved by James M. Baldwin, writing in 1893: "It remains to inquire . . . through what means or by what kind of procedure shall we investigate the matter before us in order to reach the most general and exhaustive results? . . . this problem is practically solved for us in the method of the objective sciences. For if, as has been said, psychology is a science of fact, as they are, and proceeds by the observation of a given class of facts, as they do, then the tried method procedure which they employ will be most productive here." (1893, p. 12.)

The need of experiment in psychology is exceedingly great. When we remember that, in the search for causes in the natural world, the difficulties are vastly enhanced by the fact that *single causes are never found at work alone,* and that it is the function of experiment so to eliminate agencies in a causal complex, that isolated agencies may be observed at work. . . . Antecedents and consequents are thrown into the mental life in inextricable confusion. . . . How can we single out the cause in the network, by observation. . . . Only one step can determine: the reconstruction, under artificial circumstances, of the conditions, and the endeavor to exhibit a single isolated cause. (italics ours) (1893, p. 15.)

Baldwin has here presented a rather detailed argument for the one variable design. His defense, while it is unusually explicit in the above passage, actually is but a reiteration of those highlights of that methodological rationale that we have already considered. The argument, as always, runs that

1. the causal matrix of nature is presented to the human observer in chaotic fashion, but
2. certain regularities underlie and compose this chaos, therefore
3. it is the task of science—and particularly psychology since it is faced with even more confusion than other sciences—to segment this chaos so that isolated causes and effects can be observed, and
4. the most fruitful way of accomplishing this is by the experimental-inductive methods which have already proved their worth.

Of additional interest is the fact that Mill is cited directly as providing the rules from which experimental psychology might proceed. Sully (1892) and Höffding (1893) refer their readers directly to Mill, and to Bain, for information regarding the methods of psychology. The methodology espoused by Mill had not originated with that author, and there is little doubt that it would have exerted considerable formative interest in psychology if the canons had never been formulated. The canons in themselves, however, had made sufficient impress that J. S. Mill, who, after all, was not really a psychologist, had become a sort of methodological oracle for psychology.

Baldwin's other comments were also restated by other authors. Höffding (1893) and Stout (1896) stressed the need for discovering isolated causal linkages, although the latter showed the same awareness as had Bain of the causal confusion with which the behaving organism was typically faced. Sully (1892), Ladd (1896), and Scripture (1897), all found it incumbent upon psychology to use those methods of science that had proved fruitful in the past. Sully's comment is of particular interest since he ties this obligation to the similarity of psychology's task with that of all science—that of finding essential causes.

In thus separating itself as a positive science from philosophy, psychology has placed itself more on the level of the physical sciences. Its conceptions of mental phenomena, and of laws ascertained by induction from these, have, in fact, been modeled on the pattern of conceptions reached by physical science. More particularly, in its consistent determination to deal with all mental processes as subject to the great law of causation, modern psychology has tended to assimilate itself in one important respect to the physical sciences. (1892, p. 4.)

It was this determination to follow all established sciences in the pursuit of "the great law of causation" that somehow got confused with a determination to emulate their *methods* in this pursuit.

Scripture was particularly impressed by Ebbinghaus' methodological achievements, and comments upon them in what can only be a direct paraphrase of Ebbinghaus himself.

The possibility of gaining any accurate and trustworthy knowledge concerning memory depends upon the possibility of applying what is often called the "natural science" method merely because mental science has made so little use of it. This method is essentially as follows: from the complexity of conditions surrounding a phenomenon we first exclude those that are evidently unessential; then we seek to maintain all the others unchanged except one. . . . (1897, p. 60.)

Besides the disentanglement-causality hypothesis that we have offered, it was probably also significant that the canonical methodology was often couched in systems of logic. This is true not only of Mill, for Lotze's book was a *Logic* as was Bain's. And Hobhouse in 1896 produced a summary, rationale for, and thorough-going espousal of the canons in a volume entitled the *Theory of Knowledge*. The Mill-derived procedure had thus not only proved itself pragmatically but had doubtless taken on the role as the most reasonable, rational and logical way to proceed. And if psychology were to maintain any self-respect, could it tolerate else than being logical?

In American psychology, the one variable design carried the day completely. And it was during the period from 1896 to about 1915 that one of the most influential American psychologists, Edward B. Titchener, championed this methodology so strongly.

Titchener was a student of Wundt, and he learned well the lessons taught by the master. His basic tenet was that

. . . the longer scientific observations are continued, and the more scientific methods are refined, the clearer does it become that experience is regular and orderly . . . a scientific law thus expresses a regularity, an unbroken uniformity of some aspect of experience . . . No science is as yet complete, but the formulation of a law means that the science of which it holds is complete up to a certain point. (1910, p. 5.)

Titchener's formulations are little different from those of Howard C. Warren who, though his influence on methods was of less than Titchenerian proportions, also carried Wundt's message to the experimental world.

The way to the formulation of laws, as far as Titchener was concerned, lay in carefully controlled experimentation. In his *Outline of Psychology* he describes the necessary experimentation.

"An experiment is a trial, test, or observation carefully made under certain special conditions: the object of the conditions being . . . to help the observer to rule out disturbing influences during his observations, and so to get at the desired results in a *pure* form . . . results which follow directly from the conditions laid down by us, and are not due to the operation of any unforeseen or unregulated causes." (1896, p. 35.)

Like most of his predecessors, and contemporaries, Titchener was seeking for the pure causes—the regularities underlying the chaotic flux of nature. And his methodological key to causal purity was the same as that of his teacher and of the scientific world of the day, that is, to disentangle this pure cause from all possible confusing influences.

Titchener also appealed to the methodological unity of science as a justification of his methodology. He noted that, "since all the sciences are concerned with the one world of human experience, it is natural that scientific method, to whatever aspect of experience it is applied, should be in principle the same." (1910, p. 23.) To be only "in principle the same," however, implies variance of method as a function of subject matter. And Titchener did indeed note some essential differences in the subject matter of psychology and physics. (1910, pp. 20 and 23.) After noting these rather basic differences, however, he concludes, "but, in general, the *method* of psychology is much the same as the *method* of physics." (italics ours.) The Zeitgeist had remained cordial to the methodological emulation of the natural sciences, and Titchener became one of the greatest spokesmen of them all. His four-volume Manuals (Vol. I, parts 1 and 2, 1901; Vol. II, parts 1 and 2, 1905) were perhaps the most influential experimental manuals ever written in psychology.

One of the first experimental manuals to follow Titchener's was Charles S. Myers', *Textbook of Experimental Psychology*. Here Myers

appealed for the experimental simplification at which the disentanglement of causes and thus the classical paradigm, had always been directed.
Responding to the objections which contemporaries posed to such a basis
for experimentation, Myers noted:

> To this objection we can only reply that experiment must necessarily start
> from the simplest conditions, and that just as the other abstract sciences when
> at last they are employed in applied science, approach more and more closely
> to the concrete of human experience, so psychology, once having gained the
> necessary knowledge under simpler conditions of experiment may someday
> be enabled to devise experiments more complex and more analogous to the
> conditions of workaday life. (1911, p. 188.)

Again, the awareness that the "content of human experience" was a
quality far different than that being studied by psychology, was recognized. And again, as Wundt had said long before, Myers said that
simplification must be accepted if one were to behave as a scientist.

Angell, writing in 1912, also accepted simplification as necessary to the
ability of contemporary science to deal with nature's confusion. When he
discussed how to perform a study of the effects of light upon the growth
of plants, he said: "Nature herself gives us much evidence bearing on
this matter, and yet in nature light seldom varies unaccompanied by
changes in other physical phenomena. It is combined in an almost variable way with the production of heat, and it frequently varies in a confusing manner with conditions of moisture." (1912, p. 77.)

In the face of such confusion in nature, Angell thought it extremely
important that experimentation, as a means of cutting through this
confusion, be utilized. "It is a matter of common knowledge that the
remarkable achievements of modern science are largely due to the development of experimental methods." (1912, p. 115.)

The elaboration of similar thought among the prominent psychologists
of the day can easily be continued and we shall do so for a few. The
theme on which we wish to focus is the familiar one of the basic regularity of nature covered by entangled causes, which can be neatly stripped
away through classical design.

In 1914 John B. Watson soundly criticized the then current methods
of animal experimentation for leaving too many variables uncontrolled
and speaks of the method of removing the sensory organs of the animals
as the "safest" way of making sure extraneous cues do not contaminate
the results—"were it possible in work upon certain aspects of vision to
use animals in which only the visual receptors with the necessary effectors
were functioning, our results could be obtained with far greater accuracy

than at present." (1914, p. 210). This is the search for simplicity, for disentanglement, carried to its logical end; for in such experimentation the behaving organism would be reduced to one organ system, a most artificial condition. Such was the behavioristic emphasis on control, and it was influential enough to more firmly entrench the rule of one variable as the method in American psychology.

Thus, after 50 years of psychological theorizing, the thought regarding experimentation was still Wundtian. Psychologists recognized that the human organism, which they had elected to study, was daily confronted with nature's confusing intermixture of causes and effects, yet the methods used for this study were based on a notion of eliminating confusion wherever possible. Little need for an indigenous methodology was seen.

The conflict between what psychologists saw was true of life and what they felt must be done in the laboratory is shown in the writings of one of Titchener's students, William Foster, in collaboration with Miles Tinker. They first say that "the complexity of the living organism . . . constantly forces upon the investigator the consideration of sources of error and of the methods for avoiding or measuring them and consistently leads him to look for multiple causation." (1923, p. 3.)

Both J. R. Kantor (1924, p. 14) and Robert MacDougall (1922) wrote in a vein similar to Foster and Tinker concerning the complexity of real life observations, but these two men were among the few who did not call for the blanket application of the one-variable method despite the complexity of nature. The following quote from MacDougall's *The General Problems of Psychology* has a very modern sound.

It is the first task of experimental method to eliminate the confusing multitude of factors which in ordinary experience are associated in a single concrete process, and, by an arbitrary selection of events, to secure the isolation of that element which alone is to be studied . . . It is therefore the task of experimentation to introduce an artificial simplification into the procedure of science, while retaining the essential features of the phenomenon to be investigated. It must devise a schematic representation of reality, so true to the original that the results obtained from employing this conventional rearrangement as its material shall be applicable to the event as it appears in its natural form. . . . At the same time, the ultimate criterion of method in any field of knowledge is its service in the discovery of truth. Whatever road of approach furthers that end is legitimate; science has no royal road. . . . If laboratory experimentation involves any essential disturbance of the phenomenon, the psychologist must lay aside his plans of formal simplification and study the event under its natural conditions accepting whatever complications the change introduces into his problem. (1922, pp. 351–352.)

During this period, then, MacDougall appears to be one of the few to admit that the complexity of "the event under natural conditions" may require a modification of the strict one-variable method of experimentation. The problem of precisely how to deal scientifically with "whatever complications" were introduced by studying "the event under natural conditions" remained, however. It was undoubtedly the fact that no obvious alternative presented itself that Dashiell, in the first paragraph of his *Experimental Manual in Psychology,* admonished the student that: "The essence of a scientific experiment on any phenomenon is to control all the conditions (so far as possible) keeping all constant but one. Then to vary that one to observe what other phenomena change with it (as cause or effect or co-effect). This logic will underlay all your experiments. Look for it!" (1931, p. 1.)

To summarize, from the very first, psychologists have been self-conscious about the scientific status of their discipline. Although a clear recognition of the complexity of cause-effect relations ran parallel to the awareness of the need for scientific methods, the commitment to method obscured and overran the need to cope with complexity by other means than efforts to simplify it. Toward the end of the first half of the twentieth century, however, the first definite break with this tradition occurred. It appeared in the writings of Egon Brunswik.

BRUNSWIK'S CONTRIBUTION

In the 1930's, then, MacDougall and Dashiell were among the chief proponents of the same curious paradox that we noted in the work of Wundt, Bain and Titchener. Cognizant of the chaotic flux that nature invariably presented to human observation, they wanted somehow to penetrate this confusion and to discover fundamental regularities. They doubted seriously the legitimacy of disentangling causes by experimental manipulation, and then proceeded to disentangle them anyway. It was, they believed, a decision forced by necessity—but the necessity was that of acceptable science, not that of psychology's subject matter.

In tracing the role of systematic design up to this point we are provided with an apt demonstration of the functioning of what Kuhn has recently termed "paradigms" in science. "Paradigm" is used by Kuhn to describe the fact that "some accepted examples of scientific practice —examples which include law, theory, application, and instrumentation together—provide models from which spring particular coherent traditions of scientific research." (Kuhn, 1962, p. 10.) A paradigm may thus be methodological as well as theoretical: "Paradigm procedures and applications are as necessary to science as paradigm laws and theories, and they have the same effects." (Kuhn, 1962, p. 60.) The paradigm serves a useful, indeed a requisite, function in the progress of science by providing a means by which research can be conducted in a coherent framework. The randomness is thereby taken out of scientific efforts; some direction is given as to what problems are worthy of scientific attention and how one might investigate them. But if paradigms guide, they also limit. "Inevitably they restrict the phenomenological field accessible for scientific study at any given time." (1962, p. 60.) And again, "A paradigm can even insulate the community from those socially important problems that are not reducible to the puzzle form, because they cannot be stated in terms of the conceptual and instrumental tools the paradigm supplies." (1962, p. 37.)

Kuhn's description of scientific paradigms describes quite well the functioning of psychology's principal methodological paradigm—that which we have termed systematic design. The method was seized upon by a young psychology, hungry for scientific respectability. It was believed adequate to the problems of psychology because it was adequate to the standards of science. And psychology was as yet free to define its problems in terms of a respectable methodology. Indeed as Koch observes, "At the time of its inception, *psychology was unique in the extent to which its institutionalization preceded its content and its methods preceded its problems.* If there are keys to history, this statement is surely a key to the brief history of psychology." (italics ours) (1959b, pp. 1–2.)

Paradigms in any science, once firmly implanted, become difficult to uproot, perhaps because they satisfy a scientific need—or a need of scientists—by providing systematization and by providing criteria against which scientific efforts might be weighed. Most certainly the one-variable paradigm became so established in psychology, filling a most basic need for scientific status. However vital paradigms might be they are altered; "scientific revolutions" do occur. Such revolutions become possible when some awareness of an anomaly, of a discrepancy between the paradigm and the requirements of the real world is experienced. As Kuhn (1962, p. 52) puts it, "Discovery commences with the awareness of anomaly, that is, with the recognition that nature has somehow violated the paradigm-induced expectations that govern normal science." We have seen that some awareness of anomaly between systematic design and the real world has been manifest *throughout the history of modern psychology.* From the time of Wundt, psychology has been aware that its methodological template did not quite fit the world, that it was not adequate to the subject matter that psychology must encompass. Freud provides an example of the awareness of this anomaly. Although he made no direct methodological contributions, Freud recognized that the presence of a carefully controlled stimulus could lead to various responses, and the same response could be made to various stimuli; that is, he recognized the importance of vicarious functioning. Brunswik argued that "vicarious functioning has found such sweeping and unparalleled recognition in psychoanalysis . . . that this recognition may well be considered the most important contribution of this school to psychology." (1938, p. 716.) One of the consequences of this recognition of a wide variety of vicarious mechanisms is that no single diagnostic cue is likely to have the character of foolproof evidence. Diagnosis thus possesses all the characteristics of probabilistic inference—a process which the classical design paradigm cannot adequately describe.

Despite this recognition of the anomaly between psychology's methods and its aims, the role of the classical paradigm was never seriously called into question. It was as if the anomaly, once referred to, could be put aside for some future reconciliation. The entrenchment of the paradigm, or perhaps the lack of an alternative, precluded a "revolution" or radical modification of the paradigm. Kuhn has noted that "the decision to reject one paradigm is always simultaneously the decision to accept another, and the judgment leading to that decision involves the comparison of both paradigms with nature and with each other . . . To reject one paradigm without simultaneously substituting another is to reject science itself." (1962, pp. 77–79.) Brunswik's function was to bring the anomaly into focus again, but more vividly than before—to suggest that psychology must recognize it and remedy it. Perhaps more importantly, Brunswik offered, for the first time in psychology, an alternative to the univariate paradigm. In proposing representative design as this alternative, Brunswik supplied not only a workable methodology for the "real world" but a compelling rationale, the probabilistic nature of the environment, to go with it.

Brunswik observed that "only scattered recognition had been given to the fact that object-cue and means-end relationships do not hold with the certainty obtained in the so-called laws of nature, but are rather of the character of probability relationships." (1943, p. 260.) To him the recognition of the probabilistic character of the causal relationships in the environment called for a "fundamental, all-inclusive shift in our methodological ideology regarding psychology." (1943, p. 261.) If the organism must behave in relation to nature's uncertainty, we can learn more about how he behaves by presenting him experimentally with the same kind of probabilistic environment that nature presents. He does not meet the isolated variable outside of the laboratory, why force him to deal with it within the laboratory? Furthermore, Brunswik asserts, "it can be shown that classical design does not succeed in its purpose of isolating a variable, in reality it only succeeds in tying several variables inseparably to each other, which then leads to unresolvable difficulties in interpreting the results in the sense of assigning them to certain crucial factors." (1951, pp. 213–215.)

Thus, not only does classical design attempt to force the organism to deal with an environment antithetical to the one presented by nature, but it does not really succeed in this attempt. To Brunswik, these observations pointed up the necessity of changing this methodological paradigm whose proponents were attempting to generate "strict" laws of behavior. "Classical psychology has never been able to cover more than a rather narrow and artificial segment of life by such strict laws. Generalization of the scope of psychology is a step required not only for its becoming universal in a relatively esoteric and technical sense, but for its becoming life-adequate as well." (1951, p. 214.) That Brunswik was not alone in noticing the limited generalization of psychological research in its present state is obvious from Koch's statement in Volume III of his study that

. . . it is already evident that concern with the conditions and limits of generality of lawful psychological statements is widespread and acute among the authors of these volumes . . . It is an interesting paradox that a climate in which investigators typically reported *experimental* results (in *scientific* journals) in the most "local" and situation-bound terms was at the same time one in which theorists (often the same persons) translated these findings into *theoretical* laws potentially adequate to "all behavior." (1959a, p. 749.)

In order to generate laws potentially adequate to all behavior, Brunswik proposed the use of existing correlational techniques to describe the relationship between the various stimuli present in the organism's environment, and his achievement of desired goals, between multiple cues and behavior. Such correlational techniques had been available for years, and so had been an awareness of the purpose for which Brunswik suggested their use. He was aware that Galton had seen the necessity for dealing with partial relations on a statistical basis, for he noted that the methodological shift for which he called had already occurred ". . . at the time of Galton and his followers who established correlation statistics as a particularly suitable means of quantitatively expressing ambiguous probability relationships. . . ." (1943, p. 261.) What Brunswik suggested then, was the use of correlational techniques to implement the new methodological paradigm in psychology—one which would be adequate to psychology's subject matter as well as to science. Brunswik's most original contribution to the methodological revolution, which he hoped would occur, was his insistent call for the representative design of psychological experiments. This was the paradigm that, he felt, should replace the inadequate systematic design paradigm.

Thus, if psychology is to approach the prediction of behavior across situations, if it is ever to be adequate to life, representative design must replace systematic design as the favored methodological paradigm. Kuhn (1962) has described, as mentioned above, the resistance that typically occurs whenever a replacement for a pervasively used paradigm is suggested. Brunswik himself noted that "since the statistical macroprobabilism of representative design would move psychology away from physics and other fundamental natural sciences with their nomothetic thema, considerable resistances must be expected along the way." (1956, p. 160.) Brunswik was confident that "the more palatable systematic design (would) mature into, and be superseded by, the more truthful representative design." (1955, p. 215.)

Although he labored long and arduously on behalf of representative design and attempted to convince psychologists of the incongruity between one-variable design and the subject matter of psychology, psychological methods since his death have continued much as they were before and during his life. Textbooks still do little more than paraphrase the methodological thought of Mill and largely ignore speculations about whether such methods can be legitimately applied to the subject matter of psychology. What Dewey termed "the quest for certainty" has kept psychologists from changing the methodological paradigm. However, a change may yet occur, for as Koch says, "For the first time in its history, psychology seems ready—or almost ready—to assess its goals and instrumentalities with primary reference to its own indigenous problems." (1959, p. 783.) If we are indeed sufficiently mature to make methodological decisions in terms of our subject matter, Brunswik has provided us with a choice. Until his contribution, there was, in fact, no choice.

We have attempted to document both the general acceptance of classical design in psychology and the rationale underlying this acceptance, the notion that "actual" or "pure" causes must somehow be separated within nature's causal confusion. That there was some dissatisfaction with the inability of this paradigm to deal with nature's complexity is evident. Until Brunswik's proposed "representative design," however, there existed no real alternative to classical design. It was not inevitable that a solution such as the representative sampling of a subject's environment would occur. Indeed it was not inevitable that any solution be offered, since psychologists had so long accepted the necessity of experimental disentanglement. Brunswik's unique methodological contribution to psychology was that he did not accept the inevitability of experimental isolation. Brunswik was willing, that is, to deal with nature as it presented itself to the behaving organism—in a chaotic manner. The study of "pure" causes, utterly separated from disturbing influences, might have had relevance for physical science; it was inappropriate to the subject matter of psychology.

Brunswik, then, was dealing with a problem—the chaos of nature— which had been of concern to experimental psychologists since the beginnings of their science. Whatever historical place future methodologists may accord him, there can be little contention that Brunswik offered a unique and challenging way of treating the issue. Psychology, according to Brunswik, must recognize the state of nature and treat it accordingly; causal texture must be experimentally coped with, not denied.

REFERENCES

Angell, J. K. *Chapters from modern psychology*. New York: Longmans, Green, & Co., Inc., 1918.

Bacon, F. *Novum organum*. In R. M. Hutchins (Ed.), *Great books of the western world*. Vol. 30. Chicago: Encyclopaedia Britannica, Inc., 1952.

Bain, A. *Logic*. Vols. I and II. London: Longmans, Green, Reader, & Dyer, 1870.

Baldwin, J. M. *Elements of psychology*. New York: Dryden Press, Inc., 1893.

Baldwin, J. M. *Dictionary of philosophy and psychology*. New York: Macmillan, 1911.

Boring, E. G. *A history of experimental psychology*. New York, London: D. Appleton & Company, Inc., 1929.

Brunswik, E. Organismic achievement and environmental probability. *Psychol. Rev.*, 1943, *50*, 255–272.

Brunswik, E. Notes on Hammond's analogy between "relativity and representativeness." *Phil. Sci.*, 1951, *18*, 212–217.

Brunswik, E. Representative design and probabilistic theory in a functional psychology. *Psychol. Rev.*, 1955, *62*, 193–217.

Brunswik, E. Historical and thematic relations of psychology to other sciences. *Sci. Monthly*, 1956, *83*, 151–161.

Crombie, A. C. *Medieval and early modern science*. Vols. I and II. New York: Doubleday, 1959.

Dashiell, J. P. *An experimental manual in psychology*. Cambridge, Mass.: Riverside Press, 1931.

Descartes, R. Rules for the direction of the mind. In R. M. Hutchins (Ed.), *Great books of the western world*. Vol. 31. Chicago: Encyclopaedia Britannica, Inc., 1952. (a)

Descartes, R. Discourse on the method. In R. M. Hutchins (Ed.), *Great books of the western world*. Vol. 31. Chicago: Encyclopaedia Britannica, Inc., 1952. (b)

Ebbinghaus, H. *Psychology, an elementary textbook*. Boston: Heath, 1908.

Ebbinghaus, H. *Memory*. (Tr. by H. A. Ruger and Clara E. Bussenius)

New York: Teacher's College, Columbia University, 1913.

Faraday, M. *Experimental researches in electricity*. Vol. 1. London: Quaritch, 1839.

Foster, W. S., & Tinker, M. A. *Experiments in psychology*. New York: Dryden Press, 1923.

Galileo, G. Dialogues concerning the two new schemes. In R. M. Hutchins (Ed.), *Great books of the western world*. Vol. 28. Chicago: Encyclopaedia Britannica, Inc., 1952.

Gilbert, W. On the loadstone and on the great magnet of the earth. In R. M. Hutchins (Ed.), *Great books of the western world*. Vol. 28. Chicago: Encyclopaedia Britannica, Inc., 1952.

Harvey, W. Anatomical exercises on the generation of animals. In R. M. Hutchins (Ed.), *Great books of the western world*. Vol. 28. Chicago: Encyclopaedia Britannica, Inc., 1952.

Hilgard, E. R. *Introduction to psychology*. New York: Harcourt, 1957.

Hollingworth, H. L. *Psychology, its facts and principles*. New York: D. Appleton & Co., Inc., 1928.

Jevons, W. *The principles of science*. London: Macmillan, 1873.

Kantor, J. R. *Principles of psychology*. New York: Knopf, 1924.

Koch, S. Epilogue. In S. Koch (Ed.), *Psychology: a study of a science*. Vol. 3. New York: McGraw-Hill, 1959. Pp. 729–788.   (a)

Koch, S. Toward an indigenous methodology. (mimeo), 1959.   (b)

Kuhn, T. *The structure of scientific revolutions*. Chicago: University of Chicago Press, 1962.

Lavoisier, A. Elements of chemistry. In R. M. Hutchins (Ed.), *Great books of the western world*. Vol.

45. Chicago: Encyclopaedia Britannica, Inc., 1952.

MacDougall, R. *The general problems of psychology*. New York: New York University Press, 1922.

McKeon, R. Aristotle on scientific method. *J. of the History of Ideas*, 1947, *8*, 3–45.

Mill, J. S. *A system of logic*. (8th ed.) New York: Harper and Brothers, 1882.

Moore, J. S. *Foundations of psychology*. Princeton, N.J.: Princeton University Press, 1921.

Myers, C. S. *Textbook of experimental psychology*. London: Cambridge, 1911.

Newton, I. Optics. In R. M. Hutchins (Ed.), *Great books of the western world*. Vol. 34. Chicago: Encyclopaedia Britannica, Inc., 1952.   (a)

Newton, I. Mathematical principles of natural philosophy. In R. M. Hutchins (Ed.), *Great books of the western world*. Vol. 34. Chicago: Encyclopaedia Britannica, Inc., 1952.   (b)

Pearson, K. *The life, letters, and labours of Francis Bacon*. Vol. IIIA. London: Cambridge, 1940.

Randall, J. H., Jr. The development of scientific method in the school of Padua. *J. of the History of Ideas*, 1940, *1*, 177–224.

Ribot, T. *German psychology of today*. New York: Scribner, 1886.

Scripture, E. W. *The new psychology*. London: Walter Scott, Ltd., 1897.

Sully, J. *The human mind*. London: Longmans, Green & Co., Inc., 1892.

Thorndike, L. *A history of magic and experimental science*. Vol. I–VIII. New York: Macmillan, 1923.

Titchener, E. B. *An outline of psychology*. New York: Macmillan, 1898.

Titchener, E. B. *A textbook of psy-*

chology. New York: Macmillan, 1910.

Warren, H. C. *Human psychology.* Cambridge, Mass.: Riverside Press, 1919.

Watson, J. B. *Behavior. An introduction to comparative psychology.* New York: Dryden Press, 1914.

Woodworth, R. S., and H. Schlosberg. *Experimental psychology.* New York: Holt, Rinehart and Winston, Inc., 1954.

Wundt, W. *Lectures on human and animal psychology.* (Tr. by J. E. Creighton and E. B. Titchener, 1896) New York: Macmillan, Inc., 1863.

Wundt, W. *Outlines of psychology.* (Tr. by C. H. Judd) Leipzig: W. Engelmann, 1897.

Wundt, W. *An introduction to psychology.* (Tr. by R. Pintner) London: G. Allen, 1912.

7

A Functional View of Memory

MURRAY E. JARVIK

There can be no doubt that the difference between the mind of the lowest man and that of the highest animal is immense . . . nevertheless the difference in mind between man and the higher animals, great as it is, certainly is one of degree and not of kind.

These seem like rather commonplace thoughts today, but when these words were written by Charles Darwin in *The Origin of the Species* nearly a hundred years ago, they were considered revolutionary, not to say profane and blasphemous. Yet, even today and probably forever it will be admitted by all comparative psychologists that there is a tremendous gulf separating man from the highest apes in the ability to deal with information acquired during a lifetime.

Speech, and particularly written speech, enables man to store, integrate, and transmit vast quantities of information which a chimpanzee or gorilla simply cannot handle. Certainly the most complex visual discrimination and delayed response problems that can be handled by a test-wise chimp are child's play to a human child. The ability to acquire speech, evidenced in a two-year-old child, implies the existence of a vast cerebral apparatus in humans which is lacking in all other forms of life. It is clear that learning has survival value for human beings, but it is not necessary in many present-day organisms, as frogs, worms, and amoebae testify.

There is something about the structure of man and the nature of his environment that has made it necessary for him to be able to learn and to remember so well in order to survive. The reason seems to be that man, better than any other species, is able to penetrate into and to survive in almost any type of changing environment. Other creatures remember with their genes and develop fins and wings and fur coats; but man remembers with his mind and makes clothes and uses tools and builds houses out of blocks of ice or animal skins or bamboo poles. Certainly the wasps and the bees exhibit marvelous social intelligence; the eels and the salmon have an amazing perspicacity concerning the fate of their future generations; and the cuckoo and cowbird exert an amazingly successful influence on the other birds. However, a radical environmental change would annihilate these creatures. Man can cope with severe and sudden changes in his life space by virtue of his supreme ability to learn, though the advent of an atomic war might overwhelm even this ability.

INTRODUCTION

Although Egon Brunswik's major concern was with perception, he was strongly influenced by the learning theories of his good friend, Edward C. Tolman. In 1935 with Tolman, he developed the idea that cue-object relations and means-goal relations have varying degrees of probable validity. The paper that Brunswik published in 1939, in which he examined probability as a determiner of rat behavior, foreshadowed by a decade the great interest in probability learning which occurred in experimental psychology during the fifties and which is still growing. It was Brunswik's view that probability learning was a more representative type of activity than the univocal right or wrong response approach traditionally used in learning experiments. Thus, probability learning represents a distal focusing in time which may be considered analogous and supplementary to the distal focusing in space involved, for example, in the constancy phenomena. An organism utilizes two kinds of information in dealing with the world around it: that furnished by its sensory receptors and that which is stored somewhere under its skin. Memory is the term applied both to the information that is stored and to the storage process itself. The purpose of this paper will be to examine some of the possible purposes of memory and the important adaptive role in organismic functioning played by probability learning.

DEFINITION OF MEMORY

Memory is a construct that operational psychologists do not often invoke by this name. Bartlett (1932) objected to the reification of a process he preferred to call "remembering." Warren's Dictionary of Psychology (1934) defines it as a generic term for those experiences, movements, or functions that are conditioned upon earlier experiences, movements, or functions of the organism. It can be seen that Warren's is an extremely general definition and in its broader sense would have to include all experiences, movements, and functions. A more restricted view would require that memory exists if a set of temporary stimulus conditions leaves an effect on an organism that persists a long time, perhaps indefinitely. As a corollary, one might say that if a response long separated in time from a stimulus can be found to be correlated with it, then a memory may be said to exist.

Learning is the process of establishing a memory or, in other words, a process of acquiring and retaining information. Memory, or remembering, is the process of retaining such information in a subsequently available form. In its simplest form, learning involves three steps: first, there is the acquisition of information, which may occur rapidly or slowly and always involves receptor stimulation; then, a delay period which may last anywhere from seconds to years during which retention occurs; finally, an active process of remembering involving retrieval of stored information and revealing the existence of memory by means of a performance shown to be dependent upon previous stimulation. It must be kept in mind that during all phases of learning there is constant interaction between many different kinds of materials within the organism and many different events in the environment. The number of kinds of learning which may be going on concurrently is, of course, difficult to estimate and is limited by attentional processes. Recognition, simply implying a correlation between old and new events, is certainly the most general form of remembering. Recall, which involves some form of reproduction, is a very special case involving artistic or phonetic skills. Reproduction of most forms of information that enter the nervous system is obviously impossible.

The computer engineer has a somewhat easier time of describing memory in his machines than the psychologist in his organisms since the former has a physical mechanism that he can see or feel. His description refers to some kind of storage device, be it a magnetic drum, a punched tape, or a punched card. At present the psychologist can only infer that a similar mechanism exists in the body of a remembering organism.

MEMORY AS A MECHANISM FOR ESTABLISHING DISTAL RELATIONSHIPS

Memory may be considered an extension of perception in time that enables higher organisms to predict the future. Such predictions free creatures from the stimulus-bound reflex or automatic type of behavior common in the more primitive phyla (Thorpe, 1956). It presupposes extensive and complex storage facilities in the nervous system but, unfortunately, very little is presently known about its physiological basis. As one descends the scale both in phylogeny and ontogeny, one finds that behavior of an animal is more and more dependent upon its commerce with the immediate environment. The reactions of a day-old human infant or of a frog are highly predictable, and one may, in fact, develop nomothetic laws of behavior for such creatures with a great deal of confidence. The idea of being able to construct such models of human behavior occurred to philosophers in antiquity, and such well-known examples can be seen in the work of Descartes (1664) and LaMettrie (1865). On the other hand, it can be readily seen that the stimuli impinging upon a normal adult human being have only a limited influence upon his behavior, an embarrassing state of affairs to those who would like to predict behavior accurately.

But the picture is not so bleak. There are "laws" of memory that give us some basis for prediction of learned behavior. One approach for the psychologist to take is to view his fellow human beings in their natural environment and see how they learn there.

What is the representative type of learning in the everyday life of the average individual? It is hardly the food or shock-motivated learning of the severely deprived laboratory rat. On the contrary, it would seem that there is a great deal of what might be called incidental learning and tremendous amounts of retroactive and proactive inhibition (Underwood 1957). Commonplace stimuli, such as food and clothes, are perceived and then are quickly forgotten because similar percepts encountered previously or subsequently interfere with them. News items appearing in the papers or on television are remembered for a day or two and then are superseded. The headlines of yesteryear do not change in the newspaper morgue but are rapidly obliterated from memory.

The type of experiment performed by Brunswik (1944) by sampling perceptual experiences in the day of an individual has never been systematically performed for learning. If one were to ask questions about current and aged news events from a sufficiently large sample, one could undoubtedly obtain very good learning and forgetting curves. One might find that individuals properly selected for age would remember fewer details about the Graf Zeppelin disaster today than twenty years ago. Such experiments would merely point up the importance of the interference factor in forgetting. An experiment perhaps more analogous to that of Brunswik's would require an individual to recount the events of the past twenty-four hours, much as a diarist does. The actual occurrences could then be related to the subjective recall or recognition. This would give some notion of the survival rate of different traces in the daily life of an individual.

Following Bartlett's (1932) lead, many investigators have shown how distortion or restructuring enters into memory experiments. The well-known experiments of Carmichael, Hogan, and Walter (1932), and of Hanawalt (1937) illustrate changes wrought by time. It is interesting that distortions rather than complete omissions or depletions do occur with recall. Such findings lend support to the idea that some sort of hypothesis or guessing behavior occurs during the act of remembering. There is ample evidence that even in the act of perception, cues of probabilistic value are used. So it must certainly be truer in the act of remembering when only traces of these probabilistic cues are present, cues which are necessarily less reliable, that guessing must occur.

It is interesting to note that Bartlett was advocating representative design in the study of memory, just as Brunswik did in the study of perception. He felt that instead of attempting to minimize meaningfulness, as with nonsense syllables, an attempt should be made to maximize it, and to study whatever factors might be involved in utilizing the meaningfulness of the material. The acceptance of Bartlett's view does not negate the importance of the highly controlled experiment by Ebbinghaus and his successors but emphasizes an important neglected area.

The conditions that make associations easy or difficult to form and to recapture have never been intensively investigated though they must be of fundamental importance. They undoubtedly involve what Thorndike (1932) called "belongingness." It has been demonstrated again and again that simple temporal contiguity is not sufficient to establish conditioning in either animal or man. Most animal psychologists have had the sad experience of failing to teach animals to associate what would seem to be rather obvious relationships between stimuli. Why is it that a monkey or a chimpanzee learns to discriminate two colors in very few trials if the test is presented one way and in an interminably long number of trials if presented another way (Jarvik, 1953)? Why is it that a spider monkey will make a discrimination with great alacrity if the stimuli touch, but if they are slightly separated the problem becomes insoluble (Lashley, 1949)? Under certain circumstances where conditioning can be simple for human beings, it may be impossible for a chimpanzee. What makes a relationship obvious for a subject must be related to the organization of his nervous system and the readiness that it has to accept two pieces of information as related. Certain types of learning can occur in a single trial where others take hundreds of trials before an association is established. A favorite paradigm of learning is illustrated by the child touching a burning stove experiencing pain and henceforth avoiding the stove. Essman and Jarvik (1960) investigated a rapid form of learning in mice in a situation entirely analogous to that confronting our hypothetical child. A mouse received a shock for stepping from one platform to another and usually learned in one trial to inhibit such movement. Similarly Estes and Skinner (1941), Hudson (1950), and Hunt and Brady (1955) have shown that rapid learning of a conditioned emotional experience could occur in rats.

Just why the rapid association does occur in these cases is not at all clear. The child touching the burning stove has to appreciate the fact that it is hot if he is to avoid it subsequently. He will not avoid other stimuli in the room even though they were associated in time with the burning sensation. If the stove were lukewarm or at room temperature, then certainly very little would have been learned. One of Thorndike's laws of learning, the law of intensity (1932), might be invoked to explain the remembrance of this single unpleasant experience. It is commonplace knowledge that cues are not always strong or clear. Tolerance of ambiguity is a personality factor in which Else Frenkel-Brunswik (1949) was quite interested and which is undoubtedly of importance in both perception and learning. In the usual univocal learning or discrimination problem, the law of effect will appear to be confirmed. Brunswik has pointed out (1951) that this is based upon what he called "the bias of inexhaustible supply." In fact, many animals will avoid a just previously rewarded place or stimulus and alternation tendencies are quite high in a variety of species. Such tendencies seem to be particularly great when experiments involving curiosity or exploratory tendencies are performed. Monkeys can apparently learn oddity or matching problems with equal facility. In any case, it takes time for an animal to learn the rules of a particular game unless they just happen to fit a hypothesis that it brings to the situation, that is, a built-in solution to the problem. This may be an innate tendency to deal with particular perceptual configurations or to emit motor responses of a certain type.

It has been noted that there is a phylogenetic difference in ability of animals to form learning sets (Miles, 1957). Furthermore, animals with brain lesions have difficulty not only in learning, but in learning to learn, so that amount and type of cerebral tissue is apparently responsible for disability. The evidence is very strong that the rostral portion of the cerebro-spinal axis plays a larger role in learning than does the caudal (Kellogg, 1947).

Is it possible to eliminate the learning capacity of an adult human? If this could be done selectively without interfering with other functions, it would teach us a great deal about the learning process. Defects in immediate memory have been described by Milner (1956) in patients with temporal lobe lesions but the behavior of these patients indicates that retention can occur providing interference is minimized. In an ordinary, unprotected environment recent memory is severely impaired. Nevertheless, the patient remains an intelligent functioning human being. Even if there were total destruction of immediate memory, in which case the use of language would be destroyed, those activities which did not involve the retention of long sequences of acts could be performed. Certainly eating, dressing, driving, enjoyment of television, and various forms of interpersonal relations could occur. There are, however, individuals suffering from mental deficiency or organic brain disorders who manifest impairment of such behavior (Tredgold, 1952).

Contrast the behavior that could be exhibited by a hypothetical individual in whom all learned behavior was wiped out. He would truly be reduced to the level of an animal and a rather low one at that. Individuals who once were normal may develop mental deficiency following brain damage of severe degree just as there are imbeciles who never were normal. Their behavior may be equivalent to that of a month-old infant. They have reflexes with which they were born but the impact of the world has been erased. If learning capacities are impaired in childhood, development as a functional normal human being is impossible. If they are destroyed in adulthood, the deficit is surprisingly little.

The function of memory may be said to enable the individual to absorb the information that civilization and culture provide. The rudimentary nature of subhuman culture is due in large measure to the poorly developed function of memory, even in the higher primates.

Deficiencies of memory are a commonplace part of the psychopathology of everyday life so eloquently pointed out by Sigmund Freud (1917). Repression might be considered a form of interference, but some of the complex examples of forgetting, given by the master of psychoanalysis, may not be acceptable to those accustomed to viewing logically, highly-controlled experiments. It would be hard to deny that forgetting frequently, perhaps most frequently, occurs for events that have little or no significance to an individual.

It has long been known in the field of legal testimony that the reliability of witnesses is often open to question. The reason for the confusion of witnesses usually is ascribed to forgetting, but poor performance on a memory test may be due to difficulty in acquisition, in retention, or in recognition. The degree of reconstruction of events perceived incidentally at some previous time may be rather considerable and may not be appreciated as such by the individuals doing the remembering. The reconstruction may be accompanied by considerable confidence and feelings of "déjà vu."

The nervous system has an amazing facility for improving the quality of low fidelity stimulus inputs. Visual patterns are markedly distorted in the eye, and they are reconstructed in the brain to appear perfect. Ambiguity, of course, occurs not only in sensation but in perception, and it also occurs on the efferent side of the organism. Activity may be purposive but a good deal is not. Much activity belongs in the class known as general and most kinds of free operant activity could hardly be called purposive though they may accomplish something of incidental value to the organism through luck or chance.

The perceptual constancies furnish much evidence that hints of individually limited validity when taken together may be extremely valuable in describing the real distal world. It is common experience that in memory limited cues are useful in reconstructing past events with rather satisfying faithful results. Frequently what is recalled or recognized is not what was, but what ought to have been. Let us consider, for example, the processes that are involved in memorizing a poem. If a man were to recite a poem once into a tape recorder, it could be reproduced years hence with perfect fidelity. The amount of information, however, which can be stored on such a tape is relatively limited. The nervous system or the brain obviously does not operate this way. First of all a poem is not memorized in one recitation. It is very likely that the method of recording is quite different from that which is obtained with a tape recorder. The information contained in the poem has to be fitted into a matrix that already exists and involves great efficiency or space saving in the central nervous system. It undoubtedly involves a process of recoding plus recording, as described by George Miller (1956). The unusual feat achieved by Sidney Smith in memorizing forty binary digits at a single exposure as described by Miller (1956) is probably a general model of the way in which memorizing occurs. A tape recorder does not have a limited memory span or span of apprehension as we do, but the reason for this may not be to the advantage of the machine. The tape recorder cannot intercorrelate all the information which comes into it. If it could, it would be a computer. It seems that the brain is the best kind of computer known to date, since its access time for a tremendous amount of information is exceedingly short, and its energy and space requirements are exceedingly small.

Certainly the ambiguity of cues or traces and confidence inspired by them are not perfectly related. The fictional Sherlock Holmes was able to feel that he knew a great deal more about the past life of an individual whom he encountered for the first time than could Dr. Watson. The reason for this, of course, was that Holmes was a perceptual gambler. He was willing to take the chance that the cues of limited validity really meant what he thought they did. The difference between him and his less discerning contemporaries probably lay in the feeling tone surrounding the meaning of these cues. Where they doubted, he knew. His reasoning on the basis of limited evidence was an example of what Reichenbach (1938) called concatenated inductions.

We live in what seems to be a very solid world, but the cues from which we draw this feeling are very unsubstantial. Classical psychophysics illustrates well the effect that ambiguous stimuli may have upon an individual. At threshold any type of stimulus is probabilistic in that it elicits a given response only 50 percent of the time. Just what the physiological events underlying this uncertainty are have never been adequately determined, but it would seem that fluctuation in receptor sensitivity has something to do with it (Stevens, 1961). Very likely, central fluctuations contribute to it; furthermore, noise of external origin also plays a part.

When recall or recognition is defective, the individual will ordinarily resort to guessing. A guess is a prediction based upon insufficient evidence accompanied by feelings of uncertainty. In our civilized life, guessing apparently plays less of a role than it did in more primitive forms of existence. The average individual engaged in routine work may express or experience relatively few feelings of uncertainty during the course of a day. Maximum security goes with maximum predictability and ordinarily can be found in institutional environments, such as prisons or totalitarian states. What is so unpleasant about prison where sufficient food and shelter are provided that makes it so punishing to an individual? There are individuals outside prison walls who also lead rather humdrum lives, so they may invent games to beat the boredom.

A workman with a good job, when he wakes up, knows exactly what clothes he has and what he is going to wear, what he is going to eat for breakfast, how to get from his home to work, and just what he is going to do in his routine job during the day. When he gets home one of a few varieties of food to which he is accustomed will be waiting for him on the table and he will experience no anxiety about this beforehand. His postprandial diversions may consist of reading the newspaper or looking at television and, unless he chooses to participate in a quiz program vicariously, conjecturing or predicting will occur only to a very limited extent during the course of the evening.

Of course, unpredictability varies considerably in the activities of individuals. Even in the best ordered lives, there is uncertainty about interpersonal relationships. Most people try to organize their lives so as to keep the need for guessing to a minimum, at least so far as the necessities are concerned. A fixed routine and a tendency toward compulsiveness can reduce the necessity for remembering to a minimum. Thus, when every object in a man's room has its carefully assigned place, the probability of finding it is quite high. It must be that an orderly file system is an externalization of efficient arrangement of mnemonic processes in the nervous system.

Civilization, as one of its major virtues, has tended to reduce the riskiness of life, at least so far as the individual is concerned, and consequently, gambling. The danger of accidents from atomic bombs may be quite great but individual citizens don't worry about this much because the odds are difficult to calculate. Perhaps with greater publicity, worrying will increase. A primitive native hunting in an African jungle, on the other hand, has to worry rather actively most of his day. A soldier on the battlefield or a criminal being hunted similarly has to do a good deal of guessing during the course of the day and for the same reason.

While, on one hand, the desire for security tends to minimize guessing, on the other hand, there seems to be a strong tendency *per se* to guess probably related to curiosity or playfulness. Such motivation is frequently expressed in the form of gambling in which a risk is taken with the hope of attaining some gain. Although gambling is often decried as an immoral form of activity, it nevertheless has a great popular appeal, as any visitor to Reno can testify. In its wider sense, gambling is the very basis of survival in life. Games make varying demands of skill and knowledge. A participant has to learn whether alternative responses give equivalent results. If they are unequal, then he is at a decided disadvantage if he cannot perceive this disparity.

There has been an increasing trend in recent years to derive formulae that would describe choice behavior in uncertain situations. Such models (Hake and Hyman, 1953; Bush and Mosteller, 1955; Luce, 1959; Estes, 1959), because of their statistical nature are improvements over older Hullian attempts (Hull, 1943) to arrive at universal laws of behavior. Behavioral strategy in such gambling situations has been shown to be a function of the way in which reward or punishment was delivered (Wilson and Rollin, 1959; Siegel and Goldstein, 1959). The matching of objective event probability with subjective response probability (Jarvik, 1951) has been shown to occur only under special conditions.

Games differ primarily in the amount of information a player must perceive and retain in order to characterize the risks at a given moment. In bridge or horse racing, the required skill is considerable whereas in roulette or the shell game relatively little acumen is needed. The investor in the stock exchange may freely admit that he takes as calculated a risk as the bettor at the race track, and the financial pages of a newspaper bear a striking resemblance to a racing form. The airlines passenger, the automobile rider, and the pedestrian are apt to risk their lives with less calculation. The public hardly appreciates that chance is involved in such long term risks as poisoning, heart disease, and cancer from eating certain foods and smoking, and such activities are undertaken with little trepidation.

On the other hand, even the most downtrodden clerk with the most routine job has a yen for adventure. When gambling is absent at work, it may still be pleasant at play. All games, it can be said without exception, involve an element of chance and risk, and there seems to be enjoyment associated with the taking of such risks. The risks may not be high though they may range all the way from the loss of pennies in football pools to the loss of life in dueling and Russian roulette. Similarly, entertainment, whether it be in the field of literature, drama, or comedy is more enjoyable when the climax is unexpected or at least when the possibility of guessing correctly is low. This is particularly true of detective stories. There are few experiences more boring than a joke heard twice. There are not many individuals who are willing to see a play or motion picture more than once, unless it contains so much that a subsequent viewing will be essentially a new experience. The concept of novelty implies some form of delayed matching procedure and consequently involves memory. Something will seem new if it hasn't been seen or experienced before. It may also appear new if previous knowledge of it is forgotten.

All of this implies that learning itself has a certain amount of incentive value to a higher organism. This has variously been considered under categories such as desire for novelty, curiosity, or exploratory behavior. It is, undoubtedly, in some way related to the adaptive value of learning. Certainly the individuals amongst the higher vertebrates who don't like to learn are going to die. It is important, however, to consider the motivational aspects of learning as somewhat distinct from the actual process of recording the memory.

Many mechanical forms of memory, particularly digital ones, such as punched tape or punched cards, have an almost perfect ability to reproduce what was put into them, but such is the exception rather than the rule in human memory. For one thing, input is extremely limited, as studies of Broadbent (1958) have indicated. Memory defects certainly should reveal something about the mechanisms underlying memory. The shape of the forgetting curve and Jost's law indicate that old memories are more stable than recent memories. To put it another way, Ebbing-haus's learning curve (Woodworth, 1938) shows that the forgetting function is approximately logarithmic, and this has been amply confirmed. This asymptotic relationship appears on first inspection to reflect a general phenomenon in learning and has been described by Hull as a negative growth function. To put it differently, the longer a piece of information has been remembered, the less likely it is to be forgotten. This indicates that it becomes more stable or less susceptible to disruption with age.

The form of memory defect most noticeable subjectively is that associated with the normal aging process. Where is the individual, even though he may be rather young, who does not experience difficulty in remembering names or associating them with faces? Old age provides a golden opportunity to study memory defects and gerontologists are taking advantage of it (Birren, 1959). In their severest forms, such as in Korsakow's syndrome, such defects are associated with disorientation, confabulation, and confusion (Talland, 1960). Such individuals may remember events of their childhood quite well but cannot recall things that happened just five minutes before. Thus there is some difficulty in preserving recent traces or in stabilizing recently acquired information.

What are the factors, then, responsible for forgetting? Psychologists generally agree that retroactive inhibition or interference plays an important role in this phenomenon. The now classic experiments by van Ormer (1932) and Jenkins and Dallenbach (1924) both indicated that mere passage of time was not nearly so efficient in obliterating learned material as some type of active interference by other activities. There was apparently some passive decay in both experiments even though it was slight. It would be difficult to define passive decay accurately since this would imply absence of neural activity, a condition incompatible with life. Central nervous activity can, however, be markedly depressed by general anesthetics. It is not known at present whether prolonged interference with such activity has any greater effect on retention than a brief period of depression (Gerard, 1955).

One of the interesting characteristics of memory that has not been subjected to much study, because of the difficulty in measuring it, is the feeling of familiarity that accompanies an act of recall or recognition. It has been noted by Zubin (1948) that individuals suffering from amnesia following electroconvulsive shock therapy frequently suffer from memory loss but, in addition to this, there is a feeling of unfamiliarity or a "jamais vu" phenomenon. Even though individuals may do quite well in recognition tests, they feel uncomfortable or unsure about their choices.

GENETICS—SPECIES MEMORY

The presence of memory indicates the existence of a changing environment full of information that could not be inherited efficiently. The advantage that learning ability imparts to a creature that has it should be carefully considered in any attempt to understand this function. But learning, as usually understood by psychologists and physiologists, is only a narrow concept that ignores a number of other ways in which individual organisms adapt themselves to their environment. They may form spores or develop antibodies or shed limbs to meet new exigencies. But apparently, it is with rapid learning taking place over seconds or minutes that a brain is particularly useful. This organ is apparently designed to code, store, and deliver information in a highly efficient way.

The advantage of being able to cope with a changing world by adapting to it is useful only to organisms with long life spans. Creatures with short spans may depend mainly upon genetic means for adaptation, but, even at this level, adaptive enzymes (Williams, 1959) have been shown. The alternative to learning is living in a relatively fixed environment and allowing the reflex functions of the nervous system to cope with it, like a frog, or to dispense with the nervous system altogether, like a tapeworm (Jarvik, 1960).

The information storage capacity of the nucleic acids is generally agreed to be the basis of life. This information is acquired by chance slowly over generations, and belief in the inheritance of acquired characteristics is rare though it crops up again and again. Anatomical determinism appears to be fantastically invariable; the amazing similarity of twins is good evidence of this. Adaptation to the environment develops from mutations and from recombinations made possible by sexual reproduction. Such adjustment can be considered the equivalent of either learning or forgetting. Here is a reasonable analogy between two processes that have exactly the same goal, the preservation of complex environmental information for the survival of an organism. Certainly complex forms of behavior called instinctive (Thorpe, 1956) are inherited and it seems a reasonable assumption that the determinants of these are stored in the same way in the nervous system as those of acquired behavior.

Two processes that do not necessarily involve the brain but which resemble learning are addiction and immunity. In either case, the presentation of a stimulus, in this instance a chemical, results in a modification in the organism that is revealed by altered response on the next presentation. The mechanism of addiction to narcotics, for example, is still poorly understood (Seevers, 1958), but it may be that its elucidation would reveal something about processes involved in memory. It is highly likely that morphine or heroin addiction involves long-lasting and perhaps permanent changes in synaptic transmission in the central nervous system. Changes in synaptic transmission have also been postulated (Hebb, 1949) to occur in learning. It is known, however, that changes outside the nervous system also occur as a result of morphine addiction. For example, enzymic changes in the liver (Axelrod, 1956) and even the action of isolated intestine (Paton, 1957) is modified by the chronic injection of narcotics.

The mechanism of immunity offers an example of a phenomenon that has been explained by two theories. One of these is very analogous to what could be considered to occur in learning and has been dubbed "the instructive theory" by Lederberg (Burnett, 1961). A more radical but apparently more plausible theory in view of the evidence is proposed by Burnett (1961), called the selection theory, which holds that the manufacture of antibodies is controlled by a sort of evolutionary process occurring within the body involving the survival of resistant strains of plasma cells. Interestingly, the presence of antigen kills embryonic plasma cells whereas in the mature cells it stimulates them to proliferate rapidly.

Just as Darwinian evolution would have to be a less efficient process than Lamarckian, so it would seem that the development of immunity depends to a great extent upon chance factors. Is it possible that memory also functions in a similar way? Are precursors for all the varieties of memory already present in the nervous system, and need they merely be stimulated by an environmental event that is somehow isomorphic with them? To some extent, there seems to be evidence that certain memories are hidden in the nervous system waiting for the right experience to come along and that some experiences will never be remembered simply because there are no preformed memories available for stimulation.

The fact that memory is a construct need not deter us from using the term. For many years the gene was a construct, but there was every reason for believing that the structure of this entity would be elucidated someday. Evidently some change occurs in the nervous system as a result of learning, and if only techniques in neurophysiology or histology were advanced, enough scientists would be able to see it, to examine it, to scrutinize it. After all, the only reason we assume that memory occurs is the fact that there is a correlation between past events and present events. A photograph or a high-fidelity phonograph record are memory devices used by man that furnish very high correlations between past and present events. Edison's first record, "Mary Had a Little Lamb," was decidedly low-fidelity, and yet one could be sure to what original event it was related. But the grooves on his wax cylinder can be seen today. What kind of grooves are made in the brain of a person hearing this poem?

The historian, the archeologist, and the paleontologist are all specialists in analogues of memory. Of course, they study mnemonic devices produced intentionally or accidentally by individuals preceding them, or even by nature in bygone days. The job of these experts is to reconstruct the past on the basis of such evidence as they may find. Sometimes the clues are very few. Theirs is a perception that is distal in degree. Proximal events in perception are of low reliability taken individually but are of great value taken collectively in establishing distal validity. The same situation applies in memory, which is really perception with a temporal dimension.

PHYSIOLOGY OF THE ENGRAM

One of the problems that faces the physiological psychologist who is interested in mechanisms of memory is whether retention or storage of information in the nervous system is a static affair relatively fixed in nature or is constantly changing. Considerable turnover occurs in the chemical components of cells, even in the calcium and phosphorus content of the bones. If information were retained in a fixed form, as it is on a phonograph record, then one would expect that neither subsequent activity nor the passage of time would have any influence upon it. All learning experiments, starting with Ebbinghaus, have shown conclusively that such is not the case.

There is evidence of another type, however, that passage of time may influence the stability of a trace, which may be subsumed under a theory known as consolidation theory (Mueller and Pilzecker, 1900). In humans it has been known for some time that an event that produces sudden and severe change in brain function is capable of causing retrograde amnesia. Concussion and electroconvulsive shock therapy have given rise to clinical reports of such phenomena. However, experiments with anesthetic agents (Pearlman, Sharpless, and Jarvik, 1961) have shown that apparently less damaging effects upon neural function may produce the same effect. It is difficult to find well-controlled studies on humans bearing on this point. A great many experiments conducted with animals have shown that a variety of treatments that interfere with brain function are capable of producing retrograde amnesia providing the treatment is introduced within a certain critical period of approximately fifteen to twenty minutes following the learning experience (Duncan, 1945). Basically, of course, remembering and forgetting are only the converse of each other. It would be impossible to disprove the hypothesis that everything one experiences is remembered. The facts of reminiscence show that events that apparently were forgotten can, in fact, be revived. But there are other events that are apparently irretrievably lost, at least they are never able to be brought back by whatever means are tried.

It is not utterly essential that memories or mnemonic processes be lodged in the brain. Any physical event will result in persistent effects. Scars are endowed in literature with properties of unpleasant memories. Certainly Captain Ahab's loss of a limb was a mnemonic process that helped to remind him of Moby Dick and to flavor his memory with an emotion. Anatomical changes that disturb the integrity of the organism do not necessarily describe the environment very clearly though teeth marks can have pretty good symbolic value. A lobster that regenerates a lost limb has, in a sense, forgotten it. Too much plasticity is not compatible with memory. It would be difficult to see how an amoeba could store information unless it had some rigid parts. It does have the needed rigidity in its genes. Long term or persistent memory must depend upon a structural configuration to hold it, even when temporally sequential events are being stored, but the nature of this structure still eludes us.

In the broader sense, compatible with philosophical determinism, all the events in the universe at any given moment are dependent on all preceding ones so that there is a universal memory or causation. The mere persistence of inanimate objects in a room constitutes a memory in its broad sense, a fact appreciated, for example, by Queen Victoria in mourning for Prince Albert. Practically speaking, functional relationships may be established, as the old British associationists and John Stuart Mill put it, by the principle of concomitant variation (Cohen and Nagel, 1934) or as they are more modernly known, by correlational techniques.

When a medical student chants "on old Olympus' towering top," he is using a mnemonic device. When monkeys or pigeons are trained to do delayed response tests, then they use "mediating responses" to bridge the delay in time. These are also mnemonic devices and are obviously alternatives to the mnemonic processes in the brain. Human beings use such mnemonic devices with notorious frequency; certainly writing and printing are our best examples of such. But a mnemonic device, to be efficient, has got to be capable of being integrated with those which exist in the brain. Hence the organization of these tools should teach us something about memory processes in the brain.

There is one very elementary form of behavior that appears to be related to, if it is not identical with, learning, which is instructive to consider from a probabilistic point of view. Habituation has been defined as a decremental response with repeated stimulation. It resembles sensory adaptation, and it is allied to it in function. Sensory adaptation requires the persistence of a stimulus. In the absence of a stimulus, there is return to prestimulus conditions. In habituation, the change may outlast the disappearance of the stimulus by a considerable length of time. Experimental extinction has frequently been considered a form of habituation. Habituation may also be contrasted with muscular or glandular fatigue. Repeated stimulation of a gland, for example, will produce less and less effect simply because the secretion is depleted. However, if sufficient time is allowed to elapse between stimuli for replenishment, the decrement does not occur.

A response that is habituated behaves as though the probability of the stimulus being significant were an inverse function of the stimulus rate of occurrence. This is also precisely what happens in extinction. Spontaneous recovery after a lapse of stimulus free time obeys the same probability relationship, but the rate is low. Humphrey (1930) showed that the snail, *Helix albolaris,* quickly habituates the tentacle withdrawal response to mechanical stimulation when the latter is repeatedly presented. Konorski (1948) feels that habituation is analogous to extinction and that both involve some type of inhibitory process. More recently, Sharpless and Jasper (1956) showed that habituation of the arousal response to an auditory stimulus could occur in cats even in the absence of auditory cortex. It is clear that habituation serves the purpose of preventing needless activity on the part of an organism. It would also seem that habituation can occur on the purely sensory side (Lindsley, 1960) allowing the channeling in of restricted information where it is most apt to do some good.

One may note an undercurrent of teleology running through the arguments in this paper. Such a view is consistent with the Darwinian concept that inherited mechanisms tend to survive if they are useful to the organism. The use of behavior is to enable the organism to predict and control its environment. As Brunswik (1956) put it, ". . . the perceptual system appears as a complex instrument aiming at a mapping of the distal environment into the organism. Since perception is 'persistent' and 'docile' in pursuing this aim, it fulfills Tolman's criteria for 'purposiveness' of behavior (1932, . . .)." The function of memory is to incorporate past information from the environment into the organism in order to allow it to predict the future more effectively.

SUMMARY

In 1906 Kuhlman felt that the subject's response in a task requiring him to recall visual forms, "can never be described even half correctly by calling it reproduction. It is rather a construction, not a reconstruction, a construction of a certain result that is accepted in a place of the original, and far from a reconstruction of a past perception." (Woodworth and Schlosberg, 1954). Since the function of memory is the same as that of perception, namely to adapt an individual to the outside world removed from him in time and space, memory is both selective and inductive in nature. When we remember what we ate for breakfast yesterday, we really depend upon the effects of hundreds of breakfasts in the past. It is much easier to remember breakfast than dinner because, since the former meal is generally less variable, the probability of guessing correctly is greater.

Whatever processes are involved in the formation, storage and retrieval of the trace must be related to the usefulness of the trace in survival. As with perception in general, memory is far from perfect and certainly not photographic in nature and, as Brunswik (1944) put it, ". . . the consequence is compromise and a falling short of precision but also the relative infrequency of drastic error." Access time is extremely fast compared with all but the most modern computers and compares favorably with perception or stimulus configurations physically present. In short, memory is an efficient device to enable individuals to gamble efficiently with an environment too changeable for its effects to be incorporated into genes, but stable eneugh so that its effects early in the life of an individual may be of value to him later.

REFERENCES

Axelrod, J. Possible mechanisms of tolerance to narcotic drugs. *Sci.*, 1956, *124,* 263–264.

Bartlett, F. C. *Remembering: an experimental and social study*. London: Cambridge, 1932.

Birren, J. E. *Handbook of aging and the individual*. Chicago: University of Chicago Press, 1959.

Broadbent, D. E. *Perception and communication*. New York: Pergamon, 1958.

Brunswik, E. Probability as a determiner of rat behavior. *J. exp. Psychol.*, 1939, *25*, 175–197.

Brunswik, E. Distal focussing of perception: size-constancy in a representative sample of situations. *Psychol. Monographs*, 1944, No. 254.

Brunswik, E. Note on Hammond's analogy between "relativity and representativeness." *Phil. of Sci.*, 1951, *18*, 212–217.

Brunswik, E. *Perception and the representative design of psychological experiments.* Berkeley, Calif.: University of California Press, 1956.

Burnett, F. M. Immunological recognition of self. *Sci.*, 1961, *133*, 307–311.

Bush, R. R., and F. Mosteller. *Stochastic models for learning.* New York: Wiley, 1955.

Carmichael, L., H. P. Hogan, and A. Walter. An experimental study of the effect of language on the reproduction of visually perceived forms. *J. exp. Psychol.*, 1932, *15*, 73–86.

Cohen, M. R. and E. Nagel. *An introduction to logic and scientific method.* New York: Harcourt Brace and Company, Inc., 1934.

Darwin, C. R. *The origin of the species.* New York: Modern Library, Inc., 1936.

Descartes, R. *L'homme.* Paris: Angot, 1664.

Duncan, C. P. The effect of electroshock convulsions on the maze habit in the white rat. *J. exper. Psychol.*, 1945, *35*, 267–278.

Estes, W. K. The statistical approach to learning theory. In S. Koch (Ed.), *Psychology: A study of a science.* New York: McGraw-Hill, 1959.

Estes, W. K. and B. F. Skinner. Some quantitive properties of anxiety.
J. exp. Psychol., 1941, *29*, 390–400.

Frenkel-Brunswik, E. Intolerance of ambiguity as an emotional and perceptual personality variable. *J. Pers.*, 1949, *18*, 108–143.

Freud, S. *The Psychopathology of everyday life.* New York: Macmillan, 1917.

Gerard, R. W. Biological roots of psychiatry. *Sci.*, 1955, *122*, 225–230.

Hake, H. W. and R. Hyman. Perception of the statistical structure of a random series of binary symbols. *J. exp. Psychol.*, 1953, *41*, 291–297.

Hanawalt, N. G. Memory trace for figures in recall and recognition. *Arch. Psychol.*, N.Y. 1937, No. 216.

Hebb, D. O. *The organization of behavior.* New York: Wiley, 1949.

Hudson, B. B. One trial learning in the domestic rat. *Genet. Psychol. Monogr.*, 1950, *41*, 99–143.

Hull, C. L. *Principles of behavior.* New York: D. Appleton & Co., Inc., 1943.

Humphrey, G. Le Chatelier's rule and the problem of habituation and dehabituation in *Helix albolabris. Psychol. Forsch.*, 1930, *13*, 113–27.

Hunt, H. F. and J. V. Brady. Some effects of punishment and intercurrent "anxiety" on a simple operant. *J. comp. physiol. Psychol.*, 1955, *48*, 305–310.

Jarvik, M. E. Probability learning and a negative recency effect in the serial anticipation of alternative symbols. *J. exp. Psychol.*, 1951, *41*, 291–297.

Jarvik, M. E. Discrimination of colored food and food signs by primates. *J. comp. physiol. Psychol.*, 1953, *46*, 390–392.

Jarvik, M. E. Means of integrating

approaches to human behavior. *Suppl. Dis. nerv. Syst.*, 1960, *21*, 1–14.

Jarvik, M. E., and W. B. Essman. A simple one-trial learning situation for mice. *Psychol. Rep.*, 1960, *6*, 290.

Jenkins, J. G. and K. M. Dallenbach. Oblivescence during sleep and waking. *Amer. J. Psychol.*, 1924, *35*, 605–612.

Kellogg, W. N. Is 'spinal conditioning' conditioning? Reply to 'A comment.' *J. exp. Psychol.*, 1947, *37*, 264–265.

Konorski, J. *Conditioned reflexes and neuron organization.* London: Cambridge, 1948.

Kuhlmann, F. On the analysis of the memory consciousness. *Psychol. Rev.*, 1906, *13*, 316–348.

La Mettrie, J. O. de. *L'homme, machine.* Paris: Henry, 1865.

Lashley, K. S. Persistent problems in the evolution of mind. *Quart. Rev. of Biol.*, 1949, *24*, 28–43.

Lashley, K. S. Dynamic processes in perception. In J. F. Delafresnaye (Ed.), *Brain mechanisms and consciousness.* Springfield, Ill.: Thomas Publishing, 1954.

Lindsley, D. H. Attention, consciousness, sleep and wakefulness. In J. Field (Ed.), *Handbook of Physiol.* Section 1, Neurophysiology, Vol. 111, American Physiological Society, Washington, 1960.

Luce, R. C. *Individual choice behavior: a theoretical analysis.* New York: Wiley, 1959.

Miles, R. C. Learning set formation in the squirrel monkey. *J. comp. physiol. Psychol.*, 1957, *50*, 356–357.

Miller, G. A. The magical number seven, plus or minus two: some limits on our capacity for processing information. *Psychol. Rev.*, 1956, *63*, 81–97.

Milner, B. Psychological defects produced by temporal lobe excision. *A. Res. nerv. & ment. Dis. Proc.*, 1956, *36*, 244–257.

Mueller, G. E. and A. Pilzecker. Experimentalle Beitraege zur Lehre vom Gadaechtnis. *Z. Psychol.*, 1900, *1*, 1–300.

Paton, W. D. M. The action of morphine and related substances on contraction and on acetylcholine output of coaxially stimulated guinea pig ileum. *Brit. J. Pharmacol.*, 1957, *12*, 119–127.

Pearlman, C. A. Jr., S. K. Sharpless, and M. E. Jarvik. Retrograde amnesia produced by anesthetic and convulsant agents. *J. comp. physiol. Psychol.*, 1961, *54*, 109–112.

Reichenbach, H. *Experience and prediction.* Chicago: University of Chicago Press, 1938.

Seevers, M. H. Termination of drug action by tolerance development. *Fed. Proc.*, 1958, *17*, 1175–1181.

Sharpless, S. K. and H. Jasper. Habituation of the arousal reaction. *Brain*, 1956, *79*, 655.

Siegel, S. and D. A. Goldstein. Decision making behavior in a two-choice uncertain outcome situation. *J. exp. Psychol.*, 1959, *57*, 37–42.

Stevens, S. S. To honor Fechner and repeal his law. *Sci.*, 1961, *133*, 80–86.

Talland, G. A. Psychological studies of Korsakoff's psychosis: VI. Memory and learning. *J. of nerv. and mental Dis.*, 1960, *130*, 366–385.

Thorndike, E. L. *The fundamentals of learning.* New York: Columbia University Press, 1932.

Thorpe, W. H. *Learning and instinct in animals.* Cambridge, Mass.: Harvard University Press, 1956.

Tolman, E. C. *Purposive behavior in animals and men.* New York: D. Appleton & Company, Inc., 1932.

Tolman, E. C. and E. Brunswik. The organism and the casual texture of the environment. *Psychol. Rev.,* 1935, *42,* 43–77.

Tredgold, A. F. *A textbook of mental deficiency.* Baltimore: Williams & Wilkins, 1952.

Underwood, B. J. Interference and forgetting. *Psych. Rev.,* 1957, *64,* 49–60.

Van Ormer, E. B. Retention after intervals of sleep and of waking. *Arch. Psychol.,* N. Y., 1932, *137,* 3–49.

Warren, H. C. *Dictionary of Psychology.* New York: Houghton and Mifflin, 1934.

William, R. *Biochemical individuality.* New York: Wiley, 1956.

Williams, R. T. *The metabolism of drugs, toxic substances and other organic compounds.* New York: Wiley, 1959.

Wilson, W. A. Jr. and A. R. Rollin. Two choice behavior of rhesus monkeys in a non-contingent situation. *J. exp. Psychol.,* 1959, *58,* 174–180.

Woodworth, R. S. *Experimental psychology.* New York: Dryden Press, Inc., 1938.

Woodworth, R. S. and H. Schlosberg. *Experimental psychology.* New York: Holt, Rinehart and Winston, 1954.

Zubin, J. Objective studies of disordered persons. In T. G. Andrews (Ed.), *Methods of Psychology.* New York: Wiley, 1948.

8

Concept Attainment with Probabilistic Feedback[1]

HIROSHI AZUMA
LEE J. CRONBACH

A person interprets his world with the aid of cues that have in the past been associated with certain consequences. Perception is made possible by the organism's ability to recognize signs or cues associated with, for example, size, motion, distance, or the identity of objects. Formal reasoning rests on the use of explicit classifications or conceptualizations; objects or events that have certain common consequences or properties are assigned to a class for which identifying cues are found. The cues used in these identifications are not always fully reliable as bases for judgment.

Brunswik repeatedly emphasized that adjustment to the environment requires the organism to cope with uncertain, probabilistic relations. Thus he said (1943, p. 258):

> I should like to emphasize especially . . . the necessary imperfection, inflicted upon achievements—as relations between classes—by the ambiguity in the causal texture of the environment. . . . Because of this environmental ambiguity, no matter how smoothly the organismic instruments and mechanisms may function, relationships cannot be foolproof, at least as far as those connecting with the vitally relevant more remote distal regions of the environment are concerned. This intrinsic lack of perfection, that is of univocality, will on the whole be the greater the more wide-spanning the relationships involved are. The only way in which perfection could be secured would be by control over all the remaining conditions which could possibly become relevant in the given case. This, however, is something the reacting organism cannot do for lack of time if not for other more serious reasons—and thus something which the psychologist who wishes to catch and rationally to reconstruct organismic adjustment at large, with all its faults and fallacies, should also not do.

Psychological research has only recently begun to observe in the

1. This study was carried out under contract N6ori-1834(33) with the Office of Naval Research; additional support was provided by the University of Illinois.

laboratory the human subject's response to a rich and at the same time equivocal environment. The classical concept-formation task has typically provided a stimulus rich in information, some part of which is unequivocally connected with a certain consequence. For example, all cards with red figures and two borders may be designated by E as positive instances of the concept that S is to identify, other cues—number of figures, shape of figures, and so forth—being irrelevant to the solution. Under these circumstances S can achieve perfect interpretation of the stimuli. In the traditional probability-learning experiment, the environment is equivocal but minimally informative. Every trial presents the same fixed stimulus (for example, the choice point in a T-maze or a signal lamp). There is no valid information to guide response selection save the base rates with which the alternative responses are called correct. Stimulus variation that might seem to provide relevant information is virtually absent. When stimuli vary in appearance, S can develop hypotheses about the significance of various aspects of the figures. The distinction between probabilistic and unequivocal situations may not be a useful one for the analysis of behavior.

From E's point of view, a task is deterministic if the feedback to S is wholly contingent on stimulus characteristics, and is probabilistic if the stimulus-feedback correspondence is imperfect. S, however, cannot make this distinction. He can be sure that a task is probabilistic only if the instructions warn him that it is impossible to be completely successful; otherwise, no matter how puzzling the seemingly inconsistent feedback may be, he can never be sure that he has not overlooked a rule that would solve the problem. It is philosophically sound to hypothesize that *every* phenomenon is completely determined by prior events, so that probabilistic relations arise only because some cues are indiscriminable, neglected, or incorrectly interpreted. Likewise, when confronted with a concept-attainment task, S is able to observe only equivocal, probabilistic relations (except as he may find a perfect rule for some subset of stimuli). He can be sure that the task is deterministic only after he hits upon a perfect solution. Hence, reasoning and learning in experiments from probabilistic feedback should exhibit much the same processes as occur in learning to cope with unequivocal complex environments, unless S knows that his information is incomplete.

Recently there have been experiments in which several attributes of the stimuli differ, and feedback is connected probabilistically to these attributes. From S's point of view, and therefore from the viewpoint of theory, it makes no difference whether the equivocality results from E's "calling 10 percent of S's correct responses wrong" or from his deciding *a priori* to reward response x to stimulus a 90 percent of the time.

We therefore do not distinguish "misinformative feedback" from probabilistic reinforcement.

The chief differences among the several experiments are in the nature and complexity of the stimulus displays, which may be characterized briefly as follows:

R. Goodnow (1954)   Airplanes characterized by three attributes; one or two attributes are visible on any trial. Attributes have different validities.

J. Goodnow (1955)   Complex drawings. S is to choose between two drawings alike in all respects but one; this two-valued attribute is the only relevant information.

Morin (1955)   Eight lights randomly allocated to two classes. The only cue to response is the location of the light shown on each trial.

Pishkin (1960)   Drawings differing in two, four, or six attributes; one attribute relevant.

Bourne (1962)   Like Pishkin's save for use of three attributes and a much longer training series.

In all these studies save R. Goodnow's the correct response is associated with only one single attribute. In R. Goodnow's experiment the several cues were independently associated with the correct response, so that each combination of cues had its own significance.

In the J. Goodnow, Pishkin, Bourne, and Morin studies the relevant binary attribute had a certain probability π of being associated with the former of two response categories. The Es were especially interested in the probability P of that response at the end of training. The following average values of P are reported. (Some of them, from charts, may be inexact.)

π	.50	.60	.70	.80	.90	1.00
P (Morin)	ca. .50	ca. .50	ca. .50	.75	.75	.96
P (Pishkin; one irrelevant attribute)		.45	.81	.89	.92	1.00
P (Pishkin; three irrelevant attributes)		.58	.64	.74	.99	1.00
P (Bourne)			.74	.96	1.00	1.00
P (Goodnow and Postman, last 20 trials)	.48	.55	.62	.80	.93	1.00

The data in the last line are taken from the experiment of J. Goodnow and Postman (1955); other references to this program of work are Jarrett (1951), J. Goodnow (1955), and Bruner, Goodnow, and Austin (1956). Ss were shown a complex key figure, modified in two ways. A Type-1 modification transferred a line from the right side of the key figure to the left side; Type 2 transferred a line from left to right. S was to select one of the two modifications as correct; the investigators designated the Type-1 modification as correct with probability π. The results given above are interpreted (Bruner, Goodnow, and Austin, p. 192) as indicating "event matching" in the sense that P is close to π. Indeed, the general proposition is advanced that event matching is to be expected when S thinks that the task is deterministic, that is, there is a definite rule to be discovered. But individuals did not match P to π. There were great individual differences; with π .50 to .80, the σ of the proportions was about .10 to .15. It is reported that Ss made their figure-by-figure decisions on the basis of complex hypotheses about figural cues. That is to say, the typical S constructed small classes of figures for which he considered Type-1 to be correct and other classes where he considered Type-2 correct. Naturally, with $\pi > .50$ his Type-2 classes tended to encompass fewer figures; the expected reinforcement rate for any such subhypothesis is only $1-\pi$, so that it tends to be extinguished. It is only in this way that a rough matching of P to π occurs.

R. Goodnow (1954; see Bruner, Goodnow, and Austin) presented airplane silhouettes to be categorized as X or not-X. Goodnow assigned to each attribute (wing, airscoop, or tail) a certain validity, that is, a certain probability that X would be reinforced when that attribute is present. Thus he might arrange that 67 percent of the planes having a straight wing were X. Goodnow gave 120 trials with feedback. In 60 of these, one attribute of each plane was visible. The remainder displayed two attributes whose respective associations with X could be described by probabilities 1.00-.67, 1.00-.33, .67-.67, or .67-.33 (or the complements of these). The 1.00-.33 and .67-.33 pairings involved conflicting indications, one cue implying X and the other implying not-X to be correct. Goodnow examined how often S gave the response predominantly associated with the more valid of the two indicators, the results being as follows:

	Association of Cue with X	Probability (π) of Reinforcement for X Response	Proportion (P) of (X) Responses at End of Training, Averaged over Groups of Ss
Single cue	1.00	1.00	.91
	.67	.67	.80
Consistent cues	1.00 - .67	1.00	.93
	.67 - .67	.80	.93
Conflicting cues	1.00 - .33	1.00	.87
	.67 - .33	.50	.50

The general conclusion (compare, Bruner, Goodnow, and Austin, p. 200 ff.) was that Ss tend to undervalue a thoroughly dependable cue and to place excessive reliance on a cue that is partly valid. Responses seem to have been determined by an imperfect statistical combination of cues rather than by logical deductions from observed relations; response was probabilistic even where it need not have been. In Goodnow's task, where planes with different single attributes were intermingled, the information load was too great for efficient retention and inference.

In a study resembling classical probability-learning experiments but offering slightly more stimulus information, Popper and Atkinson (1958) and Atkinson, Bogartz, and Turner (1959) presented a two-valued stimulus having no irrelevant attributes. There were two response alternatives; response 1 was reinforced following stimulus 1 with probability π_1, and following stimulus 2 with probability π_2 (not necessarily equal to $1 - \pi_1$). Attention was given to the probability of each response to each stimulus after training. For example, with $\pi_1 = .85$ and $\pi_2 = .15$, $P(R1|S1) = .91$ and $P(R1|S2) = .09$.

A quite different type of experiment initiated by Smedslund (1955) should also be mentioned. Smedslund defined a concept by a rule requiring weighted addition of three stimulus parameters. S was to estimate the numerical value appropriate to each figure, learning by trial and correction. E complicated the task further by adding a small random component in reporting the "correct" numerical value on each trial. The task proved to be exceedingly difficult, though Ss made some progress toward identifying the relevant cues. Ss were insensitive to the relative validities of the cues even after extended training. The fact that the stimulus-feedback relation was equivocal was probably not the chief source of difficulty. Unpublished studies by other workers have set a similar task, requiring addition of parameters with unequivocal feedback. In these studies also, learning was typically slow and imperfect.

In the present study we have been interested in how Ss utilize information where cues are equivocal, whereas previous workers have focused on average response rates. We present stimuli that vary along four dimensions and make two of these irrelevant. The other two dimensions are probabilistically related to the keyed response, one or the other indicating the correct response on each trial. Ordered stimulus dimensions and an ordered response scale were used in place of the two-valued attributes and responses of most other investigations. The experimental task thus more nearly reproduces in miniature the environment conceived of by Brunswik, describable in terms of variables. By using stimuli that can be readily described, we open the way for S to construe the stimulus field in some complex manner.

PROCEDURE

On each trial in this study, the stimulus figure consisted of a 2½ inch square within which appeared a small circle and cross. The figural parameters are the horizontal coordinates of circle and cross—x' and x'', respectively—and the vertical coordinates y' and y''. Each of these takes on one of four equally spaced values with equal probability. Since circle and cross never occupy the same location, 16 x 15 possible configurations constitute the universe of stimuli.

S was shown four "standard stimuli" in which both cross and circle are close to the $x = y$ diagonal, the cross appearing just above the circle. These figures, he was told, differ in a certain property k, Figure A having the smallest k-value and D the largest. S was to compare each stimulus with the standards, learning by trial and correction what characteristic(s) of the figure accounted for k. The most significant parts of the instructions were as follows:

. . . We have constructed here a simplified situation in which you are to learn how to predict something. We will obtain a score showing how rapidly you master such a problem. We will post these scores in a week or so, so that you can find out how well you succeeded. . . .

k-ness is an arbitrary characteristic we have defined. We determine k for each drawing according to a certain rule. . . .

What is it about the locations of a circle and cross that gives a figure a high k-value? . . . As you go through these items you will learn more and more clearly what gives a figure a high or low k value. It will be hard to learn well enough to judge correctly every time, but you should be able to make very good judgments after a while.

At the beginning of the test trials:

Now we want to test how much you have learned by having you make sixty-four more judgments. The scale, and the rule that determines k, are exactly the same as before. . . .

The task was thus presented to S as one in which k is completely dependent on the parameters. The level of success to be expected is ambiguous —as is also the case when a person looks for relationships in the real world.

Stimuli were presented in a booklet, each page showing six different stimuli. The training consisted of 128 trials. For purposes of discussion we shall treat groups of thirty-two responses as blocks. Within each consecutive set of sixteen stimuli, the possible combinations of x' and x''

appeared once each, making $r_{x'x''}$ zero. The distributions of y' and y'' were also rectangular and $r_{x'y'}$, $r_{x'y''}$, $r_{x''y'}$, $r_{x''y''}$ and $r_{y'y''}$ were very close to zero. Within each block, four figures appeared twice to give information on the stability of response.

Responses were made on an answer sheet mounted in the *SRA* self-scorer. When S punched a hole to indicate the alternative selected, he immediately learned whether he was right or wrong by the color seen through the punched hole. If the response was wrong, S punched further holes until a selection was confirmed. He was asked to circle the first response as he punched. A time limit of two minutes per page—that is, per six stimuli—was set. The end of each two-minute interval was indicated on a blackboard. However, Ss were told that ten minutes extra would be allowed at the end of the series; this allowed them to lag behind by a few pages. Following the training series, a test of sixty-four items was distributed; S responded without feedback.

Two groups were run at the same time. For one group k was a weighted average of x' and x''. In this report we confine our attention to the second group in which k was probabilistically related to x' and x''. (See Azuma, 1960, for analysis of Group 1 results.) There were sixteen undergraduate psychology students in Group 2; records of three of these Ss on the test trials were discarded, because they apparently communicated with Ss in Group 1 during the short interval between test and training trials.

The rule governing feedback can best be described as follows:

On Type-*A* items where circle and cross are in the same column, $k = x' = x''$. On Type-*B* items where $x' \neq x''$, on 75 percent of the stimuli selected at random $k = x'$; on the remaining stimuli $k = x''$.

The key was the same for all Ss. When a stimulus reappeared the value of k was determined at random for each occurrence separately. (There was no indication that Ss recognized these repetitions.)

Considering A and B items together, k equalled x' on 81 percent of the trials and x'' on 44 percent. The irrelevant parameters y' and y'' coincided with k on 25 percent of the trials. "Validities" of the cues may be expressed in terms of product-moment correlations:

$$r_{x'k} = .75 \, , r_{x''k} = .25 \, , r_{y'k} = .00 \, , r_{y''k} = .00.$$

If S makes his response R equal to x' on every trial, hits are maximized at 81 percent. Randomly responding by the rule E used to define k (event matching) gives 72 per cent hits on the average.

RESULTS

The conventional measure of success, number of correct responses, is not appropriate, because it is affected by the random decisions made in keying. We substitute a "hit score" to measure success over all items. For the subset of *B* items where the probability of success is the same for all items the proportion of Type-1 responses carries the desired information about success. Brunswik proposes (1956, pp. 41 ff.) correlating *S*'s response with each stimulus dimension as a way of describing the significance *S* attached to that dimension. Attribute-response contingencies Brunswik refers to as measures of "functional validity"; Bruner, Goodnow, and Austin suggest the designation "criterialities" for the relation between the response and the proximal variables. In the famous "lens model" of Brunswik where cues are seen as mediating between the distal property (for example, our *k*) and the response, "ecological validities" appraise the strength of left-side connections and "criterialities" the strength of right-side connections. We found it profitable also to analyze how *S* responded to *A* and *B* items separately. Altogether we have the following measures:

1. *Response count.* Responses were classified as follows:

	A ITEMS	B ITEMS
	$(x' = X'')$	
$R = x'$	Type 0	Type 1
$R = x''$	Type 0	Type 2
R between x' and x''	Impossible	Type 3
R outside x' and x''	Type 4	Type 4

The count of responses of each type was expressed as a percentage of the possible responses of that type.

2. *Hit score.* This is a function of the response counts, as follows:
$$\frac{\text{Type-0} + .75 \text{ Type-1} + .25 \text{ Type 2 responses}}{\text{Number of trials}}$$
This gives the proportion of hits expected on the average *over a large number of keys* randomly determined according to the rule used by *E*.

3. *Alternation rate (P).* In terms of response counts on B items,
$$P = \frac{\text{Type-1 responses}}{\text{Type-1} + \text{Type-2 responses}}$$
Such a ratio has little meaning unless *S* is truly responding x' or x'' on nearly every trial.

4. *Criteriality.* For any parameter (for example, x'), the criteriality is the product-moment correlation of that parameter with S's response R.

5. *Point of identification.* This is the point in the training series where S appears to have recognized that y' and y'' are irrelevant. It was considered that S recognized what was relevant in A items when he made nine Type-0 responses in a set of ten consecutive A trials and never subsequently fell below that rate. The first item in the first set of ten satisfying this criterion was taken as the "point of identification" for A. The first A item appears at Trial 7, which is therefore, the earliest possible point of identification. The point of identification for B is similarly the point after which nine of every ten B responses were of Type 1 or 2. The latest possible point of identification was the tenth A (or B) item from the end of the training series, namely Trial 91 for A and 118 for B.

Trend described by means. The course of learning represented in group means is reported in Table 1. For test blocks and the last training block the mean is given with the three Ss who communicated with the other group removed. It is evident that learning took place, the average hit score at the end of training being nearly as high as the value the key would have given. It also appears that Ss learned to rely more on x' than x'' and not to rely on y' and y'', but other analyses will modify this conclusion.

The typical S learned that either x' or x'' indicates the answer. Type-0

TABLE 1. MEANS OF VARIOUS STATISTICS, BY BLOCKS

| | | Response Types [a] | | | | | Criterialities [b] | | | | |
Block	Hit Score	0	1	2	3	4	x'	x''	y'	y''	P
All subjects ($N=16$)											
Training:											
1	51	69	51	31	21	15	.50	.16	.15	.25	62
2	63	90	61	30	8	7	.63	.30	.15	−.02	67
3	65	91	66	27	6	6	.68	.25	−.03	.10	68
4	69	94	74	20	7	4	.85	.18	.14	.05	78
With three subjects omitted ($N=13$)											
Training:											
4	69	93	75	20	8	4	.83	.19	.16	.05	79
Test:											
1	70	89	75	18	5	7	.81	.30	.04	.12	81
2	64	87	67	24	8	8	.81	.21	.06	−.01	74
Value given by Key [c]:											
	72	100	75	25	0	0	.75	.25	.00	.00	75

[a] Expressed as percentage of possible responses of that type
[b] Averaged through z-transformation
[c] Over the population of stimuli

responses increased rapidly from early trials. Both the criterialities and the counts of Type-1 responses indicate increasing reliance on x', with its mean criteriality at the end of training (.85) greater than its validity (.75). With regard to use of x'', the criterialities and the counts of Type-2 responses give different impressions. Type-0 responses increased, then leveled off, while Type-2 responses steadily decreased. The criteriality for x'', being a composite of these trends, rose and then fell.

On B items reliance on x'' decreased throughout training; the criteriality index does not reveal this.

Type-3 responses (intermediate between x' and x'') were nearly absent after the first block; nearly all such responses on later blocks came from a single unsuccessful S ($S10$). Type-4 responses are presumably based on irrelevant cues; they too disappeared early for all save $S10$ and $S3$.

The nature of individual performance is represented by the specimen analysis in Table 2. The criterialities imply that this S determined the relevance of x' early, paid as much attention to y' as to x'' on early blocks, and, on test blocks, ignored both x'' and y'. The response counts tell a more explicit story. A items were mastered at the outset (Type-0 responses). On B items, $S2$ gave some responses of Type 3 on Blocks 1 and 2; thereafter he gave Type-1 responses with a sprinkling of Type-2. At the end of the test, asked to state his solution rule, $S2$ responded:

TABLE 2. RECORD OF $S2$

Block	1	2	3	4	T1	T2
Criterialities						
x'	.74	.75	.88	.74	.87	.88
x''	.19	.30	.15	.26	.05	.08
y'	.24	.19	.08	−.26	.00	−.05
y''	.13	.03	.02	−.24	.17	−.08
Response counts						
Type 0	100	100	100	100	100	100
1	54	63	92	88	83	96
2	25	29	8	13	9	4
3	33	17	0	0	0	0
4	4	0	0	0	7	0
Alternation rate P						
	68	68	92	88	90	96
Hit score						
	60	66	78	77	74	80

Point of identification for A, trial 7; for B, trial 37.

"I judged the figures and gave answers according to the circle's position in the vertical column. The circle took preference over the X [cross] except where the X was high or low in the column." This rule is consistent with his frequent use of Type-0 and Type-1 responses. But his responses of Type 2 did not occur predominately when y'' was four or one. Moreover, $S2$'s responses to two of the repeated items were inconsistent, suggesting that there was no definite principle behind his occasional Type-2 responses. Introspective accounts of hypotheses often do not coincide with actual responses.

Other Ss, like $S2$, frequently mastered A items at a different time than B items. The points of identification are as follows:

S	5	16	1	13	2	14	11	4	7	12	6	15	8	9	3	10
A items	7	7	7	7	7	8	9	15	15	17	18	61	66	*	*	*
B items	6	10	14	19	37	6	11	1	1	1	19	10	62	102	*	*

* Never reached criterion

In examining these, it should be remembered that B items are three times as frequent as A items. Though the two points of identification are correlated, there are some striking discrepancies. $S4$, for example, made an x' or x'' response to all but one B item but he missed two of the first three A items (nos. 8 and 9); and $S15$ made an occasional error on A items long after he was choosing x' or x'' on B items. This seems to indicate that Ss were finding solutions for subclasses of items rather than becoming sensitive to the general statistical validities of cues.

The alternation rates at the end of training were frequently high; $P = 1.00$ on Block 4 for two Ss, and for seven more P was above .86. Averaged over all subjects $P = .78$, which might suggest event matching —but only two individuals were near the event-matching rate of .75. Five Ss had P values near .50 on Block 4. The P values after 128 trials cannot be taken as "asymptotic" performance; twelve of the sixteen Ss showed an increase in P from Block 3 to Block 4 and very likely would have moved closer to 1.00 with more training.

Several changes in P appeared during test trials. The changes were mixed in direction; the possibility that they are random fluctuations cannot be ruled out. Of particular interest is the collapse of $S9$, who shifted from $P = .61$ to $P = .09$—nearly uniform choice of x''. $S12$ also deteriorated. He consistently chose x' on the last sixteen training trials (having alternated previous to that), but on late test trials he shifted to a scattered, uncharacterizable response pattern, even missing five of the last six A items. These two Ss either "lost their grip" on the problem or stopped trying.

A study of the repeated items together with the introspective reports indicates that six of the thirteen Ss were following some rule in selecting their responses, though not with perfect consistency. The rules made reference to use of x'' under such conditions as "O and X in a diagonal relation and three spaces apart," "X in a corner," "X directly above and to the left of O," and so forth. Seven Ss were inconsistent, either alternating in a random fashion or changing their rules erratically during the test series. Consistency was most common among Ss with relatively high hit scores and alternation rates.

S typically responds x' to most items but identifies a class of exceptions to which he believes response x'' should be made. For example, $S8$ reported that x'' is correct when the cross is in the corner, and on six test items of Type B where the cross is in the corner he made four of his five Type-2 responses. This rule, however, was adopted only midway through the test; on training item 128 and on test items 28 and 30 the cross was in the corner yet he responded x'. In defining classes of exceptions Ss specify configurations of stimuli that take y information into account. Such hypotheses are of course not valid, though they may have been confirmed in some short series of trials.

DISCUSSION

When training trials are long continued, S presumably reaches a steady state in which the probabilities of the several responses no longer change. In most learning experiments the final probability of the correct response is 1.00, but with probabilistic reinforcement the asymptotic probability of the more-reinforced response may be less than 1. Though our stimuli are complex, most Ss learned early that x' or x'' is correct and on B items were thereafter in a binary-choice situation with reinforcement of x' at the rate $\pi = .75$. Previous investigators (for example, J. Goodnow) have frequently reported their results as indicating event matching, with P close to π. Some mathematical models also predict asymptotic event-matching (Bush and Mosteller, 1955, Chap. 5, 13; Estes, 1959, p. 411; Estes *et al.* 1957). R. Goodnow reported a tendency to make P greater than π (for moderate values of π), and Edwards (1956, 1961) assembled extensive evidence to support the view that the final P tends to be greater than π. Siegel (1961) adds the possibility that under some circumstances P will be less than π; he develops a formal model to represent conditions under which each of the results $P < \pi$, $P = \pi$, $\pi < P < 1$, or $P = 1$ is to be expected.

On our A items, the correct response is always Type-0, and 75 percent of Ss adhered to that response on Trials 91 ff. Four Ss failed to identify this principle or made one or two erratic responses. This result alone ($P = \pi = 1$) is consistent with any of the interpretations above. It does not confirm the "undervaluation" of a dependable cue that R. Goodnow reported; only 53 percent of his Ss made consistent use of a perfectly valid cue.

On B items, the final value of P is clearly high for most Ss, and still increasing; only two reach $P = 1.00$. This result is consistent with the Edwards conclusion that P will be above the event-matching rate, and with Siegel's argument. Bourne demonstrates that, with training continued for 600 trials, there may be an increase in the number making 100 percent use of the more likely response. With π .90 all his Ss reached $P = 1.00$; with π .80, 75 percent of Ss; and with π .70, 35 percent. Perhaps in our task where $\pi = .75$ many more Ss would attain $P = 1.00$ if given extended training.

Our result, like Bourne's, contradicts the J. Goodnow-Bruner view that approximate event matching is characteristic of "problem-solving" tasks and all-and-none behavior of "gambling" tasks. Our Ss were asked to solve a problem, and they seem to have been seeking a solution. Yet they gradually came to adopt the x' response as their basic principle, from which they departed infrequently. Many of them were close to all-and-none behavior and few were close to event-matching. So long as the problem-solving versus gambling (or deterministic versus probabilistic) distinction is defined in terms of S's mental set or other covert responses, it is unlikely to be valuable. To distinguish between tasks in terms of experimentally manipulated instructions to the S, however, may be profitable, as it was in the James-Rotter (1958) study of extinction after intermittent reinforcement and Edwards' unpublished study where some groups were led to expect misinformative feedback.

We had expected performance to remain stable on test trials, but many Ss changed their response pattern even in the absence of feedback as did $S8$, when he began to employ a configural hypothesis in the latter half of the test. $S6$ shifted from $P = .96$ on Block 4 to $P = .79$ on the test. Shifts of P upward toward all-and-none performance are offset by downward shifts. Reflection on the changes in response brings to our attention the fact that it is rational for S to introduce *untested* hypotheses on test trials if he is unwilling to settle for a hit rate of 81 percent (all-and-none response). At the end of training he is likely to have a somewhat complex hypothesis which will yield 70 percent–80 percent hits. If dissatisfied with this score, he can add some further qualifying clause to the rule. If his refinement is unrelated to the supposed principle underlying the key, his amendment of the hypothesis will not tend to lower his score. And, since S regards the alternation as systematically produced, he can reasonably hope to gain from any amendment based on some recalled stimulus-feedback coincidence.

Bruner, Goodnow, and Austin (p. 210) have argued that S often makes the less likely response in order to test some hypothesis directly. Since testing is no longer possible on test trials, they predict that reducing opportunity to validate will lead to more nearly all-and-none performance. In R. Goodnow's data this did occur; where π was .80, 82 percent of Ss had $P = 1.00$ under test conditions and 64 percent had $P = 1.00$ under training conditions. We, however, do not find greater use of all-and-none response on test trials. The conditions of the particular experiment seemingly act in subtle ways to modify Ss' strategy.

Certainly the strategic situation is not the same on training and test trials. Neither training performance nor test performance—nor the two combined—is an unequivocal indication of what has been learned. When feedback continues, S's strategy for acquiring information influences his responses. Removing feedback eliminates this influence, but S is still engaged in a game against the experimenter. Forced to respond with insufficient information, we cannot predict how he will employ his partial knowledge. The appropriate comment has already been made: "Research on behavior with reduced opportunity for validation has barely begun." (Bruner, Goodnow and Austin, p. 216.)

Within the set of B items where the response was sometimes x' and sometimes x'', our Ss characteristically devised complex rules for deciding which response to choose for each stimulus, identifying a minority class of stimuli for which the less likely response is presumed to be correct. All our observations are consistent with Edwards' (1956) description of performance in a binary-choice experiment:

[The data] all suggest that Ss make their choices on the basis of hypotheses about what the reward sequence is. Two kinds of such hypotheses can be distinguished. The first is what might be called big hypotheses: e.g., "The left button pays off far more often than the right one." The main use of big hypotheses is to rule out certain classes of small hypotheses and to make other classes of small hypotheses more probable. . . . Almost every decision is made on the basis of a small hypothesis. Since no small hypothesis can possibly be correct, Ss change their small hypotheses at frequent intervals, as the evidence against them accumulates.

This theory is plausible, but testing it is very difficult. Almost never can S

say after making a choice what the hypothesis was which led him to make it. Until someone develops a technique for finding out what these small hypotheses are, or at least for finding out when one small hypothesis is discarded and other takes its place, arguments like this one must remain speculative.

In Edwards' experiment all stimulus displays were identical; there were no figural cues on which S could rely and their hypotheses were based on response sequences. In our study with complex and variable stimuli, and in J. Goodnow's, Ss' small hypotheses were based on figural characteristics. There is no indication that they paid attention to sequences. While there are unexplained inconsistencies within the records of our Ss, a sufficient number of protocols have been "explained" to give credence to Edwards' proposition that "almost every alternation is based on a small hypothesis."

In adopting the criteriality analysis proposed by Smedslund and Bruner, Goodnow, and Austin, we had hoped to obtain useful information about S's utilization of cues and hence about his small hypotheses. This method proved not to be very enlightening. Part of the difficulty is technical; if S does not maintain the same hypothesis for a long series of trials, there are insufficient data to establish a correlation reliably. More serious is the fact that the basic model—linear correlation of response with attribute— gives a poor characterization of S's utilization of information. This is most obvious when we compare the test-trial criterialities for y' and y'' with the introspections and protocols. The mean criteriality never exceeded .12, and only rarely does an isolated individual criteriality exceed .20. Yet subject after subject states a small hypothesis in which the y coordinates figure. A zero criteriality by no means implies that an attribute is disregarded.

In the Brunswikian description of *perceptual* learning from which criteriality analysis arises, S is said gradually to capitalize upon correspondences encountered in samples from the ecological universe of stimuli. Brunswik, in thinking about such attainments as size constancy and social perception, emphasized the importance of the ecology; he saw learning as a shift in the statistical structure of S's responses to the ecology. While learning can be described in statistical terms in a concept-attainment task, S is not responding to the ecology as a whole. Instead, he cuts out of the swarm of stimuli one subset after another and forms an hypothesis regarding the subset. Cues are used twice, first in a rule that dictates subclass assignment, then in a second rule for the subclass that dictates the response. Such a system does indeed involve systematic cue-response contingencies, but the response is tied to a configuration, not to single cues. The system is certainly not linear; it is a composite of many rules, most of them nonlinear, so that there is virtually no possibility of compressing it into any single algebraic formula. To be sure, if one could identify the subclass S is using, one could determine within-subclass criterialities. But each S subdivides the stimuli differently. Our counts of "response types" come closer to summarizing performance than do the criterialities, though even they have limited value.

It seems likely that Brunswik himself would have anticipated the unsuitability of criteriality analysis for this type of concept-attainment experiment. The early Tolman-Brunswik paper (1935) apparently intended to offer a single model for all behavior including thought processes. Referring to the formation and use of "hypotheses," it said that "the essentials are the same" whether one is interpreting as a shadow an illumination gradient projected on the retina or venturing the hypothesis that all learning is based on conditioned reflexes. Brunswik's 1947 monograph (Part I of Brunswik, 1956) dealt in detail only with perceptual and judgmental problems, but it again could easily be interpreted as a program for all psychological research. It is from these papers that the application of his views to concept-attainment stemmed. But in his 1954 paper for the Montreal Congress (see Chap. 16, this volume) Brunswik forcefully distinguished perceptual from rational processes. The distinction between perception, which is intuitive and immediate, and thought which follows a well-organized single track, is again considered briefly in the 1956 additions to his monograph (pp. 89–99, 130.) Deductive thinking, by his account, is "certainty-geared," applying a rule that leads unequivocally from a few of the cues in the input to a correct or most rewarding response. Perceptual achievements are "uncertainty-geared," accepting the necessity of combining many cues that singly or together are equivocal, and of compromising among conclusions from the several fallible cue-systems. Trying to put formally and deductively what one has observed impressionistically is, he says, likely to engender distortions or misconceptions.

In concept-attainment studies S is led to think that there is a formal, perfect, solution rule; he therefore attempts to construct a rule to fit the information provided. As we have pointed out, from S's point of view this information is probabilistic whether the stimulus-feedback relations are equivocal or not, until he happens on a 100 percent correct hypothesis. Brunswik argues that S succeeds in coping with uncertainty by gradually becoming sensitive to more of the numerous relevant cues that, being redundant, support each other. But no concept-attainment experiments save R. Goodnow's and Bricker's (1955) employ redundant cues. The remaining studies have offered S a single relevant cue or a set of uncorrelated cues each of which has some degree of validity. In this situation S appears to proceed systematically rather than intuitively, forming hypotheses to fit some small series of observations and then amending them as they are contradicted. Gradual approach to 100 percent use of x' might be expected as a consequence of the disconfirmation of one after another of the plausible broad definitions of a class of stimuli for which x'' is the correct response, and, later, the disconfirmation of the plausible small-class hypotheses also.

The accumulation of studies using probabilistic reinforcement with multivariate stimuli has led to a somewhat consistent account of behavior to be expected, though no part of this account is established beyond question. Ss learn to make use of the relevant cues and not to rely directly on the irrelevant cues. This learning is slow when stimuli are complex. When two cues are in conflict, Ss tend to follow the more valid cue, reliance on that cue increasing as training progresses. S uses various cues, relevant and irrelevant, to define subclasses of stimuli within which the less valid cue should be followed. Sequential hypotheses are not used. While some studies report event matching, this seems likely to be a transient state in concept-formation tasks, reflecting only the hypotheses regarding "exceptions" that are temporarily in play.

Little is known about the conditions that cause Ss to take the intuitive-receptive attitude that one would expect to be favorable in learning multiple systems of intersubstitutable cues, or, alternatively, to continually form and reform explicit hypotheses.[2] Nor is much known about the conditions under which each of these mental sets is beneficial to learning the true cue-feedback contingencies. The most important point

2. It occurs to us that a fruitful experimental variation might be to inform S continually about his hit rate over items recently presented rather than about each single hit or miss. This follows Brunswik's proposal to emphasize the achievement of "overall statistical 'correctness' rather than single hits or misses of judgment." (1956, p. 34.) It would, we predict, produce a hit-maximizing strategy more rapidly than conventional procedures that place a premium on learning specific responses and on constructing perfectly valid small hypotheses. (An educational analogy would be to reward the pupil for using letter sequences in spelling which are commonly correct in English words regardless of their rightness in the specific word tested–compare Bruner, 1957, p. 48.) This suggestion has some resemblance to the "quickening" of feedback in the pursuit experiments of Taylor (1957), in which S is given benefit of experience he could otherwise accumulate only slowly; see also the remarks of Baker and Young (1960) on "block feedback" in the training of skills. [Cronbach's prediction has been confirmed directly in a study by Todd and Hammond; in press: Ed.]

To pursue further the analogy between tracking and concept-attainment: one might present a continuously variable display in which cross and circle are moved by cams. The S could move a level to indicate on a continuous scale the value of k at each moment, and could be given an on-target signal, perhaps through earphones. This would not allow for probabilistic feedback like that used here, but equivocality could be introduced in Smedslund's manner.

to make by way of summary is the intricacy of S's behavior when he attempts to deal rationally with an equivocal environment. Several of the facts observed in this experiment run counter to reports from other studies of concept-attainment with probabilistic feedback; much more experimentation is required to learn how results depend on experimental conditions.

REFERENCES

Atkinson, R. C., W. H. Bogartz, and R. N. Turner. Supplementary report: discrimination learning with probabilistic reinforcement schedules. *J. exp. Psychol.*, 1959, *57*, 349–350.

Azuma, H. Comparison of a correlational with a probabilistic approach to concept learning. Unpublished Ph.D. dissertation, University of Illinois, 1960.

Baker, C. H., and Phyllis Young. Feedback during training and retention of motor skills. *Canad. J. Psychol.*, 1960, *14*, 257–264.

Bourne, L. E. Personal communication, 1962.

Bricker, P. D. The identification of redundant stimulus patterns. *J. exp. Psychol.*, 1955, *49*, 73–81.

Bruner, J. S. Going beyond the information given. In H. Gruber, K. Hammond, and R. Jessor (Ed.), *Contemporary approaches to cognition.* Cambridge, Mass.: Harvard University Press, 1957, pp. 41–70.

Bruner, J. S., Jacqueline J. Goodnow, and G. A. Austin. *A study of thinking.* New York: Wiley, 1956.

Brunswik, E. Organismic achievement and environmental probability. *Psychol. Rev.*, 1943, *50*, 255–272.

Brunswik, E. Reasoning as a universal behavior model and a functional differentiation between "perception" and "thinking." Fourteenth International Congress of Psychol., Montreal, 1954.

Brunswik, E. *Perception and the representative design of psychological experiments.* Berkeley, Calif.: Univ. of California Press, 1956.

Bush, R. R., and F. Mosteller. *Stochastic models for learning.* New York: Wiley, 1955.

Edwards, W. Reward probability, amount and information as determiners of sequential two alternative decisions. *J. exp. Psychol.*, 1956, *52*, 177–189.

Edwards, W. Probability learning in 1000 trials. *J. exp. Psychol.*, 1961, *62*, 385–394.

Estes, W. K. The statistical approach to learning theory. In S. Koch (Ed.), *Psychology: a study of a science, Vol. 2.* New York: McGraw-Hill, 1959. Pp. 380–491.

Estes, W. K., C. J. Burke, R. C. Atkinson, and J. P. Frankmann. Probabilistic discrimination learning, *J. exp. Psychol.*, 1957, *54*, 233–239.

Goodnow, Jacqueline J. Determinants of choice-distribution in two-choice situations. *Amer. J. Psychol.*, 1955, *68*, 106–116.

Goodnow, Jacqueline J., and L. Postman. Learning in a two-choice probability situation with a problem-solving setting. *J. exp. Psychol.*, 1955, *49*, 16–22.

Goodnow, R. E. The utilization of partially valid cues in perceptual identification. Unpublished Ph.D. dissertation, Harvard Univ., 1954.

James, W. H., and J. B. Rotter. Partial and 100% reinforcement under chance and skill conditions. *J. exp. Psychol.,* 1958, *55,* 397–403.

Jarrett, Jacqueline J. Strategies in risk-taking situations. Unpublished Ph.D. dissertation, Radcliffe College, 1951.

Morin, R. E. Factors influencing rate and extent of learning in the presence of misinformative feedback. *J. exp. Psychol.,* 1955, *49,* 343–351.

Pishkin, Vladimir. Effects of probability of misinformation and number of irrelevant dimensions upon concept identification. *J. exp. Psychol.,* 1960, *59,* 371–378.

Popper, Juliet, and R. C. Atkinson. Discrimination learning in a verbal conditioning situation. *J. exp. Psychol.,* 1958, *56,* 21–25.

Siegel, S. Decision making and learning under varying conditions of reinforcement. *Annals N.Y. Acad. Sci.,* 1961, *89,* 766–783.

Smedslund, J. *Multiple-probability learning.* Oslo: Akademisk Forlag, 1955.

Taylor, F. V. Simplifying the controller's task through display quickening. *Occup. Psychol.,* 1957, *31,* 120–125.

Todd, F. J. and K. R. Hammond. Differential feedback in two multiple — cue probability learning tasks. (*Abstract Amer. Psychol.,* 1964, *19,* 535–536.) (*Behav. Sci.,* in press.)

Tolman, E. C., and E. Brunswik. The organism and the causal texture of the environment. *Psychol. Rev.,* 1935, *42,* 43–77.

9

$\mathcal{N}oise$ $\mathcal{R}eduction$ in $\mathcal{P}erception$ [1]

HAROLD W. HAKE
ALBERT RODWAN
DANIEL WEINTRAUB

The term, noise reduction, represents a recent acquisition from communication theory and refers to the capability of a receiving system to separate aspects of input representing signal, the intelligible or desired aspects of reception, from inputs representing noise, the perturbating or undesired aspects of reception. A communication component that accomplishes this separation and suppresses noise shows a remarkable characteristic: it has a larger signal-to-noise ratio at its output than at its input.

Egon Brunswik wrote extensively about that sort of capability of the perceiver. After identifying sources of unreliability in perception, he could not, in fact, escape the obligation to explain how this unreliability is overcome. Such an explanation is necessarily a major part of any "probabilistic" theory of perception.

In his "probabilistic functionalism," unreliability was introduced as an aspect of the proximal cues at the receptor surfaces of the perceiver. The "ecological validity" of these cues was supposedly low in that they were a mixture of reliable information about the distal stimulus in the real world and perturbating factors.

The term, perturbation, may be misleading in this context unless it is given a general definition. Brunswik was more concerned with regular perturbations of input, introduced by changes in location and orientation or illumination of the distal stimulus, than in random or "noisy" sources of error. The distinction is not a useful one here, however, and we extend the definitions of noise and perturbation to include any aspect of input other than that aspect of most interest. For example, where a perceiver

1. The research reported here and the search for perceiver models in telecommunication engineering has been supported in part by the National Science Foundation under NSF G 4840 and NSF G 16352.

attempts to judge the size of an object, unknown variations in its distance from the point of observation may represent perturbation of input.

Given this more general definition, Brunswik's "lens model" of perception becomes a description of a communications system that includes a source (the distal stimulus), a noisy channel (proximal cues), and a receiver (the perceiver). The *achievement* of the perceiver is the valid reconstruction of, or inference about, the source of his input. To be valid, the end result of the perceptual process must represent the successful separation of the reliable (or relevant) aspects of input from the noisy, unreliable (or irrelevant) aspects. Brunswik's "perceptual achievements," then, are examples of noise reduction, a capability held in common with certain communication systems.

Brunswik's understanding of this capability seems to have derived from two concepts, one old and one new. The old concept was that of Helmholtz's "unconscious inference," which attributes to the perceiver the ability to consider his inputs unconsciously and to infer the nature of the distal stimulus. This is actually a description of a possible mode of action in noise reduction but suffers from a lack of explicit detail. The new concept derived from Brunswik's familiarity with some of the work of Shannon (1949) and Norbert Wiener (1949). The development of information theory had provided a measure of the informational content of a message defined in terms of the minimum number of independent, binary, equally-likely selections required to specify it completely. An easy generalization of the term, message, to include stimulation of a perceiver, then, provided a rather powerful tool, for it made possible the specification and evaluation of the informational content of stimulation, a common characteristic of all sorts of stimulus inputs.

An interesting and important concept arose to describe the message for which more than this minimum number of selections is required in order to completely specify the message. This is the case, of course, where the selections are not independent, that is, where message units show intercorrelations. Such messages were described as *redundant*. The concept of message redundancy and its role in protecting against errors of transmission were known to Brunswik and were used as important explanatory principles in the description of the achievement of the perceiver. This is evident in a restatement of his theoretical position in the language of information theory:

Whenever the "capacity" of a channel is less than the richness of variability of the source from which it accepts messages, the channel is "overloaded." In this case no code will reduce the error frequency as low as one may please.

Shannon and Weaver point out that regardless of how clever one is with the coding process, it will always be true that after the signal is received there remains some undesirable (noise) uncertainty about what the message was.

The crux of organismic adjustment which we have studied in this book may be rephrased in quite a similar way: distal perceptual and behavioral mediation must, in the nature of things, in the general case rely on overloaded channels, and the limited dependability of all achievement mechanisms is the result of this overloading. And we must further note that at least part of the trouble lies with the overloading and noise in the external rather than the internal medium.

According to Shannon and Weaver, the chances of error can be decreased by "redundancy," however. Redundancy may be exemplified by, but is by no means restricted to, verbal repetitiveness. When there is noise there is some advantage in not using a coding process that eliminates all redundancy, for the remaining redundancy helps combat the uncertainty of transmission.

The reader will recognize that the vicariousness of psychological cues and means which we have come to acknowledge as the backbone of stabilized achievement may be viewed as a special case of receiving or sending messages through redundant, even though not literally repetitive channels. The probability of error, given by the variety of possible causes, or effects, that could result in, or be produced by, the type of event in question can thus be minimized. This is the case, for example, in the gain of the overall functional validity (.99) over the ecological validity of the major retinal cue (.70) in our representative survey of size constancy in which the organism acts as an intuitive statistician. . . . (Brunswik, 1956, pp. 142–143.)

This is essentially a suggestion about the role of input redundancy in the remarkable noise suppression that the perceiver achieves. It suffers from a notion that we all seemed to share some years ago in our early enchantment with information theory. The mistake is clearly stated in an excellent review of the subject by Frick (1959) who emphasized again that information theory is a formal rather than a substantive theory. It is an extension of correlation theory, not a model of action or behavior. It can describe quantitatively the efficiency of a perceiver's action, but it cannot alone explain how this efficiency is achieved. It can indicate that perceivers show more noise reduction for redundant inputs, but it does not suggest modes of action to account for this fact. When viewed in this way, Brunswik's statement merely says that inferences about the distal stimulus are made more effectively when proximal stimulation is redundant.

From an engineering point of view this is a deficient statement because it neglects the most critical aspect of the system, the perceiver, in which the crucial noise reduction occurs. It has been our intention to provide more explicit statements about the kind of receiver action represented in visual perception. This intention has led us to the consideration of the general principles that have been applied to the problem of suppressing noise in communication systems of all conceivable kinds.

The search for such principles leads beyond information theory to communication theory. This more general theory includes information theory, noise theory, and statistical decision theory (Goldman, 1953; Middleton, 1960). It has, as an important objective, a systematic approach to the design of optimal communication systems of various fundamental types, including physical, biophysical, and psychophysical mechanisms of communication. This objective naturally leads to the detailed consideration of principles of receiver action.

A first function of receivers in a communication channel is a familiar one, that of decoding. This is a crucial function in engineering practice because transmitted information is usually encoded at the source (transmitter) for transmission through some medium (channel). The most familiar encoding and decoding operations consist of the modulation and demodulation of a carrier.[2] In amplitude modulation (AM) radio broadcasting the receiver must detect a radio frequency carrier of constant frequency and respond to the modulation of its amplitude in time. Similarly, the frequency modulation (FM) receiver must respond to the frequency modulation of a carrier of constant amplitude. Demodulation is a common function of receivers because of the widespread use of modulated carriers as a general solution to the problem of communicating over distances through noisy channels. Because of these problems and because the methodology of modulation tends to be specific to particular engineering applications, the receiver function, demodulation, is not easy to generalize to analogous functions in human perception.

There is one exception. This is the case of speech production, where the mouth parts determining speech sounds move relatively slowly. The mouth is too small to be an efficient radiator at wavelengths corresponding to this low frequency of operation; and a much higher carrier frequency, the laryngeal tone, is generated and modulated by the articulators. In perceiving speech we respond to this modulation of the laryngeal tone. Because the tone can be efficiently radiated, the modulation carrying the information tends not to be lost in ambient noise.

However, in the case of visual perception, apart from interesting

2. Goldman (1953) defines modulation as the deviation of a signal from a prescribed standard pattern. For a typical AM radio station the standard pattern is an electromagnetic radiation of constant frequency (the carrier). The message broadcasted varies the amplitude of the carrier. Hence, the unmodulated carrier conveys no information; the information is conveyed by the departure of the carrier from its standard pattern.

speculation on the matter (for example, Attneave, 1954; Hake, 1957; Hochberg, 1953; and Rashevsky, 1955), we have difficulty in specifying the carrier, those aspects of stimulation that convey no information, from carrier modulation, those aspects of stimulation that carry the desired information. It does seem obvious, though, that the great mass of daily visual and auditory input for all of us is highly redundant and predictable. What happens in our daily worlds changes slightly from day to day and the objects and persons involved very seldom change in any marked fashion. Perhaps if all possible, conceivable, and perceivable kinds of visual inputs are considered, as much as 99 percent of normal, daily input is completely predictable. This portion could be considered to be visual "carrier"; the remaining unpredictable portion to be message. The generalized communication task of the perceiver, then, is that of separating the unpredictable (message) from the predictable (carrier), the changed from the unchanged.

As a demodulator, the receiver is part of a system designed to prevent noise sources from having any appreciable effect upon information transmission. A more interesting receiver function must occur in cases where the noise is present in a received message *after* demodulation. Some receiver component then has the task of separating that portion of the received mixture that originated at the message source from that portion of the received mixture that is attributable to sources of noise.

In certain cases this may be accomplished in a simple fashion. In the case of electromagnetic signaling, it sometimes happens that the perturbating noise average frequency or the average amplitude differs from the average values of the signal frequencies or amplitudes. The receiver may then act as a simple filter and absorb all inputs in the frequency band typical of the noise. Suppression of the noise would be satisfactory in that case, provided the noise and signal characteristics were sufficiently different. In practice this sort of signal-noise separation often forms a part of the demodulation operation at the receiver.

All similar receiver actions may be understood as examples of the occurrence of *generalized filtering,* in which the sensitivity of the receiver represents that of an absolutely tuned filter responding in a continuous way to the magnitude of the input to which it is tuned. Magnitudes of signal-to-noise ratio (S/N) at the input will show a continuous and simple relationship to magnitudes of S/N at the output of the receiver.

For example, the AM receiver tuned to a particular carrier frequency will produce, as an output, the message determining the modulation of the AM carrier. All perturbating noise will be filtered out except for noise which acts to modulate the carrier to which the receiver is tuned. Where noise is in the same frequency range as the message, the receiver does not discriminate between carrier modulation due to the message and carrier modulation due to that noise. Hence the noise will appear in the output of the receiver. If the receiver were moved away from the transmitter, more and more noise sources would act on the carrier during transmission and more and more noise would be heard in the receiver output. This continuous relationship between the S/N at the receiver input, which is decreased by moving the receiver farther away from the transmitter, and the S/N at the receiver output is shown in Figure 1 by

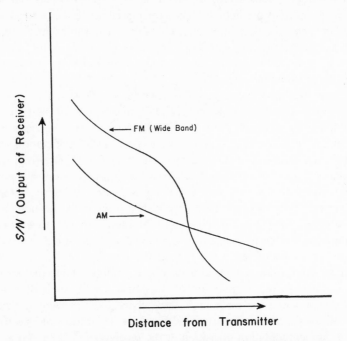

Fig. 1. The relation between the output S/N and input S/N (distance from transmitter) for AM and FM broadcast reception. The curve for the FM case illustrates noise suppression above a threshold and signal suppression below. (Stanford Goldman, Information Theory. © 1953. By permission of Prentice-Hall, Inc.)

the curve marked "AM." Such a continuous function is characteristic of receivers acting as simple filters eliminating a proportion of the undesired noise in the mixture of noise and message arriving as input. The function results from the crucial fact that, when the noise invades the range of frequencies typical of the message, the receiver cannot know which of its inputs in that range is noise and which message.

In order to act as an efficient filter, of course, the AM receiver must maintain a special sensitivity for the frequency of the carrier to which it is tuned and for the range of frequencies characteristic of the modulation due to message and a special insensitivity for all other frequencies. That is, the receiver must maintain an *absolute* calibration with respect to frequency. A receiver whose tuning (calibration) drifts with time eliminates less noise and produces less message at its output.

The suggestion is frequently made that filtering is a characteristic of human perception, that the perceiver shows special sensitivity for certain classes of inputs. The plausibility of a filtering operation in visual perception stems partly from our knowledge of receptor action. We know of the visual luminosity function, for example, which describes the relative sensitivity of the visual system for monochromatic lights. We may, therefore, consider the visual system as a filtering system, a filter peaked at 555 mμ for normal daylight vision. The principle appears, superficially, to extend to far more complex sorts of sensitivities and discriminations. Discussions of the topic of visual recognition have long included other assumptions about the occurrence of recognition by means of the correspondence between a presented stimulus and a stored standard, or "trace," of prior stimulation. The storage of standards, templates, or schemata, for comparison with stimulation has been discussed by Bartlett (1932), Vernon (1955), Attneave (1957), and Bruner (1957), among others. These discussions assume, in essence, that a complex filtering function is performed, in which the perceiver shows special sensitivity for certain inputs because of the existence of internal absolute standards matching the characteristics of these inputs.

The considerations involved in maintaining the required absolute calibration in the perceptual system have never been adequately considered, however. In fact, this complex system, which is sensitive to intensity, wavelength, and complexity of light as well as complex aspects of spatial patterning, discourages speculation about possible mechanisms. The existence of absolute calibration in human visual perception should not be taken for granted. Certainly, much of the work in this area has been devoted to the topic of explaining the lack of absolute calibration rather than its existence (Hake, 1957).

Another sort of noise reduction is possible for receivers capable of *smoothing* and *prediction* operations (Goldman, 1953; Wiener, 1949). These capabilities are most easily described in the case of univariate signals varying in time. Where a perturbating action deletes portions of such a transmitted signal, for example, receivers can be devised which are capable of supplying signal values for the missing portions of receiver input. Or, if the noise acts to alter message values, certain receivers can adjust input values to conform to most probable values. These functions require that the transmitted message show certain time-dependent characteristics, that is, that it be redundant. When a message does show such redundancies in time, receivers can use the past history of the received message to adjust input values to conform to the best predictions that can be made from a knowledge of the history of that signal (and from the history of all messages like it).

Such receivers, in effect, act to *reconstruct* a transmitted message. In describing the reconstructed message at the output of the receiver, two descriptive terms may be used: *fidelity* and *coherence*. The term, fidelity, refers to the correlation between the message as originally sent and the message as reconstructed. In perception we imply the same thing by the term *veridicality*. The coherence of the receiver output refers to a different characteristic: the *plausibility* of the reconstructed signal, the extent to which the reconstructed signal is complete and consistent with the rules of the transmission system and the language of the message. A receiver output may not be identical to the message as transmitted and yet show complete coherency.

As an example, we may think of a person trying to listen to a talker in a very noisy room. If asked to repeat what he has heard, the listener will try to produce a series of English words showing consistency with the way in which such words are used. His reconstructed message is not likely to reproduce exactly what was said, but it will be a plausible example of spoken English.

The term *coherence detection* is applied to the action of receivers that separate aspects of reception conforming to a coherence standard from aspects that do not conform. In the case of the listener described, the speech he reports hearing corresponds to a standard of coherence consisting of the probability rules governing the appearance of English speech sounds. The net effect is to show special sensitivity for the sounds occurring in temporal patterns representing the essential redundant aspects of English speech.

This special sensitivity can be made explicit. The best known experimentation relevant to the matter was produced by Miller, Bruner, and Postman (1954) who constructed words to conform to several "orders of approximation" to English words. *Zero-order* words consisted of eight letters drawn at random from the alphabet. In the *first-order* words the likelihood of appearance of each letter conformed to the relative frequency of appearance of the letters in English text. In the *second-order* words the probabilities of pairs of letters conformed to the probability of each pair in text. In the *third-order* words triads of letters conformed to the likelihood of triads in text, and so forth. Another way of describing the words is to state that, with increasing order of approximation, the words showed greater and greater coherence with English text. No actual English words were used.

When such words were flashed on a screen, one at a time, the proportions of letters correctly identified by observers were related to the order of approximation of the words. The general result is shown in Figure 2.

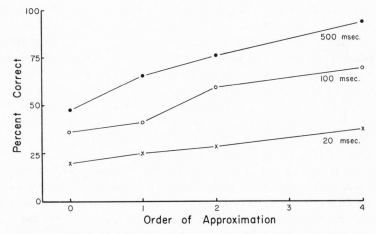

Fig. 2. A comparison of the extent to which subjects could recognize eight-letter nonsense "words" when briefly exposed. The order of approximation of the words refers to the extent to which they reflect the sequential restrictions on letter appearance in English words. (From Miller, Bruner, & Postman's "Familiarity of letter sequences and tachistoscopic identification." *J. gen. Psychol.*, 1954, 129–139.)

As a coherence-detector, the observer, whenever unable to perceive a letter presented in a flash, suggested a letter in its place. This suggested letter, since the standard of coherence is assumed to be the English language, would conform to the general probability rules determining the appearance of letters, especially in the context of any letters discernible in the flash. This is a good "guessing tactic" for guessing the missing letters of the higher-order words, but it is a less effective tactic for guessing the missing letters of the lower-order words. The sequences of letters produced by observers and the higher-order words themselves were both coherent with English; and therefore, with each other. In the case of letter sequences produced by observers trying to perceive the lower-order words, these sequences would be coherent with English text, while the stimulus words are not. Thus the verbal guessing habits of the observers can produce, at least partially, the effect shown in Figure 2 without assuming any special ability to *see* words that are coherent with English text. This is, of course, an extension of an important principle stated by Goldiamond and Hawkins (1958); and it predicts a higher score for the higher-order words than for the lower-order words even for a flash duration of zero, provided the trials are sufficiently numerous.

The discussion has emphasized the case of the univariate signal varying in time. We may speak also of coherence-detection in the case of a multivariate signal showing correlations among input values arriving simultaneously at the receiver. Receivers can be devised to show special sensitivity for coordinated variation in the several dimensions of variation of such a signal in time. This represents selectivity for redundancy evident across dimensions at any moment.

A simple example is provided by a receiver with two unidimensional channels of input and with the same signal source determining variation in the two channels. The sources of noise acting on the two channels are assumed to be random sources which tend to produce momentary values that are dissimilar and unrelated in the two channels. Such a receiver could achieve noise reduction if it accepted coordinated variation in the two channels as representing the original signal and uncoordinated variation as representing perturbation. This provides a means for discriminating between signal and noise, even though the signal and noise momentary values were in the same frequency and amplitude ranges. The addition of further redundant channels would permit still further noise reduction; these added channels would, in effect, provide further degrees of freedom for the task of detecting differences between signal and noise.

A crucial characteristic of this illustrative receiver is that it need not have a stored standard of coherence, such as the probability rules governing the generation of the original signal in time. It simply produces as a reconstructed signal whatever variation appears as the dominant, co-ordinated variation in the several input channels. Hence, it is said to have standards of coherence *imposed by input*. When the noise perturbation of the input channels is small and uncoordinated, then the original signal imposed on all channels will determine the variation in the majority of channels; that is, it will provide the standard of coherence for the receiver. When the noise perturbation is very large, however, it can effectively determine variation in all channels and provide the standard. In that case, the output of the receiver would consist entirely of noise. This illustration provides the conditions in which the *noise-improvement threshold* occurs. Above it, signal provides the standard of coherence, and noise is suppressed; below it, noise provides the standard, and signal is suppressed (Goldman, 1953).

The frequency modulation (FM) receiver acts in this way and shows a threshold of this type. It responds to the relations between the sidebands (new frequencies generated by the modulation of the carrier frequency) and the modulated carrier frequency itself. When the signal aspect of the signal and noise mixture is relatively large (large S/N) at the receiver input, the sideband frequencies vary essentially in unison with the carrier frequency. This coordinated behavior provides information about the transmitted signal and permits noise suppression, the familiar "clean-up" effect in FM reception. At some low level of the input S/N, however, the noise swamps the inputs and large amounts of signal-suppression occur. This special selectivity of the FM receiver for signals radiated from nearby transmitters and its special insensitivity for distant stations is illustrated in Figure 1. The output of the FM receiver shows noise suppression (relative to the behavior of the AM receiver at the same distance from the receiver) above a threshold value of input S/N and signal suppression below (Goldman, 1953).

The three important concepts arising in the description of FM reception are:

1. the use of coherence standards imposed by the nature of input;
2. the possibility of signal-suppression or noise-suppression because of the use of these imposed standards, and
3. the noise-improvement threshold defined between these two types of suppressive operations.

Although these concepts would seem to have important implications for the understanding of perception, they have not crucially influenced thought in psychology. Their implications have not been lost in engineering, however:

In the practical reception of signals, whether audio, television, or radar, the final human observer usually adds a large and important amount of effective noise reduction. A human observer will weight intelligible speech much higher than "gibberish" as being parts of the signal, and the human observer will even fill in the gaps where noise makes the signal unintelligible. As soon as the signal can be recognized as belonging to a customary type of communication signal, such as speech or music, the human perception mechanism gives greatly preferred weighting on the average, to true signals as compared with noise and greatly decreases the previous probability that the signal is noise fluctuation. This human "perception selectivity" is thus another example of generalized selectivity.

Perception selectivity, like other noise-reducing systems, has a threshold below which it will not operate. The threshold at which perception selectivity begins may be roughly described as the S/N level at which the signal can be recognized as belonging to the transmission "language." At this level the human perception mechanism recognizes parts of the mixed signal and noise as coming from a common origin; that is, it recognizes them as parts of a coherent signal. This level may be described as the intelligibility threshold, and is the noise-improvement threshold of a human being as a signal detector. It is probable that perception selectivity begins at a lower S/N ratio than any nonliving type of noise-improvement system so far devised. (Goldman, 1953, pp. 216–217.)

All of these concepts, of course, are not entirely new to the psychologist. The concept of noise-suppression has been a necessary one in some areas of research; that is, the study of visual acuity. Our inability to account for the fineness of visual acuity in terms of the properties of the geometric retinal image or the receptor mosaic has led to the development of several theories of visual acuity. In one way or another these theories attempt to account for the noise suppression that must occur in vision for fine detail (Senders, 1948; Falk, 1956). To date, our ability to specify the sources of noise (such as factors that blur the retinal image) has exceeded our ability to specify the mechanisms by which clarification occurs, although the recent fine work of Ratliff (1961) describes a possible neurological mechanism that could be elaborated to account for part of this effect.

The description of coherence-detection by means of a standard of coherence *supplied by input* has some familiarity also. Helson (1959) has explicitly suggested the existence of internal standards to which stimulation is referred and has specified how this standard is determined by very recent stimulation. This standard, the adaptation-level, is a simple coherence standard. Its application permits the observer to "make sense of" discrete stimulus inputs by ordering them on a dimension, or dimensions, containing the standard.

Perhaps the most intriguing concept described by Goldman is *perception selectivity*, which is suggested to operate above a threshold level of input and not below. The implication is that perceptual performance is not continuous at all levels of input. Rather there is a level of input above which one type of performance is possible and below which it is not. This is not a familiar type of threshold behavior in psychology; and, in fact, it is being discussed here at a time when even the existence of thresholds in sensory psychophysical relationships is being seriously questioned (Swets, 1961).

The threshold of perception selectivity in general can have a special definition, however, which makes it unlike the old concept of absolute threshold. Roughly, it is defined in Figure 1 by the comparison between the curve marked "AM" and the curve marked "FM." When both types of receivers are close to the transmitter, the FM receiver achieves more noise suppression. It has a higher S/N at its output, that is, shows greater "perception selectivity" for the signal. Where both receivers are distant from the transmitter, the FM receiver achieves less noise suppression than does the AM receiver. The crossover point for the two curves in this case is the noise-suppression threshold for the FM receiver, and the definition has general meaning only when the performance of the FM receiver is referred to the performance of the AM receiver.[3]

In our work reported here, we give that type of general definition to the term *perception selectivity threshold*. It refers to the point of crossover of curves describing the performance of different hypothetical perceptual mechanisms or of actual performances under different conditions of observation or stimulation. The types of simple hypothetical mechanisms explored are models based upon the crucial difference existing between the "AM" and "FM" cases that have been considered: the FM receiver acts to discriminate between momentary input values due to the action of signal and momentary input values due to the action of noise, while for momentary input values in the same frequency and amplitude ranges, the AM receiver responds to both. The implications of these two modes of action are made explicit in comparing a simple *discriminating* model and a simple *nondiscriminating* model.

THE SIMPLE PERCEPTUAL MODELS

In describing these models we imply a generalized perceptual situation in which a perceiver receives, as an input on each of a series of discrete trials, a mixture of signal (S) and noise (N).

1. On each trial the perceiver receives the combination S_jN_i; for example, $j = 1, 2,$ or 3 and $i = 1, 2,$ or 3.
2. For the sake of simplicity we assume that on half the trials the combination arrives as S_jN_i, and on the other half it arrives as N_iS_j. These two types of trials are mixed in random order. Each of the nine combinations of S_jN_i occur with equal frequency.

3. The noise suppression threshold can be defined in terms of the shape of the curve for the FM receiver alone.

The Nondiscriminating Model

In this model, the perceiver does not attempt to discriminate between S and N in the input on each trial. He simply combines their values in some way.

1. Explicitly, it is assumed that the combination of the value of S_j and the value of N_i can be perceived, while the components cannot be separately perceived. That is, the value of the combination, $S_j + N_i$, can be perceived, whereas the values S_j or N_i cannot be perceived separately.
2. The perceiver assigns one of three permissible responses to the combined value of the input. He does so by the following decision rules:

   If $S_j + N_i \leqq 3, r = 1$
   If $S_j + N_i = 4, r = 2$
   If $S_j + N_i \geqq 5, r = 3$

   This assigns responses to the combination S_jN_i as shown in Table 1.
3. Under the conditions specified, the assignment of responses to inputs during 450 trials would be as shown in Table 2. These three matrices collapse to the single matrix of Table 3, showing the relationship of r to S_j. Also shown is the definition of the *contingent uncertainty*, $U(r:S)$, a measure of the amount of nonmetric correlation between stimuli and responses (see Garner, 1962, pp. 59–62). In this case, the value of the contingent uncertainty is .4468. If the perceiver had assigned responses to the S_j as efficiently as possible, the value would be 1.5850.

TABLE 1. THE ASSIGNMENT OF RESPONSES TO THE S_jN_i BY THE NONDISCRIMINATING PERCEIVER.

		S_j		
		1	2	3
	1	r_1	r_1	r_2
N_i	2	r_1	r_2	r_3
	3	r_2	r_3	r_3

TABLE 2. THE ASSIGNMENT OF RESPONSES TO S_jN_i DURING 450 TRIALS. ASSIGNMENT RULES SHOWN IN TABLE 1.

N_1		S_j		
		1	2	3
	1	50	50	
r	2			50
	3			

N_2		S_j		
		1	2	3
	1	50		
r	2		50	
	3			50

N_3		S_j		
		1	2	3
	1			
r	2	50		
	3		50	50

TABLE 3. THE COMPUTATION OF THE CONTINGENT UNCERTAINTY, $U(r:S)$. DATA FROM TABLE 2.

		S_j			
	1	2	3		
1	100	50		$\overline{U(r)}$	$= 1.5850$
r 2	50	50	50	$\overline{U_s(r)}$	$= 1.1382$
3		50	100	$\overline{U(r:S)} =$	$.4468$

$$U(r:s) = U(r) - U_s(r)$$

The Discriminating Model

In this model the perceiver does attempt to discriminate between that aspect of input which is S and that aspect which is N. He is, however, not very good at it.

1. On each trial the perceiver, making a forced choice, must state which aspect of input is S and which is N. Since on each trial either the combination SN or else the combination NS is presented and the perceiver must state that the combination was SN or else NS, the conditions of the forced-choice method are fulfilled, and the rate at which the perceiver emits each type of response, "that aspect of input is noise" or "that aspect of input is signal," is fixed.
2. The perceiver operates with a certain hit rate (HR) and false alarm rate (FAR) in the task of identifying the aspects of input which are S and N.
$$HR = p(\text{"}S\text{"}/S)$$
where $p(\text{"}S\text{"}/S)$ is the conditional probability, given that a particular aspect of input is S, that the perceiver will identify it as S.
$$FAR = p(\text{"}S\text{"}/N)$$
where $p(\text{"}S\text{"}/N)$ is the conditional probability of noise being identified as signal. Since the situation is forced choice with two alternatives,
$$HR + FAR = 1.$$
3. We assume first that this perceiver cannot, in fact, discriminate between S and N; that is,
$$HR = FAR = .50.$$
This means that on half the trials the aspect of input, which is S, will be identified as S and on half the trials N will be identified as S. These are ("S"/S) and ("S"/N) trials, respectively. On the ("S"/S) trials, the per-

TABLE 4. THE ASSIGNMENT OF RESPONSES TO THE S_jN_i ON THE ("S"/S) TRIALS.

			S_j	
		1	2	3
	1	r_1	r_2	r_3
N_i	2	r_1	r_2	r_3
	3	r_1	r_2	r_3

ceiver assigns responses to the S_j according to the simple rule illustrated in Table 4. That is, he assigns the responses to the S_j without error. On the ("S"/N) trials, however, the perceiver unwittingly assigns responses to the N_i, as shown in Table 5. The combination of the two types of trials, in a total of 450, yields the three matrices of Table 6 and the collapsed matrix of Table 7. The computation of $U(r:S)$ for the matrix of Table 6 yields the value .3401. The perceiver who tries (and fails) to discriminate between

TABLE 5. THE ASSIGNMENT OF RESPONSES TO THE S_jN_i ON THE ("S"/N) TRIALS.

		S_j		
		1	2	3
	1	r_1	r_1	r_1
Ni	2	r_2	r_2	r_2
	3	r_3	r_3	r_3

TABLE 6. THE ASSIGNMENT OF RESPONSES TO THE S_jN_i BY THE DISCRIMINATING PERCEIVER. ASSIGNMENT RULES SHOWN IN TABLE 3 AND TABLE 4.

N_1		S_j			N_2		S_j			N_3		S_j		
		1	2	3			1	2	3			1	2	3
	1	50	25	25		1	25				1	25		
r	2		25		r	2	25	50	25	r	2		25	
	3			25		3			25		3	25	25	50

TABLE 7. THE COMPUTATION OF THE CONTINGENT UNCERTAINTY, $U(r:S)$. DATA FROM TABLE 5.

		S_j	
	1	2	3
1	100	25	25
2	25	100	25
3	25	25	100

$U(r)\ \ = 1.5850$

$U_s(r)\ = 1.2447$

$U(r:S) =\ \ .3401$

S and N does less well than the perceiver who does not make the effort and responds to the combined value of S and N.

4. However, if the discriminating perceiver gains in ability to discriminate between S and N, then he can do quite a bit better and can aspire to a performance of which the nondiscriminator is not capable. This can be demonstrated by computing values for $U(r:S)$ following the rules applied above but using values of HR in excess of .50. In Figure 3 is shown the relationship between $U(r:S)$ and HR for the discriminating perceiver. For any HR in excess of .57, the discriminating perceiver does better than the nondiscriminating perceiver. Below this crossover point, the reverse is true. The model for the discriminating perceiver illustrates the suppression of signal (due to the cases in which signal is perceived as noise) below crossover and the suppression of noise (due to the cases in which noise is identified as noise and disregarded) above crossover.

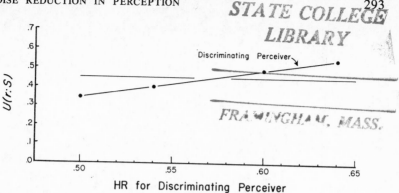

Fig. 3. A comparison of $U(r:S)$ for the *discriminating* perceiver model and the *nondiscriminating* model (horizontal line) as a function of the ability of the discriminator to distinguish between signal (S) and noise (N).

It is more interesting to study the behavior of these two models when the discriminating perceiver has a constant HR (say, $HR = .64$) and when the ability of both types of perceivers to resolve the values of S_j is varied.

1. The crucial aspect of performance is the ability to perceive the value of S_j. We term this the ability to *resolve S*. There are several ways in which this ability can be varied in the model. We chose a simple way by supposing two types of trials. In the first type, the *noiseless trials,* the value of S_j and the value of N_i can be resolved as before. Of course, the perceiver still has the task of discriminating which aspect is S and which is N. In the second type, the *noisy trials,* the value of N_i can be resolved, but not the value of S_j.
2. Five conditions are considered. In the first, all trials are noiseless. In the second condition, 76 percent of the trials are noiseless. In the third condition, 60 percent are noiseless; in the fourth, 40 percent are noiseless; and in the fifth condition, 24 percent of the trials are noiseless.
3. For the nondiscriminating perceiver, noiseless trials are assigned to the cells of Table 1, as before, in order to determine the response assignments. Noisy trials are also assigned to Table 1, but they are assigned systematically to the N_i (assigned by columns) only. Within columns, the noisy trials are assigned randomly to the rows.
4. For the discriminating perceiver we treat noiseless trials as before (Table 4 and Table 5), the number of (*"S"/S*) and (*"S"/N*) trials being determined by HR. Among the noisy trials, the HR determines a number of (*"S"/S*) trials in which signal is taken as signal. The value of S_j cannot be resolved on these trials and the response is chosen randomly. In the remaining noisy trials, the perceiver accepts N as S and so the responses are assigned as in Table 5.
5. Following those rules, a value of $U(r:S)$ was computed for each model per-

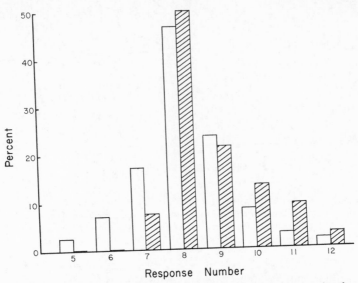

Fig. 4. Distribution in percent of responses made to stimulus card #8 when size varied alone (clear bars) and when hue varied alone (cross-hatched bars). From these distributions inferences can be made about response potentials evoked by the hue and size together. (From Eriksen & Hake, 1955, "Multidimensional stimulus differences and accuracy of discrimination," *JEP,* 1955, *50,* 153–160.)

ceiver (discriminating and nondiscriminating) and for each of the five conditions of signal resolution. These are plotted in Figure 4. The crossover effect is again evident. For series with fewer than about 60 percent noise-free trials, the nondiscriminating perceiver provides more information in his responses about S_j than does the discriminating perceiver. For series with more than 60 percent noise-free trials, the discriminating perceiver excels.

6. We present also, in Figure 5, the set of $U(r:S)$ computed for a discriminating perceiver with a HR of .60. This perceiver does less well, at his best, than the perceiver with a HR of .64, but he does better, at his worst.

In summarizing the implications of the assumptions underlying the discriminating and nondiscriminating perceiver models and their actions, it is useful to distinguish between two functions of perceivers and two principles of action.

The two functions include, first, the *discrimination* between signal input and noise input. This is the separation of input variability due to signal from the separation of input variability due to noise. The second function is that of *resolving power,* which refers to ability to identify values within the aspect of input designated as signal and within the

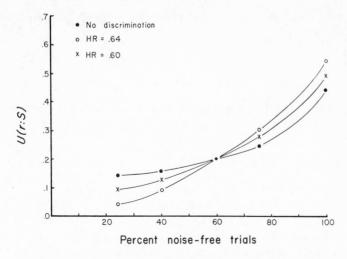

Fig. 5. A comparison of $U(r:S)$ for the *nondiscriminating* perceiver model and for two values of HR for the *discriminating* model. "Noise-free trials" refers to trials on which the value of S_j can be resolved.

aspect of input designated as noise. We have here considered two types of perceivers having the same resolving power (within each noise condition) but different abilities to discriminate between S and N. One perceiver discriminates not at all; the other discriminates with varying degrees of success.

In comparing the performances of these two simple perceiver models, two principles of action are evident:

1. When two perceivers have the same ability to discriminate between S and N, the perceiver with the better resolving power for values of S will always communicate more information about S.
2. When two perceivers have the same resolving power for values of S, the perceiver with the greater HR (ability to discriminate S from N) will communicate more information about the S if this resolving power is relatively high for both, and less information if this resolving power is relatively low for both.

The second principle is a statement of the conditions under which the *perception selectivity threshold* occurs in the performance of the simple discriminating perceiver model, relative to the performance of a perceiver model with a lower HR or relative to the performance of the nondiscriminating perceiver. These are extremely simple models operating in an elementary fashion. The principles evolved are stated in a sufficiently explicit fashion, however, to permit their extension to the performance of human observers. In any real observing situation, we need specify only:

1. What is S and what is N?
2. What is the *relative* ability of two observers to discriminate S from N?
3. What is the relative ability of two observers to resolve values of S_j?

Given these specifications, we can make some general statements about the relative abilities of observers as suppressors of noise.

THE PERFORMANCE OF REAL OBSERVERS

A familiarity with the research literature in the area of perception does not provide much that seems relevant to our topic. Research has not often been devised with the topic of noise suppression in mind. Some examples do exist in which a perceiver with a greater predicted ability to discriminate between relevant and irrelevant aspects of stimulation is shown doing a better job of providing information about the relevant aspect. However, we have restricted our consideration to situations in which a large range of perceiving conditions are considered, so that the better discriminating perceiver could be seen as doing both better and worse in providing information about the "signal" aspect of his inputs. That is, we have looked for, and have produced, perceptual situations in which the perception selectivity threshold can be demonstrated.

Absolute Judgment of Correlated Stimulus Dimensions

Eriksen and Hake (1955) demonstrated that absolute judgments of stimuli differing in two correlated dimensions were more reliable than were judgments of stimuli differing in either dimension varied alone. This was repeated here with the same result. In the multidimensional case, subjects judged stimulus cards bearing square color chips (Munsell) differing in hue and size. There were 12 cards, and each card presented a unique combination of size and hue of the chip; that is, hue and size were perfectly correlated. Absolute judgments (assigning the response numbers 1 through 12 to the cards presented in random order for 360 trials) yielded a value of 3.07 for $U(r:C)$, the contingent uncertainty between the subject's responses and the arbitrary card number. Where the cards differed only in the hue of the chip, with size of the chip held constant, $U(r:C)$ was 2.80 for the same number of trials. That is, in the task of assigning the proper response number to the cards, the addition of the size variable to the hue variable, where size and hue were perfectly correlated, was an assistance to the subject.

In accounting for this assistance, Eriksen and Hake assumed that judgment of the two dimensions on which the two cards varied was independent. The details of this assumption describe a noise-suppressive system:

1. At a given moment in time, the response tendency (rating) evoked by a magnitude on one dimension is independent of the response tendency evoked by magnitudes on other dimensions.
2. The distribution of response frequencies to a stimulus magnitude is a measure of the relative strengths of response tendencies elicited by that magnitude.
3. In the case of competing response tendencies, the stronger tendency will be evoked as a response. (1955, pp. 156–157.)

This system suppresses errors (the occurrence of a rating inappropriate for the stimulus card) because the distribution of response frequencies for a stimulus magnitude on either of the dimensions typically has a maximum for that magnitude (Fig. 5). For example, response 8 is the most likely response for the perception of both hue and size of card 8. However, if (as should occur in 16.8 percent of the appearances of card 8) the response 7 is evoked by its size, on 49.6 percent of those occasions response 8 is evoked by its hue and is the stronger tendency.

This is a simple system very much like the discriminating perceiver model considered earlier. In its most simple form the perceiver acts as though one of its inputs (hue or size) is a more reliable cue to the identity of the card. On a given trial, that dimension having the higher response tendency is designated as signal and the remaining dimension is designated as noise. The response tendency evoked by the latter is ignored. The subject's two functions on each trial, then, are:

1a. Decide which of two perfectly discriminable dimensions, hue or size, carries signal and which carries noise (which is most dependable), and
2a. resolve the value of the stimulus card by producing the response appropriate for the dimension which is considered signal.

This is not the same as the task performed by the discriminating perceiver model, but it can be shown to be completely equivalent. The perceiver model illustrates the instances in which:

1b. Signal and noise values, the S_j and the N_i, are completely uncorrelated and the perceiver discriminates to some extent between the aspect of input which is S and that which is N.

The Eriksen-Hake model illustrates the instance in which:

2b. The perceiver is completely unable to discriminate between the aspect of input which is S and that which is N, but the values of S and N, the S_j and the N_j, are at least partially correlated.

The latter statement may seem surprising, but it is true that in the Eriksen-Hake model the ability of the perceiver to discriminate between the hue and the size of the chip on each card does not help at all in discriminating which aspects reflect noise and which aspects reflect signal. And, if the correlation between S_j and N_i were reduced to zero, the subject would indeed be unable to demonstrate any noise suppression at all.

The situation in (1b) is completely describable in terms of the ability of the perceiver to discriminate between S and N. This ability can be described by the HR of the perceiver, as we did above, or by the value of $U(r{:}SN)$, which is the information transmitted by the perceiver about which aspect of input is signal and which aspect of input is noise. The situation in (2b) is completely describable in terms of the correlation between S and N. This can be provided by a product-moment correlation or by $U(S{:}N)$, the extent to which uncertainty about the momentary values of S_j is reduced by knowledge of the N_i.

As a matter of fact, either type of measure, a measure of ability to discriminate between S and N or a measure of the correlation between S and N, is equally good for describing either situation (1b) or situation (2b). The two situations are completely equivalent. The perceiver's discriminating characteristic can be described as a partial ability to discriminate between the uncorrelated dimensions S and N or else as a complete inability to discriminate between the partially correlated dimensions, S and N.[4]

The equivalence of statements (1b) and (2b) imply that, in the Eriksen-Hake judgmental situation, a decrease in the correlation between hue and size values occurring among the stimulus cards is equivalent to decreasing the ability of the subject to discriminate S from N. This correlation can be reduced by decreasing the correspondence between the hue and size of the chip. For example, in the case reported above, card 8 always presented hue 8 in combination with size 8. In the reduced correlation case, card 8 presented hue 8 in combination with size 8 half the time and in combination with size 7 half the time. With decreasing correlations, the two values of size, combined with hue 8 for card 8, became more and more divergent on the size dimension. This produces greater and greater overlap of size, each size appearing on a greater number of different cards. Thus, the hue of each card remained a perfectly reliable cue to the identity of the card but size became more ambiguous with decreasing correlation. Instead of there being just twelve cards to be

4. Or, in terms of the equivalent mixed case where the perceiver has partial ability to discriminate between partially correlated dimensions.

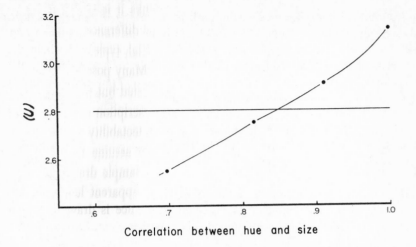

Fig. 6. Contingent uncertainty measures of performance of a subject identifying stimulus cards as a function of the product-moment correlation between the hue and the size of the color chip mounted on the card. The horizontal line represents performance when the size of the chip is constant on all cards. Each point was computed on the basis of 360 judgments.

judged, there were twenty-four, but these consisted of twelve pairs which could be identified perfectly by hue and less than perfectly by size.

The results are presented in Figure 6, with the uncertainty measure from the case where the subject judged hue alone providing a basis for comparison. The subject judging hue and size does both better and worse than the subject judging hue alone, depending upon the correlation between hue and size (or, equivalently, depending upon the subject's ability to discriminate between signal and noise). The data are interpreted to indicate that the subject judging size and hue does not give up his foolish ways and judge hue alone when the correlation between size and hue becomes less than about .85. He demonstrates instead the perception selectivity threshold defined earlier.

Absolute Judgment of Length

In the last section we considered the condition in which the correlation between stimulus values in separate dimensions could be explicitly controlled. Here we consider a condition in which the dimensions of input and their intercorrelations can be inferred only.

The situation considered is that in which a subject judges the length of a vertical line presented in the dark at a viewing distance of 2 feet. Two stimuli are used, one (*SL*) is 20 mm in height and the other (*TL*) is 20.3 mm in height. On a trial, one of these appears by itself in the dark and the subject indicates whether he thinks it is the short or the tall line. When duration of view is brief and the difference, ΔH, between *TL* and *SL* is small, the subject, from trial to trial, typically experiences a bewildering variety of apparent line lengths. Many possible sources of this variability in apparent length may be suggested but they may all be shown equivalent, in effect, to the following description of the situation in terms provided by the theory of signal detectability (Egan, 1958, Tanner, 1960; Tanner and Swets, 1954): We assume that when *SL* is presented, the experience of the subject is a sample drawn randomly from the left-hand hypothetical distribution of apparent lengths shown in Figure 7. When *TL* is presented, his experience is drawn from the

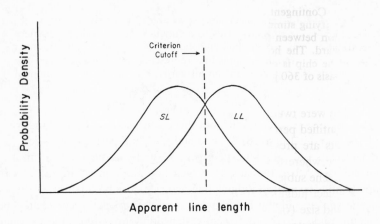

Fig. 7. The distributions of apparent line lengths from which one is sampled when either a short line (*SL*) or a tall line (*TL*) is viewed. The subject responds "long" to all apparent lengths longer than criterion cutoff and "short" otherwise.

right-hand distribution. Since there is considerable overlap in the two distributions, the subject must adopt a criterion of judgment ("criterion cutoff") and a decision rule. Apparent lengths greater than the criterion lead to the response "long." Then the ability of the subject to discriminate between *SL* and *TL* is defined by the equation

$$d' = \frac{\mu_{TL} - \mu_{SL}}{\sigma_h}$$

in which σ_h is the standard deviation of the right-hand distribution, and μ_{TL} and μ_{SL} are the means of the distributions.

These assumptions about the actions of the subject and the definition of his acuity in discriminating SL from TL actually specify the kind of perceiver the subject is. In effect, the subject makes no attempt to discriminate between aspects of his experience due to real line length, ΔH, and aspects due to the noise processes. Their effects are simply combined in some way and compared with a standard, the criterion cutoff. This conforms to the model of the nondiscriminating perceiver described earlier.

The source of the variability of experience, σ_h, when either TL or SL is presented, is a matter for speculation. The source may be considered to be some type of physiological noise. To the psychologist familiar with absolute judgments as a task, however, one likely source is the instability of the criterion cutoff itself. That is, variability of experience seems likely to be due to variation in the scale used in measuring and judging experiences. Where the instability of the cutoff, co, and the other sources of variability are independent, it does not matter which is considered to be the major source. Figure 8 shows the relationship between two views of the same problem. On the ordinate are the distributions of Figure 7, and it is assumed that σ_h is associated with some source of variability in the visual channels. On the abscissa is the hypothetical variability of the co (variability of scale). Together, these sources of variability produce the joint distributions of experiences over the plane shown. On the negative diagonal axis are the reflections of the values of the joint distributions and an absolutely stable cutoff, co'. For the distributions on the diagonal axis, we can compute a value of d'

$$d_1' = \frac{\mu_{TL}' - \mu_{SL}'}{\sigma_h'}$$

$$= \frac{TL - SL}{\sqrt{\sigma_h^2 + \sigma_{co}^2}}$$

That is, the ability of the subject may be considered as the ability to compare experiential samples drawn from the distributions on the negative diagonal with an absolutely stable co' or, equivalently, as the ability to compare samples from the more separated distributions on the ordinate with the somewhat more unstable co.

We present these two equivalent situations in this fashion to indicate the noise suppressive possibilities. Noise suppression can occur whenever the subject can manage to stabilize his judgmental criterion, co. This could be managed if input itself provided a means for the calibration of

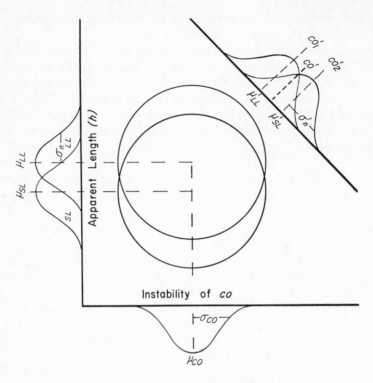

Fig. 8. The two apparent length distributions of Fig. 7 are on the ordinate and the instability of the criterion cutoff is represented on the abscissa. The resulting bivariate distributions of apparent length and cutoff instability are reflected on the diagonal axis to indicate the equivalent situation in which apparent lengths sampled from distributions with more overlap are judged relative to a stable criterion, co'. If cutoff instability and apparent length are positively correlated, then the bivariate distributions are ellipses and the reflected distributions on the diagonal axis have smaller variances. The measure, d', must then increase unless the subject also correlates the choice of his cutoff, co_1' or co_2' with the length of the stimulus line.

co. An obvious example is provided by the case in which a line of constant height is always presented along with the variable lines, SL or TL. The appearance of this constant line could provide a means for the calibration of co. If the constant-length line appeared unusually long, for example, the subject would know that lengths were being exaggerated in his experience and could adjust his co upward to compensate for this effect. This, in effect, would create a correlation between the co and experienced line height, h, *within* the joint distributions of Figure 8; and, then,

$$d_2' = \frac{\mu_{TL} - \mu_{SL}}{\sqrt{\sigma_h{}^2 + \sigma_{co}{}^2 - 2\rho_{h,co}\,\sigma_h\,\sigma_{co}}}$$

The value of d_2' depends upon the correlation, $\rho_{h,co}$, between perceived height of the stimulus line and *co within* the joint distributions of Figure 8. Where this correlation term is large, the uncontrolled variation is effectively removed from the situation.

This is suggested to be the noise-suppressive role of a constant aspect of stimulation. The subject judges the variable aspect relative to the constant aspect and this is equivalent to producing a correlation between his cutoff, *co,* and the variation of experience within stimulus states.

That is a neat trick because it means that the cutoff location becomes correlated with experienced line length without being affected by the real line length, H. A possibility of establishing such a *within* correlation without also establishing a *between* correlation exists in the experimental situation in which either *SL* or *TL* is presented in isolation, no constant aspect of stimulation being provided. The possibility arises when the subject views the stimuli binocularly.

We suppose that the aspect of variability, σ_h, may be associated with physiological processes in the visual channels and that these are at least partially independent in the two channels. Thus the "registered" line in one channel on a single trial may be larger or smaller than that in the other channel. If the subject views the stimulus line very briefly while maintaining proper fixation and accommodation, the line will be fused and only a single line experienced. With unequal registration in the two eyes some aneseikonia should result, the unequal registrations being transformed to changes in apparent orientation (tilting and leaning) of the single stimulus line seen. This provides an opportunity for the subject to distinguish between the variation in his experience due to the physiological noise processes in the two visual channels and the variation in his experience due to the actual length of the stimulus line. If ΔH is sufficiently large, his experience will be noticeably multidimensional. The noise processes in the two channels, being somewhat independent, should tend to produce variation in apparent orientation of the experienced line, while the size of the stimulus, H, leading to correlated effects in the two channels, should produce variation in the apparent length (or distance) of the stimulus. However the subject interprets the variation in his experience, with ΔH sufficiently large, he should be able to reliably identify two ways in which this variation may be classified.

The subject may then attempt to separate variation of these two sorts. He could do so, for example, by judging apparent size of the line while taking orientation into account. This would amount to an attempt to adjust the cutoff for size judgment on the basis of the apparent orientation of the line alone. With brief duration of view, or with small ΔH, it is not likely that the kinds of variation in experience, say, orientation and length of line, could be completely separated. In that case, cutoff adjustment would actually depend to some degree on perceived size as well as on perceived orientation. Conceptually this means:

1. If the subject can relate cutoff location to the experienced orientation of the line but not to its length, then

$$d_2' = \frac{\mu_{TL} - \mu_{SL}}{\sqrt{\sigma_h^2 + \sigma_{co}^2 - 2\rho_{h'co}\, \sigma_h\, \sigma_{co}}}$$

and considerable noise-suppression is possible depending upon the size of $\rho_{h,co}$.

2. If the subject relates the cut-off to experienced line length as well as to experienced line orientation, this may be conceptualized as the situation in Figure 8 when $\rho_{h'co} > 0$ but when co_1' is sometimes used when the tall stimulus is presented and co_2' is sometimes used when the short stimulus is presented. Then

$$d_2' = \frac{HR\,(\mu_{TL} - \mu_{SL}) - FAR\,(\mu_{TL} - \mu_{SL})\,^5}{\sqrt{\sigma_h^2 + \sigma_{co}^2 - 2\rho_{h'co}\, \sigma_h\, \sigma_{co}}}$$

in which $\rho_{h'co}$ depends upon the subject's ability to adjust the cut-off with respect to the experienced orientation of the line only, and HR and FAR refer to his ability to avoid adjusting the cut off location on the basis of experienced size (really, his ability to distinguish effects of H from the variation, σ_h). Where the latter ability is *nil* ($HR = .50 = FAR$), no discrimination is possible. Where this ability is perfect ($HR = 1.0$, $FAR = 0.0$), the relation between d' and d_2' (the amount of noise suppression possible) depends upon $\rho_{h'co}$.

In this conceptual scheme the possible advantage of binocular viewing is that it makes possible some discrimination between variation in experience due to real stimulus variation and variation in experience that arises from other sources. If this is the chief difference between binocular and monocular viewing in this judgmental situation, then the occurrence of a perception selectivity threshold can be predicted in the comparison of judgmental performance with binocular viewing and performance with monocular view. Binocular viewing should produce better discrimination where noise processes are relatively slight and worse discrimination where the noise processes are large.

5. Assuming that $HR + FAR = 1.0$.

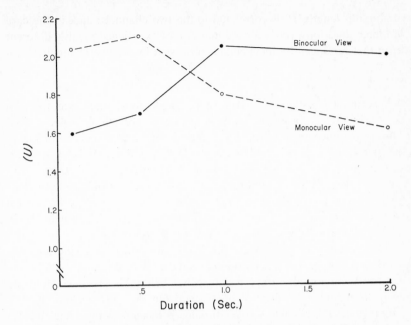

Fig. 9. Performance of a subject discriminating length of lines presented in the dark. The measure of performance is the contingent uncertainty measure and duration of view is described on the abscissa. Each point is based upon 125 trials.

In Figure 9 we present the relationship between d' and duration of view for binocular and for monocular viewing. In the case of each duration of view, 125 trials were run with $\Delta H = .3$ mm. In each trial the subject rated his confidence about whether the stimulus was tall or short and then he was told which stimulus had been presented. The tall stimulus appeared on half the trials and the identity of the stimulus on a particular trial was determined by a chance process. Between trials a very small fixation cross was fixated in the dark by the subject. For each set of 125 trials run under one of the viewing conditions and at a constant duration of view, a value of d' was computed following the methodology described by Egan (1959), Weintraub and Hake (1962), and others.

The perception selectivity threshold is evident in the comparison of the monocular and binocular conditions, suggesting that the chief difference associated with viewing conditions is a difference in ability to discriminate between real stimulus size and other factors as sources of variation in the experienced stimulus on each trial, rather than a difference in ability simply to *resolve* stimulus size. This is the logical outcome of assuming that duration-of-view controls the extent to which the effect of stimulus length, H, is correlated in the two channels; and, in the case of longer durations, produces a dimension of experience reliably different from that produced by independent processes in the two channels.

Constancy

Perceptual constancy is perhaps the single most important topic to persons interested in possible noise-suppressive operations in perception. This importance results from the supposition that a perceiver achieves the perception of objects having stable object-characteristics of size, surface color, texture, form, and so forth by suppressing all those viewing variables, such as illumination, viewing distance and angle, and so forth, which tend to alter apparent object characteristics in normal viewing. Here we describe a specific constancy-type situation in which the perception selectivity threshold can be demonstrated.

The subject looks through a small aperture down a viewing alley towards a homogeneous background located at a distance of 14 feet. He can see a horizontal surface just 6 inches below his eye and stretching away from him to a distance of 10 feet. On this surface, during each judgmental trial, a single square stimulus is located along a line running from the subject to the background. He looks at the face of the stimulus for the duration of view allowed and then judges its distance from him with the use of one of five response categories: very far, far, neither far nor near, near, very near. The stimulus squares differ in real distance and real size, there being five sizes and five distances. The five sizes are in the range from ¾ to 2 inches.

Distance 3 is always 72 inches. The other distances depend upon range. Four ranges were used and these are described in terms of the distance between adjacent possible locations of the stimuli: ½ inch, 1 inch, 2 inches, and 4 inches. For example, under the 4-inch range condition, stimulus 1 was located at 64 inches from the subject, stimulus 2 at 68 inches, 3 at 72 inches, 4 at 76 inches, and 5 at 80 inches. The five sizes and five distances combined orthogonally to produce twenty-five stimulus combinations, all presented equally often.

In considering noise-suppressive operations in this situation, two possibilities are evident:

1. If the size of the stimulus is S_j, the distance is D_i, and the stimulus combination is S_jD_i, then a special situation occurs when the perceiver cannot discriminate between S_jD_i (size j presented at distance i) and S_iD_j (size i presented at distance j). This is the situation of Table 1, in which the perceiver assigns responses to stimulus combinations without regard for which stimulus aspect is represented by rows or columns.

Real viewing of this sort must occur whenever there is no cue to the distance of the stimulus, as such, or its size. The perceiver can judge only the overall size of the combination relative to the context in which it appears. In this case the perceiver would have no hope of separating distance from size and would indiscriminately respond to both (that is, follow the "law of visual angle") in making judgments. In interpreting what was seen, the perceiver could assume the stimulus variation to be size variation, distance variation, or both, because the S_jD_i produce essentially unidimensional variation in experience. If, for example, size is the dominant aspect of real stimulus variation, the perceiver will have no basis on which to avoid experiencing this stimulus variation as *distance* variation. The introduction of greater real distance variation in the stimulus from trial to trial then would be experienced as new additional values on the same experiential dimensions and would lead to more errors because of confusion with the old values. This means that when the subject judges the *distance* of the stimulus-complexes, his responses will be most predictable when either distance or size variation is dominant from trial-to-trial in the stimulus combinations.

2. The other possibility is that the perceiver can distinguish between S_jD_i and S_iD_j. That is, his *experience* is multidimensional when stimulus variability is multidimensional. To the extent that a particular dimension of experience can be reliably associated with a particular dimension of stimulus variation, some suppression of the irrelevant dimension is then possible. Stimulus variation which is mainly size variation is less likely to be experienced as distance variation. Some limit to the perceiver's ability to keep his dimensions of experience reliably related to stimulus variation must be supposed, however. Some confusion of size and distance will occur under the special viewing conditions of the laboratory, and the extent of this confusion may be defined by the extent to which S_jD_i and S_iD_j are confused.

In the experiment described, the ability of the subject to discriminate between S_jD_i and S_iD_j was increased in two ways. In the first, the subject viewed the stimuli binocularly and the stimuli varied in size and distance. In the second, the subject viewed the stimuli monocularly but the size dimension was replaced by five values of surface characteristic (five grades of sandpaper varying in texture and color). In both of these cases, *binocular* condition or *texture* condition, the subject had a real basis for discriminating between distance variation and the irrelevant variable. In the binocular view, a larger stimulus at a greater distance would tend to be unlike any smaller stimulus at any smaller distance. In the case of the texture condition, a coarse-textured stimulus viewed at a distance would tend to be unlike any fine-textured stimulus viewed at a smaller distance. In short, these conditions would produce experiences that varied multidimensionally over trials.

The performance of the subject under those two conditions was compared with his performance under the *monocular* condition where stimuli varying in size and distance were viewed only with the dominant eye. The data are presented in Figure 10, where performance is indicated by $U(r{:}S,D)$, the extent to which the subject's distance judgments were predictable from both the size and distance (or from the texture and distance) of the stimuli. The maximum value in all cases is 2.3219.

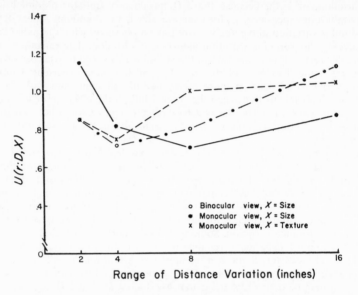

Fig. 10. Predictability of the responses of a subject judging the distance of stimuli varying also in either size or surface texture. View was either binocular or monocular and four ranges of stimulus distance were used. Each point was derived from 125 trials.

This uncertainty measure is used to indicate the total predictability of the subject's responses from both stimulus variables. This makes evident the minimum predictability that occurs for the midrange of real distance variability under the monocular condition, predictability being greatest either for a very small variation in real stimulus distance or for a very large variation in real stimulus distance. A perception selectivity threshold is described by the higher predictability of responses under the monocular condition for small distance variation and by the higher predictability of responses under the binocular and texture conditions for large distance variation. This occurs because the monocular view permits heavier response to size when the distance variation of the stimuli is small, and the binocular view, or use of textured stimuli, permits heavier response to distance alone when the distance variation of the stimuli from trial-to-trial was large.

Language Perception

In this section we consider a demonstration of the perception selectivity threshold that has been in the literature since 1954. The data describing the threshold are shown in Figure 11 and are from an experiment of Chapanis (1954) in which subjects were required to copy passages of English text from which a proportion of letters had been deleted. The deletion method was that known as the "abbreviation" method in which, after the letters are deleted, the material is collapsed together to hide the positions where letters (or spaces or punctuation marks) have been omitted. Subjects were required to copy the prose passages and to insert the missing elements as they did so. Figure 11

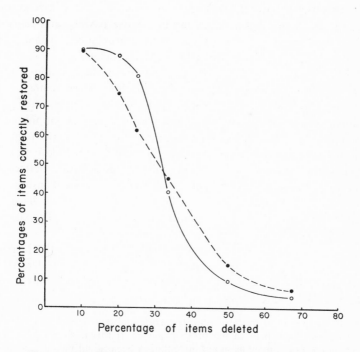

Fig. 11. Median percentages of items correctly restored by subjects copying the prose under the regular (o) and random (•) deletion conditions. (After Chapanis, 1954, "The reconstruction of abbreviated printed messages," *JEP*, 1954, *48*, 496–510.

indicates the proportion of missing elements that were restored correctly as a function of the proportion of the passages deleted and under two deletion conditions. In the first of these conditions, *random deletion,* a chance process (table of random numbers) determined the deletions. In the second, *regular deletion,* deletion of elements, was periodic. For example, under the 10 percent deletion rate, the first, eleventh, twenty-first, and so forth elements were deleted. Several passages were used and the random order determining deletions as well as the starting position for regular deletions was varied from passage to passage and from subject to subject.

This experimental situation is of special interest here because of its relevance to the ideas of Brunswik concerning the role of channel limitation in producing perceptual error. The channel in this case is the series of prose passages that the subject scans and copies. An outstanding feature of these passages is their redundancy, a term used to describe the sequential dependencies evident among letters of printed English prose. Because of these dependencies, or "context" effect, a reader can detect the fact that a letter is missing in a prose passage and suggest a good replacement. In doing so he uses the information provided by the context of the passage from which the letter was deleted.

This is the situation facing the subject under the random deletion condition. He has the double task of determining from context alone *where* the deletions occurred and *what* is missing. Under the regular deletion condition the subject has extra information about *where* the deletion has occurred, this information being provided by the regularity of the deletion process. Thus, there are here two possible kinds of perceivers who differ in their predicted ability to detect those letters that are in a particular position because of the deletion and collapsing noise process. These are the general conditions under which we have suggested that a perception selectivity threshold should occur. The situation may be understood in somewhat more detail, however.

We suggest that the curves of Figure 11 cross because the increased ability of the subject under the regular deletion condition to detect deletions is achieved at a cost. The cost is the sacrifice of some of the regularity of English letters, that is, of context:

1. There is some limit to the regularity (sequential dependencies) with which the letters can appear in the prose passages. If this limit were exceeded, they could not convey as much information because all passages would be predictable in advance to an inefficient degree.
2. Because the "channel limitation" on regularity exists, any further regularity imposed on the passages may result in some loss of the regularity that we call redundancy or context. High rates of deletion, if deletion is periodic, swamp the channel limitation for regularity and deprive the subject of his

ability to use the information otherwise present in verbal context. When rates are high and deletion regular, the most outstanding feature of the input to the subject is the deletion regularity itself. High rates that are *irregular* can be better tolerated because they are less likely to cause the channel limitation for regularity to be exceeded, that is, they interfere less with the normal redundancy of the passages.

In summary, at low deletion rates the subject under regular deletion has the advantage that both the verbal context and the deletion process provide information useful in detecting and replacing missing letters. At high deletion rates he has the disadvantage that his input is mainly the regularity of the deletion process.

These data, and those of the last section, provide a moral. We may operate upon the input to a perceiver in order to make it easier for him to discriminate between input due to "signal" and input due to "noise." Whenever we do this, we create the possibility for both a better and a worse performance. This is clearly true in the present example in which the noise aspect of input, the deletion and collapsing process, was coded (by making it regular) to permit easier detection of its effects. The coding process under high rates of deletion eliminated the redundancy of the passages, however, and increased the uncertainty of the input. This is the essential message of Egon Brunswik in the passage quoted earlier.

PERCEPTUAL IMPLICATIONS

The similarity between certain perceptual situations and the performance of communication receivers has led us to define noise-suppression in terms of the ability of the perceiver to distinguish between "noise" and "signal" rather than in terms of his ability to resolve "signal" values. This ability to distinguish between aspects of input that are relevant (or signal) and aspects of input that are irrelevant (or noise) was shown to imply a necessary and interesting perceptual result. That is, unusually poor perceptual performance (poor predictability from input states) as well as unusually good performance (good predictability from input states) are both necessary concomitants of good ability to distinguish between signal and noise. Which type of performance occurs depends upon the ability of the subject to resolve among signal values. Less ability to distinguish between signal and noise, on the other hand, means that performance is not so bad under the worst of conditions nor so very good under the best of conditions. Several instances of the occurrence of both results in the same real perceptual situations, occurrences of the *perception selectivity threshold,* were demonstrated and discussed.

Other perceptual implications of our perceiver models need to be mentioned briefly. One of these is the meaning of the perception selectivity threshold for threshold work—the measurement of recognition thresholds in brief duration tachistoscopy, for example. It seems very clear that the kind of information obtained about perceptual capacities from threshold work should be different in nature from information obtained from supra-threshold work, such as scaling procedures. Wherever perceptual performance depends upon the twin functions of *discriminating* between relevant and irrelevant aspects of stimulation and *resolving* values of the relevant aspect, then perceivers that produce the best performance under good viewing conditions will also produce the worst performance under poor conditions. That is, the most interesting perceptual mechanisms flourish only under relatively good conditions. A subject operating under threshold conditions is not a subject operating in a perceptually meaningful way. In an analogy with communication receivers, it can be said that a fine, wideband FM receiver tuned to a distant transmitter indicates little about its fantastic ability to "cleanup" the transmission of a near-by station.

A second implication concerns the concept of standards of judgment being supplied by input. In complex perceptual situations this is not an easily acceptable concept because the standards used by a subject in making momentary judgments have long been suggested to be stored standards. This depicts accurate recognition and judgment as resulting from a complex absolute calibration of many possible response-states of the perceiver relative to possible real input states. As an illustration we suggest the complex *match-mismatch* process of Bruner (1957), a modern version of the recognition process of *pair-formation* of Woods (1915) and Bartlett (1932). When restated in terms of the immense task involved in stabilizing this complex calibration with respect to the real world, the concept of stored absolute standards, at least as a sole source of calibration, becomes quite unbelievable.

Our contrasting suggestion is that standards of reference are provided, at least partially, by input variation. By operating on the basis of this input variation, the perceiver can achieve a type of calibration, *calibration-of-scale,* as one of his nonsensory roles in perception.

This was suggested, for example, in the case of the subject who was asked to judge lengths of vertical lines while looking with both eyes. It was suggested that judgments could be accurate when experiential variation due to the difference in real line lengths was great enough to be noticeably different in kind from experimental variation due to physiological processes (noise) in the visual channels. Then the length of the line in a given trial could be judged *in the context of the noise,* or *relative to the indicated extent of the noise process.* All such calibrations of scale are possible only where the perceiver can detect a difference between real inputs and scale perturbation of one kind or another. That is, the perceiver must notice more than one axis of variation in his experience and relate values of variation on one axis to values on others. Then, any indication that the distance of an object is overestimated causes the perceiver to increase his estimate of its size, for example, and any indication that the width of an object is exaggerated leads the perceiver to overestimate its height, and so forth.

Unquestionably, this process is a crucial explanation for the gain, described by Brunswik, of "the over-all functional validity" of percepts and judgment over the "ecological validity" of any of the major "retinal cues." The reliability of all cues, when sufficiently intercorrelated in experience, is simply greater than that for any cue taken individually.

Our contribution is to specify mechanisms whereby the correlation can occur and to insist that the gain does occur only above the perception selectivity threshold. Below that point the result is a loss, not a perceptual gain. But this loss below the threshold, of course, does not diminish the importance of the noise-suppression that can occur above it. When this noise suppression is sufficiently great, the perceiver can get along nicely with only very vague and poorly-defined stored standards of reference. Such vague standards can be quite acceptable provided that they can be reshaped and controlled to some extent by aspects of immediate stimulus input.

For example, a rather crude, stored standard for length of line is of no use if it varies widely from moment to moment or else simply conforms to the length registered in the visual channel. In the first case a bewildering variety of lengths would be experienced; and in the second case all lines, within wide limits, would appear to have the same length. If some aspect of input, other than that aspect being directly judged, could be used in adjusting the internal standard, then accurate judgment of length would be possible. The necessary condition is the ability of the perceiver to discriminate between two aspects of his experience: an aspect that he can use in adjusting his judgmental standard and an aspect that he must judge. We suggest that this crucial "signal-noise" separating function is possible in the perceiver whose experience is multidimensional, one dimension of experience being correctly identified as the dimension containing values to be judged and the other dimensions being used in adjusting standards of judgment. This permits noise-suppression in perception. This permits the perceiver to get along with rather poorly defined stored standards of reference, and that is a perceptual achievement of very great magnitude.

In closing, we emphasize that perceivers need not be "rational" in the sense that they always act with the conscious intent to suppress perceptual noise wherever found; rather we suggest that the noise-suppression results from the normal "nonsensory" functions of the perceiver. Swets, Tanner, and Birdsall (1961) have suggested that the psychophysical application of statistical decision theory helps make explicit a conceptual separation between those factors that influence the observer's attitudes and those that influence his sensitivity. They suggest that the former are more crucially involved in what we generally term perceptual processes, as distinguished from purely sensory mechanisms. The nonsensory aspects of perception, such as the consequences of "hits" and "false alarms," influence a single variable, the observer's criterion cutoff. A nonsensory function of the observer, then, consists in properly placing his criterion on the decision axis in order to achieve his perceptual goal.

Essentially, we are complicating this simple picture by giving the observer a more complex nonsensory task: the identification of the prominent, relevant modes of variation evident in stimulation. That is, the perceiver has the task of *locating* the axis of apparent stimulus variation in a multidimensional experiential space, if he can.

The relationship between this experienced axis of variation and real stimulus variation can achieve either of two results: it can satisfy an accuracy criterion or it can satisfy a coherence criterion. It will satisfy an accuracy criterion if it produces the desired correlation between the observer's judgments and feedback information about the stimuli being judged. A definition of the coherence criterion has been suggested by Rodwan (1961) in terms of the ability of the observer to separate as far as possible in experience clusters of *apparent* stimulus states. Specifically, he suggests Fisher's linear discriminant function as a model for the action of the observer who, in discriminating between two stimulus figures, establishes two classes of experienced figures so that the ratio of the difference *between* the centroids of these classes to the variation in experienced figures *within* classes is a maximum (see Rodwan and Hake, 1964). This best satisfies the criterion of perceptual coherence because it maximizes the ability of the observer to make his experience conform to the nature of input, namely, two input states. But it also means that the experience of the observer will be multidimensional, in order to maximize the ratio described, and this makes possible the kind of scale calibration described above. That is, the satisfaction of a coherence criterion in perception also ensures that the noise-suppression we have called scale calibration will occur if otherwise possible.

REFERENCES

Attneave, F. Some informational aspects of visual perception. *Pychol. Rev.*, 1954, *61*, 183–193.

Attneave, F. Transfer of experience with a class-schema to identification-learning of patterns and shapes. *J. exp. Psychol.*, 1957, *54*, 81–88.

Bartlett, F. C. *Remembering.* London: Cambridge, 1932.

Bruner, J. S. On perceptual readiness. *Psychol. Rev.*, 1957, *64*, 123–152.

Brunswik, E. *Perception and the representative design of psychological experiments.* Berkeley, Calif.: University of California Press, 1956.

Chapanis, A. The reconstruction of abbreviated printed messages. *J. exp. Psychol.*, 1954, *48*, 496–510.

Egan, J. P. Recognition memory and the operating characteristic. Indiana University Hearing and Communication Laboratory: *Technical Note*, AF 19(604)–1962, June, 1958.

Egan, J. P., A. I. Schulman, and G. Z. Greenberg. Operating characteristics determined by binary decisions and by ratings. *J. acoust. Soc. Amer.*, 1959, *31*, 768–773.

Eriksen, C. W., and H. W. Hake. Multidimensional stimulus differences and accuracy of discrimination. *J. exp. Psychol.*, 1955, *50*, 153–160.

Falk, J. L. Theories of visual acuity and their physiological bases. *Psychol. Bull.*, 1956, *53*, 109–133.

Frick, F. C. Information Theory. In Koch, S. (Ed.), *Psychology: A Study of a Science.* Vol. 2. New York: McGraw-Hill, 1959. Pp. 611–636.

Garner, W. R. *Uncertainty and structure as psychological concepts.* New York: John Wiley, 1962.

Goldiamond, I., and W. F. Hawkins. Vexierversuch: The log relationship between word frequency and recognition obtained in the absence of stimulus words. *J. exp. Psychol.*, 1958, *56*, 457–463.

Goldman, S. *Information theory.* Englewood Cliffs, N.J.: Prentice-Hall, 1953.

Green, D. M. Psychoacoustics and detection theory. *J. acoust. Soc. Amer.*, 1960, *32*, 1189–1203.

Hake, H. W. Contributions of psychology to the study of pattern vision. Dayton: *WADC Technical Report*, 1957, 57–621.

Helson, H. Adaptation level theory. In Koch, S. (Ed.), *Psychology: a study of a science.* New York: McGraw-Hill, 1959. Pp. 565–621.

Hochberg, J., and E. McAlister. A quantitative approach to figural "goodness." *J. exp. Psychol.*, 1953, *46*, 361–364.

Middleton, D. *An introduction to statistical communication theory.* New York: McGraw-Hill, 1960.

Miller, G. A., J. S. Bruner, and L. Postman. Familiarity of letter sequences and tachistoscopic identification. *J. gen. Psychol.*, 1954, *50*, 129–139.

Rashevsky, N. Life, information theory, and topology. *Bull. Math. Biophys.*, 1955, *17*, 229–235.

Ratliff, F. Inhibitory interaction and the detection and enhancement of contours. In Rosenblith, W. A. (Ed.), *Sensory Communication.* New York: Wiley, 1961. Pp. 183–203.

Rodwan, A. S. The linear discriminant function as a model for perception. M.A. Dissertation, the University of Illinois, 1961.

Rodwan, A. S., and H. W. Hake. The discriminant function as a model for perception. *Amer. J. Psychol.*, 1964, *77*, 380–392.

Senders, V. L. The physiological basis

of visual acuity. *Psychol. Bull.*, 1948, *45*, 465–490.

Shannon, C. E., and W. Weaver. *The mathematical theory of communication.* Urbana, Ill.: University of Illinois Press, 1949.

Swets, J. A. Detection theory and psychophysics: a review. *Psychometrika*, 1961a, *26*, 49–63.

Swets, J. A. Is there a sensory threshold? *Science*, 1961b, *134*, 168–177.

Swets, J. A., W. P. Tanner, and T. G. Birdsall. Decision processes in perception. *Psychol. Rev.*, 1961, *68*, 301–340.

Tanner, W. P. Theory of signal detectability as an interpretive tool for psychophysical data. *J. acoust. Soc. Amer.*, 1960, *32*, 1140–1147.

Tanner, W. P., and J. A. Swets. A decision-making theory of visual detection. *Psychol. Rev.*, 1954, *61*, 401–409.

Vernon, M. D. The functions of schemata in perceiving. *Psychol. Rev.*, 1955, *62*, 180–192.

Wiener, N. *Extrapolation, interpolation, and smoothing of stationary time series.* New York: Wiley, 1949.

Weintraub, D. J., and H. W. Hake. Visual discrimination, an interpretation in terms of detectability theory. *J. Opt. Soc. Amer.*, 1962, *52*, 1179–1184.

Woods, E. L. An experimental analysis of the process of recognizing. *Amer. J. Psychol.*, 1915, *26*, 313–327.

10

On the Nature of the Environment [1]

ROGER G. BARKER

Two themes stand out strongly in my memory of Kurt Lewin from the time I was a post-doctoral fellow with his group at the University of Iowa in 1935 and 1936.

One theme was Lewin's vigorous presentation of psychology as a conceptually autonomous science. In his view, psychology is independent of biology, physics, and sociology; its constructs and theories are not reducible to those of any other science. Heider (1959) has reminded us that this was a guiding conviction of Lewin from his earliest days, and that it is expressed in his theory of the life space. Kurt Lewin brought this view to Iowa, and under the impact of his brilliance and enthusiasm all who worked with him there operated within its framework. But his conception of the place of psychology among the sciences did not go unchallenged; in fact, it was an explicit and a lively issue. The philosophy of science had recently come to the University of Iowa directly from Vienna. Under these circumstances, Lewin, who would certainly have chosen to let history settle the argument, had to enter into discussions of what, for him, were the familiar issues of positivism, reductionism, and the unity of science. These discussions were landmarks of the Iowa landscape of those days and surely everyone who participated in them, even from the periphery, will always remember them.

The essence of science for Lewin was a system of explicitly stated concepts by means of which exceptionless derivations could be made. Since, in this view, the concepts of physics, biology, and sociology are incommensurable with those of psychology, he concluded that only probabilistic, empirical relations could be discovered between variables of psychology and those of other sciences. It was impossible, as he saw it, to make derivations to behavior from the nonpsychological environ-

1. This paper was originally presented as the Kurt Lewin Memorial Address for 1963. Professor Barker's address is being reprinted here (with the kind permission of the Editor of the *Journal of Social Issues*) because it presents a unique reconciliation of Brunswik's environmentalism with Lewin's interest in central processes.

ment, to use his own term, or the preperceptual or ecological environment to use Brunswik's terms.[2] It was this that made it essential for Lewin to limit psychology to an encapsulated system of purely psychological constructs.

My experience at Iowa convinced me that psychology was faced with a three-way dilemma and that it had to choose between achieving a truly Galilean psychology of precise derivations, but with the ecological environment omitted, accepting a probabilistic functionalism of the kind advocated by Brunswik, with the ecological environment included, or retreating to a fractionated psychology of specialties and microtheories without conceptual unity. I am now beginning to see the issues differently. But before turning to this, I must report another theme that is prominent in my memory of Kurt Lewin and which helps to define the issue I want to discuss.

This theme is the overriding influence of the ecological environment in Lewin's own life. How well I remember a summer day I spent with him in the Sierra Nevada mountains of California. It was a beautiful day. Then the news came over the automobile radio that Hitler's German armies had invaded Poland. This was an event in the objective geopolitical-social world; this was an occurrence in the ecological environment. It was hard, indeed, to follow Lewin's scientific tenets here. It was difficult to think that this occurrence had no certain consequences for him, or for me, or for multitudes of others for whom it had as yet no life-space representation whatever. Lewin was among those men who have had to contend in their own lives with the most striking evidence of the coercive power of the political-social environment. Indeed, two ecological realities, Jews and Nazis, were in some way causally implicated in the strange fact that Lewin was carrying on his work in an Iowa town. He recognized this, of course. He often emphasized the profound importance for people of nonpsychological events; but despite their saliency for him personally, he could not incorporate them into a science of psychology, as he understood science.

So Lewin led an uneasy life with this dilemma. He saw very clearly that an adequate applied behavioral science requires conceptual bridges between psychology and ecology, and even though his conception of science told him that this is impossible, much of his effort from the Iowa

2. *Nonpsychological environment, preperceptual environment, ecological environment* and *environment* are used interchangeably in this essay to mean the environment as described by the physical and biological sciences, and by those social sciences that are not adumbrations of individual psychology. *Psychological environment* and *life space* are used interchangeably as Lewin used them.

period onward was preoccupied with it. Sometimes he approached the psychological-ecological breach directly and explicitly, as in his gate-keeper theory of the link between food habits and food technology and economics (1951); sometimes he approached it obliquely and implicitly, as in his attempt to treat the social field as a psychological construct (1951). He seemed unable to avoid the interface between ecology and psychology and to work within his own system, as he had done in the earlier studies of tension systems, psychological satiation, and level of aspiration. I think the reason is clear: Lewin's total life experience and his conception of psychology as a science were in irreconcilable conflict. He could not ignore his life experiences, and he could not give up his conception of psychology. It was a painful conflict.

It seems to me that, as psychologists, we are all confronted with the same dilemma today. And for those with the concerns represented by the Society for the Psychological Study of Social Issues the conflict is especially crucial. The environment which man is creating for himself is surely even more threatening (and, also, more promising, if we are able to call the turns) than it was twenty-five years ago. Who can doubt that changes in our environment ranging from new levels of radiation, to increased numbers of people, to new kinds of medicines, and new kinds of social organizations, schools, and governments are inexorably changing our behavior, and that our new behavior is, in turn, altering our environment? Can this total eco-behavioral system be incorporated within an explanatory science? Can we understand and control the total array and flow of what is happening to us, or must the couplings between the environment and behavior always be dealt with fragmentally, probabilistically, empirically, and *post hoc?* It is to this problem that I should like to direct your attention today.

I shall, first, define the dilemma, or rather the dilemmas, more precisely.

PROBLEMS ALONG THE ENVIRONMENT TO ENVIRONMENT CIRCUIT

We can trace the round of events in which behavior is involved from distal objects in the ecological environment (say a fly ball in a baseball game) to proximal events at receptor surfaces (the image of the approaching ball on the retinas); to afferent, central, and efferent processes within the silent intrapersonal sector of the circuit (for example, perceiving the approaching ball); to molecular acts (for example, raising the hands) and finally to molar actions which alter the ecological environment (catching the ball). This is the environment to environment circuit, the E-E arc, which Brunswik (1955) and others (Murray, 1959; Miller, Galanter and Pribram, 1960; Zener, Gaffron, 1962) have considered the fundamental psychological datum.

I have mentioned one dilemma of the E-E arc, namely, that it involves such alien phenomena in its various parts that a conceptually univocal treatment has seemed impossible. But there are other dilemmas.

Most psychologists, including Lewin and Brunswik, have found the ecological environment on the afferent side of the person to be unstable, and to exhibit at best only statistical regularities (Brunswik, 1955; Lewin, 1951). This disordered input has confronted students of the total E-E arc with the difficult problem of accounting for its transformation within the circuit into an ordered output. In consequence, the selective and organizing powers of the intrapersonal segment of the E-E arc, which to quote Leeper, "yield relatively stable effects out of the kaleidoscopically changing stimulation they receive" (1963) (pp. 387–388), has undoubtedly claimed the greatest efforts of psychologists; here fall the problems of perception and learning. This is the second dilemma of the E-E arc.

Furthermore, it is generally agreed by students of perception and learning that the ecological environment does not demand behavior, but that it is, rather, permissive, supportive, or resistive. It is true that a language is often used that implies at least a triggering function for the ecological environment: events in the environment are said to stimulate, to evoke, to instigate behavior. And the fact that experiments are by design usually conducted within environments that are, indeed, stimulating gives support to the language used. However, the fine print of psychological theory always, so far as I have been able to determine, makes the intrapersonal sector of the arc the arbiter of what will be received as stimuli, and how it will be coded and programed in the intrapersonal sector before it emerges as output (Lawrence, 1963; Ratliff, 1962; Schoenfeld and Cumming, 1963). The simple fact is that to function as a stimulus, an environmental variable must be received by the organism. In fact, the S-R formula would be more in line with basic psychological theory if it were recast as an R-S formula: R for *reception* by the organism followed by S for *submission* of the coded information back to the environment. It is safe to say that in most psychological thinking, ecological occurrences at the afferent end of the E-E arc are assumed (a) to be indifferent to their ends via the arc, and (b) to be endowed with directedness and purpose only within the intrapersonal sector. This is the problem of motivation, and it is a third dilemma of the E-E arc.

These three dilemmas rest upon certain conceptions of the ecological environment, namely, that it is disordered, that it is without direction with respect to behavior, and that it is conceptually incommensurate with the intrapersonal sector of the E-E arc.

Since psychologists usually consider the environment only insofar as it is propaedeutic to their main concern with behavior, it would appear desirable to examine, again, the ecological segment of the E-E arc as it exists before being received, coded, and programmed within the silent intrapersonal sector of the circuit. Egon Brunswik wrote, in this connection:

... both organism and environment will have to be seen as systems, each with properties of its own, yet both hewn from basically the same block. Each has surface and depth, or overt and covert regions ... the interrelationship between the two systems has the essential characteristic of a "coming-to-terms." And this coming-to-terms is not merely a matter of the mutual boundary or surface areas. It concerns equally as much, or perhaps even more, the rapport between the central, covert layers of the two systems. It follows that, much as psychology must be concerned with the texture of the organism or of its nervous processes and must investigate them in depth, it also must be concerned with the texture of the environment as it extends in depth away from the common boundary (Brunswik, 1957, p. 5).

I raise the question then: What *is* the texture of the ecological environment?

ATTRIBUTES OF THE ECOLOGICAL ENVIRONMENT

The physical and biological sciences have amassed almost limitless information about the environment, and some of it bears directly and univocally upon the issues before us. The three environmental attributes I shall mention have been independently affirmed and reaffirmed by many observing techniques and instruments. They are far removed from the human observer; most of them are properties of the environment as revealed directly by photographic plates and recording instruments. They are elementary facts.

Order in the Preperceptual Environment

The environment as described by chemists, physicists, botanists, and astronomers is not a chaotic jumble of independent odds and ends, and it has more than statistical regularity. It consists of bounded and internally patterned units that are frequently arranged in precisely ordered arrays and sequences. The problem of identifying and classifying the parts of the environment, i.e., the taxonomic problem, is very great, but the problem is not, primarily, to bring order out of disorder. On the contrary its first task is to describe and explain the surprising structures and orders that appear in nature: within carbon atoms, within DNA molecules, within developing embryos, within oak trees, within baseball games, within hotels (if you will), within nations, within solar systems; and to account for the occasional absence of order and organization, in atomic explosions, in cancerous growths, and in social disorder.

It must be noted, however, that order and lawfulness are by no means spread uniformly across the nonpsychological world; not every entity is lawfully related to every other entity. The preperceptual world is not one system but many, and their boundaries and interconnections have to be discovered.

A frequent arrangement of ecological units is in nesting assemblies. Examples are everywhere: in a chick embryo, for example, with its organs, the cells of one of the organs, the nucleus of one of the cells, the molecular aggregates of the nucleus, the molecules of an aggregate, the atoms of one of the molecules, and the subatomic particles of an atom. A unit in the middle ranges of a nesting structure such as this, is simultaneously both circumjacent and interjacent, both whole and part, both entity and environment. An organ, the liver, for example, is whole in relation to its own component pattern of cells, and is a part in relation to the circumjacent organism that it, with other organs, composes; it forms the environment of its cells, and is, itself, environed by the organism.

Direction and Purpose in the Preperceptual Environment

Most units of the ecological environment are not directionless in relation to their parts. They are, rather, self-regulated entities (or the products of such entities) with control circuits that guide their components to characteristic states and that maintain these states within limited ranges of values in the face of disturbances. Some of the strongest forces in nature and some of the most ubiquitous patterns of events are found within ecological units: in atomic forces and in developmental sequences, for example. The new understanding of cybernetic processes makes it no longer necessary to be skeptical of the reality of target-directed systems within the ecological environment.

There are mutual causal relations up and down the nesting series in which many environmental entities occur; the preperceptual environment is made up of systems within systems. An entity in such a series both constrains and is constrained by the outside unit that surrounds it and by the inside units it surrounds. This means that entities in nesting structures are parts of their own contexts; they influence themselves through the circumjacent entities which they, in part, compose. A beam determines its own strength by its contribution to the structure into which it is built; a word defines itself by its contribution to the meaning of the sentence of which it is a part.

Incommensurability in the Preperceptual Environment

The conceptual incommensurability of phenomena which is such an obstacle to the unification of the sciences does not appear to trouble nature's units. The topologically larger units of nesting structures have, in general, greater variety among their included parts than smaller units: an organism encompasses a greater variety of structures and processes than a cell; a river is internally more varied than a brook. Within the larger units, things and events from conceptually more and more alien sciences are incorporated and regulated. In an established pond, a great variety of physical and biological entities and processes are integrated into a stable, self-regulated unit; the component, interrelated entities range from oxygen molecules to predacious-diving beetles. This suggests that within certain levels of nesting structures conceptual incommensurability of phenomena does not prevent integration and regulation. In fact, self-regulated units with widely varied component entities are, in general, more stable than units with lesser variety (Ashby, 1956).

In summary, the sciences which deal with the entities and events of the nonpsychological environment directly, and not propaedeutically as in psychology, do not find them to be chaotic or only probabilistic in their occurrence. It is within the physical and biological sciences that the greatest order and lawfulness have been discovered, an order and lawfulness much admired by psychologists. These sciences do not find environmental entities to be without direction with respect to their component parts, and conceptual incommensurability does not prevent the integration and lawful regulation of ecological entities. One cannot avoid the question, therefore: Why has psychology found the ecological environment to be so different?

Let us take seriously the discoveries of the biophysical sciences with respect to the preperceptual environment, and identify and examine the environment of behavior as they identify and examine the environments of physical or biological entities: of animals, of cells, of satellites. This is neither more nor less difficult than it is to identify and examine the habitat of an animal, the organ in which a lesion occurs, or the planetary system within which a satellite orbits. The investigator first identifies the animal, the lesion, the planet, or, in this case, the behavior unit with which he is concerned, and he then explores the surrounding area until he identifies and then examines the circumjacent environmental unit.

But first we must have a unit of behavior. One cannot study the environment of behavior in general.

THE ENVIRONMENT OF BEHAVIOR EPISODES

Psychology has been so busy selecting from, imposing upon, and rearranging the behavior of its subjects that it has until very recently neglected to note behavior's clear structure when it is not molested by tests, experiments, questionnaires and interviews. Following the basic work on behavior structure by Herbert F. Wright (Barker and Wright, 1955), Dickman (1963) has shown that people commonly see the behavior continuum in terms of the units (or their multiples) which Wright identified, namely, behavior episodes. Here, for example, are descriptive titles of consecutively occurring episodes from the behavior stream of six-year-old Belinda Bevan during a 10-minute period beginning at 2:22 p.m., on July 18, 1957 (Barker, Wright, Barker, and Schoggen, 1961):

> Watching bigger girls form a pyramid (gymnastic)
> Taking off her shoes
> Going closer to the big girls
> Putting on her shoes
> Admiring bracelet on Alice
> Poking Alice
> Looking at Winifred's ladybug
> Following Alice
> Watching boys
> Looking into porch of schoolroom
> Closing door of schoolroom
> Watching girls play hopscotch
> Giving Harry his shoe
> Getting bracelet from Alice
> Interfering in Delia's and Winifred's fight
> Admiring bracelet on Alice

Behavior episodes, such as these, are not arbitrarily imposed divisions of the behavior continuum in the way that microtome slices of tissue and mile-square sections of the earth's surface are imposed divisions. They are, rather, natural units of molar behavior (Barker, 1963) with the attributes of constancy of direction, equal potency throughout their parts, and limited size-range. Like crystals and cells which also have distinguishing general attributes and limited size-ranges, behavior episodes have as clear a position in the hierarchy of behavior units as the former have in the physical and organic hierarchies. It makes sense, therefore, to ask what units of the ecological environment encompass behavior episodes.

Consider, for example, Belinda's behavior episode, Looking at Winifred's Ladybug, from the series just given.

The record of this episode of Belinda's behavior stream reads as follows:

> Belinda ran toward Winifred from Miss Groves' room.
> Winifred had found a ladybug and was walking around with this ladybug saying, "Ladybug, ladybug, fly away home."
> Belinda went up to Winifred.
> She pulled Winifred's arm down so she could see the ladybug better.
> She smiled as she watched the beetle. She watched the ladybug for 10 or 15 seconds.

This episode constitutes an *E-E* arc originating in the ecological event, "Winifred . . . was walking around with this ladybug" and ending in the ecological events, Belinda, "pulled Winifred's arm down . . . she watched the ladybug. . . ."

The environing unit in which this episode occurred was easily identified. It extended in depth away from the junction points between Belinda and Winifred-with-the-ladybug with a characteristic pattern of people, behavior, and objects which abruptly changed at a surrounding physical wall, and at temporal beginning and end points.[3] The environmental unit was Afternoon Break, Yoredale County School Playground, North Yorkshire, England, 2:22–2:31 p.m., July 18, 1957.

We have studied many behavior episodes, and we have always found them within ecological units like the one surrounding the episode Looking at Winifred's Ladybug. We have called these ecological units *behavior settings*. Our work in Midwest, Kansas, and Yoredale, Yorkshire, has demonstrated that behavior settings can be identified and described reliably without an explicit theory and by means of a variety

3. In other cases the boundaries may not be so definite, they may in fact be boundary zones; and there are sometimes alternative bounds to an environmental unit. In these cases detailed judgments have to be made regarding the location of the boundary, but the principle does not change (see Barker and Wright, 1955).

of survey techniques. This is of some importance, we think, as an indication that behavior settings are tough, highly visible features of the ecological environment.

There is only a beginning of a scientific literature on behavior settings. Except in their applied phases, the biological and physical sciences have eschewed ecological units with human behavior as component elements. They have stopped with man-free ponds, glaciers, and lightning flashes; they have left farms, ski-jumps, and passenger trains to others. And psychology and sociology have, for the most part, shied in the other direction; they have avoided whole, unfractionated ecological units with physical objects as well as people and behavior as component parts. So behavior-setting-type units have almost completely fallen between the bio-physical and the behavioral sciences, and this has been a source of serious trouble for the ecobehavioral problem: there have been no solid empirical ecological units. Unbounded, demitheoretical, demiempirical units do not provide the firm base an empirical science must have. Floyd Allport (1961) has persuasively pointed to one difficulty of such demientities: they disappear when the attempt is made to touch them, as is essential if they are to be studied; in their place one encounters individuals. And there is another difficulty: a universal attribute of the environment of a person, whatever its other characteristics may be, is a univocal position in time and space. The units of an ecobehavioral science must have time-space loci. Behavior settings fulfill both of these requirements: they can be encountered, qua environmental units, and re-encountered; and they can be exactly located in time and space.

It is not often that a lecturer can present to his audience an example of his phenomena, whole and functioning *in situ*—not merely with a demonstration, a description, a preserved specimen, a picture, or a diagram of it. I am in the fortunate position of being able to give you, so to speak, a real behavior setting.

If you will change your attention from me to the next most inclusive, bounded unit, to the assembly of people, behavior episodes, and objects before you, you will see a behavior setting. It has the following structural attributes which you can observe directly:

1. It has a space-time locus: 3:00-3:50 p.m., September 2, 1963, Clover Room, Bellevue-Stratford Hotel, Philadelphia, Pennsylvania.
2. It is composed of a variety of interior entities and events: of people, objects (chairs, walls, a microphone, paper), behavior, (lecturing, listening, sitting), and other processes (air circulation, sound amplification).
3. Its widely different components form a bounded pattern that is easily discriminated from the pattern on the outside of the boundary.
4. Its component parts are obviously not a random arrangement of independ-

ent classes of entities; if they were, how surprising, that all the chairs are in the same position with respect to the podium, that all members of the audience happen to come to rest upon chairs, and that the lights are not helter-skelter from floor to ceiling, for example.

5. The entity before you is a part of a nesting structure; its components (for example, the chairs and people) have parts; and the setting, itself, is contained within a more comprehensive unit, the Bellevue-Stratford Hotel.

6. This unit is objective in the sense that it exists independently of anyone's perception of it, qua unit.

You will note that in these structural respects, behavior settings are identical with biophysical units.

This, then, is a behavior setting; within it is displayed, for you to see, the finer-grained texture of the environment as it extends around and away from the behavior occurring here. What is this texture and how does it affect behavior? This leads us to the more dynamic characteristics of behavior settings.

Every stable, patterned, and bounded assembly of phenomena (whether this be in the particles of milker's nodule virus, in the lines of a spectrograph, or in the position of chromosomes in meiosis) indicates that *some* regulator is operating. And where in nature is stable patterning clearer than in a baseball game, a church service, a law court, or a highway, i.e., in behavior settings? The question in all of these cases is: What is the source of the order?

It does not require systematic research to discover that the patterns of behavior settings do not inhere in the people or the objects within them. It is common observation that the *same* people and objects are transformed into different patterns as they pass from one variety of setting to another. This is exemplified by numerous pairs of behavior settings in Midwest and Yoredale with essentially the same people and objects as component parts but with quite different patterns. For example:

Church Service—Church Wedding
High School Senior Class Play—Senior Graduation
School Playground: Recess—May Fete on School Playground

It is common observation, too, that *different* sets of people and objects exhibit the same pattern within the same variety of behavior setting. This is exemplified by the almost complete turnover of persons each year in academic behavior settings, with the patterns of the settings remaining remarkably stable. One of the striking features of communities is how, year after year, they incorporate new people, despite the idiosyncratic behavior and personality traits of these people, into the characteristic patterns of their stable behavior settings: of Rotary Club meetings, of doctors' offices, of garages, of bridge clubs. Obviously, whatever it is that impresses the characteristic array and flow of behavior settings upon their interior entities and events is largely independent of the persons who participate in them.

However, these general observations do not tell us the degree of change in the behavior of *individuals* as they move from setting to setting. It is possible for the *patterns* of behavior settings to differ greatly without a similar difference in the behavior of the individuals involved. The standing behavior patterns made by the inhabitants of a track meet and by the same people as inhabitants of a ball game are quite different, yet the behavior of most of the individuals within these settings appears to be quite similar: by and large, the runners and throwers run and throw in both, and the cheerers cheer in both settings.

A considerable number of investigators have made quantitative studies of the differences in the behavior of the same persons in different behavior settings (Goffman, 1963; Gump, Schoggen, & Redl, 1963; 1957; Gump & Sutton-Smith, 1955; Jordan, 1963; Raush, Dittmann, & Taylor, 1959; 1959; 1960; Soskin & John, 1963). I shall not survey this rather extensive body of research; the findings are in general agreement on the issue of importance to us here, and they are represented by the research of Raush, Dittmann, and Taylor. Working within a therapeutic milieu with disturbed boys, these investigators found that on the behavior dimensions hostility-friendliness and dominance-passivity there was as much variation between behavior settings, with boys constant, as between boys with settings constant.

Altogether, then, there is abundant evidence that behavior settings, like many biophysical entities, are strongly self-regulated systems which regulate the behavior episodes within them as molecules regulate atoms, as organs regulate cells, and as structures regulate the beams of which they are constructed.[4] To the extent that this is true, it means that the ecological environment of behavior is not passive, is not directionless, is not chaotic or probabilistic.

THE REGULATION OF BEHAVIOR SETTINGS

But how do behavior settings regulate themselves, including the behavior episodes within them? How does "the texture of the environ-

---

4. The interdependence of their parts is of practical, methodological importance. It provides a basis for establishing the limits of behavior settings in those cases where the boundaries are obscure. (See Barker and Wright, 1955; also, Barker and Barker, 1961).

ment as it extends in depth away from the common boundary" influence individual behavior?

One can ask, of course, why one should bother with the distal texture of behavior settings. Whatever this texture may be, it ultimately has to be translated into input at the junction points with particular persons. Why not, therefore, get down to brass tacks at these junction points, that is, at the sensory surfaces?

There are a number of reasons why this cannot be done. For one thing, behavior settings have so many richly interconnected elements that their tremendous complexity at the sensory surfaces of all inhabitants concurrently cannot, at the present time, be dealt with conceptually or practically. Behavior settings are often very large systems, and simplification is necessary. But what may appear to be the most obvious simplification, namely, dealing with the input to single inhabitants, or to a sample of inhabitants, does not reveal behavior settings. It is not only in perception that the attributes of parts differ from those of the whole. In any system with interdependent parts the order obtaining at a point of the system varies with the portion of the total system within which the part is considered. It is easy to overlook how greatly attributes vary with context. Take, for example, a visual target, a spot on the tire of an automobile moving forward at a road speed of 50 miles per hour. The spot will display simultaneously the following motions:

1. a random vertical vibratory motion within the field of a stroboscope focused on the spot at a single point in the wheel's revolution;
2. a uniform circular motion of about 1000 RPM within the context of the wheel; and
3. a cyclical forward motion varying from zero to 100 miles per hour within the context of the auto-highway traction system.

The same state of affairs occurs in a behavior setting. Suppose one were to study input and output of a second baseman in a ball game. By careful observation, all incoming and outgoing balls could be tallied, timed, and their speeds and directions recorded. The input itself would be without a sensible order, and there would be no relation between baseball inputs and outputs. But within the behavior setting, baseball game, the record would be sensible, orderly and lawful. It is important to note that it is not the player who converts this into order, it is the game, the behavior setting. The player acts as the game's agent and is able to receive and throw the ball in an orderly way because the rules (the program) of the game, and all information about the momentary state of the game available to him through a variety of inputs, guide his actions. However, all the inputs and outputs of a single player, of a sample of the players, or of all the players if considered outside the context of "the game" would be without sensible order. It is important to note, too, that a much greater quantity of information would be required to discover "the game" from the inputs and outputs at the junction points with the individual players than is contained in the program of "the game" itself (Maruyama, 1963).

A special difficulty with the ecological input at the junction points with individuals arises from the difference in the temporal dimensions of the inputs at these points, that is, of the stimuli, and the behavior output with which we are concerned, that is, behavior episodes. Stimuli are very short units occurring in unpredictable sequences during the period of any episode, while episodes are much longer units with direction and interdependence from their points of origin. However, episodes are not determined by their internal states alone; they are guided in their details by the ecological environment. To predict a behavior episode it is necessary to know the prevailing conditions throughout its entire course, but the ecological input of stimuli during an episode can only be known at the completion of the episode. What is needed as an ecological anchor for behavior episodes is a stable unit with at least as long duration as episodes. Behavior settings, whole and undismantled, fulfill this minimal requirement; they are episode-sized ecological units. And behavior episodes are setting-sized behavior units.

Behavior settings do have unitary textured properties which can be dealt with as bridge builders deal with the span of a bridge rather than with its atoms. One such property is number of inhabitants. In the remainder of this paper, I shall present some evidence that this ecological variable influences individual behavior and some ideas as to how it does so.

BEHAVIOR SETTING SIZE AND INDIVIDUAL BEHAVIOR

There is evidence, some of which I have presented to you, for each of the following statements, but I shall consider them, here, as hypotheses that were investigated by the research to be reported. Behavior settings are bounded, self-regulated entities involving forces which form and maintain the component inhabitants and objects of settings in functioning patterns with stable attributes. One of the stable attributes of a setting is its functional level, and another is the optimal number of inhabitants for maintenance of this level. The optimal number of inhabitants may be precisely specified by the setting (a bridge game requires four inhabitants), or may fall within a range (a First Grade reading class in

Midwest functions well with 15 to 25 pupils). When the number of inhabitants of a behavior setting is below the optimal number (within limits), the homeostatic controls of the setting maintain the total complement and pattern of the setting's forces essentially intact, and this produces differences, in comparison with an optimally populated setting, that ramify to the level of individual behavior. The differences reach the level of individual inhabitants by two main routes, one a rather direct route involving behavior setting structure and dynamics, the other more indirect via control mechanisms. I shall consider the more direct route first.

Behavior settings with fewer than optimal inhabitants are less differentiated, and their networks of forces are interconnected through fewer junction points than otherwise equivalent settings with optimal numbers of inhabitants. It follows from this that on the level of individual dynamics, the inhabitants (that is, the junction points) of the former, or "underpopulated," settings are points of application of more behavior setting forces with wider ranges of direction than are inhabitants of the latter, or optimally populated, settings. Behavior setting forces cause participation in behavior settings, and persons and objects which receive more forces in more varied directions will participate with greater forcefulness in more varied ways. On the level of particular activities, far-reaching differences will result, all characterized by stronger motivation, greater variety, and deeper involvement in the settings with less than the optimal number of inhabitants.

When people are more than optimally abundant in behavior settings, the differences noted will be reversed.

At some point in the linkage between behavior setting population (an ecological fact) and forces upon individual inhabitants (psychological facts) a transformation from nonpsychological to psychological phenomena occurs. But in the present analysis we are not concerned with where or how this takes place, but only with the fact that as between behavior settings with the same number and pattern of forces (however the forces may operate), the settings with fewer than optimal number of inhabitants will bring more forces to bear per inhabitant in more directions than settings with an optimal or greater number of inhabitants. I have elsewhere indicated that while a person's perception is obviously involved in his degree of participation in a behavior setting, he need not be aware of the population of the setting as such (Barker, 1960). Prediction can be made from ecological facts to individual behavior via behavior settings without any knowledge of the channels or transformations involved and without previous observation of the phenomena.

The derivations from behavior setting size to individual behavior were investigated recently at the Midwest Psychological Field Station in the behavior settings of high schools. The settings were equivalent in all respects except number of inhabitants, which ranged from below to above optimal. Prototypes of the settings that were studied are the Junior Class Play of a small high school where each of the 22 members of the class participated in presenting the play to an audience of about 350 persons and the Junior Class Play of a large high school where about 100 (14 percent) of the 700 members of the class had some part in presenting the play to an audience of about 2000 persons. Only behavior settings where attendance was voluntary were included in the studies.

The data showed that the students of the small high schools, in comparison with those of the large school:

entered the same number of behavior settings (although there were fewer available),

held important, responsible, and central positions in a greater number of the settings,

experienced more attractions and more pressures toward participation in the settings,

entered a wider variety of behavior settings, and

held important, responsible, and central positions in a wider variety of the settings.

These differences were not slight. Over the seventeen-week period of the study, the students of the small high schools participated in central, responsible positions (as members of play casts, as officers of organizations, as members of athletic teams, as soloists, and so forth) in over three-and-a-half behavior settings per student, on the average (3.7), while students of the large high school participated in these important roles in 16 percent as many settings, that is, in just over one-half setting per student (0.6). The students of the small schools held central, responsible, and important positions in twice as many *varieties* of behavior settings as the students of the large school (Gump & Friesen, in press). In short, these data showed, as the theory predicted, that the students of the small high schools (with fewer than optimal inhabitants per setting) were more strongly motivated, engaged in more varied activities, and were more responsibly involved than the students of the large school (with more than optimal inhabitants per setting). These are direct symptoms of the predicted differences in the strength and range of direction of forces. There is much additional evidence from research in industry that supports the predictions (Willems, in press), and the investigations and theories of Calhoun (1963; 1956; unpublished manuscripts) on population density and behavior velocity in animals are in general accord with the predictions.

There are less direct consequences of behavior setting population differences. When the participants in behavior settings fall below the optimal number and become points of application of more forces, they have increased functional importance within settings, and the situation may be reached where everyone is a key person for the stability, and even for the survival of settings. These are ecological facts. To the degree that the inhabitants are aware of their own behavior in behavior settings their experiences will pertain to their own efforts, achievements, and contributions to the functioning of settings. In fact, Gump and Friesen (in press) found that the students of the small schools exceeded those of the large schools in satisfying experiences related to the development of competence, to being challenged, to engaging in important activities, and to being involved in group activities. When the number of inhabitants of behavior settings are greater than optimal, when there is a surplus of people, and people are the points of application of fewer forces, the functional importance of all inhabitants is reduced on the average, and the situation will be reached where almost no one will be crucially missed as a contributor to the functioning of settings. Under these circumstances, it is to be expected that the inhabitants' experiences will pertain to behavior settings as detached, independent phenomena, to the performances of others, and to their own standings in comparison with others. In fact, the students of the large school exceeded those of the small schools in number of satisfying experiences related to the vicarious enjoyment of others' activities, to being affiliated with a large institution, to learning about the school's people and affairs, and to gaining "points via participation." These data may be summarized in terms of Dembo's distinction between *asset* values and *comparative* values (1956). The small schools more frequently generated in their students self-valuations based upon how adequately the students saw themselves contributing to behavior settings, that is, being assets to settings. The large schools more frequently generated in their students self-evaluations based upon the students' perception of their standing in comparison with others. These are fundamental differences: in terms of asset values, everyone in a behavior setting can be important and successful; in terms of comparative values, only a few can be important and successful.

I shall turn next to the connection between behavior setting population and individual behavior via the regulatory systems.

The inhabitants of a behavior setting always have the potentiality, and usually the active tendency, to exhibit a greater variety of behavior than the setting requires or can tolerate. The behavior setting control mechanism reduces this variety to the amount appropriate to the setting, and maintains it within an acceptable range of values. One type of control mechanism found in connection with behavior settings is a direct, deviation-countering servo-mechanism that counteracts any deviation beyond the acceptable values; a restaurant hostess who supplies coatless patrons with "appropriate" jackets functions as a deviation-countering homeostat and exemplifies this type of control. Another frequent behavior setting control is a vetoing-type mechanism that provides just two states with respect to the variables it governs: *in* and *out* of the setting (member-nonmember, pass-fail, alive-dead, permitted-not permitted, free-trapped) (Ashby, 1956). A restaurant hostess who refuses admission to coatless, aspiring patrons exemplifies this control mechanism. In general, deviation-countering controls are more efficient, but they are more difficult to devise and more expensive to operate than vetoing regulators. The latter are abundant in nature, for example, vetoing the "unfit."

The regulation of behavior settings is usually a complex process, involving alternative mechanisms, and the continual selection of the most effective regulators for the conditions obtaining. In other words, regulation operates directly on behavior setting patterns and indirectly via the regulators themselves. In general, behavior settings with fewer than the optimal number of inhabitants must use deviation-countering control mechanisms, or they will perish; inhabitants are functionally too important to be vetoed out. I have seen a four-man baseball game of nine-year-olds tolerate and nurse along with carefully applied deviation-countering controls a four-year-old participant, or even a mother. In this case one outfielder, even an inefficient and inapt one, is likely to produce a better-functioning game than a game with no outfielder. On the other hand, if there are thirty candidates for players in the game, a better game will result with less fuss and bother if all four-year-olds, mothers, and other inapt players are vetoed out. And nine-year-olds have ways of doing this, and they regularly do it. Those vetoed out become substitutes, bat-boys, and spectators. In behavior settings with more than the optimal numbers of inhabitants, efficiency usually moves behavior settings toward veto-type control mechanism.

Both deviation-countering and vetoing controls, insofar as they are effective in stabilizing the functioning of behavior settings, apply their differing influences more frequently to marginal inhabitants, likely to engage in deviant behavior, than to focal, conformable inhabitants, unlikely to engage in deviant behavior.

In the case of the high school study we expected that deviation-countering control measures would be more frequent in the small than in the large schools, and that this excess frequency would be greater among the academically unpromising than among the academically promising students. Willems' data bear upon these issues. He called the deviation-countering influences *pressures;* they included all the forces toward participation which the subjects reported as originating outside themselves, for example, "My friend asked me to go"; "Band players were expected to come," and so forth. Over all, students of the small schools received two times as many deviation-countering influences as the students of the large school, and academically marginal students of the small schools (that is, students without academically favorable abilities and motivation) received almost five times as many deviation-countering measures as marginal students of the large school.

Both deviation-countering and vetoing control mechanisms produce uniformity of behavior, but with very different consequences for people. In settings where people are at a premium, uniformity is necessarily achieved as we have seen, by the regulating *behavior,* without limiting the interests, abilities, and motives of inhabitants. In settings where people are surplus, uniformity is achieved to a considerable degree by vetoing, not behavior, but inhabitants who exhibit deviant behavior; and this amounts, in effect, to selecting inhabitants for conformity and uniformity with respect to personality characteristics, (interests, abilities, motives). There are secondary resultants of these control processes which cannot be considered here; but it is immediately clear that the settings with fewer than optimal inhabitants, within which behavioral uniformity is engrafted upon personality diversity, are desegregated, egalitarian, functionally tolerant settings, while settings that veto the unfit and retain the fit are segregated, uniform, specialized settings.

Data were not secured upon details of the vetoing control processes in the schools. But the consequences were apparent: students who did not participate on a responsible level in any voluntary school activity, that is, that were vetoed out of all but spectator participation, constituted 2 percent of the students of the small schools, and 29 percent of the students in the large school. It is from the nonparticipating students that great numbers of school "drop-outs" come (Willems, in press).

An essential feature of the regulation of behavior settings is that there be two-way communication between a setting and its parts. In particular, it is essential that both a participant and the setting be informed of the adequacy of the participant's functioning. In general, behavior settings are lavish with alternate and emergency circuits to carry these messages. This may be illustrated on a simple, but fundamental level. It is important in a ball game that fly balls be caught, and if not caught, otherwise dealt with; so the ball catcher must know if he did actually catch the ball. Going through the motions is not enough. Consider the player at the moment when his task as a participant in the setting is precisely defined, namely, to catch a fly ball: there is the ball in the sky; the ball's image is on his retinas; his perception of the ball is veridical; the ball approaches, the player's arms raise, his catching hand encounters the ball, but feedback 1, via proprioceptive channels, reports to the player that the ball is not caught; feedback 2, via visual channels, reports that the ball is not caught, but is rolling along the ground; feedback 3, via auditory channels from the umpire, reports that the ball is not caught (and the batter safe); feedback 4, via auditory channels from the other players and spectators, reports that the ball is not caught (the batter safe and the game in jeopardy). If these channels fail to deliver the message of what happened along this E-E arc, there is delayed feedback. Feedback 5, via the manager's memory storage, his verbal mechanism, and the player's auditory channels, reports ten minutes later that the ball was not caught (the batter safe, and the game lost); finally feedback 6, via the sportswriter's story in the paper and the player's visual channels, reports five hours later that the ball was not caught (the batter safe, the game lost). The ball game takes no chances in delivering to the player the report of his behavior deviancy. Those who know the plans of the setting Baseball Game know that if the message of the noncaught ball is not received by the player immediately via feedback channels 1, 2, or 3, and if he gives no return message to the game that he has noted his behavior deviancy, the message will be greatly amplified in channels 4, 5, and 6, and radically altered from a factual message to a strong deviation-countering influence.

Behavior settings and their inhabitants are mutually, causally related. Settings have plans for their inhabitants' behavior, and inputs are activated within the limits of the settings' control systems to produce the planned behavior.[5] If one channel to this behavior is closed, the setting "searches" within the life-space arrangements of the subjects for another open circuit. This is the meaning of Willems' findings that the deviation-countering influences of behavior settings were neither uniform for all inhabitants nor randomly distributed among them, but varied systematically with the personal characteristics of the inhabitants.

From this merest beginning of an ecobehavioral science, one is tempted in many directions and challenged by many problems. But the E-E circuits of the present behavior setting inform me that it has completed

5. The term *plans* is used here as Miller, Galanter, and Pribram (1960) have defined it with reference to individuals.

this phase of its plans, and that deviation-countering homeostats are warming up. So let me close by returning briefly to Kurt Lewin's dilemma, and to our dilemma.

The conceptual breach between psychological and ecological phenomena is, of course, not closed by behavior settings, it is as great as ever. But within the behavior setting context, the problem is restated so that breach can be by-passed on certain levels: the approach is redirected from the sublime but millennial goal of developing a single conceptual system, and also from the discouraging prospect of mere empiricism, probabilism, and fractionated microsciences, to the more modest and hopeful goal of discovering general principles of ecobehavioral organization and control without regard for the conceptual or substantive content of the phenomena regulated.

The recasting of the ecobehavioral problem does not abandon a first approximation to Kurt Lewin's conception of science: it does not abandon derivations; and the life space remains intact. Within a behavior setting a person contributes to the setting by which he, himself, is constrained. The life space is the means by which the setting secures the behavior appropriate to it. And in this connection, it is important to note that in any self-regulated system variety within the system is necessary if varied disturbances outside the system are to be countered. This is true of behavior settings, too, diversity of life space among the inhabitants of a setting makes possible behavior setting *unity* and *stability*. One problem of an ecobehavioral science, is to investigate how diversity and uniformity on the level of persons contributes to the unity and stability of behavior settings. In the past, important resources of psychology have been committed to the development of vetoing regulators which reduce diversity within settings. There is great need now to understand how the powerful deviation-countering control mechanism of behavior settings can produce unity and stability in conjunction with variety among its inhabitants.

Behavior settings have their roots in Kurt Lewin's conceptions of quasi-stable equilibria, in his treatment of parts and wholes, in his concern for the total situation, in his teaching that theory always must defer to data, and in his preoccupation with the ecobehavioral problem. How greatly the plant that has grown from these roots would have benefitted from his cultivation and pruning! Whether or not behavior settings prove to be a fruitful approach to the ecobehavioral problem, they serve at least to continue Lewin's multidirectional approach to it, and to emphasize the crucial importance of the ecobehavioral problem for the science of psychology.

REFERENCES

Allport, F. The contemporary appraisal of an old problem. *Contemp. Psychol.*, 1961, *6*, 195–196.

Ashby, W. R. *An introduction to cybernetics.* New York: Wiley, 1956.

Barker, R. G. Ecology and motivation. In M. Jones (Ed.), *Nebraska symposium on motivation.* Lincoln, Neb.: University of Nebraska Press, 1960. Pp. 1–49.

Barker, R. G. (Ed.). *The stream of behavior.* New York: Appleton, 1963.

Barker, R. G., and Louise S. Barker. Behavior units for the comparative study of cultures. In B. Kaplan (Ed.), *Studying personality cross-culturally.* New York: Harper & Row, 1961. Pp. 457–476.

Barker, R. G., and H. F. Wright. *Midwest and its children.* New York: Harper & Row, 1955.

Barker, R. G., H. F. Wright, Louise S. Barker, and Maxine F. Schoggen. *Specimen records of American and English children.* Lawrence, Kans.: University of Kansas Press, 1961.

Brunswik, E. *The conceptual framework of psychology.* Chicago: University of Chicago Press, 1955.

Brunswik, E. Scope and aspects of the cognitive problem. In H. Gruber, R. Jessor and K. Hammond (Eds.), *Cognition: the Colorado symposium.* Cambridge, Mass.: Harvard University Press, 1957. Pp. 5–31.

Calhoun, J. B. A comparative study of the social behavior of two inbred strains of house mice. *Ecological Monogr.*, 1956, *26*, 81–103.

Calhoun, J. B. Population density and social pathology. In L. Duhl (Ed.), *The urban condition.* New York: Basic Books, 1963. Pp. 33–43.

Calhoun, J. B. Unpublished manuscripts.

Dembo, Tamara, Gloria L. Leviton, and Beatrice A. Wright. Adjustment to misfortune—a problem of social psychological rehabilitation. *Artificial Limbs,* 1956, *3*, 4–62.

Dickman, H. The perception of behavioral units. In R. Barker (Ed.), *The stream of behavior.* New York: Appleton, 1963. Pp. 23–41.

Goffman, E. *Behavior in public places.* New York: Free Press, 1963.

Gump, P. V., and W. V. Friesen. Satisfactions derived by Juniors from nonclass settings of large and small high schools. In R. G. Barker and P. V. Gump, *Big school, small school.* Stanford, Calif.: Stanford University Press, (in press).

Gump, P., P. Schoggen, and F. Redl. The camp milieu and its immediate effects. *J. soc. Issues,* 1957, *13*, 40–46.

Gump, P. V., P. Schoggen, and F. Redl. The behavior of the same child in different milieus. In R. Barker (Ed.), *The stream of behavior.* New York: Appleton, 1963. Pp. 169–202.

Gump, P., and B. Sutton-Smith. The it role in children's games. *The Group,* 1955, *17*, 3–8.

Heider, F. On Lewin's methods and theory. *J. soc. Issues,* 1959, *13*, pp. 1–13.

Jordan, N. Some formal characteristics of the behavior of two disturbed boys. In R. Barker (Ed.), *The stream of behavior.* New York: Appleton, 1963. Pp. 203–218.

Lawrence, D. H. The nature of a stimulus: some relationships between learning and perception. In S. Koch (Ed.), *Psychology: a study of a science.* New York: McGraw-Hill, 1963, Vol. 5. Pp. 179–212.

Leeper, R. W. Learning and the fields of perception, motivation, and personality. In S. Koch (Ed.), *Psychology: a study of a science.* New York: McGraw-Hill, 1963, Vol. 5. Pp. 365–487.

Lewin, K. Defining the "field at a given time." *Field theory in social science.* New York: Harper & Row, 1951. Pp. 43–59.

Lewin, K. Forces behind food habits and methods of change. In D. Cartwright (Ed.), *Field theory in social science.* New York. Harper & Row, 1951. Pp. 170–187.

Lewin, K. Frontiers in group dynamics. *Field theory in social science.* New York: Harper & Row, 1951. Pp. 188–237.

Maruyama, M. The second cybernetics: deviation-amplifying mutual causal processes. *Amer. Scientist,* 1963, *51,* 164–179.

Miller, G. A., E. Galanter, and K. H. Pribram. *Plans and the structure of behavior.* New York: Holt, Rinehart and Winston, Inc., 1960.

Murray, H. A. Preparations for the scaffold of a comprehensive system. In S. Koch (Ed.), *Psychology: a study of a science.* New York: McGraw-Hill, 1959, Vol. 3. Pp. 7–54.

Ratliff, F. Some interrelations among physics, physiology, and psychology. In S. Koch (Ed.), *Psychology: a study of a science.* New York: McGraw-Hill, 1962, Vol. 4. Pp. 417–482.

Raush, H. L., A. T. Dittmann, and T. J. Taylor. The interpersonal behav-ior of children in residential treatment. *J. abnorm. soc. Psychol.,* 1959, *58,* 9–27.

Raush, H. L., A. T. Dittmann, and T. J. Taylor. Person, setting and change in social interaction. *Human Relat.,* 1959, *12,* No. 4, 361–378.

Raush, H. L., A. T. Dittmann, and T. J. Taylor. Person, setting, and change in social interaction: II. A normal control study. *Human Relat.,* 1960, *13,* No. 4, 305–332.

Schoenfeld, W. N., and W. W. Cumming. Behavior and perception. In S. Koch (Ed.), *Psychology: a study of a science.* New York: McGraw-Hill, 1963, Vol. 5. Pp. 213–252.

Soskin, W., and Vera P. John. The study of spontaneous talk. In R. Barker (Ed.), *The stream of behavior.* New York: Appleton, 1963. Pp. 228–282.

Willems, E. P. Forces toward participation in behavior settings of small and large schools. In R. G. Barker and P. V. Gump, (Eds.), *Big school, small school.* Stanford, Calif.: Stanford University Press, (in press).

Willems, E. P. Review of research. In R. G. Barker and P. V. Gump, (Eds.), *Big school, small school.* Stanford, Calif.: Stanford University Press, (in press).

Zener, K., and Mercedes Gaffron. Perceptual experiences: an analysis of its relation to the external world through internal processings. In S. Koch (Ed.), *Psychology: a study of a science.* New York: McGraw-Hill, 1962, Vol. 4. Pp. 516–618.

11

Simulation: The Construction and Use of Functioning Models in International Relations [1]

WAYMAN J. CROW

Simulation is defined as the construction and operation of models, usually reduced in scale from the size or complexity of the situation being modeled. Simulation has had a long history in the physical sciences, particularly in engineering, where the construction of harbor models has aided the understanding of erosion by tidal currents and the use of scale models in wind tunnels has benefited aerodynamics. Simulation has only recently been used in the social sciences. [2]

According to Sigmund Koch (1959), we are ending a whole phase in the history of psychology. The waning influence of Freud and of postulational behaviorism on the thinking of American psychologists has led to a flourishing of new methods, new approaches, and a willingness to extend the scientific approach to problems of great complexity. Simulation in the behavioral sciences is part of this next phase and has been influenced by developments in the laboratory study of small groups, interest in formal, theoretical and mathematical models, the availability of high-speed computers, the concern for systems analysis and operations research, decision and game theory, and the attempt to extend research methods across disciplinary lines. Simulation as part of a new virility has understandably been almost exclusively influenced by the demands of the subject matter studied (business situations, air defense systems, and so

1. The research reported was supported by Project Michaelson, NOTS, China Lake, California.
2. Shubik (1960) has presented a useful bibliography and Guetzkow's book (1962) of readings contains representative simulations in the fields of psychology, sociology, political science, economics, and education.

forth); consideration of its methodological presuppositions or epistemological roots has received less attention.

It will be contended in this paper that the simulation approach to international relations is not only compatible with Egon Brunswik's theoretical orientation, but that the simulation approach has much to gain from it. The theoretical congruence between the simulation approach and Brunswik's probabilistic functionalism is therefore not the only interest—such denotations should also serve useful purposes for simulation research efforts.

There are two reasons for theoretical interest in the relation between Brunswik's orientation and the simulation approach to international relations. The first, as mentioned above, is that the orienting attitudes and conceptual structures adopted in simulation research have tended to arise naturally from the context of the problems dealt with, rather than as a self-conscious application of a systematic methodological viewpoint. Whatever Brunswik's success might have been, he made a great effort to impress psychologists with the necessity for becoming self-conscious of the appropriateness of method with respect to the research problem. Secondly, simulation has developed on the periphery of the main body of psychological theory, and therefore Brunswik's ideas were less likely to have been encountered. In the development of his theory Brunswik relied heavily upon historical analysis of psychology particularly as embodied in perceptual problems. It may be for this reason, as well as for the fact that his empirical research was primarily in the area of perception, that his concern for social psychology and related areas is less well known. The congruence in outlook that appears to have arisen from the consideration of new problems in relative isolation from Brunswik's ideas supports his prediction of a gradual but inevitable convergence toward a functionalist formulation.

It may serve a useful purpose to make explicit the relationship between probabilistic functionalism and simulation research. The application of a systematic theoretical viewpoint may clarify existing problems in simulation and orient future developments.

The presentation proceeds as follows:

1. A description of the Inter-Nation Simulation is presented to provide illustrative materials;
2. An application of this simulation in a research study is described for the same purpose;
3. Specific aspects of probabilistic functionalism are related to the simulation and its research uses, and
4. Two issues in simulation research are examined in the context of Brunswik's orientation.

DESCRIPTION OF
THE INTER-NATION SIMULATION

The Inter-Nation Simulation (INS) as developed by Harold Guetzkow and his colleagues at Northwestern University (Guetzkow, *et al.,* 1962) involves the creation of a world of fictitious nations. These nations are operated by people, the decision-makers, within the rules laid down by the design of the system. The worlds used in the author's research at the Western Behavioral Sciences Institute were composed of five nations, and each nation had three decision-makers. These fifteen decision-makers operated their nations in a series of twelve to fifteen seventy-minute periods. During the seventy-minute periods the decision-makers allocated their resources to the production of consumer goods, armaments, and so forth, made war and defense plans, and attempted to arrange trade agreements with the decision-makers in other nations. They could do this by sending written messages or through conferences. They sent representatives to the meetings of an International Organization and learned of events occurring in the world by reading copies of the *World Times,* a newspaper published each period by the experimenter. These activities produced consequences that were calculated by the experimenters according to preset functional relations among the variables of the system. At the beginning of each seventy-minute period the decision-makers were given new values representing the consequences of their decisions. These numerical values indicated changes in economic and military strength and the satisfaction that the hypothetical people in their nation had with these consequences.

Basic Capabilities and Generation Rates, Trade, Aid, and Alliance are resources available or potentially available to the decision-maker and constitute the raw materials he has to work with to further whatever goals he chooses for his nation. He may use these resources to produce a variety of values. He can produce Consumption Satisfaction Units, Research and Development Projects, more Basic Capability Units, Conventional and Nuclear Force Capability Units and Strength.

The use of the nation's resources to produce these values results in consequences that change the position of the nation at the start of the next seventy-minute period. The Basic Capability and Force Capability Units that are produced are added to those existing at the beginning of the period after a certain proportion has been deducted representing depreciation and operating costs. Other consequences are more complex and affect the position of the decision-maker in relation to the hypothetical population of his nation. This population is represented in the INS by the concept of Validators.

In the INS the Validators are represented by preset functional relations between two sets of variables representing the Validators' satisfaction with national security and with consumption level. These functions are represented by computations made by the experimenter.

The decisions made by the decision-makers of one nation affect the internal affairs of another nation. It is clear that a decision made by one nation to enter or not to enter into Trade, Aid, or Alliance with another nation can affect the Validator Satisfaction in that nation. Less obvious may be the effect of the decision made in one nation to increase Force Capability. This can lower Validator Satisfaction with respect to National Security in a second nation by changing that nation's Relative Strength. The same effect can result within an alliance if one member decreases its armaments or suffers losses due to revolution. It is an important aspect of the simulation that through this interdependency the decisions of another nation can seriously jeopardize the security of a nation's decision-makers in retaining their jobs.

In general, the retention of office depends upon the extent to which the decision-makers of a nation satisfy their validators as indicated by the level of Overall Validator Satisfaction.

Two types of office-holding determination are made by the experimenter—determination for orderly change in office and determination for disorderly change. The determination for orderly change takes place periodically (every two or three periods) as determined beforehand by the experimenter and corresponds to elections or the orderly transfer of power as occurs in the ascension to the throne of an hereditary monarch.

Determination of a disorderly change in office can occur in any period. Whenever Validator Satisfaction drops below an established level the revolution threshold is reached and a determination of the probability of a revolution is made.

If a decision-maker loses office through revolution or through orderly change, he is replaced in the simulation with another participant. Other details involving the richness of the simulation have been omitted.

This then is the system in which the decision-maker operates in Inter-Nation Simulation. He has available certain resources that he uses to produce economic and military values. The production of these values entails consequences in regard to the Validators' satisfaction with their standard of living and national security. These consequences entail further consequences with respect to revolution or orderly change and determine whether the decision-maker retains or loses his office and whether or not there is economic and military growth or stagnation in his nation. The intranational properties must be rich enough to provide an adequate setting for the major theoretical focus, which is the interactions among the national units.

Some additional features should be mentioned. Each period, the decision-maker completes a War Plan indicating his strategy and response should he make war or be attacked. Decision-makers may issue press releases to the *World Times* thus providing an outlet for propaganda. The face-to-face conferences are usually tape-recorded and the decision-makers use written forms for their decisions. International agreements and communication within and between nations are also on written message forms. One copy of all regular messages goes to the *World Times*. These records are available to the experimenter to analyze and provide one major source of data. The experimenter may require the participants to answer questionnaires, to write a History of the World or perform other tasks which provide additional data for analysis.

A STUDY USING THE INTER-NATION SIMULATION [3]

The particular strategy used in the study was Charles Osgood's (1963) Graduated Reciprocation in Tension Reduction—GRIT. In this strategy a nation follows a policy of initiating a series of unilateral moves graduated from low to high risk. These acts must be perceived by the opponent as reducing his external threat so that they invite reciprocation and the reduction of international tensions while at the same time they must not endanger the basic security of the nation following the policy.

In our effort to determine the feasibility of using the INS to perform experiments regarding this strategy a "World" of five nations was established. This world had two major powers, OMNE and UTRO, and three lesser powers: ERGA who was allied with OMNE, and ALGO and INGO who were allied with UTRO.

In order to intervene in the system to produce tension, the experimenters secured the cooperation of the participant who was the central decision-maker (CDM) of the nation OMNE. He was told that from time to time he would be requested to take special actions that no one else was to know about.

In order to provide a measure of the effects of the experimenter's

3. Lawrence N. Solomon was coprincipal investigator with the author in this study. See Crow and Solomon (1962) and Crow (1963) for further details.

interventions and to know the appropriate time to introduce the GRIT strategy, a period by period monitoring of the tension level in the world as perceived by the participants was carried out. Each period the participants responded to questions regarding their perception of the likelihood that war would occur, of the trust being shown among nations, and so forth. The results from these questions were combined for all decision-makers and served as the tension index.

The tension level as shown in Figure 1 built up to a peak as a result of

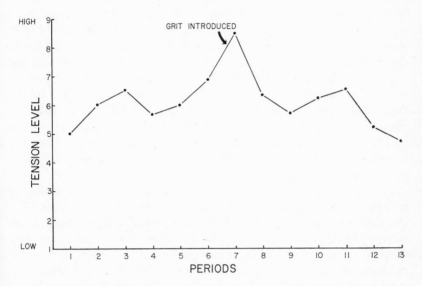

Fig. 1. General tension level. CDM—means of all nations and all scales.

the tension-inducing moves, then decreased following the introduction of the GRIT strategy and tension was at its lowest level at the time the world ended. In a complete experiment, which was not run, these results would be compared to control runs—identical, except that the strategy would not be introduced.

PROBABILISTIC FUNCTIONALISM RELATED TO SIMULATION AND ITS RESEARCH USES

International relations research faces two major obstacles in its progress toward scientific maturity:

A. The enlargement of its objective methodology; and
B. The construction of a conceptual model adequate to the complexity of the relations among nations.

Objective Methodology

Brunswik's observations regarding the requirements of objectivity for psychology may be equally cogent for international relations. The requirements for objectivity are relatively simple—there must be consistency both for the successive observations of a single individual and among the observations of different individuals. Political scientists have been restricted in their efforts to develop their science by a limited objective methodology and the technical difficulties in executing it. Regularities in the phenomena of international relations are difficult to detect with the method of historical analysis because information regarding repetition is often unavailable. This limitation is only partly circumvented by the "case study" method, and both methods lack the ability to produce the phenomena repeatedly at a time when the scientist is prepared to observe it. The scientist is further handicapped because the valuable insights and hypotheses given by these techniques have not been subsequently subjected to rigorous examination.

However, adherence to objectivity does *not* carry with it commitment to other aims and procedures developed by the older sciences. The spectacular success of classical physics recommended it as a model to be followed in other content areas. Classical physics was characterized by the conceptual analysis of matter into small particles—elementarism; the synthesis of these elements in accordance with strict and universally valid laws—nomothetic aim; and preoccupation with the specific mechanism producing observed regularities—reductionism. The imitation of these other aims and procedures of physics has long retarded the development of theory and research in psychology and may be equally stultifying in the development of an empirically based science of international relations.

"In present psychological discussion it is often forgotten that the requirement for scientific exactitude is relatively modest and does not include the reductionist-nomothetic-systematic syndromes which some psychologists have adopted under the spell of a somewhat stereotyped image of physics." (Brunswik, 1956, p. 144.)

Imitation of elementarism in psychology has led to the analysis of behavior into reflexes and conditioned reflexes. Imitation of the nomothetic aim has led to the search for strict and universal laws of conditioning and to the relative neglect or rejection of probabilistic generalizations about behavior. However, probability laws may be just as objective and precise as strict laws and more applicable to the complexity of the relations among nations. Imitation of the reductionist aim in psychology has led to a search for the underlying mechanisms and pathways of mediation of observed stimulus-response relationships and their reduction in the direction of the more fundamental laws of physiology. Under this impetus psychology has increasingly overemphasized its *biological* science content to the detriment of the challenge to psychology inherent in the full range of human activities. It would be unfortunate, and ironic, if the study of international relations were to be sidetracked in the future by an attempted reduction to psychological laws. Particularly so because the new "behavioral approach" in Political Science is just now emerging from a decade-long controversy (Snyder, 1962).

All scientific disciplines must adopt objective methods of observation and communication. Sometimes, unfortunately, other features of the older sciences are mistakenly viewed as additional requirements. Such notions may have been a stumbling block in the development of a *science* of international relations by making such a goal seem unobtainable. Each scientific discipline must be faithful to the requirements of its subject matter and borrowings from other disciplines, particularly whole strategies of research, must be critically examined. Whether or not the borrowings apply should become a matter of empirical fact rather than doctrine.

In extending objective methodology through simulation, a model is created in the laboratory, a model that hopefully mirrors the natural world and lends itself to rigorous objective analysis. It is in this attempt to construct a functioning model that congruence with probabilistic functionalism is most evident.

Construction of a Conceptual Model

Basic to the entire structure of Brunswik's approach is the methodological postulate of behavior-research isomorphism. It is a restatement of Spinoza's credo that the order or pattern of research ideas or design should be the same as the pattern of the thing studied. "Research," wrote Brunswik, "may be said to have reached an adequate, 'functional' or 'molar' level of complexity only if it parallels, and is thus capable of representing behavior in all its essential features." (Brunswik, 1952, p. 25). Once this position is assumed then choice points at critical junctures of the development of theory and method are influenced to a great degree. In viewing behavior in grossly descriptive terms and thus noting its essential features, one chooses the concept that most closely parallels the behavior.

Simulators appear to function as if they had adopted the postulate of behavior-research isomorphism, as indicated by the following quotations:

Developing a model involves abstracting from reality those components and relationships which are hypothesized as *crucial to what is being modeled*. (Brody, 1963, p. 2; emphasis added.)

The central problem inherent in all simulation processes, and in all model building as well, is that of adequate reproduction of the real system. (Dawson, 1963, p. 13.)

Events, as recorded in all their variety in historical and contemporary documents, are the usual basis for the development of theory about relations among nations. . . . Such theory building—consisting of the development of adequate concepts and the relation to these concepts to each other in propositions—must encompass *the welter of facts from life situations*. . . . Simulation is an operating representation of *central features of reality*. (Guetzkow, 1963, pp. 82–83; emphasis added.)

Together, these two kinds of factors and their relationships produce an operating environment for the decision-makers which is designed to be isomorphic to the environment in which foreign policy decision-makers operate within the system of nations of the world. (Guetzkow, 1963, p. 104.)

In following the postulate of behavior-research isomorphism in psychology Brunswik noted that the most prominent descriptive feature of behavior was distal focusing—the convergence of originally diverse and unrelated events toward a characteristic integrated pattern—"the organism is a catalyst of the environment." Two major features are involved in this pattern. The first is called terminal reference—the "purposiveness" inherent in all behavior. The second feature is the variety of "means" available and utilized in persistence toward the goal, called vicarious functioning. Since behavior is focused upon achievement then research should be focused upon achievement and since the organism utilizes an intersubstitutable array of means to achievement, research should be designed to represent this feature of behavior. Such appears to be the case with the INS.

In describing the genesis of the INS, Noel reports that "we were all steeped in the literature of international relations." (Guetzkow, 1963,

p. 70.) Guetzkow mentions the propositional inventory of international relations done by Denis A. Sullivan which "helped guide my selection of key variables." (Guetzkow, 1962, p. 82.) [4] In this search for the central features of the reality of international relations the major feature selected was decision-making—a functional concept. The decision-maker is the catalyst in international relations. This focus is revealed in the fact that without exception all variables in the system described in the preceding section are linked to decision-making. The variables of the system and the relationships as programed in it, define the opportunities and restraints of the decision-making environment. Guetzkow indicates this orientation when he notes, "But the deeper source for this work is found in the developments in decision-making, as exemplified in the work of Simon and Snyder." (Guetzkow, 1962, p. 83.)

Participants in the INS are given a lengthy orientation to acquaint them with the characteristics of the system. They are then purposefully left free to pursue their own goals as decision-makers for their nations. They bring with them their own values and ideas regarding the conduct of relations among nations; in other words, their own distal focusing. Given the starting condition, for example, initial basic capabilities, already established alliances, and so forth, the decision-maker is free to move in the direction of the achievement of his goals, utilizing the variety of cues and means available. His terminal reference may be long-range, such as economic development of his nation, world domination, or peaceful co-existence. Shorter-ranged focusing of his behavior is forced by the seventy-minute periods that require him to allocate his resources regularly.

He must focus upon the environmental parameters as embedded in the system and as revealed to him in the orientation. From the written messages he receives from other decision-makers he may evaluate the intentions of a potential opponent or ally, thus utilizing these cues to guide him in the selection of "means" to an end. He is free to select from a wide variety of means. In working toward economic development, for example, he may invest in the generation of basic capability units, research and development projects, perhaps incur the risk of lowered validator satisfaction by diverting resources from the generation of consumption satisfaction units or from the production of force capability units. He may alternatively arrange for trade, aid, or a loan, a change in alliance, or the reduction of world tensions through disarmament agree-

4. It should be noted that this corresponds in an informal way with the "canvassing of outpost variables" advocated by Brunswik.

ments, in order to free resources. He may select any combination of these potentially adaptive means or none of them.

The preceding discussion has indicated that simulators have followed the major orienting attitudes of probabilistic functionalism with respect to behavior—research isomorphism, terminal focus, and vicarious functioning. The elaboration of this perspective into probabilistic functionalism as a systematic position involves:

a. use of adaptive significance as the criterion of significant problems;
b. focus upon environmental regularities as the external potential available for organismic functioning;
c. recognition that relationships are necessarily probabilistic because of the uncertainties inherent in environmental situations;
d. relegation of the specific mechanism of mediation to secondary consideration.

The use of adaptive significance as the criterion of significant problems

Only those variables that relate to the restraints and supports for decision-making are included in the INS. Many aspects of reality are omitted: for example, the different nations do not have different languages, there is no geography, the specific mechanisms of obtaining office are left unspecified, and so forth. To be sure, the adequacy of the selection and omission of variables is open to question, particularly at this stage of the development of the INS. However, the adaptive significance of each variable should be determined prior to its inclusion.

Focus on environmental regularities

The programed relations among the variables of the system indicate focus upon environmental regularities as the external potential available for organismic functioning. For example, validator satisfaction increases as a function of the excess of consumption satisfaction units remaining in a nation over and above the amount necessary to maintain the population at a subsistence level. Another example is that 1 nuclear force capability unit will destroy 1000 basic capability units in a target nation. The adequacy of the programed relationships in the simulation environment is in doubt; for example, the nuclear destroy ratio is based on unclassified government information only. However, the intent is clear—to provide the decision-maker with the best system of restraints and opportunities in his simulation environment that the present state of theory and knowledge of real world environmental regularities will permit.

Recognition that relationships are necessarily probabilistic

There is a widespread use of stochastic processes and Monte Carlo methods in the programed relations among the variables of the simulation. For example, the amount of payoff received from an investment in a research and development project is determined by a roll of the dice. At a period of orderly determination of office holding, a decision-maker with a very high probability of retaining his office might still lose it if an improbable number were to be selected from the table of random numbers. Comparable improbable events in the real world might be a scandal in the immediate family of the decision-maker or the occurrence of *two* heart attacks. Another manner in which the decision-maker faces an "uncertainty-geared environment," to use Brunswik's phrase, stems from the interdependency of his decisions with the decisions of the leaders in other nations. Does an avowal of peaceful intentions indicate a relaxation of tensions or the prelude to a surprise attack? Are one's smaller allies maintaining the maximum expense of the economic burdens of armaments that their nations can stand, as their leaders maintain, or could they do more?

The use of probabilistic features in the programed relations among the variables in the simulation is necessary because the functional equations are not completely known, nor would it be possible to include all of them in the system. Even if the precise functional relations were known it would not be desirable to include them—to do so would make the environment unrepresentative of the environment faced by real decision-makers. As with the source of uncertainty arising from the other decision-makers in the system, information is of limited *availability* as well as of limited trustworthiness. To quote Brunswik, "The environment to which the organism must adjust presents itself as semierratic and therefore all functional psychology is inherently probabilistic. . . ." (1955, p. 193).

An extended discussion of this point is needed because the nomothetic bias is so ingrained in scientific thinking as to almost require a conscious exercise of will to escape it even temporarily. The probabilistic viewpoint does not deny the existence of universal and strict laws, as Brunswik indicates in reply to Krech:

Contrary to what he imputes, I *do* believe that God does *not* gamble. . . . But the crucial point is that while God may not gamble, animals and humans do, and that they cannot help but to gamble in an ecology that is of essence only partly accessible to their foresight. And although an infinite and omniscient intellect could operate by law and ratiocination alone, as a psychologist even such a being would have to follow the methodological postulate of behavior-research isomorphism and operate at the probabilistic level of discourse. (Brunswik, 1955, p. 236.)

Knowledge of the exact and universal physical laws of triangulation which underlie the perception of physical distance are unknown so far as an actual perceiver is concerned. To use another example, it is possible using strict physical laws to predict the future position of a physical object at a future time, if the initial position, velocity, and direction are known. Baseball players should be able to develop fool-proof predictability and be able to hit a home run every time at bat. They do not develop this ability, of course, because the necessary information is not available to them. Instead, batters develop nervous mannerisms and superstitions, and managers develop strategies colorfully described as "playing the percentages." Another aspect of the issue is illuminated by an example from telecommunication engineering. In overloaded channels in which the capacity of the channel is less than the richness of variability of the message source, it has been shown that it is impossible to devise a system that will remove all uncertainty (Shannon and Weaver, 1949. See also Brunswik, 1956, p. 142). This indicates that even if the information needed to apply strict lawfulness were available to a decision-maker the environment would still remain uncertain because of the impossibility of processing it.

Relegation of the specific mechanism of mediation to secondary consideration

Nomothetic aim, reductionism and elementarism intermesh in that the search for strict laws requires a complete step-by-step linkage of causal elements. Less-than-perfect functional relationships spur the investigator on toward scrutiny of smaller and smaller details of mediation. Less than one-to-one observed regularities are reduced to their elements in the service of a search for strict laws.

Ignoring the empirical facts about the accessibility and uncertainty of the environment (detailed above) in order to retain a nomothetic aim can lead to limited progress in severely restricted content areas. It leads eventually to futility or to conceptual systems that are grotesque caricatures of human functioning. Simulators would do well to resist the allures of such physicalistic imitation or the proddings of their nomothetically oriented colleagues and would do well to relegate mediation to secondary consideration. The argument for the inclusion of mediational detail on the basis of completeness or realism is illusory. Simulators should bypass mediational detail to concentrate upon the more important objective which is to be certain that the *central* features of international relations are encompassed and that the relationships specified among them are adequate approximations of the real system.

TWO ISSUES IN SIMULATION RESEARCH EXAMINED IN THE CONTEXT OF BRUNSWIK'S ORIENTATION

The major question facing the INS is the evaluation of its adequacy as a model of the real world—its representativeness. The second question involves the use of simulations in research designs.

Representativeness

The most widely known aspect of Brunswik's thinking is probably his insistence that we should sample the environment as well as the individual. The two questions most frequently asked about the INS are: How closely does the INS mirror the real world? and, Are the decision-makers in INS studies like real world decision-makers? The first question concerns ecological generality. Ecology is defined as the natural-cultural habitat of an individual or group. The second question concerns populational generality.

Ecological generality

One major purpose of research using INS is in the development and testing of the model itself as a theory of international relations. Simulation models can be checked for their correspondence to reality through three general approaches.

The first is to simulate some known past historical event in order to compare simulation results with historical results. An example is found in the work of the Hermanns (1963) who simulated the events leading up to the outbreak of World War I and whose work included an intriguing first attempt to match the personalities of real world leaders.

After reading personal documents, biographies, and so forth, of several real world leaders of that time, the investigators completed a battery of personality tests, seeking to answer the questions the way the world leaders would have answered them if they had taken the tests. The same tests were administered to a large group of high school seniors, and those having personality profiles matching the World War I leaders were used as decision-makers in the INS. The results regarding the correspondence of the simulation run and the real world historical events were encouraging but lack the necessary replications to be considered evidence.

The second approach is to anticipate history and to simulate events that are expected to occur in the near future. One then waits for the real world events to unfold in order to check the simulation results. An example is the work of Richard Brody (1963) who introduced a spread of nuclear weapons into ongoing simulations in order to test hypotheses regarding alliance patterns. When real world events unfold he will be able to check his results—making Dr. Brody the only person known to the author who is impatiently awaiting the spread of nuclear weapons.

Another study using the same general approach is presently underway at Northwestern University under the direction of Dr. Dorothy Meier. In this study simulations are constructed to run from the present time to several months in the future. The correspondence of simulation results to real world events can thus be checked in a short time-span.

The third approach for checking the adequacy of the model is to seek evidence for each of its subparts. Of particular importance are the functions specified by the model in linking the variables together. Rigorous examination of existing theoretical and empirical findings is needed. For example, in the INS validator satisfaction with respect to the level of consumer goods is given equal weight to validator satisfaction with respect to national security. Evidence should be accumulated to support this weighting or a more accurate approximation.

In each of these three approaches confidence in the ecological generality of the INS will grow as evidence accumulates and as revealed inadequacies are dealt with through revision of the model. How representative of the real world is the INS? We do not know. The work has just begun and the necessary results are not yet available.

It is necessary to be explicit at this point to avoid misunderstanding. There may exist a tendency to introduce a "double standard" regarding the question of whether principles tested and confirmed by a particular research technique are applicable to more complex situations. There is an inclination to exempt the older, classical methods from the same question that is pursued vigorously with methods bearing surface resemblances to reality. Actually all methods have an equal burden of proof and the answer in final analysis is an empirical answer. The approach in answering this question for the INS has been outlined above. It justifiably should be spared the heated criticisms of experimental "purists" until their own preferred methods have adequately shouldered the same burden.

Populational generality

The participants in the INS studies are like those in most studies in the behavioral sciences—they are characterized more by their availability than by their representativeness. They have been high school and college students and navy recruits for the most part. Only a limited number of foreign students and foreign service officers have been used.

However, the approach, at present, is simply not well enough developed to justify a request for the time of high level decision-makers. There appears to be a growing interest in the government in research relevant to international tensions, and so there is reason to believe that cooperation will be obtained when such an effort becomes justifiable.

It is little consolation to know that you stand with your colleagues on the same thin ice with regard to populational representativeness. This is particularly true for the simulator of international relations who walks on the same thin ice carrying a heavier burden. The burden is heavier because national decision-makers are a highly selected and presumably unique group. It is important that the question of population generality be carefully stated. The question is frequently asked, "Can you predict the actions of real world leaders from results obtained using Naval recruits?" Phrased in this way the question is inappropriately exacting. Predictions of the behavior of a single individual from the best psychological test data are precarious and even the "exact" sciences use safety factors in the order of seven to one when applied to bridge building. This is due to the uncertainty in predicting the load-bearing capabilities of individual steel beams. Predictions are limited to probable outcomes in all cases. What is needed is to discover and verify principles of decision-making behavior. Once known, the applicability of these principles to a specific real world context and personality will for a long time, perhaps forever, remain an art. An art that at present can profit greatly from even slight reductions in probable error.

Simulation is at the stage of development where principles investigated in studies using samples from homogeneous populations can fruitfully be tested for their populational generality. Preliminary work is underway to investigate the effects of selected personality variables upon the outcomes of simulation runs. INS studies using participants from other cultures are also planned. From such efforts answers may be found to the questions: Which principles remain constant and which ones change as populations of participants change? Which personality and cultural characteristics are significant determiners of simulation outcomes?

The Use of Simulation in Research Designs

Simulations may be used as a method of controlling and manipulating variables in order to test hypotheses—that is, as a central element in experimental designs. With this use, it serves the same function as a t-maze, Skinner box, or the laboratory use of small groups. For this purpose one sets aside temporarily the question of the correspondence of the simulation to the real world in the same way that experimenters set aside the question of whether or not the t-maze or the presentation of nonsense syllables on a memory drum is an adequate simulation of real life learning situations.

There has been some confusion regarding the use of the Inter-Nation Simulation in experiments, which arises from an attempt to distinguish between *quasi* or *pseudo* experiments and "true" experiments. Helmer and Rescher (1959) identify pseudo-experiments as those carried out in the model and not in reality. But this distinction has led to the errone-ous statement that experiments as such cannot be carried out using a simulation.

In his examination of formal psychological theories Brunswik noted that nomothetic rigor is often purchased at the price of withdrawal within boundaries lacking adequate scope—they become in his term "encapsu-lated." This concept is useful in clarifying the issue of pseudo-experi-ments. Experiments carried out solely in the model are encapsulated. Feedback loops are self-contained within such systems and do not pass out into the surroundings where there can be ecological involvement. However, simulations can be made part of a larger system and therefore the answers to predictive problems are not preset.

The term "pseudo-experiment" could be a useful distinction if it were restricted to mean the introduction of changes in a model in order to determine the effects of the change on other parts of the model. However, it would perhaps avoid confusion if the term "experiment" were not used at all, if instead one talked about "tuning" a model or "logical explora-tion" of a model in the same way that one determines the consequences of a change in an assumption on a mathematic system. The intent is to learn more about the internal workings of the model and conclusions are restricted to it.

To clarify the issue, consider the following two research designs:

1. In a multiple t-maze learning situation after animals reach a certain cri-terion, say 80 percent correct turns, electric shock will be introduced into the incorrect alleys. The performance of the animals under this experi-mental condition is then compared to the performance of animals under the same conditions except that shock is not introduced.

2. In the Inter-Nation Simulation after a certain level of perceived tension has been reached, a particular strategy is introduced. The performance of the decision-makers under this experimental condition is then compared to the performance of decision-makers under the same conditions except that the strategy is not introduced.

While these two designs may differ in details such as the precision of controls, they are not fundamentally different and both must be considered as "true" experiments or both must be considered as "pseudo" experiments. To consider them both "pseudo" experiments violates customary usage, and there can be no "true" experiments at all if they must be carried out in reality in order to qualify. All experimentation involves abstracting from reality—some intervention into the natural flow of events. Otherwise, the term experimentation does not apply, and one speaks instead of a field study.

In concluding this attempt to relate the method of simulation research to Brunswik's probabilistic functionalism, it is important to stress, even to exaggerate, the potentiality inherent in this new approach. In the past few years a surprising number of behavioral scientists have turned their attention and research efforts towards the problems of international tensions. This event in itself represents a shaking-loose from the restrictions of aim and scope, characteristic of the traditional orientation in political science and psychology. But this flood of ingenuity and hope can be dammed and diverted by the hostility of a conventionally-minded majority. Insistence on the conventional approach can shunt this new potential into a tedious reenactment of the search for strict laws. Those continuing to work within the framework of the "tried and true" approach to the scientific endeavor can nevertheless nurture an exciting potentiality by giving supportive counsel to new approaches no matter how unconventionally risky or brash they may seem to be.

It has been the purpose of this chapter to link one of these new approaches, simulation research, to Brunswik's orientation. His orientation involves functionalism—focus on life-relevant problems and probabilism —recognition of an uncertain environment. The expression "our chances for survival" translates directly into the terms of probabilistic functionalism.

REFERENCES

Brody, R. A. Political games for model construction in international relations. In H. Guetzkow, *et al.* (Eds.), *The use of simulation for* *teaching and research in international relations.* Englewood Cliffs, N.J.: Prentice-Hall, 1963, 190– 223.

Brunswik, E. *Perception and the representative design of psychological experiments*. Berkeley, Calif.: University of California Press, 1947.

Brunswik, E. *The conceptual framework of psychology*. Chicago, Ill.: University of Chicago Press, 1952.

Brunswik, E. In defense of probabilistic functionalism: a reply. *Psychol. Rev.*, 1955, *62*, 236–242.

Brunswik, E. Representative design and probabilistic theory in a functional psychology. *Psychol. Rev.*, 1955, *62*, 193–217.

Crow, W. J., and L. N. Solomon. A simulation study of strategic doctrines, La Jolla, Calif., Western Behavioral Sciences Inst., 1962 (mimeo).

Crow, W. J. A study of strategic doctrines using the Inter-Nation Simulation. *J. confl. Res.*, 1963, *7*, 580–589.

Dawson, R. Simulation in the social sciences. In H. Guetzkow (Ed.), *Simulation in social science: readings*. Englewood Cliffs, N. J.: Prentice-Hall, 1962, 1–15.

Guetzkow, H. (Ed.) *Simulation in social science: readings*. Englewood Cliffs, N. J.: Prentice-Hall, 1962.

Guetzkow, H. A use of simulation in the study of inter-nation relations In H. Guetzkow (Ed.), *Simulation in social science: readings*. Engle-wood Cliffs, N. J.: Prentice-Hall, 1962, 82–93.

Guetzkow, H., et al. *Simulation in international relations: developments for research and teaching*. Englewood Cliffs, N. J.: Prentice-Hall, 1963.

Helmer, O., and N. Rescher. On the epistemology of the inexact sciences. *Mgmt. Sci.*, 1959, *6*, 25–52.

Hermann, C. F., and Margaret G. Hermann. On the possible use of historical data for validation study of the Inter-Nation Simulation. Northwestern Univer.: Program of Graduate Training and Research in International Relations, January, 1962.

Koch, S. Introduction to study I. Conceptual and systematic. In S. Koch (Ed.), *Psychology: a study of a science*, Vol. 1. New York: McGraw-Hill, 1959, 19–40.

Osgood, C. E. *An alternative to war or surrender*. Urbana, Ill.: Illini Books, 1962.

Shannon, C. E. and W. Weaver. *Mathematical theory of communication*. Urbana, Ill.: University of Illinois Press, 1949.

Snyder, R. C. Experimental techniques and political analysis: some reflections in the context of concern over behavioral approaches. *Ann. Amer. Acad. Pol. Soc. Sci.* Monogr., Philadelphia, 1962.

II
CRITICISMS

12

Representative Sampling and the Purposes of Perceptual Research: Pictures of the World, and the World of Pictures [1]

JULIAN HOCHBERG

The most important questions to ask about any scientific endeavor concern what sorts of factual questions should be asked. These methodological issues are usually most difficult to face. Since the piecemeal demise of "structuralism"—which was the effort to build all behavior around mental content and to build all mental content up out of a finite set of ideas of sensation (and memories of previous sensations)—the most consistent and painstaking attempt to construct a programmatic methodology, taking full account of the failure of past purposes, was that made by Egon Brunswik.

Brunswik tried to answer basic questions of method and purpose that others have left implicit. His most important proposal was, I believe, that of "representative design," but the usefulness of this answer depends upon the precise questions that are being asked (and upon the purposes for which the data are sought). Although the difficulties that Brunswik faced will not go away merely by our ignoring them, the particular solutions that he proposed are not always applicable, and it will pay to identify the areas in which they are.

THE NEED FOR REPRESENTATIVE DESIGN

Brunswik demonstrated the need for "representative design" most clearly, I think, in the series of four experiments that comprise the

1. This paper was written in the course of an inquiry in pictorial perception supported by NSF GB71.

361

framework of *Systematic and representative design of psychological experiments* (1956). Each is described in turn below.

Experimental Design, Type A

The structuralist psychophysical program of research is exemplified by the Galton Bar experiment:

Two lengths of rod are presented against homogeneous backgrounds, which isolate them from contaminating influences. There is only one independent variable, the length of the Variable bar, which the observer compares to the Standard bar viewed from the same distance, by one of the traditional psychophysical procedures. The dependent variables are the *precision* and *accuracy* of size-estimation (measured, respectively, in *DL*s, that is, the minimum change in length that is required for the observer to recognize that a difference exists, and *PSE*s, that is, the actual physical lengths at which observers judge the two lengths to be equal). Statistics measures appear in the analyses of these data only as error terms, to be minimized and avoided.

The only systematic purposes for undertaking such research are:

1. These data (the *DL*s) might be treated as elementary perceptual experiences (*sensations*) out of which to construct the perception of other (less artificial) situations in which we might be interested: this was the structuralist enterprise, and, for a variety of reasons, is no longer *explicitly* considered seriously.
2. These situations might reveal the organism's performance under the best and simplest conditions; knowing such "simple psychophysics," we are presumably in a better position to attack "more complex" problems, and, eventually, even those of daily encounter.

Brunswik is fighting no straw man here. The literature still abounds in "detection thresholds" and scales obtained from isolated points or patches of light, and in interminable debates over "subceptual" thresholds, with little or no attempt to set either a purpose or a future to such undertakings.

It is perfectly true, of course, that any scientist hopes that the psychometric functions obtained in the Galton Bar situation will eventually be explainable by the same overall laws that will explain other and more generally interesting perceptual phenomena, and that lawful relationships may (and, in some sense, "should") be studied *wherever* they occur. But it is also true that, when these univariate "detection" experiments were really in their ascendancy, there was a clear and definite conceptual structure in terms of which they could be regarded as the "simplest cases," as the building blocks out of which all else could be built, and *this belief is no longer considered tenable.*

Hence, it becomes incumbent on the researcher in this area to inquire into, and report upon *the generalizability of his findings to other situations,* that is, either to show the precise sense in which we may again regard these as "simple" starting points or, if they are not to be so regarded, what the program of research is, from which these studies derive their programmatic meaning.

Brunswik is unassailably correct, here, it seems to me, and one can only hope that this point eventually sinks in. It is too easy to find writers quoting Brunswik's methodological dicta with apparent reverence, in a paper dedicated to, say, experimentally demonstrating the effects of "needs" upon size-judgment thresholds, ignoring the fact that only the repudiated decades of structuralism provide some purpose to the experimental demonstration. Brunswik himself held that such threshold-data cannot provide starting points that are "simple" in any sense of the word, for reasons that become clear when we consider the second experiment in his heuristic series:

Experimental Design, Type B

The *"Gestalt* problems" appear with "multidimentional psychophysics"; if the simple Galton bar gains "arrowheads," thus destroying the "isolation" of the bars, we obtain the famous Muller-Lyer "illusion": in the Galton bar, the lengths of the bars, and the sizes of the adjacent areas impinging on the bars, had been "artificially tied" together, that is, *area* and *length* were automatically covaried in strict proportionality. In consequence, their relative importance as stimulus variables in determining the apparent lengths of the lines, could not be evaluated. In the Muller-Lyer experiment, if we vary lengths and areas independently by varying the angles made by the "arrowheads," the adjacent *area* is shown to be at least as predictive of the observers' judgments of the lengths of the lines, as is the variable of *length,* itself.

Here is the main problem to which "representative design" is addressed.

The structuralist assumption was this: that we can vary one dimension of stimulation (and its corresponding dimension of response) at a time, *and that we can readily identify the two psychophysically-related dimensions which are being varied:* ". . . length . . . is apt to be singled out by the classical experimenter as the independent variable, both by virtue of its introspective prominence as what may be called the 'figural variable' and by virtue of its being the most conveniently manipulable or measurable aspect of the situation." (Brunswik, 1956, pp. 16ff.) The apparently-simple experiment pretends to be "univariate" but is in reality "clustervariate" (that is, covarying length and area, among other variables, in an arbitrarily-tied fashion), concealing the real complexity of the psychophysical determinant of apparent length. Only by issuing a host of unexplicated but irredeemable promissory notes can we relate the artificial structure of the traditional psychophysical experiment, to the world in which the organism normally functions.

Brunswik does not really inquire into the Gestalt-problem proper, here: somewhat prematurely, he accepts a version of the classical "confusion theory" (Woodworth, 1938, p. 645), that is, that apparent length is simply a compromise between the two alternative possible "poles of intention" (that is, the independent variables of *length* and *area*). Although it is presented almost as a methodological principle, however, this is merely one *theory* about an illusion. This apparently simple handling of the Gestalt problem is in reality as much an example of inadequate ecological sampling, as was the structuralist Galton bar experiment. The problems of explaining the illusions, which Brunswik dismisses as questions of "merely mediating" variables, are clearly more than that: they have methodological implications in themselves, as Brunswik's use of this one indicates. Brunswik's writings are not mere exercises in logic: his methodology was based on research findings, and his prescriptions have to be reviewed in that context. Brunswik was more interested in being able to predict the observer's general *achievement* in responding to the distal variable of length, embedded as it is among other variables, than in being able to "explain" the illusion. However, the measure of "achievement" one employs depends upon the particular theory and illusion chosen, and this "illusion" is no more representative than the Galton bar. The Muller-Lyer pattern has punctured one psychophysical hypothesis (that is, that apparent length is a simple function of physical length), but it has not established another one in its place, nor has it shown that another hypothesis cannot be offered.

Experimental Design, Type B, was presented to show that *factorial design* (that is, the simultaneous manipulation of two or more independent variables) is necessary to disclose the *interaction* of length and area to be the effective variable, and to reveal failure of the "univariate" psychophysical theory. However, if we had started with this complex *interaction* itself as our independent variable, a univariate design would have been sufficient throughout (this, as we shall see, is Gibson's strategy). Factorial designs are not *necessary* for "multivariate psychophysics"; are they always *sufficient* to insure recognition of the true variables at work? No: factorial designs guarantee immunity from artificially-tied variables only if experiments could be performed in which all possible variables could be simultaneously and independently varied over their entire ranges.

But this cannot, of course, be done. Some basis for choice must be found, and this is why "ecological sampling" is such an important concept; it allows us to choose those combinations (and levels) of variables for study, that we are likely to encounter in future use of the data we have found. An explicit attempt to do this appears in the next experiment.

Experimental Design, Type C

"Achievement" comes more clearly to the fore as the purpose of research, in the Size Constancy experiment: in the "illusions" of Experimental Design, Type B, observers made "errors" in length or size judgment, which were in correspondence neither with the retinal images (*proximal* stimulus variables) nor with the object lengths (the *distal* stimulus variables); these two sets of variables had been manipulated in unison in both of the first experiments. Now, in real life, since the size of the retinal image is a function of both the distal size of the object and of the distance from the eye at which that object is placed, the two sets of variables can be "untied" (that is, varied independently) by setting the standard at one distance and the variable at another, and by requiring the observer to bring the two to apparent equality. This act— the untying of the proximal size from the distal size—reveals another striking discrepancy between the proximal stimulus and the psychophysical judgment. The Brunswik ratio (or the "constancy ratio") measures the extent to which the judgment of equality can be predicted from the two variables of proximal and distal size: If perception of equality were completely determined by the proximal stimulus measures, the constancy ratio would be 0.00; if it were completely determined by the distal stimulus measures, the ratio would be 1.00. The fact that constancy ratios are commonly closer to 1.00 than to 0.00 is very important in Brunswik's argument in favor of the necessity of representative design, for three reasons:

1. This fact, that our judgments correspond to the constant, stable distal object, rather than to their changing proximal projections, is a widespread characteristic of our perception of things. Measures of the physical object provide us with a more reliable basis for predicting judgments in *natural situations,* than do measures of the proximal stimulation that falls upon the receptor organs, or than do the traditional approaches to psychophysics that strove to discover the chains of causal connections within the organism. We need a broad, organismic functionalism that will enable us

to predict observers' perceptual achievement, from our measures of objects in their natural contexts.

2. If perceptual achievement were perfect, there would be no problems for perception psychologists to study: perception would reflect completely the stimulating environment, and, to predict what people see, we would need only to know what the world is like. However, constancy ratios are *not* 1.00, and we cannot predict responses unequivocally from our knowledge of the (distal) stimulus. Thus, Brunswik maintains, we must be content with discovering probabilistic relationships only; stimulus-response probabilities vary with individual differences in perceptual abilities, with different attitudes, with different choices of experimental procedure, and so forth. There will always be variability in our data, and failures in our predictions. Why, in the face of such variability, can we not simply try to find a new set of variables? Because ". . . . the alleged unidimensionality of the classical experiment . . . must appear fallacious. . . . It is obviously in the nature of things that not all variables except one be held constant, if only the scope of experimental observation is extended beyond the immediate conditions . . . (which) must be done if the goal is an inventory of the gross efficiency of organismic functioning . . . rather than a study of the 'fundamental' minutiae of organismic technology." (Brunswik, 1956, p. 20.)

    We will see that this assertion has been challenged as being more the result of an inadequate analysis of the proximal stimulus distribution than an "atheoretical" methodological conclusion, and that this error in analysis, in turn, was a consequence of Brunswik's unrepresentative sampling of the stimulus environment.

3. The classical theories of psychophysical relationships were erroneous overgeneralizations from inadequate samplings of stimulus-combinations. However, we cannot simply test *every* conceivable situation to avoid overgeneralization: to what variables, and in what directions, should we extend research? Brunswik's answer is that we should sample the universe of situations *representatively*, that is, ". . . representative sampling is extended from the subjects to the objects, from the individuals to the stimulus situations . . . and psychology is conceived of as a fundamentally statistical discipline throughout its entire domain," with "functional validity taking its place alongside . . . test validity," and it ". . . becomes possible to ascertain the 'ecological generality' or 'applicability,' of a result along with its counterpart, populational generality or reliability . . . bringing to convergence European academic with Anglo-American statistical tradition." (Brunswik, 1956, p. 58.) We can, in short, minimize our errors in prediction, *and attach known error terms to those predictions, by the suitable sampling of our experimental situations to reflect the environments to which we wish to generalize our findings.*

This is an immensely bold suggestion and, even if we have to limit it severely, as I think we shall, it is more constructive and revolutionary in its potential effects than has yet been realized in any field of perceptual research.

How is such sampling to be performed?

In an early size-constancy experiment which Brunswik devoted to this attempt, the two variables of *proximal size* and *bodily size* were not systematically varied by the experimenter, but were ". . . randomly sampled from the normal environment of a university student, stopped in her daily routine . . . to write down her estimates of the extension that happened to be most prominently attended to by her as 'figure' in her visual field of the moment, as well as of other elements of the situation, shifting from one of five attitudes to another." (Brunswik, 1956, p. 44.) What can we do with the resulting data? "If such a program were carried out on a variety of functional topics, a subject . . . could then be described in his relationships to the world by a set of correlation coefficients . . . From the coefficients describing these relationships one would, of course, not be able to predict correctness of orientation in the environment with certainty in any particular instance. But they definitely would give an overall relative frequency ('probability') of adequate contact with vitally relevant variables, which may be a much more relevant type of information than certainty with respect to relatively insignificant instances or details." (Brunswik, 1956, p. 48.)

DIFFICULTIES IN ECOLOGICAL SAMPLING: ATTENTIONAL, ATTITUDINAL, AND CONCEPTUAL

Attentional

The observer's "attention" was used to define the set of distal objects that comprise the ecological sample in the representative survey of Experimental Design, Type C. Is the subject a reliable source of such information? Recent comparisons of subjects' judgments of where they are attending, with eye-movement records, grossly confirm this assumption, but we need more precise information (Hochberg and Brooks, 1962).

Will different observers sample the environment, by their fixation-sequences, in similar ways? Will even a single observer generate a determinable frequency distribution? There is now some good evidence supporting this (Brooks, 1961)—but all obtained under the same task, namely, "pay attention to your attention." Brunswik was well aware of the dangers of generalizing from one attitude to another, and he tried to obtain each observation under a number of different instructor-induced attitudes (five, in his experiment). He made no attempt at a *sampling* of possible attitudes or tasks, however, and this provides our next difficulty:

Attitudinal

Do subjects look at the same things in their environment when they are periodically being stopped for questioning, as when they are pursuing some more normal task? Even if they do, are the judgments that are made in the course of some instrumental activity, and that are expressed in terms of such activity, (for example, threading an automobile through a gap in the traffic) the same as those expressed as verbal opinions? (This, of course, is the problem faced by the social psychologist who tries to base his predictions of subjects' behavior—for example, voting—on the answers they have put to questionnaires.) We have some reason to believe (Smith and Smith, 1960) that verbal judgments are not, in general, good predictors of spatial behaviors, but these samples of tasks also cover a restricted range of possible behaviors.

The only criterion that would suffice to test the validity of this kind of sampling procedure, would be *the actual performances of those specific tasks to which one wants to generalize* (for example, driving ability in traffic), and it then becomes gratuitous to try to interpose a laboratory questioning procedure to try to discover what the subject "perceives." That is, if we have followed Brunswik this far, it seems to me that we must be prepared to go farther: *if our criterion is only functionalistic achievement, with no concern for "mediating mechanisms," the entire purpose of perceptual research becomes unclear. What we should study, by this reasoning, is spatial performance—not perceptual observations.*

Conceptual

If we consider the population of normal *situations* to which we propose to generalize, the sampling in this size-constancy experiment is inadequate to Brunswik's purposes since "normal" observations are made by a locomoting observer in a world that provides most of the information about the distal environment *in direct consequence of that locomotion:*

The systematic examination of such motion-dependent information comes from Gibson, who would deny that such measurements of the proximal stimulus-pattern as can be achieved by a stationary judgment point have any relevance to the variables from which the size judgment should, most naturally, be predicted: the relevant variables are the higher-order invariants and stimulus-gradients that confront the normal observer-in-motion (Gibson, 1959). These variables of proximal stimulation are, to all practical purposes, *perfectly* correlated with the distances, sizes, and so forth, of distal events, and therefore provide (essentially) *certain, rather than probabilistic, information about the sizes and distances in the distal world confronting the observer.* Whether or not real observers do in fact make use of this potentially-usable information, remains a question that has by no means been answered, and there are considerable difficulties with Gibson's approach that accrue from an inability to discriminate in advance between those situations that will in fact generate illusions and errors, and those which will occasion more-or-less veridical perception.

There is good reason to doubt (Smith and Smith) that observers do utilize all of this potential information, and to the extent that environments differ in the availability of these "higher-order" cues, some kind of ecological sampling will be needed before Gibson's hypotheses can be fully tested or used (Hochberg and Smith, 1955). But a fundamental difference remains: Gibson has shown that one *can* still propose a psychophysics in which the only use of statistics is to handle errors. And this reveals two limitations of the representative sampling procedure undertaken by Brunswik.

The first limitation is this: the arguments that representative sampling is a methodologically necessary consequence of the "inevitably probabilistic" relationships between proximal stimuli and distal world, are overgeneralizations. These arguments are based upon a vulnerable psychophysical theory, not upon some unassailable deductions from some logical structure, nor upon a firm empirical foundation.

The second limitation is that "representative sampling" is no substitute for a theory of what to look for: Brunswik's theory about what he considered to be an adequate sampling procedure, what he accepted as an adequate representative sampling procedure, limited the variables his measures could discover, just as surely as did the limitations of the "univariate" design of Experimental Design, Type A (1956, p. 12).

Thus, instead of the usual tasks that confront observers, Brunswik's sample more closely approximated a study of *still pictures:* "In the statistical survey of size constancy . . . . It was decided to postpone investigation of the effectiveness of the distance cues . . . . It was emphasized, however, that an investigation of this type of mediational problem . . . would have been quite possible if, say, the situations of the survey had been photographed from the place where the subject stood *(thus establishing a duplicate of retinal configurations) and these records had been subjected to further scrutiny"* (italics mine). This is precisely what Gibson would deny as providing an adequate sampling of the "distance criteria," at all. But to Brunswik the momentary picture, and its independent parts, comprise the population of independent proximal variables to be sampled: "An analysis of . . . the ecological validity of distance cues, is undertaken in a forthcoming study by . . . Seidner, who uses randomly selected pictures from a popular magazine and randomly selected places . . . within these pictures." Examination of the various traditional pictorial cues of depth (that is, ways of rendering distance on a picture) ". . . suggest the following ecological validities, that is, correlations of the real distances in the situations photographed . . . with the actual location, color, and so forth, of their projections in the photographs." (Brunswik, 1956, p. 49.)

What population of stimuli does such a sample represent? In what sense are these measures called "ecological" validities? Since we see a bias appearing in Brunswik's sampling procedure (p. 10), can we find some precautions that will insure representativeness? Before we attempt to deal with these questions, let us consider the last experiment in Brunswik's series, in which they receive much firmer answers:

Experimental Design, Type D

This was concerned with the "social perception of traits" (from photographs): here, the stimulus objects, as well as the observers, are persons. The basic problem is, how well can observers judge such "covert distal" traits as "intelligence," "honesty," and so forth, from faces. If the only stimuli being judged were an American banker and an Australian aborigine, in their native garb, we could not conclude much about the judgment of, say, intelligence, no matter how large and representative the sample of the *observers*. Some form of representative sampling is thus as necessary for the stimulus-objects, as it is for the observers.

This experiment provides explicit measures of all of the kinds of generalization we might wish to make, in relatively unambiguous form. Let us consider several of the eight different uses to which Brunswik puts the correlation coefficient here, the purposes to which they can be used, and the assumptions necessary before those purposes can be safely attempted.

Populational generalizations

Consider first the traditional question of *interobserver reliability:* within what probable error can we expect to obtain the same findings with new groups of observers? As long as we have sampled our group of observers randomly from some population having a known distribution, we can make our predictions with a well-defined expectation of error. Here, the sampling procedure by which we draw our observers from the population of people whose performance we wish to predict, simply need follow one of the standard survey or sampling procedures.

Attitudinal generalizations

To what extent can a judgment that was obtained with one task or attitude be relied upon as a predictor of some other behavior? This problem is relatively unbothersome with respect to stimulus sampling, in this experiment, since the sample of stimuli (that is, people to be judged) can be set up independently of the attitudes of the judges: at least we know that this sample of stimuli does not itself depend upon the task of the judges in this experiment, as it did in the case of the size-constancy experiment (1956, pp. 43–48).

Measures of achievement

Of these, *functional validity* is central: this measures extent to which the observer responds to the variable to be judged—in this experiment, the actual measured intelligence of the persons who are being judged. Such abilities are limited by:

Ecological generalizations

The observer cannot possibly do better in judging the environment, than the consistency of the environment itself permits. Brunswik has defined two critical measures of environmental consistency: The *ecological reliability* measures the consistency of any measure of the stimulus object (for example, how reliable is the IQ in the population from which our sample was drawn?). The *ecological validity* measures the extent to which we can predict one stimulus variable by measuring another (for example, in this experiment, the correlations between, say, the forehead-height of the stimulus-objects, and their IQs).

Note that in the situations described in (4), our measures of stimulus-populations are the counterparts of those obtained with the populations of observers, in (1). That is, the necessary generalizations can be made only to the extent to which the experimental measures are obtained from samples that were randomly selected from populations with known distributions. In this "social perception" experiment, we can do this (at least ideally) because our stimuli are people, having known distribution characteristics. We can thus (again, at least in principle) consider the attempt at representative sampling of stimulus situations to be meaningful.

We can also see a clear way to do this for other objects with determinate distributions: trees, handwriting, voices, cats, and so forth—objects whose distributions we can know or estimate, whose definitions as a class are not subject to the task and differential attention of the subject. Is there any general way in which we can do the same for size-constancy and space-perception experimentation?

What is wrong with the technique of sampling published pictures?

Why Pictures Are Not Representative Samples of the World of Proximal Stimulation

In the research we have considered, Brunswik has used *pictures* (or approximations-to-pictures) as the populations of environments from which sampling was undertaken. We have seen that this can be challenged as being unrelated to the proximal stimulus confronting the eye in the normal observer-environment relationship. Moreover, while Gibson's "higher-order variables" do depend upon some small degree of implicit ecological sampling (for example, the approximate homogeneity of texture-distributions, and the expectation of surface-continuity and structural rigidity in the normal environment), the determinacy of the proximal-distal relationship in Gibson's system (as opposed to the probabilistic uncertainty postulated by Brunswik) places no premium upon what would be incredibly expensive surveys to obtain representative ecological information. When Gibson's research has generated enough information about the degree of error that we should expect to obtain in different kinds of environment (which it does not as yet provide), some form of representative sampling will again be in order. I think that we will have, at that time, a "complete" theoretical approach to the problems of space perception. At present, we have three components for such an approach, none of which are ready for attempts at integration: the Gestalt insights in intrastimulus dependencies; Brunswik's representative functionalism with its focus on the importance of the distal stimulus and on the purposes for which research is being undertaken; and Gibson's "higher-order psychophysics" which, discarding the "simple elements" of psychophysics (which were only superficially simple), seeks to discover new dimensions of proximal stimulation, which are in correspondence with both the distal world to which the organism must adapt and with (at least) the "veridical" or accurate components of response.

Brunswik has been sampling, not proximal stimuli, but a special class of distal objects, *pictures*. Examining the samplings of pictures, we shall see that these have no stateable relationship to the normal tridimensional world, no relationship that will permit generalization from one to the other to be made. Consider Brunswik's later attempt to deal with the Gestalt problem:

One of the best known of the organizational principles of human perception . . . is the factor of . . . "proximity." According to this principle, the two constituent items in pairs of dots or parallel lines will the more tend to be united in a common perceptual "figure" the closer to each other they are in the visual field. . . . The functionalist must ask whether or not organization by nearness is biologically useful. Such usefulness would be given if, more often than not, parallels close to each other in the visual field could be traced to the common boundaries of a mechanically coherent, manipulable object . . . The problem of the ecological validity of nearness (or proximity) can be answered only by representative sampling the existing ecology.

Brunswik and Kamiya attempted to approximate such a sample with the use of seven shots from a well-known motion picture reproduced in a popular magazine and covering a well-distributed variety of common-life situations . . . pairs of adjacent straight (or near-straight) parallels . . . were considered . . . from the proximal point of view, their separations were classified in eight distance categories. . . . From the distal point of view the pairs were classified dichotomously (A) as forming joint contour(s) of a bilaterally exposed permanent mechanical unit or (B) as falling into any one of a group of other alternatives having in common a more incidental and behaviorally less relevant origin of the separation. (Brunswik, 1956, pp. 119-120.)

Low point-biserial correlations were found, and "The proof, just reported, of the existence of such a validity at least for one of the Gestalt factors of organization opens up the possibility of viewing the stimulus configuration involved in this factor, proximity, as a cue acquired by generalized probability learning." (Brunswik, 1956, p. 122.)

Now I cannot accept this conclusion even if I were prepared to consider pictures as being equivalent to proximal stimulation (which, for reasons considered above, I am not). There is an important and revealing inadequacy in the sampling procedure that was employed: "Proximity" was not measured in any way that would allow generalizations to be made upon which to base conclusions about "probability learning." The viewpoints from which the pictures were taken, were certainly not a representative sample of the world. They are not randomly sampled, either, because they were chosen by the cameraman from a population of possible camera positions, by an editor from a population of pictures submitted to him, and both of these "human filters" were at some pains to eliminate those pictures that are confusing, misleading or unpleasing. This is not an erratic sampling, either: *to the extent that cameraman and editor have based their selective procedures upon the proper use of "proximity"* (that is, to avoid "shots" in which close parallels on the picture are *not* part of the same portrayed object), *whether through intuition or precept, we have measured only the operation of this Gestalt factor in the behavior of those editors, not its occurrence in the ecology.*

This is the problem of the interaction of observer on the one hand, and the defined ecology on the other, which we have encountered before (p. 43). It will and must appear whenever we try to define a population of stimuli that is set off from the rest of the possible populations of stimuli by the fact that it confronts the observer as a result of the observer's own tasks and actions. It has occurred here because Brunswik and Kamiya merely replaced the tasks of the "normal" observer, to whose environment they wished to generalize, by the tasks of the cameraman and editor and, inadventently, the tasks of the latter include a component (that of selecting "good pictures" to put on paper) which completely confounds the meaning of the results.

We have no reason to believe in advance that any such set of measures will comprise a stochastic process with definable transition probabilities, since at any point in the series of measures, some new decision may be reached, some motive may be "triggered," some total of confirming or disconfirming observations with respect to some organismic "hypothesis" may be exceeded, and the task of "searching the environment" will proceed along some new line, generating a new population of selected stimuli. Moreover, even if we find, empirically, that the particular set of measures we have started to sample (for example, the pictures sampled by Seidner, or by Brunswik and Kamiya) does generate a simple and usable frequency distribution, we need some independent means of designating the bounds of that population: does this distribution encompass *all* magazine pictures? *all* pictures? *all* pictures to be published within the next decade? the next century? In addition, we need some means of determining the probability that any subject sampled from some population of observers will be confronting that population of stimuli with some one task of a possible population of tasks. Not only is such a sampling operation truly a formidable task: it first demands a solution to just about all of the other problems in psychology as well, and offers no advance prospect of being statistically applicable, even then.

Can we then put more modest requirements upon the "ecological sampling" procedures? To do so, we will have to make explicit the *purposes* for which one seeks the sample, in terms of which purposes we can then judge the adequacy of any ecological sampling technique.

THE THREE PURPOSES OF REPRESENTATIVE ECOLOGICAL SAMPLING

Even approximations to representative design are not cheap: "Representative design in its full scope requires not only a basic theoretical and methodological restructuring but is a formidable task in practice as well. Ideally, it would take concerted research projects of a magnitude hitherto unheard of in experimental psychology." (Brunswik, 1956, p. viii.) The purposes for which such a design should be employed, therefore, must be examined, and the extent to which those purposes can be met, must be evaluated in each case of research. This is particularly important when we remember that any procedure that falls short of an impossibly-complete representative design, is still subject to biases, and may lead to unfounded confidence in false conclusions.

Ecological sampling was proposed for three partially-separable purposes, as far as I can discern:

The Test and Use of Probabilistic Empiricism

Empiristic associationism is an ancient solution to many of the problems of visual perception. Of all of its proponents, only Brunswik followed up its implications fully: it is a predictive theory only if we know the world to which the organism has been exposed, and the nature of the associations that would be built upon that world of confrontations. Brunswik inclined toward a specific empiristic theory that called for ecological sampling as a means of understanding the nature of what each and every creature had learned from its environment: the theory is that organisms are "probability learners," and the "perceptual system as an intuitive statistician" produces "Perception":

. . . that relatively primitive, partly autonomous, institutionalized, ratiomorphic (reason-like) subsystem of cognitions which achieves prompt and richly detailed orientation habitually concerning the vitally relevant, mostly distal aspects of the environment on the basis of mutually vicarious, relatively restricted and stereotyped, insufficient evidence in uncertainly-geared interaction and compromise, seemingly following the highest probability for smallness of error at the expense of the highest frequency of precision. (Brunswik, 1956, p. 146.)

Whether or not one accepts this theory (and I think that recent research makes its ontogenetic components doubtful, Hochberg, 1962), *it is only a theory, and does not constitute a methodological basis for such a consequential methodological decision.* If it is our aim to obtain a catalog of the frequencies with which various situations have confronted the organism in order that a probabilistic empiricism will be able to predict the learned perceptual habits of the organism from this catalog, we are not going to be able to accomplish that goal by any simple ecological sampling, as we have seen. The main obstacle is that we cannot say anything about the proximal stimuli, or "cues," to which the organism has been exposed, merely by knowing the ecological distributions normal to its environment. Only if we assume that each point in a sphere surrounding the head of the developing organism always enjoys and maintains an equal likelihood of fixation can we reason directly from ecological distribution to learned probabilities. Moreover, in order for such ontogenetic historical probabilities to be of any use to the scientist in predicting any subject's perceptual achievements, they would have to be common to an entire population of subjects, and, if this were so, the uniformities of adult perceptual behavior would have to be more economically measurable *in their own right,* anyway. (Hochberg, 1957.)

The Discovery of Unfounded Generalizations

A second reason for adopting representative instead of systematic research design, is to locate the critical tests by which to deflate any unfounded generalizations that may have been based upon too-narrow samplings of variables, and to provide insight into the multivariate nature of what may at first appear to be univariate psychophysical relationships (pp. 362; 363). *Factorial* designs are usually proposed to remedy this narrowness, but, as we have seen (p. 364), and as Brunswik argued (1956, p. 110), the use of factorial design is no substitute for representative ecological sampling in this respect, and may be just as misleading as univariate designs.

Closely related to this purpose, is the necessity for obtaining stimuli that are *not* selected according to some experimenter's bias: in testing individual differences, we know well that if we wish to demonstrate a correlation between skin color and intelligence, we must prevent the experimenter from choosing individuals with exactly such a correlation built into his selection procedure. Similarly, in the design of perceptual research, the experimenter cannot help being an observer as well, while he is selecting his stimuli, and some precaution against biased selection is frequently necessary. (However, we should notice that such precaution would be equally-well accomplished by *any* procedure that is arbitrary and out of the experimenter's control.)

To meet these requirements, however, *we need not seek ecological samples which are even approximately representative of frequency of occurrence.* All that we must have is enough of a sampling of each of the extreme combinations of variables that can occur in the populations of situations to which we wish to predict, to enable us to test the generality of the theory upon which the prediction is to be based. At its extreme, such an ecological sample, which might be used in a systematic rather than a representative design, would include any hypothetical representative samples as subsets. As long as we have a theory (and we have seen above that there is no escaping this necessity in some form), and as long as we stand ready to face up to any reliable failure of prediction—regardless of how unlikely we would be to encounter the circumstances in which that failure would be met in the "normal random course of events"—our ecological sampling need only be adequately representative in *range* of multivariate combination, not representative in *frequency*, for the population of situations to which we wish to be able to generalize. The "illusion" of Experimental Design, Type B, does not have to be particularly prevalent in our environment, in order to reveal the inadequacy of the theory concealed in Experimental Design, Type A, but it *does* have to have been sampled and noted.

The Estimation of Errors-of-Generalization

The most important and promising reason for undertaking representative sampling, but the most difficult goal to achieve except in certain special cases (compare pp. 370), is to provide an estimate of the probable error that will obtain for any prediction that will be made in the future. The possibility of attaching some known confidence level is essential to any scientific *prediction* "unless one is willing to go into plausibility generalizations—always precarious in nature—or satisfied with results confined to a self-created ivory-tower ecology. . . ." (Brunswik, 1956, p. 110.) This is easy to do with new stimulus situations only if the prediction is made on the basis of samples obtained from the same population of stimuli (having known distribution characteristics) to which we wish to predict. Unfortunately, we cannot just simply *assert* that any set of measures made upon the world of stimulus-objects will suffice to fill this requirement, as we have seen on p. 373. What made the use of representative sampling meaningful in Experimental Design, Type D, was the independently-definable nature of the stimulus-population, and the bound that could be set to the population about which we were attempting to generalize. No differential psychologist would seriously undertake to shape a prediction for "just any individual at all," regardless of where we get him, and the same modesty has to attend our attempts to generalize to situations.

It seems to me that there are two classes of situation-sets that we can restrict enough to make such generalizations possible. The first class is defined by a set of behaviors to which we want to predict; the second is defined by a set of arbitrarily-generated stimulus populations that we can define. The first class requires the use of a psychological theory in order to step to new stimulus situations, while, symmetrically, the second can be related to new behaviors only through a psychological theory:

Behavior-Defined Ecological Samples

If a particular distribution of stimuli is defined by some kind of behavior (for example, magazine-reading, lathe-operating, and so forth), and this class of behavior has some intrinsic functionalist interest to us —which it should have if we are to study it at all, since we will not be able to do more than make predictions *within* the ecological sample defined by this behavior—we can enumerate the kinds of stimuli to which subjects do expose themselves in the course of that behavior. The Seidner study may give useful information about the "popular magazine" populations during the period of the study, even if it is not relatable to the ecology of the distal objects being represented, and it certainly tells us what to expect from the organisms who edit (and perhaps about those who purchase) that magazine. On the other hand, the editors who produce this world of pictures may change, or readers may switch to different browsing patterns. We have to remember that our ecological samples are specific to the behaviors by which they are defined, and so such samples have to be of interest in their own right. If a particular distribution of stimuli is defined, in this fashion, by some practical application or need (be it industrial, commercial, or whatever), we know two things about the data we draw from that distribution.

First, the configurations of variables are relevant to a large population of observers and situations. This may not be a good guide to representativeness in the statistical sense, but it seems to have some inescapable minimum value in the functional sense, and this, to anyone of even mildly functionalist bent, suggests that here we will get good raw material from which to construct theories that will transcend the bounds of purely statistical, inductive attempts at generalization. Second, with no other basis for selecting stimulus-populations to study, it seems only reasonable to select those areas in which to work, in which society will encourage other workers to labor, else we stand little chance of amassing enough sampling data to permit a reasonably general theory to emerge.

I think that this criterion would have met with Brunswik's approval (1956, p. 110): it sets its sights on cataloging achievement-in-certaindefined-situations, rather than seeking information applicable to man-ingeneral in the world-in-general, and this seems congenial to the Brunswikian *Weltanschauung*. The second alternative sampling procedure can also be supported from his writings (Brunswik, 1934).

Artificially-Generated Stimulus Sets and "Local Laws"

A second solution is to draw random samples from a population whose limits and distribution characteristics we can specify because the population is artificially generated. Thus, we can make up rules by which we can obtain *nonsense shapes* (Attneave and Arnoult, 1956), *schematic faces* (Brunswik and Reiter, 1937), or *randomly-viewed projections of randomly-constructed objects* (Hochberg, 1962b, p. 48). By drawing random samples from such populations, we accomplish two things: First, we eliminate experimenter bias in the selection of the stimuli being used to test any particular hypothesis, and, to the extent that these samples are representative in *range* of the distributions that we normally expect to encounter, they will serve this purpose well. Second, we can determine the error that attaches to any generalization we make about each such population. Such stimulus-populations can be valuable research tools in the same sense that nonsense syllables make good research tools for some purposes (compare Vanderplas and Garvin, 1959). However, we obviously cannot consider such samples to be representative of what any observer will confront in his normal behavior. In Brunswik's terms, ". . . ecological types of generalizations . . . requires the presence of an ecological universe from which the stimuli have been sampled . . . an *N*, that is, a sample in the representative sense; . . . an *M*, that is, a mere multitude of cases . . . is an artificial universe in itself, but this rechristening will not add to its generalization potential." (1956, p. 108.) All that we can do with these findings, is to construct some theory in terms of which all of the *relevant* (as we decide relevance) variables are similar for the artificially-constructed population, and the ones to be encountered in the kinds of behaviors to which we are interested in generalizing, and then attempt to test that *theory* by choosing some arbitrary (but not necessarily representative) samples of that second population for cross-validation purposes.

In short, in both kinds of attempt to attach error-terms to whatever generalizations we may make, we have no *general* procedure by which we can apply those error terms outside of narrowly-defined populations of situations—*except in terms of some theory which will relate one set of circumstances to another: and there is as yet no sense in which we can attach an over-all error term to such a conceptual structure itself, no matter how "formidable" a project is undertaken.*

SUMMARY AND CONCLUSIONS

Ecological sampling of experimental situations is necessary to prevent overgeneralizations about what comprises the inventory of important psychophysical variables. However, what we accept as "adequately representative" is not independent of the particular theories we bring to be tested by the sampling procedure. Part of the "probablism" that appeared to make fully representative sampling inescapably necessary results from two theoretical assumptions ("cue-independence in a stationary proximal projection," and "probabilistic empiricism"), instead of from methodological principle: if we construct theories that are not themselves inherently probabilistic and ambiguous in the predictions they produce (for example, Gibson's "higher-order variables of potential information"), or in the kind of information they require, the *kind* of ecological sampling that is necessary changes correspondingly. Otherwise, testing theories, as distinguished from sampling organismic "achievement," requires merely that the test conditions represent the *range* of stimulus variation, *not* the shape of its distribution. For purposes of attaching error-terms to predictions, fully representative ecological sampling would be required, but this kind of sampling is only possible in very restricted ways. Defined populations that will permit such error-terms to be estimated can be sampled for "natural" behaviors in which we are interested, or for artificially-generated stimulus sets; however, such estimated errors do not automatically apply outside the defined sets. Representative design must test, but cannot in general replace, theories about the perceptual process.

REFERENCES

Attneave, F. and M. D. Arnoult. The quantitative study of shape and pattern perception. *Psychol. Bull.,* 1956, *53,* 452–471.

Brunswik, E. *Wahrnehmung und gegenstandswelt*. Vienna: Deuticke, 1934.

Brunswik, E. *The conceptual framework of psychology*. Chicago: University of Chicago Press, 1952.

Brunswik, E. *Perception and the representative design of psychological experiments*. Berkeley, Calif.: University of California Press, 1956.

Brunswik, E. and J. Kamiya. Ecological cue-validity of "proximity" and of other Gestalt factors. *Amer. J. Psychol.,* 1953, *66,* 20–32.

Brunswik, E. and L. Reiter. Eindrukscharaktere schematisierter gesichter. *Zeitschrift f. Psychol.,* 1937, *142,* 67–134.

Gibson, J. *The perception of the visual world*. Boston: Houghton Mifflin, 1950.

Gibson, J. Visually controlled locomotion and visual orientation in animals. *Brit J. Psychol.,* 1958, *49,* 182–194.

Hochberg, J. Spatial representation: Theme 10. *Proc. Int. Congr. Psychol.,* 1957.

Hochberg, J. Nativism and empiricism in perception. In L. Postman (Ed)., *Psychology in the making*. New York: Knopf, 1962.   (a)

Hochberg, J. The psychophysics of pictorial perception. *Audio-Visual Communication Review,* 1962, *10,* 22–54.   (b)

Hochberg, J., and V. Brooks. The psychophysics of form: reversible perspective drawings of spatial objects. *Amer. J. Psychol.,* 1960, *73,* 337–354.

Hochberg, J. and V. Brooks. The prediction of visual attention to design and paintings. *Amer. Psychol.,* 1962, *17* (abstract).

Hochberg, J. and O. Smith. Landing strip markings and the "expansion pattern": I. Program, preliminary analysis, and apparatus. *Perc. mot. Skills,* 1955, *5,* 81–92.

Smith, O. and P. Smith. Ball-Throwing responses to photographically portrayed targets. *J. exp. Psychol.,* 1961, *62,* 223-233.

Vanderplas, J. and E. Garvin. The association value of random shapes. *J. exp. Psychol.,* 1959, *57,* 147–154.

Woodworth, R. *Experimental psychology.* New York: Holt, 1938.

13

Constancy and Conservation: A Comparison of the Systems of Brunswik and Piaget[1]

JAN SMEDSLUND

Egon Brunswik's "Psychologie vom Gegenstand her" and Jean Piaget's "Psychologie génétique" represent two of the most systematic and explicit attempts that have been made to create a completely general conceptual frame of reference for psychology. This paper will explore some of their differences and similarities, and discuss the points where they complement or contradict each other. In this process of comparison we shall focus upon seven closely related problem areas: the delimitation of the response, the delimitation of what is intended, the feedback process, the role of the external world in psychology, the process of acquisition, static and dynamic descriptions, achievement and structure.

Brunswik and Piaget both emphasize the idea of organisms as "stabilizers" of events and relationships (Brunswik, 1952, pp. 19–20; Piaget, 1952a, pp. 5–7); Brunswik's thinking in this respect is typically represented by the core-concept of *constancy,* Piaget's by *conservation.* The stress on *invariance over changes* is an important similarity between the two authors, and distinguishes them from the *S-R* psychologies whose unit of behavior is the connection between a specific *S*-class and a specific *R*-class.

Constancy is frequently exemplified in Brunswik's writings by the experiments on the perception of *object size.* The determination of size constancy may involve the following typical procedure: the subject is shown a stick at some distance and is asked to indicate which one of a

1. The author is indebted to Professor Kenneth R. Hammond and to the participants of an advanced seminar in psychological theory at the University of Colorado, for highly stimulating and helpful comments. At an earlier stage in the preparation of the manuscript, cand. psychol. Finn Tschundi, Oslo, provided some important criticisms.

series of model sticks is exactly as long as the distant one. The difference in length between the chosen model stick and the distant stick is then measured. It turns out that over a wide range of conditions these differences are very small, that is, size is correctly estimated in spite of variations in distance. The methodology and rationale of these experiments is discussed in great detail in Brunswik (1934; 1956).

In order to facilitate the comparison with Brunswik, Piaget's core concept will be exemplified by his studies of *size-conservation*. (See Piaget, Inhelder and Szeminska, 1960, pp. 95–103.) The subject is shown two equally long sticks placed side by side in such a way that the equality is immediately recognized. Then one of the sticks is moved slightly and the subject is asked whether the sticks are now equally long or whether one of them (and which one) is longer. Size conservation is said to be present when the subject continues to assert that the two sticks have the same length. It turns out that young children frequently do not possess size conservation. The 50 percent level of acquisition is situated at eight years (Vinh-Bang, 1959).

It should be noted that the above choice of typical experiments is somewhat arbitrary and that it merely serves to illustrate how the core-concepts may be defined operationally. The "psychologies" that are built around these two concepts are in many ways strikingly similar. However, they also have some marked differences, both complementary and contradictory. A study of these differences may be of value in laying the ground for further and still more general theoretical developments.

THE DELIMITATION OF THE RESPONSE

In contradistinction to classical *S-R* psychology, Brunswik and Piaget both strongly emphasize the complete ambiguity of a single observation of a response in a stimulus-situation, with given antecedent stimulus-situations. On the basis of one observation one cannot know *what* the subject is doing, and any physicalistic description of actual movements and stimulations will remain quite arbitrary.

In their discussion of this general diagnostic problem the two writers focus on different but complementary aspects. Brunswik is much concerned with the problem of delimiting the variables of the external situation that determine the response. These are the variables of which behavior is a "constant function" or with which it is highly correlated. The difficulty in delimiting the focus of behavior is at a maximum when the stimulus variables are completely "tied" and is decreased when they are varied independently. As an example of an experiment containing this ambiguity, Brunswik describes a study of size perception with the Galton bar (Brunswik, 1956, pp. 12–14). In this experiment the distal and proximal variables of size are completely "tied" and one cannot know upon which one the response depends. Smedslund (1953) and Campbell (1954) have expanded Brunswik's line of reasoning into the area of learning, "the problem of what is learned."

In an exactly parallel way Brunswik argues that one cannot infer from a single observation to the invariant aspects of the response itself. This can only be done by observing a series of responses in the same and in varying proximal stimulus-situations. A good example is the instance of avoidance conditioning where the subject, given a certain position of the hand, apparently has learned to extend his finger. The description "the subject has learned to *extend* his finger" turns out to be premature, since, with a different hand position, the subject also flexes his finger in response to the conditioned stimulus (Wickens, 1938).

In addition to pointing out the ambiguity of inference from single observations and constant situations, Brunswik puts forth the thesis that, in general, the proximal/peripheral region is a chaotic one, and that invariant relationships are only found between the distal and central regions. Responses are most fruitfully characterized by their convergence on certain distal objects or situations, what Brunswik termed psychology in terms of objects.

Piaget also stresses the fundamental ambiguity of the single observation of an act and its consequences. He writes: "Now, an operational act may, in its content, closely resemble an intuitive act, a sensori-motor or perceptual act and even an instinctive act; a geometrical figure may thus be the product of a logical construction, a preoperational intuition, a perception, an automatic habit and even a building instinct." (Piaget, 1950.)

In general, Piaget is considerably less explicit than Brunswik in problems of response diagnosis. However, in the given quotation and in other passages, he seems to complete Brunswik's point of view by adding a new dimension. He seems to argue that even though a set of responses involving varying muscular innervations and varying initial proximal stimulus-conditions, always result in a given geometrical figure (distal focus), there still remains some important ambiguity. This ambiguity refers to the response system of which the observed responses form a part. The instinctive nest building in the form of a geometrical figure obviously is part of a behavior system with very different properties from those involved when a high school student construes the same figure on the basis of Euclid. Among such properties one may mention: resistance to extinction, susceptibility to temporary inhibition, verbal control, dependence on stimulus-variations, ability to vary the properties of the figure, ability to vary its position, ability to combine the construction of the figure with other acts, ability to analyze the part-responses involved in the construction, and so forth. Whereas Brunswik has been concerned with the delimitation of the distal focus of a set of responses, Piaget seems to stress the importance of the pattern of *possible distal focuses* to which any individual focus belongs. To Piaget, a complete characterization of a set of responses includes not only a specification of its focus, but also of the pattern of response dispositions of which it forms a part.

One may conclude that although both writers stress the complexity of defining a response, they have been concerned with partly different aspects of the diagnostic problem.

THE DELIMITATION OF
WHAT IS INTENDED

Purposiveness or intentionality is generally accepted as an important descriptive feature of behavior, and is an integral aspect of our everyday perceptions of other people. It is of some interest to compare Brunswik's and Piaget's analysis of the criteria of intention.

To Brunswik the delimitation of the response seems to be identical with the delimitation of what is intended. In other words, in Brunswik's system responses are described in terms of their intention. By studying the covariation of a given response category with various environmental variables one may determine what is intended. Often there are several variables having a correlation with the responses. Brunswik mentions the perception of number as an example of such multipolar intention systems (Brunswik, 1934, pp. 140–150). Judgments of number are not only correlated with the actual number of objects, but also to some extent with the *size* of the elements and with the *value* of the elements (stamps). This is expressed by Brunswik in stating that the subject typically achieves a kind of "intermediary object" which does not correspond exactly to any single environmental entity. In such cases, he suggests that the object with which behavior *correlates most highly* over varying conditions should be regarded as the intended object (Brunswik, 1934, p. 185).

In contradistinction to Brunswik, Piaget has not been very much concerned specifically with the criteria of intentionality. Thus one has to try to infer such criteria from his theoretical model, with the aid of such scattered references to intentionality as may be found in his writings.

A basic concept in Piaget's system is the *schema* or assimilatory schema (the model of assimilation and accommodation will be described in the section on the feedback process). The existence and delimitation of a schema is inferred from any recurrent pattern of activity of the subject. Schemata typically contain sub-schemata and are imbedded in more general schemata. A response is defined by specification of more or less extensive parts of the system of schemata to which it belongs (compare the preceding section).

In a recent article Piaget describes the relationship between the concept of schema and the current notions of motive and interest (and thereby intentionality) as follows:

> . . . an assimilatory schema involves a structure (cognitive aspect) and a dynamics (affective aspect), but in continuous and indissociable forms. . . . From this point of view, a motive is nothing but the conative or affective aspect of a schema, claiming its normal nourishment, that is, objects which it can assimilate; and interest . . . is the affective relation between the motive and the object that may satisfy it. To say that the subject is interested in a result or an object thus means that he assimilates it or anticipates an assimilation and to say that he needs it means that he has schemata which demand its utilization. (Piaget, 1959, pp. 46–47; translated from French.)

From this and other passages (see particularly Piaget, 1949a, vol. 3, pp. 131–186) one may infer with some assurance that for Piaget the delimitation of what is intended coincides with the delimitation of the schema activated at a given time, for example, with the delimitation of the response. The following passage supports this interpretation:

"Finality is thus to be conceived not as a special category, but as the subjective translation of a process of putting into equilibrium which itself does not imply finality but simply the general distinction between real equilibria and the ideal equilibrium." (Piaget, 1952a, p. 11.)

Since equilibrium means stability, this means that when intention is fulfilled the corresponding schema is stable and when intention is not fulfilled the schema is unstable. Consequently, since the schema refers to a recurrent pattern of activity, it is reasonable to infer that when a pattern of activity is repeated a second time without any modification, the intention was fulfilled the first time, whereas if the pattern is modified, the intention was not fulfilled.

The matter may be clarified with the help of some very simple expectancy terms. Let P_1 and P_2 symbolize two perceptions and R_1 symbolize some overt behavior. What is intended by 0 when he reacts with R_1 to P_1? The criterion mentioned above implies that if $P_1 - R_1 - P_2$

occurs and if P_1 is followed by R_1 the next time it occurs, then P_2 was intended by 0 and the schema is $P_1 - R_1 - P_2$. On the other hand, if P_1 is not followed by R_1 the next time, one may infer that P_2 was not intended by 0 (was not part of the original schema beginning with $P_1 - R_1$).

This formulation of a feedback-criterion of intentionality has at least two inherent limitations. First, it should be noted that many fulfillments of an intention modify the environment and/or the person in such ways that the original starting point (here P_1) cannot occur again. Secondly, the schema may be part of a more complex superordinate schema, for example, a generalized expectancy of "never twice in the same way," which means that the achievement of the intention will not maintain the elementary schema ($P_1 - R_1 - P_2$). To some extent both these limitations may be surmounted if more superordinate schemata are taken into account in the analysis. In conclusion one interpretation of Piaget's position defines fulfillment vs. nonfulfillment of intention in terms of the *stability* of a schema or system of schemata. Both authors seem to assert that the operational delimitations of what a subject is doing and of what he is intending are identical. Neither of them goes very far into the complexities of the diagnostic problems involved.[2] Brunswik relies on a covariance criterion, whereas Piaget apparently has in mind a stability or feedback criterion. These criteria are equivalent, since repeated maintaining feedback effects from a distal focus, will lead to statistical convergence of behavior on this focus. Conversely, disrupting feedback effects will prevent repetition and consequently convergence. The difference between the convergence and the feedback criteria of intention is closely related to Brunswik's and Piaget's preference for different kinds of data. See the section on static and dynamic descriptions.

THE FEEDBACK PROCESS

Both theorists include the feedback from the environment in their conceptual scheme, but their treatment of the process is somewhat different.

The feedback is introduced in Brunswik's lens model as follows:

A semicircular arrow is appended in the figure to the terminal focus to indicate that lens patterns do not stand in isolation but are apt to reflect back upon

2. It should be noted that by identifying what the subject is doing and what he is intending, both authors fail to deal with the important distinction between "can" and "try." See Heider, 1958.

the organism in a future state in what is now sometimes called a "feedback" loop . . ., such as when arriving at the food is followed by satisfaction and reinforcement of the preceding behavior ("law of effect"). . . . Further lens patterns may be involved in this process. (Brunswik, 1952, p. 20.)

Throughout his writings Brunswik seemed to adopt the common assumption that responses are ultimately corrected and improved as a function of some kind of direct contact with the relevant aspects of the environment. By observing how things actually are, the person becomes able to act and judge with ever increasing accuracy. Since Brunswik has written so little explicitly about the problem of the feedback process, and since he sometimes refers to complications in these effects (see the last sentence in the quotation above), the interpretation of his position remains a little indefinite. One may only state that in his writings and experiments, he implicitly seemed to accept a simple empiricism (feedback from direct contact with an external reality) and that he at least never attacked such a point of view.

The problem of the nature of the feedback from the environment has been central in Piaget's thinking and has resulted in his assimilation/accommodation model of organismic adaptation, which he introduces in the following way:

Now, to avoid the difficulties of teleological language, adaptation must be described as an equilibrium between the action of the organism on the environment and vice versa. Taking the term in its broadest sense, "assimilation" may be used to describe the action of the organism on surrounding objects, in so far as this action depends on previous behavior involving the same or similar objects. In fact every relation between a living being and its environment has this particular characteristic: the former, instead of submitting passively to the latter, modifies it by imposing on it a certain structure of its own. It is in this way that, physiologically, the organism absorbs substances and changes them into something compatible with its own substance. Now, psychologically the same is true, except that the modifications with which it is then concerned are no longer of a physicochemical order, but entirely functional, and are determined by movement, perception or the interplay of real or potential actions (conceptual operations, and so forth). Mental assimilation is thus the incorporation of objects into patterns of behavior, these patterns being none other than the whole gamut of actions capable of active repetition.

Conversely, the environment acts on the organism and, following the practice of biologists, we can describe this converse action by the term "accommodation," *it being understood that the individual never suffers the impact of surrounding stimuli as such* (italics ours), but they simply modify the assimilatory cycle by accommodating him to themselves. Psychologically, we again find the same process in the sense that the pressure of circumstances always leads, not to a passive submission to them, but to a simple modification of the action affecting them. This being so, we can then define adaptation as an equilibrium between assimilation and accommodation, which amounts to the same as an equilibrium of interaction between subject and object. (Piaget, 1950, pp. 7–8.)

For more recent and technical presentations of the model, see Piaget (1957; 1958).

From this and other passages in Piaget's writings it is clear that assimilation is a general term covering not only "perception" and "interpretation," but also such things as "skill" or the active manipulation of the environment. In general it is the active or passive incorporation of the environment into the subject's system of schemata. The term accommodation is intended to cover the feedback effects of the environment on the subject. However, Piaget also uses the term in sentences such as "the mutual accommodation of schemata to each other." Here he refers to such things as the coordination of movements and perceptions and the reorganization of thinking in the direction of greater internal consistency and economy. In this context accommodation becomes synonymous with equilibration or the tendency towards what he calls "the accord of thought with itself."

When it comes to the feedback from the environment, there are two main conceptual alternatives. One of them is to assume that the "real" structure of the environment (as measured by the experimenter) makes an impact on the subject and modifies and controls his ways of assimilation. This interpretation has been widely accepted, apparently also by Brunswik. The other alternative, suggested by Piaget, is to regard accommodation to the environment as being a process of mutual adjustment of the various assimilatory schemata activated by stimulation from the environment. From this point of view the environment is fundamentally treated as an X ("das Ding an sich") which is merely known as a source of independent causation. The usual description of the feedback in terms of the ordinary (more or less physicalistic) intersubjective language is seen as involving the basic fallacy of reifying and absolutizing one preferred way of construing the environment.

Piaget's interpretation of the feedback process has three implications which differentiate it from a simple empiricism.

The first is that some aspects of the external stimulation give rise to no feedback effects since they are not assimilated into any schema. This is not to be confused with a filter theory that concerns aspects of stimulation that are partly assimilated and *by virtue of this* can be filtered out.

The second is that since assimilatory schemata always have some kind of spatio-temporally distal reference, there is never any simple recording of events, but always some element of interpretation or inference.

The third implication is that modifications of the assimilatory cycles need not occur only as a function of disturbances induced by outside stimulation, but may as well result from a purely *internal conflict* between different schemata.

The second of these implications will be exemplified and discussed below, and the other two in the section on acquisition. Let us consider a size perception study, where the experimenter informs the subject of the correctness of a judgment and then presents the same distal object once more. Normally, the auditory stimuli from the experimenter will have a pronounced effect on the subject's next judgment of the same object. However, one may conceive of subjects who will fail to change their judgments, for various trivial reasons such as not being able to understand the experimenter's language or because they think it is an experiment on deceit, and that the experimenter is lying. These possible exceptions are theoretically important since they reveal that the feedback does not stem directly from the auditory stimuli, but from the subject's *interpretation* (perception) of them. Like the perception of the visual stimuli from the object (P_1), the perception of the auditory stimuli from the experimenter (P_2) is dependent on other perceptions. Thus, the information from an assistant that the experimenter is not trying to deceive (P_3), may again render P_2 influential on P_1. Finally, if the subject happens to read in a journal in the laboratory that deceit with the cooperation of the assistants is customary in this type of experiment (P_4), this may cancel the reinforcing effect of P_3 on P_2's influence on P_1, and so forth.

This reinforcing and weakening effect of perceptions on each other is equally prevalent when we turn to the subject's attempts to verify his judgments more directly. He may take the distal stick, place it side by side with one of the comparison sticks, conclude that they are equally long, and then replace the distal stick in its former position. At first view, this may look like a direct confrontation with solid external reality. However, it is easy to show that the perception of the stimuli from the comparison of the sticks will have a feedback effect on the judgments only given certain interpretations of the situation. As we have already mentioned, preschool children frequently assert that although the two sticks are equally long when placed side by side, one of them becomes longer when it is moved to another position (Piaget, Inhelder and Szeminska, 1960, pp. 95–103). This reveals that the adult's perception of the outcome of the comparison rests upon the hidden assumption of size-conservation. If he is informed that one of the sticks is expanding rapidly from the heat of his hand, his interpretation of the stimuli from the two sticks side by side will change completely.

Thus it appears that it is not the physical stimuli themselves that induce feedback effects, but the subject's *perception* (assimilation) of them. Since each perception in turn is dependent on feedback from other perceptions, we may assume that, in principle, all reinforcement is of indefinitely high order, and frequently circular. Our perceptions form a vast system of interdependencies and there is no such thing as a simple unconditional registration of external facts. Even the simple case of perceiving a pinpoint of light in complete darkness is not a case of mere recording of external fact. Even a pinpoint of light is judged as having a position in the horizontal-vertical plane, a distance, an intensity, a color, it is seen as moving or unmoving, it varies or does not vary in intensity, color, distance, it has some kind of origin, it is visible to one eye or to both, and so forth. Any judgment about this light is subject to reinforcement by other perceptions relating to the various categories of judgment. Even the simple statement that there is a light out there is likely to be revised if one is informed that one is being hypnotized, suffering from a brain disease or being electrically stimulated in the visual cortex.

Apparently, feedback effects always are contingent upon the subject's assimilation of the situation, which is equivalent to stating that accommodation consists in the mutual adjustment of assimilatory schemata to each other. This is entirely in line with current developments of the theory of observation in modern philosophy.

To summarize, Brunswik was never much occupied with the problem of the feedback process and frequently seemed to adopt a straightforward empiricist point of view. In Piaget's system the feedback process is analyzed in great detail, and it is argued that the input from the environment influences the subject only as it is assimilated into his schemata. The relationship between any external event and the way it is assimilated by the subject is in principle indeterminate, in other words there are no external "facts" that are directly "recorded" by the subject in a mechanical fashion; interpretation and inferences always intervene.

THE ROLE OF THE EXTERNAL WORLD IN PSYCHOLOGY

As a correlate to the analysis of the feedback process, the role of the external intersubjective world in both systems will be briefly described. Despite their differences in conceptualizing the feedback process, not only Brunswik, but also Piaget, retains a place for stimulus-description in reporting an experiment.

We will first review Brunswik's position. As a part of his program to study the relationship between behavior and objects, he discusses the epistemological status of these two realms as they have been gradually differentiated. He describes one aspect of the development of psychology as a progressive "differentiation within the originally unstructured field of naive personal experience." (1952, p. 8.) He mentions Democritus' scepticism of sensory qualities and Locke's distinction between primary and secondary qualities, the former being more objective and reliable, the latter being more subjective and unreliable. Finally, the modern psychologist makes a clear distinction between perception and external reality, or between responses and stimuli.

"For the psychologist, perceptual thing-impressions or their physiological counterparts—or the ensuing overt verbal or behavioral manifestations—are definitely 'responses' to be contrasted with stimuli. The distinction which Carnap draws between 'predicates of the thing-language' and 'perception terms' can be maintained only if the former are restricted to data of measurement, which often seems tacitly implied." (Brunswik, 1952, p. 8.)

Furthermore, he suggests that objectivity may be defined in terms of the degree of interpersonal observational reliability, and that the observations of spatiotemporal coincidences play such a prominent role precisely because they are unsurpassed with respect to interpersonal reliability.

In order to analyze behavioral achievements it becomes important to describe the surrounding external world. The layers of the environment that concern ordinary human adaptation are much too molar to interest physical scientists, and have been left largely unexplored to the present time. The study of the psychologically relevant environment was labeled *ecology* by Brunswik (in analogy with the corresponding biological notion), and was considered by him to be an important and integral part of psychology. By studying the causal texture of the environment one is enabled to evaluate the efficiency of actual behavioral adjustments, both with respect to utilization of cues and means and with respect to distal achievement. An example of this kind of research is the study of the ecological validity of "proximity." (Brunswik and Kamiya, 1953.) In summary, Brunswik's position means that the objective external environment should be an integral part of every psychological description.

Piaget's position on this question is quite complex: The subject is continuously assimilating the input into his schemata and accommodating them to each other. The activated schemata define the situation as it exists *for him*. As to the objective external situation, Piaget stresses the relativity and constant development of our collective notions of reality (Piaget, 1960, pp. 114–115) and points out that all we have is an increasingly complex system of interpretations of the elusive "das Ding an sich." The implication of this is that one should not reify the experimenter's construction of the situation, and that the subject is not confronted with the end-products of the experiment's cognitive processes. In this connection it should be instructive to quote Piaget's discussion of the task of visual exploration of a simple figure.

Let us discuss the following two problems: why do we see a single perceptually unchanging figure, while exploring a figure or object with changing points of fixation (unchanging in position (unmoving) and in qualitative and metric properties . . ;) and why does this unchanging figure lead to a more exact judgment (particularly with respect to the length of its lines and their proportions) than in the case of a single centration?
To both of these questions the answer of realism naturally appears to be the simplest: the figure is perceived as being unmoving and unchanging because it is so in reality, and we perceive its properties more exactly, because we observe it more closely! (italics ours) But "in reality" means physically, that is, a certain number of intellectual operations in fact make it possible for us to think that the figure is neither displaced nor modified in its metrical properties. However, from a genetical point of view we know very well that this invariance of position involves the "group of displacements," that is, a structure which . . . belongs to a higher level than that of perception. As to the invariance of metrical properties . . . , it also depends on operational mechanisms . . . much more complex than the perceptual processes. *To depend on what is the "real" figure, is thus to refer to a level of conceptual knowledge . . . which does not suffice to take account of the elementary perceptual processes . . .* (italics ours). Thus one has to explain the permanence of the perceived figure's position, form and dimensions without leaving the field of purely perceptual relations. (Piaget, 1958, pp. 72–73; translated from French.)

In this special case, Piaget strongly advocates psychological analysis without reference to the external physical situation, since the latter is the product of cognitive processes, more complex than the ones under investigation. In most of Piaget's studies both independent and dependent variables are response-defined. The only exception is his theory of elementary perception where proximal stimulation is the main independent variable. Although the physical environment usually is excluded from his theory, Piaget describes his experimental situations in physicalistic terms.

Like all other experimenters he accepts the following well known elementary inference on the basis of objective stimulus-conditions: *If two proximal stimulus situations are physically identical, no subject will be able to discriminate between them.* This inference is the basis for the operational definition of *psychological change.* If the subject's behavior changes from one presentation of a proximal stimulus situation to the next, then the change must derive from a change within him which is not dependent on any change in outside stimulation. In intersubjective comparisons the same procedure defines *individual differences*.

This inference reflects the necessary working assumption that the "grain" of the objective physical world as we conceive it today, always is finer than the "grain" of any subject's world. Briefly, *the intersubjective physical descriptions are employed in psychology in order to control the input from outside the subject, enabling one to eliminate irrelevant external influence and to single out psychological change and difference for study*. This description also makes replication by other experimenters possible. In spite of this method of input-control, Piaget's system except in the case of elementary perception is a Response-Response psychology, whereas Brunswik's system clearly is an Object-Response psychology.

THE PROCESS OF ACQUISITION

After the preceding discussion of the feedback from the environment, the positions of Brunswik and Piaget should be clear also in the case of acquisition, which is a process composed of many elementary feedback effects. The two models would seem to imply respectively a direct recording of environmental events and trends (empiricism), and a process of differentiation combination and mutual accommodation of assimilatory schemata.

At this point it should be emphasized that no psychologist (including Brunswik) has ever maintained a *consistent* empiricism. It has always been admitted that there are frequent instances where the feedback from the external stimuli is modified by perception, motivation, and so forth. The difference between Piaget's position and an empiricism of the type advocated by Brunswik is that according to the latter a direct impact of the structure of the external reality on the subject occurs in sufficiently simple and unambiguous situations, whereas Piaget denies this.

Brunswik's empiricist position is clearly apparent in his heavy reliance on probability learning as an explanatory device. He conceived of it as a very sensitive recording of objective probabilities, and even ventured to explain the Gestalt law of "proximity" as a result of probability learning of certain cues of very low ecological validity (Brunswik and Kamiya, 1953). The assumption of high sensitivity to ecological validities has not been consistently confirmed. (See, for example, Smedslund, 1955.)

There are two main predictions based on Piaget's assimilation/accommodation model, which differentiates it from empiricism.

1. Subjects may not learn at all in the presence of relevant inputs in very simple stimulus-situations, if they do not possess schemata for assimilating these inputs in certain ways.
2. Subjects may learn in the absence of relevant inputs by reorganization and mutual accommodation of conflicting assimilatory schemata.

The meaning of these two points may also be expressed as follows: *Given adequate motivation and attention, the occurrence of objectively adequate inputs (stimulation and reinforcement) is neither a sufficient, nor a necessary condition for learning.*

Three recent studies relevant to point 1 will be described, which all show approximately zero effects of repeated presentations of relevant external stimuli.

The first is a study of multiple-probability learning (Smedslund, 1962). The stimulus material contained two relevant cues with a multiple validity of .90, and two irrelevant cues. The cue-values were different positions of complex visual figures, and under these conditions most of the subjects were completely unable to improve their judgments of the distal variable, even after as many as 4800 presentations of the stimulus material. Apparently, the presence of highly valid cues (and high motivation) is not a sufficient condition for probability learning.

An experiment by Greco (1959) compared the learning of children from six to eleven years and adults. The material consisted of large and small boxes of cardboard, the large ones composed by two small boxes placed and glued together on top of each other. Both types of boxes contained drawers that could be pushed in both directions (like a matchbox). In the large double boxes only the upper drawer was utilized. In the small boxes a blue bead was glued to the inside in one end of the drawer and a red bead in the other end. In the large boxes there were either blue or red beads in both ends of the drawer. The subject was permitted to look into one end of the drawer and was asked to predict the color in the other end. Thus, in the large double boxes the rule was identity in color, whereas the rule for the small, single boxes was difference in color. The results showed that only one of twelve subjects below seven years was able to learn the rule within 100 presentations, all the subjects between seven and eleven years learned the rule (with an average of 27 presentations), and the adults (with a few exceptions) found the rule within 10 presentations. Greco pointed out that these variations in ability to assimilate a simple empirical trend, corresponded to certain differences in the mental structure of the age groups. It has been shown (Piaget, 1950) that children acquire the ability to multiply classes around seven years, and this ability seems to be necessary in order to solve Greco's problem inductively (large versus small boxes *x* red versus blue beads). Furthermore, it is known that the ability to analyze combinatorial structures and to proceed hypothetico-deductively is developed around eleven-twelve years. This presumably enabled the adults to find the correct solution after a few presentations.

Finally, we will briefly mention a study of our own (Smedslund, 1963a) inspired by certain earlier results by Piaget and Inhelder (1956, pp. 443–496). The experiment concerned children's conceptions of the spatial orientations of the water surface in a bottle that is tilted in various ways. Children below seven years frequently have no idea of the horizontality of the water surface, as judged by their drawings and by their choice among drawn model figures. A group of five- to six-year-old children who did not have the notion of horizontality of water surface, were allowed to observe the actual water surface in a bottle that was tilted systematically in various ways. After this, the children were immediately retested on drawings and on choice of model figures. The results show very little or no improvement, probably because the children did not seem to relate the water surface to the horizontal surface of the table. The seemingly simple "recording" or "observation" of the objective water surface, actually presupposes a complex system of schemata relating to such concepts as "straight line," "angle," "parallelity," and so forth. Only when the subject has a schema of horizontality, will he be able to notice deviations from horizontality in his own drawings or in the model figures, and accommodate his behavior accordingly.

Observations of this type would seem to create difficulties for a simple empiricist conception of feedback effects, since they show no impact of environmental structure in very simple physical situations.

Point 2 above, represents Piaget's most radical departure from empiricist learning theory, since it admits the possibility of acquisitions without direct stimulus support. In some experiments on the learning of conservation of substance (Smedslund, 1961b, 1961c) it has been possible to demonstrate the existence of such a process.

A subject is said to have conservation of substance when he thinks that the amount of substance in an object necessarily must remain unchanged during changes in its form, as long as nothing is added or taken away. The 50 percent level of acquisition of this notion is reached somewhere between six and eight years, depending on the particular experimental conditions (Smedslund, in press) (Vinh-Bang, 1959).

In one of the experiments the material was piles of small colored pieces of linoleum (½ x ½ cm, forty-eight pieces in each pile). In a typical item in the training sessions, the subject was shown two piles and was told that they contained the same amount of material. Then one of the piles was deformed into a "sausage," a "ring," a long "snake," and so forth, and the subject (without conservation) said that there was now more material in one of the piles than in the other. Then a piece was added to or taken away from one of the piles, and the subject was again asked to judge the relative amount of material in the two piles. If the subject, for example, had said that the "sausage" contained more material, and a piece was then taken away from it, that is, the amount was diminished, there would obviously be a conflict between the schema of deformation (more in the sausage) and the schema of addition/subtraction (less in the sausage). The training sessions consisted in letting the subject solve a series of problems of this and similar types. Care was taken to avoid all differential reinforcement of answers and the experimenter tried to maintain a completely neutral attitude to all the subject's responses. The external stimuli offered only ambiguous cues to the amount of material. As far as is known the only source of change was the continual conflict between the schema of addition/subtraction and the schema of deformations. In this particular experiment, altogether eight of fifteen subjects changed their behavior dramatically and suddenly, sometimes with signs of vivid insight and satisfaction. Their most cogent argument for giving up the deformation schema was: "Oh, I know it must be the same amount all the time, *because we did not add or take anything away!*" Since external reinforcement seemed to be absent, the observed changes appear to reflect a process of inner conflict resolution and fall under the category that Piaget has labeled "the accord of thought with itself." The recent book of Berlyne (1960) provides an interesting theoretical background for these findings.

Tentatively one may conclude that many data create difficulties for a direct empiricist interpretation of the processes of acquisition as sometimes implied by Brunswik. Apparently Piaget's model can handle such data easily, at least in a general programmatic way.

STATIC VERSUS DYNAMIC DESCRIPTIONS

There is one conspicuous difference between Brunswik and Piaget, which stands in comparative isolation from the other aspects of their systems, namely their consistent use of static versus dynamic description. The unit of static description is an instance of behavior at a given moment; the unit of dynamic description is a continuous period of behavior. The static description does not involve *time* and *change,* whereas this is the defining characteristic of dynamic descriptions.

Brunswik's functional unit of behavior is defined statistically both with respect to achievement and macromediation. It is built on correlations between sets of response-measurements and sets of proximal and distal stimulus-measurements. Each of these response-stimulus couples represents an unchanging isolated situation, in the sense that it does not involve observation of variations of responding and stimulation over time, and is not related by the subject to the other situations. The situations are related to each other only by the experimenter who groups them together for purposes of computation. There is no transition between one situation and another and their temporal order is irrelevant, that is, it may be permutated in any way without affecting the resulting correlation. This is generally true of the concept of constancy and of Brunswik's treatment of perception. However, it is equally valid in his descriptions of overt behavior and of thinking. He has published one study of rat learning (Brunswik, 1939), where the main descriptive categories are *percentage* of choices of alternative pathways. In another study (Brunswik, 1956, pp. 89–93) perception and thinking are compared in terms of *error distribution.* Perceptual judgments were found to be scattered rather close to the "correct" value, whereas the reasoned judgments were either completely correct or way off the mark. Again, the basic descriptive categories are *frequencies* of various responses, and no reference to changes and time is involved.

In his treatment of learning, Brunswik compares statistical measures derived from the same type of data, at different times. The dynamic character of Piaget's descriptions is clearly apparent in the core-concept of conservation. This concept is defined by the identity of certain responses before and after changes in the perceptual aspects of the situation. Similar observations are involved in the study of the moral behavior of children. The children become able to maintain certain inner standards or principles, in spite of varying external "temptations." In both cases continuous series of behaviors are observed.

The same emphasis on continuous observation over periods of time can be found in Piaget's treatment of behavior at the adolescent and adult levels of development. In the study of notions of permutation the subject may be asked, for example, to show all the ways in which four objects may be placed in a row (ABCD, BACD, BCAD, BCDA, and so forth). Here the situation is assimilated into a network of "possibilities" that may be materialized by active manipulation or by outside agencies. The network is maintained throughout any changes in the actual arrangement, as long as no objects are taken away or added. Instead of the conservation of an actual dispositional property (concrete thinking), we may here talk of the conservation of hypothetical possibilities (abstract or formal thinking) (Inhelder and Piaget, 1958).

The dynamic character of Piaget's descriptions is evident also in his analysis of lower developmental levels. If a desired toy is hidden behind a pillow, it ceases to exist psychologically to a child who has not yet acquired the elementary notion of objects. When this notion is acquired, the child searches for the object behind the pillow; the object still exists to him although it has changed from a visible to an invisible mode (Piaget, 1956, pp. 3–96). A still more elementary level is exemplified by simple perceptual activity, such as exploring a figure visually. The continuous input changes are compensated and balanced, and the result is an approximately unchanged and unmoving configuration.

In summary, Brunswik describes behavior by grouping together unrelated momentary events into a statistical composite measure, whereas Piaget studies degree and scope of stabilization over continuous periods of observation.

ACHIEVEMENT AND STRUCTURE

Brunswik was primarily interested in the study of *achievements,* whereas Piaget has stressed the patterning of psychological activities (structure). However, both these aspects are an integral part of the subject matter of psychology, and it is important to study more directly how the two theorists incorporate them in their systems. Brunswik's treatment of achievement has already been described: the degree of achievement is measured by the degree of correspondence between the results of behavior and the objective goal situation or focus.

Piaget's system contains two types of achievement, namely what he calls *"the accord of thought with things"* and *"the accord of thought with itself."* (Piaget 1952a, p. 8.) The first of these categories corresponds superficially to Brunswik's concept of achievement, but the second has no counterpart in the "psychology in terms of objects."

However, it should be noted that Piaget's "accord of thought with things" does not involve a direct comparison between behavior and the objective reality. It refers to the degree of correspondence between assimilatory schemata which are evoked by external stimulation; it is a correspondence between the *perception* of the size of a distal object, and a subsequent *perception* of the same object placed side by side with the object of comparison.

The "accord of thought with itself" refers to the degree of internal consistency and coordination of behavioral schemata (rationality). We will give two examples of this type of achievement:

Preschool children usually lack so-called transitivity of weight; accepting that object A weighs more than object B, and that B weighs more than C, they feel quite free to predict that C is heavier than A (Piaget and Inhelder, 1941). No amount of empirical evidence seems to lead them to understand that the relationship between A and C is determined by the relationships between A and B and between B and C (Smedslund, 1959; 1963b).

Some years later, children begin to relate these relationships to each other, and arrive at transitivity of weight, as being a kind of inner necessity.

The same development occurs in the case of classes. After having accepted that all the pearls in a heap are made of wood, and that most of the wooden pearls are brown and a few are white, five- to six-year-old children proceed to assert that there are more brown pearls than wooden pearls. Some years later most children feel that the preceding statements are incompatible, and that there *necessarily* must be more wooden pearls than brown ones (Piaget and Inhelder 1959). This achievement of "logical truth" is of central importance in Piaget's theory of development.

We will now turn to the problem of structure, or the network of behavioral dispositions. Brunswik stresses the importance of studying macromediation, that is, the more molar aspects of the strategies whereby achievement is effected. His model for this is the lens-model of "Oderverbindungen" or habit-family and cue-family hierarchies. The subject is able to stabilize vital relationships by means of processes of *vicarious mediation*. Each of the alternatively functioning channels of mediation is essentially isolated from the others except for the commonality in focus, and the only factor that may change such a pattern of mediation is the achievement versus nonachievement of the goal or of subgoals. The only exception to this isolation of the mediation channels is implied in Brunswik's occasional descriptions of motor coordination and the use of multiple cues simultaneously. A Brunswikian physicist would be one who vicariously applies the corpuscle theory and the wave theory to the phenomena of light and who will change his approach only when facing contrary experimental evidence. The Piagetean physicist in addition to this will also be worried by the inconsistency in his theoretical framework and will work towards a unified theory (accord of thought with itself). Brunswik does not discuss the property of reversibility of operations that is so prominent in Piaget's system.

In summary, the lens model represents a structure that has a limited amount of combinativity (motor-coordination and cue-combination), extensive associativity (vicarious functioning), and which is essentially irreversible.

Here we can give only an extremely condensed account of some main aspects of Piaget's structural models. For complete descriptions, see Piaget (1949b, 1952b, 1957) and Inhelder and Piaget (1958, pp. 245–350).

The mental structure of children is seen as developing toward ever more inclusive and stabilized systems characterized by a progressively more complete *combinativity, associativity,* and *reversibility*. In his analysis of behavioral structures during the first eighteen months of life Piaget arrives at a picture closely resembling the lens model. He describes the gradual development of limited forms of combinativity and vicarious functioning and the general lack of reversibility (as witnessed by the absence of very elementary forms of conservation, such as the conservation of objects). Since Brunswik has been mostly concerned with perception, which is the dominant mode of cognizance at this early age, the convergence of the two systems is encouraging and easily understood. The fact that Brunswik did not develop structural models that would cover later states of development, also seems to reflect his relative lack of concern with thinking in its various forms.

At the level of symbolic representation Piaget discerns three main stages of development.

1. Level I (prelogical thinking, two to seven, eight years). The combinativity, associativity and reversibility of mental operations are as yet generally incomplete. For example, the subject may be able to classify objects into the class A and class $-A$ (not A), and likewise to classify the same objects into class B and class $-B$. But they are not yet able to combine the two classifications mentally and to sort according to two criteria simultaneously. Nor are they able to consider simultaneously a class and one of its subclasses (for example, the wooden pearls and the brown wooden pearls). The latter failure is due to the absence of reversibility; the operation of dividing a class into subclasses is not balanced by a potential inverse operation of joining the subclasses together into the original class, which is a necessary condition for keeping in mind the class and the subclass simultaneously.

2. Level II (concrete logic, seven, eight to eleven, twelve years). Mental operations are grouped together in inclusive and stable systems of simple and double classifications, seriations, correspondences, and numbers. Transitivity of assymmetrical and symmetrical relations is achieved ($A > B.B > C$: $\supset$:$A > C$, $A = B.$ $B = C$: $\supset$:$A = C$) and the subjects become able to consider simultaneously a class and its subclasses. At this state also double classification becomes possible, and the two elementary classifications ($A.$ $-A$) and ($B.$ $-B$) yield the four subclasses ($A.B$) ($A.-B$) ($-A.B$) ($-A.-B$).

3. Level III (formal logic from eleven, twelve years). At this stage the subject becomes able to operate with purely *hypothetical relationships* and to *reflect,* that is, to think about his own more elementary mental operations. In the case of the double classification, the subject becomes able to consider all the *possible* relationships between the two classes. There are sixteen possible patterns of combination of the four elementary subclasses $(A.B)$ $(-A.B)$ $(A.-B)$ $(-A.-B)$. Thus, the presence of $(A.B)$, $(-A.B)$, and $(-A.-B)$ with $(A.-B)$ absent, corresponds to the implication $(A \supset B)$, the existence of only $(A.B)$ and $(-A.-B)$ with the absence of $(-A.B)$ and $(A.-B)$ means the equivalence $(A = B)$, and so forth.

To summarize, Brunswik's structural model is closely similar to Piaget's analysis of behavior during the first eighteen months of life. The later stages of development, involving increasing degrees of reversibility, are not covered by Brunswik, probably because of his nearly exclusive concern with perceptual processes.

CONCLUDING REMARKS

The systems of Brunswik and Piaget have been compared on a number of specific points. In this section a brief comparison will be attempted in more general terms.

There is one important characteristic common to Brunswik and Piaget that gives them an important place in contemporary psychology. This is their persistent and unusually penetrating analysis of the most general and fundamental problems of psychology, and their recognition that we have barely started the difficult search for a fruitful conceptualization. Their common aim has been "to determine the structural and functional properties of the unit of behavior *in abstract terms."* (Brunswik 1952, p. 92; italics ours.) Both had an extensive background in the philosophy and history of science, and were trained in and enthusiastic about the new experimental science of psychology. Their early divergence and later development has an obvious and interesting relationship to respectively German logical empiricism in Vienna and French rationalist philosophy in Geneva, but this lies outside the scope of the present paper. The common interest in the theory of knowledge also seems to have contributed to the fact that the resulting systems became *cognitive,* containing only sketchy outlines of how to cope with affective-motivational aspects of behavior.

There are three salient major differences between the two psychologists: One is the difference in basic epistemology, Brunswik being close to logical empiricism and Piaget having formulated his own system. Another difference is that Brunswik has been primarily "method-centered," criticizing and improving experimental design, whereas Piaget has been primarily "content-centered," trying to describe mental structures with little regard for strict methodology. A third important difference lies in the field of research; Brunswik was nearly exclusively working in the field of perception, mostly with adult subjects, whereas Piaget has been doing extensive research both on perception and cognition, but mostly with children. The impact of these differences can be traced throughout the more specific points that have been mentioned.

In evaluating the two contributions it should finally be noticed that Brunswik has presented a methodological program without a specific psychological theory, whereas Piaget has presented a psychological theory with a relatively weak methodological foundation. This has made the comparison somewhat difficult.

We hope that this treatment, however incomplete and abbreviated, will be an incitement to continue the work of the two great psychologists and to unravel those unconscious conceptual tangles that still block the progress towards psychological knowledge.

REFERENCES

Berlyne, D. *Conflict arousal and curiosity*. New York: McGraw-Hill, 1960.

Brunswik, E. *Wahrnehmung und Gegenstandswelt. Grundlegung einer Psychologie vom Gegenstand her*. Wien: Deuticke, 1934.

Brunswik, E. Probability as a determiner of rat behavior. *J. exp. Psychol.*, 1939, *25*, 175–197.

Brunswik, E. *The conceptual framework of psychology*. Chicago: University of Chicago Press, 1952.

Brunswik, E. *Perception and the representative design of psychological experiments*. Berkeley, Calif.: University of California Press, 1956.

Brunswik, E., and J. Kamiya. Ecological cue-validity of "proximity" and of other gestalt factors. *Amer. J. Psychol.*, 1953, *66*, 20–32.

Campbell, D. T. Operational delineation of "what is learned via the transposition experiment." *Psychol. Rev.*, 1954, *61*, 167–174.

Greco, P. Induction, deduction et apprentissage. In *Études d'épistémologie génétique,* Vol. 10. Paris:

Presses Universitaires de France, 1959. Pp. 3–59.

Heider, F. *The psychology of interpersonal relations*. New York: Wiley, 1958.

Inhelder, B., and J. Piaget. *The growth of logical thinking from childhood to adolescence*. New York: Basic Books, 1958.

Piaget, J. *Introduction à l'épistémologie génétique*. Paris: Presses Universitaires de France, 1949. 3 vols. (a)

Piaget, J. *Traité de logique. Essai de logistique opératoire*. Paris: Colin, 1949. (b)

Piaget, J. *The psychology of intelligence*. London: Routledge, 1950.

Piaget, J. *The origins of intelligence in children*. New York: International Universities, 1952. (a)

Piaget, J. *Essai sur les transformations des opérations logiques. Les 256 opérations ternaires de la logique bivalente des propositions*. Paris: Presses Universitaires de France, 1952. (b)

Piaget, J. *The construction of reality*

in the child. New York: Basic Books, 1956.

Piaget, J. Logique et équilibre dans les comportements du sujet. In *Études d'épistémologie génétique.* Vol. 2. Paris: Presses Universitaires de France, 1956. Pp. 25–117.

Piaget, J. Assimilation et connaissance. In *Études d'épistémologie génétique.* Vol. 5. Paris: Presses Universitaires de France, 1958. Pp. 49–108.

Piaget, J. Apprentissage et connaissance. In *Études d'épistémologie génétique.* Vol. 7. Paris: Presses Universitaires de France, 1959. Pp. 21–67.

Piaget, J. La portée psychologique et épistémologique des essais neohulliens de D. Berlyne. In *Études d'épistémologie génétique.* Vol. 12. Paris: Presses Universitaires de France, 1960. Pp. 105–123.

Piaget J., and B. Inhelder. *Le developpement des quantités ches l'enfant.* Neuchâtel: Delachaux et Niestlé, 1941.

Piaget, J., and B. Inhelder. *The child's conception of space.* London: Routledge, 1956.

Piaget, J., and B. Inhelder. *La genèsè des structures logiques élémentaires. Classifications et sériations.* Neuchâtel: Delachaux et Niestlé, 1959.

Piaget, J., B. Inhelder, and A. Szeminska. *The child's conception of geometry.* New York: Basic Books, 1960.

Smedslund, J. The problem of "what is learned?" *Psychol. Rev.,* 1953, *60,* 157–158.

Smedslund, J. Multiple-probability learning. Oslo: Oslo University Press, 1955.

Smedslund, J. Apprentissage des notions de la conservation et de la transitivité du poids. In *Études d'épistémologie génétique.* Vol. 9. Paris: Presses Universitaires de France, 1959. Pp. 85–124.

Smedslund, J. The acquisition of conservation of substance and weight in children. V. Practice in conflict-situations without external reinforcement. *Scand. J. Psychol.,* 1961, *2,* 156–160.   (a)

Smedslund, J. The acquisition of conservation of substance and weight in children. VI. Practice on continuous *v.* discontinuous material in problem situations without external reinforcement. *Scand. J. Psychol.,* 1961, *2,* 203–210.   (b)

Smedslund, J. The utilization of probabilistic cues after 1100 and 4800 stimulus-presentations. *Acta Psychologica,* 1962, 383–386.

Smedslund, J. The effects of observation on children's representation of the spatial orientation of a water surface. *J. genet. Psychol.,* 1963, *102,* 195–201.   (a)

Smedslund, J. The acquisition of transitivity of weight in children. *J. genet. Psychol.,* 1963, *104,* 245–255.   (b)

Smedslund, J. Concrete reasoning. A study of intellectual development. *Child Develpm. Monogr.,* in press.

Vinh-Bang. Évolution des conduites et apprentissage. In *Études d'épistémologie génétique.* Vol. 9. Paris: Presses Universitaires de France, 1959. Pp. 3–13.

Wickens, D. D. The transference of conditioned excitation and conditioned inhibition from one muscle group to the antagonistic muscle group. *J. exp. Psychol.,* 1938, *22,* 101–123.

14

A Critical Consideration of Egon Brunswik's Probabilistic Functionalism

ROBERT WARD LEEPER

THE CIRCUMSTANCES AND NATURE OF THE PRESENT PAPER

Early in 1954, a letter from Gardner Murphy invited me to join Egon Brunswik and himself in one of the symposia at the International Congress of Psychology at Montreal in the following June. The symposium was to have the cosmic-sounding title, "The Relation of the Person to His Environment." Murphy's paper was to deal with concepts of the boundaries between the person and the environment, Brunswik's with his ideas of similarities and differences between thinking and perception as "ratiomorphic" types of functioning. My own paper, Murphy proposed, might examine the implications of field theory for psychology.

In the half-year that followed, the three of us did a lot of exchanging of suggestions and criticisms on our preliminary drafts. In this period, I soon became convinced that, instead of dealing with the topic that Gardner Murphy had originally suggested to me, my paper might more appropriately provide a commentary on Brunswik's ideas. This was eventually its form.

After the Congress, Murphy's paper was published (1956); but Brunswik's paper, now included in the present volume, was never published, and my commentary on it similarly was never submitted for publication. (For abstracts, see Brunswik (1955a) and Leeper (1955).)

My failure to publish this paper left me with a feeling of unmet obligation. The preparation for this symposium not only had necessitated a more intensive study of Brunswik's ideas than most psychologists have been able to make, but also had given me an unusual opportunity to get

405

acquainted with Brunswik's thinking in almost the last year of his life. My further acquaintance with Brunswik's publications, furthermore, convinced me that there was some considerable need not only for some clearer and simpler statement of Brunswik's main ideas, but also for a critical re-examination of those ideas on the basis of a wider array of examples than Brunswik commonly had used.

In the period since the Congress in 1954, three important sets of material have been published that add very significantly to the papers dealing with Brunswik's work. These are:

1. The several papers—and especially those from Brunswik—published in the *Psychological Review* in 1955 from a Symposium on the Probability Approach in Psychology at the University of California in Berkeley in July, 1953;
2. Brunswik's *Perception and the Representative Design of Psychological Experiments,* published posthumously in 1956;
3. The summary of Brunswik's ideas and research by Leo Postman and Edward Tolman in Volume 1 of Sigmund Koch's *Psychology: A Study of a Science* (1959).

These publications, it seems to me, still leave a great need for clarification and critical discussion of Brunswik's contributions, but they certainly put us into a much more favorable situation for such an attempt now than we were in 1954. Also, in my own personal case, it has been possible to give a much longer consideration of Brunswik's ideas than I could in 1954. Consequently, although the present paper attempts the same type of role that my briefer paper tried to serve at the Montreal Congress, it has attempted a more inclusive discussion of Brunswik's work, even that it by no means covers all aspects of that.

To some persons, it will probably seem inappropriate for a paper in a memorial volume to be as bluntly critical as the present paper will be on a number of scores or for it to suggest that there are so many points where Brunswik's ideas need to be rounded out into a more comprehensive psychological theory. Such criticisms and suggestions may seem inappropriate not merely because there is no opportunity for Brunswik to reply and correct those points where I may have failed to catch the intent of his writing, but also because such a paper may seem inconsistent with the customary tone and purpose of such memorial volumes. However, what seems most important is that our present discussions should take Brunswik's ideas really seriously and try to find some means whereby they can be brought into the main streams of contemporary psychology. It seems that Brunswik truly was making some very important and original contributions. But it also seems that, if these contributions are not to be lost to most psychologists, we must get a much clearer idea of what they are, what their strengths and limitations are, and what modifications and developments they might receive.

In our discussions of these matters, there is obviously a basic difference between Egon Brunswik and myself. Brunswik was primarily a creative worker—not only in theoretical matters, but also in his ability to move naturally back and forth between theoretical discussions and ingenious experimental work suited to yield striking demonstrations of his concepts. But he was relatively unconcerned with trying to make his presentations simple or clear. The important task, as he saw things, was to develop and state some fundamentally new modes of thought. In our correspondence about the Montreal symposium, I urged various clarifications of his paper, particularly to take into account the fact that many of his audience would be persons for whom English would be a more or less unfamiliar language. He acceded to some suggestions regarding the length and complexity of his sentences, but for the most part he waved such suggestions aside. "If you are going to present difficult ideas," he finally declared, "you simply have to present them in difficult terms."

My own tendencies are different. For one thing, I am convinced that, when a person is dealing with complicated theoretical issues, he needs to try to state things in the simplest possible terms, because I am convinced that a theoretical worker, otherwise, is likely to create difficulties not only for other persons, but also for himself. For another thing, I have a basic distrust of long logical leaps that do not come down fairly often to make sure that they are keeping contact with a broad base of empirical realities. I feel that there may be some gains from trying to approach Brunswik's work with these different major objectives. But, even if so, it can easily be seen that the difference in possible contribution is the difference between the person who is primarily engaged in creative work and the other person who, if he is making any theoretical contribution at all, is doing so merely through tidying up the contributions of others. I hope the present paper may have some contribution of this latter sort. At the same time, I realize that cleaning women sometimes throw away some extremely useful things and sometimes rearrange objects in some awfully odd ways. Maybe this will happen in the following. The risk must be taken, however, because it is important that Brunswik's ideas not be relegated to some museum, but be brought into the living give-and-take of psychological controversy, involving them in the dialectic process that Boring so often has praised, especially in his years as editor of Contemporary Psychology. As Boring has said, such vigorous discussion is probably indispensable for bringing out the important potentialities of any complex body of thought. Such considerations, then, have prompted the character of the present paper.

THE LIMITED USE OF BRUNSWIK'S IDEAS

It may be that I underestimate the degree to which Brunswik's ideas have been studied and used by psychologists. However, it seems safe to say that only a very small percentage of psychologists have anything except some very general and frequently rather inaccurate impressions regarding Brunswik's contributions. As far as I can judge, both from printed statements about Brunswik's work and from querying a number of psychologists about this topic, the common conception of Brunswik's work, insofar as this work is known at all, is made up of the following impressions:

Impression 1

Brunswik was somewhat of a bridge between the older psychology of Germany and Austria, on the one hand, with its main emphasis on perceptual phenomena, and American experimental psychology, on the other hand, with its stress on learning and with its predominantly biological and objective orientation. His influence probably came partly through his contributions to Tolman's thinking. This relationship and also the perceptual ancestry of his thinking probably indicate that it is more soft-minded than the usual American tradition.

Impression 2

Brunswik was much interested in the philosophy-of-science viewpoint which developed in Vienna. Hence, he may have played some part in producing some of the present background assumptions of much of American psychology. However, since the pronouncements of this philosophy of science turn out to be more equivocal than originally had been claimed, they are less revolutionary than was expected, and this phase of Brunswik's contribution may be mostly just of historical interest rather than something significant for current psychology.

Impression 3

Brunswik spoke a lot about the need for "representative design" in psychological research, but the meaning of this is rather obscure. It may be mainly an advocacy of use of real-life situations as much as possible and a disparagement of artificial laboratory situations. This, in turn must mean that he had some old-fashioned sentimental resistance to the necessary methods of scientific work.

Impression 4

Brunswik spoke a lot about the value of correlational studies of perception and perhaps of other sorts of phenomena. This had something to do with his desire to demonstrate that perception is generally a fairly accurate process. However, it is hard to see what significance such correlational methods might have, other than their lending some support to this very general point.

Impression 5

In general, then, Brunswik probably proposed no ideas that are not fairly well represented in our present-day thought in experimental psychology. Any careful study of his writings may perhaps safely be left to those who are primarily interested in the history of psychology.

If the above is even an approximation of the thinking of the majority of psychologists, it means that there are some recognizable points of relationship between this image of Brunswik's work and the actual facts of the matter. But it also means that there has been a very inadequate grasping and utilization of Brunswik's concepts. If such actually is the case, and if there is danger that it may continue, it is important to try to learn why there has been this limited use of Brunswik's contributions, and it is important to try to counteract these factors.

SOME MAIN REASONS FOR THIS LIMITED UNDERSTANDING

There have been, I believe, four main factors that have tended to account for the limited understanding and use of Brunswik's contributions. These seem to be the following:

1. Brunswik was contributing some genuinely new ideas on certain scores, and these were ideas, in many cases, which were not in keeping with the Zeitgeist, as Boring calls it (1955), of the age in which they occurred. For one thing, he was stressing perceptual problems in a period in which American psychology had not yet overcome its behavioristic prejudices against working on perceptual phenomena because of their earlier alignment with discussions of subjective experience and introspective or phenomenological methods of observation. For another thing, he was proposing some new means of thinking about perception and about other phenomena. He was using concepts that the majority of us

had not practiced with. He had developed some rather well-chosen terms for referring to these concepts, but these terms also were unfamiliar to us. Consequently, his writings presented some inevitable difficulties such as one ought reasonably to expect when a new conceptual system and a new terminology are proposed. Part of the difficulties of communication were inevitable. They were difficulties such as always will be met whenever any worker proposes some fundamentally new modes of thought.

2. Other difficulties in understanding Brunswik's proposals came simply from difficulties of style. A great deal of the difficulty comes from the compactness with which Brunswik wrote and from the large number of technical terms that he characteristically crammed into single sentences. There are difficulties, too, from the cumbersome and involved character of many of his sentences. If I were to try here to document adequately such statements, it would require a considerable sample, and there is no space or point in that. But, I believe that any reader can establish this point for himself by turning to the several papers from Brunswik that have been printed in this volume, including the papers he wrote for presentation at meetings. These were not papers that a listener could read and reread, and they ought to have been simpler than the printed papers. But they are papers, like the rest of Brunswik's writing, which require rereading after rereading before one gets each part sufficiently well mastered to grasp, adequately, the larger units of thought.

I know in my own experience that I have had to read and reread Brunswik's papers a number of times, working slowly to relate his statements to background material that I could call to mind, before I could get a clear and usable understanding of much of what he was saying. His writing is rewarding with such repeated reading. It is not like writing which seems very impressive on first acquaintance, but which becomes less impressive the more carefully one analyzes its logic. Brunswik "wears well," as one might say. But it is not writing that communicates much to those who feel that they must read it rapidly or read it merely one or two times.

3. Even though Brunswik did a magnificent job in delineating some of the main historical trends of psychology, especially in his monograph on "The Conceptual Framework of Psychology" (1952), there are occasional respects in which Brunswik doubtless has struck the advocates of other points of view as having misunderstood some parts of their interpretations. For instance, speaking of Adler's work, Brunswik said: ". . . Adler's major contribution, the attempt to shift earlier reduction schemes from the sex drive to the desire for mastery and prestige, is merely a change of content." (1952, p. 60.) On this, it might well be

maintained that the concept of personality as basically a matter of a learned "life style" is a much more fundamental contribution.

In speaking about Gestalt psychology, Brunswik spoke about it as recognizing vicarious functioning through the principle of transposition. But, he added:

"Since this principle of 'transposition' ignores 'families' of cues the members of which do not formally resemble each other but are held together merely by association . . ., recognition of vicariousness remains limited to one of its comparatively trivial aspects. . . ." (1952, p. 62.) A Gestaltist would feel troubled by this for, even though he would agree that it is appropriate to speak about transposition only when the equivalence between two patterns of stimulation is one that is independent of training, this point does not at all mean that Gestalt theory is unconcerned about other equivalences that are learned. The work of Köhler with chimpanzees, for instance, certainly involved lots of instances where chimpanzees had to learn that one object or one method of dealing with things was equivalent to some other. Similarly, a Gestaltist would be troubled by Brunswik's characterization of their work as having been concerned particularly with ambiguity and illusion, as being almost solely subjectivistic or phenomenalistic in approach, and of having a mode of approach in which ". . . the intricate problems of psycho-environmental (central-distal) stimulus-response coordination are, by both Köhler and Koffka, summarily dismissed by allusions to a vaguely conceived kind of pre-established harmony (or extended isomorphism) between the structural principles of the surroundings and the field dynamics within the organism." (1952, p. 63.) It is true, for instance, that Gestalt psychologists have spent much time in studies of perceptual illusions, but the reason for this interest has been the desire to learn how it is possible for the organism to perceive veridically so many features of its environment. The work with illusions, for example, helps to eliminate the overly simple principle that people otherwise tend to trust that we perceive things as we do because the perceptual mechanisms merely reflect external realities or peripheral stimulation.

In the same way, an S-R psychologist might feel uncomfortable about Brunswik's description of the work of Watson and Hull as having been concerned, not with the stimulus situation and with the results of behavior, but with correlations between receptor events and happenings in the effector organs. Such a theorist might well say, "True enough, Watson typically talked in these terms, but his experimental work of course was rarely in those terms—he described, for example, the apparatus in which he placed the animals he tested, and he described the errors they made and the successful reaching of goal-boxes. So, he was not mainly dealing with 'proximal-proximal' relationships!"

In the huge territory that Brunswik described in his aim to portray the gradual convergence of psychological theory and research toward its current character, such errors of characterization, if indeed they are such, are relatively infrequent by comparison with the very penetrating and informative statements on a vast and complex array of types of work. However, I believe it still is true that a number of other groups of psychologists have felt that, at some points, Brunswik was describing their work in terms that were not valid.

4. Another factor that has produced some considerable degree of difficulty in understanding and using Brunswik's ideas is that, with a number of his major concepts, Brunswik had not yet worked out the implications of his thinking nearly as adequately as they will need to be worked out. In a number of cases, key terms are inadequately defined. In a number of matters, the meaning or implication of major principles is not explored with more than one or a few examples in each case. Even when Brunswik wrote about some matters repeatedly, the successive discussions tended to repeat the examples and make essentially the same statements that already had been given in previous discussions. Consequently, some degree of confusion and uncertainty prevails at a number of points.

For example, the term "ecology" is a key term for Brunswik. Representative research design calls for a representative sampling of situations from an "ecology" or "natural-cultural habitat." But, what is an ecology or natural-cultural habitat? Postman and Tolman, in the paper in which they attempted to summarize Brunswik's views in Koch's volume, said:

> "Representative design" thus refers to investigations in which the external ecology of the organism is studied in a sample of situations. . . . It must also be emphasized that representative design does not refer to the sampling of *variables*. . . . When variables are sampled, there are as many universes as there are variables. But there is only one universe of environmental situations; that is, there is only one ecology for a given organism. (1959, p. 521.)

One might well wonder whether this was Brunswik's intent. When a person moves from a farm to a city, or is confined in jail, or finishes medical school and starts his practice, does he still have the same ecology? To the best of my knowledge, Brunswik's papers do not give anything that explicitly and clearly answers this question. My own impression is that Brunswik felt that an individual might be considered from the standpoint of various ecologies. Thus, speaking about his own experiment on size constancy, he said: "More drastic misestimates of size, such as of the moon, are probably mostly cases of going beyond the confines of the ecology of manipulable things." (1965, p. 489.) Now, if there is an ecology of manipulable things for a given person, there must also be another ecology that includes the moon, sun, stars, clouds, and flashes of lightning. There presumably would be other ecologies.

Even though this term was so central for Brunswik's major discussions, he did not state, however, how he would have dealt with questions such as these.

Another instance concerns the functions governed by the "lens model." As will be explained later, it seems that there were two types of examples that Brunswik used in speaking about this concept. He moved back and forth between these two types of examples without raising the question of whether two somewhat different sets of phenomena might be involved in them.

Brunswik's general idea of a need for a broad sampling-base for psychological generalizations ought to have led him to consider a wide array of examples for each major proposition that he was making. Instead, the successive discussions in different articles and monographs tended to repeat the same examples presented previously in the same context. From this, it has been more difficult for other psychologists to see what possibilities there were in Brunswik's concepts.

On a good many of these points, I think that part of the origin of these difficulties was the fact that Brunswik worked more nearly alone—with less interaction with other psychologists—than would have been optimal for the development and clarification of his proposals. It would have been better if his work could have been the center of a more lively and extensive series of controversies. There was some of such, as in the July 1953, with its two papers by Brunswik (1955b, 1955c) and the critical papers by Postman (1955), Hilgard (1955), Krech (1955), Feigl (1955), and Hammond (1955). But there was less of this than there should have been. It would have been better if more discussion could have occurred while it could have had the criticisms and reactions of Brunswik. That is now impossible. But, in the lack of that, it seems to me that the most genuine tribute to him that we can give is to be as vigorous and forthright in our criticisms and in our proposals for revision of his work as we can be. Hence the character of the present paper.

THE MAIN SUBSTANTIVE IDEAS FROM BRUNSWIK

To set the stage for the later evaluations and revisions that I will suggest, there are some advantages in grouping Brunswik's concepts as falling within two different groups. In the first place, Brunswik proposed a number of fundamental concepts regarding the nature of the phenomena that psychology is investigating empirically. In the second place, taking into consideration the nature of psychological phenomena, he felt that a number of rather distinctive methodological principles ought to be recognized and used by psychologists. In some ways, it seems he was more interested in such methodological problems than in empirical questions. But, if so, this was only because he felt that empirical research will be wasteful and inefficient until it is based on methodological principles appropriate to the subject-matter of psychology, methodological principles founded, not primarily on logical or philosophical grounds, but by reference to the nature of psychological phenomena. Brunswik spoke of this relationship as "the methodological postulate of behavior-research isomorphism." Thus:

> . . . one may . . . demand that the "order," or pattern, of research "ideas," or design, should be the same as the pattern of the "things" studied, which in our case is behavior. Research may be said to have reached an adequate, "functional," or "molar" level of complexity only if it parallels, and is thus capable of representing, behavior in all its essential features. We may call this the methodological postulate of behavior-research isomorphism. (1952, p. 25.)

In line with this mode of thinking, let us speak first of the relatively empirical or substantive principles that Brunswik emphasized. His most important principles seem to me to be the following. Let us state them without any attempt, for the present, to evaluate them.

(1) *The Adaptive Significance of Behavior and of Psychological Processes.* Psychologists need to adopt the general biological evolutionary point of view. Psychological processes are mainly a means of biological adaption, mainly matters of "the readjustive value of behavior in coming to terms with the physical or social environment," to quote from the last paper which Brunswik gave (in December, 1954, before the Section on History and Philosophy of Science of the AAAS).

(2) *The Dependence of Adaptation on Responses Related to Things Distant in Time and/or Space.* As Brunswik phrased it, "Forced to react quickly or within reasonable limits of time, it (the organism) must respond before direct contact with the relevant remote conditions in the environment, such as foodstuffs or traps, friends or enemies, can be established." (1952, p. 22.) Particularly is this true with man and the other higher animals. Their biological survival depends on their taking into account the relatively remote factors that they can take into account because of their fine distance receptors, their great learning ability, and their capacity for social communication.

(3) *The Limited Ecological Validity of the Cues and Means Which Must Be Used in Dealing with Remote Factors.*   This molding of behavior to deal with factors remote in space and/or time has to depend on factors that are of imperfect ecological validity—that is, that are more or less unreliably related to the objective factors and possible distal achievements that are the really important things for the organism. Even though some cues are more nearly valid than are others, none are absolutely trustworthy, and no means that the organism can use can be counted on as having utterly invariable results.

(4) *Lens Functioning as an Aid in Dealing with Such a World.* In this semierratic world, organisms are helped by their use of processes that may be understood to some extent by means of a "lens model" of organismic functioning. Just as a lens permits a camera to take a picture in relatively dim light because it takes scattering bundles of rays of light and refocuses each bundle on a point on the film, so the lens-functioning of the organism permits multiple use of cues (or means), thereby permitting better information (or more certain action) than the organism could achieve merely through one cue (or means) or another. Also, just as a lens would permit the use of a narrow beam of light focused only on *any* part of a lens, rather than requiring that the same part of the lens would be used in each case, so also does the lens-functioning of the organism make possible a vicarious substitution of one means or cue for another. Thus, if two people cannot communicate verbally with each other because they speak different languages, they may revert to gestures or to some other means of communication. Consequently, even though the organism lives in a world that is extremely heterogeneous, there is more stability in the achievements of the organism than we could expect were it not for this lens phenomenon.[1]

(5) *The Organism's Need of Dealing in Terms of Probabilities.*   Even with this lens-functioning, however, the organism cannot be sure of effective adaptation. The best that the organism can do is to live in terms of probabilities of different costs and different possible gains. Some highly unlikely reward may still be worth struggling for, and some highly unlikely disaster may be worth guarding against, but what the organism must always do is to try to live in terms of the best estimates of "probability times cost" and "probability times possible rewards."

(6) *The Ratiomorphic Character of Cognitive Processes.*   It would be a mistake to understand psychological processes in rationalistic

1. It may seem that, in this discussion of the lens model, I am introducing a number of revisions into Brunswik's concepts, rather than merely summarizing them. However, these are the ideas that are implicit, it seems to me, in Brunswik's examples and abstract statements on this matter.

or intellectualistic terms. But, in some more basic biological sense, psychological processes nevertheless are something which ". . . involves the particular type of orderly interaction we find best exemplified in syllogistic reasoning or in mathematical calculation." (1965, p. 487.) For example, the individual might have learned that, when he hears thunder, he may also expect some rain. From this general premise, and from noting at a given time that there is some thunder, he will tend to anticipate that rain is likely to come soon. The same holds true when a number of cues are taken into consideration and when some compromise is reached with regard to the divergent testimony they give. The organism bases its behavior on reasoning-like combinations of premises to reach conclusions.

(7) *The Lack of Complete Equivalence of Different Lens-Functions.*   As we have mentioned above, Brunswik placed major emphasis on the idea that the organism needs to be described by a "lens model" or needs to be understood as capable of "vicarious mediation" or utilization of any of a number of cues or means required to attain required ends under varying conditions. However, Brunswik did not regard the "lens" as a completely perfect means of substitution of one cue or means for another. As he said, "Imperfections of achievement may in part be ascribable to the 'lens' itself, that is, to the organism as an imperfect machine." (1952, p. 23.) He spoke particularly, in his last writings, of some differences that he believed tended to come in consequence of whether the individual tended to make a judgment about an environmental situation by means of sensory perceptions or by means of "thinking." This would be merely one instance of a host of examples of the fact that, when the organism chooses to use one means of response rather than another, some variations in the distal achievement or behavior-results will come because of the particular means chosen.

(8) *The Importance of Situational Determinants of Behavior.* Psychology cannot be made up solely of principles to the effect that such and such species of organisms (or types of individuals) tend to show such and such behavior. Must of our empirical research, and probably even the greatest part of that empirical research, needs to be concerned with questions about what situational factors produce what effects. As Brunswik said:

It may well be that in many contexts individuals in a population are more homogeneous or stereotyped than are situations in an ecology, and that the ascertainment of ecological generality may be a more challenging [and profitable] task than that of responder-populational generality. . . . Ebbinghaus needed only himself as a subject to lay the foundation for much of modern learning theory. . . . (1955b, p. 202.)

In general, in these principles, Brunswik was emphasizing the idea that the specific means by which the organism adapts do not matter very much. There is more stability in what the organism accomplishes than in the means which the organism uses to accomplish such things. There is more stability in what the organism accomplishes than in the cues by which it judges what it has to cope with.

THE MAIN METHODOLOGICAL PRINCIPLES FROM BRUNSWIK

From such concepts about the nature of psychological processes, Brunswik derived various propositions regarding how psychologists ought to proceed in their work of research and theory-construction. As I understand his methodological principles, his main proposals were the following:

(1) *We Need an Adequate Basis of Sampling for Whatever Abstract Principles We Propose.*   The material with which we are working in psychological research is not like some chemical that can be secured in some purified form. Instead, there is almost infinite variety in the situations in which behavior occurs. Hence, we cannot take some one or some few samples of some broad class of situations and be sure, from our observation with such inadequate samples, that what has been manifested there, even if quite clearly and significantly, will also be manifested by other examples from the range of situations that would be covered by the abstract principles that we are tempted to use in reporting our results.

Psychologists have learned, Brunswik said, that a research worker must be careful to get adequate samples of types of individuals whom he wishes to compare. But we have been very negligent (perhaps because of the huge labor that this rule would involve) of the fact that, when we talk about the effects of different types of situations, we need some adequate sampling of them just as truly as we need some sampling of individuals. The logic of the two matters is the same. Thus:

Everyone knows that encountering, say, a wife who is taller than her husband . . . does not justify the inference that wives . . . are always, or are overwhelmingly (or, Brunswik might have said, frequently), taller than their husbands. . . . What the instances mentioned do demonstrate, however, is . . . that it is possible for a wife to be taller than her husband. . . .

(In the same way, since experimental research typically involves merely a standardized sample of a certain type of situation,) Experiments in the biological and social sciences are often formally analogous to the instances referred to above, . . . they do demonstrate a mere possibility. . . . (1956b, p. 54.)

It is difficult, however, for psychologists to make their conclusions as modest as their evidence. To guard against the temptations of over-generalization, we must realize that there is a sampling problem involved whenever we make abstract statements.

(2) *Representative Sampling of Natural-Cultural Habitats as Essential for Significant Quantitative Principles.* Psychology needs quantitative principles. It is not sufficient merely to know that "this factor has this type of influence in some situations." But, if we are to have good quantitative principles, this calls for much more than just demonstrating a "statistically significant difference" or a "statistically significant correlation." Something like that is merely the prelude for other work to determine quantitative relations. Particularly, any quantitative statement needs to be based on evidence sufficient to indicate the relative weight of some factor in a universe of situations which can be effectively described so that other workers—whether in other research or in practical applications of such rules—can know what domain the quantitative generalization applies to.

Such domains could be defined artificially or arbitrarily, but the work of psychology would be endless if this were our procedure. Instead, we need to deal with domains defined in some more externally given fashion. Hence we need to deal with the natural-cultural habitats or ecologies of organisms. Our studies need to give us a representative sampling (whether by random sampling or by some more stratified means) from such domains. Out of such representative sampling—and only by this means—can we get the data that will permit us to make good quantitative principles.

(3) *The Further Reasons for Representative Research Design.* The reason for working with natural-cultural habitats or ecologies is more than just the need for drawing samples from domains that can be meaningfully specified. Representative research design involves working with real-life situations, as contrasted with the artificially simplified and stereotyped situations generally used in experimental studies (in "systematic research design," as Brunswik terms it). The use of such real-life situations has three virtues.

a. The different variables in real-life situations are merely irregularly related to each other. Unlike what is true of the majority of experiments on learning, for example, there is no one action in real life that will always be rewarded, and no discriminable cue that always will indicate the same referent. A sampling of real-life situations gives an opportunity for the organism to demonstrate its modes of functioning in probabilistic situations.

b. Because real-life situations have not been artificially simplified, they offer abundant opportunity for the organism to display the phenomenon of vicarious functioning.

c. In representative design, real-life situations have not been artificially simplified, with some variables eliminated from the situation. Hence these situations permit interactional effects to occur which we need to learn about.

Such considerations are important, Brunswik said, because the need
in psychology is not solely for ". . . rigor of fact-finding, inference, and
communication," but is a need also "to establish exact study on an adequate level of complexity." (1952, p. 1.)

(4) *Psychology Needs to Seek for Probabilistic Laws.* A
search for strict laws—a use of the "nomothetic approach," as Brunswik
defines this—is appropriate in some other sciences. It would be appropriate also in psychology if it were feasible for psychologists to make
allowance for all the many chance influences that occur in the objective
environments with which the organism is dealing. If psychologists were
omniscient, superhuman, they conceivably could have all the data for
predicting that, in a given case, the behavior of the organism actually
would produce such and such unusual effects because of the chance
variations of conditions affecting the validities of cues and/or means.
But, neither the organism nor the psychologist can predict the chance
developments that will occur in real-life situations. Hence, the organism
has to deal with its environment in terms of probabilities. The psychologist also, in trying to understand the functioning of that organism has
to work in terms of probabilistic laws that will take into account the uncertainties in the cues that the organism will receive and the uncertainties
in the means that it employs to try to attain its ends. Psychology should
try to estimate these probabilities as precisely and exactly as possible,
just as it is true that studies of parent-child relationships should attempt
to determine as precisely as possible what the correlation, say, is apt to
be between the characteristics of parents and the characteristics of offspring. But these probabilistic laws will be descriptive merely of the
probabilities for any given individual, just as statements in genetics attempt to state the probabilities that dominant or recessive traits will show
in an offspring of parents of a given genetic type. It is unrealistic to
believe that we can ever make definite and exact predictions of what a
given organism will do in a given situation, just as it is impossible to
predict what set of chromosomes will be selected by the reduction-
division of a given reproductive cell. We can attempt to estimate probabilities exactly, but this is basically different from attempting to form
strict laws. Psychological laws must be based on studies of situations
which involve the same sorts of uncertain relationships that exist in
abstractly described ecologies.

(5) *Psychological Research and Theory Ought to Deal Mainly
with Distal-Distal Relationships.* At quite a few points, Brunswik's

statements either *appear* to call for casting psychological principles in terms of statements about the relationships of "distal focal variables" (relationships of environmental situations to behavior products) or quite unmistakably advocate this sort of formulation.

Thus, what seems a very clear advocacy of distal-distal principles is given in the concluding chapter, on "Convergence toward an objective functional approach," in his monograph on "The Conceptual Framework of Psychology." Referring first to some earlier writing by himself in 1934, Brunswik said:

> The present writer has spoken of a "psychology in terms of objects" . . . in which organisms are described, and differentiated from one another, by reference to the—predominantly distal—stimulus or result variables with which they have "attained" stabilized relationships. By applying this approach to distal-to-distal functional arcs bridging over the entire organism without descending into it [see Fig. 1, Chap. 1, this volume, Ed.], one may further gain in scope and at the same time get around the hazardous construction of intervening variables. . . . In specifying this proposal by urging positive ascertainment of focusing, and of the width of vicarious functioning in the proximal versus the distal region(s), we can avoid focal-arc atomism (sec. 8) in spite of the ignoring of intraorganismic mediation. The full-fledged pattern of functionalistic research can be realized in this manner, thus removing what must seem the most cogent basis for criticism of the empty-organism approach. (1952, p. 72.)

Various other statements by Brunswik might very easily be understood in the same sense of advocacy of "distal-to-distal functional arcs bridging over the entire organism without descending into it." Thus, in a much earlier paper, Brunswik said:

> Thus, both for reception and for action, it turns out that the special manner in which any thing is mediated (or done) is not especially essential or significant. One and the same means-object may be represented at different times by very different stimulus configurations. And one and the same goals may be reached equally well by very different kinds of movements and means-object manipulations. . . . The really significant question always is: What are the kinds of such objects and final goal-effects which the organism is able to attain independently of all the varying circumstances with a relatively large degree of accuracy and probability . . . ? (1936, p. 125.)

In his final paper in December, 1954, Brunswik said:

> We have conjectured that the emphasis on wide-spanning functional correlations at the expense of attention to the intervening technologic detail is one of the major characteristics that distinguishes psychology from its predecessors

. . . the functional arcs that span toward, and gain their feedback from the remote, "distal" environment . . . are the really important arcs. (p. 509.)

Many other quotations could be given that similarly would tend to leave the impression that Brunswik favored the same proposal advocated by B. F. Skinner (1950, 1957)—that psychology ought to avoid any development of inferences regarding intervening processes or variables, ought to have nothing to do with any supposed introspective data, and ought instead to formulate its principles solely in terms of "functional relationships" between objectively observable situations and objectively observable behavioral results.

(6) *Psychological Research and Theory Ought Generally to Take the Form, Not of Distal-Distal Principles, but of Distal-Central, Central-Distal, or Distal-Central-Distal Principles.*   To make this statement, and to submit it as descriptive of Brunswik's thinking rather than as a possible alternative to it, is to hazard a more controversial description of Brunswik's ideas than has been the case in any of the rest of this paper. But, even though I have arrived at this conclusion only in the very last possible moment for revision of this paper, I believe the evidence is very clearcut that indicates that this was Brunswik's basic mode of thought, even though he expressed it sometimes in ways that could be understood in different terms from those he meant.

Let me review the reasons for picturing this as Brunswik's main conception. We may note, first of all, that he deplored "hostility to theory and to central inference." (1952, pp. 47–49.) He saw such hostility to inferential concepts as a mark of immature thinking about the philosophy of science. He felt that much of the avoidance of inferential terms has been a consequence of fear of not escaping the subjectivist connotations of older psychology, and he felt that such tactics involve the cost of losing the "heuristic advantages to be gained from the 'apperceptive mass' attached to traditional terms. . . ." (1952, pp. 44–47.)

In the second place, we may note that Brunswik spoke of the lens model as a means of conceiving the relationships between "focal variables" rather than necessarily between distal factors. For example, in the section of his 1952 monograph where he spoke of "Stabilized achievement and vicarious mediation," (1952, pp. 16–21), he ended this section with a discussion entitled "Central-distal versus peripheral focusing of achievement." In this, he made what I now regard as a really crucial statement of his outlook:

Recent psychology has shown that variables located in certain "areas," "layers," or "regions" of the environment or of the organism seem more often to be focal than those in others. Some of the most crucial changes of emphasis in contemporary psychology are based on the recognition of the relatively nonfocal, vicarious, "generalized" role of the sensory as well as of the motor periphery, coupled with the comparatively focal character of the central as well as the distal regions, both situational and historical, in the case of the higher animals at least. (1952, p. 21.)

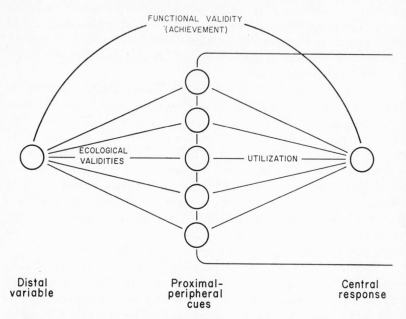

Fig. 1. Diagram given by Brunswik to illustrate "the lens model as applied to perceptual constancy." (Adapted from E. Brunswik. Representative design and probabilistic theory in a functional psychology. *Psychol. Rev.*, 1955, *62*, 193–217.)

As expressing this conception, it is worthwhile to examine carefully Figure 1, which reproduces what Brunswik gave in a diagram of "the lens model as applied to perceptual constancy." (1955a, Fig. 8, p. 206.) In this diagram, it is to be noted that the one focal variable is the distal variable, the other is marked as the "central response."

One might ask, "Why didn't Brunswik treat the individual's judgment of the size of an object as a distal variable, since, of course, Brunswik was recording the overt judging response of the person? Why speak about 'central responses' when what was observed by the experimenter was the final behavior product (for example, the subject's saying '8 feet')?"

In a certain sense, of course, the implications of this question are unimpeachable. But, it seems that Brunswik's view could be stated, in reply, in some such terms as these: "When we have a person look at an object and make a judgment about its size, he might indicate his judgment or his perception of its size by any of a long series of means. He might reply orally, he might write down his estimate in numbers, he might raise his hand to indicate the size of the object, he might compare the object with some other object, he might make a line on the ground with his foot, he might check one item from a multiple-choice question, and so forth. So, there is a great deal of possible vicarious mediation in his indication of what he sees. But, since there are such high correlations between the estimates that he would communicate by such different means, we are forced to infer that there had been some focal variable within the organism, some central response, which then could furnish the basis for any of a great diversity of forms of producing an effect on his environment (in this case, for communicating his judgment to the experimenter)."

In line with this thinking, we might well say that Brunswik's conception would be expressed somewhat more fully, not by the diagram given in Figure 1, but by the somewhat more elaborate diagram which I propose in Figure 2. I do not know of any *diagram* in Brunswik's writings which exactly corresponds to this particular diagram, but Brunswik's Fig. 1, Chap. 1 and his comments on it are quite close. And, many parts of his discussion apparently assume this sort of thing. His sympathetic comments about Tolman's work, for instance, suggest this form

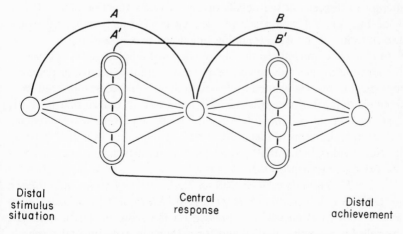

Fig. 2. The double-lens model which seems to be required to portray diagrammatically the basic model which Brunswik's discussions implied.

of statement (1952, pp. 67–70). His very sympathetic comments about the inferences in psychoanalytic theory regarding motives, defense mechanisms, and personality structure also are in line with this conception.

Now, if we go back to the quotation made above from Brunswik's 1936 paper, we can see that this quotation can be understood in terms of such a double-lens model. Furthermore, when one reads Brunswik's papers with this conception in mind, one realizes that, when he spoke about "wide-spanning functional arcs" or "wide-spanning functional correlations," the context typically reveals that he was speaking, not about distal-to-distal relationships, but about relationships between distal and central factors, or about distal relationships as mediated by such and such central responses. I am reminded by all this of a correction which he jotted in the margin of a letter that he sent to me on May 19, 1954, when we were corresponding about the paper that he was to present at the International Congress of Psychology a month later. In dictating the letter he had apparently said that ". . . our symposium . . . concentrates on distal-distal (S-R) problems exclusively, so far as I can see." In the margin, however, he added the word "central" to change this to "distal-central-distal" problems.

One other way that Brunswik expressed the sort of thing that is represented by Figure 2 is that he spoke frequently about the need for "macro-mediational studies"—studies that would be planned "from above" through previous observations of "distal-distal" relationships. The distinction he drew between such macro-mediational studies and reductive-nomothetic-systematic attempts is that such studies would not attempt to dissect out the details of the two lens functions (the A' and B' of Fig. 2), but would accept such vicarious functioning and would deal in terms of the wide-spanning functional arcs A and B.

In all such comments as the above, we must emphasize that Brunswik did not want to speak about central processes in introspective or phenomenological terms. He wanted to deal with them as processes inferred from objective data. But, nevertheless, it is important to realize that his basic mode of thought was not one of talking about perceptual phenomena, for example, in terms of distal-distal relationships, but in a different way dictated by his belief that it was efficient to develop concepts about intervening central processes.

(7) *There Is a Place Also for Reductive and Systematic Studies, but Only as Quite Accessory to Studies Which Permit Vicarious Mediation.* When Brunswik was pressed on the score of whether he saw any role for reductive studies and for systematic experimental research, he insisted that he saw these as having certain important functions, but

that their relative role had been vastly overemphasized. In the 1953 symposium, for example, after some vigorous criticism by the other discussants, Brunswik included the following statement in his final *In Defense of Probabilistic Functionalism: A Reply:*

> Probabilistic functionalism is not . . . hostile to reduction. It merely places correlational achievement-mapping of generalized functional arcs at the top of a hierarchical pyramid . . .; this is followed by the macro-mediational analysis of vicarious attainment strategy. As to the third level in this pyramid, the reductive study of micro-mediational tactics, I agree with Professor Hilgard that this and the entire nomothetic approach should not be "replaced" by the probabilistic approach of the two top levels, although I would like to place reductionism in a marginal position to psychology unless it is executed in firm contact with the two functional aims. In order to reduce, we must know what to reduce. We must reduce "from above," that is, starting from such high-complexity functional units as the lens model. . . .
> The nomothetic-reductionist-systematic type of approach has in the past been overstressed at the expense of the probabilistic-functional-representative approach. . . . We have had all of the former and nothing of the latter for too long. Now we must balance psychology in the molar and molecular realm. (1955b, p. 237.)

In the course of our preparation of papers for the 1954 International Congress, I got very much the same comment from Brunswik when I urged that there were many values in mediational studies and that most of his own work actually was mediational or reductive, including his paper at this Congress. Brunswik's comment was essentially that he "of course" recognized the need of mediational studies to round out our psychological knowledge and to permit us to make more discriminating predictions, but that psychologists had been giving a one-sided emphasis on systematic research and that he probably had slipped into a too-strong emphasis on nonmediational studies to try to redress the balance. If such is the case—and Brunswik certainly stated it in very clear terms—it calls for a revision of many of the pronouncements from Brunswik regarding the proper methodology for psychology.

(8) *The Prime Importance of Partial-Correlation Methods as a Means of Analysis.* Despite what has been said in the preceding section, most of the statements Brunswik made regarding the analysis of significant factors in complex situations have placed emphasis on partial correlation as the means of answering questions of *"how?"* Thus, he said:

> The challenge of further isolation (of significant variables) must be met by after-the-fact, mathematical means, as in the study of individual differences. For example, we may use partial correlation as a mathematical means of holding constant a certain variable. . . . It must also be noted that, in contradistinc-

tion to systematic design, the process of analysis may be stopped at any point, falling back on the nonreductive aim of functional research, together with the assurance that the unresolved part of the associations is safely within the fold of the ecology to which the investigation has been geared from the beginning. (1955b, pp. 202–203.)

In such generalized statements about methodology, therefore, Brunswik was not describing the sort of work that he had done on perception versus thinking, on the role of different probabilities of reward in animal learning, and on the learning of perceptual cues. Instead, he was calling for a more consistent use of representative design than his own research actually demonstrated.

A TENTATIVE PRELIMINARY EVALUATION OF THESE PRINCIPLES FROM BRUNSWIK

The main difficulty with Brunswik's proposals, it seems to me, is that he has overstated his case. He has drawn too sharp a contrast between his own proposals and those advanced by other psychologists. He has not made sufficient use of his own precept that, before one makes broad generalizations, he ought to have a very careful and extensive sampling of the instances such as the generalization purports to cover, and that from this sampling he ought to see whether there is a sufficient basis for the broad and strong statement that he is inclined to make. Furthermore, because he did not try to canvass a wide diversity of examples, he did not locate and correct some serious shortcomings in the definitions of some of his key terms (as in the case of the term "ecology," which we already have discussed).

Because of the overgeneralizations in Brunswik's writings, these writings tend to invite criticisms and perhaps overstatements on the opposite side, and the constructive gains that might have come from Brunswik's work are in danger of being lost. Perhaps even at that, the strategy that he adopted, probably quite unintentionally, may have been more worth using than a strategy of much more careful statements. Maybe it is true that new proposals have to be exaggerated in order that they gain attention and consideration. Or, perhaps it is inevitable that, as Boring has suggested in two of his last papers (1954, 1955), it is more or less inevitable that truly creative persons have a strong measure of egoistic interest, and some lack of appreciation of the contributions of others, else they are not likely to have the strong motivation needed for the development and presentation of some new ideas or findings.

My own basic conviction, though, is that overstatements are risky—

that they too much tend to invite countercriticism and counterattacks and that, in the hurly-burly of this, the important positive contributions get trampled and lost. And, in Brunswik's case, as I have said above, I think there are some highly worthwhile original proposals. Consequently, I think it is very important to re-examine Brunswik's principles, asking how we can state them in some more justified fashion and how we can show their organic relations to various other bodies of thought. The following discussion will be attempting to give a sort of restatement that I believe is demanded in the light of some broader sampling of materials from which to reason.

Most of the points that will be discussed are methodological points. Some points about the nature of psychological phenomena will be included in the discussion of these as needed, and then the discussion will end on several points where the main concern is just with empirical hypotheses.

SOME MORE SPECIFIC PROPOSALS ON A NUMBER OF MAIN CONCEPTS FROM BRUNSWIK

(1) *The Need for Adequate Sampling for Any Abstract Statements.*   Perhaps the most important concept from Brunswik, it seems to me, is his very general methodological point that we must be careful not to make abstract statements that are broader than our sampling of cases really would warrant. As he said, as cited above, a research study in a very restricted experimental situation may be sufficient to establish the point that a certain relationship exists in at least that one instance, just as the data on a single couple can establish the point that it is possible for a wife to be taller than her husband. Furthermore, as Brunswik said,

Quite often the demonstration of a mere possibility . . . is all that is necessary and desired of a piece of research, and may be fully sufficient to establish tentatively a principle for purposes of further verification and thus to stimulate further research; in all cases of this kind the systematic experiment is in place and may save the burdens that would go with a proof of ecological generality. In other cases, a systematic experiment may serve to exclude certain trivial factors from the explanation of a phenomenon. (1956b, p. 55.)

However, if we make statements of some other sort, such as that "all cases of . . . involve . . .," or "most cases of . . . involve . . .," we **must** have adequate sampling of instances to warrant such statements. Brunswik has rendered an extremely important service in calling our attention to the fact that sampling theory is just as relevant and just as indispensable when we make abstract statements about types of situations as when we make abstract statements about types of persons or types of organisms of any sort.

(2) *The Need for Representative Sampling as a Basis for Generalized Quantitative Principles.*   This seems to me like another excellent principle from Brunswik. Brunswik did well to point out that the task required by representative research design is a very huge task, but that it is a task that we cannot shirk if we want to make abstract statements of a meaningful quantitative sort about the relative contributions of different factors to some sort of behavior or achievement. The demonstration of quantitative relationships within a particular experimental situation is merely a first step in developing an adequate quantitative principle. Until we get the means to specify some larger domain of situations of which that experimental situation is an example, and until we have secured a representative sampling of instances from that larger domain, we really do not have an *abstract* principle of a quantitative sort, but merely a quantitative finding applicable to that one instance, comparable to the finding that "it is possible, judging from this one married couple, for a wife to be 14.7 percent taller than her husband."

As said earlier, the domains that we sample by research could be defined artificially or arbitrarily, but the work of psychology would be endless if we followed this procedure. Instead of that, we need to get domains which are worth talking about, worth knowing about, and yet which can be identified clearly enough so that other workers can know what we have undertaken to sample. Then, by some technique or other, whether by random sampling or stratified sampling or whatever, we need to get a representative sampling of instances from that domain; otherwise our quantitative statements cannot be used.

(3) *The Importance in Psychology, however, of Qualitative Principles.*   As in the quotation given above, Brunswik has granted clearly that there can be some real value in research that proves nothing more than that a certain factor can exert a certain type of influence in a certain direction. But, in his discussions of psychological theory, Brunswik has not adequately indicated, it seems to me, how important are such qualitative principles in psychology (and in other sciences) and how much of psychological knowledge, at least for some long period, must consist solely of such qualitative principles.

For many purposes, we are not greatly concerned about the details of quantitative relationships, but wish only to know that such and such a factor has such and such an influence in at least some cases. This is not to say that we will not be interested in quantitative knowledge as soon as it can be acquired. But, in the meantime, a more sketchy sort of knowledge can have great value. Much of medical knowledge, for instance, is of this sort, and yet is quite valuable in spite of limitations of a quantitative sort. For example, there must surely be individual differences in susceptibility to scurvy or pellagra under conditions of vitamin deficiency, but it is not very important, practically speaking, to know about these differences. Once the qualitative principle has been established—that such diseases can come from certain nutritional deficiencies and that they may be prevented or cured by such and such means—this knowledge easily can be used by employing diets that have some considerable margin of safety in them, and most of the value can thus be attained that could come through much more elaborate quantitative knowledge.

In the same way, a great many psychological problems could be dealt with more successfully and intelligently if we but knew the types of factors that are important and the directions in which their influences are exerted. It is a good thing for us to develop these principles into as nearly adequate quantitative principles as we can, and hence it is important for us, as we were saying above, to get as adequate a sampling-basis as we can for our generalized statements. But, useful and important knowledge does not start merely with the kind of knowledge that can be secured only through representative sampling.

(4) *The Importance in Psychology of a Sampling Procedure More Economical than Representative Sampling.*   Particularly as related to human life, since cultural factors can so enormously change human behavior, but also because human beings are adapted for living under such a terrific diversity of natural environments, and because the world in which we live is so infinitely complex and variegated, it is an extremely difficult thing to get any adequate representative sampling of "natural-cultural habitats" of human beings. But, we ought not to proceed as though our choice had to be a selection between representative sampling, on the one hand, and no significant breadth of sampling, on the other hand. There is another method of sampling that can be used quite economically and which is adequate for testing certain sorts of generalizations, at least in rough and tentative ways. We might speak of this method as a technique of "testing the limits," borrowing a term from Rorschach work.

For example, when a psychologist is tempted to generalize, from research with a particular situation, that "all learning requires an intent to learn," the danger is that he may be extending his finding to a vastly larger area than is justified. The thing for him to do, then, is to consider other instances of learning that seem least likely to exemplify the influence that he observed in his particular experiment. He might ask whether we can plausibly maintain that animals have an intent to learn. If he decides that such extreme instances seem to indicate that he has overgeneralized, then he may try to locate some more restricted category within the field of learning, so that he may test whether he can find some more modest but still fairly large territory where he will find no exceptions (even in seemingly extreme instances within that category). By such successive retreats from his extreme instances, he may ultimately find some rough indication of the limits of application of his finding. Or, he may demonstrate to himself that he cannot identify any basis for telling when the principle applies and when it doesn't, and may realize that he has to come to such a conclusion as, "Under some conditions, which I have not found the means of specifying, learning requires an intent to learn."

Brunswik to some extent illustrated the use of this method of sampling in connection with his experiment on perception versus thinking. In the specific instance that he used, it seemed that thinking tended to yield a high proportion of exactly correct answers, along with many gross errors in other cases, because of a tendency for thinking to take merely one single track *or* another in trying to reach a solution of the task. Perceptual judgments, on the other hand, all tended to be at least approximately correct through some multiple use of cues or a multiple-track type of approach.

In assessing the significance of his study, however, Brunswik did not depend merely on his one study. As he summarized the matter:

Ending on a note of caution, we should like to stress that the representativeness of our two versions of a common cognitive task is open to some doubt. Many specific conditions could be listed under which it is perception which is bizarre while it is thinking which is mellow and given to compromise. Aside from deductive considerations, only representative design could definitely prove us right or wrong in our conjecture that the juxtaposition which we have presented is more typical than its reverse. (1956b, p. 93.)

In judgments about the intelligence of a person, for instance, our *thinking* certainly tends to use multiple cues. On the other hand, when a person looks at a TAT card, he tends to *perceive* it as clearly and obviously portraying one sort of personal situation rather than another—something much like what Brunswik has spoken of as the single-track switching that may be more typical of thinking. Furthermore, when people do engage in thinking which is clearly single-track, we cannot count on its being accurate in any case, because it may be using faulty premises. Thus, in the old days of blood-letting in medicine, the major premise on which the practice depended was that "People who are ill are suffering from bad blood."

My impression is, however, that, although Brunswik recognized some of these considerations that can be urged against taking his experimental results as illustrative of perception and thinking more generally, he also tended to speak at various points about this study as though his data were more representative than we have a basis for believing that they are. For, if there are such exceptions as mentioned above, it is only in some special sense that he could have been justified in using, in the title of his Montreal paper, the expression ". . . a Functional Differentiation between 'Perception' and 'Thinking.' " If the conclusion is that the two different types of distribution of errors are found *only in general* to differentiate between perception and thinking, as Brunswik is saying, then it must follow that he was using some more fundamental means of saying what phenomena should be classed as perceptions and which as instances of thinking. *And,* one wonders, then, whether we ought not to challenge the traditional means of classification and propose some new classification that would cut across the old categories. He may have had this in mind, in part, in using the two terms (in parts of this same discussion) of "certainty-geared interactions" and "uncertainty-geared interactions." But it is hard to see that these terms are warranted when we find that he spoke as follows:

". . . certainty-geared interaction may go wrong . . . when the single cues representing the constituent variables are not in reality foolproof, that is, when certainty-geared interaction lacks its necessary counterpart in the ecology. Take here the earlier confinement of airplane altimetry to the air-pressure cue, and the resultant crashes of planes in mountainsides whenever the cue was misleading." (1965, p. 490.) Still further, we cannot say that explicit logical thought of a single-track sort would be geared at least to propositions which the individual would regard as certainties, even when these are not actually such. In many cases, an individual knows that some course of action has merely a faint hope of success, and yet he uses it because it seems less uncertain than other possible courses of action.

(5) *The Question of the Proper Type of Laws for Psychologists to Strive for.*   The preceding discussion leads us to another methodological point stressed by Brunswik, but which seems in need of

revision. Brunswik frequently drew a contrast between the physical sciences, which he saw as seeking for strict laws, and psychology, which he said must search merely for probabilistic laws.

Rather than portraying this question as an all-or-none matter, it seems to me that Brunswik would have done better to speak of this question as a question of a continuum. What we want in psychology would be categories and principles which, although cast in highly abstract form, would enable us to make as nearly precise predictions as possible. So, in our consideration of instances of perception and thinking, if we find that there are merely general tendencies for thinking and perception to yield the sorts of pattern of errors that were found in Brunswik's experiments, this knowledge is more uncertain than we wish, even though it has some value. What we naturally try to do is to reclassify the various instances of cognitive processes and see whether we can find some different classes where we can anticipate, with higher likelihood, the two sorts of patterns of performance which Brunswik described. When there are so many uncontrollable factors both within the organism and within the environment, we cannot hope to reach the point where our predictions can be precise in individual cases; but we at least are seeking for laws that will be as precise as possible.

As long as some large assortment of unidentified conditions remains constant, we can predict quite definitely, of course, what a single individual will do—we can predict what he will eat for breakfast, what route he will follow in going to work, and what words he will mispronounce. But such predictions are of little use for psychology. Precision of that sort is unimportant in a science, because sciences are basically efforts to develop highly abstract knowledge, which will facilitate dealing with new instances. When the world and the organisms in it are so complex, and when there is so much loose play in the separate parts of each, it seems inevitable, all right, that psychological laws must be probabilistic. But, as Brunswik emphasized at one point, at least, so are many of the laws of physics. The gas law of physics, for instance, is merely a statement of a statistical likelihood. The important point is not simply that we must deal in probabilistic laws; the point is also that we want to make these laws as nearly exact or strict as we can.

(6) *The Need for a More Functional Concept of Ecologies.* I have mentioned, above, the lack of any sufficient indication of how Brunswik meant the term "ecology" to be applied. It is, nevertheless, a key term. If we are to hold, as Brunswik did, that behavior is a function of complex situations and that we ought to emphasize representative research design—that is, the study of a representative sampling of real-life

situations from an ecology or natural-cultural habitat in each case—we have got to have some better meaning for this term. There can be no proceeding with representative research design if we cannot say what the ecologies are that such research should sample.

On this problem I think that we need to work backwards from a consideration of the point discussed in the previous section—namely, that we want the means to make predictions that will be as nearly exact as possible. If this point be granted, then it would follow from this that, whenever we get some additional knowledge which enables us to specify a highly important parameter, this gives us the means of defining an ecology about which it will be worth our while to study and generalize.

Take the example of size-constancy which Brunswik mentioned so frequently. In the experiment which he performed, no object that was viewed was more than about 2 miles away. Within that range, the product-moment correlation between the log of measured bodily size and the log of estimated bodily size was .987 for one individual, .993 for another. But these data were gathered during the daytime, and there was no opportunity for estimates of the size of stars. Suppose the individual studied had been an old-time shepherd or an ancient Polynesian mariner steering his course by the stars. In such a case, lacking our modern knowledge of the distance and size of stars, such persons would have made extreme errors, and the product-moment correlation that included such instances would have tended even to be negative. But, what interest would there be in such a correlation? The main fact would still be, somewhat as Brunswik said, that those old-time individuals still would have made highly accurate size-judgments regarding near-by objects, just as modern men do, and that the estimates regarding the size of stars belong in a special class, which we need to discuss separately. Hence, there is some point for the expression that Brunswik used in his Montreal paper when he spoke of "the ecology of manipulable things."

But, if we proceed in this fashion, as I believe it would be quite necessary for us to do, it seems that it leads to quite a different basic mode of thought from that which Brunswik usually implied. It means that the definition or identification of any ecology is not prior to knowledge of cause-and-effect relationships, but would be affected by whatever knowledge we had which would warrant separating off some category of cases as ones significantly different, on the average, from other cases. Within the ecology thus separated off, we still would have the question, "What are the relative weights of the various uncontrolled factors in determining the effects seen?" or the question, "How accurate, for example, are judgments of intelligence (or size or monetary value and so forth) within the limits of the situations thus separated off?" But we would be depending on our earlier partial knowledge of such cases to help us separate off those cases that are functionally similar to one another in some important ways. Otherwise we cannot get abstract principles well adapted to our objective of providing the means for relatively precise predictions.

The situation faced by psychology is basically the same as the situation faced by an individual with reference to the life situations to which he must learn how to respond as well as possible. He has to learn that the behavior that is effective in one type of situation is not effective in another, and that the factors that are very highly correlated with success in one type situation have only a much lower correlation with success in a different type of situation. In each type of situation, there will be variations that will go beyond what he can anticipate; but the individual nevertheless could well express the lessons from his learning by saying, "I have learned that, at different points, I am in such and such different ecologies, and I've had to learn different laws about how to proceed and what to expect in those different ecologies. My knowledge still is probabilistic, but it is a darn sight better when I recognize these different settings in which I'm operating than when I disregard them or do not know about them." In the same way, although it is true that psychology wants to describe ecologies in more abstract terms than the individual person would be likely to do, the attainment of good explanations by psychology depends on the recognition of a great host of ecologies, separated out by some understanding of the key factors operating in various life situations, even for a given individual.

(7) *The Limitations of Partial Correlation as a Means of Developing and Testing Hypotheses about Functional Relationships.* As said previously, Brunswik decried the general stress on experimental or systematic research because he believed that it accomplishes only what can be done, and in a safer fashion, by mathematical analysis "after the fact," using partial-correlation techniques to keep other factors constant and to determine whether a particular factor is one from which some predictions can be made. Thus, replying to some criticisms from Postman in the 1953 symposium, he said:

"Since, in principle, under representative design all variables are allowed to vary and none are held constant artificially, their role can be ascertained after the fact. For the same reason, there is a gain rather than a loss of information, contrary to what Postman seems to fear." (1955b, p. 239). In his main paper in the same symposium, Brunswik compared systematic research to soap operas and popular novels and movies. All of these deal in clichés, in cases ". . . by no means impossible or nonexistent, but made prominent out of all proportion to its frequency, and to the detriment of all other types of incident." (1955b, p. 215.) Because of this, Brunswik said,

. . . the suspicion arises that the didactic role which systematic experimentation obviously plays in the mental economy of the scientist, by virtue of the simplicity and order it both requires in the design and furnishes in the result, may outweigh the fact-finding competence of systematically designed experiments. . . .

The main function both of art and of systematic experimentation, then, is to shake and mold us by exaggeration and extreme correlation or absence of correlation. But exaggeration is distortion, and this distortion must, in science, eventually be resolved by allowing the more palatable systematic design (of research) to mature into, and to be superseded by, the more truthful representative design (1955b, p. 215.)

Part of this interpretation we may agree with. As has already been said, it seems quite appropriate to say that good quantitative principles can be based only on representative sampling of the ecologies to which they are supposed to apply. But, the other implications of this interpretation are ones we must reject. What can the statement mean that "Since, in principle, under representative design all variables are allowed to vary and none are held constant artificially, their role can be ascertained after the fact"? After what "fact"? Put in plainer words, the question is, "After we have conducted a series of observations and measurements, and have recorded our data, can we then go back and tease out some relationships which we had not even suspected might exist?"

It seems to me that the answer to this question is quite different from what Brunswik implied. *Sometimes* the data will have included material from which additional relationships can be discovered. But the fact that a huge number of variables had been present in different quantities and in different timing does not mean at all that a research worker will have noted those variables or that he will have record that such and such values for them were associated with such and such values on other variables.

When we go back over the history of scientific work, whether in psychology or medicine or physiology or whatever other field, it seems that almost no principles have been discovered, or hypotheses developed, by mathematical analysis after the fact—that is, after the data have been gathered. The work of scientific discovery depends mainly on one or the other of two special origins of hypotheses. One origin is chance observations in which certain factors have been related to each other in some exaggerated or unusual and hence striking way, as when Semmelweiss in the 1840's got his clue to the cause of child-bed fever when one of the other physicians died, with the typical symptoms of this disease, within four days after having cut his hand with a scalpel during the course of an autopsy on the body of a woman who had died from this disease. The other main origin is deductive reasoning, arguing more by analogy, as it were, from general premises that reach out into a wider territory than actually had been established up to that point.

With either of such origins for his hypothesis, the scientific worker then admittedly arranges conditions in a fashion intended to exaggerate the hypothesized relationship. He wants the situation to be didactic— that is, he wants it to teach him something, wants it to establish or give fairly clear disproof of a *qualitative* finding. The early workers on beriberi, for example, expected that the disease probably was communicated from one person to another, but when they arranged conditions so as to accentuate the likelihood of such transmission, it did not occur. Hence they had to turn from this hypothesis, whereas a representative research design might have given rather ambiguous testimony on this score. They had to have some other chance conditions which gave them the altogether unexpected idea that the disease came from diets heavy in the use of polished rice. The same point could be illustrated through reference to Harlow's work on the effects of certain factors in the experience of infant monkeys, or in any number of other psychological studies.

Admittedly, as said before, the determination of quantitative relationships calls for the representative sampling which Brunswik has emphasized. But Brunswik has misjudged, it seems to me, in saying that the original development of hypotheses can come by partial-correlation techniques, and in speaking disparagingly about other methods as didactic, exaggerating, artificial, and so on. I believe that the consideration of a wide sampling of scientific work suggests that the original development of hypotheses and original demonstration that "there really is something there" have to come by these means in most instances.

(8) *The Limitations of Distal-Distal Studies as Compared with Mediational Studies.*   As has been said, Brunswik seemed generally (except when he was pressed with criticisms of this proposal) to prefer to picture the main work of psychology as the development of concepts about distal-distal relationships.

There certainly are many problems that can be cast in such terms. Many practical questions can be well phrased in this way. For example, the question whether a reduction in the maximum speed on highways would reduce accidents can be answered by studying the accident rates under two different laws. Valuable facts can be learned without having to get any light on why the rate is different under one law than under another. Similarly, changes of industrial productivity can be demonstrated under different conditions of temperature, humidity, and lighting without bothering to ask why the productivity changes with changes in these environmental conditions.

Not only practical questions, but many straight research questions can be phrased in this fashion. Skinner, for instance, has demonstrated important differences of performance under different schedules of reinforcement in lever-moving experiments with rats and pigeons.

In fact, the possible case for distal-distal formulations may be made to sound fairly impressive by pointing out that, in almost all of psychological research, the observational data are concerned solely with distal stimulus situations and distal achievements. From this, the argument can be raised, "Since almost all of the data in psychological research are data on distal factors, nothing can be added by trying to develop constructs about the processes which intervene between the distal stimulus situation and the distal achievement."

However, here again, before we draw such sweeping conclusions, we need to see what sort of sampling we have for our generalization. To begin with, we can note that observation of proximal responses often is important. The skillful athletic coach does not observe merely whether the athlete clears the bar in a pole-vault, but *how* he does it. The same for the violin teacher, the teacher of typing, or the foreman training men in laying bricks. In social psychology, it has been found important to study the different observable techniques that different leaders use in trying to get things done by a group, rather than study just the assignment of task and the final group accomplishment.

In the field of cognitive processes, there is increasing evidence that there are important effects that come from the type of cognitive activity in which the individual engages in trying to cope with a complex problem. Brunswik's own experiment on perception versus thinking was a demonstration that those two different cognitive activities in that situation yielded different sorts of judgments. The work of Bruner, Goodnow, and Austin on different strategies in concept formation revealed the same point in their situation (1956). Many other studies of thinking, such as those by Katona (1940), Hanfmann (1941), and Bouthilet (see Leeper, 1951, p. 745), have established the same point.

Consequently, it seems clear that psychology would deprive itself of valuable information if it confined itself solely to distal-distal formulations. Distal-distal studies are valuable means of *initial* exploration of complex phenomena. But, except as they lead on into more differentiating mediational concepts, they leave us with rougher functional correlations than, at least for many purposes, we need to develop.

(9) *The Need to Elaborate the Lens Model.*   In many contexts, when Brunswik spoke about the lens model he was speaking about the capacity of the organism to combine evidence from several cues to reach some better representation of some feature of the environment. At other points, instead of speaking about such multiple use, he was speaking about the organism's capacity to choose between one means and another and yet work toward the attainment of some common end in all of the different cases. Brunswik seemed to move back and forth between the two concepts as though he saw them as indistinguishable. Thus, in his final monograph, he said:

> The limitations in the dependability of single-cue variables force an uncertainty-geared probabilistic strategy upon perception. In order to improve the cognitive "wager" . . . the perceptual system must accumulate and combine cues. Thus we arrive at a more complete understanding of the principle of mutual substitutability or "vicarious functioning" of means (or cues) which Hunter, Tolman . . . and most other behaviorists looking for a structural criterion have incorporated into their basic definitions of behavior or purpose. . . . (1956b, pp. 140–141.)

Now, it may be that the combining of different cues (or means) is like the phenomenon of choosing between alternative possible means. But the "choosing between" in the case of means would seem a closer parallel to those cases in which the organism shifts from one single cue (or group of cues) to another and yet continues to make much the same "cognitive wager." And, on the side of the use of cues would seem to be the fact that the organism often acts redundantly to make more certain that the intended effect will be realized. The small child, for example, not merely tells its mother by words that he wants to go home, he also tugs at her hand.

It would seem as though Brunswik is quite right in saying that these two things have some abstract quality in common, and may both deserve to be designated by some common term such as "lens functions." But, there may be some important differences between them, too. The shift from one means to another without sacrifice of the end to be attained is something which calls for a consideration of cybernetic mechanisms (goal expectations, motives, purposes, or whatever we choose to call them). This may be the same phenomenon, entirely, that is involved in the multiple use of cues. I want merely to suggest, however, that the appreciation of some important similarities should not divert us from trying to find out whether, in some other respects, we have two significantly different operations here.

(10) *The Need for a More Adequate Exploration of the Implications of the Ratiomorphic Model and of Alternatives to It.* Brunswik emphasized the ratiomorphic model as one of his main proposals. But, he did not go very far in spelling out what he meant by it. He indicated that it definitely was not a rationalistic or intellectualistic construct, and that it did not imply that cognitive processes necessarily were completely accurate. He also suggested that behavior, and more particularly cognitive activity, including both perception and thinking, ". . . involves the particular type of orderly interaction we find best exemplified in syllogistic reasoning or in mathematical calculation." (1965, p. 487.) That is, I suppose we might say, cognitive processes are ones that utilize not only the particular conditions observed at the moment, but also more general premises or beliefs derived from earlier experiences. The individual notes not merely the apparent blueness of the tree-covered hill that he sees, but also takes advantage of some generalization that he has developed that tree-covered hills look blue only under such and such conditions of distance and/or illumination. The use of such considerations may be an extremely swift process, as in spatial perceptions, or a more slow-moving process, as in much of explicit logical thought. But, in either case, a conclusion is drawn whose validity can be checked, or, in principle, might be checked, against the independent reality that is portrayed.

This is a proposal of considerable interest, but it leaves us with hardly more than the beginning of work on the question of how all this is accomplished. Brunswik might have replied to such a criticism by saying that, in a distal-arc functionalism, there is no need to ask about the "how" of things. But, as we have seen, Brunswik was not content to leave any question in this way. His more fundamental proposal has been that distal-distal studies would identify various phenomena in need of more careful study and that a more adequate understanding might then be secured by mediational studies planned "from above."

Let us illustrate the problem, taking a couple of instances that illustrate some rather common phenomena. Suppose we have people look steadily at such a drawing as that shown in Figure 3. At least after staring at this for a short time, people find it impossible to continue seeing it as a merely two-dimensional drawing. They find it impossible to stare at it for longer periods of time without having it reverse in perspective. Furthermore, the rectangular pieces are not seen as lying in the same plane—

instead, it is as though the person were seeing a rectangular strip of paper that had been folded, with somewhat different angles at different points, along lines at right angles to the long edges of the rectangular strip.

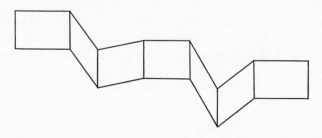

Fig. 3. A simple visual figure that illustrates the ambiguities in the proposition that perceptions are "ratiomorphic."

Now, it might be said, "This perception is ratiomorphic, because people, at least in a civilized environment, have more dealings with objects which have 90-degree corners than with objects with any other sort of corner. What the person is doing is seeing the drawing in such a way that it could be a strip of paper creased in such a right-angle way."

But, this doesn't get us very far. The individual also has had a lot of experience that acquaints him with the fact that the surface of a sheet of paper is merely two-dimensional and with the fact that a drawing on such a sheet of paper does not shift from one moment to another. Why would it be, then, that the individual perceives or "draws his reasoning-like conclusion" from one sort of background-knowledge or training rather than from another? Merely to say that such perceptions are ratiomorphic or reasoning-like does not carry us very far, but presumably some other principles can be found that will enable us to say that one sort of effect rather than another will occur.

Take another instance: any worker in the field of personality is well acquainted with the fact that an emotionally maladjusted person often responds as though he were reasoning from premises that he knows are false and that he rejects under other circumstances. For example, a person may commonly feel and say, "I'm worthless; I do more harm than good; it would be better if I did not try to accomplish things because I create more difficulties than I make contributions to counterbalance them."

In such a case, the person may have quite sufficient ability to recognize that all persons have real limitations, and he may be very discriminating in his judgment of the balance of good and bad in other persons and even in himself when he is considering his life in a reflective mood. He has other premises from which he might reason, therefore. But, if his common emotional responses are reasoning-like, they must be derived from premises other than he respects intellectually. Or, he may accept some social or religious philosophy which actually cannot be the set of premises from which his actual interpersonal relationships must be derived.

There are instances such as an experienced touch-typist can testify to. If such a typist has covers over his various keys, he will not be able to look at the keyboard and say what keys can be used for different purposes—which is the back-spacer rather than the margin-release, which is the key for the hyphen, which for the asterisk, and so on. But he can put his hands on the keyboard and demonstrate by his finger movements that, in some sense, his psychological processes are such as though he were saying, "Such and such a key has the asterisk mark on it which can be used after depressing the shift key; I want to type the asterisk; therefore that key is the one to hit." He does not go through such a process now. So, what point would there be to saying that his behavior is syllogistic-like?

What I am saying, to put it more briefly, is that our psychological concepts need to be, in great part, something much more specific than a ratiomorphic model, as developed only by a few brief comments, provides us with. We need a whole series of more differentiated concepts about perceptual processes, learning, the use of habits, motivation, selective forgetting, and other matters. In such a more developed theory, what would tend to be found, I suspect, is that reasoning and reasoning-like processes are merely special cases of some more general phenomenon or principle. But, to make some good judgment about this, we cannot leave either the ratiomorphic model or such a possible alternative model in such a very indefinite form as Brunswik left his concept. The implications of theoretical concepts must be spelled out in much greater detail.

(11) *The Need for Considering the Possibility of Highly Selective Organizing Characteristics of Cognitive Processes.* As we said at the start of the summary of Brunswik's main concepts, one main principle that he espoused was that our methodological and broad conceptual principles ought to be decided in the light of the nature of psychological phenomena, rather than as *a priori* philosophical principles. In keeping with this spirit, there is a problem to which Brunswik ought to have given major attention, but on which his views are indicated only in rather un-

certain indirect ways. In part, this is the problem of whether inner psychological processes can be predicted at all precisely from outer environmental influences, or at least from exact information about receptor stimulations. In part, it is the further question whether, if cognitive processes cannot be very definitely predicted from such means, whether there are other means of learning what cognitive organizations have been produced and whether such knowledge can be important in predicting what will occur in different stimulus situations.

It may be that cognitive processes are highly correlated with, or highly predictable from, the distal conditions that have affected the individual, at least provided we take into account not merely the current distal conditions but also the earlier distal conditions from which various habits might have been formed. On the other hand, it may be that cognitive processes depend on selective organizing activity to such an extent, and these in turn depend on essentially chance factors to such an extent, that we cannot achieve a satisfactory means of predicting behavior just by studying distal-distal relationships, but must center much of our research and theory on problems of how to judge what mediating processes occur within different individuals, as Lewin emphasized (1943).

Clearly, with any species that has great learning ability, there can be no sufficient predictability of behavior merely from the immediate stimulus situation affecting the organism. The whole significance of learning is that it makes the organism able to respond to a situation in a manner different from that which would be manifested if earlier learning situations had been different. We could find endless examples of the fact that people from different cultures respond to the same objective situations in different ways and even that different individuals in the same culture, or from the same family, for that matter, make different responses to the same kind of situation.

However, the possibility still remains that, provided earlier stimulus situations also are taken into account, the behavior of the organism may be highly predictable from the whole sequence of stimulus situations that the organism has met. Such was the view in Clark Hull's theory, for instance. Hull believed in stating his principles in terms of inferences about habit-strength, reaction-potential, reactive inhibition, and so on, rather than merely in terms of distal-distal relationships. But, the use of such mediational concepts in Hull's approach was not terribly essential, because Hull believed that these inferred factors or intervening variables could be estimated fairly closely by taking into account the relative numbers of reinforcements and non-reinforcements, the timing and intensity of various stimulations, the quantity and biological appropriateness of reinforcements for the species in question, and a few other such factors. What is inner, Hull essentially was saying, may be fairly well predicted from these refined measures of what has been outer.

In general, Brunswik's discussions of perception and judgment were a good deal in this same vein. *When Brunswik spoke about the multiple cues available to the organism in any situation, he did not generally put emphasis on the idea that the organism might select certain cues rather than others, or that different individuals might use quite different cues and make quite different cognitive responses in the same objective situation.* Instead, with his lens model, he put emphasis on the tendency of the organism to *combine* various cues in order to reach some better over-all judgment. In his discussions of size constancy, for instance, he placed considerable emphasis on the very high correspondence between the individual's perceptual judgments and the properties of external realities.

When he discussed judgments of intelligence and personality, Brunswik stressed evidence that different judges tend to use somewhat different bases of judgment, tend to differ in the weights they assign different cues, and even sometimes treat some cues as though they were positively correlated with the trait to be judged when, in actuality, the correlation is negative. Still, the general impression that Brunswik tended to convey was that such differences were somewhat minor matters—that, even though different judges might differ in the accuracy of their judgments, there would tend to be a good deal of agreement. Brunswik generally was speaking as though the organism tends to perceive things in about the terms that the ecological validities of those things would warrant.

Let me make two quotations from Brunswik to illustrate what I mean. These quotations, from his two last publications, both have reference to the same experiment of 1953.

This writer and Kamiya . . . have demonstrated (with the use of $N = 892$ separations between adjacent parallel lines in a roughly "proportionate" sample of shots from a current motion picture) that the long-recognized gestalt factor of "proximity" posesses a certain modest ($r = .12$) but statistically significant ecological validity as an indicator of mechanical object unity. Its utilization as an organizing principle for perceptual "figures" is thus a probabilistically adjustive mechanism. The realization of this fact may help to open the door for a possible "reduction" of the hitherto unabsorbed gestalt dynamics into learning theory. (1955b, p. 241.)

Later, speaking of the same study, he remarked:

Since . . . all ecological validities represent a challenge to the organism for utilization, and since it appears that certain cues are on the average being utilized roughly in proportion to the degree of their validity . . . our findings lend plausibility-support to a viewing of the Gestalt factors as cases of successful cue-utilization subsumable under the principles of learning theory. (1956b, pp. 122-123.)

The physiological hypothesis that would be consistent with such views by Hull and by Brunswik is the idea that the nerve impulses that arrive in the brain from any peripheral stimulation arrive in the brain as basically independent travellers and continue to exert influences in the brain in the same way. As Hull phrased the matter,

"According to the 'law of reinforcement' . . . every one of the receptor discharges and receptor-discharge perseverations active at the time that the to-be-conditioned reaction occurs must acquire an increment of habit strength. . . ." (1943, p. 206.)

The alternative to this sort of proposal is that which has been urged, even if in somewhat different terms in the different cases, by Lashley (1938, 1942, 1960), Tolman (1948), Köhler (1929), Köhler and Adams (1958), Bruner (1957), and Leeper (1963). The fundamental proposal of this alternative view is, in the first place, that the functional units of brain activity are not the individual nerve impulses, but complex dynamically organized processes. According to this view, the outstanding fact about the brain is that it takes the incoming nerve impulses and makes new functional units of a much larger scope out of them—functional units that stress certain properties of peripheral stimulation and leave other properties unrepresented, just as a radio amplifies some wave-lengths of what comes in from the antenna and leaves other wave-lengths weak and ineffective. In the second place, the essence of this alternative view is that there are many factors that, practically speaking, are chance factors, but which are powerful determinants of what perceptual organization occurs. In the third place, this alternative interpretation suggests that it is possible, frequently, to find what perceptual or cognitive organization has in fact occurred and that this knowledge can be extremely important in predicting what particular effects will be seen in the life of the particular individual in different objective situations.

In other words, according to this view the processes involved in the formation of cognitive processes are somewhat analogous to those that determine the shapes of snowflakes. All snowflakes are made up of about the same materials and get formed under very nearly similar circumstances, and yet they are of most diverse types. They do have some internal dynamic organization so that each snowflake builds itself symmetrically, yet different snowflakes become more or less different from one another under "almost identical" conditions.

Let me illustrate concretely what I mean, using Boring's "wife-and-mother-in-law" figure which I employed in an experiment reported in 1935. We can dictate pretty heavily what the individual will see in such a *vieldeutig* stimulus-figure, either by drawing the figure so that it favors one possible organization rather than another or by giving some prior training with such loaded examples. Or, as Botwinick, Robbin, and Brinley (1959) have demonstrated, there are some personal characteristics that may exert some degree of influence on what will be seen, as through the fact that the age of the perceiver tends to be related to the age of the person perceived from such drawings. But, aside from such loading of the dice, it seems that it is almost a chance affair as to which organization a given individual will get with the Boring figure. Yet, in any case, the individual does get one clearcut organization or another, and, if we wish to make predictions about details of his behavior with reference to the figure, it is worthwhile to learn what perceptual organization he achieved. We can ask him, for instance, to point to the tip of the nose of the person he sees. Depending on what he does, we can then predict whether he will report that the mouth is visible or hidden, we can predict roughly what age he will judge the woman to be, we can judge what details he might gloss over if he were copying the drawing, and so on. The perceptual organization is decisive for all of these further aspects of his overt behavior. On the other hand, if one knew merely that the person had been presented with the Boring figure as distal material, even on some series of trials, the only prediction that could well be made is that the person might show one pattern of responses *or* the other.

Now, is such an ambiguous figure a good paradigm of the environmental situations which the individual meets? Are most environmental situations thus ambiguous, *vieldeutig,* ambivalent, or are most situations *eindeutig* except for minor shadings of the perceptual or cognitive responses they evoke?

I think Brunswik's discussions tend to suggest that such a stimulus-material is an oddity. Most of the stimulus-materials which we perceive, I think he would have said, we perceive in a veridical fashion. We perceive trees as trees, rain as rain, books as books, and so on through the great host of everyday environmental realities.

For many common stimulus-materials, one might agree. However, if we want to base our portrayal, not on some limited sampling of situations, but on some broader sampling, I believe we need also to take account of those more complex and subtle situations that are important for personality functioning and for our more complex social processes. Particularly in them, as Peter Madison and I have urged in our discussion of personality (1959, Ch. 6), it seems extremely important that such situations typically are, in high degree, *vieldeutig* situations. The situation that brings a sense of panic to one person brings a sense of security to another; the behavior or personality characteristic that one person views with shame is viewed with pride by another person, and so on down the line. The tactics that one nation sees as buttressing its national honor and international standing are seen by another nation as the poorest possible course of action.

I do not mean to imply, of course, that it is impossible for us to make considerable progress—or even great progress—toward learning what objective training conditions or learning situations tend to produce one such personality effect rather than another. We have made some progress on this task already, and it is important to push our research as vigorously as possible. But, what I do mean to imply is that:

1. complex life situations, such as are involved in the learning of personality habits, are extremely complex situations, with very inconsistent and conflicting relationships in them (as Brunswik expressed it, with very low ecological validities for most factors); and
2. in such situations, the individual tends to crystallize certain perceptions and concepts rather than others, selectively stressing certain things and neglecting other things, constructing certain patterns rather than others, and then subsequently tending to perceive what confirms what he already has learned to perceive.

In such situations, and with such processes operating, it seems that distal-distal studies, even when they take into account earlier learning situations as well as the current stimulus situation, can yield no more than very rough predictive principles. It seems to me, therefore, that our concepts in psychology generally need to be mediational principles, rather than distal-arc principles. The latter may have value as a prelude to other work, as Brunswik said, but I think that his tendency to stress distal-arc studies as strongly as he did came in part because of implicit acceptance of an interpretation of cognitive activity that had undue faith in the degree to which cognitions correspond with ecological validities.

How are we to decide between different alternative possibilities like these? How are we to determine the areas in which such examples as the Boring figure would be a valuable paradigm and those other areas in which its implication would be misleading?

On this basic conceptual problem, I think we are driven back to a basic principle of Brunswik. We cannot decide such questions merely by examples or by experimental evidence which indicates that such and such effects can occur as possibilities. We are concerned with a quantitative question, with a problem of the degree to which some example is representative. And, when we are faced with questions like this, a really satisfactory answer cannot be secured except by a type of research method that we tend not to use because it presents us with such a high task—namely, the method of representative research design.

There are some very important values, therefore, in a number of important concepts which Brunswik hammered out. I believe that the major concepts, however, can be adapted into a primarily mediational type of approach to psychology. Indeed, beyond that, I believe that they can be adapted, and need to be adapted, into a primarily perceptual or cognitive type of approach to psychology, and I believe that much of Brunswik's own research actually was in this direction. There are some important modifications at some points, however, to permit this graft to "take" and grow rather than to be rejected or neglected.

SUMMARY

The present paper is a development from one which I presented in a symposium shared with Egon Brunswik and Gardner Murphy at the International Congress of Psychology at Montreal in 1954. My paper in that symposium was primarily a commentary on Brunswik's paper, now printed for the first time in the present volume, and on his ideas more generally. In the study and discussions preceding that symposium, I became convinced that Brunswik typically had not been expressing the underlying trend of his thinking and that, for an adequate utilization of his contributions by psychology, he should be presenting a somewhat different formulation than he usually urged. In rewriting my paper for this eventual publication, I have become more convinced than ever that some considerable reformulations are necessary to permit optimal use of Brunswik's contributions. This paper has attempted to sketch some of these main points.

Brunswik's work has been less discussed and less used by psychologists than should have been the case. Most psychologists have had only a vague idea of what he stood for. They have not had the means of assimilating the major contributions from it. In turn, the limited attention to Brunswik's ideas during his lifetime prevented him from receiving the healthy criticism and from making some of the revisions and restatements that he might have made otherwise. It is important now to try to make up for what might better have occurred earlier.

Several factors helped to account for this relative neglect. Brunswik's emphasis on perceptual phenomena and on probabilistic considerations was not much in keeping with the *Zeitgeist* of American psychology during most of his life, even though there has been more congruence in the last ten years or so. His ideas and terms were new enough that, combined with his terse and difficult style, they made his writings and papers difficult to understand and criticize. The amount of influence of Brunswik's writings has probably been limited as well by another factor—to wit, that other psychologists have felt that various of Brunswik's descriptions of their concepts did not correspond with the real intent of those concepts. Further difficulties have existed because Brunswik did not spell out adequately the meaning of some of the crucial terms that he used. There were various factors, therefore, which perhaps make it understandable that there has been merely a limited discussion of his concepts. They have considerable significance for psychology, however, and this earlier paucity of discussion should be remedied.

In summarizing Brunswik's main ideas, it is worthwhile to group them under two headings. In many ways, Brunswik seemed more interested in broad methodological questions, or the problems of theory-construction, than in more particular empirical questions. However, his view was that certain methodological principles were important, not because of any *a priori* philosophical analysis of science in general, but because of certain empirically demonstrable points about the nature of psychological processes and about the nature of environmental factors related to those processes. Any discussion of his system, therefore, needs to rest on a discussion of his psychological assumptions.

Some main points that Brunswik emphasized regarding psychological phenomena were these: Psychological processes are adaptive biological processes. Very commonly, they are means of dealing with things distant in time and/or space. The cues on which the organism has to depend in such dealings are always of limited ecological validity, and the means which the organism must use to try to produce the environmental effects are of limited validity, too. In this situation, the higher organisms, especially, have achieved increased effectiveness through a means of functioning best described by a "lens model." Organisms have the means for multiple use of cues and means, and they have the capacity for choosing between alternative possible means for attaining any particular objective. In all of such responding, because of the limited ecological validities of cues and means, the organism is dealing with probabilistic situations rather than with the highly invariant situations that we tend to set up in experimental research because of considerations of expediency and because of our desire to establish strict laws of behavior. In their cognitive activity, organisms are engaged in processes that are basically reasoning-like or ratiomorphic. Despite the fact that this is true both of perception and of thinking, there probably are important functional differences between these two sub-types of cognitive activity, and we should explore these differences. The lens functions are not completely equivalent to one another.

On the side of methodological principles, Brunswik urged that such empirically demonstrable points regarding psychological phenomena create a need for certain related ideas about the proper procedures for psychological research and theorizing. More particularly, some of the main points he advocated were as follows: Any abstract statement must rest on some adequate sampling of the domain that it purports to cover. Since most psychological propositions speak about types or classes of situations, we must have adequate samples of such classes or domains of situations. Particularly for any adequate quantitative principles in psychology, we need to have a representative sampling of natural-cultural habitats or ecologies of the organisms considered. In the representative research design which we ought to use for such purposes, we ought to deal with real-life situations; these involve the probabilistic features which psychological processes actually have to be concerned with; they also give wide opportunity for significant lens functioning; and they permit a study of interactional effects generally eliminated in experimental situations. From psychological research, it would be a mistake to expect that we can achieve strict laws—the probabilistic nature of what the organism must deal with signifies, in turn, that our laws can only be probabilistic laws. Because of the capacity of organisms for vicarious or lens functioning, psychological research should not generally be concerned with process details or intervening processes, but should generally be concerned with relationships between distal stimulus situations and distal achievements. However, after distal-distal studies have defined problems that might be given more intensive study, there is a need for systematic or analytical research guided by such prior exploration "from above." Even so, the main means of analysis of more particular factors should be partial-correlation studies of distal-distal data.

These major concepts from Brunswik are a stimulating and significant set of proposals. Some of Brunswik's concepts and some of his terminology ought to become part of our common psychological heritage. However, any adequate use of Brunswik's contributions is not apt to be made until we re-examine his notions and remove from them the over-generalizations that he sometimes made and spell out more clearly the implications of some of his principles.

The point from Brunswik on which there should be least argument, though it is a principle widely neglected in the theorizing of psychologists, is that abstract generalizations should be restricted to what the sampling of situations actually gives a research worker some good warrant for saying. A point of almost equally obvious character is that, for significant quantitative principles of any abstract sort, as contrasted with quantitative principles related merely to particular experimental situations, we will have to make the very ambitious studies suggested by Brunswik's concept of representative research design.

In Brunswik's discussions, however, there is not sufficient indication of the value of *qualitative* principles in psychology—principles identifying certain variables as having certain relationships to other variables, but not attempting to estimate the quantitative aspects of these relationships. Brunswik ought also to have indicated that, as a means of testing many abstract statements, it is possible to use a much more economical means of sampling than representative sampling. A considerable degree of testing can be done by a technical examining of extreme or possible limiting cases.

There can be no doubt but that, as Brunswik said, the predictions from psychological principles cannot be better than probabilistic statements. There are so many uncontrollable factors both within the organism and within the environment that predictions cannot be exact. However, the contrast that Brunswik drew between probabilistic laws and strict laws was overstated. Even though the predictions in psychology must be probabilistic, our aim remains that of learning to understand as many variables and relationships as possible, and in as definite terms as possible, so that our predictions can become as nearly precise as we can make them. In our search for such relatively more precise means of prediction, we need to investigate a great diversity of different ecologies for different purposes. Different ecologies cannot be identified satisfactorily in any *a priori* manner; the reason we group some set of situations together as falling within some type of natural-cultural habitat is that we know, from our understanding of significant causal factors, that this is a set of situations worth studying separately from other sets of situations. Therefore, systematic research often needs to be the prelude to definition of ecologies and to the planning of representative research, rather than always the reverse of this.

When Brunswik proposed that partial-correlational analysis would be the chief means of teasing out special factors, he was proposing an idea that might seem feasible on first consideration; however, even though a wealth of factors may have been present in the situations studied by representative research, the investigator typically would not have noted the presence of most of such factors, and his records would typically not contain the data from which such heuristically noteworthy analyses could be made "after the fact," as Brunswik expressed it. Instead of speaking so disparagingly of case-material and of experimental methods as exaggerating, distorting, didactic, Brunswik might well have said that the original identification of significant variables and relationships commonly has to come through contact with unusual situations that involve some relationship in some unusually clear or exaggerated fashion.

Studies of distal-distal relationships can have many values, especially for exploratory investigation and for rough practical purposes. However, the lens-functions of the organism fall so short of complete equivalence that it is very important for psychologists to explore mediating or intervening processes as well as the more broad-arching distal relationships. Actually, a great portion of Brunswik's own research was concerned with mediating processes.

An example of the more detailed analysis that is needed is the point that Brunswik's discussions of the lens model covered two partly different phenomena: on the one hand, the *combining* of different cues or means to gain more assurance than could come through any *either-or* selections; on the other hand, the selecting or *choosing between* one cue or means and another.

There is need of much analytical work in psychology. It does not take us very far, for example, to say that cognitive processes are ratiomorphic or reasoning-like; we need to understand how to predict whether the organism, as one might say, will reason from one set of premises rather than from another, or will engage in a reasoning-like process that stresses certain factors rather than others.

Brunswik did not give much attention to the question of whether many stimulus situations have the potentiality of supporting, in different individuals, or in the same individual at different times, drastically different cognitive processes analogous to the widely different perceptions that can occur with reversible illusions and other ambiguous figures. It may be that such examples are oddities. On the other hand, it may be that, especially in such fields as those of personality and social psychology, almost all situations are highly *vieldeutig* or ambiguous. In such fields it may be of major importance to realize that cognitive processes tend to select only a portion of the cues that might be used and tend to construct dynamically organized processes that differ enormously from person to person and from culture to culture. If this is in truth a widespread phenomenon, it would mean that Brunswik ought not to have placed so much stress on studies of distal-distal relationships, but ought to have placed much more emphasis on the idea that he expressed at some points that cognitive processes are a means of producing, within the organism, a representation of the objective environment, and that many of our formulations need to be distal-central-distal formulations, rather than distal-distal formulations. The extent to which there is some occurrence of markedly different representations of the environment within different individuals, even under what seem like very similar training situations, is something that we can determine only by extensive empirical study. Only by some more adequate representative sampling of life situations can we determine the degree to which the character of cognitive processes justifies a distal-distal type of approach or the degree to which, on the contrary, we will need to make mediational studies and use mediational concepts such as are suggested by cognitive studies with ambiguous stimulus materials.

There may be a number of changes and refinements, therefore, that ought to be made in Brunswik's principles. However, it is well worth the labor to make any such changes, because Brunswik has given us a considerable number of concepts that are indispensable to help psychology become a more mature and careful field of scientific work.

REFERENCES

Bergman, G. Review of Brunswik's The conceptual framework of psychology. *Psychol. Bull.*, 1952, *49*, 654–656.

Boring, E. G. Psychological factors in the scientific process. *Amer. Scientist*, 1954, *42*, 639–645.

Boring, E. G. Dual role of the Zeitgeist in scientific creativity. *Scient. Monthly*, 1955, *80*, 101–106.

Botwinick, J., J. S. Robbin, and F. J. Brinley. Reorganization of perceptions with age. *J. Geront.*, 1959, *14*, 85–88.

Bruner, J. S. On perceptual readiness. *Psychol. Rev.*, 1957, *64*, 123–152.

Bruner, J. S., J. J. Goodnow, and G. A. Austin. *A study of thinking.* New York: Wiley, 1956.

Brunswik, E. Psychology in terms of objects. In H. W. Hill (Ed.), *Proc. 25th Anniv. Celebr. Inaug. Grad. Stud.* Los Angeles: University of

Southern California Press, 1936. Pp. 122–126. Reprinted in M. Marx (Ed.) *Psychological Theory.* New York: Macmillan, 1951. Pp. 386–391.

Brunswik, E. Probability as a determiner of rat behavior. *J. exper. Psychol.*, 1939, *25*, 175–197.

Brunswik, E. Note on Hammond's analogy between "relativity and representativeness." *Phil. Sci.*, 1951, *18*, 212–217.

Brunswik, E. *The conceptual framework of psychology.* Chicago: University of Chicago Press, 1952.

Brunswik, E. Representative design and probabilistic theory in a functional psychology. *Psychol. Rev.*, 1955, *62*, 193–217.   (a)

Brunswik, E. In defense of probabilistic functionalism: a reply. *Psychol. Rev.*, 1955, *62*, 236–242.   (b)

Brunswik, E. Historical and thematic relations of psychology to other sciences. *Sci. Monthly*, 1956, *83*, 151–161. (a)

Brunswik, E. *Perception and the representative design of psychological experiments*. Berkeley, Calif.: University of California Press, 1956. (b)

Brunswik, E. Reasoning as a universal behavior model and a functional differentiation between "perception" and "thinking." This volume.

Brunswik, E. and J. Kamiya. Ecological cue-validity of "proximity" and of other gestalt factors. *Amer. J. Psychol.*, 1953, *66*, 20–32.

Feigl, H. Functionalism, psychological theory, and the uniting sciences: some discussion remarks. *Psychol. Rev.*, 1955, *62*, 232–235.

Hammond, K. R. Probabilistic functioning and the clinical method. *Psychol. Rev.*, 1955, *62*, 255–262.

Hanfmann, E. A study of personal patterns in an intellectual performance. *Character & Pers.*, 1941, *9*, 315–325.

Hilgard, E. R. Discussion of probabilistic functionalism. *Psychol. Rev.*, 1955, *62*, 226–228.

Hull, C. L. *Principles of behavior*. New York: Appleton-Century-Crofts, Inc., 1943.

Katona, G. *Organizing and memorizing*. New York: Columbia Univer. Press, 1940.

Köhler, W. *Gestalt psychology*. New York: Liveright, 1929.

Köhler, W. and P. A. Adams. Perception and attention. *Amer. J. Psychol.*, 1958, *71*, 489–503.

Krech, D. Discussion: theory and reductionism. *Psychol. Rev.*, 1955, *62*, 229–231.

Lashley, K. S. The mechanism of vision: XV. Preliminary studies of the rat's capacity for detail vision.

J. gen. Psychol., 1938, *18*, 123–193.

Lashley, K. S. An examination of the "continuity theory" as applied to discrimination learning. *J. gen. Psychol.*, 1942, *26*, 241–265.

Lashley, K. S. Cerebral organization and behavior. In F. Beach *et al.* (Eds.), *The neuropsychology of Lashley*. New York: McGraw-Hill, 1960.

Leeper, R. W. A study of a neglected portion of the field of learning—the development of sensory organization. *J. genet. Psychol.*, 1935, *46*, 41–75.

Leeper, R. W. Cognitive processes, in S. S. Stevens (Ed.), *Handbook of experimental psychology*. New York: Wiley, 1951. Pp. 730–757.

Leeper, R. W. Complex intermediate processes between situation and response: their methodological implications. *Acta Psychol.*, 1955, *11*, 110–111.

Leeper, R. W. Learning and the fields of perception, motivation, and personality. In S. Koch (Ed.), *Psychology: a study of a science*. Vol. 5. New York: McGraw-Hill, 1963. Pp. 365–487.

Leeper, R. and P. Madison. *Toward understanding human personalities*. New York: Appleton, 1959.

Lewin, K. Defining the "field at a given time." *Psychol. Rev.*, 1943, *50*, 292–310.

Murphy, G. The boundaries between the person and the world. *Brit. J. Psychol.*, 1956, *47*, 88–94.

Postman, L. The probability approach and nomothetic theory. *Psychol. Rev.*, 1955, *62*, 218–225.

Postman, L. and E. Tolman. Brunswik's probabilistic functionalism. In S. Koch (Ed.), *Psychology: a study of a science*, Vol. 1. New York: McGraw-Hill, 1959. Pp. 502–564.

Skinner, B. F. Are theories of learning necessary? *Psychol. Rev.*, 1950,
57, 193–216.

Skinner, B. F. The experimental analysis of behavior. *Amer. Scientist*,
1957, *45*, 343–371.

Tolman, E. C. Cognitive maps in
rats and men. *Psychol. Rev.*, 1948,
55, 189–208.

Tolman, E. C. and E. Brunswik. The
organism and the causal texture of
the environment. *Psychol. Rev.*,
1935, *42*, 43–77.

III
SELECTED PAPERS
BY BRUNSWIK

15

The Organism and the Causal
Texture of the Environment [1]

EDWARD C. TOLMAN
EGON BRUNSWIK

*Having found that our previous separate investigations had led us quite in-
dependently of one another to a common point of view as to the general
nature of psychology, we decided upon this joint article.*

I

Each of us has come to envisage psychology as primarily concerned
with the methods of response of the organism to two characteristic
features of the environment. The first of these features lies in the fact that
the environment is a *causal texture* (*Kausalgefüge*) [2] in which different
events are regularly dependent upon each other. And because of the
presence of such *causal couplings* (*Kausalkoppelungen*), actually existing
in their environments, organisms come to accept one event as a *local
representative* (*Stellvertreter*) for another event. It is by the use of such
acceptances or assertions of local representatives that organisms come to
steer their ways through that complex network of events, stimuli and
happenings, which surrounds them. By means of such *local representation* (*Stellvertretung*) the organism comes to operate in the presence of
the local representative in a manner more or less appropriate to the fact

1. This article was written during a relatively long stay of the one author,
Tolman, in Vienna in 1933–1935 (and was originally printed in the *Psychological
Review* in 1935, *42,* 43–77. A somewhat different version under the title *"Das
Lebewesen im Kausalgefüge seiner Umgebung"* will, it is hoped, appear later in
German. The authors have sought throughout to bring their two sets of terminol-
ogies into correspondence. The parallel German terms are presented here in
parentheses.
2. For the term "texture" as well as for advice on various other English terms
we wish to express special indebtedness to Professor S. C. Pepper. (See also Pepper,
1934.)

of a more distant object or situation, that is, the *entity represented* (*das Vertretene*).[3]

The second feature of the environment to which the organism also adjusts is the fact that such causal connections are probably always to some degree *equivocal* (*mehrdeutig*). Types of local representatives are, that is, not connected in simple one-one, *univocal* (*eindeutig*) fashion, with the types of entities represented. Any one type of local representative is found to be causally connected with differing frequencies with more than one kind of entity represented and vice versa. And it is indeed, we would assert, this very *equivocality* (*Mehrdeutigkeit*) in the causal "representation"—strands in the environment that lend to the psychological activities of organisms many of their most outstanding characteristics.

It appears also that, whereas the one of us, Tolman (1932), was led to emphasize these two facts of *local representation* and of *equivocality* (*Mehrdeutigkeit*) by a study of the relations of *means-objects* (*Mittelgegenstände*) to *ends* (*Zielgegenstände*) in the learning activities of rats, the other, Brunswik (1934a), was led to emphasize these same concepts as a result of an examination of the relations of *stimulus cues or signs* (*Reize als Anzeichen*) to *Gegenstände*[4] as a result of a study of the

---

3. The first modern psychologist to suggest the universal importance of this principle of "representation"—the scholastic *"aliquid stat pro aliquo"*—for *all* psychological phenomena was Karl Bühler (1929). He has emphasized, in particular, the "sign" function of local representatives in their different forms, that is, as *"signals"* for action and as *"Anzeichen"* in reception. He has made an especially important analysis of the sign function of *"symbols"* in his psychology of speech (1934).

For another modern emphasis on the sign-function in perception and thought see Ogden and Richards (1925).

4. The word *"Gegenstand"* has been employed by Brunswik (1934a) and will herein be further employed to designate, not complete environmental objects or bodies in their concrete totalities, but single object-characters abstracted from such total bodies. Such abstracted characters are conceived and defined in completely objective fashion. They are discovered and identified by processes of measurement and computation as these latter are carried out either by physics or by the more ordinary procedures of practical life. And it appears thus that in any single total *behavior-object* (*Körper, "Ding"*) there intersect numerous simple *Gegenstände*, such, for example, as: size, form, reflection-coefficient for light waves (that is, physical "color"), hardness, weight, density, volume, chemical characteristics, and so forth. All these properties might at different occasions (in different life-contexts) become in different manner biologically important, or, to use the concept of Karl Buhler, become in different manner *"abstractively relevant."* From this standpoint the properties of a means-object, characterized previously by Tolman as *discriminanda, manipulanda, utilitanda,* are to be conceived as groups of *Gegenstände*, which are different with respect to their abstract relevancy for the organism. (Compare Ogden and Richards, 1925, Chapter 3.)

Further, because of its generality and abstractness this word *Gegenstand* can be

relations involved in the "Konstanz"—phenomenon in human perception.[5]

We observe animals making and using tools, entering paths, ingesting food, avoiding dangerous objects, and the like. But in each such case the tools, the paths, the foods, the dangerous objects are behaved to only because of their role as means-objects. They are behaved to, that is, in their roles as the most probable "local representatives" whereby to reach or avoid such and such more ultimate, "represented" positive or negative, goals. For it is the reaching or avoiding of these more distant represented goals that are of final importance to the organism. And further, we also observe these same animals, responding selectively, (and perhaps in the ordinary case relatively correctly), to immediate entities (for example, the detailed structure of light-wave bundles, and the like) in their turn, as the most probable local representatives, that is, cues, for such tools, paths, foods, dangerous objects, and so forth. And here also, it is the character of these more distant "represented" objects that have the greater determining significance for the organism. Light-wave bundles, and the like, are to be correctly selected as the most probable local representatives, that is, as cues, for such and such object-characters, just as the latter must themselves be correctly selected as the best local representatives (that is, as means-objects) for the finally to-be-reached or to-be-avoided goals. Without the ability to rely on these two successive types of local representation no higher forms of organism could have developed and successfully survived.

Finally, it is to be pointed out that because of the equivocality (*Mehrdeutigkeit*) that always to some degree obtains in both such steps, that is, in the relations between cues and means-Gegenstande and in those between the latter and goals, the organism is led in both instances to the assertion of "hypotheses." That is, whether in the process of selecting the correct means-object (Gegenstand-complex) to reach a

---

used not only for the properties of *means*-objects but also for the *cue*-properties of peripheral stimulation processes (for example, intensity, form, or size of the projection of an object at the retina, the visual angle, and so forth) as well as for such internal events or states as goal-satiation, and the life,—in short, for everything, which can be defined in terms of physics (or geometry, and so forth) and which is, therefore, capable of objective measurement.

5. It should also be noted that of the two of us it was primarily Brunswik (1934a, pp. 29ff.) who previously emphasized the importance of the feature of equivocality (*Mehrdeutigkeit*) in the environmental causal couplings. This sort of *Mehrdeutigkeit* is, of course, not to be confused with the possibility of a subjective "*Gestalt-mehrdeutigkeit*," that is, with the fact—first emphasized by Benussi—that one and the same stimulus-configuration may on different occasions be responded to by quite different perceptual impressions.

given goal or in that of selecting the correct cue-Gegenstände for perceptually identifying a means-Gegenstand, the organism is forced to venture an hypothesis.[6] We would here introduce, that is, the term hypothesis as not only appropriate and inevitable for the case of discursive thought, for which it was originally coined, but also for such simpler lower-order situations as are here involved in immediate perception and in the simpler sorts of means-end activities. Thus, whether the case be that of a father, who, as a result of his reading and previous experimentation, ventures a discursive verbalized hypothesis to the effect that the conditioned reflex is the fundamental principle of all learning and proceeds thereupon to try to make his children love Latin as a substitute-stimulus for chocolates; or whether it be that of a rat, who, from having been run through a discrimination-box and having found the lighted alley always open, tends "hypothetically" to choose this alley continuously for some time afterwards (whether or not the latter then still leads to food); or whether, finally, it be that of a monkey or a human being who, upon having projected upon his retina the characteristically fuzzy grading-off edge of a dark area, sees this dark area as a shadow and not as a separate spot with a blacker surface quality; the essentials are the same. In each such case the organism behaves "as though." That is, he ventures an hypothesis. He may be right; but he may also be wrong. A fuzzy edge in the given case may surround not a shadow, but a spot with separate surface-color.[7] The lighted door, in the given instance, may lead, not to food, but to electric shock. The giving of Latin before chocolate may result not in the child's coming to love Latin, but merely in an unpleasant propensity to secrete saliva while studying Latin.

An hypothesis "asserts" that a given "a" is the local representative of a given "b." But the connections between types of local representative and types of entities represented are, as we have said, practically never "one-one." Any given type of "a" is probably always capable of being in varying degrees the representative of a number of different types of "b." Any given type of "b" is probably always capable of being represented with different degrees of frequency by each of a number of different types of "a." Any particular hypothesis, therefore, that a given "a" on a given occasion means a given type of "b" will have only a certain probability of being valid. The degree to which such an hypothesis will

6. This use of the term "hypothesis" in a purely *objective* sense was first made by Krechevsky (1932) and has since also received the approval of Claparède (1934). The objective earmark for such hypotheses lies in the appearance of systematic rather than chance distributions of behavior.

7. For all the various possibilities in this sort of situation see Kardos (1934).

tend to be valid or merely superficial and hasty will vary with the degree to which, "normally," the given type of cue-Gegenstand does tend to be coupled in "relatively one-one" that is, *univocal, (eindeutig)* fashion with the given type of to-be-perceived (*intendiert*) means-Gegenstand or upon the degree to which the latter does tend to be normally coupled in "relatively" one-one fashion with the given type of goal-Gegenstand.

As we have indicated, it is to be one of the main tasks of this essay to indicate the further significance for the psychologies of perception and of means-end action of just such lacks of complete *univocality*.

But first we wish to present a single simplified scheme for combining perception and means-end action into one picture (on the oversimple assumption of univocality).

II

Figure 1 is a diagram to represent the combined perceptual and means-end activities of an organism. This diagram involves the simple but incorrect assumption (to be corrected by later diagrams) of solely univocal, one-one (*eindeutig*) correspondences between goals and

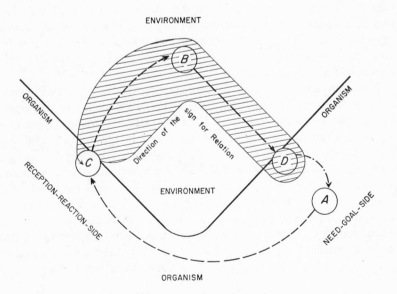

Fig. 1. Organism and behavior object—with assumption of univ-ocal, one-one, couplings between cues, means-objects and goals. The cognitive lasso principle.

means-objects and between the latter and cues. In this figure the area above the v-shaped continuous line (that is, a "v" with a curved bottom) represents the environment, whereas the area below this line represents the organism. Let us suppose that *b* indicates a *behavior-object* (*Hantier-barerkirper*) that is, a possible means-object in the visual field, for example, food, which, as such, as the characteristic that it is an appropriate possible cause (with the cooperation of the organism) for resultant satiation, *d*. Independently of the organism this object *b* radiates causal trains, for example, light-waves, in many directions. And part of these lead (continuous arrow *bc*) to the sensory surface of the organism. Let us assume, further, that other objects of the same variety as *b* have previously sent visual influences of this same sort to the organism. And let us also suppose that previous trial and error activities on the part of the organism have demonstrated the *behavior-manipulability* (*Hantierungstauglichkeit*) of these *b* sorts of object. And, finally, let us suppose that the outcome of such behavior-manipulations led in each past case to satiation *d,* that is, let us suppose previous experience by the organism of the *utilitability* (*Erfolgstauglichkeit*) of things like *b*. The total organized experience resulting from all these previous causal currents means the present readiness of a system of "hypotheses" concerning the various different actual or possible causal chains connected with *b*— that is, as to the probable suitability of any new *b* as a means for reaching, that is, as a cause for resulting *d* and also as to the fact that the given peripheral stimulus at *c* probably results from (has probably been caused by) a *b* sort of object.

If, now, as a result of some internal activity, say hunger *a,* there comes an influence from the *need-goal-side* (*Bedarf-Erfolgseite*) of the organism to the *reception-reaction-side* of the latter (broken arrow *ac*), resulting in an opening of sense-organs and in the activation of this hypothesis-system, this latter together with the peripheral stimulus-configuration coming from *b* will lead to a reactional event, *c*. In this reactional event, *c,* the peripheral stimulus has assumed the function of a *sign, cue,* (*Anzeichen*) indicating an actual *b* and "transitively" through *b,* a possible final *d*. In this event, *c* the total past and present causal complex—indicated in the diagram as surrounded by the dotted loop—is anticipatively *lassoed* (*Lassoprinzip*). *C* thus has the character of a *sign-gestalt* (*Zeichengestalt*).[8] It appears, therefore, further, that if

8. Previously Tolman used (1932; 1933) the term "sign-gestalt-expectation" for the organic event and the term sign-gestalt for the objective environmental complex corresponding (in the case of correct behavior) to this organic event. Here, however, it seems simpler for the term sign-gestalt-expectation to be omitted and

the situation be one of univocal relations or, that is, if it be a situation in which the anticipatory achievement of the lasso will be in all cases of this type correct, then it can be said that the means-object and also the goal have been by means of this lasso or sign-gestalt, *intentionally attained* (*intentional erreicht*) (Brunswik, 1934a).[9]

We note next that broken arrows indicate those causal chains in which the activity of the organism itself is necessary. Thus the broken arrow *cb* (issuing from the sign-gestalt *c*) is intended to depict the actual manipulation of *b,* grasping, eating, and so forth. And the outcome of this manipulation of *b* is indicated by the broken arrow *bd*. This latter action is to be conceived as resulting out of such manipulation, that is, as occurring without further independent activity on the part of the organism and it brings about the final goal situation *d*. Finally, after the attainment of *d,* there will occur, after some interval of time, a new appearance in the organism of the need *a* (broken line *da*). And thereupon the whole circular process will once again be set into action.

III

Figure 1 presented the scheme of an organism in its environment for a very simple case—namely, that in which one step only is involved both on the left-hand and on the right-hand sides of the diagram. But organisms often meet situations involving a succession of cues or a succession of means-objects or both. Figure 2 is, therefore, now presented to show types of further extension of the diagram that are necessary for cases involving more than one step between cue and behavior-object or between the latter and the final goal.

---

to use the term sign-gestalt for the organic event alone. The environmental entity or entities (with reference to which the organic event—the sign-gestalt—occurs) are, as we are emphasizing throughout this article, to be conceived and described as simply some area within a total environmental causal texture. Such an area will contain as its most essential feature strands of "local representation."

9. It should be pointed out that one of the important features of the type of psychology here being argued for is that it demands and makes possible a characterization of the fundamental capacities of the organism in terms of the types of object and goal which the given organism is capable of thus "intentionally attaining." It is this feature which Brunswik had in mind when he called his a *"Gegenstand-psychology"* (*Psychologie vom Gegenstand her*), that is, a psychology from the standpoint of the organism's ability intentionally to attain Gegenstände. This type of an objective psychology is outlined theoretically in (Brunswik, 1934a; 1934b). An article in English concerning the main experimental results and the fundamental concepts is also in preparation.

For another somewhat related treatment of the interconnection of the organism with its environment see the "Umweltlehre" of Uexkull (1909).

The nature and meaning of Figure 2 will be understood most easily
if you apply it to a concrete example. Let us suppose that the organism
in question is a child in his crib and that the object b is a piece of chocolate. We shall suppose further, however, that the latter is beyond the
child's own reach.[10] He requires, therefore, some second object as a

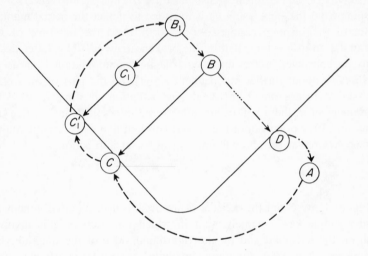

Fig. 2. Example of lengthened means-goal and cue-means
chains.

secondary means to the chocolate. And let us suppose further that there
are in the room both good-willed and less favorably willed individuals.
The child can use the assistance to be provided by the good will of one
of these good-willed individuals. This good will will serve, in short, as
the second means-object b_1, suitable for achieving the first means-object
(the chocolate, b). But this good will b_1, this secondary means-object,
lies shut-up within the psycho-neural make-up of the other individual. It
can send no direct cues to the sense organs of the child. The perception
of it has to be mediated causally through some external characteristics
in the other person's face. The facial expression of the other individual
must, in short, serve as an intermediate cue c_1 between the final cues c'_1
on the child's retina and the ultimately to-be-perceived means-object b_1

10. If the child were able to reach the chocolate himself, the *adbc* part of Figure
2 would suffice. The whole situation would in fact reduce again to that represented
in Figure 1.

—the good will (or the bad will) of the other individual. Such an example, thus, presents a double step on both the reception-side and the means-side of the activity. The retinal effects on the child's eyes serve as local representatives, signs, for the facial expression of the individual. And this facial expression as a local representative serves in its turn as a sign, (or sign-system) for the will (good or bad) of the other individual. Again, on the right-hand side of the diagram, the will of the other individual is a local representative of, and the means to, the presence of the chocolate, and then this chocolate is, in its turn, the local representative of and the means to final satiation.

It is evident that the general scheme of Figure 2 could be extended indefinitely to allow for long trains of intervening means-objects or long trains of intervening cues, or both. Or again, it could easily be modified to allow for various special types of case such, for example, as that in which two means-objects have to be behaved to simultaneously—or in which one and the same object will serve both as secondary cue and as secondary means.[11]

Consider now still another type of possible extension of the original diagram that may also sometimes be needed. It must be noted, namely, that any single behavior-object such as *b* must in reality be conceived as subdivisible into three distinguishable aspects. The first of these parts or aspects (groups of Gengenstände) (see Figure 3), we shall designate as the *discriminanda*-properties of such an object. These discriminanda would be such properties (Gegenstände) as the object's color, shape, size, and so forth, which are the relatively direct causes of the immediate sensory cues. They are the properties whereby the object is differentiated, discriminated from other objects. As the second part or aspect of a single behavior object, we would designate its *manipulanda*-properties. The manipulanda of an object are, so-to-speak, its essential, behavioral core. They are the properties that make possible and support actual behavioral manipulations. They are the object's grasp-ableness, pick-up-ableness, chew-ableness, sit-on-ableness, run-through-ableness, and the like. Finally, as the third aspect or part of a behavior-object, we have what we shall designate as its *utilitanda*-properties. The utilitanda of a behavior-object lie, so-to-speak, on that side of it, which points towards further means-objects or towards an ultimate goal. They are the ways in which the object, given the manipulanda, or its manipulanda and discriminanda combined, can be useful as a means for getting to further objects and

11. An example for this latter would be paper currency, which, at least in former times, served both as a cue for and a means to gold.

goals. Thus, for example, a behavior-object such as a maze alley that has the manipulanda of run-through-ableness will, as such, also have the utilitanda of leading to objects that are distant in space. Or a behavior-object such as a piece of chocolate will have, by virtue of its manipulanda

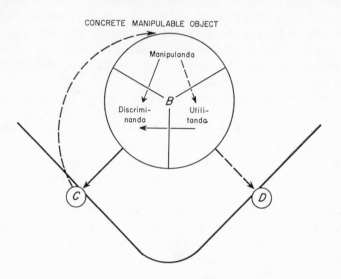

Fig. 3. Aspects within the single behavior-object.

character as something chewable, the utilitanda character of something that will lead towards a full stomach. Or, still again, the behavior-object, the good will of another individual, will have, by virtue of its manipulanda character of possessing a substitute pair of hands and feet, the utilitanda character of bringing about the reaching of objects which from the position of the original organism are, as such, unattainable. Or, again, a picture that has both the discriminanda properties of a certain pattern of color and the manipulanda properties of thinness and hang-up-ableness will have the utilitanda-properties of aiding in the establishment of a particular setup for a certain type of aesthetic satiation.[12]

It is to be noted, however, that in this discussion and in Figure 3 we have again been assuming for simplicity's sake only univocal relations. But such univocal relations do not really obtain. Quite different discriminanda may be coupled on different occasions with one and the same

12. The terms "discriminanda" and "manipulanda" have already previously been used by Tolman (1932; 1933). The term "utilitanda" is here, however, now suggested to designate what previously (see especially Tolman, 1933) were called "means-relations."

manipulanda. Apples are sometimes red but they are also sometimes yellow. And one and the same discriminanda will on different occasions be used as signs of different manipulanda. Brown is sometimes coupled with and used as a sign of chocolate, but at other times it is coupled with and used as a sign of, say, a negro skin. Similarly, the relations between manipulanda and utilitanda may be equally *equivocal* (*mehrdeutig*). Thus, for example, the run-through-ableness of a maze-alley does probably in somewhat more than 50 percent of the time have the utilitanda character of getting the organism on towards some further place. But it by no means always has that character, as witness the case of blinds, whose very definition is that they do not thus get an organism on.

A completely adequate diagram of the individual behavior-object, and of these its three aspects would have to allow for such internal equivocalities. It would have to be built up, that is, on somewhat the same plan as Figure 4, which we shall come to in the next section.[13]

Finally, before passing on to the next section, we would like here also to point out that just the reverse of the general types of situation allowed for by Figures 2 and 3 also occur. That is, not only are there cases in which the chain between c and d must be depicted as lengthened, but there are also cases in which this chain is to be conceived as shortened —with fewer, or no, intermediate steps. Thus, in sufficiently primitive, or young, organisms the appropriate diagram would seem to be one in which the arrows in Figure 1 are contracted into a single one running directly from d to c. That is, in such cases response to cue, manipulation of means and achievement of the goal telescope into but one single process.

For example, Charlotte Bühler and her co-workers Ripin and Hetzer (1930) and Rubinow and Frankl (1934) have followed the development of the feeding responses in infants. The very youngest infants responded to the actual touch of the nipple only. But gradually with increasing age the babies began to respond with sucking movements to the laying on of the bib, then later to the approach of any sort of a pointed object. Until finally at about eight months they responded to the presence of a nipple plus a white fluid and to that only. Only at this last stage would the introduction into our diagram of the independent inter-

13. This is perhaps also the place to point out that within the organism there will also be equivocalities as to goals. Professor Charlotte Bühler has pointed this out to us. It leads to such questions as the operation of such fictive goals positive or negative as general "expansion" or general "restriction" of life. (Compare Charlotte Bühler (1931) which with varying degrees of equivocality may perhaps control the more immediate direct goals. See in this connection also the distinction between superordinate and subordinate goals in Tolman, (1932) pp. 28ff.)

mediate *hantierbarer Körper b* as in Figure 1 seem to be needed or appropriate.

We will turn now in the next section to an expansion of Figure 1 to allow for the sorts of complication that arise upon the introduction of nonunivocalities between means-objects and goals and between cues and means-objects.

IV

Figure 1 presented the situation for the organism upon an assumption of univocal couplings of means-Gegenstand to cue-Gegenstand and of means-Gegenstand to goal-Gegenstand. But such an assumption is in reality never realized. The whole uncertainty of knowledge and behavior arises just out of such *equivocality* (*Mehrdeutigkeit*) in the causal surroundings.

Consider for a moment the nature of the causal connections in the physical world independent of organisms. We observe that, whenever any individual event occurs, a more or less extended complex of many independent part causes must have been existentially operative. Further, any specific type of an event will on different occasions and in different places have different causes, or more exactly speaking, different total complexes of part causes. And also, vice versa, any given type of an event will itself operate as a part cause on different occasions and in different places for the production of different final total events. The causal interweavings of unit events among one another are thus, in both directions, equivocal. But some of these connections will be more probable than others.[14]

Exactly this same sort of causal equivocality must be applied, now, to the sets of causal chains—those between goals and means and between cues and Gegenstände—in which we are specifically interested. In order, however, not to overcomplicate the discussion, we shall consider only a limited number of the actual possibilities.

Let us examine, first, the right-hand side of Figure 4. It will be observed that we have depicted one positive goal and several negative goals.[15]

14. Concerning the nature of the causal structure of the world in general, see H. Reichenbach (1925) and H. Bergmann (1929).

15. The concept of negative goals is to be conceived here as including not only actually injurious consequences such as real physical injury but also cases which involve, merely undue expenditures of time or energy in the reaching of positive goals.

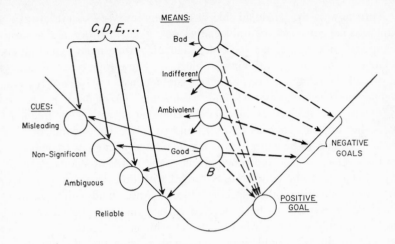

Fig. 4. Paradigm: Four types of goal-means relation; four types of means-cue relation.

Further, we have shown only four main types of means-object relative to such goals. These four are to be designated as: *good, ambivalent, indifferent, and bad* (*gutes, ambivalentes, indifferentes, schlechtes Mittel*). The "good" means-object may be conceived as one which, if manipulated, will tend to lead in a relatively high percentage of instances (say up to 95 percent; [16] heavy arrow) to the positive goal and in only a relatively small number of instances (say 15 percent; thin arrow) to a negative goal. An "ambivalent" means-object is to be conceived as a type that will lead with a relatively high probability (that is, with high frequency) to the positive goal but one which may also lead with a relatively high probability to one or more negative goals. An "indifferent" means-object is to be defined as one that will lead with but very little probability, that is, frequency, either to the positive goal or to a negative goal. And, finally, a "bad" means-object is one which will lead with high probability to the positive goal. Finally, we would throw out the suggestion that the "ambivalent" types of means and the "bad" types of means are in some situations (especially, if the negative goals are very intense) to be grouped together under one head and labeled "dangers." For both types will trend to lead with high frequency (heavy arrows) to negative goals.

16. The fact that we have chosen examples of percentages that total more than 100 is to allow for the fact that often one and the same types of means-object is capable of leading simultaneously both to the positive and to the negative goals.

Turn now to the left-hand side of the diagram. We observe at once a similar analogous lack of univocality. But again in order not to over-complicate the figure, we have depicted only four main types of cue relative to the one "good" means-object, *B*. These four types of cue we have called "reliable" (*verlässlich*), "ambiguous" (*zweideutig*), "non-significant" (*bedeutungsarm*), and "misleading" (*irreführend*). The first type is to be conceived as capable of being caused with great frequency by "other objects" such as *C, D, E,* and so forth. The second, or "ambiguous" cue is to be conceived as a type caused with great frequency by both the given object and other objects. The third, or "nonsignificant" type of cue, is to be conceived as caused with little frequency by either the given object or other specific objects. And, finally, the fourth or "misleading" type is to be conceived as one that may be caused with little frequency by the given object and with great frequency by other objects. Again, we would throw out the suggestion that the ambiguous and the misleading cues may for some individuals and under some con-ditions constitute a rather special common group to be designated as "hazardous." For both types of cue present a high degree of probability of leading the individual astray, that is, of having been caused by other objects, *C, D, E,* and so forth, instead of the to-be-sought for good means-object *B*. (Hazardous cues would thus be analogous to "danger-ous" means-objects.)

Considering now both sides of the diagram it appears at once that the psychological success of an organism will depend (1) upon its ability to pick out "good" means-objects for reaching the positive goal and (2) upon its ability to select the reliable cues for this good means-object. An organism will be successful in so far as it can do both.

But let us indicate the real significance and experimental fruitfulness of these classifications of means and cues by turning to some concrete examples.

V

Let us illustrate, first, the right-hand side of the diagram. We may take a case of learning in rats.

Imagine a maze, and let us suppose it somewhat unusual in type in that it has choice-points of the two sorts shown in Figures 5A and 5B. Suppose, that is, that each choice-point has four alleys, instead of the usual two, issuing from it. Two of these always point south and two north. Further, one alley in each pair is always lighted and the other dark, and one has an electrified grill and the other, no such grill. Fur-

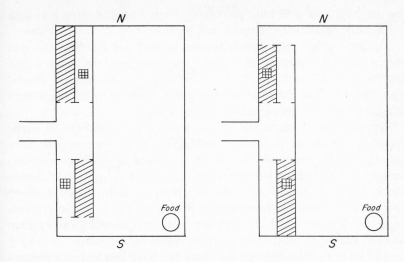

Fig. 5. Schematic maze for the purpose of illustrating the four basic types of means-object.

ther, in the cases of the 5A choice-points both the two south-pointing alleys will lead on, whereas both the two north-point alleys will be blinds. Also in the 5A type of choice-point both the lighted alleys will have electric shocks and the dark alleys will have no shocks. In the cases of the 5B choice-points, on the other hand, everything will be just reversed; the north-pointing alleys will lead on and the dark alleys will provide the shocks.

Consider, now, a particular maze in which most of the choice-points are of the 5A type and only a few are of the 5B type. We see at once that in such a maze, the south-pointing dark alleys are "good"; for they will lead with a high degree of frequency to the positive goal, food (that is, heavy broken arrow from good means to positive goal as shown on the right-hand side of Figure 4) and with practically no frequency to either of the negative goals (electric shock) or undue exertion (that is, blinds). (See thin broken arrow.) The south-pointing lighted alleys will be "ambivalent," for they will lead with a high degree of frequency both to the positive goal, food, heavy broken arrow, and to the negative goal, electric shock (also heavy broken arrow). The north-pointing dark alleys will be "indifferent" for they will lead with little frequency to the positive goal, food (thin broken arrow) and with practically no frequency to the worse of the two negative goals—electric shock, also thin broken arrow. And the north-pointing lighted alleys will be "bad" for they will lead with little probability (heavy broken arrow) to both the negative goals, electric shock and blind.

The interesting experimental question is: how will the rats behave in such a maze? Will they pick the "good" alleys and avoid the "ambivalent," the "indifferent" and the "bad"? Obviously the answer will depend upon the nature of their innate propensities, their previous experiences and their stage of learning in this particular maze.

Suppose that all the rats to be used in the experiment have an innate propensity to choose dark alleys rather than light. And suppose, also, that this innate propensity has been reinforced by specific preceding training in a discrimination box where light alleys always led to electric shock. Suppose, in short, that the rats bring to such a maze a strong "hypothesis," based partly on innate endowment and partly on previous experiences, to the effect that dark alleys, as such, have a greater probability to leading to good consequences than do lighted alleys.

And let us likewise suppose that these rats have also all had a preliminary feeding-period in the south-east corner of the room—that is, in the actual spot where the food box in the maze proper is placed. Also, let us suppose this corner of the room to be in some way distinctly characterized, by virtue, perhaps, of the visual features on the ceiling, or because of odors coming from it, or in some other way. Let us suppose, in short, that the rats also bring a second "hypothesis" to the effect that food lies southward and that south-pointing alleys should, as such, be better than north-pointing alleys.

Rats bringing the above hypotheses and presented to the above sort of a maze should, right from the beginning, and without the need of any new learning, behave relatively "correctly"—that is, they should at once choose the "good" dark south-pointing alleys most frequently and the "bad" lighted north-pointing alleys least frequently. And presumably they should choose the "ambivalent" lighted south-pointing alleys and the "indifferent" dark north-pointing alleys with some sort of in-between frequencies. It is to be noted, however, there are as yet in the literature no experiments that give exact information as to the two latter sorts of possibility. We do not know, for example, whether the rats will show a greater preference, or lack of preference, for the "indifferent" dark north-pointing alleys, which have only a small probability of being either very good or very bad, or the "ambivalent" lighted south-pointing alleys which have quite a high probability of being very good but also a high probability of being very bad. The possibility and desirability of further experimentation on such a point as this at once suggests itself. And such future experimentation might well prove extraordinarily suggestive. It might even prove a way of differentiating emotional dispositions. Thus, for example, the rat who tended to prefer "indifferent" means to "ambivalent" ones might perhaps be defined as "cautious," whereas the one who tended to prefer "ambivalent" means to "indifferent" ones could perhaps be designated as "courageous" or "dare-devilish." And, granting such definitions, then, such a set-up would also allow us to investigate the effects of such factors as degrees of hunger, or varying degrees of having been "blocked" (in Lewin's sense) and the like, upon such emotional states. Indeed, a whole array of possibilities of this general sort for future research suggest themselves.

Or, again, we may turn, now, to the consideration of other types of experiment. These would be experiments in which the total maze would not, as above, agree with the rats' initial hypotheses but in which the rats would have to acquire a new hypothesis (that is, to learn). Two subtypes of case present themselves. On the one hand, there would be the type of experiment in which the detailed hypotheses that the rats brought with them were definitely wrong. And, on the other hand, there would be the type of experiment in which the animals brought no detailed hypotheses but merely a very general hypothesis that expressed itself as an initial readiness to explore equally all alleys. (Note: This latter would be the perfect pure case of trial and error learning.)

To illustrate the former type, let us imagine a situation similar to that previously described save that the actual maze connections would be arranged just oppositely. That is, imagine a maze in which the great majority of choice-points will be like that in Figure 5B and only a few like that in Figure 5A. To such a maze the rats, with their innate propensities and previous experience just as before, will bring absolutely wrong hypotheses. What will they do? Obviously they will learn. That is, although they will begin by selecting the objectively "bad" alleys and avoiding the objectively "good" alleys, soon they will begin to correct these initial selections and to acquire the necessary new hypotheses.[17] But the specifically new and interesting question, which experimentation will have to answer, is in what order will the old hypotheses—that is, the old order of selection of blinds, drop out? What will be the intervening phases of relative preference for the different types of alley through which the animals will pass? Again a whole series of new experiments suggests itself.

Consider now the second subtype of experiment—that in which the

17. The definition of learning as essentially the correction of old hypotheses and the formation of new ones has already previously been suggested by Tolman and Krechevsky (1933).

rat brings no specific hypotheses as to the north-pointingness nor as to lightness or darkness, but exhibits merely an initial equal readiness for all four types of alleys, that is, what we may call the "pure" case of so-called trial and error. What will be the order of learning in such a case? Will the rats drop out the "bad" alleys first, and then the "ambivalent" and then the "indifferent"? Or will they follow some other order? Again important further experiments are needed.[18]

The above must suffice to illustrate the significance, experimentally, of a classification of means-objects based on the probability-relations between such means-objects and goals. We will turn, now, in the next section to illustrations of the experimental significance of the analagous classification of cues, that is, to illustrations of the left-hand side of Figure 4.

VI

We may imagine a case in which the "good" means-object in the particular instance must possess the property (Gegenstand) of lying at a certain specific spatial distance from the organism. That is, the organism, if it is to be successful, must be able to select correctly the "reliable" visual cues for *third-dimensional depths*. It must be able to distinguish between such "reliable" cues and those which instead are merely "ambiguous," "non-significant," or even "misleading."

As, perhaps, the best example of *reliable* cues for the visual perception of the third dimension, we might take (for organisms with binocular vision) *biretinal disparity*. Differences of third-dimensional depth in the environment are projected differently into the two eyes. And the extent and nature of these differences is utilized by the organism as a cue for the perception of distance. But, although such biretinal differences do usually stand in almost univocal correspondence with actual differences of distance (relative to the point of fixation), this is by no means always the case. For by means of a stereoscope one can also provoke, as a result of pictures that are really flat, just these same biretinal differences. In this latter case the flat pictures produce biretinal effects that "normally" are produced only by real differences of third-dimensional depth. But such instances are obviously artificial and exceptional and have but a low degree of "general" probability. They are none the less possible, and this possibility is cared for in Figure 4 by the faint causal

18. The experiments in the literature that seem already to have made a beginning attack upon such problems as those suggested in this section are those of Hamilton (1916), Kuo (1922), and Patrick (1934a; 1934b).

line debouching into reliable cues from "other possible objects" *C, D, E.*
. . .

Further, the fact that a stereoscope is able to arouse impressions of
the third dimension means that the perceptual system as such continues
to adhere quite blindly to the hypothesis that biretinal disparity is necessarily a cue for third-dimensional depth. And the perceptual system
does thus adhere to this hypothesis even when the presence of the stereoscope is an added item among the perceptual data. The perceptual apparatus is, in other words, by itself relatively shortsighted and superficial.
It is incapable, at least without specific training, of separating out the
case where biretinal disparity occurs by itself unaccompanied by a stereoscope from that in which there is the added perceptual data coming from
the stereoscope. The perceptual apparatus is incapable of reacting to the
former case as indicating with a high probability real third dimension
and to the latter as indicating with high probability mere flat pictures.
For such a prompt differentiation the superior and more fundamentally
accurate processes of discursive thought appear to be required.

Again, let us also note that just the reverse sort of situation can also
occur. Biretinal disparity cannot only be artificially produced, as by a
stereoscope, but it can also be artificially destroyed. Consider, for example, the case in which a scene is observed not directly but in the finder
of a camera. In this sort of a setup the effect upon the two retinas is
that coming from a flat plane. There is no biretinal disparity although
there are real differences of third-dimensional depth. In other words,
biretinal disparity can not only have other causes than real depth in the
environment, but real depth can under special, although "normally"
improbable, conditions fail to produce biretinal disparity. Thus, even
for this example of a very *reliable* type of cue, there still obtains some
degree of equivocality in both directions—in the directions both from
Gegenstand as cause to cue as effect and from cue as effect to Gegenstand
as cause.

Let us consider next an example of *ambiguous* cues for third-dimensional depth. Ambiguous cues we have defined as ones which, though also
frequently induced by the given type of Gegenstand, are of less certain
value in that they can likewise frequently result from other Gegenstände
than the one in question. An especially good example of such cues relative to third-dimensional distances is *perspective*. Let us explicate. Many
objects—especially those common in civilized environments—tend to be
right-angled, or to be bound by parallel lines, or to occur in rows made
up of individual items all of equal size. Consider, for example, such
objects as: streets, sidewalks, house facades, single windows and rows

of windows, corridors, rooms, pieces of furniture and the like. Such single objects or series of objects are, however, very often presented to the organism at an angle, that is, not as face on but as stretching off into a third dimension. Thus it happens that distorted angles and distorted size relations (converging lines and trapezoidal forms, and so forth) result with great frequency from differences of third-dimensional depth and the perceptual apparatus comes to use these distorted forms as distance criteria. More often, however, than was true for biretinal disparity, these distance criteria of "distorted forms" can also result from other causes than actual third-dimensional depth. Such forms can also be produced with great ease artificially—as for example, by a mere pair of carelessly drawn converging lines. And, likewise, there actually exist in the world many objects whose surfaces are really trapezoidal, diamond-shaped and the like. So that these latter objects even when face forward produce "distorted" images. Indeed many of the familiar optical illusions are cases in which just such "distortions" in actually flat surfaces are interpreted as stretching-off into the third dimension.

To return now to Figure 4 we find this equivocality whereby distorted images can be produced very frequently either by really right-angled objects, rows of equal objects, objects with parallel boundaries stretching off into the distance, on the one hand, or by really distorted objects and artificial objects, on the other, allowed for by the forking of the causal lines that debouch into "ambiguous" cues. And both of the two branches of this fork are drawn with heavy lines. That is, in terms of our example, the cue of distorted retinal images may result with about equal and relatively great probabilities either from true stretching-off into the third dimension, on the one hand, or from actually distorted objects or from mere drawings, on the other.

In other words, a pure reliance upon perspective as a depth criterion necessarily leads to many mistakes (illusions). All the cases where appearances of depth are produced solely by drawings fall into this group. Consider, for example, Figure 6. The row of three angles appears quite strikingly as a chain of three mountains really equal in size but extending back into the third dimension. But it is to be noted that when these curves do thus appear, it means that the perceptual apparatus has overgeneralized. For in nature there is no very great tendency for rows of mountains equal in size to stretch away from one as so often happens for windows, trees and the like. In fact, the most frequent tendency in nature would seem to be for the nearer mountains (seen as they usually are from the plain) to be actually the smaller. Or, again, consider the other part of Figure 6. If the two adjacent parallelograms are seen as an open book, the perceptual apparatus has again over-generalized. For it has assumed that these angles, and perhaps all angles of this kind, are in nature really right angles. In a word, too great a reliance upon the ambiguous cues of perspective always means laziness and overgeneralization on the part of the perceptual apparatus.

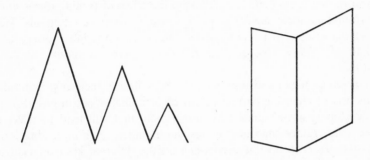

Fig. 6. Failures of perception due to the persistent functions of hypotheses appropriate only in cases of real perspective.

Let us consider, now, an example of *nonsignificant* cues for third-dimensional distances. A relatively good instance is that of *number of intermediate objects*. It appears that the more such intermediate objects there are between an observer and the main object, the further off the latter tends to appear. And in actual nature there is, of course, some probability that a longer distance will, in truth, be filled with more intermediate entities than a shorter distance. But there is also some probability that more intermediate objects may mean (result from) something other than greater distance. Intermediate objects will often lie so that the eye cannot detect them. And in any case, it is obvious that in nature there is no such constant relationship between number of intermediate objects and distance as there tends to be between biretinal disparity and distance. The cue of number of intermediate objects is then a good example of a relatively *nonsignificant* cue. (See again Fig. 4.)

Turn now to *misleading cues*. A relatively good example was found in the work of Holaday on the Konstanz-phenomenon in the perception of size (1934, p. 454). In this investigation it so happened that in the main experiment, while working with certain definite distances, of the two objects to be compared, the left-hand object was definitely nearer than the other. As a result, in a subsidiary experiment under conditions of poor visibility, the left-hand object was now really the farther away, the subject, because of his preceding training, with the same general range of distances, continued to see it, the left-hand object, appeared nearer. In other words, the effect of the preceding training in the main experiment made the left portion of the given object (under conditions of poor visibility) appear the nearer. Analogous results appeared also in the work of Eissler (1933, p. 259) on the effect of turning forms out of the frontal parallel plane. Such perseverations (with resulting misleading cues) likewise seem to be frequent and well-known in experiments on weight perception. (See also Izzet, 1934, p. 316; Brunswik, 1934a, p. 120.)

To sum up for this section, we would emphasize, then, that in addition to its task of choosing correct means-objects, the organism has also that of developing an adequate reception system that will tend to select reliable cues, rather than ambiguous, nonsignificant, or misleading ones. And its task is to do this even when all the different kinds of cues are present and competing with one another. The investigation of the degree and manner in which the perceptual system can or cannot do this as well as of its capacity for learning, sets the stage for many important further experimental investigations.[19]

VII

In the two preceding sections we have presented examples to illustrate experimentally the different classes of means-objects and cues. We have seen that these classes are defined by the respective strengths of the causal probability lines between such types of means-objects and the plus and minus goals, and between the former and types of cues. Any type of means-object has certain specific probabilities (given the causal structure of the particular environment) of serving as a frequent means for reaching the desired positive goal, and it also has certain specific probabilities of leading rather to one or more of the negative goals. Similarly, any given type of cue has (given the causal structure of the environment) specific, respective, probabilities of having been caused by one Gegenstand or other.

The organism's task is thus, as we have seen, always that of picking out the means-objects and the cues that have the high probability-lines (in the given case) of leading to the required goals and to the appro-

19. Some beginnings in this direction were, in fact, contained in the investigations of Holaday (1934), Eissler (1933), and Izzet (1934). For still more recent investigations in the same direction see likewise Brunswik (1934a).

priate means-Gegenstände. But the next point, and the one which we especially wish to bring to the fore in this section, lies in the further fact that the values of these probability-lines are not fixed once and forever for all environments. A means-object, such as a dark alley, which is "good"—that is, has a strong probability of not leading to the negative goal of injury—in an environment of "free nature" may be "bad"— that is, have strong probability of leading to a negative goal such, say, as that of an electric shock—in the special environment of a particular animal laboratory. Similarly, a cue such as bi-retinal disparity, which has a strong probability of having been caused by a true third-dimensional depth in the ordinary environment may have a very small probability of having been so caused in the more special environment of a psychological laboratory that frequently includes, as it does, stereoscopes and other "artificial" devices in front of the eyes.

It appears, however, that an organism usually tends to bring with it to any given new environment a set of already prepared hypotheses. These hypotheses result from its innate make-up and from its previous experiences of "normal" average environments. That is, it will bring with it expectations based on heredity and early experience that certain types of means-object tend most frequently to serve as causes (routes) to positive goals and that other types tend most frequently as routes to negative goals. And, similarly, it brings from heredity and early experience a propensity to expect types of sensory data as having been most frequently caused by certain types of Gegenstände and as having been infrequently caused by certain other types of Gegenstände. But the particular actual environmental setup may not correspond to the "normal" average environment. God, or the experimenter, may have introduced rather unique and special causal corrections. In such special cases the organism must adjust itself to the new differentiating features and revamp its hypotheses accordingly.

For example, we have supposed that rats, by virtue of innate endowment or of their previous general experience of "normal" spatial environments, tend to bring with them to any maze the hypothesis that south-pointing alleys have, as means-objects, a very great probability of leading towards the south side of the room. But in a given particular maze it may have been established by the experimenter that, contrary to such "normal" probability, the south-pointing alleys shall, in this special case, have a greater probability of leading to the north side of the room and, *vice versa,* that the north-pointing alleys shall in this instance have a greater probability of leading to the south side of the room. It appears therefore that, if the rats are finally to be successful in this particular maze, they must be able to discover further identifying features that differentiate this maze from the "normal" one. And they must attach their new hypotheses to these further features. If they can do this, then when such further features are present, they will react to the south-pointing alleys as having the higher probability of leading north and to the north-pointing as having the higher probability of leading south. And only when such special further features are absent will they revert to the more general hypotheses—suitable for "normal" mazes and "normal" environments in general—that south-pointing ways have the higher probabilities of reaching the south and that north-pointing ways have the higher probabilities of getting to the north.

Or, similarly, we may suppose that a binocular organism tends (on the basis of innate endowment and early childhood experience) to bring to the perception of the third dimension an hypothesis to the effect that "normally" biretinal disparity, as a cue, had a high probability of having been caused by and, therefore, of meaning, third dimensional depth. But, in the very special laboratory environments that include stereoscopes, bi-retinal disparity often has a low probability of having been caused by real third-dimensional depth and may, therefore, become by itself a misleading cue. The binocular perceptual apparatus must, in such a case, correct its initial hypothesis, which was only appropriate for "normal" environments, by including, if it can, within its cue-system, the further features as to the presence or absence of a stereoscope. But, as we saw above, the perceptual system by itself seems unable to do this. The organism, to be successful, must in this situation resort to that more elaborate apparatus which we call discursive thought. That is, in this example, the further specifications of the hypotheses needed by the organism for successful immediate adaptations require the cooperation of something more than the purely perceptual apparatus.

Or consider the reverse sort of case. A normally relatively bad means-object for getting to the south side of the room is, as we have said, a north-pointing alley. But under the special "arbitrary" conditions set up by a particular experimenter this round-about route may become a very good means-object for getting there. It appears, indeed, from experiments by Gilhousen [20] that rats which are overtrained on such round-

---

20. Gilhousen (1931; 1933). For other experiments on overtraining and fixation see also Hamilton and Ellis (1933a; 1933b), Krechevsky and Honzik (1932), Hamilton and Krechevsky (1933), Elliott (1934) and Everall (in press). Indeed, it would seem that what Kohler (1925) has designated as "bad" errors (as distinct from "good" errors) are also of the nature of what we are here calling "fixations" resulting from overtraining.

about routes in a special setup may become so "fixated" on the north-pointing roundabout route that they will persist for a long time continuing to try to take it even after it is no longer the correct route. In other words, they can become so over-trained for the special case that when the special conditions of that case no longer apply, they are unable to drop this special hypothesis.

Similarly, a normally very misleading cue for any specific third-dimensional nearness such as the cue of "being the left-hand one" of two objects, can, as we have seen, under the very special conditions of a particular experiment, become a relatively good "reliable" cue. Further, it appeared, however, that the perceptual system can become so over-trained for this special case that when later the requisite special conditions are no longer present the individual may, if the visibility conditions are poor, continue to see the left-hand object at a certain distance even though it is no longer so. The perceptual apparatus in such a case has also become, by overtraining, "fixated" on left-handedness as the appropriate and sufficient cue for a certain distance. But if the individual is, under more "normal" conditions to behave correctly, his perceptual apparatus must be able to abandon this overfixated hypothesis. The persistence of the latter is an evidence that the organism has become lazy and has dropped out some of the essential features of its original "normal" cue system.

To sum up, we may say, in general, that in the selection both of the means-objects that have high probabilities and of the cues that have high probabilities the organism responds in the form of hypotheses. The organism brings with it these hypotheses from innate endowment and from previous experience. The hypotheses tend to be correct for "normal" average environments. When, however, the probabilities in the particular environment are not those of a "normal" or average environment, then the organism, if it is not to go under, must acquire new hypotheses. Further, it appears that this new environment may differ from the "normal" either by being more general, or by being more specific, or by being equally, but differently, specific. And still further it appears that in any of these three types of cases the new hypotheses, which must be achieved, require the organism to take into its cue-system and into its selection of means-objects further identifying features. Learning, whether in the perceptual system or in the means-end system, is just such an acquiring of new hypotheses. But, and this is biologically the most important point, such new hypotheses should be attached to the specific identifying features of the particular situations to which they are appropriate. The organism should, that is, become docile to a very developed and subtle system of sensory cues—in a way which allows it, for example, to respond differently to one and the same part-cue of biretinal disparity according to whether or not the further part-cues presented by a stereoscope are or are not so present.[21] And, similarly, it must also be docile to a very wide and subtle set of means-object differentiations. It must be able, for example, to distinguish the particular north-pointing maze-alley in some particular maze, which, as such, leads south from other ordinary north-pointing alleys that are "normal" and lead north.

Thus the wholly successful organism would be one that brings, innately, normally "good" means-end hypotheses and normally "reliable" perceptual hypotheses; but which can immediately modify these innate hypotheses to suit the special conditions of a special environment; which can note and include in its cue-system and in its means-end-system the presence of the further identifying features of these special environments. But further, such an organism must also, if it is to be completely successful, be equally able at once to drop out such new hypotheses when the special features as to cue or means are no longer present.

In the case of ordinary trial-and-error learning (whether perceptual or means-end) the new features are noted and the new hypotheses acquired only under the hard taskmaster of actual bitter behavior. In the case of "insight" learning the new features are noted and the requisite new hypotheses are evoked as a result of innate endowment and general experience before they have ever actually—behaviorally—been put to the test. In the case of unmodifiable instinct the new features are never noted and the new hypotheses never acquired; the organism continues to behave in the old fashion and goes under. In the case of motivational and emotional inadequacies the organism is either overhasty or overlazy

21. Or to take, perhaps, a better example for this case of becoming docile to a very developed and subtle system of sensory cues, it appears that this is just what has happened in the case of the so-called Konstanz-phenomenon in the perception of size, color, and the like—thus, for example, to take the case of size-perception, it appears that the organism has developed an extraordinary ability and propensity to perceive, as intentionally attained Gegenstand, the "real" size of an object independent of enormous differences in the size of the visual angle, which this object presents to the eye when at different distances away. But this means simply that the organism has come to include in its cue system visual angle plus one or more reliable distance criteria. Every type of perceptual *"Ding-konstanz"* depends in fact upon just such a mutual working together of a variety of cues (for example, direct retinal effects of size, color, and so forth; distance criteria; direction criteria; illumination criteria, and so forth.) Compare in this connection the discussion of Brunswik and Kardos (1929) of the *"Zweifaktorenansatz"* of K. Buhler and the considerations concerning the equivocality of single stimuli by Heider (1930) and also by Brunswik and Kardos (1929).

in making observations of the new cue-features and the new means-features and in developing the requisite new, more adequate hypotheses.

Indeed, we would like to add, as a final word, the suggestion that all the problems of psychology—not only those of visual perception and of learning—but all the more general problems of instinct, insight, learning, intelligence, motivation, personality, and emotion all center around this one general feature of the given organism's abilities and tendencies for adjusting to these actual causal textures—these actual probabilities as to causal couplings.

VIII

In conclusion, we would summarize as follows:

1. The environment of an organism has the character of a complex *causal texture* (*Kausalgefüge*) in which certain objects may function as the *local representatives* (*die Stellvertreter*) of other objects; these latter to be known as the *entities represented* (*die Vertretenen*).

2. This function of local representation has, however, two subvarieties.
   A. On the one hand, objects or situations may function as local representatives of others in that they provide (with the cooperation of the organism) *means-objects* (*Mittelgegenstände*) to the others; these latter to be known as the *goals* (*Zielgegenstände*).
   B. On the other hand, objects or events may also function as local representatives for others in that, being themselves caused by such other objects or events, they serve as cues (*Anzeichen*) for the latter. These latter, in their turn, would then be known as the *Gegenstände* relative to such cues.

3. The simplest paradigm involving these two kinds of local representation will be one in which an organism is presented with a single *behavior-object* (*hantierbarer Körper*). This behavior-object is to be conceived as lying "in between" the *need-goal side* (*Bedarf-Erfolg-Seite*) and the reception-reaction-side of the organism. And, as so lying, it may function causally in two ways:
   A. This object can (with the cooperation of the organism) function as the means-object for the reaching of some goal.
   B. This object can also send out causal trains which may be picked up as cues by the reception-reaction-side of the organism. These cues will, then, function to represent the Gegenstande, which make up the object

4. These resulting cues, considered as a reactional event, may be said anticipatively to *"lasso"* (*Lasso-principle, that is, sign-gestalt*) the present causal complex on the basis of past causal complexes. In other words, such cue-Gegenstände will be responded to as presenting then and there an actual instance of the given type of means-Gegenstand and as also presenting (transitively) through this means-Gegenstand the possibility of a type of final goal-Gegenstand.

5. But such a paradigm with only one behavior-object between goal and cues is for some types of situation too simple and for others too complex.

    A. In many actual situations there may be more than one successive means-object and more than one successive cue-object. But such cases, although the picture must be complicated to allow for them, do not introduce anything new in principle.

    B. It also appears that such a single intervening behavior-object (Gegenstand-complex) may have three, somewhat independently variable and distinguishable aspects. These are to be designated as its *discriminanda*, its *manipulanda* and its *utilitanda*. These further complicate the picture but they do not demand anything fundamentally new in principle.

    C. Finally, there are other types of situation, obtaining for very young or for very primitive organisms, in which there are no distinct intervening Gegenstände, as such, between cues and goals. The whole picture must in such cases be conceived as telescoped.

6. It appears now, further, that the causal couplings between goal and means or between the latter and cue (or between different aspects within any one of these) are seldom, if ever, *univocal* (*eindeutig*). For it appears that any given type of goal will be capable of being causally reached by more than one type of means-object. And, vice versa, any given type of means-object will be capable of leading to more than one type of goal. Similarly, any given type of means-object can cause more than one kind of sensory cue and any one type of cue can be caused by more than one type of means-object.

7. Such *equivocality* (*Mehrdeutigkeit*) brings it about that the organism has to venture hypotheses as to what the given means-object will "most probably" lead to in the way of goals or as to what type of means-Gegenstand the given cues have with "most probability" been caused by. (Such hypotheses are always capable of purely objective definition.)

8. Further analyses of the actual types of probability-relation, which may obtain suggest preliminary, and it would seem experimentally fruitful, classifications of means-objects into the four types: *good, ambivalent, indifferent, and bad* (*gutes, ambivalentes, indifferentes and schlectes Mittel*) and of cues into the four types: *reliable, ambiguous, nonsignificant and misleading* (*verelässliches, zweideutiges, bedeutungsarmes and irreführendes Anzeichen*).

9. It appears that the organism's task, in any given case, is to correct whatever hypotheses it brings with it to fit the real probabilities of the actually presented setup.

10. The organism brings hypotheses based on innate endowment and previous experience, which tend to be suitable to the probability-relations of "normal" environments. But in any actual given environment these "normal" probability-relations may not hold.

11. If, therefore, it is to be successful, the organism must eventually develop both cue-systems and means-object systems which are, at one and the same time, both wide and inclusive and yet full of very fine discriminations.

12. Finally, it appears that the study of the organism's abilities and propensities in the development and operation of such cue-systems and mean-end systems and resultant hypotheses involves not only the problems of perception and of means-end learning, but also those of instinct, memory, insight, intellect, emotion—in short, perhaps, all the problems of pyschology.

REFERENCES

Bergmann, H. Der Kampf um das Kausalgesetz in der jüngsten Physik, Braunschweig: Vieweg, 1929.

Brunswik, E., und L. Kardos. Das Duplizitätsprinzip in der Theorie der Farbenwahrnehmung, Zsch. f. Psychol., 1929, 111, 307–320.

Brunswik, E. Wahrnehmung und Gegenstandswelt, Grundlegung einer Psychologie vom Gegenstand her, Leipzig und Wien: Deuticke, 1934. (a)

Brunswik, E. Psychologie vom Gegenstand her, Eighth Internat. Congress of Philosophy, 1934, Prague: Orbis. (b)

Bühler, Charlotte. Kindheit und Jugend, (Genese des Bewusstseins) 3rd edition, Leipzig: Hirzel, 1931.

Bühler, Charlotte. Der menschliche Lebenslauf als psychologisches Problem, Leipzig: Hirzel, 1933.

Bühler, Karl. Die Krise der Psychologie, 2d edition, Jena: G. Fischer, 1929.

Bühler, Karl. Sprachtheorie, Die Darstellungsfunktion der Sprache, Jena: G. Fischer, 1934.

Claparède, E. La genèse de l'hypothèse, Arch. de Psychol., 1934, 24, 1–155.

Eissler, K. Die Gestaltkonstanz der Sehdinge, No. 3 of: Untersuchungen uber Wahrnehmungsgegenstände, ed. by E. Brunswik, Arch. f. d. ges. Psychol., 1933, 88, 487–550.

Elliott, M. H. The effect of hunger on variability of performance. Amer. J. Psychol., 1934, 46, 107–112.

Everall, Eleanor. Perseveration in the rat. J. Comp. Psychol., in press.

Gilhousen, H. C. An investigation of "insight" in rats. Science, 1931, 73, 711–712.

Gilhousen, H. C. Fixation of excess distance patterns in the white rats. J. comp. Psychol., 1933, 16, 1–24.

Hamilton, G. V. A study of perseverance reactions in primates and rodents. Behav. Monog., 1916, 3, no. 2.

Hamilton, J. A., and W. D. Ellis. Behavior constancy in rats. J. genet. Psychol., 1933, 42, 120–139. (a)

Hamilton, J. A. and W. D. Ellis. Persistence and behavior constancy. J. genet. Psychol., 1933, 42, 140–153. (b)

Hamilton, J. A. and I. Krechevsky. Studies in the effect of shock upon behavior plasticity in the rat. J. comp. Psychol., 1933, 16, 237–254.

Heider, F. Die Leistung des Wahrnehmungssystems. Zsch. f. Psychol., 1930, 114, 371–394.

Holaday, B. E. Die Grossenkonstanz, der Sehdinge. No. 2 of: Unters. ub. Wahrnehmungsgegenstände, ed. by E. Brunswik. Arch. f. d. ges. Psychol., 1934, 88, 419–486.

Izzet, T. Gewicht und Dichte als Gegenstände der Wahrnehmung. No. 6 of: Unters. üb. Wahrnehmungsgegenstände, ed. by E. Brunswik.

Arch. f. d. ges. Psychol., 1934, *91*, 305–318.

Kardos, L. Ding und Schatten, Eine experimentelle Untersuchung über die Grundlagen des Farbensehens. *Zsch. f. Psychol., Erganzungsband 23*, 1934.

Krechevsky, I. "Hypotheses" versus "chance" in the presolution period in sensory discrimination learning. *Univer. Calif. Publ. Psychol.*, 1932, *6*, 27–44.

Krechevsky, I. and C. H. Honzik. Fixation in the rat. *Univ. Calif. Publ. Psychol.*, 1932, *6*, 13–26.

Kohler, W. *The mentality of apes.* New York: Harcourt, 1925.

Kuo, Z. Y. The nature of unsuccessful acts and their order of elimination. *J. comp. Psychol.*, 1922, *2*, 1–27.

Odgen, C. K. and I. A. Richards. *The meaning of meaning.* New York: Harcourt, 1925.

Patrick, J. R. Studies in rational behavior and emotional excitement: I. Rational behavior in human subjects. *J. comp. Psychol.*, 1934, *18*, 1–22.

Patrick, J. R. Studies in rational behavior and emotional excitement: II. The effect of emotional excitement on rational behavior in human subjects, *J. comp. Psychol.*, 1934, *18*, 153–196.

Pepper, S. C. The conceptual framework of Tolman's purposive behaviorism, *Psychol. Rev.*, 1934, *41*, 108–133.

Reichenbach, H. Die Kausalstruktur der Welt und der Unterschied von Vergangenheit und Zukunft. *Bayerischer Akademiebericht,* 1925.

Ripin, R. und H. Hetzer. Frühestes Lernen des Säuglings in der Ernährungs-situation. *Zsch. f. Psychol.*, 1930, 118.

Rubinow, O. und L. Frankl. Die erste Dingauffassung beim Säugling; Reaktionen auf Wahrnehmung der Flasche. Mit Einleitung und Schluss von Ch. Bühler. *Zsch. f. Psychol.*, 1934, *133*, 1–71.

Tolman, E. C. *Purposive behavior in animals and men.* New York: The Century Co., 1932.

Tolman, E. C. Gestalt and signgestalt. *Psychol. Rev.*, 1933, *40*, 391–411.

Tolman, E. C. and I. Krechevsky. Means-end-readiness and hypothesis—a contribution to comparative psychology. *Psychol. Rev.*, 1933, *40*, 60–70.

Uexkull, J. V. Umwelt und Innenwelt der Tiere. Berlin: Springer, 1909.

16

Reasoning as a Universal Behavior Model and a Functional Differentiation between "Perception" and "Thinking" [1]

EGON BRUNSWIK

From the dawn of science, efforts have not ceased to conceive of man as a rational being. One of the sources of this belief must be seen in the explicit or tacit realization of the fact that adjustment and the struggle for existence require some form of rebuilding of the surroundings within the organism so that orientation and anticipation can take place.

For any system, such construction or extrapolation beyond its boundaries involves integrative interaction within the system. What is more, it involves the particular type of orderly interaction we find best exemplified in syllogistic reasoning or in mathematical calculation.

In order that such a procedure be perfectly realized, general regularities must first be extracted from the environment. An extreme, explicitly rational case of such law-stating, or nomothetic, behavior is that of the physicist. To make prediction with certainty from physical law, however, the environment must be a "controlled" one; that is, added information of an enumerative, geographic kind is needed. Only then may information be called "sufficient." As an example, take range-finding by triangulation. Distance, D, may thus be univocally obtained by application of the laws of geometrical optics, provided that the extrasystemic medium is controlled as to its relevant characteristics, such as the absence or presence of optical inhomogeneities. From D we may proceed to the construction of the size of a distant body, B, by incorporating its direct retinal projection, P, within our input material and by using the law of proportionality of B to P and to the distance D. The important point is that under controlled application of physical law the dependability of each of the two proximal cues, P and D_c, is theoretically perfect, and thus one single cue for each constituent variable seems sufficient. The construction process within the

1. Read at the International Congress of Psychology in Montreal, 1954.

system, then, merely needs to duplicate the environmental laws cited. Such a machine-like interaction in a single-track net within the responding system may be labeled "certainty-geared" interaction or strategy.

Assume now that prior information falls short of the physicist's perfect penetration of environmental texture so that strict laws have not yet been discovered and extraneous control has not yet been established. If past information centers on a limited universe, such as on a more or less circumscribed natural-cultural habitat or "ecology," however, confinement may be taken as a vague substitute for knowledge of law and for the often cumbersome direct control of the medium. Extraction of semi-erratic yet stereotyped regularities of limited range of application and usually quite limited statistical dependability or "ecological validity" is possible as a first approximation, thus saving on complexity and time at the expense of dependability. An example is the perceptual depth-cue known as linear perspective. In our technological ecology parallel lines are frequent and are often viewed under an angle. Thus there is a relatively high probability that convergent lines in the retinal picture have been caused by parallels leading into depth; but at the same time this is by no means certain. In the ecology of the jungle with its relative absence of parallelism and of standardized body sizes the same cue is ecologically much less valid. (It must be stressed that even such triangulation cues as binocular disparity or binocular convergence have limited ecological validity if the external medium lapses from control, witness the viewing of reality through flat pictures, or its reverse, the faking of reality in the stereoscope.)

The low ecological validity of single cue variables is not entirely beyond remedy, however. It may be compensated for to some extent by the use of multiple systems of mutually substitutable, or "vicarious," cues. The resulting multiple track mediation nets may be called "probability-geared" or "uncertainty-geared" interactions. Instead of one foolproof cue for D, the system now utilizes a whole family of cues of more or less limited trustworthiness (D_u, D'_u, and so forth); the construction of B from these cues together with P may be further aided by more direct probability cues for B itself, based on, say, familiar shape-color-size combinations (B_u, B'_u, and so forth).

Let us now turn to a concrete case in which our task of ascertaining the size of a distant body, B, has been presented once as a typical life-near experiment on perceptual size-constancy, and once as a typical explicit arithmetic reasoning problem with univocal indications about P and D. There were twenty-eight and twenty-seven subjects, respectively, and "8 cm." was the correct answer in both cases. The perceptual variant of our task is characterized (1) by a relative paucity of on-the-dot precise estimates; but this counterbalanced by (2) a relatively compact distribution of errors, and (3) a relative freedom from grossly absurd errors. The seeming perfection of arithmetic inference, on the other hand, proves in practice to be highly vulnerable. While it is true that there is (1) a relatively large proportion of ideally accurate answers, and (2) these answers stand out sharply as an isolated bar without contamination by near-misses, there is (3) occasional error so bizarre—for example, 4800 cm.—that only the choice of a logarithmic scale, and one of considerable horizontal spread at that, was able to accommodate them.

Attempting now to backward infer strategy from achievement it is suggested that our soft and smudgy yet organic "perceptual" error profile is the result of the check-and-balance system of probability-geared multiple-track mediation. The key to both the high precision and the erratic mistakes of the ratiocination variant, on the other hand, may be sought in a presumed natural affinity of "thinking" with single-track nets; the errors here appear based not so much on the dynamic confluxions inherent in perceptual cue-rivalry and compromise but rather on relatively mechanical derailments into certain major substitute tracks, such as the one involving the finding of the retinal or picture equivalent, P, or of the most likely mean intuitive estimate, b. In the Wurzburg tradition these inadvertent task substitutions may be subsumable under Otto Selz's law of partial effectiveness of a task (*Gesetz der Teilwirksamkeit der Aufgabe*).

Our concrete examples are rather obvious and certainly not representative of "perception" versus "thinking" at large. Yet a beginning must be made toward an objective explication of the age old yet hitherto rather introspectionistic or speculative, and thus precarious distinction between these traditional major sub-systems of cognition. That intuitive perception is relatively instantaneous, uses vicarious cues and is mostly not quite accurate is common knowledge. It may be added that in a study employing "representative design," that is, a large sample of everyday situations drawn from the ecology of an adult subject, the errors as to size were found not to surpass about three- to four-fold over- or underestimation, thus covering a total range of about one logarithmic unit or one power of ten. (Even in such grossly atypical schemes as the Ames' distorted room the error seems to keep within similar bounds.) (More drastic misestimates of size, such as of the moon, are probably mostly cases of going beyond the confines of the ecology of manipulable things; if we were to take the trouble of transferring Katz's modes of appearance from color to size, such perceptions may likely turn out to be kept in suspense phenomenologically by an insubstantial, field-like rather than thing-like appearance.)

While we may thus find perception fairly uniformly exhibiting the probability-geared strategy, "thinking" in the customary sense of the term is without doubt much less homogeneous. There obviously are many cases of so-called thinking, which also use the weighing of vicarious or competitive multiple evidence. Our example was one of routine application of deductive reasoning; as we have learned from Gestalt psychology, creative thinking is probably much more perception-like. Yet there undoubtedly is a certain core province of thought or of the "intellect" which is single-track in the manner of our concrete example and thus is like the gift of Prometheus: highly potent and beneficial, or else disastrous without the benefit of adequate warning. We all remember our school days when the question was, for example, how long it would take to fill a reservoir by means of three instead of two tubes of certain specified diameters, and we came out with such absurd answers as a billion years or a millionth of a second. Probably we should include here much of the allegedly logico-deductive and thus allegedly unambiguous "intuition of essences" or *Wesensschau.*

The perils of entrusting decision making to linear single-cue systems in which the throwing of a switch threatens collapse are brought home more in earnest when we remember that certainty-geared interaction may go wrong not only as to deductive routines but also on the inductive leg of the inferential process. This is the case when the single cues representing the constituent variables are not in reality foolproof, that is, when certainty-geared interaction lacks its necessary counterpart in the ecology. Take here the earlier confinement of airplane altimetry to the air-pressure cue, and the resultant crashes of planes in mountainsides whenever the cue was misleading. Of still greater general import are some of the artificialities of the prevalent highly orderly or "systematic" research designs which, as can be shown, are intimately affiliated with the overestimation of lawfulness as an instrument of knowledge; in medical or social application this has resulted in jerky successions of striking hits and dangerous gross aberrations in an adjustment process that is "hard" and often narrow or unimaginative.

Although certainty-geared strategy was found to duplicate the rigorous texture of general law, and uncertainty-geared strategy the textural potential of a more confined and more specific yet at the same time more varied body of informational input, from the "reductive" point of view, they both fall under the model of reasoning-type inferences. We may label this reduction of cognitive functions, and thus indirectly of behavior, to a common model of reasoning "ratiomorphism." (The Latin-Greek hybrid composition of the term will perhaps be forgiven in the light of such famous precedents as Auguste Comte's coining of the term "sociology.") Only by at least implicit recognition of this underlying communality are we enabled to proceed to differentiation between relatively autonomous cognitive subsystems at the more molar level of strategy and of achievement. In this light perception and the different varieties of thinking begin to reveal themselves as but different forms of imperfect reasoning, each with its own particular brands of virtues and of "stupidity," if the term be permitted. (All intuition and all irrationality thus appear but as aspects of rationality.)

Perhaps the most sweeping ratiomorphic model directly applied to organismic processes comes from McCulloch and Pitts; these cyberneticists and mathematical biophysicists have likened all nervous activity, with its all-or-none principle, to Boolean algebra and the traditional two-valued, "true-false" logic, and have proceeded to develop a theory of nervous nets from this basic scheme. Within cybernetics at large, our case of certainty-geared ratiocination is explicated by the standard use of calculating machines whereby the representational control of the input is tacitly entrusted to the extraneous human operator and single-track nets appear sufficient for the remaining, chiefly deductive leg of the construction process; switching errors inside the machine are then the major source of failure. Intuitive perception, on the other hand, seems to make use of some probabilistic features incorporated in inductive cybernetic "predictors." Still better, we may compare probability-geared strategy with telecommunication through a semierratic, "noisy" extrasystemic medium. Under these conditions "redundancy" has been acknowledged by Shannon and Weaver as an effective countermeasure; and redundancy is in fact but a rudimentary form of vicarious cue mediation. Ashby has recently recognized "vicarious function" as a characteristic of "ultrastable systems," although for the present this recognition is probably no more than a glow on the horizon so far as the actual elaboration of working models of adequate complexity on the part of cyberneticists is concerned.

As of the more general recognition of the probabilistic character of perception, William James has spoken of perception as being "of probable things"; more recently, Thurstone has characterized perception as that function which is "based on insufficient evidence." The related conception of the perceptual system as intuitive statistician was to my knowledge first cast into mathematical language by Thorndike as early as 1920. Hofstatter in Vienna demonstrated that such statistical properties as means or sigmas could be intuitively appraised in a manner comparable to the perceptual constancies. Attneave has recently scrutinized the capacity of the perceptual system to choose from a variety of equally possible hypotheses in a complex process of quasi-statistical intuition.

In his Sensation and Perception in the History of Experimental Psychology, Boring has correctly interpreted the speaker's point of view of the mid-thirties as a "modern equivalent" of Helmholtz's theory of unconscious inference. I should like to stress the phrase "modern equivalent." (As is probably true for most recurrences in history, there is a spiral development toward synthesis at a higher level; in our case, this is given by a raise in the level of objectivity.) We have shifted from Helmholtz's predominately introspectionistic conscious versus unconscious dimension (and his stress on sensation) to the functional level, (involving both a statistical comparison of achievement distributions and a retracing of differences between cognitive subsystems in the underlying rational or quasi-rational strategy.) In our present probabilistic functionalism, perception is operationally redefined as a special form of automatic, semistereotyped, imperfect reasoning. As Eleanor Gibson has recently observed, most other post-Gestalt psychological theories of perception are likewise patterned upon inductive reasoning, the many existing differences in outlook notwithstanding. Among them is the transactionism of Ames and the Princeton group, and the hypothesis-information theory of Bruner and Postman.

Piaget's contention of the intellect as a reversible and of perception as an irreversible type of process are obviously also related to our treatment of cognitive functions, although it must be stressed that Piaget seeks the source of the statistical nature of perception within the organism and its Gestalt-type confluxion interactions while we see the root of the predicament in the vicissitudes of the ecology. (Michotte's combination of the term "phenomenal" with the abstract category of "causality" is another example of the rapprochement of perception and thinking, a rapprochement that makes their functional distinction both easier and more necessary.) (As everywhere, Galileanization of the originally Aristotelian dichotomies between the various cognitive subfunctions, as effected by the shift from phenomenology to a functional tracing process, may be the best way to clear the atmosphere.)

Another independent line of approach combines implications of such heterogeneous background elements as Carnap's stress on the "rational reconstruction" of the world in the framework of logical positivism and Freud's idea that the appearance of one manifestation of a latent factor may make the appearance of alternate symptoms unnecessary. This synthesis has been effected by Else Frenkel-Brunswik when she introduced multiple correlation into the operational reconstruction of clinical intuitions of "motivation" based on "behavior"; this technique is particularly appropriate by virtue of its sensitivity to the negative intercorrelations among alternate manifestations—or cues—which must be expected on psychoanalytic (as well as perhaps also on functional) grounds in any personality material.

In an unpublished study of clinical intuition in the interpretation of the Rorschach test conducted at Colorado, Hammond and Todd have described striking instances of unawareness of the cues actually used by the raters, of concentration on single cues, and of reversals of cue-validities in the response. With a slant more toward experimental psychology, Smedslund at Oslo has studied multiple probability learning of new perceptual cues, and has independently come to some similar conclusions regarding the occurrence of distortive cue-utilization. In both cases it seems to be the restriction of evidence, or the shrinkage from pliable vicariousness toward a single-track type of mediation, in short from a perception-type to a ratiocination-type of approach where only the former is applicable, which lies at the core of inappropriateness, in some cases perhaps even of neurosis. Again we are reminded of Else Frenkel-Brunswik's work, in this case of her concept of "intolerance of ambiguity."

The trend toward rational explication is in evidence in the emotional-conative field also, witness such systematic efforts as Leeper's emphasis on the constructive function of the emotions and David Rapaport's rational model of psychoanalytic mechanisms.

A few final words on the relation of our ratiomorphic unification-diversification scheme to Gestalt psychology. "Atomistic" cues, generalized probability learning which is essentially "blind," and other such paraphernalia we must use in the rational explication of perception are probably not to the liking of the Gestaltists. The law of Pragnanz, and with it the problem of illusion, continues to emerge as the heart of the Gestalt school; at least this is so if we take Metzger's reaction to Rausch's work—which is the first major postwar German development in Gestalt psychology—as an indication. From our point of view, such confluxion dynamisms are but side aspects of rivalry, compromise, and related features of uncertainty-geared interaction, regardless of their potency within the intrasystemic field. Perception must not so much be "good," it must be "true"; and while the two sometimes coincide, this is by no means always and by no means necessarily so.

A point of agreement with Gestalt psychology nonetheless emerges from the fact that in problem-solving the literal untruth of "good form" changes into the more profound, instrumental truth of creative restructuring; it is here that "perception" and "thinking" come closest to meeting on common ground. Perhaps the most cogent point of sympathy with Gestalt psychology derives from the fact that it has brought to successful conclusion what Murphy, in his History of Psychology, has called the shift from focal to marginal consciousness. In doing so, Gestalt psychology has paved the way for the vindication of the more primordial, more organic, more biological of the cognitive functions—perception—against the rationalistic overvaluation of the intellect.

This vindication of perception has been the major purpose of this paper also. In a way we may even summarize our considerations by saying that ratiomorphism as we have defined it is far from being rationalism or intellectualism; on the contrary, ratiomorphic reduction seems to us the best instrument for the overcoming of rationalism and for the establishment of an encompassing empiricistic outlook on the problem of cognition.

17

Historical and Thematic Relations of Psychology to other Sciences [1]

EGON BRUNSWIK

Not quite a century has passed since experimental psychology began, in Gustav Theodor Fechner's treatise on the "psychophysics" of sensation in 1860, to emancipate itself as a science. The emancipation has taken place relative to the purely speculative approach of philosophy, on the one hand, and relative to the confinement to the human or animal body imposed within psychology's closest antecedent among the sciences, physiology, on the other. And not quite half a century has elapsed since John B. Watson, in 1913, suggested that psychology abandon its original subjectivistic or introspectionistic concern with sensation and other data of consciousness and concentrate on the "behavior" of the organism as a physical body in a physical environment. Thus psychology was to be placed fully under the auspices of the methodologically most rigorous of its older sister disciplines, physics.

In the light of a comparative science, psychology stands at the crossroads as perhaps none of the other disciplines does. I shall stress especially its relationships to the physical and biological sciences, including some of the relatively "lowbrow" cultural disciplines such as economics.

FROM PHYSIOLOGY TO PHYSIOLOGICAL PSYCHOLOGY

The emergence of what we may call the specific "thema" of psychology is best discussed by contrasting the physiological psychology of today with the physiology from which it has sprung. Some of the major physiological discoveries of the first half of the nineteenth century were more or less directly at the doorstep of psychology. Among these were the Bell-Magendie law, which asserts the structural and functional discreteness of

1. Read at the AAAS meetings in Berkeley, 1954, and later published in the *Scientific Monthly* 1956, *83*, 151–161; reprinted here with the kind permission of the American Association for the Advancement of Science.

the sensory and motor nerves, and the law of specific sense or nerve energies by Charles Bell, Johannes Muller, and Helmholtz, which recognizes the dependence of sensation on the receiving organism. Still another discovery, the establishment of the rate of nervous impulse by Muller and by Helmholtz, best represents the step-by-step tracing of internal processes, which is so characteristic of physiology; this is symbolized by the straight line in diagram A of Table 1.

TABLE 1. THE EMERGENCE OF PHYSIOLOGICAL PSYCHOLOGY FROM PHYSIOLOGY.

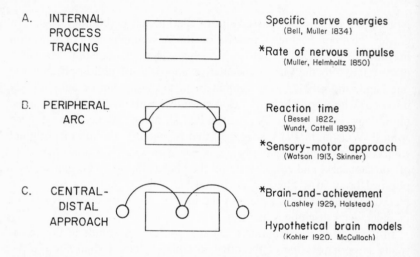

A. INTERNAL   Specific nerve energies
    PROCESS   (Bell, Muller 1834)
    TRACING   *Rate of nervous impulse
                                          (Muller, Helmholtz 1850)

B. PERIPHERAL   Reaction time
    ARC   (Bessel 1822,
                                          Wundt, Cattell 1893)
                                        *Sensory-motor approach
                                          (Watson 1913, Skinner)

C. CENTRAL-   *Brain-and-achievement
    DISTAL   (Lashley 1929, Halstead)
    APPROACH   Hypothetical brain models
                                          (Kohler 1920. McCulloch)

Compare this pattern with the counterpart of rate of nervous impulse in psychology proper, reaction time. The distinguishing characteristic of problems of this latter kind is the concentration on the over-all functional correlation of sensory input and motor output without primary concern for the details of the mediating process. This correlational peripheralism is described by the bridgelike arc in schema B of Table 1. In line with its gross, achievement-oriented character, the study of reaction time received its first impetus from difficulties with observational error in astronomy raised by Bessel in the 1820's; later it became a favorite of Wilhelm Wundt, the founder of the first psychological laboratory at Leipzig in 1879, and of his American assistant, James McKeen Cattell, who applied it to his differential-psychological testing research at Columbia University.

The direct physical observability of both stimulus and response renders the study of reaction time a nineteenth century rudimentary anticipation of Watson's sensory-motor behaviorism and of Bekhterev's concurrent reflexology. Most importantly, Fechner's psychophysics shared with the study of reaction time a relational rather than a process-centered emphasis. This was manifested in the famous Weber-Fechner law, which expresses sensation as a direct mathematical function of the external stimulus. The fact that psychophysics is being considered almost unanimously the birth cry of psychology proper must be ascribed to this correlational feature.

Various conditioning and higher learning problems have recently been treated under the sensory-motor reflex schema by Skinner and others. Critics have bemoaned the fact that this approach, cutting short as it does from input to output, tends to bypass the brain; and the dean of historians of psychology, Edwin G. Boring, has criticized it as a "psychology of the empty organism." (Boring, 1949.)

In the development of physiological psychology, the possibility of such an accusation is circumvented by the emergence of a third type of approach that at the same time does away with peripheralism in its various forms. It is described in Table 1 under diagram C. Occurrences in the brain—that is, "central" factors—are directly correlated with relatively remote, or "distal," results of behavior ("achievements"), such as the reaching of the end of mazes of varying intricacy by a rat (right arc; the arc to the left is shown to indicate that abstraction and related cognitive extrapolations into the causal ancestry of the stimulus impact are inseparably intertwined with all brain-and-achievement studies).

Foreshadowed by Gall's notorious "phrenology" in the early nineteenth century and by Flourens' pioneering of brain extirpation experiments soon thereafter, the central-distal approach reached its full scope in the brain-lesion study in rats by Lashley in 1929 (Lashley, 1929). The same year brought Berger's report on brain waves and thus the beginning of electroencephalography with its wide use in modern psychiatry. More recently, Halstead has applied the statistical tool of factor analysis to the study of brain and intelligence at the human level (Halstead, 1947). In contrast, the 1860's and 1870's witnessed the peripheralistically conceived brain-localization studies of Broca and of Fritsch and Hitzig in which the more narrowly sensory or motor aspects were stressed at the expense of organization and integration.

Of considerably shorter history than the empirical brain-and-achievement studies are the largely hypothetical studies of the brain, which began with Kohler's theory of dynamic brain fields or "physical Gestalten" in 1920 (Kohler, 1955). While the Gestalt-psychological approach is more purely central rather than genuinely central-distal, the distal, adjustmental aspects have come to share the limelight in the study of "teleological mechanisms" by McCulloch and other cyberneticists (Annu. N. Y. Acad. Sci., 1948).

PSYCHOLOGY AND THE ANCIENT SPECULATIVE UNITY OF SCIENCE

One of the most prominent problems of a comparative science of science is that of the unity of the sciences (Brunswik, 1952). Most scientists agree that there must be unity with respect to the objectivity of both observation and the procedural aspects of theory construction. Physiological psychology and the school of behaviorism are primarily dedicated to the unification of psychology with the natural sciences along these lines. Equally important as the procedural unification is the thematic diversification of the sciences, however. I have therefore made it a point to begin these considerations with an example of such diversification of psychology from a neighboring discipline.

Close inspection shows (Brunswik, 1952) the considerable inhibitions stemming from vested intellectual interests that must be overcome to achieve such differentiation among the sciences. We must be on guard against excessive thematic unity, especially if we are concerned with a younger discipline growing up in the shadow of overwhelming parent sciences.

Formidable and even grotesque examples of an excessive unity of a highly uncritical kind can be brought forth from ancient science. An example involving the psychology both of sensation and of personality along with physics and physiology is presented in Table 2. For the most part the schema is based on the pre-Socratic cosmology of Empedocles and on the humoral doctrine of four temperaments of Hippocrates and Galen; the last two columns are relatively modern elaborations (see Allport, 1937, pp. 63ff). The original dichotomies are developed into quadripartite systems either by doubling or by compounding so that a modicum of differentiation is achieved.

From the systematic point of view, two features must be especially emphasized in connection with Table 2. One is the arbitrariness of classification as revealed most drastically by the presence of alternative sets of columns for the same subject matter—for example, a double dichotomy and a partly conflicting compound dichotomy for the sensory qualities. (We may add that another of the pre-Socratics, Anaximander, chose air to be cold rather than dry.)

The other feature noteworthy in Table 2 is the apparent ease of

TABLE 2. SIMPLE AND COMPOUND DICHOTOMIES AND A RESULTANT PERVASIVE SYSTEM OF CORRESPONDING QUADRIPARTITE SCHEMES IN ANCIENT PHYSICS AND PHYSIOLOGY AND IN PERSONALITY PSYCHOLOGY.

PHYSICS	SENSORY PSYCHOLOGY			PHYSIOLOGY	PERSONALITY PSYCHOLOGY			
Cosmic elements	Dichotomies of qualities			Humors	Temperaments and their behavioral aspects		Compound dichotomies	
	(Alternatives:)						*(Alternatives:)*	
	Double Compound						Emotional response	Affective tone
(a)	(b)	(c)		(d)	(e)	(f)	(g)	(h)
Air	Dry	Warm-Moist		Blood	Sanguine	Hopeful	Weak-Strong	Pleasant-Excited
Earth	Cold	Cold-Dry		Black bile (Spleen)	Melancholic	Sad	Strong-Slow	Unpleasant-Calm
Fire	Warm	Warm-Dry		Yellow bile	Choleric	Irascible	Strong-Quick	Unpleasant-Excited
Water	Moist	Cold-Moist		Phlegm (Mucus)	Phlegmatic	Apathetic	Weak-Slow	Pleasant-Calm

transfer of fourness from one area to another in the manner of an absolute one-to-one correspondence. Different areas of knowledge, capable of independent approach, are thus thrown together indiscriminately by means of vague analogy; this is comparable to what such child psychologists as Piaget or Heins Werner have described as synocretic or diffuse modes of thought (for a recent summary, see M. Scheerer in *Handbook of Social Psychology*, G. Lindzey, Ed., 1954).

More specifically, Gestalt psychologists have criticized the ready assumption of a strict correspondence between physical stimuli and sensory qualities as an undue "constancy hypothesis." It is in this surreptitious manner that physics and sensory psychology (Table 2, columns a to c) become symmetrical and thus, in effect, merge into one. It is even difficult to reconstruct which of the two areas of knowledge has the observational primacy over the other, although it is evident that there is a good deal of give and take.

In philosophy, it is easily seen that the implied operational indistinguishability of matter and mind (in this case, sensation) constitutes, or at least reinforces, naïve realism; or else, by way of the horizontal dichotomy between columns, it helps to put dualism on an absolute basis. Once the constancy hypothesis of the coordination of the two realms has given rise to the accusation of "unnecessary duplication" (as in Occam's razor), this dualism in turn readily changes into either materialistic or idealistic monism. The regularity and symmetry, which result from easy transfer and carry with them the flavor of Pythagorean number mystics, may be criticized on the same grounds of subjectivism on which Schopenhauer criticized Kant's compulsive filling of all the plots in his 3x4 table of categories.

(In experimental psychology, the adoption of the constancy hypothesis in its radical form would lead to the obliteration of the stimulus-response problem of psychophysics which, as we have seen, lies at the roots of modern psychology; it would even lead to the at least theoretical impossibility of acknowledging any kind of illusion—as it has come close to doing in Locke's doctrine of primary qualities, such as size, shape or motion.)

Both the arbitrariness and the easy transfer that characterize early stages of science are further revealed in the fact that some systems are not dichotomous or fourfold but three-, five-, or seven-fold. In his capacity as a psychologist, Plato distinguished three major faculties (reason, emotion, and desire, the latter including the lowly sensation); he localized them in a corresponding hierarchy of physiological centers (brain, heart, and liver or "phern"—that is, diaphragm); and he further distinguished three corresponding sociopolitical personality types (philosopher, warrior, and worker). The ancient Chinese favored a five-fold scheme. In the doctrine of cosmic elements, the air of the Greeks is replaced by metal, and wood is added as a fifth element; the scheme is syncretically generalized to five tastes, five intestines, five sentiments, five poisons, five planets, five dynasties, and so forth (Forke, 1925). The relative merits of the various base numbers are not discussed here, although it may be granted that some of them are not without a realistic basis in certain limited areas (such as twoness for sex, threeness for man between input and output or the healthy medium between extremes, and so forth).

RELATIVE LEVEL OF
MATURITY OF PSYCHOLOGY

As has been noted in passing, the most distinctly psychological aspects of the doctrine of four temperaments have outlasted their counterparts in physics and physiology by centuries if not millenniums. Furthermore, this doctrine has flourished in much greater variety and thus is fraught with more ambiguity than its long-vanished correspondents in the natural sciences. Columns g and h of Table 2 show only two of the kinds of compound dichotomies usually suggested, both conceived in the Wundtian three-dimensional theory of emotion; Herbart used a combination of strong-weak and pleasant-unpleasant instead. There are at least sixteen major thinkers who expended their efforts on the four temperaments in a feast of arbitrary classification. Among the persons concerned were Kant and such serious experimental psychologists of the past as Ribot, Kulpe, Ebbinghaus, Hoffding, and Meumann; on the contemporary scene we find the well-known German typologist, Ludwig Klages (for further discussion and sources, see Allport, 1937, pp. 63ff). This suggests that the relative youth of psychology is matched, at least in the personality area concerned, by a backwardness in its categorical structure, or "modes of thought."

In investigating the question of the relative maturity of psychology further, we note that dichotomizing and related forms of absolute classification, as well as their formalistic-syncretic transfer to other areas, are but two of several aspects of a broader prescientific syndrome. Auguste Comte put his finger on this syndrome in his distinction between what he called the metaphysical and the positive stages of science; with an eye on the special situation in psychology, Kurt Lewin, somewhat similarly, distinguished between Aristotelian and Galilean modes of thought

(Lewin, 1935). According to Lewin, progress from the former to the latter mode involves any or all of the following, partly overlapping shifts: from dichotomies to gradations, from qualitative appearance to quantitative reality, from subjective speculation to objectivism, from classification to causation, from phenotype to genotype, from static existence to dynamic flow, from surface to depth, and from disjointed description to the "nomothetic" search for laws.

We may try to assess the standing of psychology among the sciences by listing a few of the most crucial shifts in these respects (Table 3). Perhaps the earliest shift from phenotypical quality to genotypical quan-

TABLE 3. SHIFT IN MODES OF CLASSIFICATION AND OUTLOOK FROM THE SUBJECTIVE-QUALITATIVE-PHENOTYPICAL-STATIC ("ARISTOTELIAN") TO THE OBJECTIVE-QUANTITATIVE-GENOTYPICAL-DYNAMIC ("GALILEAN") SYNDROME.

Physics (Elements)	Astronomy	Anatomy-Physiology	Biology	Psychiatry	Psychology
Empedocles 5th B.C.					
Democritus 4th B.C.					
	Ptolemy 2nd A.D.				
	Copernicus 1530				
		Vesalius 1543			
		Harvey 1628			
			Linnaeus 1738		
			Darwin 1859		
				Kraepelin 1883	
				Freud 1900	
					Titchener 1901
					Lewin 1935

tity concerns physics. From Empedocles' qualitatively conceived four-fold scheme mentioned in a previous paragraph, the doctrine of elements moved on toward an essentially modern conception of physical reality in Democritus' atomic theory that stressed shape and size instead of sensation. This theory is far from free of subjective speculation or contamination by direct perceptual appearances (especially "synesthesia" from the tactile-kinesthetic sphere), to be sure, but the step from surface to underlying reality and from dichotomy to gradation is taken at least in intent. The step from perceptual appearances to an indirect, abstract construction of a much more dynamically conceived reality was next made in astronomy with the shift from the perceptually dominated geocentric to the nomothetically more economical Copernican system.

The biological sciences followed with the shift from static anatomy to dynamic physiology as epitomized by Harvey's discovery of the circulation of the blood, and with the shift from Linnaeus' phenotypical taxonomy to Darwin's genotypical evolutionary classification in botany and zoology. Transitions between dichotomizing and gradations also occurred—for example, when in the Middle Ages the four humors were ranked according to their "degree" of aliveness (Leake, personal communication).

Confirming our suspicion, we note that corresponding steps in the psychological disciplines follow much later, mostly within the memory of ourselves or of our immediate elders. In psychiatry, there is a tradition of static description and cataloging which began in the early seventeenth century with Robert Burton's revealingly titled *Anatomy of Melancholy,* which continued with Pinel—the man who freed the insane from prison during the French revolution—and was still in evidence in Kraepelin until it was broken by Freud's "depth-psychological" revision of psychiatric classification, notably in the doctrine of neurosis. In psychology proper, there is the shift from Wundt's and Titchener's so-called "existential" inventory and description of sensory experiences to Lewin's more dispositionally conceived notions of the internal psychological "field." Instead of Lewin, I might have mentioned some of his older Gestalt-psychological colleagues, notably Wertheimer and Kohler. Beginning in the 1910's, these workers set out to work on the intrinsic central dynamics of perception, and of thinking and problem solving; by virtue of their introspectionistic orientation, they are more comparable to Wundt and Titchener than to the more behaviorally oriented Lewin. Indeed, the simile has sometimes been used that while Titchener tried to dissect consciousness analytically like an anatomist, and his "sensations" thus are no better than a carcass of experience, Gestaltists, with their

"phenomenology" are more like physiologists in that they keep consciousness alive while studying it.

As in all structural interpretations of history, a table of examples can
be no substitute for full documentation. Indeed, Hippocrates' humoral
underpinning of the doctrine of temperaments may be set parallel to
Democritus' geometric underpinning of the elements and offered as
demonstration of the fact that at least part of psychology showed objec-
tivistic intent as early as did physics. Yet humoral doctrine is physiology,
not psychology; nor would the fact that much of ancient psychology was
behavioristic from the outset change our impression that, in the handling
of the actual problems in the area, relatively primitive patterns of thought
were the rule. I have already mentioned in discussing Table 2 that
syncretic dichotomizing persists much longer and flourishes more abun-
dantly in the psychological doctrine of the four temperaments than it does
in the corresponding doctrines of the four physical elements or of the four
physiological humors. We may further remind ourselves of the fact that
in the social sciences—in many ways still younger than psychology—
elaborate dichotomous schemes are still in vogue in some quarters right
under our eyes—for example, in the work of Talcott Parsons.

DEPENDENCE OF PSYCHOLOGY ON
THE NATURAL SCIENCES

Next we turn to more direct cross-disciplinary comparisons that involve historical phase differences with respect to comparable categories
and in which psychology appears at the receiving end. For chronologically
arranged evidence, we may turn to Table 4. This table concentrates on the
experimental and differential-psychological developments that constitute
the core of modern psychology; developments in physiological and ab-
normal psychology which are incorporated in some of the preceding tables
have been played down or omitted. Special emphasis is given to conceptual outlook and methodology.

Our first consideration concerns the law-stating or nomothetic approach; it is traced at the left side of the table. While the actual establishment of natural law as it has been able to stand the test of time was
brought about in astronomy and physics during the seventeenth century,
psychology had to wait until Fechner (1860) for the beginnings of the
experimental-nomothetic treatment of sensation, and until Ebbinghaus
(1885) for that of memory by association. Solid arrows indicating these
cross-disciplinary infusions generally point downward in a telltale manner
in the respective parts of the table. Thus axiomatization, or more gen-

TABLE 4. SCIENTIFIC BACKGROUND AND CROSS-DISCIPLINARY RELATIONS OF PSYCHOLOGY WITH SPECIFIC EMPHASIS ON GENERAL SYSTEMATIC ISOMORPHISMS AND ON METHODOLOGY.

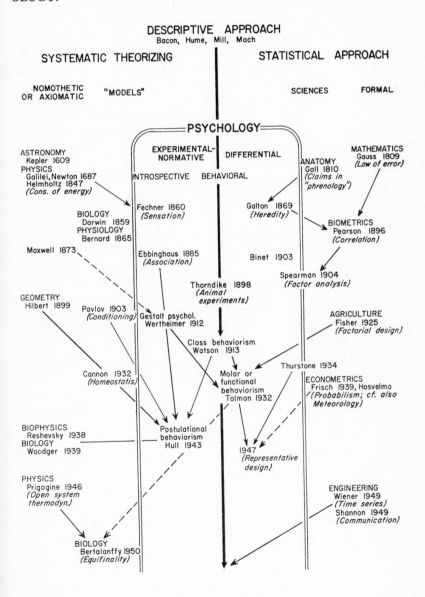

erally what Feigl called higher-order theory (Feigl, 1949), was brought about in physics by Newton; much less impressive attempts in psychology —further preceded and indeed prompted by Hilbert's axiomatization of geometry and by Woodger's efforts toward an axiomatization of biology (as his contribution to the *International Encyclopedia of Unified Science*) —had to wait until the work of Hull and his associates in the 1940's (Hull, 1940, 1943). A perusal of the writings of such nomothetically oriented psychologists as Hull or Lewin reveals that the ostensible classic among physical laws, the law of falling bodies, is invoked as an exemplar with almost monotonous regularity.

The nomothetic ideal is paramount not only in the classical phase of experimental psychology in the nineteenth century and in the recent postulational behaviorism of Hull but also in Gestalt psychology and in the physiological theory of Gestalt referred to earlier in this article. Frequent reference to "dynamics" in a brain "field" suggests analogies to Maxwell's electromagnetic field theory. Warnings pointing out that gravitation also acts in a field, have been sounded against pressing this analogy; a broken, rather than solid, arrow has therefore been used in Table 4. The fact remains, however, that the revolutionary element in Gestalt psychology is the breaking away from elementism and associationism and that the "machinelike" models to which these conceptions can be traced largely originated in classical mechanics. In addition, the coexistence of associationistic and of field-dynamic principles in modern psychological theory in certain ways resembles the duality of gravitation and electromagnetism of which modern physics has so long been tolerant.

The twenty-odd years about the turn of the century were a particularly turbulent phase in the development of psychology—so much so that Karl Bühler has spoken of them as the constructive crisis of psychology (Bühler, 1929). Gestalt psychology and classical behaviorism are but two especially clear-cut of at least four new psychological movements that sprang up in that period.

Another of these new movements is psychoanalysis. It shares with Gestalt psychology the insistence on the finding of regularities of a more complex scope. Freud, who had a distinguished active career in physiology prior to developing his dynamic theory of personality was, as was documented by Siegfried Bernfeld (Bernfeld, 1944), strongly influenced by the physical thinking of his time. He was strongly influenced by Helmholtz's principle of conservation of energy in developing his basic models. As was further demonstrated by Else Frenkel-Brunswik at the joint symposium of the AAAS with the Institute for the Unity of Science in Boston in 1954 (Frenkel-Brunswik, 1954), Freud had a keen sense of the basic requirements of the philosophy of science, popular belief to the contrary notwithstanding.

In Watson's classical behaviorism, we note that its primary concern was the fulfillment of the physicalistic ideal of observational precision. In the American psychology of this period, the desire for fact-finding and the fear of the dangers of speculation temporarily took precedence over the nomothetic aim and led to a form of descriptive empiricism or factualism that had the earmarks of Bacon's "simple enumeration" or of the early antitheoretical positivism of Comte or Mach. In stressing fact more than law, the prime urgency of the "general" was challenged in favor of the "particular," and thus a first inroad was made on the nomothetic ideal of science insofar as it concerns psychology. As I will try to show in the next section, psychology seems to drift toward a course halfway between factualism and nomotheticism—that is, toward probabilism.

Two lines of development issue from classical behaviorism. One is the formalized, nomothetic behaviorism of Hull and his associates at Yale, which I have already mentioned. The other and more radical departure is the "purposive" behaviorism of Edward C. Tolman at the University of California (Tolman, 1932). It is best introduced by first referring to the fourth of the major crisis schools, frequently called American functionalism. Historically, this school precedes, parallels, and is about to outlive classical behaviorism. Under the influence of Darwin and other evolutionists, functionalism is characterized mainly by an emphasis on the readjustive value of behavior in coming to terms with the physical or social environment. An early representative was Thorndike with his problem-solving experiments with animals and his "trial-and-error" principle. In contrast to frequency of repetition, which played such a large part in the nonsense syllable experiments of Ebbinghaus and the "conditioning" experiments of the Russian physiologist, Pavlov, Thorndike stressed the importance of success and reward in learning ("law of effect").

Tolman's purposive behaviorism combines the constructive elements of classical behaviorism with those of functionalism and of Gestalt psychology in a program of animal and human experimentation and theory that is both "objective" and "molar." Its redefinition of purpose is operational, stressing the reaching of common end-stages from a set of differing initial or mediating stages. Thus it is not less or more "teleological" in the objectionable, vitalistic sense than Wiener's and McCulloch's cybernetics.

Convergence with a further type of influence from systematic theorizing in the physical sciences may develop if von Bertalanffy's attempted reduction of biological "equifinality," and thus of purposive behavior to Prigogine's new open-system thermodynamics (von Bertalanffy, 1950) should obtain the approval of physicists and biologists. It is one of the intrinsic limitations of high-complexity disciplines, such as psychology, that final judgment of reductive theory of this kind must remain outside its province. Since the verdict of history is not yet in, I have bracketed these developments in Table 4.

Claude Bernard's and Cannon's ideas on homeostasis have received increased attention in functional psychology, and Ashby has used them in his *Design for a Brain* (1952). Ashby's book is part of a current vogue in brain models which has developed out of the earlier examples I have mentioned in connection with physiological psychology and which has recently received a further impetus from the interest in the engineering problems of complex calculating machines. With a more distinctly nomothetic slant, Rashevsky and his associates at the University of Chicago (1948) have produced biophysical mathematical models that promise to be fruitful up to the level of social psychology and perhaps even in history.

Much of the work just mentioned, notably that on homeostasis and mathematical biophysics, proceeds under the assumption of a widespread isomorphy among outwardly diverse types of processes. Von Bertalanffy has, therefore, suggested the concerted development of a "general systems theory" (*Human Biology,* 1951). Such a theory could achieve a great deal toward the unification of the sciences under the auspices of the nomothetic-reductive approach that is so closely associated with the history of the natural sciences.

DIVERSIFICATION OF PSYCHOLOGY AS A PROBABILISTIC SCIENCE

At this point, we must pause and take a look at the foundations of our discipline. There is nothing in the development of science that will inspire paralyzing awe and induce adolescent dependence as much as will a headway in modes of conceptualization such as the natural sciences have been found to possess in relation to psychology. We must, therefore, be more on guard against the intrusion of policies that are alien to our basic problems. In particular, we must ask ourselves whether the following of the nomothetic lead is an unmixed blessing for psychology.

Let us fall back on the thema of psychology as we have tried to develop it in analyzing the differences between physiology and physiological psychology. We have conjectured that the emphasis on widespanning functional correlations at the expense of attention to the intervening technological detail is one of the major characteristics that distinguishes psychology from its predecessors (diagram C of Table 1). Tolman's molar behaviorism, and parallel developments in the study of perceptual "thing-constancy," can be shown to fall in essentially the same pattern, the fact notwithstanding that the focus in the central region remains hypothetical (Brunswik 1952; Tolman, 1935).

On further analysis, we note that the functional arcs that span toward, and gain their feedback from, the remote, "distal" environment—and these are the really important arcs—become entangled with the exigencies and risks inherent in the environment. So long as the organism does not develop, or fails in a given context to utilize completely, the powers of a fullfledged physicist observer and analyst, his environment remains for all practical purposes a semierratic medium; it is no more than partially controlled and no more than probabilistically predictable. The functional approach in psychology must take cognizance of this basic limitation of the adjustive apparatus; it must link behavior and environment statistically in bivariate or multivariate correlation rather than with the predominant emphasis on strict law, which we have inherited from physics.

It is perhaps more accurate to say that the nomothetic ideology was influenced by a somewhat naïve and outdated high-school-type, thematic cliche of physics, which some of us have tacitly carried with us in the process of developing psychology into a science. As need not be reiterated here, physics itself has become statistical in the meantime. Yet we must not fall for easy analogy; we must make it clear that the statistical mechanics and quantum theory, being of a microscopic character, has little to do with the probabilism of functional psychology. Since the individual case or instance does not lose its identity in psychology, our form of probabilism is macroscopic rather than microscopic and thus of much greater consequence in the actual execution of our discipline.

The use of bivariate correlation statistics is most obviously inevitable in the study of individual differences. In reality, the two have developed in close contact with one another; I have, therefore, grouped them together on the right side of Table 4 rather than placing the statistical approach where it belongs—that is, halfway between the nomothetic and the purely fact-descriptive approach.

As long as correlation statistics were not available, problems of differential psychology were treated with an air of absoluteness that reminds one of the nomothetic approach. One of the most grotesque products of this would-be type of correlational study was the so-called "phrenology" of the anatomist, Gall, who tried to link mental faculties to the shape of the skull on the basis of the most casuistic evidence.

Psychology has from its beginnings been intertwined with statistics and its active development in a variety of ways. Classical psychophysics is closely linked to the study of unidimensional error distribution and thus to Laplace and Gauss, notably in such American psychophysicists as James McKeen Cattell. Bivariate correlation statistics was first introduced by Galton and Pearson and may even be considered to be a direct joint product of biometrics and psychometrics. The factor analysis of Spearman, of Thurstone, and of others is even more a distinctly differential-psychological development. Because of the partly mathematical character of most of these developments, I have placed them somewhere between differential psychology and formal statistics in Table 4. For the first time in this analysis, we witness a give-and-take between psychology and other disciplines (as brought out by the zig-zag course of arrows in the table); we may take this as an added omen of the inherently statistical character of psychology as a whole, briefly deduced in a preceding paragraph.

While statistical correlation and factoring, including the attendant representative sampling of individuals from a population, have traditionally been recognized as necessary in the area of individual differences as they occur in intelligence or personality testing, the possibility of studying the broader functional organism-environment relationships by these statistical methods has long been ignored. In certain essential respects, this even holds true for R. A. Fisher's factorial design and analysis of variance (1935). The variables and their levels of strength are still arbitrarily selected rather than naturally sampled; hence the results are subject to severe limitations of generalizability. By allowing multivariate analysis, however, Fisher's methods are definitely superior to the older univariate designs, especially in the study of problems of higher complexity. It is, therefore, not astonishing that their first transfer from their original domain, agriculture, to psychology (Crutchfield and Tolman, 1940) fell within the framework of Tolman's molar-functional study of behavior; their use has since rapidly expanded over wide areas of experimental psychology.

To obviate the intrinsic shortcomings of the artificial, "systematic" designs of which factorial design is but an elaborate case, I have advocated that in psychological research not only individuals be representatively sampled from well-defined "populations" but also stimulus situations from well-defined natural-cultural "ecologies" (Brunswik, 1947; 1949); only by such "representative design" of experiments can ecological generalizability of functional regularities of behavior and adaptation be ascertained. Representative sampling of situations from the ecology allows us to take cognizance of the occasional major failures that result from the fallibility of perceptual cues or behavioral means while at the same time fully recognizing the favorable cases also. Generalization of the achieved degree of success to the ecology as a whole becomes possible with the use of the routine technical criteria for sampling statistics hitherto confined to differential psychology. Since representative design has so far been used only in a limited set of contexts, it has been bracketed in Table 4.

As was pointed out by Hammond (1951; 1954), certain parallels can be drawn between the situation created in psychology by representative design and the situation created in physics by relativity theory. In both cases, an earlier overgeneralization of classical results obtained within a limited type of universe is corrected. As has been pointed out by Hammond in a different context, factorial design is geared to the manufacturing type of problem situation that prevails in agriculture, while the organically developed natural-cultural range of generalization to which psychology must aspire demands other methods. As in the example from antiquity, which was discussed in the second section, we are faced with a warning against the uncritical transplantation of content-alien themas or instrumental scaffoldings, at least as long as we wish to prize and uphold our indigenous thematic identity above all else.

Perhaps the first to see that psychology was not a "fundamental" discipline in the sense of the standard natural sciences was the Columbia psychologist, Woodworth (1918). Representative design and the resultant probabilistic functionalism are nothing but the consistent projection of such a belief onto the plane of methodology and explicit theorizing. Since the statistical macroprobabilism of representative design would move psychology away from physics and other fundamental natural sciences with their nomothetic thema, considerable resistances must be expected along the way. (A recent symposium in which I defended my views against such advocates of the nomothetic-reductionist point of view in psychology as L. Postman, E. R. Hilgard, D. Krech, and H. Feigl has been published in *Psychol. Rev.,* 1955.)

Our thematic submissiveness to the physical sciences may be more readily overcome if we can show that the proposed reorientation would bring psychology closer to other, perhaps less glamorous but no less urgent or real, natural and social sciences in which macroprobabilism has long been recognized as a legitimate attitude. Prominent among these admittedly and recognizably statistical disciplines are meteorology (for an outline of statistical procedures in meteorology, see H. R. Byers, *General Meteorology,* 1944, pp. 486ff.) and economics insofar as they use autocorrelation and intercorrelation, as theoretically stressed especially by Wiener (1949), for probability prediction. Economics deserves special attention in view of the reinforcement that the statistical conception has received in the Norwegian school of econometrics, notably by Haavelmo (1944). Within still another discipline, communication theory —as cast into mathematical form by Claude Shannon, with psychologically cogent commentary by Warren Weaver (1949)—the study of message transmission through semierratic external media comes very close to the psychological problem of the anticipation of, and adjustment to, a distant world. Communication and psychological functioning also have in common the use of redundancy as a means of overcoming the low predictive probability of single signals of these instrumentalities (Brunswik, 1952, Chapter 2, and Section 23). In probabilistic functionalism this low predictive probability finds its counterpart in the limited "ecological validity" of cues or means, and the place of redundancy is taken by intersubstitutability or "vicarious functioning."

CONCLUSION

The growing strength of behaviorism has long assured that the core of a procedural physicalism and thus of the essential operational aspects of the unity of science are rapidly becoming a matter of course in psychology. The time has come when unity of science is best served by stressing the thematic differentiation among the sciences within the overall unity. In carrying this diversification to its logical conclusion, psychology emerges as a macrostatistical discipline, thus acquiring not only distinct thematic identity but also internal methodological unity. The acceptance of this probabilistic functionalism and of the attendant representative design of research may be facilitated, both inside and outside psychology, by a comparative methodology involving sciences of all shadings. The best way to emancipate psychology from the suggestive power of those nomothetic-reductionist natural sciences in the shadow of which it began its development is to demonstrate its structural affinity with disciplines already recognized as statistical in character.

REFERENCES

Allport, G. W. *Personality.* New York: Holt, 1937.

Ashby, W. R. *Design for a brain.* New York: Wiley, 1952.

Boring, E. G. *History of experimental psychology.* (2nd ed.) New York: Appleton, 1950.

Brunswik, E. *The conceptual frame-*

work of psychology. Chicago: University of Chicago Press, 1952.

Brunswik, E. *Perception and the representative design of experiments.* Berkeley, Calif.: University of California Press, 1956.

Brunswik, Else F. Psychoanalysis and the unity of science. *Proc. Am. Acad. Arts and Sci.,* 1954, No. 80.

Bühler, K. *Die krise der psychologie.* (2nd ed.) Jena, Germany: Gustave Fischer Verlagbuchhandlung, 1929.

Byers, H. R. *General meteorology.* New York: McGraw-Hill, 1944.

Crutchfield, R. S., and E. C. Tolman. Multiple-variable design for experiments involving interaction of behavior. *Psychol. Rev.,* 1940, *47,* 38–42.

Feigl, H. Some remarks on the meaning of scientific explanation. In H. Feigl and W. Sellars (Eds.), *Readings in philosophical analysis.* New York: Appleton, 1949. Pp. 510–514.

Fisher, R. A. *Design of experiments.* Edinburgh: Oliver & Boyd, 1935.

Forke, A. *The world conception of the Chinese.* London: *Probathain,* 1925.

Haavelmo, T. Probability approach in econometrics. *Econometrica,* Suppl., 1944.

Halstead, W. C. *Brain and intelligence.* Chicago: University of Chicago Press, 1947.

Hammond, K. R. Relativity and representativeness. *Phil. Sci.,* 1951, *18,* 208–211.

Hammond, K. R. Representative vs. systematic design in clinical psychology. *Psychol. Bull.,* 1954, *51,* 150–159.

Hull, C. L., *et al. Mathematico-deductive theory of rote learning.* New Haven, Conn.: Yale University Press, 1940.

Hull, C. L. *Principles of behavior.* New York: D. Appleton-Century Company, Inc., 1943.

Kohler, W. *Gestalt psychology.* New York: Liveright, 1947.

Lashley, K. S. *Brain mechanisms and intelligence.* Chicago: University of Chicago Press, 1929.

Leake, C. D. Personal communication.

Lewin, K. *Dynamic theory of personality.* New York: McGraw-Hill, 1935.

Rashevsky, N. *Mathematical biophysics.* Chicago: University of Chicago Press, 1948.

Scheerer, M. Cognitive theory. In G. Lindzey (Ed.), *Handbook of social psychology.* Vol. 1. New York: Addison-Wesley, 1954.

Shannon, C .E., and W. Weaver. *Mathematical theory of communication.* Urbana, Ill.: University of Illinois Press, 1949.

Symposium on the probability approach in psychology. *Psychol. Rev.,* 1955, *62,* 193–242.

Tolman, E. C. *Purposive behavior in animals and men.* New York: Century, 1932.

Tolman, E. C., and E. Brunswik. The organism and the causal texture of the environment. *Psychol. Rev.,* 1935, *42,* 43–77.

Von Bertalanffy, L., *et al.* General systems theory. *Human Biology,* 1951, *23,* 302.

Wiener, N. *Extrapolation, interpolation, and smoothing of stationary time series.* New York: Wiley, 1949.

Woodworth, R. S. *Dynamic psychology.* New York: Columbia University Press, 1918.

18

Samples of Egon Brunswik's Early Conceptualizations

Translated by

LEWIS W. BRANDT

TRANSLATOR'S NOTE

Brunswik greatly exploits the highly synthetic character of the German language by constantly creating his own combined forms. He thereby follows a tradition in which Nietzsche was perhaps the greatest poetic expert. Furthermore, Brunswik practices stylistic conciseness by bringing large numbers of thoughts into one and the same sentence. English is a much more analytic language than German, however; therefore, both words and sentences from the original must often be broken up in the English translation.

I have tried to restrict my footnotes to a minimum. Wherever I consider an explanation for the English reader unavoidable, the footnote is followed by my initials in order to distinguish it from footnotes in the German text.

It should be noted that the word "correlation" as it appears in this translation does not refer to a mathematical correlation (except in the one instance where this is spelled out). It is used in connection with the central problem with which Brunswik deals in his book, namely the tieing, linking, or coupling together of an object with what I have translated as the "immediate percept" (which is closer to Brunswik's German term than either "percepts" or "sense data" would be). Also, in the translation "psychology in terms of objects" as used by Brunswik in his English works stands for the more exact "psychology from the point of view of the object."

We wish to express our gratitude to Deuticke for permission to reprint pages 95–105, 222–225, and 231–234 from E. Brunswik's *Wahrnehmung und Gegenstandswelt*. Vienna: 1934.

New York City, July 1962   Lewis W. Brandt

MULTIPLE MEDIATION OF OBJECTS IN PERCEPTION

Bühler's Duplicity Principle as a
Basic Conceptual Model for the
Realization of the Constancy of Things

This section deals mainly with *questions of explanation,* particularly with the problem concerning the functional possibilities that may produce the constancy of things. How does perception reach bodily objects and how does it correctly (or approximately) recognize their properties?

From the beginning, we could characterize the examples from size and color perception, which we mainly used for our reasoning up to this point, in about the following way: If we select the "circumstances" under which bodies are observed—in our examples, the distance or the illumination—in different ways, then the stimulus effects that issue from them and hit our sense organ are not unequivocally linked to the physical properties of the bodies themselves. To the contrary, the extension of the projection of the body upon the retina varies with the distance and its intensity with the intensity of the illumination.

In a situation in which bodies of different distance or illumination are to be compared as to their size and color, in the main, two following alternatives result: one either intends to compare the stimulus effects as to their properties, or one intends to compare the bodies themselves. The first alternative does not require any complicated adjustment of the apparatus of perception; we said, in this respect, that intentionally the projective values are easily attainable. The second alternative, however, requires that the difference in circumstances be "accounted for," and therefore it requires a specific performance of the instrument of perception. As a rule, properties of bodies are thus attained with greater difficulty than their projected values.[1]

We reason here as follows: immediate percepts as far as they derive at all from influences of the environment, can, in the final analysis, lean only upon those offshoots of the events in the environment that impinge upon the sense organs, namely upon *stimuli.*

Suppose we had reached by means of perception the properties of bodies without error. This would mean that there are immediate percepts

1. In order to avoid any misunderstandings we repeat that "easy" and "difficult" in this context do not express the subjectively experienced degree of difficulty in perceiving but indicate the objective requirements made of the instrument of perception.

or reactions that are unequivocally correlated with them. For example, the verbal response "6 cm" would be given by a subject again and again when, but only when, the viewed body actually has a length of 6 cm; and, above all, this must be so, independent of the distance of the body.

The difficulty now lies in the fact that we do not find any single stimulus that satisfies this unequivocal correlation between the subject-link and the object-link. For, the only immediate influences of the body (that is, the object) upon the organism, namely the projections on the retina, always change with the distance.

We find a way out only by looking no longer for individual stimuli but for stimulus *complexes* whose internal relations follow this correlation.[2]

Such a complex requires, however, *at least a second stimulus factor besides the projection of the body itself.* Evidently, such a stimulus factor is ideally usable by us only when it is *unequivocally correlated with the respective circumstance* (distance, illumination). As indicated above, the properties of bodies can be described as functions of their direct projective influences and the circumstances.

Let us assume there exists a stimulus that is unequivocally correlated with distance or illumination. Such a stimulus would, together with the "direct" (as Kardos uses the term), that is, projective stimulus influences coming from the bodies, constitute a stimulus basis that, *in its internal relations,* in other words, as a whole, was unequivocally correlated with the body properties on the one hand, and with the corresponding subject links on the other.

Body size is always given by the *product e' tan ϕ.* In other instances, concerning albedo, for example, the *quotient* from the two stimuli values mediates the correlation of subject link and object link by being itself correlated with both. (Albedo is actually defined by the quotient from two intensities of radiation.) In every similar case, some *mathematical function* of the two stimuli plays this role of mediator. Later on, we shall refer to various other functions of this kind in our examples.

Again, the question of whether stimuli that are unequivocally correlated with such circumstances as distance, illumination, and so forth, really exist may be set aside. We are interested only in the fact that they

2. Kardos, whose ideas are close to ours in this context, raises the problem "how the unequivocal correlation of two manifolds can be realized *through a less dimensional manifoldness of stimuli."* The difficulty could be overcome, if *"different pairs of influences* originating from reflected and from incident rays of light always corresponded to different degrees of albedo."

(or stimuli complexes) ought to exist, if it be possible for us to intentionally attain properties of bodies *totally* (which implies always). We also disregard here whether such stimuli, if they exist, are truly used by the instrument of perception completely or incompletely, in the sense of seeing things as constant, as well as the question of the form in which this utilization operates.

The twofoldedness of the stimulus basis for the perception of properties of bodies, a perception which is independent of circumstances as described by us, is thus a logical requirement that may be propounded independent of any experience relative to the realization of the constancy of things. Karl Bühler expressed this in his *general duplicity principle*,[3] which must be applied also in many instances of (approximate) constancy of phenomenal motives of things. That is, variant immediate percepts can also correspond to invariant properties of bodies [4] only if both the direct indices of projection and the indices of circumstances are at our disposal in the form of peripheral stimuli. We see the significance of the duplicity principle in the emphasis placed on twofoldedness of the stimulus basis required for perception of body color, that is, on the paired structure as such. Even more significant is the fact that the special *sign* character *of each one* of these two stimuli is given its rightful place, and the list of all factors that may at all be considered to take over this sign function is immediately constructed for all phenomenal areas.

Properties of radiation processes may confront the organism as immediate percepts through a single stimulus. (At least in vision) properties of bodies require always at least two and generally more stimuli to become immediate percepts. This fact may also be expressed as follows: For properties of radiation processes the mediation is simple, while for properties of bodies it is complex. In this context, by mediation we mean those processes that are causally located between object link and subject link.

Multiple mediation has the following characteristics: If we follow the mediating causal processes individually from their origin, they first

3. K. Bühler, Erscheinungsweisen, p. 141: "The twofoldedness of the effect as such . . . is the main point here." *viz.* L. Kardos, Die "Konstanz" phänomenaler Dingmomente, *Beitr. z. Problemgeschichte* d. Psychol. (Bühler-Festschrift). Jena, 1929 and E. Brunswik and L. Kardos, Duplizitätsprinzip. Bühler's duplicity principle may be distinguished from von Kries' duplicity theory (function of rods and cones in the retina) and also from the possibilities which Bühler himself considered in his above mentioned book as special elaborations.

4. E. R. Jaensch emphasizes particularly the concept of invariance. (Zur Grundlegung der Wertlehre als Wirklichkeitswissenschaft, *Arch. f.d. ges. Psychol., 77,* 1930.)

"evaporate"; that is, they in no way indicate that later on an event (the subject-link of the intentional relationship), which is unequivocally correlated with the point of departure (the object-link, the property of the body) will ever happen again. Indeed, if, in this stage, we make a tranverse section through the causal chains which issue from the body, or even from its illumination, and in which the causal chains exert effects as stimuli, we find, as stated above, no single event that could be unequivocally correlated with the body property. *Therefore, the correlation between the two events occurs through a leaplike bridging of a causal intermediary layer whose individual elements take no part in this correlation.*

Metaphorically speaking, the further mediation process then proceeds within the organism through *recollection, binding together and melting together into a single effect,* so to speak, of those *splintered effects,* including even those which are separated in time.[5]

The form this process takes can be compared with the effect of a condensing lens upon light rays (see Fig. 1). A point *P* emits rays into all directions. Looked at in isolation, each individual ray could originate from any odd point on its backward extension. This means that it is not unequivocally correlated with its place of origin. When two or more of these diverging rays impinge upon a condensing lens, they are bent together in such a way that they meet again in one point. This one point is then unequivocally coordinated with the point of origin of the radiation. It is then and only then in one and the same place, if the origin of the radiation is not moved. Thus, there exists after all an effect that is unequivocally coordinated with the radiating point, while this was not the case for each individual mediating partial process. We ascertained the same facts in principle for multiple intentional mediation.

The example of the lens must, of course, be considered *only to be an analogy.* The analogy exists only insofar as the various stimuli which make the perception of things possible originate in a spatially limited layer and are reunited, as in a focus in an immediate percept (for ex-

5. Bertrand Russell, in a very strange manner, makes the idea of *collecting effects* into a general characteristic of subjectivity (*The analysis of mind.* London: Macmillan, 1925). The selection of effects that appear (in the course of time) at a definite individual place, for example, at the "passive" place of a nervous system, that is, a "biography," instead of collecting the causal emanations from the position of an "active" place, is essential for the "psychic" point of view. We then localize at the latter place a "piece of matter." The place becomes our "object." We believe we do not go too far in assuming that this idea remained incomplete only because the facts of thing constancy were not sufficiently before Russell. Other basic thoughts, too, did not ripen or were lost in the woods for the same reason. Only the special peculiarity of collecting effects creates the characteristic of something psychic. (Regarding Russell see Cassirer, Jahrb. d. Phil., III, 1917, p. 47ff.)

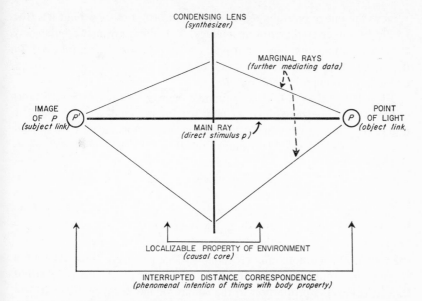

Fig. 1. Schema of sythesizing process through a simple optical system and through the function of perception. (See Fritz Heider, Die Leistung des Wahrnehmungssystems, Z. f. *Psychol., 114,* p. 381, regarding the correlations of systems indicated by the arrows.)

ample, living experience of color) or reaction (judgment about the color), which presents itself clearly as a closed unit. In size or form perception, the effects frequently originate rather clearly from one place, namely from the body itself. The twofoldedness can, then, perhaps, be seen in the simple extension of the projection, on the one hand, and in the values for the cross disparity that occurs due to binocular vision, on the other hand (*viz.* the contributions to our series by Holaday and Eissler). In color constancy, the closer or farther spatial environment, as the case may be, probably participates more than in size constancy in bringing about the second factor, namely the event that mediates the illumination. As mentioned earlier, a large number of "criteria" enter into account here. One can attempt to investigate these factors more closely experimentally and to compare their effectiveness and reliability.

One may assume, however, that the devices that unite these ramifications into a single final effect, are concretely quite different from the workings of a condensing lens. It is true that the eye itself contains a condensing lens, and one could imagine that the distance be unequivocally given as a stimulus condition, for example, through the tension of the lens muscles which, with changes in the distance of the body always refocus the image onto the retina (and not in front of or behind it). This would be rather similar to our analogy. Yet, there are many indications that "accommodation" does not play an important role as a criterion for depth, but that other factors enter that are less closely related to our example from experimental physics.

Even if we assume that accommodation were a fully usable distance criterion, it would explain only how a stimulus comes about which is unequivocally correlated with the circumstance, "distance." It would not explain, however, why this stimulus, together with the one of the projection of the body, causes the size impression to be that of a constant thing. It was exactly this function for which our example of the lens was to give a formal analogy.

In another simpler respect however, the eye lens as such leads to important correlations between extra- and intra-somatic events, for example, to a sharp coordination of points between a fixated area and the retina. Furthermore, any reflecting surface generally illuminates other surfaces in accordance with the law of the spread of effects in space, that is, in inverse proportion to the square of the distance. Thus it does by no means illuminate all surrounding surfaces to the same degree. The eye lens corrects this by letting the effects of surfaces that reflect from further away, fall on a correspondingly smaller part of the retina. The two manifolds of objects *"surface brightness* of a reflecting surface" and *"strength of illumination* of the retina due to the radiation issuing from that reflecting surface" are *strictly correlated* with each other, so strictly that in all our considerations we could take one instead of the other without making a mistake. This is another particularly beautiful example of the ambiguity of the nomenclature of the poles of intention. People are generally much too little aware of how often strictly correlated objects are unnoticeably taken for one another.

We do not know in detail how the instrument of perception exercises its function of collecting and transforming when it brings about a perception of things that is independent of the circumstances. Earlier, we mentioned the analogy with the lever that, according to its length, gives a stimulus of sometimes more and sometimes less *"weight,"* that is, transforms it in accordance with the indications of the circumstances. That too, of course, is only an analogy. Similarly, we must consider it to be an "as if" when we say that the instrument of perception fulfills the *function of an intellectual operation* in accounting for the circumstances. Phenomenally nothing of this is noticeable, and functionally we may assume only a relationship to exist, but not identity in kind.

Fortunately, we need not rack our brains about the *how* of the mediation. It is sufficient that it, in fact, occurs in perception and that we can imagine physical and psychological *models* that operate similarly. Thus we are not tempted to blame mysterious agents for the occurrence of the constancy of things.

In order to point out the ability of the instrument of perception to recollect effects issuing from the situation and to work them into unified immediate percepts about the properties of bodies, we may call it (perception) a "synthesizer". Transforming divergence into convergence, the instrument of perception reflects the diverging causal processes in the manner of a mirror image, as illustrated in this section and earlier in this book. Usually, *only organisms* with their equipment that is specially created for this purpose, or tools made by organisms, are capable of such accomplishments. To intend and to intentionally attain is a privilege of living beings. Perception achieves a *subjective picture* of the environment through somatic processes, *a restitution of the objective equations of bodies that had disappeared in the stimulus layer.* The adjustment to properties of bodies, hence can also be designated as a specific kind of *synthetic adjustment.* In a different way, for example, by splitting undifferentiated "brightness" into whiteness of the thing and phenomenal brightness of illumination, the transformation is at the same time dividing as well. Hence, we may speak also about an organization in the sense of a production of higher order combinations with simultaneous differentiation or, in short, about a synthetic-analytic articulation. (See Brunswik, 11. Kongrebber, p. 54.)

The "cooperation of soul and external object" which the ancients already considered perception, and the "autoactivity of the soul" which Tetens mentioned, are already exhaustively treated by the habitual articulating manner of transformation [6] of the "aiming body organs" as Karl Bühler calls the "sense"-instruments.

---

6. Evidently, in earlier stages of *development,* for example, in more primitive animals, the synthesis for thing constancy is not yet or only partially completed. Beyrl, Klimpfinger and myself have pursued this question in *human* development. Size, form, and color constancy show a corresponding *rhythmic increase* from relatively low values in 2 to 3 year olds (91, 13, and 26 respectively) to optimal performance in 10 to 15 year olds (99, about 50, and about 43 respectively). In educated adults (with the exception of specialists in looking such as hunters and painters) perceptual constancy is again *somewhat lower* than in adolescents or in uneducated people (namely 96, 32–40, and 40). This regress of perception is, however, probably made up for by correcting, critical-discursive agencies which consciously continue the transformation and further improve the total performance. (Holaday could ascertain that through a change from naive perception to an *"attitude of competition"* the quality of size estimation can be improved from 82.3 to 92.7 or with instruction to compare the projection values from 28.5 to 13.3, that is, for both intentional kinds of set by one half of the unachieved remainder.— Holaday, Beverly E., Die Grobenkonstanz der Sehdinge bei Variation der inneren und auberen Wahrnehmungsbedingungen. Arch. f. d. ges. Psychol., *88,* 1933.)

A word concerning the problem of *genetic primacy of unitary apprehension*. It is doubtlessly correct that the "analytical" organization of wholes, which is superimposed upon simple synthesis, advanced further into details on higher rather than on intermediary steps of development. Hence, regress uncovers in the first place only uniform-chaotic-complex-qualitative or possibly even "physiognomic" forms of reaction. In most of the paradigmatic instances, the regress cannot be pushed beyond this intermediary step in the phenomenal sphere; yet, we must assume beyond it and at the very beginning a *presynthetic stage* (see Klimpfinger, Sylvia, Ueber den Einflub von Einstellung und Uebung auf die Gestalkonstanz. Arch. f. d. ges. Psychol., *88, 1933.* Vol. 4 of the Untersuchungen Uber Wahrnehmung edited by Egon Brunswik, p. 592ff) in the sense of Kant's thesis of the synthetic character of the unity of apperception. In the assumed presynthetic stage, excitations due to the juxtaposition of stimuli still exist relatively loosely side by side and reactions of individuals also occur more towards details than in relation to the overall situation. In the genetic study of thing constancy the presynthetic steps that precede the articulated wholeness of the finished world of things become even sometimes explicitly tangible. (Geist, Entw., p. 134.) One need not assume (like Husserl) further special "meaning-giving acts." Intention is, if we transpose a definition by Charlotte Bühler to perception, nothing but the "admission to action according to its kind." Actual spontaneity is limited to putting into action by means of an intentional set one of the prepared kinds of admission and transformation of effects.[7]

Thing constancy, which is brought about by the natural-synthetic set of every day life and which we met already in several forms, has, as one can now see clearly, nothing to do with the so-called "constancy assumption" for which earlier psychologies have often been reproached, and according to which molecularly conceived individual sensations are said to stand in a fixed correlation with individual stimuli. To the contrary, intentional correlation with the stimulus characteristics of the distant body even requires a loosening of the relationship of the immediate percept to the retinal projections of bodies.

Organisms can bring about an unequivocal existential coordination between an extraorganismic and an intraorganismic manifold in which the intermediary causal processes do not partake in terms of their ele-

---

7. Hering has already indicated, from the viewpoint of a causal orientation, that in this way the layer of the thing gets preference in relation to the layer of the stimulus: "Vision is not seeing light rays but seeing the properties of things themselves." (Grundzuge der Lehre vom Lichtsinn, in: Graefe-Samisch, Handbuch der gesamten Augenheilkunde, 12, p. 8.)

ments; that is, they produce between layers of reality correlations that leap across the intermediary layers. We noted this fact in our discussion of the relational properties of the intentional relationship by saying that the intentional coordination is an "interruptable" correlation. It is interruptable in the sense that its single-meaningness [8] is preserved even when the object moves away from immediate causal proximity—in other words, direct stimulability [9] persists following separation, even when the direct causal connection is interrupted and makes room for perception of something at a distance. As long as such an interruption has not been tried out, one cannot decide whether the corresponding object has been intentionally attained to some degree.

The intentional correlation that was earlier recognized as a special case of coexistence from a theoretical viewpoint of relations can like any regular coexistence be used as a sign relationship. The organism creates for itself an internal (intranervous) sign system for the spatio-temporally close, distant and farthest environment. This system stands in a definite way in causal connection with itself. The organism creates this sign system by apprehending aggregates of signs (that is, nothing else but *possible effects* from a distance) [10] and transforms them into sign units for objects that are relevant for survival. In this way, the organism extends its world functionally and phenomenally far beyond the limits set by its skin.

SPATIAL DISTANCE—CAUSAL DISTANCE— "INTENTIONAL DEPTH"

The environment of an organism may be conceived as being in causal layers in relation to the organism itself. All processes, which as stimuli

8. Eindeutigkeit = the property of having a single meaning; this is the noun derived from the adjective translated by "unequivocal." The German adjective means literally "having a single meaning." Since this concept is central in Brunswik's work, I made up the above neologism the meaning of which should be self-evident. (L. W. B.)

9. Reizfähigkeit = the property of being capable of stimulating. (L. W. B.)

10. There has to be at least *one indication* for each *constituent part* of an object (for example, for reflected and direct light for albedo, for projection value and distance for body size, for width, depth and heights for volume of a block and so forth). However, as a rule, the sign itself is combined with vicarious, but not always equally reliable, other indications for the same item into an or-combination.*

* Parallel to the German term Und-Verbindung which means additive combination, enumeration and is best rendered in English by "hyphenation," Brunswik writes here "Oder-Verbindung," which means a grouping of alternatives and corresponds to Piaget's "two-way classificatory systems, expressing quality correspondences" (Piaget, Jean. *Logic and Psychology*. New York: Basic Books, 1957. Introduction by W. Mays on p. xii.). (L.W.B.)

influence the organism, can be causally followed backward. We thus proceed from causally closer layers of what is happening to causally more and more distant ones. Sometimes, but not always, this will imply also a special movement away from the organism.

If, for example, we follow backwards the causal chain of the radiation processes that hit our eyes, we attain as the next important stage "behind" the stimuli, the bodies with their properties, for example, their size or their reflective capacity for light. If we go from there still further causally backwards, we reach the light source, which illuminates the body. Often, the latter is situated closer in space to the organism than the illuminated body, although it is causally farther away. The concept "causal space" is related to functional space, and it is opposed to topologic-geometrical space.

The stimulus is causally closest to the organism. It lies, so to speak, in *causal immediacy* before the latter. The stimulus object is *directly stimulative*.[11] At the same time, it can be attained intentionally particularly "easily," that is, in a straightforward way and without multiple mediation. No intricate device is necessary for the production of subject links that can be unequivocally coordinate with the stimulus object. We want to express these two facts also by saying that in the intentional attainment of the stimuli the "intentional depth" (or "intentional distance") is *small*.[12] The properties of bodies are, however, generally lying one step further away.[13] They are only indirectly stimulative and must be *multi-*

11. i.e. *capable of stimulating without intermediary*. (L. W. B.)

12. Karl Buhler introduced in his *Krise der Psychologie* (Jena, 1929, p. 63) the concept of *depth of perception* to which our concept of intentional depth is closely related. Jacoby's concept of "gnoseologic depth of reach" seems to lie in a similar direction but belongs in an entirely different conceptual frame.

13. This is to be understood as follows: The body property "reflective power" (coefficient of reflection) is, for example, defined as *statement of a condition*. "If one lets light fall upon the body, so-and-so percent of the light is reflected." This statement of condition is valid for a definite *place* in space, namely the surface of the body. We could also say that at the given location lies a definite *causal core* which alters any radiation in a definite manner, forces its characteristic upon the radiation, and thereby becomes the *"object body-color."* The *radiation after reflection* by the surface of the thing is the last stage of the process which is decisive for the stimulus; the *transformation while reflecting* which is characteristic of the properties of the material of bodies, is the penultimate stop; the *radiation before reflection* is the last but two; and the light source, which again may be considered as a causal core, then lies even another step causally farther. Albedo as such is not at all capable of stimulating unless indirectly mediated by radiation. Probably the problem of color constancy is so particularly complicated because of this kind of complete dependence upon causal off-shoots.

We are aware of the fact that this grading is, from the point of view of physics, *fariously mediated as described by the duplicity principle.* Thus, they are by one degree more "difficult", that is, *more intricate* intentionally to attain than stimulus properties. Expressing this more briefly, we say that things belong to an intentionally farther layer of reality [14] than stimuli.

The concept of intentional depth thus refers in the first place to what we designated above as degree of difficulty, or more correctly, to the degree of intricacy brought about by the necessity of synthesizing on a multiple mediation basis. The term "degree of difficulty" is open to misunderstanding. It could easily be understood in the sense of a subjectively experienced difficulty, that is, as a deviation from the habitual (yet not simple) intentional direction. The term intentional depth avoids this disadvantage.

Intentional Depth Does Not Mean the Same as Causal Distance

Causally distant objects may have relatively little intentional depth. For example, illumination is indeed causally farther than the thing but

---

somewhat crude and superficial, but it seems to serve our purposes well. For it indicates which layers of the environment are contacted by those processes which eventually reach us as stimuli and how they can be correspondingly causally *ordered.*

See Heider, Fritz, Ding und Medium, Symposiun I, 1927, where properties of things and mediating processes are confronted with each other; similarly another paper by Heider, Die Leistung des Wahrnehmung systems, *Z. f. Psychol.,* 114, 1930, where the idea of a correspondence between the world of things and the system of perception is also described; Kardos uses the concepts "layer of reality" and "intentional depth."

14. Thouless (Phenomenal Regression to the "real" Object, *Brit. J. Psychol., 21, 22,* 1931/1932) describes the facts of thing constancy as "phenomenal regression to the real object" and also expresses with this terminology the structure in layers that the world has with regard to our perceptual system. We should prefer to replace the attribute "phenomenal" by "functional" in order to indicate that, in proceeding into greater intentional depth, the primary issue is the appearance of a layer of immediate percepts which stands in unequivocal correlation to the respective kind of objects, while it is less important that the immediate percepts themselves take on a different character (for example, a phenomenal character of things). Here, like in the entire German literature on the subject, one still finds the identification of the descriptive and functional viewpoints which Koffka and Frenkel rightfully criticized. In reality, the impression of the thing and thing constancy merely correlate, but do not strictly correspond to each other, according to our more recent findings. Katz and Jaensch emphasized the "intentional Character" of color constancy (and hence also of *thing perception).* Jaensch, E.R., Untersuchungen uber Grundfragen der Akustik und Tonpsychologie, Leipzig, 1929, p. VIII and Katz, D., Der Aufbau Farbwelt, Z. F. Psychol., Erg. -Bd. 7, 2. Aufl., 1930, p. 119.

has less intentional depth because it enters (relatively directly) into the mediation of body properties.[15] The reverse situation happens too; for example, specific gravity is a causally more immediate object but of greater intentional depth than absolute weight. The difference between intentional depth and causal distance will become even clearer later on.[16]

In general, we may say that *of two objects the one which appears in the mediation of the other must always be considered as intentionally closer.* This is evident after what was said above, since for the latter of the two objects the mediation is somewhat more complex and goes through more layers.

Since intentional depth is not identical with causal distance, it is even less so with *spatial distance.* For example, bodies that are at various distances from us are all at the same intentional distance. On the other hand, absolute weight and specific gravity are at the same spatial distance but at different intentional distances. In the same way, we refer to an "intermediate"-object only metaphorically and not literally.[17]

Before concluding this section we would like to touch upon an important question *from the psychology of experience,* which belongs in this context. In case an object of greater intentional depth is intentionally attained, that is, if immediate percepts or reactions are reversibly unequivocally coordinated with it, must there also exist immediate percepts that can be unequivocally coordinated with the mediating objects? In other words, is it necessary that, for example, if size constancy exists, the distance and the projection values be given also in consciousness?

Results from experimental psychology and, to a certain extent, every day life experiences as well, indicate that such is not the case. Projection values in particular show the *tendency not only to enter but also to be submerged in the mediation process.*[18] Among the subjectively most diffi-

15. In the instance of color perception, approximately the following situation arises: Of the two objects which partake in the mediation of albedo "reflected radiation" is causally closer than albedo, and "illumination" is causally farther. The body surface albedo causes the intensity of illumination to become intensity of reflected radiation insofar as the illuminating light hits the respective body. Thus, the body surface albedo enters the radiation process in the middle. Illumination as such then enters the mediation process once more via another route. (see p. 8ff.)

16. This refers to a section which is not included in the present excerpt. (L. W. B.)

17. Brunswik uses the preposition Zwischen "between." This preposition, which can be translated as "intermediate" or in German can be used as a prefix like "under" in English. The confusion between literal and metaphorical meanings would, therefore, in German be more probable than in English. (L. W. B.)

18. The submergence of mediation processes * as functional mediators is a phenomenon that is well known in other contexts. For example, we learn nothing directly about the state and the often very remote arrangement of the muscle

cult tasks to be accomplished is the making conscious even only for an instant, of projection values (more precisely of their relationships). Nor are the circumstantial data always conscious;[19] and even when they are, they do at least not always enter the mediation process as they are given. Especially in the area of shape constancy a *paradoxical relationship* can often be demonstrated between the conscious impression of a rotation and shape constancy—shape constancy despite the impression of a frontal-parallel position and contrariwise the lack of any shape constancy in the face of an impression of rotation (see Eissler, Kurt, Die Gestaltkonstanz bei Variation der Objekte und ihrer Einwirkungsweise auf den Wahrnehmenden, *op. cit.,* p. 528ff. and Klimpfinger, *op. cit.;* in Holaday *op. cit.,* p. 457ff.). Similar observations are reported from the area of size constancy.

The question as to whether intentional depth arises out of the lived-through experience[20] itself belongs also in the realm of qualitative analysis of lived-through experience. No doubt something like a *personally experienced intentional depth exists,* that is, momentary consciousness of being related to this or that object layer. But this knowledge[21] may, of course, deceive us just as we can be mistaken concerning intended or intentionally attained objects in general; the former instance is perhaps a little less blatant, because it concerns merely *general phenomenal levels of objectivity* of impressions and not special kinds of objects within a specific object layer. Holaday could, for example, ascertain a correlation between bodily impression *of things* and high size constancy on the one hand and not-thing-like *figural* impression

---

groups which implement the movement of our limbs, but we experience only the effect as such. Similarly, we know usually (perpendicular vision!) nothing about the position of the stimulated points on the retina without indirect observation or instruction, and so forth. Generally speaking, there exists a tendency to neglect intentional circumstances of approachability in relation to *organ states* of one's own body whenever they are as such inconsequential and are mere intermediary stages for the process of acquiring knowledge.

* The older expression for "submerging in the mediation process" is something like: "to remain unconscious and yet to manifest itself." The prefix Brunswik uses here means "passing through." These are thus stages through which the process of acquiring knowledge merely passes. (L. W. B.)

19. Regarding the progressive disappearance of originally mediating content of consciousness see for example, B. B. Erdmann, *Reproduktionspsychologie,* 1920.

20. Erlebnis is interchangeably translated as "lived through experience" and "personal experience." Erfahrung appears only at the beginning of the preceding paragraph and is there translated by "results . . . and . . . experiences." (L.W.B.)

21. Brunswik uses here Bewubtsein in the sense of "knowledge" while he usually uses it in the sense of "consciousness." (L. W. B.)

and projective vision on the other (*op. cit.,* p. 457). But it was after all only a mathematical correlation and not strict correlation of the *impression* of things with a functional attainment of the corresponding object level. (See also Eissler *op. cit.,* p. 541ff.)

MULTI-POLAR INTENTION SYSTEM

Perception Versus Inductive-Deductive Procedures

In connection with the discussion of the efficiency of social perception, it may be worthwhile to compare once more the advantages of perception, on the one hand, with a measuring-constructive "inductive procedure" (Bühler), that is, of thinking, on the other. Which one of the two functions attains its object more completely and more frequently?

In the first place, thinking has an inestimable advantage over perception: it is not "trained," but immediately adaptable to all circumstances; it is not diffuse, but analytical. Hence, it alone is fit for the transformation of results of measurements into the only reliably objective knowledge. However, to this end, the cumbersome procedure of measuring is required, combined with positional changes of the person acquiring the knowledge of the thing; instruments and previous determinations concerning the causal connections (in mediate measuring) are also necessary. In brief, this procedure for obtaining the empirical source is unwieldy.

Provided the empirical material (the totality of available stimuli) is to be kept the same for both functions (that is, one must remain in one single place), which function is then more efficacious?

Two cases can be distinguished. In the first one, the basis for mediation is not highly manifold and complex, as, for example, it is in the observation of things. Here, the more ensuring, more critical, more circumspect, and slower proceeding of deductive reasoning is superior to a precipitate and blindly-mechanically functioning perception. Thus, according to the experiments by Holaday, for example, thinking by means of reasoning and general knowledge may notice that the distance was underestimated, and it can correct the impression of the apparent size in the direction of a better intentional attainment of the intended object. To be sure, in the example given, a correction is made only of an already existing result of perception. Yet, the mere fact that such a correction is correct most of the time indicates the superiority of thinking in this instance.

The situation is different in the second case. Here the basis for mediation is *very extensive, many-shaded, and very ramified in time and space*. This is the case, for example, in the perception of the attitudes of other people. Here, thinking is decidedly at a disadvantage: its resources of utilized criteria are too limited and the range up to which a synthesis (a "combined view" of data to be used for mediation) can grow is too narrow. Thinking preserves the ponderance of transformation proper for the procedure of measuring and for similar empirical methods of collecting data. One might say it preserves a bureaucratic trait in so far as every single datum must first be nicely registered by itself and can only then be forwarded, whereas perception does not insist upon making the mediation conscious.

Above all, the wide range and the correspondingly wide ramification and subtlety of the basis for mediation seem to be the factors that make the ingenious intuitiveness of perception possible, and due to which perception frequently surpasses discursive thinking by far in such complex areas as the knowledge of people. Perception takes into account much that thinking is too ponderous to be able to incorporate into the mediation. In many cases, perception will not correct such omissions— as it does in the perception of things—but it will only make matters worse (for example, by artificially overemphasizing some criteria).

Perception must be considered more *primitive* than thinking even though it is more efficacious in difficult areas that are not yet accessible to thinking and even though thinking is the younger of the two from the point of view of genetic epistemology. For perception operates with less adequate means than thinking does; namely, with unreliable indications, which can be gained from a distance, from a single location, and without entering into the structural details of things. It accepts these indications unreflectively and in a fixed uniformity for what is indicated. It does so much as if it had been trained by strict drill.[22] At best, it lets these indications be displaced by others in blind competition. Thus, despite its greater "genius," it is the less intelligent function of the two, the one which can be more easily deceived than thinking, which is more cautious and which, instead, rather saves itself perplexity and uncertainty.

However, when thinking is rash, it may be subject to gross errors too, and perhaps frequently even to more gross ones than is perception. The term "partial effectiveness" of part of a task, which *Selz*[23] introduced to

22. The German word here translated as "trained" is the word used in connection with the training of animals in the circus. (L. W. B.)

23. Selz, O., *Zur Psychologie des produktiven Denkens und des Irrtums*. Bonn, 1922.

designate the mistakes (errors) that appear in the solutions of logical problems, also seems to fit our situation: in the process of solving problems through thinking, frequently only part of the usable basis for mediation becomes effective, and this may lead to gross distortions.

Perception and thinking both serve the same task of the organism: to know its environment. Both operate with basically the same means as we demonstrated. They are analogous functions, but perception must be considered to be the more primitive of the two. *As to their functions, both present a process using circumstantial evidence.* This process becomes *explicitly conscious in thinking,* but in *perception* is largely *stereotyped* once and for all and *submerged in mediation.*

Usually perception is intellectualized in an explanatory fashion—that is, in order to understand perception, something is borrowed from thinking. This procedure is phenomenologically incorrect but functionally at least partially correct. But it is not only possible to find in perception qualities that one considered to belong to thinking; almost the reverse is also possible, namely to find qualities of perception where one saw thinking: *thoughts* [24] that enter consciousness spontaneously may perhaps more justifiably be considered to be the content of perception rather than of thought; obviousness, too, is a living experience whose origin must be looked for in perception.

Similarly, some theoreticians consider the psychoanalytic solution of a complex, through making it conscious, as a regrouping or a new perception. The yet unsolved inner situation is the result of some definite stupidity of character that may be compared to the diffuse-uncritical blindness of perception, as when confusion, displacement, and substitution mechanisms, as well as inappropriate motives, creep in, and these impurities "remain unconscious," that is, submerged in their role as mediators.

Thus, looking more closely, we see that the lines between thinking and perception become vague and entangled, as happens so often in the analysis of neighboring areas. At the same time, the phenomenological difference between "perceptible" (anschaulich) and "imperceptible" (unanschaulich) loses its sharpness. The question may remain unanswered as to whether social perceptions and those of mental constructs should be called perceptible-like perceptions of things. One will not do so,

24. "Einfälle," which Brill mistranslated in Freud as "free associations," are thoughts that occur to a person spontaneously without relationship to anything going on in consciousness prior to their occurrence. See Brandt, Lewis W., Some Notes on English Freudian Terminology, *J. Amer. Psychoanalytic Assn.* 1961, *9,* 331–339. (L. W. B.)

if one has become accustomed—as is frequently the case—to understanding as perceptible experiences those which can be described in the terminology of the perception of things. On the other hand, one will do so if one makes one's decision concerning the perceptive-imperceptive primarily on the basis of the general uniformity and immediacy, the clarity and qualitative demonstrability of lived-through experiences.

CONCLUSION: EXTENSION OF OBJECT-PSYCHOLOGY TO THE ENTIRE FIELD OF PSYCHOLOGY

Our considerations were developed mainly by means of examples drawn from the area of perception. However, we had already stated in the introduction that the facts from other areas of Psychology could be dealt with basically in the same manner. During the course of our investigation, we were repeatedly confronted with relationships and connections with other areas. The question as to whether external situations could arouse identical impressions or identical reactions (actions) seemed of secondary importance. A clear-cut line between perception and action could not be drawn. Thus, a bridge to the psychology of will was built. In this connection, the question may be asked as to whether or not we reached the goals that we set for ourselves. We now move from the phenomenal area of cognitive, responsive intentionality to the one of pragmatic intention. The latter can be treated in an analogous way, since it is here that the concept of something intentionally attained or accessible finally regains its original meaning. The only thing of importance is to discover in the present, the past, or the future those objective situations that are unambiguously linked to a specific action or reaction (in the widest sense of that word, that is, a subject-term [25]) irrespective of whether those objective situations exist independently or are brought about by ourselves.

Looking at the protocols of investigations from the psychology of thought, it often seems that this area, more than any other, is obligated to pursue a psychology in terms of objects. The description of the experience, a description that in itself is already extremely difficult and frequently not easily understandable intersubjectively, often consists of nothing but the naming of the intended object: a "knowledge about" this or that seems to be given, which often confronts any attempt toward

---

25. "Subjektsglied" is the most general term for the reaction in an organism as opposed to the "Gegenglied," the most general term for what happens in the environment of the organism. (L. W. B.)

a presentation in the usual terminology of the psychology of experience with an invincible resistance and which can be resolved only through recourse to the object.[26] The question arises whether the entire series of various phenomenal "representatives" of the objects of thought which appear in the protocols, for example, of concepts and other formations in the realm of ideas, leads to the same consequences as the abstract definition of the respective object; or whether here, too, those strange, diffuse phenomenal mixtures appear between the object and communication (of the respective representation), which we recognized as a characteristic of perception. Thinking, too, is probably to a large extent contaminated, adheres to exemplifications, and so forth, and is directed by them. Obviously the attempt to solve these problems would lead us deeply into questions about the nature of the objects of thought in general and of their relationship to their representation. Because of the difficulties and stagnation in which the experientially oriented psychology of thinking finds itself, we emphasize the advantages inherent in treating the thought process from the point of view of the kinds of objects that are intentionally attained or made attainable through its contents. In the course of our investigations this, too, shall be attempted through the experimental determination of the usage of the defined terms.[27] An important, but also particularly difficult question that is closely related to those just touched upon, concerns the objects that are intentionally attained through ideas.

Finally, what are the possibilities regarding a psychology of emotions in terms of objects? Emotions are characterized as lived-through experiences of the position taken. Their intended object is, in the sense of this definition, the useful and the noxious as such, wherever, howsoever, and

---

26. v. Bühler, Gedanken.-v. also E. Husserl, Epilogue to my "Ideen zu einer reinen Phänomenologie," Jahrb. f. Philos. u. phänomenolog. Forsch. *11*, 1930, p. 567.-The "separability" (in terms of lived-through experience) of the immanent," "intentional" object from the content seldom exists even in the realm of the facts of perception; therefore, "imageless" thought is perhaps nothing else and not "more" than the "immanently conscious" object of thinking. Hence, the "recourse to the object" is not yet "psychology in terms of objects" but the only adequate description of the contents of introspection. As far as it concerns itself with thinking, a "psychology in terms of objects" directs itself at the necessarily mediate determination of the intentionally attained object. These objects whose attainment is intended in each act of thought are considered by us to be something entirely different from the actual experience of thinking. Yet we do not disregard their "ideality" (formality). Thus, our hunch concerning the identity of imageless thought and immanent objects of thinking has nothing to do with psychologism.

27. The material errors of discursive-conceptual thinking ought to be treated as analogous to the investigations of perception. They must be considered as approaching the best, and seldom attained, moments of critical thinking.

to whatever they may be found to be linked. These emotions then, are again properties of things—they should better be called possible effects [28] —which also must always be related to the momentary or the general need of the individual. Thus any position taken must in itself contain as output a cognition that concerns the relationship of the utility of a fact to the organism as a whole.[29] Hence, emotions too are intentional and may or may not attain their object. We know that they frequently mislead us regarding the usefulness or noxiousness of a particular event. It thus becomes evident that a psychology of emotions in terms of objects would also be worthwhile.

We are of the opinion that *all areas of psychology may be studied from the points of view and by the methods of investigation of a "psychology in terms of objects."* We also believe that a turn towards this exact-objectivistic direction of psychology would offer many advantages and bring the solution of many problems closer to us. All these efforts would have the following in common: In order to describe all forms of behavior of the organism in all their expressions, those objects or situations must be studied that are intentionally attained through these forms, that is, which are unambiguously linked to them in the manner characteristic of the intentional relationship.

In the area of perception, it might have been possible to avoid the introduction of a new terminology by the usage of such common expressions as "correctly estimated," "illusion brought about by extraneous factors," and so forth. We had, however, two reasons for redefining the concept of intentionality by means of an objective-type term and for making it into the central term of a system of terminology. First, we believe that the importance of the life-preserving function of the organism can be most effectively presented in this manner for the perceptual system too, irrespective of the conceptual unity of the presentation. Second, only

28. Helmholtz stated in his Reden und Vortrage (Braunschweig 1896, p. 321) That "every property or quality of an object is in reality nothing but the capability of exercising an effect."

29. The emphasis on the cognitive aspect of emotions shows the merits of F. Krueger's theory of emotions (Das Wesen der Gefühle, 3rd ed., Leipzig 1930) which, following Cornelius, considers emotions as nothing but qualities of complexes of the total experience of the moment in opposition to the objectively experienced contents of knowledge which are mere extrapolations. Brentano has claimed that emotions have intentionality and contain an evaluation. Meinong even introduces special objects—"Dignitative"—which emotions are said to grasp (Emot. Präs. §11). The frequent objections to an intentionality of emotions are explainable by the correct observation that at least the so-called sensational emotions do not consciously "mean" anything and thus have no "immanent" object. However, our objectivised approach of Intentionality remains unchanged by this fact.

through this emphasis on what is important is it possible to create a sufficiently unified terminology for the entire prospective field of inquiry of a "psychology in terms of objects." Hence, we did not use the less ambiguous but more epistemologically involved word "gnoseologic" instead of "intentional."

In our opinion, the essential characteristic of any intentionality approach is its *twofoldness*. By this, we mean the continuously executed evaluation of what is factual by means of what is "correct;" in other words, the projection of the output onto the ideal output in terms of the object. We believe that, heretofore, psychology has dealt with its phenomena too much in themselves and for themselves, too much as "immanent." It is true that, at all times and within the broadest framework, "correct" and illusory perceptions, knowledge and error, correctly directed and unsuccessful action, and successful and unsuccessful works were distinguished from each other and kept apart on the basis of their characteristics. Yet, the structure of the phenomenon, of the fact as such, occupied the center of interest. Nor did psychology lack an *internal* structure: attempts were made to draw conclusions from behavior and activity to lived-through experience and vice versa. However, we are not referring to this kind of manifold organization, since what it unites still belongs as a whole in the area of "subject-terms." If psychology, as a whole, and in its general conceptual development, does not take further steps beyond this overall area, it will remain monistic in its basic conceptualization, and will remain an *open system* which makes impossible an understanding of the essentially intentional, twofold-meaning structure of psychic events.

Brentano and *Husserl* have used an intentionality approach, but they did not quite reach objective reality. The attempt remained fettered to "egology" and thus had to collapse without bearing fruit.

A "psychology in terms of objects" intends to shift the emphasis from the side of the subject to that of the object. For this psychology, the object world is the pillar on which psychology must concretely rest. The relationship of the subject to the world—a relationship which philosophers and psychologists have always seen and considered to be essential —shall here be moved into the center, and a quantitatively implemented system of psychology shall be erected upon it.

Appendix

Zur entwicklung der albedowahrnehmung (Concerning the development of albedo perception). *Zschr. f. Psychol.*, 1928, **109**, 40–115.

(und L. Kardos.) Das duplizitatsprinzip in der theorie der farbenwahrnehmung (The duplicity principle in the theory of color perception). *Zschr. f. Psychol.*, 1929, **111**, 307–320.

(und H. Kindermann.) Eidetik bei taubstummen jugendlichen (Eidetics in deaf-mute juveniles). *Zschr. f. angew. Psychol.*, 1929, **34**, 244–274.

Prinzipienfragen der Gestalttheorie (Systematic questions of Gestalt theory). In E. Brunswik, C. Buhler, H. Hetzer, *et al.* (Eds.), *Beitrage zur problemgeschichte der psychologie: festschrift zu Karl Buhler's 50 geburtstag.* Jena: Fischer, 1929. Pp. V + 258.

Uber farben-grossen und Gestaltkonstanz in der jugend (On the constancy of color, size, and Gestalt in youth). In H. Volkelt (Ed.), *Bericht uber den XI kongress fur experimentelle psychologie.* Jena: Fischer, 1930. Pp. 52–56.

Experimente uber kritik: ein beitrag zur entwicklungs-psychologie des Denkens (Experiments on criticism: a contribution to the developmental psychology of thinking). In G. Kafka (Ed.), *Bericht uber den XII kongress der Deutschen gesellschaft fur psychologie.* Jena: Fischer, 1932. Pp. 300–305.

(mit L. Goldscheider, und E. Pilek.) Untersuchungen zur entwicklung des gedachtnisses bei knaben und madched vom 6–18 jahren (Investigation in the development of memory with boys and girls aged 6–18 years). *Zschr. f. angew. Psychol. Beiheft 64*, 1932, VIII + 158.

Die zuganglichkeit von gegenstanden fur die wahrnehmung und deren quantitative bestimmung (The accessibility of objects for perception and their quantitative determination) in Untersuchungen uber wahrnehmungs gegenstande (Studies concerning the objects of perception). *Arch. f. die ges. Psychol.*, 1932, **88**, 377–418.

Flacheninhalt und volumen als gegenstanden der wahrnehmung (Surface dimension and volume as objects of perception). In *Bericht uber den XIII kongress der Deutschen gesellschaft fur psychologie.* Jena: Fischer, 1934. Pp. 120–123.

Wahrnehmung und gegenstandswelt: grundlegung einer psychologie vom gegenstand her (Perception and the world of objects: the foundations of a psychology in terms of objects). Leipzig und Wien: Deuticke, 1934.

Experimentelle psychologie in demonstrationen (Experimental psychology in demonstrations). Vienna: Springer, 1935.

Tolman, E., The organism and the causal texture of the environment. *Psychol. Rev.*, 1935, **42**, 43–77.

Prufung und ubung hoherer wahrnehmungsleistungen (dingkonstanz) (The verification and use of higher achievements of perception—thing constancy). Prague: *C. R. 8 Conf.*

int. Psychotech., 1935, 684–689.

Psychologie als objektive beziehungswissenschaft (Psychology as an objective science of relations). *Actualites Sci.*, 1935, **389**, 7.

Psychologie vom gegenstand her (und) discussion (Psychology in terms of objects [and] discussion). In *VIII*ᵉ *congres international de philosophie a Prague*. Prague: Orbis, 1936.

Psychology in terms of objects. In H. W. Hill (Ed.), *Proceedings of the 25th Anniversary Celebration of the Inauguration of Graduate Studies*. University of Southern California, 1936. Pp. 122–126.

and R. Cruikshank. Perceptual size-constancy in early infancy. *Psychol. Bull.*, 1937, **34**, 713–714.

und L. Reiter. Eindruckscharaktere schematisierter gesichter (Impression-characteristics of schematized faces). *Zschr. fur Psychol.*, 1938, **142**, 67–134.

Die eingliederung der psychologie in die exakten wissenschaften (The position of psychology within the exact sciences). *Einheitswissenschaft*, 1938, **6**, 17–34.

Das induktionsprinzip in der wahrnehmung (The principle of induction in perception). In H. Pieron, I. Meyerson (Eds.), *XI*ᵉ *congres international de psychologie*. Paris: Alcan, 1938.

Psychology as a science of objective relations. *Phil. of Sci.*, 1938, **4**, 227–260.

The conceptual focus of some psychological systems. *Journal of Unified Science (Erkenntnis)*, 1939, **8**, 36–49. Also in M. H. Marx (Ed.), *Theories in contemporary psychology*. New York: Macmillan, 1936. Pp. 226–237. (Paper sent in for the Fourth International Congress for the Unity of Science, Cambridge, England, 1938.)

Perceptual characteristics of schematized human figures. *Psychol. Bull.*, 1939, **36**, 553.

Probability as a determiner of rat behavior. *J. exp. Psychol.*, 1939, **25**, 175–197.

A random sample of estimated sizes and their relation to corresponding size measurements. *Psychol. Bull.*, 1940, **37**, 585–586.

Thing constancy as measured by correlation coefficients. *Psychol. Rev.*, 1940, **47**, 69–78.

Perceptual size constancy in life situations. *Psychol. Bull.*, 1941, **38**, 611–612.

Organismic achievement and environmental probability. *Psychol. Rev.*, 1943, **50**, 255–272. (Part of "Symposium on Psychology and Scientific Method," held in 1941. Other speakers were C. Hull and K. Lewin. Reported as "The Probability Point of View" in M. H. Marx (Ed.), *Psychological theory*. New York: Macmillan, 1951. Pp. 188–202.

Distal focussing of perception: size-constancy in a representative sample of situations. *Psychol. Monogr.*, 1944, Whole No. 254.

Social perception of traits from photographs. *Psychol. Bull.*, 1945, **42**, 535–536.

Four types of experiment. *Amer. Psychologist*, 1946, **1**, 457.

Points of view. In P. L. Harriman (Ed.), *Encyclopedia of Psychology*. New York: Philosophical Library, Inc., 1946. Pp. 523–537.

Systematic and representative design of psychological experiments: with results in physical and social perception. Berkeley: University of California Press, 1947. Pp. VI + 60. (Published also in J. Neyman [Ed.], *Proceedings of the Berkeley symposium on mathematical statistics and probability*. Held at the

Statistical Laboratory, Department of Mathematics, University of California, August 13–18, 1945, and Jan. 27–29, 1946. Berkeley: University of California Press, 1949. See 1956.)

Statistical separation of perception, thinking and attitudes. *Amer. Psychologist*, 1948, **3**, 342.

Discussion: remarks on functionalism in perception. *J. Personality*, 1949, **18**, 56–65. (A contribution to a "Symposium on Personal and Social Factors in Perception" at the Denver meeting of the American Psychological Association. Also in J. S. Bruner, and D. Krech (Eds.), *Perception and personality: a symposium*. Durham, N. C.: Duke University Press, 1950. Pp. 56–65.)

Note on Hammond's analogy between "relativity and representativeness." *Phil. Sci.*, 1951, **18**, 212–217.

and H. Herma. Probability learning of perceptual cues in the establishment of a weight illusion. *J. exp. Psychol.*, 1951, **41**, 281–290.

The conceptual framework of psychology. In *International Encyclopedia of Unified Science*. Vol. 1, No. 10. Chicago: University of Chicago Press, 1952. Pp. IV + 102. (Pre-publication announced as *Methodological Foundations of Psychology* and earlier as E. Brunswik and A. Ness, *Theory of Behavior*).

and J. Kamiya. Ecological cue-validity of "proximity" and other Gestalt factors. *Amer. J. Psychol.*, 1953, **66**, 20–32.

"Ratiomorphic" models of perception and thinking. In N. Maillouw (Ed.), *Proc. 14th Internat. Congress psychol. Montreal, 1954*. Amsterdam: North Holland Pub. Co., 1955. (Published also in *Acta Psychologia*, 1955, **11**, 108–109.)

Representative design and probabilistic theory in a functional psychology. *Psychol. Rev.*, 1955, **62**, 193–217. (a)

In defense of probabilistic functionalism: a reply. *Psychol. Rev.*, 1955, **62**, 236–242. (b)

(1955 (a) and (b) are adapted from contributions to the first part of a "Symposium on the Probability Approach in Psychology" held under the chairmanship of Edward C. Tolman, at the Berkeley Conference for the Unity of Science, University of California, July 1953. Other speakers were L. Postman, E. R. Hilgard, D. Krech, H. Feigl.)

Historical and thematic relations of psychology to other sciences. *Sci. Mon.*, 1956, **83**, 151–161.

Perception and the representative design of psychological experiments. (2d ed.) Berkeley and Los Angeles: University of California Press, 1956. (Part I is a reprint of 1947, Part II is entitled: Perception: the ecological generality of its distal aim.)

Ontogenetic and other developmental parallels to the history of science. In H. Evans (Ed.), *Men and moments in the history of science*. Seattle: University of Washington Press, 1959. Pp. 3–21.

Author Index

Subject Index

Achievement, accord, 399–400; and evolution, 85–87; and functional efficiency, 175; limits of, 71–75; and multifinality, 157–158; probabilistic character of, 36

Acquisition, theories of, 394–397

Adaptation, criterion of problem significance, 350, 414; and memory, 237–238; probabilistic character of, 415

Agreement and differences, method of, 208, 210, 214

Analysis of variance, 510; assimilation/accommodation model, 388–391; predictions from, 394–397

Astronomy, pattern matching in, 94–96

Behavior, adaptive significance of, 414; control of, deviation countering, 334–335, 337—veto, 334–335, 337; maps of, 91–92; nomothetic, 487–488; probabilistic character of, 115; situational determinants of, 416; units of, 324–337—dynamic, 398–399, functional, 109, 398, static, 398

Behavior episodes, 324–325; and stimuli input, 330

Behavior-manipulability, 462

Behavior-object, 462; aspects of, 484; properties of, discriminanda, 464–467, 484—manipulanda, 465–467, 484, utilanda, 465–467, 484

Behavior-research isomorphism, 110, 352, 414; and simulation, 347–348

Behavior settings, 325–337; control mechanism of, 333–335; distal texture of, 329; and individual behavior, 328; regulation of, 328–330; size of, 330–337; structural attributes of, 326–327; as systems, 328

Behaviorism, molar, 509; nomothetic, 55–56, 507; purposive, 507

Bender-Gestalt Tests, 45–47

Birentinal disparity, ecological validity of, 474–475

Brain activity, functional units of, 444

Causal connections, 457; equivocality of, 458, 468, 484

Causal texture, equivocality of, 258, 468–470

Causality, impersonal, 150—multifinality in, 156; personal, equifinality of, 150–151, 153, 155–156—local character of, 149–151, and multifinality, 157, and perception, 151–155, unifinality of, 153

Central phenomena, invariance of, 52

Central processes, 41–47

Central-Distal relations, 43, 45, 421–424, 497

Classical design of experiments, 63–66, 204–205; and multiple causation, 206–207; see also One-variable

Cognition, ratiomorphic character of, 38, 49, 415–416, 448–449, 491; organizing characteristics, 441–446

Coherence, perceptual, criterion of, 314; detection of, 284–286

Communication theory, 280, 512

Compromise, perceptual, 39–41, 169, 254

Computer simulation, and environment, 26, 34

Concept attainment, and criteriality analysis, 272–273; deterministic, 259; probabilistic, 259–275; and hypothesis testing, 270–274

Concomitant variation, method of, 210, 221

Conflict, cognitive, 75

Conservation, of hypothetical possibilities, 399; of size, 383, 390; of substance, 396–399

Constancy, 35, 482, 515; and compromise, 169; and noise suppression, 306–309; size, 40–41, 365, 382–383; thing, 515—and constancy assumption, 522, development of, 521; value, 40–41

Criteriality analysis, 272–273

Cue-family hierarchies, 30, 112

Cue-means, chains of, 464–465

545